Human
Experimental
Psychology

Human Experimental Psychology

Margaret W. Matlin
State University of New York at Geneseo

Brooks/Cole Publishing Company
Monterey, California
A Division of Wadsworth, Inc.

Consulting Editor: Edward L. Walker

Printed in the United States of America

10 9 8 7 6 5 4 3 2 1

Library of Congress Cataloging in Publication Data

Matlin, Margaret W.
    Human experimental psychology.
    Bibliography: p. 447
    Includes indexes.
    1. Psychology, Experimental.   2. Human experi-
mentation in psychology.   I. Title.
BF181.M35   150'.7'24   78-31173
ISBN 0-8185-0330-0

Acquisition Editor: *William H. Hicks*
Manuscript Editor: *Margaret C. Tropp*
Production Editor: *Robert Rowland*
Interior and Cover Design: *Katherine Minerva*
Illustrations: *Lori Gilbo*
Typesetting: *Holmes Composition Service*

This book is dedicated to
Harry K. Wong, Leonard M. Horowitz, and Robert B. Zajonc,
whose enthusiasm for research and teaching was infectious.

Preface

Textbook writers typically feel compelled to explain why their own book is different from all others on the market. I feel the same compulsion, particularly because I believe that this textbook is *not* merely a repackaging of other experimental-psychology textbooks under a different-colored cover.

After inspecting the current offering of textbooks in experimental psychology, I realized that there was no appropriate textbook for many (perhaps most) of the students who actually take courses in experimental psychology. Only a very small percentage of students pursue graduate work in experimental psychology; most probably apply experimental psychology in areas such as counseling, education, and business. These students would be unlikely to use information about research areas such as animal learning or physiological psychology, or methodological refinements such as the 12 different kinds of two-group designs. Furthermore, the level of available books is too high for average students. I have tried to address these problems in the following way:

1. The book includes chapters on five research areas. Without attention to both design and content, the student is left either with the rationale for experiments but no concept of what they produce, or with the conclusions of experiments but no idea of how they were obtained.
2. The research-area chapters—perception, memory, language, cognition, and motivation—deal with human behavior rather than animal behavior.
3. Two chapters useful to everyone working with humans have been included—a chapter on the social psychology of the experiment and a chapter on the ethical treatment of human subjects. These chapters will also be valuable to students pursuing work in areas of psychology such as personality, social psychology, and developmental psychology.
4. I have tried to make the writing as clear and basic as possible, following the American Psychological Association's warning to avoid artificial scientific style and excessive qualification in writing.
5. The book contains many examples from everyday life to illustrate various principles. There are also some easy informal experiments you can try that do not require any elaborate equipment.

As you look at the table of contents, you will notice that the book is divided into two main sections. The first section focuses on the techniques and tools of experimental methods. Chapters 1 and 2 are concerned mainly with designing experiments. Chapters 3 and 4 discuss social and ethical complications that often arise when human subjects are used. A Japanese movie, *Late Autumn,* contains the remarkable line: "It's people who tend to complicate life. Life itself is simple." The same could be said about experimental design! Chapters 5 and 6 acquaint readers with two kinds of tools—psychological scaling and psychophysics—that are also essential to many areas outside of experimental psychology.

The second half of the book examines five research areas in experimental psychology. Each of the chapters discusses several of the methodological issues presented in the first half of the book. Intentionally, these chapters concern "higher mental processes" rather than areas of human behavior such as psychomotor skills or conditioning. Also, I prefer to discuss a few experiments in detail rather than a large number in summary. Unfortunately, this meant that many important topics could not be covered. Thus, these five chapters should be viewed as covering typical research, rather than constituting a review of the literature.

Two other points should be mentioned. The first concerns statistics. Some psychology departments require statistics as a prerequisite for experimental psychology, while some do not. This book does not assume a prior knowledge of statistics, and the few statistical terms that are used are footnoted. A brief statistics appendix at the end of the book provides enough information to help students perform common analyses. A step-by-step approach with examples makes this appendix easy for beginning students to use.

The second point concerns terminology. Whenever new terms are introduced in the text, they are made obvious by the use of **boldface type**. Part of the learning involved in any new subject is a familiarity with the vocabulary. Drawing attention to a new word when it is discussed in the text should be more helpful than a glossary isolated at the end of the book.

I find experimental psychology to be a fascinating and challenging area. I hope that I can successfully convey this enthusiasm!

The three people to whom I have dedicated this book inspired me at various points in my involvement with research. Harry K. Wong was my first mentor and introduced me to my first research project. Leonard M. Horowitz, of Stanford University, impressed me with the clarity and organization of his lectures and kindled my interest in memory research. Robert B. Zajonc, my dissertation chairman at the University of Michigan, served as an ideal role model with his awesome breadth of knowledge in experimental and social psychology. The words and ideas of other professors also helped me in writing this book: Gordon Bower, Douglas Lawrence, and Eleanor Maccoby of Stanford University, and Eugene Burnstein, Robyn Dawes, Edwin Martin, Arthur Melton, Richard Pew, Edward Walker, and Daniel Weintraub of the University of Michigan.

Concrete help on this book came from many sources. Two graduate students at SUNY Geneseo worked diligently on this project. Christine Beard assembled the permissions forms, helped compile the bibliography, and checked my statistical calculations. She also read every word of the manuscript and made excellent suggestions for revisions. Valerie Gawron also helped compile the bibliography.

Brooks/Cole is my idea of a model publishing company. Everyone who has worked with me on this book has been skilled, efficient, and friendly. I would like to thank Bill Hicks, who provided abundant guidance and encouragement as well as numerous suggestions that helped turn an idea into a manuscript, and Vena Dyer, Administrative Assistant, who I suspect is Wonder Woman in disguise. Micky Lawler, Bob Rowland, and Peggy Tropp worked wonders on the production end of the manuscript, bringing clarity out of many tangled sentences. C. Deborah Laughton, Jamie Brooks, Katherine Minerva, and Richard Verduin, also should receive special thanks.

Edward Walker, Brooks/Cole's consulting editor, offered considerable guidance in the technique of writing a textbook, as well as specific factual information from his knowledge of experimental psychology. A number of reviewers deserve my gratitude for their conscientious examination of the manuscript. I would like to thank Dr. S. Joyce Brotsky of California State University, Dr. John Haralson of California State University, Dr. Stuart A. Karabenick of Eastern Michigan University, Dr. Marigold Linton of the University of Utah, Dr. Donald E. Moss of the University of Texas at El Paso, David B. Volckmann of Whittier College, and Dr. Eugene Zechmeister of Loyola University.

Finally, I would like to thank my husband, Arnie, and my daughters, Beth and Sally, for providing help, love, warmth, enthusiasm, and appreciation.

Margaret W. Matlin

Contents

xi

2 Performing and Reporting the Experiment 38

3 Social Aspects of the Psychology Experiment   104

4 Ethical Aspects of the Psychology Experiment   135

5 Psychological Scaling Methods   158

Part 1

The Methodology of Experimental Psychology: Techniques and Tools

1

Concepts in Experimental Design

3

This is a book about research in psychology. We will examine how psychologists design research and what tools they use. Also, we'll discuss the products of their research: knowledge about how humans see, learn, talk, think, and act.

Students often think that research is an extremely esoteric activity, conducted only by scholarly-looking people wearing white lab coats who use equipment borrowed from the sets of the movie *2001*. Furthermore, they suspect that the topics of research must be very far removed from ordinary human experience. This picture is misleading. In fact, psychologists often conduct research on the kinds of things you wonder about in everyday life. For example, you might wonder if you would learn your French vocabulary better if you studied for ten minutes on each of four evenings rather than studying the entire list in one evening. You might wonder if you tend to eat less when a cold prevents you from smelling the food. You might wonder if soft music on the radio will hinder your performance on a set of statistics problems. Questions like these have also intrigued psychologists.

Psychological research and everyday speculation do not really differ with regard to the type of question asked. Instead, the difference lies in the approach to the problem. Everyday speculation typically uses a single demonstration and informal observation, whereas psychological research uses repeated demonstrations and formal, systematic observation. As a consequence, the conclusions we reach in everyday life are necessarily tentative and ambiguous, whereas the conclusions we reach in psychological research can be much firmer.

One of my own typical "everyday speculations" may help to illustrate this point. Recently, I was teaching a course in statistics, and the class was going badly. The students looked grumpy, asked questions about concepts they should have mastered, and performed poorly on the tests. I speculated that the narrow, dark classroom might be responsible for our problems, so we switched to a bright, airy room. The students looked happier, they seemed to ask better questions, and they performed well on the tests! It was tempting to conclude that students learn better in bright, airy rooms.

Unfortunately, however, my conclusion had to remain tentative because there were many other possible explanations for the "miracle cure." By the time we changed classrooms, several of the students who were having the most difficulty had dropped the course: my samples were different for the two conditions. We may also have covered easier material in the new room: the material was different for the two conditions. Furthermore, after several weeks in the dark room, I anticipated poor performance, whereas I believed the students would do well in the new, brighter surroundings: my expectations were different for the two conditions. Also, the students were in the dark room for the first six weeks and in the light room for the last eight weeks: the length of their experience with statistics was different for the two conditions. You can probably think of many other ways in which the two conditions may have differed.

As you can see, the conclusion that the classroom surroundings produced the change in performance was really quite shaky. In real life, the situation could not be controlled very carefully. Consequently, there were many other factors that could have been responsible for the improved performance, and I could not conclude that the change in the classroom caused a change in the performance. Psychologists could conduct research on this question, but they would have to be fastidiously careful to control for other contaminating factors.

Let's begin our exploration of experimental psychology with an introduction to the various scientific methods that psychologists use. As you will see, most of these methods use careful observation with no attempt to *change* behavior. These methods may yield insights, but the conclusions must often remain tentative. In contrast, the experimental method introduces systematic manipulation, controls, and careful measurement. Consequently, we can be more confident about the cause-and-effect conclusions based on this method.

Different as the various scientific methods are, however, they all share a common goal: they are all searching for the truth. That phrase may sound very pompous, but it is accurate. Psychologists want to find out the truth about the factors that are related to behavior. If some factor—say, noise intensity—does influence behavior, they want to conclude that there is indeed a relationship. However, if noise intensity does not influence behavior, they want to conclude that there is no support for the proposed relationship. Unfortunately, there are dozens of complicating factors that make the search for truth quite difficult in psychology. A major portion of this book concentrates on examining those factors. As we will see in the next few pages, each of the research approaches has its own kind of complicating factors.

RESEARCH APPROACHES

There are several different methods for conducting studies in psychology. Most of this textbook concerns the experimental method, but psychologists often use other research methods—including naturalistic observation, the survey method, the correlational method, and the case history—to discover information about human beings. Each of these methods will be discussed briefly in this section. In a later chapter on psycholinguistics (Chapter 9), we will focus once again on the issue of research approaches, offering several examples of each of these methods as they have been used in research on the psychology of language.

As you read about each research method, think about the kinds of conclusions you can draw from the data obtained—specifically, whether you can conclude that one factor *caused* a behavior to occur. When we consider the experimental method, we will see that this notion of causality is crucial. The experimental method involves the systematic manipulation of factors. If only one factor is allowed to change, and if the subjects' behavior changes when that factor is changed, then we can be reasonably confident that there is a cause-and-effect relationship between that factor and the behavior change.

The Naturalistic-Observation Method

The term **naturalistic observation** means exactly that: the careful observation of behavior in a natural setting. The observation is typically very detailed, and it may continue for a long period of time. Naturalistic observation is frequently used in **ethology**, which is the study of animal behavior in natural settings. For example, an ethologist may hide out in the bushes for hours or days watching the rufous-sided towhee go about its activities. The ethologist may gather very detailed, complete records of the mating habits, the nesting patterns, the rearing of the young—all the observable behaviors of the rufous-sided towhee. Strange as it may seem, ethologists and psychologists have not been as energetic in applying this technique to the study of human beings.

One excellent example of the use of naturalistic observation is the record of a typical day in the life of a 7-year-old boy. Barker and Wright (1951) wrote a delightful book which simply describes in detail everything that a boy named Raymond did during one day in his life. Here, for example, is what Raymond did between 8:27 and 8:28 in the morning:

> Raymond ambled along the top of the wall until he came to the benches that were grouped together on one corner of the courthouse lawn.
>
> He sat down on one of the benches with a pleasant, relaxed expression.
>
> He rocked the bench back and forth for a few seconds, sitting with his hands stretched out and holding the edges of the bench to brace himself. His feet were out in front of him, flat on the ground.
>
> He hummed a little to himself, very softly, contentedly.
>
> He jumped up and began rocking the bench as he stood on the ground at one end of it. He held onto the seat and the back and pushed the bench back and forth [pp. 50–51].

As you can see, the naturalistic-observation method calls for a careful recording of all activities as they occur spontaneously. The observer may record language one moment, then physical movement, then quiet play; observation is not restricted to a particular category.

One important aspect of naturalistic observation is that the observer must try valiantly to stay out of the way and not influence the organism's normal activities. This is a more difficult task than it might seem. I remember a project we were assigned as undergraduates in a child-psychology course. It sounded simple: all we had to do was observe a child in a typical setting for 15 minutes. I came in, clipboard in hand, ready to sit quietly in a corner while 3-year-old John continued to play normally with his toys in his bedroom. No such luck! John found my clipboard and me far more interesting, and he came over to visit and ask questions. Clearly, this was no sample of "natural behavior." The naturalistic observation technique raises an interesting problem to which we will return later in this chapter: how can we measure a behavior without altering the behavior through the measuring process?

Underwood (1966) has pointed out another problem with the naturalistic-observation method. With this method, it is difficult to determine cause-and-effect relationships; all we have is a list of events, connected in time. For example, we might record one event "child's mother enters the room" and then another event, one second later, "child runs to hide behind the sofa." We have evidence for a *time* relationship, but not a *causal* relationship; we cannot say that the child's mother entering the room *caused* the hiding. In reality, another factor might have caused the hiding.

Thus, the aim of naturalistic observation is description rather than an understanding of causality. The naturalistic observation method provides a rich source of observations of behavior as it occurs naturally, but it typically does not allow us to interpret that behavior. The only reliable way to establish a causal relationship is to observe that the cause leads to the effect on many separate occasions, and to observe that, when the cause is absent, the effect is absent as well. In naturalistic observation, subjects usually do not cooperate by repeating behaviors many times while you are watching. Notice, however, that the naturalistic-observation method may provide some ideas or hypotheses that can be tested later using the experimental method.

Another term that is often used interchangeably with naturalistic observation is **field study**. This term, commonly used in social psychology, usually refers to observation in a natural setting that does not change the behavior of the people being observed. In a **field experiment**, however, psychologists go out into a "real-life" setting, but they somehow try to provoke a particular behavior. In this case, they are no longer merely observers: they want to see whether the deliberate manipulation of certain variables will influence behavior. The field experiment, therefore, combines naturalistic observation with the experimental method.

Wispé and Freshley (1971), for example, devised a field-experiment technique called "the broken-bag caper." In this technique, a young woman, who is an accomplice of the experimenter, stands at the exit of a supermarket with a bag of groceries. At a designated moment, she lets the bag slip and tear, spilling her groceries on the floor. The experimenter observes who comes to help her and notes whether the helping behavior is related to certain characteristics of the accomplice. It is field experiments like this one that make some psychologists reluctant to help anyone in distress in a university town; they are convinced it's part of someone's master's thesis!

Many psychologists argue that the results of field research (either field studies or field experiments) are more generalizable to real-life situations than are the results of more traditional, laboratory methods of experimental psychology. They contend that behavior in "real life" is quite different from behavior in the unnatural setting of a laboratory. That argument has some merit, as an example cited by Zimbardo (1969) demonstrates. Zimbardo describes the typical results found in the laboratory on motor tasks such as the pursuit-rotor (where the subject must keep a pointer on a moving target): after an hour, subjects are fatigued, bored, and inaccurate. However, in a field study, volunteer drivers were ordered to drive at high speeds for 24 consecutive hours, and the researchers failed to find evidence of fatigue. In Chapter 3, we will consider other evidence that research in the laboratory often does not match research in the field. However, we must again recall a clear disadvantage to field-research techniques: it is difficult to establish cause-and-effect relationships, particularly because variables cannot be controlled with precision in field research. This point will become clearer in the section on the experimental method.

The Survey Method

In the **survey method**, a researcher selects a group of people and asks them questions. Sometimes the format is a written questionnaire; sometimes it is a face-to-face interview. Typically, the respondents supply some demographic information, such as their sex, age, marital status, income, education, race, or political preference. For example, Lin and Ensel (1976) conducted a door-to-door survey of people's fear of a variety of institutions. They found that the most fear-arousing institutions are the Internal Revenue Service and door-to-door salesmen, whereas the least fear-arousing institutions are bus drivers and library personnel.

In general, survey methods are used in social psychology and sociology, rather than in areas of experimental psychology such as perception and learning. For more details on this method, you should consult textbooks oriented specifically to those fields (such as Babbie's *The Practice of Social Research*, 1975, Chapter 11).

The Correlational Method

In the **correlational method**, psychologists try to determine if two measures are related. They gather two measures on each individual and try to determine whether there is some systematic pattern in the data—whether there is a **correlation**. A correlation may be positive: a person who receives a high number on measure A generally receives a high number on measure B, whereas a person who receives a low number on measure A generally receives a low number on measure B. A correlation may also be negative: a person who receives a high number on measure A generally receives a low number on measure B, whereas a person who receives a low number on measure A generally receives a high number on measure B. Positive and negative correlations are illustrated in Figure 1-1.

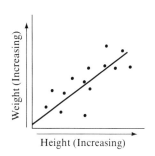

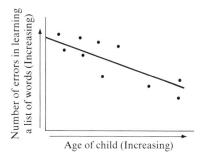

A. Positive correlation   B. Negative correlation

Figure 1-1. Examples of positive and negative correlations.

Many psychologists use the correlational method in their research. For example, Clarkson, Vogel, Broverman, Broverman, and Rosenkrantz (1970) studied a group of mothers to determine whether family size was correlated with self-concept. They found a negative correlation between family size and feelings of competence: women who had fewer children saw themselves as more competent.

The phrase "Correlation is not necessarily causation!" is something that every instructor of experimental psychology chants at least once a semester. Just because two factors go together does not mean that one causes the other. It *may* be that factor A causes factor B. However, it may be that factor B causes factor A. Finally, a third (perhaps unidentified) factor may cause both A and B. For example, let's consider those results on family size and feelings of competence. It may be that small family size causes feelings of competence: women may come to feel less competent as they have more children (A causes B). It may be that feelings of competence cause small family size: the feeling of competence may produce a wish for freedom and a desire not to be "tied down" by a large family (B causes A). However, it may be that a third factor causes both A and B. For example, social class might be relevant: upper social-class status may create more feelings of competence, and it may also encourage smaller family size. We will see many examples of the "Correlation is not necessarily causation" problem throughout the last five chapters of this book, particularly in Chapters 9 (Psycholinguistics) and 11 (Motivation).

We have said that the correlational method produces difficulties because the nature of the causality cannot be identified. Why would anyone want to use it, then? Sometimes researchers use the correlational method in order to gather data because it would be unethical to use the experimental method and *manipulate* one of the variables. For example, newspaper articles have recently noted that there is a correlation between wife-beating and the husband's having been an abused child. The methodologically ideal experiment would require one group of children to be raised normally and another group of children to be given the experimental treatment—abuse. The experimenter would then record the number of wife-beaters in each group when the subjects reached maturity. In a case such as this, the ethical advantage of the correlational method is obvious.

Other researchers use the correlational method because the data are often readily available and can be used with very little effort. Cronbach (1957) has stated this option most colorfully:

> The correlational method, for its part, can study what man has not learned to control or can never hope to control. Nature has been experimenting since the beginning of time, with a boldness and complexity far beyond the resources of science. The correlator's mission is to observe and organize the data from Nature's experiments. As a minimum outcome, such correlations improve immediate decisions and guide experimentation. At the best, a Newton, a Lyell, or a Darwin can align the correlations into a substantial theory [p. 672].

Finally, the correlational method is useful to researchers in the area of applied psychology. These researchers may not care about the specific nature of the causality because their primary concern may simply be accuracy of prediction. They may be very pleased to know that two measures "go together," and they may not need to know *why*. For example, Martin (1977) cites some research on motorcycle accidents conducted by the U.S. Army, in which researchers investigated whether the number of accidents was correlated with other variables such as socioeconomic level and age. They discovered that the best predictor, in fact, was the number of tattoos the rider had! (Incidentally, can you figure out why tattoos would be correlated with accidents?)

An important adaptation of the correlational method is called **multiple regression**. Although a detailed consideration of this statistical procedure is beyond the scope of this book, an understanding of the function of multiple regression will be useful if you encounter the term in journal articles. The correlational method attempts to relate one measure, A, to another measure, B; multiple regression attempts to relate many measures—A_1, A_2, A_3 and so on—to measure B. For example, Astin (1975) examined how various factors are related to the likelihood that a student will drop out of school. By using multiple-regression analyses, he established that many factors are related to the drop-out rate, including having relatively uneducated parents, not having a job, living at home, and having a low grade-point average. Other factors, such as tuition fees and the similarity of other students, were found to be unimportant.

The advantage of multiple regression is that it can often eliminate irrelevant variables. For example, measure A_1 may not really be directly related to measure B. However, it may *appear* to be related because measure A_1 is correlated with measure A_2, and measure A_2 is correlated with measure B. The results of a multiple-regression analysis will tell us that measure A_1 is not really important.

Indeed, you may come across studies that use other kinds of analyses, in which stronger conclusions might have been drawn by means of multiple regression. For example, a paper by Naeye, Ladis, and Drage (1976) examined characteristics of parents that might be related to infants' dying from the "sudden infant death syndrome." In a number of individual tests, they found that the incidence of this syndrome was related to social class, race, education, and marital status. Perhaps if they had done a multiple-regression analysis, the results might have shown that one of the factors (say, race) was not really important, but only appeared to be important because it was related to other factors, such as social class and education.

Another adaptation of the correlational method is called the **archival method**. This method uses data that have already been collected in order to test new hypotheses. (In a way, it's like recycling used bottles!) For example, in the chapter on motivation, we'll look at archival approaches to achievement motivation. In one study, McClelland (1961) speculated that a society's need for achievement was correlated with its economic development. To demonstrate his point, he measured need for achievement by seeing how often the children's literature of a given country mentioned the need to achieve success. Then he measured economic development by going to a second kind of archival record, the records of growth in electricity production. The two measures were significantly correlated.

The archival method can also use previous research from psychology journals as an archival source. For example, Underwood (1957) wanted to see whether there was a relationship between the number of word lists a subject had learned previously and the number of words recalled on the current list. He examined the literature and recorded two numbers for each study—the number of previous lists the subjects had learned and the number of words the subjects recalled from the current list. He found that people recalled less when they had learned a large number of previous lists. We will consider the implications of these results in the chapter on human memory.

Notice that in the archival method, the experimenters do not deal directly with the subjects, but only with their data. They never see a subject face to face! An advantage to this approach is that the experimenters' expectancies are less likely to influence the results (a problem we will consider in Chapter 3). A disadvantage is that the previous researchers, on whom experimenters must rely, may not have gathered precisely the kind of data they would like to have, using the conditions they would have chosen.

The Case-Study Method

The **case-study** or **case-history** technique is an in-depth study of one person. Typically, the case study stresses individual differences, or how this particular person is different from other people. The method frequently involves an examination of the important events in the person's life, and it may involve interviews with the person's friends and relatives. Case studies may also involve the use of information from standardized tests.

Students in my educational psychology class are always impressed with a Russian mnemonist named Shereshevskii, whose case history was reported by Luria (1968). A mnemonist is someone who uses mnemonic tricks, or memory devices, to remember huge amounts of material. For example, Shereshevskii was presented with a mathematical formula with perhaps 20 long terms that looked like these:

$$N \cdot \sqrt{d^2 \cdot x \ \frac{85}{vx}} \cdot \sqrt{\frac{276^2 \cdot 86x}{n^2v \cdot \pi \, 264}}$$

He looked at the formula for about 5–7 minutes and made up a story to code it into his memory. The story for the first segment of the equation involved an imaginary person named Neiman (N) who came out and poked with his stick (·).He looked at a dried-up old tree, and this reminded him of a root ($\sqrt{\ }$). Neiman said it was no wonder this tree was withered because it was already standing when he built these houses, these two here (d^2), and again he poked with his stick (·). He said that the houses were so old that a cross (x) should be placed on them. This would give a great return on his original capital, because he had invested 85,000 rubles (85) in building them. A roof finishes off the building (_____), and down below a man is standing and playing a harmonica (vx). Half an hour later, Shereshevskii was able to recall the entire formula. More surprisingly, he still recalled it perfectly 15 years later.

Clearly, the case history can present rich details about the life of a single person. However, it does not allow us to conclude anything firm about people in general. Furthermore, the researcher might show certain kinds of biases, presenting some information to make a point and leaving out other information. The "truth," therefore, may be somewhat distorted.

The Experimental Method

All the methods we have examined so far involve the careful observation and recording of behavior. What are the essential features of the **experimental method** that differentiate it from these other methods? Why does the experimental method allow us to draw cause-and-effect conclusions, whereas the other methods do not?

The systematic manipulation of variables. Unlike the other methods, the experimental method involves the systematic manipulation of variables. A **variable** is a set of conditions in an experiment that are changed or can be changed (Wilkening, 1973). "Amount of noise" is an example of a variable, because the amount of noise in a laboratory is one of the sets of conditions that can be changed. An experimenter can change the amount of noise by presenting loud noise for some subjects, soft noise for other subjects, and no noise for still other subjects.

To **manipulate** means to change—in this case, to change something about the organisms we are studying or about stimuli relevant to those organisms. Notice that the concept of *change* is unique to the experimental method: with naturalistic observation, for example, our objective was to observe without changing. In the simplest kind of experiment using the experimental method, we have two conditions. One condition, the **control condition**, is left unchanged. The other condition, the **experimental condition**, is changed in some way: a particular variable is present in the experimental condition that is absent in the control condition. To select an example from everyday life, you might suspect that you eat less when you can't smell food because one week, when you were healthy (control condition), you ate more than the next week, when a cold prevented your smelling (experimental condition).

Now let's look at the word **systematic**. To be systematic is to be orderly, and the experimental method specifies a particular kind of orderliness. Specifically, we must change only one variable at a time: the experimental and control conditions must be identical in all other respects except for the one variable we are studying. In the experiments we conduct in everyday life, we are seldom systematic. In the "eating experiment," for example, there are many, many variables that are different for the two conditions—not just the presence or absence of smell. Other aspects of the cold might suppress your hunger. The food might be different in the two conditions, as might be the surroundings and the people eating with you. If nothing else, you are several days older in the experimental condition!

Developmental psychologists have discovered that the concept of systematic manipulation cannot be mastered by young children. For example, if you hand a 7-year-old a pendulum and ask her to discover what factor or factors determine the speed of the pendulum's swing, the child might proceed as shown in Figure 1-2. First, she might use a long string and drop a heavy weight from

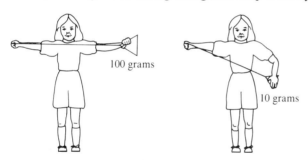

Trial 1. Long string, heavy weight, maximum height.   Trial 2. Short string, light weight, intermediate height.

Figure 1-2. A young child is unable to solve a problem by manipulating only one variable at a time.

high up. On the second trial, she might use a short string and drop a light weight from an intermediate height. Notice, however, that there are three variables— string length, heaviness of the weight, and height of release—that are different for the two trials. If she finds that the speed of the pendulum's swing is different for the two trials, she will not be able to draw any conclusions about the specific *cause* of the difference. The cause could be any one of the three variables, or it could be a combination of these variables. In fact, it is not until adolescence that children understand that they can ultimately solve the problem only by manipulating one variable at a time.

When there is only one variable that is different for the control and experimental conditions, we say that we have a well-controlled experiment.

The problem of controlling an experiment is one that we will reconsider in detail in Chapter 2 when we discuss particular variables that need to be controlled and particular control techniques. However, let's consider one example from a hypothetical experiment to see why the control problem is so critical.

Let us suppose that you are interested in the influence of another person's presence on learning a list of words. Ideally, subjects in the control condition learn the list in the normal fashion, but only *one* critical variable—another person in the room—is added for subjects in the experimental condition. Why do you need to be so compulsive about making sure that the critical variable is the only thing that is different between the control group and the experimental conditions? The reason is that when you're all done with the experiment, you'll need to draw conclusions, and the conclusions will be ambiguous and uncertain unless that critical variable was the only thing that was different for the two conditions.

For example, in that idealized learning experiment, the only variable that differed for the two conditions was the presence or absence of the other person. However, suppose you had been sloppy in designing the experiment, as illustrated in Figure 1–3. Let's say that in the experimental condition, you knocked

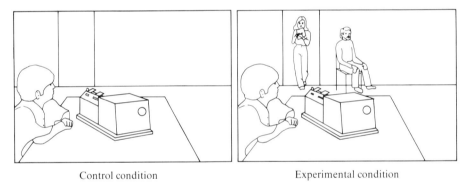

Control condition   Experimental condition

Figure 1-3. An example of a confounded experiment.

on the door, came in, introduced the stranger, and left. In the control condition, however, you ignored the subject completely: you did not knock on the door, you did not enter, and you said nothing. Yes, the stranger is present in one condition and absent in another, but there are many other variables that also differ in the control and experimental conditions.

Now suppose you inspect your data and you find that subjects learned the lists much faster in the experimental condition. That's all very nice, except that you cannot put your finger on the specific variable that caused the experimental group's performance to differ from that of the control group. Yes, it could be the fact that the stranger was present for the experimental group and absent for the control group. However, it also could be your knocking on the door, your coming in, or your talking that somehow changed the experimental group, perhaps motivating them to learn better. These uncontrolled factors, present in one condition but absent in the other, are known as **confounding variables**. Confounding variables and other details are exactly what distinguish a bad experiment from a good one. We will consider confounding variables again in Chapter 2 when we discuss how they should be handled in designing an experiment. In Chapter 8, we will look at the problem of confounding variables in studies on memory.

If an organism's behavior changes consistently as one variable is changed, then we can be reasonably confident that this variable caused the change in behavior. For example, if some subjects learn lists of words without another person present (control condition) and other subjects learn the same lists with another person present (experimental condition), and we find that learning is consistently better in the experimental condition, then we can state with reasonable certainty that a change in one variable (presence or absence of another person) caused a change in another variable (the measure of learning).

The measurement of variables. So far, we have seen that the experimental method involves the systematic manipulation of variables. The experimental method also involves the careful *measurement* of variables. We need to attach numbers to the behavior of our subjects. Notice that the naturalistic-observation method and the case study typically make no attempt to translate behavior into numbers; the correlational method and the survey method, however, usually share this characteristic of measurement with the experimental method.

In designing an experiment, you need to decide what kind of numbers you will assign to behavior. For example, if you are studying memory, you must figure out how you will measure memory. You must begin by choosing appropriate *operational definitions*. An **operational definition** is one that defines a concept in terms of the operations used to measure that concept. For example, your operational definition of memory might be "the number of words perfectly recalled five minutes after the list was presented." What operations did you use to measure the concept of learning? You waited five minutes before asking the subject to recall the words, and you counted the number of words that were perfectly recalled. A different operational definition might specify a different waiting period, ask the subjects to demonstrate their memory in terms of recognition, or count the number of words that were at least partially recalled (see Table 1–1). An operational definition specifies exactly what we mean by a particular concept. It does not define a concept in terms of other abstract concepts; rather, it concretely tells us what we have to do to *measure* that concept.

Table 1–1. Suppose you are examining memory, using this list of 12 words. How many different operational definitions can you suggest for the concept *memory*?

cookie	light	table
toe	dentist	windows
ink	human	paper
tree	house	after

Think for a moment about why we need operational definitions. Suppose you would like to study infants' preferences for various shapes. You propose that infants prefer complex shapes. In this case, you need operational definitions for both *preference* and *complexity*. You might define shape complexity by asking 20 adults to rate each shape on a seven-point scale, such that a rating of 1 equals ''very complex'' and 7 equals ''very simple.'' You might define preference in terms of the number of seconds each shape is looked at by an infant when it is held 100 cm from the infant's eyes. As you can see, specifying the operational definitions forces you to think carefully about the basic elements of the variables you are exploring. An operational definition makes it perfectly clear to you—and to the rest of the world—how you intend to measure the concepts you are examining. You can't fudge by giving such a general definition that no one could challenge you!

The problem for you personally, however, is that people might not agree that your operational definitions were well-chosen. For example, they might say that adults' ratings of complexity might not be appropriate for an infant. They might also say that your operational definition of preference has some problems: just because infants look at one object longer than another does not mean that they *prefer* it; in fact, they may be looking at the object to figure out what frightening thing it might do to them. While it might be personally embarrassing to have someone challenge your operational definition, perhaps claiming that their operational definition has more merit, it's healthier for the welfare of psychology to have definitions that are so specific that we can all figure out what they mean and can challenge them if we think they are inappropriate.

The choice of operational definitions, needless to say, can influence the kind of results you obtain. Suppose you are studying love relationships, and you must arrive at an operational definition to measure how much love someone feels toward someone else. If you define love as ''admiration for person X,'' you will probably obtain different results than if you define love as ''changes in heart rate when person X enters the room.'' You will probably find still different results if you define love as ''the extent to which person X occupies a central, important position in the subject's life.'' The use of different operational definitions can easily lead to different conclusions in psychological research.

Thus, two essential attributes of the experimental method are systematic manipulation of variables and measurement of variables. Now, let us consider the matter of experimental design in greater detail. We begin with the hypothesis. Then we will talk about the independent variable, the dependent variable, and drawing conclusions about the relationship between the two. Finally, at the end of the chapter, we will look at more complex kinds of experimental designs.

THE HYPOTHESIS

A **hypothesis** is a tentative law or a tentative explanation. It is a hunch we have, whether from observation, reasoning, or theory. However, the hypothesis has not achieved the formality of a law, because it has not been frequently tested. In contrast, a scientific **law** is a statement of regular, predictable relationships among observable variables (Marx, 1963); this relationship *has* been frequently demonstrated.

A hypothesis is a statement of what you expect to happen if certain conditions are true. A hypothesis can be stated in an "if . . . then" format: *if* certain conditions are true, *then* certain things will happen. The hypothesis tells what kind of relationship you expect to find between two kinds of variables— the independent variable and the dependent variable.

The **independent variable** is the variable that the experimenters manipulate: they decide how much of that variable to present to the subject. For example, an independent variable in one experiment might be the presence or absence of another person while the subject is working on a task. In another experiment, the independent variable might be the amount of time that has passed since a person last ate. The independent variable is described in the *if* part of the "if . . . then" statement of the hypothesis. For example, in the hypothesis "If another person is present, then the subject will learn faster," the independent variable is the presence or absence of another person.

The **dependent variable** concerns the responses that the subject makes; it is the set of measures describing the subject's behavior. The dependent variable is described in the *then* part of the "if . . . then" statement of the hypothesis. In the example above, the dependent variable is the set of measures we obtain on the subject's learning in the different conditions. The dependent variable *depends* upon the value of the independent variable. For example, the amount learned (dependent variable) *depends* upon whether another person is present or not (independent variable).

Table 1–2 gives some examples of hypotheses and specifies the independent and dependent variables represented by each hypothesis.

Before turning to a more detailed discussion of the independent variables, we need to introduce one more basic term, **functional relationship**. When the independent variable has an influence on the dependent variable, we say that there is a functional relationship between the two variables.

THE INDEPENDENT VARIABLE

Independent variables can be divided into four different categories: **stimulus characteristics, environmental characteristics, manipulated subject differences,** and **subject characteristics.** A brief discussion of each of these categories will help you appreciate the variety of independent variables that can be studied in experimental psychology. Chapter 10, on cognition, is organized according to these four categories of independent variables, and we will consider a large number of examples at that time.

The first three categories are the classic kinds of independent variables because experimenters can manipulate them systematically. Subject characteristics should be treated as a special case, because experimenters cannot *manipulate* or change these variables. As a result, confounding variables present many problems.

Table 1–2. Examples of hypotheses, specifying independent and dependent variables.

Hypothesis	Independent Variable	Dependent Variable
1. If another person is present ....then the subject will learn faster.	Presence or absence of another person	Measure of learning (e.g., number of trials necessary to learn the list)
2. If a room is quiet ....then the subject will solve problems more accurately.	Amount of noise	Number of errors made on problem-solving tasks
3. If a nonsense figure is familiar ..then the subjects will prefer it to other items.	Familiarity of figure	Measure of preference (e.g., rating of figure)
4. If a child has had special language tutoring..............then the child will use longer sentences.	Presence or absence of tutoring	Length of sentences
5. If a line is bordered by arrowheads.................then the subject will perceive it to be shorter.	Presence or absence of borders	Measure of perceived length

18

Stimulus Characteristics

In every experiment, stimuli are presented to subjects, and the subjects must respond. Psychologists frequently study whether characteristics of the stimulus influence the nature of the response. For example, in a psycholinguistics experiment, we might be interested in determining whether the form of a sentence (active versus passive, positive versus negative) influences how quickly the sentence can be matched to a picture. In a verbal-learning experiment, we might want to know whether the familiarity of English-word stimuli influences how easily they can be learned. Finally, in a perception experiment, we might examine whether the angle of the arrows in the Müller-Lyer illusion influences the degree of distortion in the illusion.

Environmental Characteristics

Characteristics of the setting of an experiment can be used as independent variables. For example, we might contrast performance in neat, orderly, laboratory settings with performance in messy, unprofessional settings. We can also examine the influence of temperature on behavior. The presence or absence of another person, the example we discussed earlier, is another instance of an environmental characteristic. Variables that are physical parts of the task are classified as stimulus characteristics; other physical variables are classified as environmental characteristics.

Manipulated Subject Differences

In studies of manipulated subject differences, we take groups of subjects that are initially equivalent, and we experimentally create differences after the subjects arrive in the laboratory. Very often, we use different instructions to groups of subjects in order to create differences. For example, we might instruct some subjects simply to memorize a list of paired words, while we instruct other subjects to visualize each pair of words in some sort of vivid interaction. The two groups of subjects may have been identical when they came to the experiment, but they are different after they have received the instructions. If the experimenter in this kind of study has been careful to assign subjects randomly to the two conditions and to keep all other variables constant except for the instructions, then confounding variables should not present problems.

Notice that the three kinds of independent variables discussed so far all permit systematic manipulation of the independent variable. The groups of subjects are equivalent to begin with, and the experimenters change the variable they are interested in studying. They may change the characteristics of the stimuli that the subjects are exposed to. They may change the characteristics of the subjects' environment. They may produce other differences among subjects in terms of their expectations, knowledge, or instructional set. In all of these cases, then, the experimenter has control over the independent variable. The situation is different for subject characteristics.

People who come to an experiment differ from each other in many ways. Obviously, some are male and some are female. Subjects may also vary on other demographic characteristics, such as age, marital status, socioeconomic class, education, and so forth. Furthermore, subjects may vary in their personality characteristics. Some may be "sensitizers," who seek out emotional stimuli, and some may be "repressors," who avoid emotional stimuli. Some may be high on a Machiavellian scale and will use any method to "get ahead," while others may be low. Some may have internal locus of control, believing that they are responsible for what happens to them, while others may have external locus of control, believing that other people and things determine what happens to them.

It seems, then, that there are some independent variables that we cannot freely manipulate. For example, we cannot really *manipulate* the sex of the subject. However, we are able to select the subjects, for example, so that half are males and half are females. We may also select subjects, on the basis of a test given before the experiment, so that half are sensitizers and half are repressors.

Notice, however, that when we examine subject characteristics, there may be a number of confounding variables that we cannot control as carefully as we can when variables are actively manipulated. For example, suppose we are studying self-esteem. We give a test to measure self-esteem, and on the basis of the scores we select a high-self-esteem group and a low-self-esteem group. The problem is that the high-self-esteem group may differ from the low-self-esteem group on variables other than self-esteem. In particular, the low-self-esteem group may include a large proportion of females and lower-socioeconomic-class persons than does the high-self-esteem group. Remember that in an ideal experiment, there is only one variable that is different for the two conditions. In this case, however, there might be several variables that are different for the two conditions. Suppose that we found a difference in behavior for our two groups. Could it be due to the difference in self-esteem? Yes, but it also could be due to differences in the sex ratio or to the differences in social class. In other words, we wouldn't be able to identify the exact *cause* of the difference. Researchers who are interested in subject characteristics must be particularly careful to match their subjects in terms of other potentially confounding variables.

Psychologists disagree about the classification of research conducted on subject characteristics. Some consider these studies to be a special case of the correlational method, because researchers merely measure an existing characteristic and relate that characteristic to the subjects' behavior. I prefer to follow in the tradition of Underwood (1966) and consider studies on subject characteristics to be a special case of the experimental method. These studies cannot be categorized as classic examples of the experimental method, because *manipulation* is not involved. However, the experimenters can conduct the studies systematically by selecting specified numbers of subjects within each category and carefully controlling confounding variables.

As we saw earlier, the dependent variable is the behavior of the subject, rather than the variable manipulated by the experimenter. Part of the chapter on motivation examines the wide variety of dependent variables that have been studied in sensory-deprivation experiments. The chapter on perception focuses on the challenge of measuring the dependent variable. Because the perceptual processes—such as seeing, hearing, and smelling—are normally private ones, psychologists encounter difficulties in trying to measure them. Thus, we will be considering the dependent variable frequently in the second part of this book.

There are a number of issues that must be considered in a discussion of the dependent variable. In general, these issues concern the identification of a dependent variable that reflects what we want it to reflect. In our search for the truth about variables that influence behavior, we must be confident that we are measuring that behavior with extreme care.

Reliability

Reliability means consistency. When we say that a test is reliable, we mean that the same person consistently receives approximately the same score every time the test is administered. In contrast, a test is unreliable if a person's score varies from one administration to the next—being high on one occasion and low on another. To reflect what we want it to reflect, a dependent variable must be reliable; if it is inconsistent—sometimes high and sometimes low—then it is worthless. An example of a reliability problem, involving the measurement of achievement motivation, is discussed in Chapter 11.

Experimental psychologists also confront the reliability problem when they measure the consistency with which a dependent variable is recorded. For example, a researcher might measure the length of time that passes between the end of the stimulus and the beginning of the subject's response. To make certain that these measurements have been consistent, he or she might ask a colleague to repeat the measurements. If the two sets of measurements are correlated, say, +.95 (close to a perfect correlation), the researcher can be confident that the recordings are highly reliable.

Validity

For a test to be **valid**, it must measure what it is intended to measure, rather than some other attribute. An intelligence test, for example, should measure intelligence—and not some other irrelevant quality.

It is important to realize that a test can be reliable but invalid. A graduate student, Cathy Thomas, once provided an excellent example of this problem. She devised the Thomas Quick Test of Intelligence, which consists of a single item: "What do you like to put on your hamburger?" People who like nothing on their hamburgers receive a score of 0; those who like pickles, onions, ketchup, and cheese receive a score of 4—the total number of items they specify. The higher the score, the higher is the subject's intelligence. This test is probably highly reliable, because people are consistent in listing what they like on their hamburgers. However, you'll probably agree that the test is not a valid test of intelligence. It is measuring *something* with great reliability—but that something is not the thing that it purports to be measuring.

In experimental psychology, we say that a dependent variable is valid if it is a reasonable example of the concept that it is supposed to define. There are several ways to measure the validity of a concept. One way is to show that the dependent variable is highly correlated with other established dependent variables that have been used in previous research concerning the concept. Another way is to show that the dependent variable is influenced by factors that ought to influence the variable. In assessing the validity of a test of achievement motivation, for example, psychologists found that achievement-oriented settings produced higher scores on the test than did relaxed settings—suggesting that the test probably was a realistic reflection of achievement motivation.

The concept of validity is an important one in experimental psychology, because we would like our measures to reflect true values, rather than irrelevant, contaminating factors. Several of the methodology chapters in this book focus on this problem of reflecting true values. In Chapter 3, for example, we will see that psychologists are concerned that their measures might be contaminated by social factors. In Chapter 5, we will see that psychologists using scales must be careful that their measures are not contaminated by certain rating tendencies. In Chapter 6, we will see that psychophysicists are concerned that their measures of thresholds might be contaminated by still other factors. Invalid measures—measures that reflect something irrelevant—can disrupt the search for truth.

The kind of validity we have been discussing so far is known as *internal validity* (Campbell & Stanley, 1963). A measure has high **internal validity** if an observed effect has been caused by the experimental variable, rather than by irrelevant, contaminating variables. In contrast, if subjects in instructional condition A perform better than those in instructional condition B because they are more intelligent—because the experimenter did not equate the groups at the beginning—then these results have low internal validity. The observed effect has been caused by an extraneous variable.

Campbell and Stanley also discuss another kind of validity, called *external validity*. **External validity** means that the results of the experiment can be applied to others who did not take part in the experiment. For example, an experiment conducted only on upper-middle-class, Latin-American, identical twins living in Poughkeepsie, New York, would have lower external validity than a study conducted on a wide variety of different subjects. As we will see in Chapter 3, experiments are typically conducted using college students; for this reason, their external validity may sometimes be suspect.

Now let us consider two other concepts that are related to validity: the **response-measure problem** and **unobtrusive measures**. When an experiment has a response-measure problem, the dependent variable underestimates the abilities of the subject, and, therefore, the results are not valid. Unobtrusive measures are used to avoid a second kind of validity problem—that of measuring the reaction to the measurement process itself, rather than the behavior we are trying to measure.

The response-measure problem. A researcher, anxious to identify where the hearing organs are located on the cricket, devised the following experiment. He trained a cricket so that it would jump whenever he gave the command "Jump!" Then the researcher carefully removed the front legs from the cricket, leaving the back legs intact. He issued the command "Jump!" and the cricket jumped. Clearly, the hearing organs were not located in the front legs. Then the researcher carefully removed the back legs and issued the command "Jump!" Lo and behold, the cricket did not jump. The researcher therefore concluded that the cricket's hearing organs are located in its back legs.

This story, hopefully fictional, was told by my high school biology teacher to illustrate the response-measure problem—the problem that occurs when the dependent variable does not adequately measure the true abilities of the subject. The choice of an inappropriate response measure causes the researcher to draw the wrong conclusions: the subject may be quite competent (hearing the command), but the researcher cannot know this unless the subject is physically capable of performing the required response (jumping).

In human experimental psychology, the problem is particularly important when infants and children are used as subjects. In a study testing depth perception in infants, for example, one object was placed near the infant and another object was placed far away. The experimenter chose accuracy of reaching behavior as the dependent variable. Because the infants reached equally often for the near and the far object, the study concluded that the infants had not developed depth perception. This study is plagued by the response-measure problem: young infants simply aren't able to reach very precisely. In reality, the infants may well have noted the difference in distance between the near and the far objects, but their reaching was so clumsy that their perceptual abilities were underestimated.

The response-measure problem arises because in psychology we often try to measure covert processes (what goes on in the organism's head) rather than overt processes (those activities that can be readily observed). If only we could hop inside someone's head, attach a meter at the appropriate place, and directly measure those covert processes! Instead, we have to be content with taking those covert processes and trying to make them overt; we must try to translate thoughts and attitudes into behaviors and activities—without losing too much in the translation. Lashley (1960) notes that when an animal fails in a task, it is not safe to conclude that it lacks the capacity for that task, unless we can be certain that the question was properly asked. The warning applies equally to the study of humans. "Do infants have depth perception, as shown by their reaching patterns?" is an example of an improperly asked question.

Unobtrusive measures. Webb, Campbell, Schwartz, and Sechrest (1966) argue that psychologists' measurements are often invalid for another reason: measurements are frequently **reactive**. The problem is that subjects react in a certain way to being measured, and when they react, they change the measure itself. Consequently, the measure is invalid: it isn't measuring what it's supposed to measure, but something else instead—a reaction to the measurement process.

Suppose a psychologist used a movie camera to record social-interaction patterns in the student union. In all probability, the camera could not record your normal, daily behavior in the union. Instead, it would record your reaction to the movie camera. Furthermore, the exact nature of your reactions would depend on the cues you received from this "measurement device." Imagine how you might react if the camera were labeled "City Police." How about if it were labeled "NBC" or "Columbia University Project on Crowding Behavior"? It's an intriguing and difficult problem: by the measurement process we change the very behavior we are trying to measure!

Webb, et al. (1966) propose that researchers make more frequent use of **unobtrusive measures**—measures that can be obtained without the subjects' being aware that they are being measured. Arguing that unobtrusive measures are more valid than reactive measures, they offer a number of clever suggestions:

> The floor tiles around the hatching-chick exhibit at Chicago's Museum of Science and Industry must be replaced every six weeks. Tiles in other parts of the museum need not be replaced for years. The selective erosion of tiles, indexed by the replacement rate, is a measure of the relative popularity of exhibits.
>
> The accretion rate is another measure. One investigator wanted to learn the level of whisky consumption in a town which was officially "dry." He did so by counting empty bottles in ashcans.
>
> The degree of fear induced by a ghost-story-telling session can be measured by noting the shrinking diameter of a circle of seated children [p. 2].

The advantage of each of these three measures is that it can be obtained without the subjects' awareness of the measurement process. Contrast these measures with reactive measures of the same attributes. If we wanted to measure the interest level of various exhibits at the museum, we could distribute a questionnaire and ask people to rate the exhibits; however, people might respond the way they think they *should* respond, rather than the way they really feel. Undoubtedly, a door-to-door survey of whisky-drinking habits in a dry town would seriously misrepresent the true consumption. Similarly, asking children about their fears would underrepresent true fear, as children generally wish to appear braver than they really are.

It is worth noting, however, that unobtrusive measures are not necessarily free of the validity problem. Tile replacement, for example, might reflect other, irrelevant variables, such as closeness to the museum entrance. Nonetheless, unobtrusive measures do avoid the problem of people responding on the basis of social desirability rather than their true feelings.

Watch for unobtrusive measures in the last five chapters of this book. In a study described in Chapter 11, for example, Schachter, Goldman, and Gordon (1968) wanted to see whether the eating habits of obese and normal people were different. They told subjects that they would be participating in an experiment on the effects of tactile stimulation on taste, and they supplied subjects with various crackers and with rating scales on which to record their judgments of the crackers' saltiness, garlic flavor, and so forth. The subjects were told to taste as many crackers of each type as they wished. Meanwhile, the experimenters counted the number of crackers eaten. Subjects were probably not aware that their total cracker consumption was being measured.

Sensitivity

In addition to being reliable and valid, the dependent variable should also be **sensitive**. A dependent variable is sensitive if a change in the independent variable is mirrored by a change in the dependent variable; a dependent variable is insensitive if we can manipulate the independent variable without any change in the dependent variable.

Two examples of insensitivity are colorfully labeled the *ceiling effect* and the *floor effect*. The **ceiling effect** occurs when a task is so simple that performance remains very high for all levels of the independent variable. In a sense, performance has reached a ceiling, and it can go no higher. I once encountered a ceiling effect when I was trying to measure recall for English words: virtually everyone recalled all the words. The next time around, I wanted to make the task even more difficult so that recall would be poorer. I was too successful, and I encountered a floor effect: very few of the subjects recalled any of the words. The **floor effect** occurs when the task is so difficult that performance remains very low for all levels of the independent variable. A sensitive dependent variable must avoid either of these two extremes, aiming for the region where people perform moderately well.

We have seen that the choice of the dependent variable is a particularly important facet of the search for the truth about behavior. If experimenters choose a dependent variable that is not reliable, that is not valid, or that is not sensitive, they may be misled. Unfortunately, they will draw the wrong conclusion about the factors that influence behavior. Their conclusions will reflect methodological problems in their experiment, rather than reflecting reality.

Multiple Dependent Variables

You know that the dependent variable should be reliable, valid, and sensitive (which sounds like a variation on the Girl Scout Law). However, there is still one problem. Before you start the experiment, often you cannot predict which of your potential dependent variables is the most reliable, valid, and sensitive. One solution to this problem is to use several dependent variables.

For example, in discussing operational definitions, we said that we could measure infants' preferences for various shapes by observing how long the infant looked at each shape. However, researchers might feel uneasy about using that measure as the only index of preference. They might wish to add other dependent variables, such as number of vocalizations, amount of smiling, or changes in body movement.

The choice of appropriate dependent variables is particularly critical in psychology because we are frequently trying to measure psychological reactions we cannot see—reactions such as preference or love or anxiety. Since we cannot measure these covert processes directly, the best we can hope for is a good translation of those covert processes into observable dependent variables. Thus, it is often preferable to use multiple dependent variables, because many translations can give a more complete picture of reality than one translation alone.

ESTABLISHING FUNCTIONAL RELATIONSHIPS

How do we decide whether an independent variable has an influence on the dependent variable—whether there is a functional relationship between the two variables? This process involves comparing the data we have gathered with the hypothesis we have proposed. If the data are consistent with the hypothesis, we say that our data support the hypothesis. If they are inconsistent, we say that they fail to support the hypothesis. It is important to note, incidentally, that if we accept the hypothesis, we do *not* say "The data *prove* that our hypothesis is correct." In psychology, we can never prove that a hypothesis is correct; we can only provide support for a hypothesis. The word *prove* implies that the results will always hold true. In geometry, you can prove that the sum of the interior angles in a triangle is 180°. That is true today, and it will still be true ten years from now. However, if you repeat your psychology experiment ten years from now (or even tomorrow), you may not find the same results that you found today.

To determine whether the results are consistent with the hypothesis, you need to use statistical analysis. Examples of the major statistical tests can be found in the Appendix to this book; for a more detailed introduction to statistics, see Kirk (1978).

Statistical analysis can reveal many different kinds of relationships between the independent variable and the dependent variable (see Figure 1–4). In some cases, a straight line can be used to summarize the relationship, as shown in Examples A and B. In other cases, the relationship may be more complex. In Examples C and D, a curved line summarizes the relationship: for some values of the independent variable, the dependent variable *increases* as the independent variable increases, but for other values of the independent variable, the dependent variable *decreases* as the independent variable increases. Finally, in Example E, there is no readily identifiable relationship between the independent variable and the dependent variable.

It is important to recall, however, that experimenters do not always reach the correct conclusions about whether there is a relationship between the independent and the dependent variables. Psychologists conduct experiments to find out the truth about behavior, but for numerous reasons—such as too few subjects in the experiment or too much variability in the testing conditions—

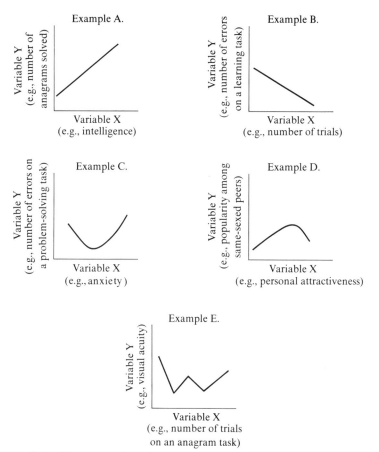

Figure 1-4. Five examples of different kinds of relationships between an independent variable (*x*) and a dependent variable (*y*).

their search for truth is not always successful. Two kinds of incorrect conclusions are known as Type I (or alpha) errors and Type II (or beta) errors (see Table 1–3). When experimenters make a **Type I error**, the data lead them to conclude that a relationship exists when, in fact, there is no relationship. A **Type II error** is just the opposite: experimenters conclude that the data do not support the hypothesized relationship when, in fact, there is a relationship. Understanding the concept of Type I and Type II errors is important as a corrective to the blindly optimistic view that scientists always draw the correct conclusions about patterns in nature.

A discussion of the relationship between the independent and the dependent variables must also include the **law of parsimony**. This scientific law states that "the simplest approach is the best, all other things being equal" (Wilkening, 1973, p. 97). In other words, a simple explanation of the data is better than a more complex explanation. Sometimes, unfortunately, the simplest explanation of the data is that there is no identifiable relationship between the independent and the dependent variables.

Table 1–3. Seeking the truth: four possible outcomes.

The Experimenter Concludes	*The Truth Is*	
	Performance in the control condition equals performance in the experimental condition	Performance in the control condition does *not* equal performance in the experimental condition
Performance in the control condition equals performance in the experimental condition	Experimenter reaches correct conclusion	Type II error
Performance in the control condition does *not* equal performance in the experimental condition	Type I error	Experimenter reaches correct conclusion

MORE COMPLEX EXPERIMENTAL DESIGNS

So far, our discussion of the experimental method has been quite simple. One group of subjects is exposed to a particular variable (for example, another person in the room), and another group of subjects is not (no other person in the room). However, psychology experiments are seldom that simple. The next time you are in the library, pull out a psychology journal and glance through the articles to see what kinds of designs are used in current research. You'll rarely find a single control group and a single experimental group. The purpose of this section is to show you two ways in which more complex experiments can be conducted.

More Than Two Levels of the Independent Variable

One way of making an experiment more complex is to use more than two levels of the independent variable. When we have only two conditions or treatments in our independent variable, we say that we have two levels of that variable. For example, if one group (the experimental group) receives praise while they are learning and another group (the control group) receives no praise, the experiment involves two levels of praise. In the same experiment, however, we might decide to use, say, four conditions: no praise, praise on every 10th response ("low praise"), praise on every 5th response ("moderate praise"), and praise on every response ("high praise"). Experimenters can include as many levels of the independent variable as they choose.

Factorial Designs

All of the experiments we have discussed so far have involved only one independent variable (for example, presence or absence of another person, or amount of praise). In many studies, however, experimenters use two or more independent variables, with each variable represented by two or more levels. This type of study—which typically uses all possible combinations of the levels of the independent variables—is known as a **factorial design**.

Suppose, for example, we are interested in studying the ways in which recall is influenced by two independent variables: praise and sex of subject. If we decide to use only two levels of the praise variable, we end up with four different conditions: (1) praise, female; (2) praise, male; (3) no praise, female; (4) no praise, male. A design with two independent variables can be conveniently represented by a matrix like the one shown in Table 1–4.

Table 1–4. Simple matrix showing mean number of words correctly recalled as a function of condition and sex. (The **mean** is a statistical term calculated by adding all the scores together and dividing the sum by the number of scores.)

Condition	Female	Male	Overall Mean	
Praise	14.2	13.8	14.0	
No praise	11.6	11.8	11.7	
Overall Mean	12.9	12.8		

Naturally, we can have more than two levels for each of our two independent variables. Try making a matrix for an experiment in which your independent variables are age (1, 2, 3, and 4 years old) and setting (home, laboratory, and a familiar daycare center), and the dependent variable is the number of vocalizations in a 10-minute period. Make up some representative numbers to fill the cells of the matrix. Notice that you end up with a total of 12 conditions (4 times 3).

There is no reason to restrict the experimental design to only two independent variables. In reading journal articles, you may find experiments that are quite complex, involving several different variables. Suppose, in the word-recall experiment, we decide to study a total of four variables. In addition to the praise condition and sex of subject, we might also consider characteristics of the stimuli (high-arousal words versus low-arousal words) and characteristics of the praise-giver (formal versus informal). If we use only two levels of each variable, the experiment will include a total of 16 (2^4) conditions. This experiment would be referred to as a $2 \times 2 \times 2 \times 2$ ("2 by 2 by 2 by 2") design because it has two levels for each of four variables.

As you can imagine, it often becomes difficult to keep track of all the conditions when the experiment includes many variables. A two-dimensional matrix works nicely if you have only two variables, but a four-dimensional matrix is hard to imagine! Therefore, it is usually most convenient to represent all the conditions by means of a branching diagram that looks like an upside-down tree, as shown in Figure 1–5. Note that you can identify each of the 16 conditions in this example by tracing along the various branches of the diagram.

For the record, we could easily expand this design to include more than two levels of each variable. A design that included four praise conditions, two

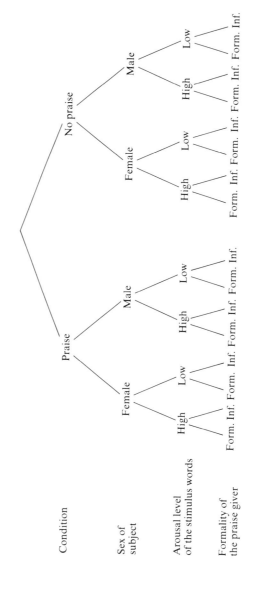

Figure 1-5. Branching diagram representing a hypothetical experiment with four independent variables.

sex-of-subject conditions, four characteristics-of-stimuli conditions, and three characteristics-of-praiser conditions (a $4 \times 2 \times 4 \times 3$ design) would involve a total of 96 different conditions!

In reality, experimental designs seldom become *that* complex. Psychologists don't typically select variables at random, "just to see what happens." More often, they confine themselves to two or three independent variables. By way of example, let me describe briefly an experiment of my own (Matlin, 1975), in which I asked subjects to estimate how often certain words occurred in the English language. In this experiment, I used a total of three variables.

The first variable was the type of instructions. Some subjects received instructions that said they should estimate frequency of usage in terms of how often they, personally, might have seen the words in the last year. Other subjects received instructions that said they should estimate frequency of usage in terms of how often a language expert might have encountered the words in an examination of books and magazines. Thus, there were two levels of the instruction variable. The second variable was the pleasantness of the words they were judging: as established by a separate group of raters, some of the words were pleasant, some were neutral, and some were unpleasant. Thus, there were three levels of the pleasantness variable. The third variable was the true frequency of the words, as established by a word-frequency count that will be discussed in Chapter 8 (Kučera & Francis, 1967). I included seven levels of the frequency variable. Thus, the experiment used a $2 \times 3 \times 7$ design, represented in Figure 1–6.

Why did I choose these three variables? My primary concern was word pleasantness: would people think that pleasant words were more frequent than less pleasant words (even though the objective frequency was equivalent)? It seemed, however, that the answer to this question might depend on the instructions they received. Perhaps people might think that they, personally, saw pleasant words more frequently, but that an "objective" person, such as a language expert, might not. Rather than doing two separate experiments, I simply added another variable to the experiment. Now I could have done the experiment with a large number of equally frequent words. If I found that word pleasantness affected frequency estimates for this particular group of words, however, I wouldn't know whether the effect held true only for words of that frequency, or whether it held true for a wider range of English words. Therefore, I included seven categories of frequency, from very rare words (such as *tacit* and *reverie*) to quite common words (such as *road* and *murder*). I used a wide range of frequencies so that I could establish whether there was **generality** across all frequency categories—that is, whether the effect held true under a wide range of circumstances, rather than being limited to only a small category of stimuli.

After collecting data from a factorial-design experiment, researchers perform a statistical analysis called *analysis of variance* (see Appendix for an overview of analysis of variance with one independent variable; for analysis of variance in factorial-design experiments, consult Kirk, 1968).

One important type of information provided by analysis of variance concerns the main effects. A main effect tells us whether a particular independent

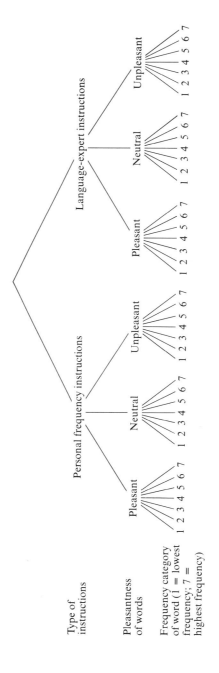

Figure 1-6. Design of an experiment in estimating the frequency of English words.

variable has a simple, overall influence on the dependent variable. It is derived by comparing the means for the dependent variable corresponding to each level of the independent variable. In Table 1–4, for example, we can examine two main effects—one for each of the independent variables. What is the main effect of sex? Overall, the females recalled 12.9 words, and the males recalled 12.8 words: the main effect of sex does not seem to have a significant influence on recall. How about the main effect of praise? Overall, the subjects in the praise condition recalled 14.0 words, and the subjects in the no-praise condition recalled 11.7 words. We cannot be certain without a statistical analysis, but it seems that the main effect of praise does influence recall.

Note that when we examine the main effects, we "collapse" across the levels of the other variables. For example, when we examined the main effect of sex, we averaged together the praise and the no-praise conditions for the females to obtain a mean of 12.9. The same process for the males yielded a mean of 12.8. In examining the main effect of sex, we asked, "Forgetting about the fact that each of the sexes was split into two conditions, is there any overall tendency for males to differ from females?"

In addition to the main effects for each independent variable, analysis of variance in a factorial-design experiment provides information concerning interactions between independent variables. This is one of the advantages of a factorial design and will be discussed in some detail.

Interactions between Independent Variables

Let's suppose that our experiment involves a 2 × 2 design, which means that we have two conditions for each of two independent variables: sex (male and female) and age (8 years old and 16 years old). The dependent variable is some measure of achievement motivation (the tendency to seek success in achievement situations). Suppose that we measure the average achievement-motivation score for each of the four groups of subjects and obtain the data shown in Figure 1–7.

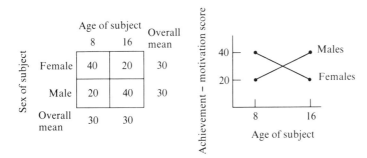

Figure 1-7. Results of a hypothetical experiment in which there is an interaction.

What do these data show? First, let's look at the main effects. Is the main effect of sex significant here? It isn't in these data, because the overall mean for females is 30, and the overall mean for males is also 30. Is the main effect of age significant? Again, it is not, because the overall mean for 8-year-olds is 30, and the overall mean for 16-year-olds is 30.

Do we conclude, therefore, that nothing interesting is happening in our data? No, because it looks as though females get *lower* scores as they grow older, whereas males get *higher* scores as they grow older. Although there are no significant main effects in these data, there is a significant *interaction*. An **interaction** means that a variable has different effects on different conditions. In the female condition, higher age is associated with lower achievement motivation; in the male condition, higher age is associated with higher achievement motivation. Thus, the variable of age has different effects for the two sexes.

If the variable of age had the *same* effect for males and for females, then the data might be as shown in Figure 1–8. In this case, we say that there is no interaction. (Note, however, that here the main effects of sex and age both appear to be significant.)

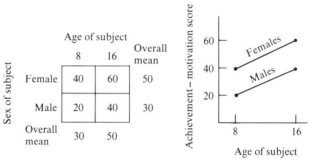

Figure 1-8. Results of a hypothetical experiment in which there is *no* interaction.

An interaction shows up when a variable improves performance in one condition but worsens performance in another condition. An interaction also shows up when a variable changes performance in one condition (whether for better or worse) but has no effect on the other conditions. The important thing to notice is whether the effect is *different* for the two conditions.

A factorial analysis of variance must be performed to determine whether an interaction is statistically significant. Informally, however, you can get a general indication of the presence or absence of an interaction by looking at a graph of the data. If the lines for the two conditions are parallel, (as in Figure 1–8), there is no interaction: the variable has the same effect on the different conditions. If the lines are not parallel, the difference in their slopes suggests a different effect for the two conditions—in other words, an interaction. In Figure 1–7, this difference is particularly striking because one slope is positive and the other negative. Figure 1-9 shows examples of graphs in which there is no interaction.

As noted earlier, an interaction can also show up when a variable changes performance in one condition and has no effect on the other condition. An example of this kind of interaction appears in Figure 1–10. In this study, the

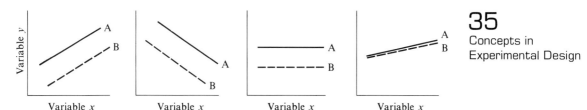

Figure 1-9. Examples of graphs in which there is no interaction. In all of these examples, the lines representing the two conditions are parallel.

experimenters have arranged for a male student (a **confederate,** or person paid to help in the experiment) to be waiting on a bench when a "real" subject arrives for the experiment. A conspicuous sign reads "Please have a seat." When the subject sits down on the bench, the experimenters note how far the subject is sitting from the confederate. There are two independent variables in this experiment: sex of subject (male and female) and attractiveness of male confederate (attractive and unattractive). The results show that attractiveness of the confederate *does* have an effect when the subjects are female, but does *not* have an effect when the subjects are male. There is an interaction: the attractiveness-of-confederate variable has different effects on the different sexes.

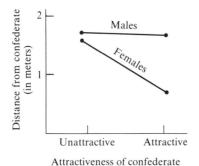

Figure 1-10. Distance that males and females sit from an unattractive or attractive male confederate: a two-way interaction.

Interactions do not need to be confined to simple 2 × 2 designs. We can have interactions for data in which there are more than two levels of the independent variable. For example, Figure 1–11 shows part of the results for the word-frequency experiment discussed earlier. Subjects in both conditions gave lower frequency estimates for neutral words (such as *road*) than for pleasant words (such as *sunshine*) or unpleasant words (such as *murder*). However, notice that this tendency is much more marked for subjects in the personal-instructions condition than for subjects in the language-expert-instructions condition. Subjects are reasonably confident that they personally encounter neutral words less frequently, but they are more objective in supplying estimates for the "language expert." Thus, the two V-shaped curves are not parallel.

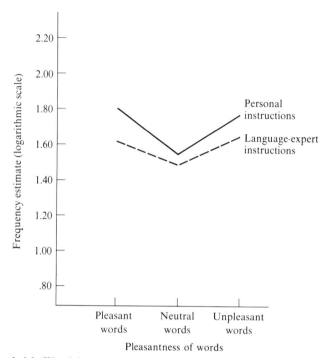

Figure 1-11. Word-frequency estimates for pleasant, neutral, and unpleasant words, as a function of two kinds of instructions: a two-way interaction.

So far, we have been discussing two-way interactions involving only two independent variables, but higher-order interactions—three-way or even four-way—are also possible. Let's consider an example of a three-way interaction. Suppose we add a third variable to the sitting-next-to-the-confederate experiment. In addition to attractiveness of the confederate and sex of the subject, we will also include age of the subject as a variable, contrasting college-age subjects with elderly subjects. The results might be as shown in Figure 1-12.

Three-way interactions are sometimes complex to describe; let's give it a try. Here we see that sex and attractiveness interact for young subjects, but not

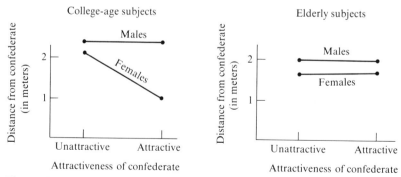

Figure 1-12. Distance that males and females sit from an unattractive or attractive confederate, as a function of subjects' age: a three-way interaction.

for elderly subjects. Notice that for college-age subjects, females react differently from males to the attractiveness of a male confederate. For elderly subjects, however, females and males are similarly unaffected by the attractiveness of the confederate. In actual studies, researchers are sometimes unable to find a clear pattern that can explain why a three-way interaction showed up in their data. Statements such as "No clear explanation for the three-way interaction could be discovered" sometimes appear in journal articles.

In the last five chapters of the book, we will frequently pause to point out an interaction. Often, there will be a graph to show you more vividly how the interaction works. You might glance through these last chapters now, looking for examples of interactions. Pay particular attention to the beginning section of Chapter 11.

Interactions are important because psychology is a subtle science. Often, we do not find simple, main effects. A variable may have one kind of effect on one condition and another kind of effect on another condition. Part of the challenge of research in psychology comes from trying to find reasons for these kinds of apparent inconsistencies.

SUMMARY

1. The naturalistic-observation method involves the careful observation of behavior in a natural setting. The observer tries to record normal activities without interfering.
2. In the survey method, the researcher selects a group of people and asks them questions.
3. The correlational method is used to determine if two measures are related. It cannot establish which measure is the cause and which is the effect.
4. The case-study method involves an in-depth study of one person, typically stressing how this person differs from other people.
5. The experimental method manipulates variables systematically and uses operational definitions to specify how the variables will be measured.
6. A hypothesis is a statement of what we expect to happen if certain conditions are true.
7. The independent variable concerns the conditions that the experimenter manipulates; the dependent variable concerns the responses that the subject gives.
8. There are four kinds of independent variables: stimulus characteristics, environmental characteristics, manipulated subject differences, and subject characteristics. Only the first three categories are used in "true experiments," because subject differences cannot really be manipulated.
9. The dependent variable should be reliable, valid, and sensitive.
10. Psychologists typically use designs more complex than the classic two-group design. They can test more than two levels of the independent variable, and they can use factorial designs, in which they examine two or more independent variables.
11. Factorial designs allow us to study interactions as well as main effects. In an interaction, a variable has different effects on different conditions.

2

Performing and Reporting the Experiment

OUTLINE

The purpose of Chapter 1 was to acquaint you with the general concepts and principles of experimental psychology. We discussed the basic design of psychology experiments, and we considered the general attributes of "good" experiments.

Chapter 2 is a "how to" chapter—practical and "nitty-gritty." If you were going to perform an experiment and write it up, how would you proceed? We will consider the steps in chronological order, from finding an idea for an experiment to writing a summary of the experiment. In the last portion of the chapter, I'll describe an actual experiment, as a concrete example of the way research might proceed.

DERIVING THE HYPOTHESIS

Suppose you sat down in your experimental-psychology class next Tuesday, and the professor told you to find your own hypothesis that could be tested in a psychology experiment. How would you find an idea, and how would you turn that idea into an experiment? Let's consider these first two steps in the sequence of performing a psychology experiment.

Finding the Idea for an Experiment

Let's look at five sources of ideas for psychology experiments: observation, past research, theory, curiosity, and applied problems. It is important to note, however, that these categories are not mutually exclusive: an idea may easily be inspired by two or more of these sources.

Observation. By now, you have had perhaps 20 years of experience in observing human behavior. Do not underestimate the value of this experience as a rich source of ideas for experiments!

Once a year, I teach a course in Psychology of Women, for which a research project is required. I specify, to the students' horror, that this means "go out and look at some aspect of behavior" and not "go look it up in the library." Every year, several students sit mournfully in my office complaining that they don't have any ideas for their project. The experience is frustrating for me, too, because I *know* they have ideas; they are simply reluctant to acknowledge that any of these informal ideas can be nurtured into something that has this incredibly formal name—a hypothesis. In their 20 years of experience as human beings, these students have made numerous informal observations about differences in the behavior of men and women, and most of these observations could be tested in an experiment. Generally, after about five minutes of coaxing, students will admit that they do have an idea, though they don't think it is very good. In all likelihood, the idea *is* a good one, and it can be transformed into a hypothesis. This year, for example, a few of the ideas studied were: (1) Do women stand closer to other women than men stand to other men? (The student thought of this idea when she looked at people in a crowd.) (2) Do women look for different qualities in a spouse than men do?

(The student thought of this idea in a late-night talk with her roommate.) (3) Do women hold fewer offices in student government than men do? (The student thought of this idea as she looked around a student council meeting at her predominantly female college.)

Students often assume that any idea they find through informal observation has already been tested many times. Although this is frequently the case, there are exceptions. For example, there is an informal observation captured by the popular saying "Time goes more quickly when you're having lots of fun." It seems that there are no studies in the published literature that directly test this hypothesis!

Chapter 1 mentioned that the naturalistic-observation method frequently produces ideas that can be tested more formally in a later experiment. Thus, formal observation, as well as informal observation, can be a source of hypotheses. Harry Harlow (1957), whose research on motherless monkeys may be familiar to you, has described how observation can gradually change into experimentation:

> At the present time, for example, we are interested in tracing the development of various patterns of emotional behavior in the rhesus monkey. We began by looking for response patterns which might fit into this rather broad category and noting the kinds of situations which elicited such behavior. But this observational study, like almost any observational study, is gradually taking on the characteristics of an experiment. As we gain sophistication about the monkey's emotional responses, we become more selective in the patterns which we observe, and we define our various dependent variables with increasing precision in the expectation of getting increased reliability. We learn what independent variables might be profitably exploited and gradually arrive at crude scales for quantifying these variables. We know at this point that we are using the experimental method, but we are not sure at exactly what stage the transition occurred p. 490 .

Past research. Psychologists probably derive most of their ideas from previous research, either their own or research that has been reported by others. This is one reason why the first research project frequently seems the hardest, and later research ideas come more quickly: once you try one experiment, that experiment suggests many others.

B. F. Skinner (1956) wrote an interesting paper that describes the way his own research frequently suggested other hypotheses. For example, when his apparatus for delivering food reinforcement broke down, Skinner discovered the principle of extinction. Without reinforcement, the rats responded less and eventually stopped responding altogether. At first, Skinner treated this as a defect, and quickly fixed the apparatus. In later research, however, he deliberately stopped the reinforcement and examined extinction more formally. Similarly, on another occasion, Skinner was busily making little food pellets to be delivered as reinforcement to his rats. It was a beautiful afternoon, and he had just calculated that the supply of pellets would be exhausted by Monday unless he spent all afternoon and evening making pellets. At that point, he asked himself why *every* press of the lever had to be reinforced. He decided to supply only one pellet every minute, and he found that the response rate remained high and stable. The principle of periodic reinforcement was thus discovered quite by accident, in the process of conducting other research. In later experiments, he studied the principle more formally.

Let's discuss three ways in which previous research can suggest ideas for research. One way is a *replication experiment*. A **replication** is a repetition of an experiment that has already been performed. The purpose of a replication is to test the reliability of the earlier results. A perfect replication would try to use an identical subject population, identical equipment, and identical surroundings. If a replication is successful in obtaining the same results as the original experiment, we can be reasonably confident that those earlier results were not simply a fluke.

Psychologists seldom perform replication experiments that are exact duplications of earlier experiments. One practical reason for this avoidance of replication experiments is that psychology journals are reluctant to publish studies that are exact replications, with no new variables or new strategies added. Some psychologists have argued, however, that replications should be performed and published more often. If this happened, they argue, we could be more certain that our results are reliable before they are accepted as "fact." To answer this plea, the Journal Supplement Abstract Service of the American Psychological Association welcomes well-designed replication experiments in its publication, *Catalog of Selected Documents in Psychology*.

Another way in which previous research can suggest ideas for research is through *contradictory results*. A psychologist, in reviewing the literature in an area of interest, may find that some studies show one kind of result, whereas other studies show precisely the opposite. These contradictory results may suggest a hypothesis. Perhaps the nature of the results depends on which operational definition the experimenter chooses for the dependent variable, or perhaps there is an interaction, with the independent variable influencing behavior in different ways for different conditions.

Still another way in which previous research can suggest ideas for research is through *extending the range* of the study. If a particular effect has been demonstrated by one researcher, another researcher may want to test the generality of these findings. Will the effect hold true for another kind of subject? Will it hold true for another kind of stimulus, or another kind of environment, or another kind of instructions? Recall our discussion of the different kinds of independent variables in Chapter 1. That list can also serve as a source of ideas for variables that can be changed when experimenters want to extend the generality of previous findings. Thus, experimenters can extend the range of a study by varying the experimental conditions.

Experimenters can also extend the range of a study by extending the levels of the independent variable. Will the effect hold true when more extreme levels of the independent variable are used? In one study, for example, Zajonc (1968b) found that the more often people saw an item, the better they liked it. His results showed that people who saw a long nonsense word 25 times liked it better than if they had seen it only once or twice. Now, wouldn't you imagine that there would be some limit to this effect? Zajonc, Crandall, Kail, and Swap (1974) extended the limits on this earlier study by presenting stimuli as frequently as 243 times. To everyone's surprise, these very frequent items were still liked best. When researchers extend the levels of the independent variables, we say that they are looking for **boundary conditions,** or borderlines within which an effect holds true.

Theory. Another common source of ideas for hypotheses is a theory of interest to the experimenter. The term **theory,** according to Marx (1963), has several different meanings, but the most common one seems to be "a group of logically organized . . . laws" (p. 9). Generally, then, a theory is broader in scope than a single law. More details on the use of theories can be found in a book by D. W. Martin (1977).

Several portions of the last five chapters of this book discuss research that is designed to test theories. For example, the theory of achievement motivation, discussed in Chapter 11, makes several predictions about the relationship between achievement motivation and variables such as task difficulty, and researchers have designed experiments to test these hypotheses. Chapter 8, on memory and verbal learning, is organized according to the theory that memory processes are different for items that are to be stored for a few seconds than for items that are to be stored for long periods of time. An alternative theory proposes, however, that memory duration is irrelevant—it doesn't matter how long an item is to be stored. Part of Chapter 8 discusses the experiments that have been conducted to support one theory or the other.

Sometimes the theory takes the form of a model. A **model** is a set of ideas borrowed from another area—such as computer systems—to demonstrate how humans or animals might operate. In Chapter 9, on psycholinguistics, we will examine the search for a model to describe the way people store sentences in memory.

The researcher who finds ideas for experiments from theories typically also is influenced by past research; as I said, the sources of ideas are not mutually exclusive.

Curiosity. Let's not underestimate the power of curiosity as an inspiration for research ideas. Psychologists often are interested in a particular independent variable, and they are curious to see what kind of behavior that variable might influence. For example, I was once interested in word length as a variable, and so I tried to determine whether word length was related to short-term memory (Matlin, 1976). Other psychologists are interested in a particular behavior, and they are curious to find independent variables that might influence that behavior. A colleague of mine was interested in personal space, or the distance between two standing people, and so she decided to see whether independent variables such as sex and anxiety were related to personal space (Gawron, 1977). Research in the "curiosity" category is generally **nontheoretical**—not guided by a particular theory.

Applied problems. Frequently, research is inspired by a real-life problem that needs to be solved. Contemporary problems in areas such as mental health, peace studies, and education are being tackled by psychologists. The relatively greater interest in applied problems is reflected in the amount of money spent on research in this area. Between 1967 and 1977, the amount of money (adjusted for inflation) spent on applied research increased about 2%; during the same period, the amount of money spent on basic research declined about 35% (R.C. Atkinson, 1977).

Many psychologists who are well known for their basic research have become prominent in the area of applied research. For example, George Miller, whose work on the limitations of memory we will consider in Chapter 8, proclaimed in 1969:

> In the years immediately ahead we must not only extend ourselves and deepen our understanding of mental and behavioral phenomena, but we must somehow incorporate our hard-won knowledge more effectively into the vast social changes we all know are coming [p. 1063].

Donald Broadbent, who likewise conducted basic research in human memory, has also worked on specific applied problems—including where the control knobs should be placed in airplanes and whether English people would make fewer mistakes with dollars and cents than with pounds, shillings, and pence (Evans, 1977). Finally, B.F. Skinner, whose basic research on reinforcement principles was discussed earlier in this chapter, is well known for his development of teaching machines.

Systematic versus nonsystematic approaches. Whether your principal source is observation, theory, or applied problems, is it best to be systematic in the search for new research ideas? There is no simple answer to this question. Certainly, the stereotype of the research process is that a psychologist sits down, freshly sharpened pencil in hand, to design a hypothesis based on previous research. However, this systematic approach is only one style. The other approach, perhaps just as common, is what Lyons (1965) calls the "semiplanned accident." Skinner's discovery of the principles of extinction and periodic reinforcement certainly qualify as "semiplanned accidents." In fact, Skinner (1956) has summarized this strategy in a research principle of his own: "When you run onto something interesting, drop everything else and study it" (p. 223).

A group of prominent psychologists met in 1959 to discuss how graduate students should be trained to do research in psychology. They began by describing the stereotype of the systematic researcher:

> Crucial experiments growing out of previous findings, elaborated by self-conscious and prescient genius, are performed with great precision. The results are subjected to the closest scrutiny. . . . Finally the now confirmed discovery is inserted in a systematized lattice of already available knowledge to complete for posterity a forward step, however small, toward man's mastery of the unknown [Taylor et al., 1959, p. 169].

In reality, however, they concluded, researchers are typically much less systematic:

Actually, the process of doing research . . . is a rather informal, often illogical and sometimes messy-looking affair. It includes a great deal of floundering around in the empirical world, sometimes dignified by names like "pilot studies" and "exploratory research." Somewhere and somehow in the process of floundering, the research worker will get an idea. In fact, he will get many ideas. On largely intuitive grounds he will reject most of his ideas and will accept others as the basis for extended work [p. 169].

Clearly, this second approach is the more difficult to describe. It is also certainly the more difficult to try to teach to beginning researchers. Consequently, Taylor et al. conclude that future researchers can learn best in "apprenticeships" in which they can watch and participate in ongoing research. Lacking such an opportunity, beginning researchers might well begin by gathering research ideas systematically, being flexible enough to set these ideas aside if other ideas look far more interesting. A book edited by Siegel and Zeigler (1976) gives some additional hints for less systematic strategies in obtaining research ideas. In that book, some prominent psychologists describe how they do research and how the direction of that research often changes.

Turning an Idea into a Hypothesis

For an idea to achieve the formality of a hypothesis, it must be *testable*. You might be gazing at your sleeping cat and wonder idly whether, if your cat drank a gin-and-tonic, it would be more likely to dream about mice. Now this idea is interesting. It can also be stated in hypothesis form: *If* a cat ingests a gin-and-tonic, *then* it is more likely to dream about mice. However, the idea is not testable, given the current state of the art on animal dreams. Testability, according to Marx (1963), is one of the most important characteristics of a hypothesis.

Other ideas may be testable, but not *practical*. For example, you might have an idea that six years of one-to-one training on a daily basis, four hours a day, will substantially raise the IQs of mentally retarded children. While that version of the research idea is not practical, the idea could be tested in a modified form.

After determining that your idea is both testable and practical, you can state the idea in hypothesis form—a form that specifies the relationship you expect to find between your independent and dependent variables. The challenge comes in translating the variables into operational definitions; we will discuss this process in later sections.

REVIEWING THE LITERATURE

In the previous section, we talked about past research as a source of new ideas for experiments. Often, then, a review of the literature is one good way to derive hypotheses. Many times, however, the hypothesis occurs first, particularly when the hypothesis is inspired by informal observation or curiosity. In that case, the psychologist still must examine the psychology journals and books to see whether similar studies have already been done. The number of psychology journals is astounding; there is clearly an "information explosion" here!

Unfortunately, there is a good chance that the experiment you have in mind has already been done. One of the bleakest moments in my career as a psychologist concerned the word-frequency-estimation experiment described in the first chapter. I had conscientiously spent days searching through the literature in this area and had concluded that the relationship between pleasantness and estimated frequency had not been examined in English words. Accordingly, I spent months conducting the study and analyzing the data. Imagine, then, my distress when I was working on another project and found an article titled "Values and Estimation of Word Frequency" by Milburn and Bell (1972), a study reasonably similar to my own. Obviously, even my conscientious search had not been careful enough!

Typically, the purpose of a literature review is not simply to see whether a study has been conducted before. More often, a literature review uncovers similar studies that may clarify theoretical issues and provide ideas on techniques that you might use. In short, a literature review provides an overview of knowledge about a research area.

The first step in a psychology literature review is to consult *Psychological Abstracts*. This valuable periodical summarizes articles from hundreds of journals in psychology and other related fields. Most of the journals are from the United States, but you will also notice journals from other English-speaking countries as well as translations of abstracts from foreign-language journals.

Psychological Abstracts is published once a month, and each issue contains an index of authors and subject areas. A complete index of authors and subjects is published every six months, and it is easier to use these volumes than to look through the many individual indexes. In addition, a cumulative index appears approximately every three years, and this larger index is an even more efficient tool for wading through the years of research on a topic.

Psychological Abstracts is somewhat difficult to use, but it is essential for anyone doing research to grapple with this resource. Generally, you find the "subject index" volumes and search for your topic. The title of each relevant study will be listed, together with a number. The number refers to an entry in another volume. When you look up this entry, you will find a listing of the authors, their institution, the title of the article, the exact citation for the journal in which it appeared, and a summary of the article. Here is an example:

12361. **Horowitz, Leonard M. et al.** (Stanford U) **On the identification of warded-off mental contents: An empirical and methodological contribution.** *Journal of Abnormal Psychology*, 1975(Oct), Vol. 84(5), 545–558.—The basic assumption behind psychoanalytic psychotherapy is that mental contents that were once warded off come to emerge in the course of a successful treatment. This paper focuses on specific contents which a male patient in his mid-20's became aware of during a psychoanalytic treatment. Study 1 describes the method for identifying warded-off contents: Themes were identified that emerged for the 1st time between Hours 41 and 100; then 20 clinicians read the process notes of the 1st 10 hrs of treatment and judged which of the newly emerging themes had previously been warded off. The judges' ratings were highly reliable and case specific. Studies 2 and 3 validated the ratings (a) by assessing the patient's discomfort when warded-off themes emerged and (b) by examining relevant changes in the patient's memories of early events. Finally, Study 4 explored certain conditions involving the patient-therapist interaction that facilitate the emergence of warded-off contents. (22 ref)—*Journal abstract.*

If the abstract seems relevant, look for the article. Even if this particular article isn't helpful, it will contain a bibliography, and some of the articles listed there could be useful.

Some libraries also have another extremely valuable resource: *Science Citation Index* and *Social Sciences Citation Index*. Psychology takes up only a small portion of the (literally) millions of citations in these indexes, but this resource can perform a service for you that *Psychological Abstracts* lacks. If you have found a journal article that is particularly relevant, you may want to see whether anyone else has done related research since that article was published. The *Citation Indexes* will list all articles that cite your article in their bibliographies. If these later articles have cited your article, they will probably be relevant for your research. The Citation Indexes are quite easy to use and are generally accompanied by instruction sheets.

In many cases, however, your hypothesis is rather vague, and it seems premature to plunge into *Psychological Abstracts* until the topic is more specific. A useful resource in this dilemma is *Annual Review of Psychology,* a series that is typically shelved with the psychology books in the library. One volume of this resource has been published every year since 1950, and each volume contains many topics that are intermediate in specificity—such as Developmental Psychology, The Sense of Smell, Scaling, and Psychology of Women—covering a period of several years in the psychology literature. In addition, two journals, *Psychological Review* and *Psychological Bulletin,* contain reviews of the literature in more specific areas—for example, ''The Socialization of Achievement Orientation in Females'' (Stein & Bailey, 1973). In using these three resources, however, keep in mind that the reviews may be selective, and many relevant studies may have been excluded.

You may also want to search for relevant books. A search through the library card catalog may help you locate several books that could be useful. However, keep in mind that books are unlikely to provide a complete review of the recent literature; for that, you'll need to master *Psychological Abstracts.*

Another good way of finding out the most recent work in a specific area is to write to an ''expert.'' If your research involves an extension of the work of someone else, you should write to that person. He or she is likely to be doing further work in this area, or to know whom else you should contact. While it is an imposition to exploit ''big name'' psychologists by asking them to do a literature review for you, a psychologist in your specific area of research will probably be interested in your project.

One final recourse is one that is not really recommended: searching through the back volumes of likely journals. Chances are that this will be far less efficient. However, there is a slight possibility that you might find a relevant article, and this article can lead you to other articles. It's back to that old familiar chorus again: to make a complete review of the literature, you'll need to master *Psychological Abstracts*.

Once you have your idea and have completed the literature search, you can begin to design your experiment. Let's begin by looking at the independent and dependent variables.

THE INDEPENDENT VARIABLE

Here we will discuss the details of several problems that concern the independent variable—the variable that the experimenter manipulates. We will begin with the selection of levels for the independent variable; later we will discuss between-subjects, within-subjects, and matched-subjects manipulations of the independent variable.

Selection of Levels for the Independent Variable

In Chapter 1, we discussed the importance of translating a variable into an operational definition—a definition that forces psychologists to state precisely what operations they will perform in order to measure the variable. Fortunately, the operational definition for the independent variable generally causes fewer problems than the operational definition for the dependent variable.

A bigger problem is the selection of levels for the independent variable. How many levels should be selected, and what should be the values for the levels? In Chapter 1, we saw that psychologists often study more than two levels of the independent variable. For example, rather than studying simply a "praise" and a "no praise" condition, the psychologist might examine four conditions—"high praise," "moderate praise," "low praise," and "no praise." One reason why we usually avoid using only two levels is that with two levels, we obtain only two points on a graph. Although it may be tempting to draw a straight line between those two points, we cannot be confident that a straight line reflects the true relationship between our variables.

Let's imagine that four psychologists want to study the relationship between anxiety and performance on a problem-solving task, manipulating anxiety by varying the instructions. Let's suppose that each psychologist decides to study only two levels of anxiety and that the psychologists differ in terms of the amount of anxiety they produce in their "high anxiety" or "low anxiety" conditions. For example, Psychologist A might produce rather low anxiety in both groups, whereas Psychologist B might produce rather high anxiety in both groups. Suppose that all four psychologists perform the experiment and plot their two points on graphs. Then each one—inappropriately—connects the two points with a straight line, as shown in Figure 2-1.

Psychologist A concludes there is a strong, positive relationship between anxiety and performance: the more anxiety, the better the performance. Psychologist B concludes that there is a strong, negative relationship between anxiety and performance: the more anxiety, the poorer the performance. Psy-

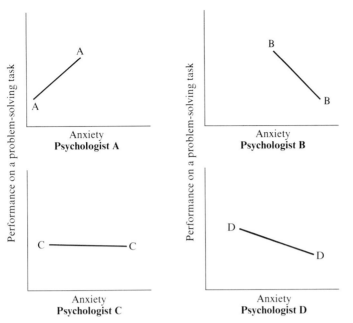

Figure 2-1. Hypothetical results of an experiment on the relationship between anxiety and performance, as conducted by four different psychologists, each using only two levels of anxiety.

chologist C concludes that there is no relationship between anxiety and performance. Psychologist D concludes that there is a weak, negative relationship between anxiety and performance.

The point is clear: with only two points, you can't get the "big picture" of reality. In fact, if we were to collect the observations of all four psychologists and make a composite graph, based on all eight data points, it would look like Figure 2-2. This example of a distorted picture of reality is like the children's fable about three blind men examining an elephant. The first man, touching the leg, is convinced that it is a tree. The second man, feeling the trunk, insists that it is a huge snake. The third man, grasping the tail, protests that it is a rope. Whether the object is an elephant or an independent variable, the best way to get a good picture of reality is to try many different viewpoints.

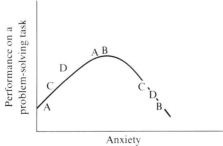

Figure 2-2. Composite graph of results of four different experiments illustrated in Figure 2-1.

At the same time that you are deciding on the number of levels of the independent variable, you must also decide on the range of the independent variable. How far apart should the levels be? The answer to this question involves finding the "golden mean" between insufficient separation of the levels and too much separation of the levels.

On the one hand, you do not want to select levels that are extremely close together. A researcher investigating the relationship between anxiety and performance illustrated in Figure 2-2, for example, would be unwise to choose two levels of anxiety that are so close together that they correspond to only a few millimeters difference on the graph. There is no portion of that curve for which such a small difference in the independent variable could have a significant influence on the dependent variable. According to this rule of **sufficient separation,** you should choose values of the independent variable that are reasonably far apart. (Naturally, what is "reasonable" depends on the experiment and may have to be discovered by trial and error.)

Psychologists sometimes ignore this rule of sufficient separation. In studies concerning the effects of word pleasantness on memory, for example, researchers typically select words that are pleasant, neutral, and unpleasant. However, some people have selected the words—perhaps by accident—so that the unpleasant words are really only mildly unpleasant (such as "swamp") and the pleasant words are really only mildly pleasant (such as "house"). When the experiment is performed, it appears that pleasantness has no influence on memory. However, if they had selected truly unpleasant words (such as "murder") and truly pleasant words (such as "happy"), then a difference would probably have emerged. Figure 2-3 shows how the rule of adequate

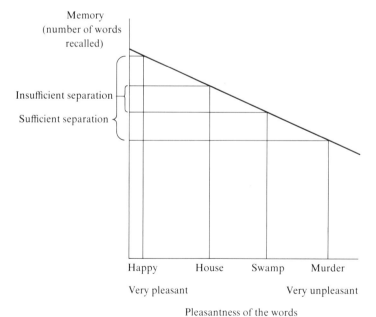

Figure 2-3. Hypothetical relationship between the pleasantness of words and memory.

separation can be applied to the hypothetical relationship between pleasantness and memory.

The problem of sufficient separation is a problem particularly for researchers in personality and social psychology, who frequently seek to manipulate an independent variable that is covert—it cannot be seen. For example, a team of psychologists may wish to examine whether anxiety influences some dependent variable—say, the desire to wait with other people rather than alone. The independent variable to be manipulated is anxiety. Suppose their results show that people in the condition called "high anxiety" were no more likely to prefer waiting with others than people in the condition called "low anxiety." It is possible that the experiment did not show the desired effect because the manipulation of anxiety was really ineffective—that is, the two groups did not truly differ from each other in anxiety. For this reason, psychologists sometimes make a **manipulation check**—an assessment of the independent variable, made during or immediately after the experiment, to determine whether the manipulation of the independent variable was successful. These checks are used to determine whether groups that *should* be different from each other really *are* different. Most often, manipulation checks take the form of rating scales (which we will consider in Chapter 5). For example, the researchers might ask a number of questions such as "How anxious did you feel after you heard the instructions?" and "How nervous did you feel about what would happen next?" Subjects are asked to respond using scales with the endpoints labeled "Very much" and "Not at all." If the responses of the high-anxiety group differ significantly from the responses of the low-anxiety group, the researchers can be confident that they have produced sufficient separation between their two groups.

We have seen that psychologists must be concerned about sufficient separation. On the other hand, it is sometimes a mistake to have *too* much separation between the levels of the independent variable. You want the levels to be within the normal range of human experience. For example, if you wanted to study the effects of room temperature on motivation, it would be a mistake to choose only two levels, such as $-5°C$ and $50°C$. The below-freezing temperature would cause subjects to ignore the motivation task and curl up tightly to conserve their body heat (or else to leave the experiment), and this is probably not an aspect of temperature that we would find interesting. More moderate temperatures, perhaps between $10°C$ and $40°C$, would be better values to study. Also, there are ethical problems with extreme values, which we will consider in Chapter 4. In summary, try to select levels of the independent variable that are far enough apart to influence the dependent variable, but not so far apart that they fall outside the realm of normal human experience.

In some cases, our concern with the independent variable is finished as soon as we have selected the levels of the variable. For example, if we are studying the Müller-Lyer illusion (see the illustration in Figure 7-17) and our independent variable is the angle of the arrowhead, the selection of angles of $30°$, $45°$, and $60°$ identifies exactly what our stimuli will be. In many other cases, however, we must then select the specific stimuli that will represent each level of the independent variable. For example, in the study described in Chapter 1 on word-frequency estimation (Matlin, 1975), I needed to select a number of pleasant, neutral, and unpleasant words for each frequency level. It would have been a serious mistake to select, for example, only the word *reverie* to represent the pleasant, least frequent words. It would be just as difficult to generalize from the results of a single word as it would be to generalize from the results of a single subject. Instead, ten words were selected for each category. For the pleasant, least frequent category, for example, the words were: *deity, admires, humour, nourishing, truthful, beatific, charisma, lovingly, reverie,* and *gardenia*.

The selection of a number of stimuli to represent each level of the independent variable is called **stimulus sampling.** The object of stimulus sampling is to obtain an unbiased selection of stimuli of a specified kind. In this context, unbiased means that the stimuli are selected either at random or according to an objective (rather than subjective) system. Stimulus sampling is most effective if an adequate number of stimuli are selected for each level of the independent variable.

It sounds obvious that researchers should choose a substantial number of stimuli to represent each level. However, this rule is often violated. For example, a study on word associations tested the hypothesis that the word associations to pleasant words are more closely related to each other than are the word associations to unpleasant words. Unfortunately, the researcher tested only one pleasant word and one unpleasant word. The results of that study are of extremely limited usefulness because it would be ridiculous to claim that the pleasant word was representative of all pleasant words and the unpleasant word was representative of all unpleasant words. The moral of the story is to select a reasonable number of stimuli for each level of the independent variable. What is ''reasonable'' will depend on the availability of stimuli and the desired length of the experiment, but you might aim for 10–20 if you are dealing with stimuli such as English words.

Between-Subjects and Within-Subjects Designs

Remember the experiment in which subjects learn words either with another person present or alone? That independent variable, presence of another person, can be manipulated either between subjects or within subjects. In a **between-subjects design,** one group of subjects learns words with another person present, and an entirely different group of subjects learns words alone. It is important to notice that the subjects do *not* ever switch conditions and serve in the other condition. In a **within-subjects design,** the same group of subjects serve in *both* conditions: sometimes they learn with another person present, and sometimes they learn alone. These two basic designs are represented in Table 2-1. Between-subjects designs are also called **between-group** or **independent-group designs.** Within-subjects designs are also called **within-group** or **repeated-measures designs.**

Table 2-1. Examples of between-subjects and within-subjects designs for a hypothetical experiment in which a subject learns a list of words either alone or with another person present.

Experimental Condition (Another person present)	Control Condition (Subject learns alone)
Joe Simpson	Karen White
Mary Rogers	Harold Anderson
Susan Smith	Sarah Long
Andy Weiss	Elizabeth Douglas
Nancy Tomlin	Sam Baker
Bill Jones	Arnold Major

a. Between-subjects design, with six different subjects in each group.

Experimental Condition (Another person present)	Control Condition (Subject learns alone)
Joe Simpson	Joe Simpson
Mary Rogers	Mary Rogers
Susan Smith	Susan Smith
Andy Weiss	Andy Weiss
Nancy Tomlin	Nancy Tomlin
Bill Jones	Bill Jones

b. Within-subjects design, with all six subjects serving in each condition.

Quite clearly, the decision to choose a between-subjects or a within-subjects design influences the whole structure of the experiment. That decision will also influence the kind of confounding variables you must be concerned about, as we will see later in the chapter. How do you decide which type of design to use? The decision rests on a careful consideration of the advantages and disadvantages of the two designs in light of your particular experiment.

Advantages and disadvantages. Let's approach this problem by discussing the advantages and disadvantages of the within-subjects design. First, let's consider the advantages:

1. You don't need as many subjects for a within-subjects design, because you obtain several measures from each subject. Thus, the within-subjects design may save time and subject resources. This may be an important consideration if the instructions and training period are lengthy; then it seems a pity to go through perhaps half an hour of preparation to obtain one single measure, as you would in a between-subjects design. Also, the number of possible subjects may be limited. For example, if you want to study blind students or patients with a particular syndrome, there may not be enough subjects to divide them into separate groups. In experimental-psychology labs, students generally serve as subjects, and an enrollment of fewer than 40 students sometimes forces the instructor to use a within-subjects design in the experiments.

2. Stages of practice can best be studied in a within-subjects design. Suppose you would like to study how subjects learn a list of English words, and you decide to examine ten learning trials. On each trial, subjects see the list and then try to recall the words. It is by far the most efficient to study a single group of subjects and to record the number of words they recall on every trial. You *could* do a between-subjects design, but consider how wasteful it would be: you would need to run ten groups of subjects, with each group studying the list for a different number of trials.

3. A within-subjects design assures that the groups are equivalent in ability, demographic characteristics, and personality characteristics. The groups *have* to be equivalent because the same people participate in each group. In contrast, the between-subjects design assigns subjects randomly to all groups. Random assignment, as we will see later in this chapter, generally produces roughly equivalent groups (just as a randomly tossed coin produces roughly equivalent numbers of heads and tails). However, by chance, the groups may end up being significantly different (just as, by chance, you may end up with 35 heads and 65 tails if you toss a coin 100 times). If you know that the groups are equivalent to begin with—as you know in a within-subjects design—then you know that any differences you discover after the experimental treatment are due to the independent variable, rather than to differences in the subjects' original characteristics.

4. A within-subjects design has reduced variability; for example, the $s_{\bar{D}}$ (the standard error of the difference scores)[1] is typically smaller in a within-subjects design than in a between-subjects design. Consequently, you may be more likely to find a statistically significant difference between your conditions. A person is likely to be reasonably consistent in his or her performance: someone who is a slow learner when learning alone is likely to be a slow learner when learning with someone else present. In a within-subjects design, therefore, you can statistically subtract for the variability due to individual differences. The advantage of reduced variability is particularly important if you are studying an area in which individual differences are very strong. For example, in a time-estimation experiment, you might instruct a subject to tell you when three minutes are up. One subject might say "stop" after 90 seconds, while others might say "stop" after 150, 200, and 400 seconds. The individual differences might be so enormous that they would overwhelm any modest influence of the independent variable. Table 2-2 shows how an experiment might produce significant results if a within-subjects design were used but insignificant results if a between-subjects design were used.

Please do not conclude that a within-subjects design must therefore be the answer to every experimental psychologist's dream! There are clear disadvantages that are sufficient to make some psychologists abandon within-subjects designs altogether. The disadvantages of the within-subjects design—and, hence, the advantages of the between-subjects design—have been the topic of heated discussion in the psychology literature in recent years. In general, the disadvantages revolve around the fact that in a within-subjects design, perfor-

---

[1] This is a statistical term describing the variability of the average difference between two groups. The smaller the $s_{\bar{D}}$, the more likely you are to have a significant difference between your groups. For further details, see the Appendix.

Table 2-2. Comparison of between-subjects and within-subjects designs, using a hypothetical experiment in which subjects are asked to estimate time while performing familiar and unfamiliar tasks. Note that the $s_{\bar{D}}$ is much smaller in the within-subjects design, and consequently the t is much larger. See the Appendix for step-by-step analyses.

Time Estimates for a Three-Minute Period

Familiar Task			*Unfamiliar Task*		
Subject	1	350	Subject	7	50
	2	150		8	150
	3	100		9	250
	4	250		10	300
	5	300		11	200
	6	200		12	100
	$\bar{X}_F = 225$			$\bar{X}_U = 175$	

Calculations

$$s_{\bar{D}} = 53.8$$
$$t = \frac{\bar{D}}{s_{\bar{D}}} = \frac{50}{53.8} = .93$$
$$t(10) = .93, p > .10$$

a. Between-subjects design, in which the difference between the two conditions is 50 seconds, but this difference is not significant because of the large individual differences.

Time Estimates for a Three-Minute Period

Familiar Task			*Unfamiliar Task*
Subject	1	350	310
	2	300	250
	3	250	190
	4	200	150
	5	150	80
	6	100	70
	$\bar{X}_F = 225$		$\bar{X}_U = 175$

Calculations

$$s_{\bar{D}} = 5.8$$
$$t = \frac{\bar{D}}{s_{\bar{D}}} = \frac{50}{5.8} = 8.56$$
$$t(5) = 8.56, p < .01$$

b. Within-subjects design, in which the difference between the two conditions is also 50 seconds, but the difference is significant because the statistical analysis subtracts for individual differences.

mance in one condition may affect performance in another condition. These disadvantages have been summarized nicely by Greenwald (1976):

1. A within-subjects design may be confounded with regard to *practice*. We will discuss this problem in much more detail later, but consider this example.

Suppose you are studying the effects of praise on performance in a ring-toss task. You first test the subjects in a no-praise condition, and then test the subjects in a praise condition. What can you conclude if they perform better in the praise condition? Nothing, because in the praise condition they have not only had praise, they have also had more practice. Performance in the first condition influenced performance in the second condition, and the subjects in your two conditions are not comparable. This disadvantage can be corrected by a procedure called counterbalancing, which we will discuss later. Incidentally, while the second group in this experiment may have the advantage of practice, they may have the disadvantage of *fatigue:* once again, the subjects in the two conditions are not comparable.

2. A within-subjects design may raise a problem of *sensitization,* particularly if the experiment involves deception. If the subjects have noticed the true purpose of the experiment while participating in one condition, they can no longer serve as naive subjects in another condition. Remember the "broken bag caper" discussed in Chapter 1 as an example of a field experiment? Quite obviously, people who have been subjects in that experiment would be suspicious if they saw another shopper's bag break one minute later. Greenwald discusses methods of reducing the sensitization problem, which generally involve better camouflages.

3. A within-subjects design may present a problem of *carry-over.* In some situations, the effects of one treatment persist too long, and they may influence performance in another treatment. This problem is particularly obvious in drug studies: you cannot test performance first in the drug condition and then in a no-drug condition, because traces of the drug may still be present during the second period. (You can't even solve the problem by always testing performance in the no-drug condition first, because then you will be confounding condition with practice, as mentioned earlier.) Greenwald suggests that this problem can be remedied by waiting a long time between conditions. Still, an experimenter might be concerned that the drug might have long-lasting effects.

4. A final disadvantage has been suggested by Poulton (1973), who says that the within-subjects design may produce unwanted *range effects.* In a **range effect,** a subject's responses will be influenced by the fact that he or she has been exposed to a range of stimuli, rather than just a single stimulus. Thus, we may not be measuring the subject's "pure" response; once again, performance in one condition may affect performance in another condition. For example, your reaction time to a particular meaningful word may be different if all the other words on the list are meaningful, rather than if all the other words differ widely in meaningfulness.

Greenwald (1976) discusses all these disadvantages and concludes that there actually is an advantage to these disadvantages! Although the within-subjects method often makes it difficult for the researcher to decide which variable is really influencing the results (because of the danger of confounding factors), the within-subjects method is often more true to life. In real life, for example, range effects occur frequently: we don't have to recall only a single word; we have to recall a word that appears in the context of other words.

So, which should you use, a within-subjects or a between-subjects design? The answer depends on your resources—both time and subjects—the extent of individual differences, the nature of the research problem, and the possibility of combating problems of practice, sensitization, carry-over, and range. In a few cases, the theory you are testing may dictate which design you choose; for example, a theory that involves individuals' comparisons of stimuli might need to be tested with a within-subjects design. One other option is to do *both* a within-subjects and a between-subjects experiment and compare the results. Erlebacher (1977) provides details on this kind of approach, in which researchers essentially add "design type" as an additional independent variable in their experiment.

Matched-subjects designs. There is a third alternative, besides the within-subjects and the between-subjects designs: you can use a **matched-subjects design.** In a matched-subjects design, you try to assign subjects so that every subject in one group is matched with another subject of equivalent characteristics in each of the other groups. For example, if you want to study time estimation, you can first match your subjects in terms of a time-estimation pretest. On the basis of their pretest scores, you can assign subjects so that every subject in one condition is matched with someone in the other condition, as illustrated in Table 2-3.

Table 2-3. An example of matched-subjects design, using a hypothetical experiment in which subjects are asked to estimate time while performing familiar and unfamiliar tasks. The subjects are first matched, pair-wise, by obtaining time judgments on an irrelevant task; these numbers appear in parentheses. The difference between the conditions is significant, because the matched-subjects design allows us to match subjects who are similar in judgment patterns and subtract in the statistical analysis for individual differences. However, the matching is not as perfect as if we had used a within-subjects design (where subjects are essentially matched with themselves). Consequently, the difference is not as significant as in Table 2-2(b). See the Appendix for a step-by-step analysis.

	Familiar Task	Unfamiliar Task
Subject Pair	1. A. S. (360) 350	T. R. (350) 310
	2. N. K. (300) 300	L. N. (310) 220
	3. M. W. (255) 250	A. H. (240) 210
	4. S. E. (185) 200	E. M. (200) 120
	5. D. S. (150) 150	P. D. (140) 120
	6. V. G. (90) 100	W. U. (100) 70
	$\overline{X}_F = 225$	$\overline{X}_U = 175$

Calculations

$s_{\overline{D}} = 8.3$

$$t = \frac{\overline{D}}{s_{\overline{D}}} = \frac{50}{8.3} = 6.06$$

$t(5) = 6.06, p < .01$

The matched-subjects design offers many of the advantages of the within-subjects design, while avoiding many of its disadvantages. On the one hand, the groups are reasonably equivalent to begin with, and you can statistically subtract for the variability due to individual differences. On the other hand, because each subject participates in only one condition, you avoid the problems of practice, sensitization, carry-over, and range—problems that plague the within-subjects design.

How do you decide what characteristics to use in matching subjects? This is a difficult decision, because you may not know what characteristics will be relevant in your experiment. However, try to think of the characteristics that are likely to be correlated with your dependent variable. Will sex, age, intelligence, education, some particular ability, or some particular personality characteristic be correlated with the behavior you are trying to measure? Quite clearly, a literature review is helpful in locating the relevant characteristics. Often, subjects can be matched on the basis of characteristics they bring to the laboratory (such as sex, age, or grade-point average). Other times, you may want to give a pretest, like the one suggested in the time-estimation example. However, pretesting has its drawbacks, too. You may sensitize the subject, introducing a problem similar to the one associated with within-subjects designs. In summary, the matched-subjects design has advantages and it avoids some other disadvantages, but it raises some problems of its own, including the selection of relevant characteristics and the drawbacks of pretesting.

We will consider between-subjects, within-subjects, and matched-subjects designs once again when we look at sensory-deprivation studies (Chapter 11). Researchers in that area have to consider carefully the advantages and disadvantages of the three options and the methodological problems arising from each.

Mixed designs. So far, we have been discussing the treatment of a single independent variable: should that variable be manipulated between subjects or within subjects? However, as we noted in the last chapter, an experimenter usually studies several independent variables. Very often, an experimenter will manipulate one or more variables between subjects and one or more variables within subjects. These designs are called **mixed designs.** For example, look back at the experiment on word-frequency estimation diagrammed in Figure 1-6. Here, the instructions variable was manipulated between subjects, whereas word frequency and word pleasantness were manipulated within subjects. Whereas each subject participated in *either* the personal or the expert-instructions condition—but not both—each subject participated in *all* word-frequency and *all* pleasantness conditions.

CONFOUNDING VARIABLES AND CONTROL

Confounding variables—uncontrolled factors that are present for one condition of the independent variable but absent for other conditions—were discussed in Chapter 1. Confounding variables make it difficult to interpret the results of an experiment. If we find a difference in the dependent variable, it may be due to the independent variable, but it may also be due to a confounding variable that increases the difference between the conditions. In another experiment, if we find *no* difference in the dependent variable, this may be due to a confounding variable that *decreases* the difference between the conditions. The important thing to remember is that confounding variables contaminate the results, and experimenters must make stalwart efforts to eliminate them.

The example of confounding that I usually describe to my experimental-psychology class is one that comes from *Time* magazine (1976) rather than a professional journal. The Pepsi-Cola company decided to conduct its own tests to see whether people preferred Pepsi or the nation's leading soft drink, Coca-Cola. They assembled their subjects—who all claimed to prefer Coke to Pepsi—and allowed them to sample the two drinks. The labels were removed from the drinks: and Coke was served in a glass marked *Q,* and Pepsi was served in a glass marked *M*. The results showed that more than half of the subjects preferred Pepsi! Hopefully, you'll see that there is a confounding variable: the letter *Q* versus the letter *M*. The drinkers may have preferred glass *M* to glass *Q* because of the independent variable—the contents of the glass. However, the preference may have been due to the confounding variable: subjects may prefer the letter *M* to the letter *Q*. In fact, the Coca-Cola company was quite eager to point out this confounding variable. In their own tests, they poured Coke into *both* glasses, glass *M* and glass *Q*. Their subjects preferred the Coke in glass *M* to the Coke in glass *Q*. To my knowledge, the companies still haven't conducted the ideal experiment. (We'll consider suggestions for an ideal experiment later in this chapter.)

Systematic Variance versus Error Variance

Suppose we conduct the experiment on the effects of an audience on subjects' learning. When we look at the learning scores, we find variability. The scores clearly differ from one another, and they can differ for as many as three different reasons.

Two of the reasons are concerned with **systematic variance.** This means that there are consistent differences *between* the two groups. One kind of systematic variance is due to the *effects of the independent variable* we are studying. This is the kind of variance that we want. The larger this kind of variance is, the stronger is the influence of the independent variable on the dependent variable. In the learning experiment, we would hope to find that our independent variable, presence or absence of an audience, produces a great deal of variance in the independent variable.

The second kind of systematic variance is due to the *effects of the confounding variable*. Clearly, we don't want this kind of variance. The larger this kind of variance is, the stronger are the influences of the confounding variables. This kind of variance serves to drive the average scores in the two conditions further apart when they should be close together, or to drive the average scores closer together when they should be far apart. Variance because of a confounding variable only serves to obscure the effects of the independent variable.

In addition to systematic variance—the differences between groups—scores also differ from one another because of **error variance**—the differences in scores *within* each group. People in the audience-present condition differ from one another; people in the audience-absent condition also differ from other members of the same condition. We don't want error variance, because it creates ''noise'' and makes it difficult to see whether the independent variable has any influence on the dependent variable. A 10-point difference between our two groups may be very large if scores within each group differ from one another only by, say, 5 points. However, that 10-point difference is miniscule if scores within each group differ from each other by, say, 50 points.

In a well-designed experiment, the experimenters try to maximize the variance that can be attributed to the independent variable. To this end, as we have seen, they should ensure sufficient separation between the values of the independent variable, and they should choose more than two values for the independent variable. At the same time, they should try to minimize the variance caused by confounding variables. The rest of this section will be devoted to ways of minimizing this type of variance.

Experimenters should also try to minimize error variance. The best way to decide how to minimize error variance is to review the various kinds of independent variables and ask how each type of variable can be standardized as much as possible. Thus, the more similar the stimuli are to one another, the less error variability they will produce. The same is true for environmental characteristics: if you test one subject in the laboratory and the next subject in a dormitory room, their scores will surely differ. Variables involved with manipulated subject differences should also be standardized: for example, the same instructions should be delivered in the same manner to all subjects. Finally, subject characteristics should be reasonably similar for all members of one condition: if the members of one condition of a problem-solving study varied in age from 6 to 13, there would be enormous error variance.

Now let us concentrate on the type of variance that is due to confounding variables. First we will look at the variety of confounding variables, and then we'll discuss some ways to handle the problem.

Kinds of Confounding Variables

Let's divide the kinds of confounding variables into four categories—the same four we used to classify independent variables. Whenever you conduct an experiment, you should review these four sources of confounding variables to see whether any of them are lurking in your experiment.

Stimulus confounding variables. The Pepsi/Coke experiment is an example of a stimulus confounding variable. In that case, there was something about the stimulus that was different for the two conditions. In a well-controlled experiment, all irrelevant stimulus variables must be identical for all conditions.

The problem of stimulus confounding variables is a frequent one in verbal-learning experiments, because many stimulus characteristics are correlated with other stimulus characteristics. We will encounter this problem in

Chapter 8 when we examine how word meaningfulness, pleasantness, frequency, and imagery are intertwined. The results of an experiment investigating one of these variables remain uninterpretable unless the experimenter has controlled for the other three variables.

Environmental confounding variables. An environmental confounding variable is introduced whenever some aspect of the setting is different for each of the conditions. This type of confounding variable was encountered in Chapter 1: an experimenter entering the room in the experimental condition but not in the control condition. Experimenters typically conduct experiments in laboratories in order to avoid many environmental confounding variables. Picture a room in the psychology laboratory at your college, and compare it to the student union. If you tried to conduct an experiment in the student union, there would be *hundreds* of variables that would be beyond your control and might be systematically different for your experimental conditions. There might be a record playing on the audio system, a friend of the subject might wander by, a dog might come up and want to be petted, a conversation between other students might begin nearby. In the laboratory, at least, it's relatively quiet and free of irrelevant stimuli.

Even so, think of the number of variables that could be relevant in your experiment, even if you are using a laboratory setting: room temperature, lighting, direction the subject is facing, how far away the subject is from the equipment, other equipment in the room, and how long the subject takes on a given trial. None of these variables is interesting to you in this particular experiment, yet you must make sure that there is no environmental variable that might be correlated with your dependent variable that is systematically different for your conditions.

Among the environmental confounding variables, one of the most troublesome is order. For example, suppose you wanted to conduct the ideal Pepsi/Coke experiment, and you decided to place the Pepsi on the right and the Coke on the left. This experiment still would not be ideal because your independent variable is confounded with spatial order: subjects might systematically prefer items in the right-hand position. Suppose you decided instead to have them taste Pepsi first and Coke second. This experiment would be similarly flawed because the independent variable is confounded with temporal order: subjects might systematically prefer items they judge last. (Order effects in psychological judgments are discussed in more detail in later chapters.)

Order is likely to be a confounding variable in verbal learning, too. As we will see in Chapter 8, items at the beginning and end of the list are learned more readily than items in the middle of the list. Order is a factor that must be fastidiously eliminated as a confounding variable, so that all stimuli occur equally often in all orders. (We will discuss the mechanics of this counterbalancing procedure shortly.)

Manipulated-differences confounding variables. Another type of confounding occurs when you treat groups of subjects differently on attributes other than your independent variable. For example, suppose you want to test the effects of a special remedial program for preschool children, and you work with the experimental group of subjects for several hours a day, leaving the control group to continue their normal living. If you find a difference in their performance later on, is that difference due to the specific program or to the fact that the experimental group received more attention? The subjects' knowledge that they are participating in an experiment may be sufficient to motivate them to perform better.

A particular kind of manipulated-differences confounding variable arises in drug studies. Suppose Group A receives a pill, while Group B receives no pill. If we find a difference in their performance later, it may be due to the contents of the pill, but it may also be due to the difference in their expectations. Group A expected some kind of change to occur because of the pill, whereas Group B had no such expectations. Ideally, the experimenter should give Group B a **placebo**—a pill made of sugar or some other inactive material. Subjects are not told the contents of the pill they swallow, and all subjects receive the same instructions. Thus, the two groups are equivalent in their expectations. Trouton (1957) has pointed out that placebos can produce physical and psychological changes, presumably through a change in expectations. Specifically, placebos have been effective in the relief of coughing, tension, asthma attacks, hay fever, and headaches. Placebos have also caused depression, sleeping problems, stomach ailments, and even severe skin problems. The sugar pill seems to be a new miracle drug, though it often has worrisome side effects! We will discuss expectations in more detail in the next chapter; for now, let's simply stress caution in matching conditions for expectations.

Subject confounding variables. The number of potential subject confounding variables is one reason why psychologists find it difficult to study subject characteristics as independent variables. Recall the discussion of this problem in Chapter 1. Other variables, which are correlated with the independent variable we are examining, may really be responsible for the differences in the dependent variable. For example, a group that is high in achievement motivation may differ from a group that is low in achievement motivation in terms of intelligence and social class—as well as in achievement motivation. A good knowledge of the literature will help you to identify what other characteristics are related to the independent variable you are studying and whether these characteristics are related to the dependent variable.

Subject confounding variables should concern you even if the independent variable you are studying is a stimulus characteristic, an environmental characteristic, or a manipulated subject difference. If you know that your dependent variable is influenced by any subject characteristic, then you must take precautions so that your groups are equivalent with respect to that characteristic. For example, suppose you are studying verbal learning under two kinds of instructions (a manipulated-subject-difference experiment). If Group A has 75% males and Group B has 25% males, any difference in their performance may be due to differences in the sex ratio rather than differences in the instructions.

Subject confounding variables can sneak in when you don't expect them. For example, suppose you are performing a manipulated-subject-difference experiment, and you test all of the subjects in Group A before you test any of the subjects in Group B. Weigel, Weigel, and Hebert (1971) have pointed out a problem with this arrangement: subjects who participate in experiments at the beginning of the term are surprisingly different from subjects who participate at the end of the term. Specifically, students with better study habits and attitudes sign up early in the term; those with poorer study habits and attitudes wait until the end of the term. Any difference in the performance of your two groups may be due to the original differences in the kinds of subjects in the two groups. Clearly, a carefully designed study requires that equal numbers of Group A and Group B subjects be tested in the early and late stages of testing.

How to Handle Confounding Variables

Once you have identified the confounding variables, what do you do next? Basically, you have four choices: (1) you can let the variable vary randomly; (2) you can keep the variable constant; (3) you can counterbalance; or (4) you can control statistically.

Random variation. Generally, you can choose to let the variable vary randomly if you have decided that the variable should not have a significant influence on the behavior you are studying. For example, you may let the variable "distance away from the equipment" vary randomly in a concept-formation experiment. Some subjects may sit up close and others several inches farther away, but you do not specify the distance for any of the subjects. You assume that the average difference for one group will be equal to the average difference for the other group, or that—if there is a difference—distance is unrelated to performance in this task.

Keeping the variable constant. If the variable may have an important influence on the behavior you are studying, and if it is logistically possible, you should try to keep the variable constant for all conditions. For example, a verbal-learning experiment should be controlled by having the lists of words equated for all irrelevant variables. A study on word meaningfulness should use lists that differ in meaningfulness but are equivalent with respect to other factors, such as frequency, pleasantness, and imagery.

Major environmental variables, such as lighting and the direction the subject is facing, should be kept constant for all the conditions; the lights are turned on to the fullest, for example, and the subject always faces the door. You should control for major subject confounding variables by making sure that the groups are equivalent with respect to characteristics you consider important; in an experiment on achievement motivation, for example, intelligence and social class should be equal for all groups. Manipulated-differences confounding variables can be handled by making certain that all groups are treated the same: the control group of preschool children should receive the same amount of attention as the experimental group. Your goal is to avoid systematic differences between the groups.

Counterbalancing. **Counterbalancing** is a specific control technique that handles problems with order. The purpose of counterbalancing is to make certain that all conditions occur equally often in all possible orders. This control is necessary because people change as a result of the passage of time and as a result of experience. Subjects are different at the end of an experiment than they were at the beginning. If we ignore this difference, we introduce a confounding variable.

Let's suppose that we are interested in studying the effects of praise on performance in a ring-toss game. Let's suppose that we are sloppy, and all of the subjects take part in the control condition (no praise) first and the experimental condition (praise) second. Suppose that we notice that the subjects perform better in the experimental condition. We simply cannot draw conclusions about the cause for their superior performance. It may be the praise, but it may be the order: performance improves with practice, and the experimental subjects had more practice. In fact, praise might be entirely irrelevant: the confounding effect of order may make us conclude that a relationship exists when, in truth, there is none.

Just as often, the confounding effect of order can make us conclude that a relationship does *not* exist when, in truth, there is a relationship. Let us imagine that praise really does influence ring-toss performance. Imagine, for example, that people throw an average of three more correct shots (out of 20) with praise than without praise. However, suppose a sloppy experimenter tests all subjects first in the praise condition and second in the no-praise condition. Furthermore, suppose that people normally throw an average of three more correct shots on trials 21–40 than they do on trials 1–20, simply because they have had more practice. As Figure 2-4 shows, the advantage of extra practice would exactly cancel the disadvantage of no praise on trials 21–40. The experimenter concludes—incorrectly—that praise has no influence on performance.

Instead, we should use counterbalancing in order to balance presentation order and experimental condition. A common kind of counterbalancing involves an AB order for one group of subjects and a BA order for the other group. One group participates in the praise condition first (A) and the no-praise condition second (B); the other group participates in the no-praise condition first (B) and the praise condition second (A). This type of counterbalancing, illustrated in Figure 2-5, distributes the effects of practice equally across the two conditions.

The ideal answer to the Pepsi/Coke battle, incidentally, seems to lie in appropriate counterbalancing. One-half of the drinkers sip Pepsi first and Coke second; the other half of the drinkers sip Coke first and Pepsi second. None of the glasses is labeled. Order effects would cancel out, and there would be no opportunity for labeling preferences. We could combine both groups of drinkers and determine whether there is, in fact, any overall preference.

For counterbalancing to work properly, the transfer from one condition to another should be symmetric (the same in both directions). In contrast, **asymmetric transfer** occurs when the effect of having the experimental condition precede the control condition is different from the effect of having the control condition precede the experimental condition. For example, suppose

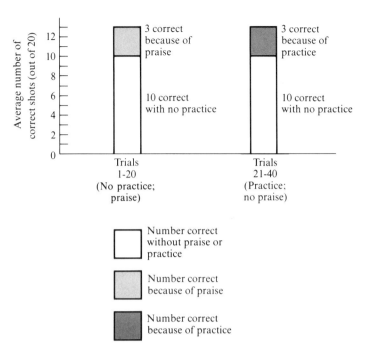

Figure 2-4. An example of an experiment that is confounded with respect to task order. The advantage of practice in Trials 21–40 conceals the fact that praise has a real effect on performance.

we want to compare memory for pairs of words in two conditions. In the control condition, we give no special instructions. In the experimental condition, we tell subjects to try to visualize the pairs of words in vivid interaction. One group of subjects (Group A) receives control instructions for the first half of the experiment and "visualizing" instructions for the second half. The other group of subjects (Group B) receives "visualizing" instructions for the first half of the experiment and control instructions for the second half. The problem is that Group B cannot *undo* their visualizing instructions and return to the normal, control instructions: these subjects will probably still continue to visualize the pairs of words. They will show carry-over from the experimental to the control conditions. In contrast, Group A will probably show no carry-over from the control to the experimental conditions. The carry-over, or transfer, is asymmetric. In situations where you have reason to suspect asymmetric transfer, you should use a between-subjects or a matched-subjects design, in which counterbalancing is not necessary.

So far, we have been talking about temporal counterbalancing, or balancing order in *time*. Spatial counterbalancing, or balancing order in *space,* must be used whenever performance or judgments are measured for objects arranged in space. As we will see in Chapter 6, if we want a subject to judge which stimulus is longer, a standard line or a comparison line, the standard must appear on the left side half of the time and on the right side half of the time.

The kind of counterbalancing that we have discussed so far has used two separate groups, one tested in the order AB and the other tested in the order

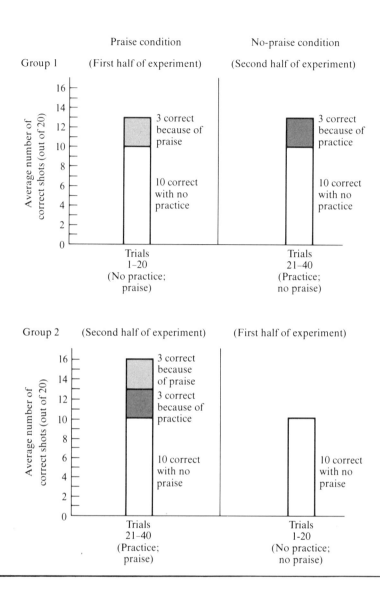

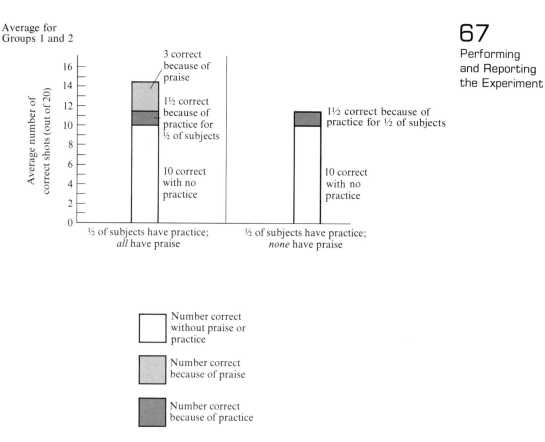

Figure 2-5. An example of an experiment in which task order and experimental condition are counterbalanced. Counterbalancing distributes the effects of practice at ring tossing equally across the praise and the no-praise conditions. Consequently, the influence of praise is revealed when we combine Groups 1 and 2. We see that, when practice is equal for the two conditions, subjects throw an average of three more correct shots with praise than without praise.

time passes. Subjects become exhausted, and their motivation to do well decreases. In fact, the ABBA kind of counterbalancing should not be used in a ring-toss experiment, because subjects would probably do best at the middle of the session. This would give a boost to the two B conditions relative to the beginning and ending A conditions.

Experimental design becomes even more complex if there are more than two conditions that must be counterbalanced. In order to have **complete counterbalancing,** each condition must occur equally often at each position, and each condition must precede and follow the others an equal number of times. These stipulations are easy to meet with only two conditions. If half the subjects are tested in the order AB and the other half in the order BA, then conditions A and B occur equally often in each position, and B precedes A as often as B follows A. With three conditions, however, six groups are necessary to meet the stipulations:

ABC
ACB
BAC
BCA
CBA
CAB

One-sixth of the subjects are assigned to each of the six groups, and each group takes part in the three conditions in the specified order.

Matters become increasingly complicated as the number of conditions increases. The formula for the number of necessary groups is $n!$, or "n-factorial," which equals $(n)(n-1)(n-2) . . .(1)$. When the number of conditions (n) is 4, there must be $4 \times 3 \times 2 \times 1$, or 24 groups, which is enough groups to drive most experimental psychologists to contemplate switching to clinical psychology. There is an alternative, however, called **incomplete counterbalancing,** which has only one requirement: each condition must occur equally often at each position.

The **Latin-square counterbalancing method** is one kind of incomplete counterbalancing; with this method, each condition occurs only *once* at each position. For example, with four conditions, we could run four groups, each containing one-fourth of the subjects:

ABCD
BDAC
CADB
DCBA

Notice as you look down the columns of letters that each letter appears only once in each column. That means that each condition occurs only once at each of the four positions. The Latin-square method is generally considered to be an acceptable way to simplify an experiment and still take care of order effects.

Statistical control. One final control technique for handling confounding variables can be used after the experiment is completely finished. There are statistical tools that allow experimenters to control statistically for variables that could not be controlled experimentally. One technique is called **analysis of covariance** (see Appendix); the other is **multiple regression,** which was mentioned in Chapter 1. Multiple regression proved useful, for example, in an experiment (Matlin & Underhill, 1978) where it was impossible to construct a list of pleasant words that matched a list of unpleasant words with respect to word frequency. (Pleasant words usually have a higher frequency.) Therefore, we conducted the experiment with unmatched lists. In the subsequent multiple regression analysis, we used word pleasantness as one independent variable and word frequency as a second independent variable. The multiple regression analysis told us the independent contributions of each of these two variables. Thus, a statistical analysis removed a confounding variable.

Analysis of covariance and multiple regression are complex kinds of analyses generally taught at the advanced graduate level. However, you may well come across them in journal articles. Therefore, you should understand their purpose: to control for variables using statistical tools and to tell what influence each independent variable has upon the dependent variable, after controlling for the other variables.

THE DEPENDENT VARIABLE

Much of the information on the dependent variable has been covered in detail in Chapter 1. In that chapter, we discussed the general requirements for a dependent variable—that it must be reliable, valid, and sensitive. We also discussed two issues under the topic of validity: the response measure problem and unobtrusive measures. Finally, we considered the use of multiple dependent variables in order to provide a complete picture of psychological processes.

It is important to consider these general concepts when you are thinking about your dependent variable. However, there are several other items that fall into the "nitty-gritty" category that must also be taken into account. In general, these items are concerned with operationalizing the dependent variable and summarizing the observations.

The Operational Definition

As we discussed earlier, the advantage of an operational definition is that it forces experimenters to decide precisely what they mean when they use a concept. For example, we cannot simply state that a variable will influence memory: we need to state what kind of memory we mean. A variable might have a very great influence on one kind of memory and very little influence on another kind of memory. Instead of "memory," then, we might say "the number of words correctly recalled" or "the number of words correctly recognized."

The choice of the operational definition can determine the nature of the results. For example, Bower and Winzenz (1970) found that the instructions to the subjects had an influence on memory when memory was defined in terms of "the number of words correctly recalled," but that instructions had little influence on memory when memory was defined in terms of "the number of words correctly recognized."

However, the operational definition should be made even more specific than this. "The number of words correctly recalled" is not complete enough because we must specify precisely what we mean by the word *correctly*. What if the word on the list was *slowly* and the subject says *slow*? Is that correct? Is it correct if the subject substitutes *sunshine* for *sunlight?*

You may decide that the response must be absolutely the same as the original word in order to call it correct. Alternately, you may decide that slight deviations (specifically, when one word is a derivation of the other word) are permissible. You must also make another decision about the operational definition: does *correctly* mean not only that the words must be recalled perfectly, but that the order of words in recall must be identical to the order in which they originally appeared? Deciding about the criteria for correctness forces you to think about what aspects of memory you consider essential. If you decide, for example, that *slow* is an acceptable variation of *slowly,* you are saying that you are interested in memory for the basic meaning of a word rather than the correct storage of the entire word.

The operational definition may take several different forms. So far, we have considered only **response frequency,** or the number of words recalled. This is certainly the most common format for the dependent variable in verbal-learning studies. However, a verbal-learning researcher might also consider using **response latency,** or the delay prior to the production of a response. It is possible that response latency might be a sensitive measure of the effects of a particular independent variable, and two groups might be equivalent in response frequency but different in response latency. Response latency is often used in word-association research, where long delays before responding are presumed to reflect psychological conflict about the word. It is also used in cognition research, where decision time or solution time is measured.

The **magnitude** of the response, or the size of the response, is another format for the dependent variable. Research in attitudes commonly uses this measure. For example, subjects may be asked to rate how much they like a particular item. Chapter 5, on scaling methods, considers this topic in detail. In addition, the magnitude of physical responses can also be measured. Does a child press a bar harder to see a complex stimulus than a simple stimulus? Does a college student give the response more loudly when another person is present?

Response duration, or how long the response lasts, is another format for the dependent variable. Do people look at neutral pictures longer than at ego-threatening pictures? Do obese people spend more time eating than normal people? Does a rat press a bar in a Skinner box longer during extinction than during acquisition?

Summarizing the Observations

Before you begin to run the first subject in your experiment, you must consider what your data will look like. You should try to be very concrete at this stage: make up numbers to represent the responses of an ideal subject, supplied in the same format that your "real" subjects will use. Sometimes these data will be in a format appropriate for immediate statistical analysis. However, sometimes there will be an overwhelming number of observations, and you may realize that the numbers must be summarized before plugging them into the correct statistical test.

At this stage—before you collect any data— you must consider the kind of statistical analysis you plan to use to decide whether your findings are significant. (A brief description of several common statistical analyses can be found in the Appendix.) Decisions on the design of the experiment and the kind of statistical analysis used must go hand-in-hand. Occasionally, experimenters get so excited about trying a new experiment that they forget this step. At the end of the experiment, they find that the data they have collected simply do not allow them to draw the kinds of conclusions they wanted to draw.

SUBJECTS

So far, we have been concerned with the *things* of an experiment. Now, let's focus on the people in the experiment. We will be concerned here with human subjects; animal subjects are considered in detail in other textbooks (see, for example, Sidowski, 1966). The issues we will consider are sampling techniques, subject loss, sample size, and random assignment.

Sampling Techniques

In most cases, you cannot examine an entire population of subjects. Instead, you study part of the population, which is called a **sample.** After studying that sample, you will make generalizations that you will apply back to the whole population.

In order to make generalizations from the sample back to the population, it is necessary that the sample be representative of the population. In **representative sampling,** the sample must represent the characteristics of the population from which the sample is taken. In other words, we want characteristics to be present in the sample to the same extent that they are present in the population. If the sample includes too many of one kind of people, or not enough of another kind, then the sample is not representative, and we cannot necessarily claim that the results hold true for the general population.

If we fail to find a representative sample, we say that we have a **biased sample.** For example, if we are interested in the opinions of American adults on gun regulations and we send a questionnaire only to members of the National Rifle Association, we will end up with a biased sample. Perhaps we can generalize our results to apply to members of the N.R.A., but we cannot claim that our results can be generalized to all American adults. The survey would lack external validity. (Remember? This means that the results can be applied to other situations or populations.)

It is important to keep in mind that you must limit your statements to the kinds of subjects you are studying. If you have conducted your experiments on college students, then your statements must be limited to college students, not extended to ''humans'' or ''humans between the ages of 17 and 21.'' Because you selected your sample from the population of college students, your generalizations can only be applied with confidence to that population—college students.

In the next chapter, we'll talk more about the populations of subjects that psychologists typically study and how these populations are unusual. If you wish your statements to apply to a large segment of the human population, then you must consider venturing beyond the college-student subject pool. Furthermore, some areas of research only sample a small, unusual portion of that population of college students. For example, in the chapter on motivation, we will consider the kind of people who sign up for sensory-deprivation experiments. These people are different from other college students; for one thing, they are above average in "thrill-seeking." Consequently, the results cannot be generalized to apply to all college students, let alone to all people. The studies tell us how people who are high in thrill-seeking react to sensory deprivation, but we cannot legitimately argue that these results are equally applicable to all people.

There are two basic techniques for obtaining representative samples. In **random sampling,** every person in the population has an equal chance of participating in the experiment. This means that you use a carefully specified, unbiased system to decide who will be in your sample. One way to do this is to use a table of random numbers, such as those in the appendix of statistics books, and figure out a system so that the numbers correspond to the people in the population. Then you select numbers from the table, and you pick the individuals who correspond to those numbers.

Stratified sampling is a more systematic way of ensuring that several of the characteristics of the population are represented in the sample. The experimenters first identify the characteristics that they believe to be relevant to their study; then they carefully select specified numbers of people who have these characteristics. For example, you might do a nationwide survey on political opinions, selecting a sample of 5000 people to represent the population. You might select the sample so that it is representative of the following characteristics: sex, age, political affiliation, education, and income. Stratified sampling is used in the public-opinion polls whose results you often see in newspapers. It is also used to predict the outcome of elections. More details on the technique are available in Babbie (1975).

Subject Loss

One way in which a sample can become biased is by subject loss, or dropout. Let's imagine that you are conducting an experiment for which subjects must show up five days in a row in order to complete the study. You specify that any subjects who fail to show up on even one of those dates will have their data left out of the final analysis. Think about the group of subjects whose data are kept: they will be a highly unusual, motivated group. Clearly, they will not be representative of the entire population. Therefore, it would be unwise to conclude that the results of your study apply to all college students.

An example of this situation appears in the motivation literature as summarized by Donelson and Gullahorn (1977). A number of studies have shown that warm, nurturant mothers have daughters who are low achievers, whereas less affectionate, "hostile" mothers have daughters who are high achievers. If we interpret the results of those studies at face value, we might conclude that every mother should be throwing her daughter out into the snow at a tender age. However, on closer inspection, we see that these studies were longitudinal studies, requiring many years of periodic participation. Most mothers would drop out of extended studies of this kind. Mothers unusual enough to participate in such lengthy studies are highly unlikely to be characterized by extreme hostility and rejection. These "hostile" mothers may have been among the least warm mothers in this very unusual, limited-range sample, but they would not be considered particularly hostile relative to the entire population of mothers in the United States. (Incidentally, can you figure out a possible interpretation for the results?)

Subject dropout can be a particular problem in studies with infants. What do you do if you have your equipment all ready to go, you are sitting there with your freshly sharpened pencil ready to record the data—and the infant either falls asleep or else wails inconsolably? Most researchers, in despair, do not finish running that subject, and they lose those data. Sigman, Kopp, Parmelee, and Jeffrey (1973) argue that it is a poor policy to discard subjects who do not remain alert for the duration of the experiment. They found that babies who were most likely to alter their mood (from alert to crying, for example) during the course of testing for reflexes were more attentive to visual stimuli than those who remained in the same mood. Consequently, if you discard babies who start to cry, you may be discarding the ones who would be most attentive. As a result, you may end up with an unusual sample of infants.

Subject dropout is a problem that is often overwhelming when researchers use questionnaires: every person who does not return the questionnaire can be considered a dropout. Imagine how many returned questionnaires you might receive if you sent a questionnaire to every adult resident in your town. Even if you stamped the return envelope, only a small percentage of the people would be motivated enough to fill it out and return it. The responses in the questionnaires would give you a very distorted picture of reality and might lead you to the wrong conclusion.

In summary, the loss of a small number of subjects is not harmful, but the loss of a substantial portion of the subjects can produce two serious problems: (1) You may end up with a biased sample, with only unusual people remaining in the study. The results would then lack generality, and the external validity of the study is threatened. (2) You may have a higher dropout rate in one of the experimental groups than in the other groups. If a particular kind of person is most likely to drop out, you may end up with groups that are not equivalent. Thus, the internal validity of the study would be threatened.

Sample Size

How many subjects should you select for your study? A large sample size is desirable because it reduces the likelihood of a Type II error. In other words, with large samples, you are better able to detect true differences between your conditions instead of concluding "no difference" by mistake. For example, the *t* test (see Appendix) is typically used to determine whether the difference between two groups is significant: the larger the *t*, the more likely it is that the difference is statistically significant. Here is the formula for *t*:

$$t = \frac{\bar{X}_c - \bar{X}_e}{\dfrac{1}{\sqrt{N}}(s_D)}$$

In this formula, as *N* becomes larger, *t* becomes larger. For example, suppose the difference between the means $(X_c - \bar{X}_e)$ equals 10 and the standard deviation of the difference scores[2] (s_D) equals 30. If the number of subjects (N) is 9, then *t* is only 1.00. (Try that calculation yourself.) However, if the number of subjects is raised to 100, and everything else stays the same, *t* becomes 3.33. Furthermore, as a "double bonus," a larger *N* allows you to use a more lenient cutoff in the *t* tables, which makes it even more likely to conclude that you have a significant difference. For example, to be significant at the .05 level, you need a *t* of only 1.98 with 100 subjects, but you need a *t* exceeding 2.31 with 9 subjects.

On the other hand, there is a problem with a large sample size. We must be cautious in interpreting the results from large samples, because a very small difference between two groups can produce statistical significance. Suppose you read in the newspaper that Vitamin C has been found to raise IQs. Studies were conducted in which 1000 children were given daily doses of Vitamin C, while 1000 children in a control group were given placebos; after six months, the Vitamin C group's IQs were 3 points higher. Yes, that difference would be *statistically* significant. However, it would not be *scientifically* significant: 3 points is not very important when you consider the variability of IQ scores. Also, it would not be *practically* significant: families would be unlikely to give Vitamin C to their children in the hope of raising their IQs by 3 points.

Psychologists therefore try to select sample sizes that are large enough to reveal an important difference, but not so large that a small difference is blown out of proportion. For human subjects, you might aim for about 20 subjects in each group.

A knowledge of the importance of sample size can help you when you are reviewing the literature. If you read that a particular independent variable has no effect on the dependent variable, be suspicious if the sample size is *small:* there may not have been a large enough sample to reveal an important difference. If an independent variable does have an effect on the dependent variable, be suspicious if the sample size is extremely *large:* with a huge sample, small differences that are not scientifically significant become statistically significant.

Some psychologists have a different approach to sample size: they perform experiments using just one subject. They argue that single-subject exper-

---

[2] A **difference score** tells us how much someone's performance in the experimental condition differs from his or her performance in the control condition. A **standard deviation** is a measure of variability. Thus, the **standard deviation of the difference scores** tells us how much the difference scores vary from one subject to the next.

iments are superior to large-sample experiments because individual performance tends to be obscured or lost when you look only at data from a group. The single-subject technique is particularly popular among psychologists interested in operant conditioning; it is described in detail in Sidman (1960), Christensen (1977), and Hersen and Barlow (1976). In general, many of the procedures for the single-subject technique are similar to those used in large-sample experiments. Rather than many subjects each being tested a few times, in this design a single subject is tested many times.

Random Assignment

In the classic experimental setup, we have a control group and an experimental group. Something is changed for the experimental group, while the control group remains the same. Then we measure the dependent variable for each group. If the measurements differ, we reason that the difference in the treatments produced the difference in the dependent variable. However, the logic of the design rests upon the assumption that the two groups were equivalent to begin with. Sometimes psychologists ensure that their groups are equivalent by matching the subjects beforehand on relevant characteristics. More often, they assign subjects to the conditions randomly.

Random assignment means that you use a carefully specified, unbiased system to decide which person goes into which condition or group; this system must be governed by the laws of chance, rather than by subjective factors or bias. For example, you might toss a coin to determine who should be in the control group and who should be in the experimental group. Prior to the subject's arrival, a coin is tossed. If it's "heads," the subject is in the control group; if it's "tails," the subject is in the experimental group. Since random assignment is governed by the laws of chance (tossing a coin or the equivalent), and since chance should lead to a roughly equal distribution of characteristics, you can be reasonably confident that characteristics of the subjects are distributed equally between the two groups. Thus, the two groups of subjects should be roughly equivalent in terms of characteristics such as sex, age, intelligence, and personality attributes.

Let's consider an example of nonrandom assignment. Suppose we are conducting an experiment to test the effects of classroom setting—open classroom versus traditional classroom—on creativity. Let's say that we allow the students' parents to decide which classroom their children will be enrolled in. In so doing, we are violating the rules of random assignment, because a *biased* system is being used to decide which child will be assigned to which condition. Probably, more conservative parents will choose the traditional classroom, whereas less conservative parents will choose the open classroom. If the children resemble their parents, the two classes will be substantially different at the beginning of the experiment. If the groups differ at the beginning of the experiment, we have a confounded experiment. Whenever we allow the subjects (or someone responsible for them) to select their own condition, we violate the rules of random assignment.

Another requirement of the rules of random assignment is that each subject's assignment to a condition must be independent of every other subject's assignment. When you toss a coin, each toss is independent of the toss that preceded and the toss that follows. Similarly, the assignment of one subject should not be influenced by the assignment of another subject. For example, you should not let Mary Jones go into Condition A simply because she wants to be with her friend Susan Smith in that condition. A coin should be tossed separately to determine the assignment of each of the two subjects.

Let's consider an example that violates the independence rule. Imagine that you are going to conduct an experiment in which you test subjects in two introductory psychology classes at your college. The students in Class A, you decide, are in the experimental condition, and the students in Class B are in the control condition. In this example, the assignments are made as a group; they are *not* independent of one another. The experiment might be seriously confounded. For instance, Class A might meet at 8:00 A.M. and Class B at 2:00 P.M. People who sign up for 8:00 classes are probably very different from those who sign up for 2:00 classes! Consequently, a difference in the performance of the two groups might be due to initially different characteristics rather than the experimental manipulation.

What techniques can we use to assure that our subjects are randomly assigned, thus avoiding initial differences between the groups? Sometimes, psychologists will toss a coin. Other times, they place numbers on pieces of paper, with each number corresponding to an experimental condition. Another way is to use a table of random numbers and devise a system so that numbers correspond to experimental conditions. The important point is that the process by which the numbers are selected must be random, rather than having a systematic pattern or bias.

How does random assignment work when you are using a matched-subjects design? Remember that this is the kind of design in which, for example, pairs of subjects are matched in terms of some attribute that is related to the dependent variable. It is important to remember that the assignment of each member of the pair to a condition must be random. Therefore, you must devise some random system. The name of each member of the pair could be written on a slip of paper, for example, and the two slips tossed together. The experimenter might specify that the name selected first will be assigned to the control condition, whereas the name remaining will be assigned to the experimental condition.

One other point must be mentioned in connection with random assignment. Do you recall that we noted the special problems involved in experiments using subject characteristics as an independent variable? Now that you know about random assignment, you can see that random assignment *cannot* be used in subject-characteristic experiments. If you are studying the subject characteristic of age, for example, you cannot randomly assign the 8-year-olds and the 16-year-olds to the two age conditions. Similarly, an experiment on self-esteem assigns those with high scores to the high-self-esteem condition and those with low scores to the low-self-esteem condition. Because we cannot assign the subjects randomly, we cannot assume that all the other characteristics of subjects are randomly divided between the two conditions. If there are characteristics that are systematically related to the independent variable we are studying, then the two groups will differ from each other unless we take special precautions. In a "true experiment," where we can use random assignment, we *can* assume that these other characteristics will be randomly divided between the two conditions. Consequently, we can assume that the conditions will be equivalent at the beginning of the experiment, and that any differences in the dependent variable will be due to the independent variable rather than due to initial differences in the conditions.

OTHER CONSIDERATIONS IN PERFORMING AN EXPERIMENT

Four other aspects of an experiment remain to be discussed: the instructions, the apparatus, the pilot study, and debriefing the subjects. Few experimental psychologists find these areas the most exciting, yet their careful design is critical for a well-conducted experiment.

The Instructions

Instructions tell subjects what to do or what to pay attention to. In some cases, instructions can encourage or motivate subjects to do their best.

Above all, instructions have to be carefully written in order to make the subject's task as clear as possible. Think back to an experiment you may have participated in, perhaps as a student in introductory psychology. Recall your reactions when you entered the laboratory and sat down. You may have had so many thoughts in mind that you found it hard to concentrate on the instructions. They may have sounded so complicated that it was hard to know what to do. Keep in mind your own reactions when you sit down to write instructions for other subjects in an experiment.

Clear instructions are particularly important because any ambiguities will produce unwanted variability in the subjects' performances. If instructions are so unclear that subjects don't know how to interpret them, they will typically make up their own instructions. Obviously, subjects can make up a wide variety of instructions, and their performances will be likely to vary accordingly. Unwanted variability makes it less likely that you will find significant results.

Two tricks seem to help in writing clear instructions. First, set them aside after writing them, and then read them aloud several days later. A sentence that seemed perfectly lucid on a Tuesday may seem like gibberish on a Friday, particularly when you force yourself to read it out loud. Second, pretest the instructions on several subjects. This might be done even before you run the pilot study (which we'll discuss shortly) if you are not familiar with writing instructions.

You will need to make two decisions regarding instructions. First, what format should you use: should they be written down, read aloud to the subject by the experimenter, or tape-recorded? Second, how much of the experiment should you describe to the subjects before they begin? Too little information leaves the subject guessing what aspect of performance should be emphasized (for example, speed versus accuracy), whereas too much information may allow the subject to guess your hypothesis—a problem we will consider in Chapter 3. No hard-and-fast rules can be given for these decisions, but discussion with others who have conducted research in your area should be helpful.

Here are some very specific hints that may help you write clear instructions that subjects should understand:

1. Begin the instructions with some general statements to catch the subjects' attention and encourage them to attend to what follows; some phrase such as "please pay close attention to these instructions" might be included. Avoid beginning the instructions with an important sentence; you can test this rule by asking yourself whether the subject could understand the task if the first sentence were missed entirely.
2. If the instructions are written, underline the most crucial points. If they are to be read (either directly by the experimenter or on a tape recording), stress these points by appropriate pauses and by changing your intonation.
3. At the end of the instructions, summarize the most crucial points.
4. After the instructions have been given, ask if there are any questions.
5. If feasible, include a short practice period to determine if the subjects understand the instructions and to correct any misunderstandings they might have.

For an example of instructions actually used in a recent experiment, turn to the "Case History of an Experiment" at the end of this chapter (Table 2-5).

The Apparatus

The term **apparatus** refers to the equipment used in an experiment to present the material and to record the subject's behavior. The equipment may be very elaborate, designed especially for the current experiment. It may be a standard piece of equipment, such as a memory drum (which we'll discuss in Chapter 8) or a tachistoscope (which we'll discuss in Chapter 7), that is used in many different experiments. Finally, it may be extremely simple and readily available: stimuli may be presented on index cards and the data recorded with a pencil and paper.

Detailed consideration of different kinds of apparatus is beyond the scope of this textbook. However, a textbook by Avery and Cross (1978) contains an excellent discussion of apparatus used by researchers in a number of different areas: perception, perceptual-motor skills, physiological psychology, learning (both animal and human), cognition, and social psychology. In addition, the *American Psychologist* periodically publishes a special issue on instrumentation in psychology. (**Instrumentation** is a synonym for apparatus.) For example, the March 1975 issue contains articles on computer technology and bio-psychology. Finally, a journal called *Behavior Research Methods and Instrumentation* publishes articles on new techniques and apparatus.

The Pilot Study

A **pilot study** is a pretest of the experiment that is conducted before you begin the major experiment. The pilot study determines whether the major experiment has any real problems or rough spots. The pilot study uses the same instructions and apparatus as the major experiment, but it generally tests only a small number of subjects in each condition. A pilot study does not typically stand on its own merits; instead, it gathers information about unexplored territory.

It is particularly important to run a pilot study if the experiment is not a replication, if it uses a technique that the experimenter is unfamiliar with, if the task might be difficult for the subjects, or if it uses equipment that might cause problems. In summary, run a pilot study whenever there are many unknowns.

Clearly, the pilot study may take some extra time—time that you may resent spending if you are anxious to begin gathering data for the major experiment. The pilot study may show that the experiment runs very smoothly, in which case you simultaneously rejoice at the easy task ahead and lament the lost time. However, it may show that subjects take far longer than you had anticipated on the experiment, that they do not understand the instructions, or that the independent variable—in its current form—has absolutely no effect on behavior. In such cases, you will want to correct the problem before beginning the major experiment.

A pilot study may save you time and money in the long run, because you can avoid running dozens of subjects for a study that was not appropriately constructed. I vividly recall a study I conducted as an undergraduate laboratory assistant. We were testing the effects of a particular series of drugs on audiogenic seizures in mice. We had purchased a large number of expensive mice specially bred so that they go into a seizure—somewhat similar to an epileptic seizure—whenever they hear a noise of a particular frequency, such as a doorbell. Twenty-four hours before they were to be tested, we injected one kind of drug. Twelve hours later, we injected a second kind of drug. Ten minutes before testing, we injected a third kind of drug into their tail veins. (Imagine an 8-gram mouse; now imagine the tail of an 8-gram mouse; now imagine the vein on the tail of an 8-gram mouse. . . .) Then we placed the mice in the special apparatus and rang the doorbell. About four hours before testing, however, we realized that the experiment was futile. The animals lay there dazed and limp; none of them could possibly find the energy to have a seizure. The combination and dosages of the drugs had been inappropriate. Clearly, a pilot study with two or three mice would have saved us considerable financial loss, time loss, and aggravation!

Debriefing the Subjects

After each subject has been tested, the experimenter must **debrief,** or explain what the experiment was about. This may be a short verbal explanation, or it may be a more formal brief written report. The point is that subjects have donated their time to help you in your research, and you must reciprocate by making the experience educational for them. They need to know what hypotheses you were testing and how the tasks were related to the hypotheses. Any deceptions also must be explained. Obviously, this should not be a lengthy, detailed discourse; it should be material appropriate for your audience. We will discuss in Chapter 4 why this debriefing process is ethically necessary. For now, we will simply stress that debriefing is an essential part of every experiment involving human beings.

REPORTING THE EXPERIMENT

So far, the research activity we have examined has been a rather private business. Experimenters bury themselves in the library with past volumes of *Psychological Abstracts* and then quietly design their experiments. No one other than a few colleagues—and, of course, the subjects—knows anything about the research. The purpose of reporting the experiment is to make this information public, by sharing the results with the scientific community.

The American Psychological Association, which is the major professional organization for psychologists in this country, specifies a particular style that is to be used in reporting experiments. This style is described in a small book called, appropriately enough, *Publication Manual of the American Psychological Association* (American Psychological Association, 1974). Psychologists must use this specific style whenever they submit articles to the journals published by the APA or to the dozens of other journals that have adopted APA style.

Why does nearly every experimental-psychology textbook include a section on APA style? Some of you may become professional psychologists, and it is important to begin practicing the "official" style patterns as an undergraduate. Most of you will be asked to write a research report in your experimental psychology course. Since you will have to follow some format there, you would do best to learn the most widely accepted format. Finally, an understanding of APA style can help you to become a more intelligent consumer of psychological research: when you read a journal article, you will know the precise location of each of the different kinds of information about the study.

We'll begin by describing the different sections of the research report. Then we'll consider a few hints on typing format and writing style. After that, we'll examine a case history of a study that has just been completed. Finally, we will look at a sample research report.

The Parts of the Manuscript

The various parts of the research report follow each other with all the predictability of a situation comedy. We'll consider them, one by one, in the order in which they appear.

The title. The title, quite simply, tells people what your study is about. It summarizes the main idea of your study, generally using a maximum of 15 words.

Many people, glancing through the pages of a journal, will only notice the title. Keep this in mind when you are choosing the title for your report. Specifically, you should choose a title that can stand by itself, so that a reader knows the general nature of your study without having to read a word of the report. In practice, it may be best to leave the title for last, even though it will appear first. Because this is such a crucial part of your manuscript, you need a complete understanding of your study before you select a title.

Often, a good title will state clearly the independent and dependent variables—for example, "The Effect of A upon B." (Please don't take this title too literally! The first time I taught experimental psychology, one of my students handed in a laboratory report titled "The Effect of A upon B.") Avoid using empty phrases such as "A Study of" or "An Experiment About." The key to writing an effective title is to summarize all the important information without making it cumbersome or awkward. Turn to the references at the end of this book to see examples of a wide variety of titles.

The author's name and affiliation. This section contains no surprises. The only potential difficulty is deciding which authors should be listed and in what order. APA policy states: "Authorship should be limited to those who have made substantial scientific contributions to the study" (1974, p. 14). The order of authorship is generally determined by the size of the contribution, with the person who made the largest contribution listed first. As you can perhaps imagine, mature adults have been known to fight over who will be listed as first author.

The formal name of your institution should be listed as your affiliation; students are as entitled to use this affiliation as are faculty members. If you have changed institutions since you completed your work, you can list your current affiliation in a footnote.

The abstract. This section is a brief summary of the purpose and findings of your study. Like the title, it must be able to stand alone and provide a clear picture of what you have done. Keep in mind that a person in search of a relevant article is most likely to begin with *Psychological Abstracts,* and your abstract section will be reprinted there. Does that abstract provide a concise summary of the most important aspects of your study?

Psychologists often find it easiest to leave the abstract, as well as the title, until after the article is finished. Even though it appears at the beginning, you will have a better perspective on your study after you have written the main part of the manuscript. Another trick is to give the abstract to someone else to read. (Actually, it is best to have someone else read the entire report, if you can persuade anyone to do so.) This outside person can help you decide whether the abstract makes sense and can stand on its own.

The abstract should include a brief summary of the problem, methods, results, and conclusions. It should describe the number, type, age, and sex of the subjects you used. It should also summarize the research design and apparatus, as well as the results. Finally, it should mention conclusions drawn from the results. All of this must be contained in a single paragraph that is only 100–175 words long! (Abstracts for papers to be presented at psychological conventions are often limited to 50 words, which makes abstract writing into a contest in telegraphese!)

The introduction. The introduction presents the problem; it tells the reader why you decided to do the study. The introduction relates the previous literature to your problem and relates your problem to the research design you have chosen. The introduction is not labeled, since its purpose is obvious.

The introduction usually begins with a paragraph about the research topic. It may include a description of the research area, if it is likely to be unfamiliar to many readers. The trick is to write a paragraph that will entice someone who doesn't know the area, without insulting the professional who has already written three articles on the same topic.

An important part of the introduction is the literature review. You do not need to provide a complete historical review here, though you may want to refer to a review article on the topic if there is a recent one available. You should include several selected studies that are relevant to your specific topic, but avoid citing references that are only tangentially related. None of the studies needs to be discussed in detail.

After discussing the literature, you should point out the relationship between past work and your present study. Then, you can write more specifically about your own study. You can state your hypotheses, discuss your independent and dependent variables, and describe briefly the task that the subjects will perform.

The introduction should be reasonably concise. If an introduction meanders, the reader will never make it to the methods section.

The methods section. The methods section tells the reader what you did and how you did it. You may want to write this section first, because it is very straightforward and because these details must be written up quickly before they fade from memory. Two months later, you may not remember the speed with which the words were presented, the amount of time you allowed for recall, or the sexes of the subjects, unless you have been careful to write down all the information.

You should describe the method in enough detail that an experienced researcher could replicate the study if desired. This section also allows the reader to decide whether your methods were appropriate. You must be careful to include important information without burdening the reader with trivial details. The methods section is typically divided into several smaller sections. The specific sections used will depend on the precise nature of your study; one or more of them may be eliminated if inappropriate to the particular study.

1. *Subjects.* In this section, you must describe how many subjects you tested and who they were. You should also describe how you selected them: did they

volunteer, were they members of a class, were they members of an introductory-psychology subject pool? Any payments or credits should also be mentioned, as well as important demographic characteristics, such as age and sex. These factors may influence the results of your study, and another researcher wishing to replicate your study would need to test similar subjects. Finally, you should explain any subject loss. Were there any subjects who did not complete the experiment? Were there any whose data were not included because they did not follow instructions? You should be prepared to defend the elimination of any data from your study, so that it does not appear that you simply dropped data that did not support your hypothesis!

2. *Design*. This section is optional, but it can help prevent confusion if your study has a large number of independent variables or many dependent measures. The design section provides an overview of your variables. It also mentions the number of levels for each variable. Finally, it should state whether, for each variable, you used a between-subjects or a within-subjects design.

3. *Apparatus*. This section describes your equipment, listing the supplier's name and the model number. Occasionally, if the equipment is unusual, a drawing or a photograph may be included.

4. *Material*. This section may replace or be combined with the apparatus section. In this section, you describe questionnaires or tests. The way in which stimuli were chosen can also be discussed here. For example, you might describe how you selected English-word stimuli for a concept-learning experiment.

5. *Procedure*. This section summarizes each step in the research procedure. It is usually best to proceed chronologically, from the time that the subjects begin until they have finished. Psychologists typically write this section from the viewpoint of the subject, because information about what the subject does is more useful than how the experimenter administers the study. This section also includes a summary of the instructions to the subjects, counterbalancing techniques, and control features in the experiment.

The results section. The results section describes what the data looked like and what statistical analyses you used. Begin by discussing the main effects of your independent variables, and then proceed to the interactions. Remember that you want the reader to emerge from the results section with an understanding of the important findings of your experiment, rather than a dazed sense of despair at the confusion of numbers.

Let's talk about the presentation of statistics in the results section. Beginning writers are often so overwhelmed by having to do statistical tests and report them correctly that they forget to tell the reader verbally about the nature of their findings. Specifically, do not merely report a difference, but report the *direction* of the difference. For example, "Subjects learned words faster in the together condition than in the alone condition, $t(28) = 2.97$, $p < .01$" tells the reader far more than "Performance in the together condition differed significantly from performance in the alone condition, $t(28) = 2.97$, $p < .01$."

Note the style in which statistical analyses are presented. According to APA style, the statistics follow the sentence and are preceded by a comma. You specify the test you used, then the degrees of freedom, the value you calculated, and the level of significance. Similarly, the results of an analysis of variance should be reported: "Age significantly influenced speed, $F(3, 48) = 10.34$, $p<.05$." Notice that all statistical symbols—t, p, F—are italicized; in a manuscript, you indicate this by *underlining* the letter. Finally, you do not need to describe the formula for the statistical test unless it is something exotic.

When should you use tables and figures? Keep in mind that both tables and figures are expensive to reproduce; this cost must be weighed against the virtues of a nonverbal format. If your important data consist of two or three means, then there is no reason for a table or a figure. If you have a larger number of means to report, then you should consider using a table or a figure.

Whenever you include a table or a figure, be sure to refer to it in the text of your article: "As shown in Table 1, . . ." or "Boys performed better than girls (see Figure 1)." Then, at the point in the article where you want the table or figure to appear, type the following phrase, set off by lines and centered:

Insert Table 1 about here

An example of a table is given in Table 2-4. Notice that the title is as descriptive as possible, and that lines are used to separate the sections of the table.

Table 2-4. An example of a table prepared according to APA style.

Table 1. Mean Number of Words As a Function of Age and Number of Repetitions

Age of subjects	Number of repetitions of list			
	1	2	4	8
7	5	6	7	9
8	6	7	8	9
9	6	8	8	10

Note. Maximum score = 12 words.

When do you use a figure rather than a table? Tables give exact values and are suitable for presenting main effects. Figures are the best way to present interactions, because the reader can readily note that the lines are not parallel.

Examples of figures appear frequently in the last five chapters of this book. Typically, the independent variable appears on the horizontal axis, and the dependent variable appears on the vertical axis. If you have two independent variables and you would like to show how they interact, you must decide which of the variables will appear on the horizontal axis and which will be represented by two or more lines in the figure itself. The choice is sometimes arbitrary. However, if one of the variables is continuous (that is, fractions in between two integers are permissible, such as 8.45), that variable is best represented on the horizontal axis. Turn back, for example, to Figure 1-7: notice that "age of subject" appears on the horizontal axis, while "sex of subject" is represented by two lines in the figure. Pay particular attention to labeling both of the axes, listing the units in which each quantity is measured. Lightly pencil the figure number on the back of each figure, and type the figure caption, or title, on a separate page.

Generally, a professional graphic artist must prepare any figures that are to be submitted for publication. Details on the preparation of figures can be found in the APA Manual (1974, pp. 50–55).

The discussion section. Notice that the results section merely presents the results; it does not discuss them. You save these remarks for the discussion section; here, you evaluate and explain your findings.

The discussion section should begin with a statement about whether the results support your original hypotheses. You may also discuss how your results are similar to—or different from—the results obtained by other researchers. The challenge comes in trying to determine what differences in your methodology may have produced differences in the results. Sometimes the factors may be extremely subtle—as in a case of nonreplication described by Cronbach (1975). Researchers had found that mice would sleep for about 35 minutes after receiving a particular drug. In another laboratory, however, they revived in only 16 minutes. After diligent detective work, it was discovered that the new mice were housed with red-cedar bedding—rather than birch bedding—and this had changed the way in which the drug was metabolized!

In the discussion section, you may examine possible shortcomings of the study. However, this section should not be a public confession. You should also entertain any alternative hypotheses that might explain your results. (To entertain a hypothesis means, in psychological jargon, to consider a hypothesis; it does not mean—as the phrase suggests—that you need to offer it fine wine and soft music or perhaps a good French movie.)

If your results are not significant, do not try to rationalize these results and argue that they really support the hypothesis. Nonsignificance means that any difference between your groups could be due to chance. Furthermore, if your results just miss the accepted level of significance—for example, $p < .11$—you must face reality and state that your results were not significant. It is not appropriate to note that the results were "almost significant" and then write in the discussion section that the results "almost confirmed" the hypothesis.

Keep in mind that the major purpose of the discussion section is to talk about how your study has contributed to the knowledge of the subject area: what questions has your study answered?

The references. Every publication that you have cited in the text of your article must be listed in a separate section labeled *References*. The references should be arranged in alphabetical order and presented in the standard APA format; see the references at the back of this book for an extended list of examples. (Once again, to indicate italics, simply underline the words.) In the text, these references are cited by author's last name and year of publication; for example, (Oskamp, 1965).

In addition to published, accessible articles and books, you may want to refer to reports that have not been published or widely circulated, studies in progress, or papers presented at conventions. These references are placed on a separate page labeled Reference Notes, arranged in the order in which they are cited, and numbered (see APA, 1974, pp. 65–67, for examples). In the text, they are cited by author's last name and note number; for example, (Smith, Note 1).

Typing Format

The manuscript should be typed on heavy (*not* erasable) bond paper. Double-space everything (including footnotes and references), leaving margins of 2.5–4 cm (1–1½ inches) on all four sides of the page. Indent the first line of every paragraph, except for the abstract, which should be typed as a solid block. In typing references, indent every line of a citation *except* the first.

Begin each part of the manuscript on a new page, and arrange the parts in the following order:

Cover page
Abstract
Text
Reference notes
References
Footnotes
Tables (each on a separate page)
Figure captions
Figures (each on a separate page)

The sample report at the end of this chapter illustrates the correct typing format in detail. Note that each page is numbered except for the cover sheet and figures. Above each page number, type the first two or three words of the title. This **identifier** will prove useful if the pages of your manuscript should become separated. This identifier is different from the shortened title, called the **running head,** that appears on the cover sheet of your manuscript. If your paper is published, the running head will appear at the top of each page of the journal article. When you are typing the manuscript, however, it only needs to appear on the cover sheet. The length of a running head must be limited to 50 letters and spaces.

The typing of headings is often confusing to beginning writers. Each main heading (such as Methods) should be centered and underlined, with the initial letter of all main words capitalized. Secondary headings (such as Subjects, Design, Apparatus) should be typed flush with the left margin and underlined, again with initial letters of the main words capitalized.

In studying the sample report, note also the following points:

1. In citing references in text, use author's last name and year or note number, as appropriate. If the author is mentioned in the sentence, give only the year or note number in parentheses: "As Skinner (1956) observed. . . ."

2. Short quotations can be included in the text of your report, bounded by quotation marks; for example, Smith (1968) reported, "Meaningfulness influences recall when long delay periods are used, but it has no effects with short delay periods" (p. 179). Quotations that would require more than three typed lines should be set off in indented block form without quotation marks. Be sure to include page references for direct quotations.

3. Explain any abbreviations that are not standard. It may be helpful to abbreviate any long terms that appear frequently throughout your report, giving the abbreviation in parentheses the first time. The abbreviations E for experimenter and S for subject—used in journal articles prior to 1970—are no longer accepted. More explicit items, such as *students, children,* or *rats,* may be used instead of *subjects.*

4. All measurement must be expressed in the metric system.

5. Numbers present many problems. Typically, words are used to express the numbers zero through nine and any number that begins a sentence. Higher numbers are expressed in figures, as are all ages and certain other categories of numbers (see APA, 1974, p. 42, for more detailed rules).

Writing Style

Unfortunately, an experimental-psychology textbook cannot aspire to teach writing style to its readers. However, there are several general guidelines for good scientific writing that ought to be borne in mind as you write your report.

1. Present your ideas in an orderly fashion, using well-organized sentences and paragraphs.

2. Keep your writing simple and concise. Where possible, choose short, common words over long, technical ones. (Students writing laboratory reports frequently think they will sound more professional if they "utilize" rather than "use" a certain design, for example. The best scientific writing, however, is the most natural and straightforward.)

3. Avoid ambiguity. If you use the word *this,* for example, be sure that the referent is clear.

4. Aim for readability and a smooth flow of ideas. Often, it is helpful to set the manuscript aside for several days and then reread it with a fresh and open mind.

In addition, there are a number of specific guidelines for writing style listed in the APA Manual:

1. Use the past tense to review the literature and describe the experimental design; use the present tense to discuss results that are right in front of the reader. Do not shift back and forth between the past and present tenses.

2. The words *data, criteria,* and *phenomena* are plural: "The criteria were. . . ."

3. Avoid the passive voice. "The subjects received questionnaires" is better than "Questionnaires were handed out to the subjects."

4. You may use the first person, I, in moderation when appropriate. "I thought it would be advisable" is much more readable than the awkward, impersonal phrase "It was thought that it would be advisable." Other disciplines some-

times frown on the use of *I,* but psychology, appropriately enough, acknowledges that authors have thoughts and opinions.

5. Avoid sexist language. Psychologists have been in the forefront of the movement to make language apply to both sexes, rather than to males only. In 1977, the American Psychological Association issued a change sheet to its manual, titled *Guidelines for Nonsexist Language in APA Journals,* which suggests a number of ways to overcome certain difficulties in the English language. If you are referring to all people, for example, use the words *person, individual,* or *human being* rather than the generic *man.* Similarly, you should avoid the generic pronouns *he, him,* and *his.* This can often be accomplished by rephrasing the sentence in the plural or by eliminating the pronoun altogether. For other specific suggestions, see the APA Guidelines (1977b).

A CASE HISTORY OF AN EXPERIMENT

It may be useful at this point to describe a small, simple experiment that I recently completed with a graduate student, showing how we found the idea for the study, designed the experiment, and wrote the report.

At the meeting of the Eastern Psychological Association in 1977, Dr. Kathleen Grady presented a paper called *The Belief in Sex Differences,* in which she argued that people notice the sex of people far more frequently than they notice other attributes. I was in the audience and found the paper extremely interesting. Furthermore, I had just finished writing a book about how pleasant information is processed more accurately than less pleasant information (Matlin & Stang, 1978): pleasant information is retained, whereas unpleasant information is lost. Grady's study seemed to show a similar kind of selectivity: the sex of a person is noticed, whereas other information about the person is lost.

I thought about Grady's study for several months. One evening, it occurred to me that people might *remember,* as well as notice, sex better than other attributes. How could I test it in a laboratory setting? I could use pictures, but then how would I represent other attributes, such as age and race, with the same intensity, or obviousness, as sex? Age might be less conspicuous, and race might be more conspicuous. I decided that the only way to make the attributes equivalent was to use words, rather than pictures, and have them paired with a name. For example, a subject would see the last name *Jones* paired with the attributes *old, female,* and *White.* Later, I could test memory for these attributes by presenting *Jones* and asking for the attributes.

At this point, I met a graduate student in our department, Deborah Greive, and we worked out the details of the experiment together. First, we needed to consider the independent variable—attribute of the stimulus. Sex had to be one of the attributes, but we needed to decide on two other conspicuous attributes. (We were limited to two others because we knew we would be using a memory drum with four openings, one for the name, and three for the attributes.) We decided that age and race would be the most interesting.

We also decided to include a second independent variable—sex of the subject. Some earlier literature had demonstrated that males were more stereotyped in their thinking than females, and we wondered if we might find a sex-by-attribute interaction. Thus, we hypothesized that males might recall sex better than age or race to a greater extent than females.

We decided to use a mixed design, with one variable manipulated between subjects and the other within subjects. Quite obviously, sex of subjects would have to be a between-subjects variable; males and females could not switch conditions in the middle of the study! We decided to make attribute a within-subjects variable, with all subjects participating in all attribute conditions. This way, we would use fewer subjects and reduce the variability due to individual differences in recall scores; the disadvantages of working with a within-subjects variable did not seem applicable to this particular study.

The most serious kind of confounding variable we had to combat was the problem of order. Suppose that the attributes were always listed in the order *age, sex, race* as in the example *old, female, White*. That order would give an advantage to the first and last in the list; recall is relatively poor for items in the middle. Therefore, we had to counterbalance the order of the attributes, so that each order appeared equally often. There were six possible arrangements for the three attributes, and we used each arrangement twice, making a total of 12 different stimuli.

We were also concerned with another kind of confounding. Suppose on our list the name *Smith* appeared with the attributes *young, female, White,* and—perhaps without our knowledge—a prominent student on campus was a young Black woman named Ann Smith. Subjects might recall the age and sex but make an error on the race. Thus, an unfortunate chance combination of attributes with a name might lead us to incorrect conclusions. To minimize this type of problem, we designed two different lists of names and attributes, thereby decreasing the effect of any chance combinations.

Now we needed to devise an operational definition for our dependent variable, memory. The general definition was easy: memory would be the number of times each attribute was correctly recalled. Each attribute appeared 12 times; therefore, the maximum possible score was 12. "Correctly" was also easy to define: synonyms could be acceptable substitutes because we were interested in the meaning of the attribute rather than the word itself. Thus, *man* could substitute for *male,* and *elderly* could substitute for *old.* However, how long should the delay be before recall? From earlier work, I had discovered that selectivity didn't work unless there was at least a 1-minute delay between exposure and recall. Somewhat arbitrarily, we chose a 5-minute delay.

We decided to use subjects from the introductory-psychology pool and planned to aim for 48 students, 24 males and 24 females. The instructions for the experiment appear in Table 2-5. The apparatus was a standard memory drum from our verbal-learning laboratory.

We knew we needed to run a pilot study, primarily because we wanted to avoid either a ceiling effect or a floor effect. Subjects could receive a maximum score of 12, but by chance alone they were likely to guess six attributes correctly. Thus, we didn't have much leeway. We ran a pilot study to determine whether the 5-minute delay made the task too easy (with subjects receiving scores around 12) or too hard (with subjects receiving scores around 6). Ms.

Table 2-5. An example of instructions read to subjects (Greive & Matlin, 1978).

"Here are the instructions for this experiment."

"I am going to show you some information on the memory drum. When I turn it on, you'll see a person's last name, together with three words that describe that person. For example, you might see this. . . ."

[Turn on memory drum, which rotates to reveal an example.

SIMS   UGLY   POOR   SMART

Then turn off.]

"This would mean that *SIMS* is a person who is ugly and poor and smart."

"I am going to show you a number of names. Each of the names will be followed by three words describing that person."

"Here's what I want you to do. When you see an item, I want you to make a picture in your mind of what that person looks like. For example, try to picture a person whose last name is SIMS who looks ugly and poor and smart. Try to *see* what SIMS would look like in your imagination."

"Do you have any questions?"

"OK, I'll start showing you the names. Remember that you should try to imagine what each person looks like."

[Expose all 12 items.]

"OK, now I want you to try something different. Here are some anagrams that I want you to unscramble. Each of these anagrams can be unscrambled into a word. Please go at your own rate."

[Hand them a sheet of paper containing scrambled words. Allow them 2 minutes to work on the task.]

"OK, now I want you to remember the characteristics of each of the people whose names you learned earlier. In this booklet, I have listed the names. Below each name are three blanks. I want you to list, in any order you wish, the three words you saw with each name. Do you have any questions?"

"Remember, you can list the words in any order you want—they don't have to be in the order you saw them in, originally."

[Hand them an answer booklet and allow them to take as much time as they like.]

"OK, now I would like you to take these three cards and arrange them in the order you would use them together in everyday English."

[Hand them three index cards, printed with the words, WHITE, MALE, and YOUNG.]

Greive tested eight subjects and found that they received scores around 7. Therefore, we reduced the delay period to 2 minutes, so that recall would be substantially better than chance.

The pilot study revealed no other problems, and Ms. Greive began to run the "real" subjects. There is a well-known rule in experiments that something always goes wrong. We did not encounter any major disasters, but we did encounter a minor disaster: a snowfall that closed the school. Since this was the last week in which subjects could participate in experiments, we finished the experiment four subjects short of our goal of 48.

On the following pages is a report of this experiment. If a picture is worth 1000 words, then this example should be helpful in clarifying the thousands of words written about APA format. Notice, incidentally, that our hypotheses were not confirmed; therefore, a major part of the paper is devoted to figuring out reasons for the discrepancy.

Is Sex a Memorable Attribute?

Deborah M. Greive and Margaret W. Matlin

State University of New York at Geneseo

Runninghead: Is Sex a Memorable Attribute?

Is Sex a Memorable Attribute?

1

Abstract

Previous research has demonstrated that sex is noticed more than other attributes.
This study tested whether sex is remembered better than two other important attributes,
age and race. A total of 44 subjects (22 males and 22 females) saw last names
associated with three attributes (example: JONES BLACK FEMALE YOUNG) and were
asked to recall the attributes 2 minutes later. The results showed that all
three attributes were recalled equally well. However, age and race were recalled
prior to sex, perhaps reflecting linguistic habits. No evidence was found for
selective memory for sex.

Is Sex a Memorable Attribute?

2

Is Sex a Memorable Attribute?

Sex seems to be an important demographic attribute. We categorize people on
the basis of sex, and discrepancies between expected sex and true sex bother us.
Grady (Note 1) has demonstrated that people notice sex. In a field study, she asked
people to describe the person who had sold them a subway token. The respondents
always mentioned the sex of the seller. Furthermore, they were always accurate in
their recollection of sex, and they always supplied sex either first or second in
their list of characteristics.

In a second study, Grady (Note 1) showed subjects 10 pictures of people's faces.
The pictures differed with respect to sex, hair color, clothing color, and the presence
or absence of hats and glasses. The attributes differed in their distribution; for
example, there were five males and five females, but there was only one blonde and
nine dark-haired persons. The subjects' task was to describe a specified target
to a partner, using as few clues as possible. Mathematically, the most efficient
strategy would be to supply a distinctive clue, such as hair color if the blonde were
specified. However, 60% of the subjects supplied female and male clues first. Thus,
Grady's studies show that selectivity seems to operate in the processing of
information about sex.

Erdelyi (1974) presented an information-processing model of selectivity in
which he outlined how central, cognitive control mechanisms could encourage
selectivity at each of the stages in the processing of information. The second
author has found this model useful in explaining selectivity in favor of pleasant
information (Matlin & Stang, 1978): pleasant information seems to be processed
more accurately and more efficiently than less pleasant information in the stages of
stimulus selection, perceptual processes, encoding, short-term memory, rehearsal,
long-term memory, and output.

Is Sex a Memorable Attribute?

3

We believe that this model of selectivity can be applied to the processing of information about attributes. For example, Grady's studies showed that information about sex was reported more frequently than other information. In terms of Erdelyi's model, selectivity appears to operate during perceptual processes. It seems worthwhile to examine other stages in the processing of information in order to determine the generality of selectivity. Do all processes favor information about sex, or does this selectivity apply primarily to perceptual processes?

The present study examined selectivity in memory and compared the recall of information about sex with the recall of information about age and race. Our memory task paired a last name--for example, JONES--with three attributes--for example, BLACK, FEMALE, YOUNG--and compared recall for these three attributes. We hypothesized that sex would be recalled more accurately than age and race, and that sex would be listed prior to age and race during recall. We also hypothesized that males would demonstrate selective recall for information about sex to a greater extent than females, because previous research had frequently shown that males are more sex-stereotyped than females (for example, Donelson & Gullahorn, 1977, pp. 124-134; Fagot, 1974; Lynn, 1959; Nadelman, 1974; Rubin, Provenzano, & Luria, 1974).

Method

Subjects

The subjects were 44 undergraduates (22 females and 22 males) who received research credit in introductory psychology for participating in the experiment. Each subject was tested individually.

Design

The experiment used a 3 x 2 x 2 design, with three levels of category (sex, age, and race), and two levels of sex of subject and list. Category was a within-subjects variable; sex and list were between-subjects variables.

Is Sex a Memorable Attribute?

4

Apparatus

A Lafayette memory drum, model 2303C, was used to present the lists to the subjects. Each item (for example, JONES BLACK FEMALE YOUNG) was presented in its entirety for 8 seconds, with an 8-second interval between items.

Material

We selected 12 common last names from the Rochester telephone book, eliminating those names that might be associated with a particular sex (Allen, Marshall), age (Young), or race or ethnic origin (Black, Klein, Leone). Each name was assigned to a three-attribute set, using the following procedure. First, the order of the three attributes was counterbalanced: each of the six possible orders of sex, age, and race was listed twice without designating the specific dimension of the attribute (for example, AGE, SEX, RACE). Next, one order was randomly assigned to each last name, and these four-item combinations were placed in random order in a 12-item list. Finally, a coin was tossed to determine the dimension of each attribute (for example, heads = old, tails = young), with the specification that the final list should contain six males and six females, six young people and six old people, and six Black people and six White people. Two such lists were constructed in order to minimize the impact of any accidentally meaningful combinations of names with attributes.

Procedure

Subjects were informed that they would see lines of words on the memory drum, with each line consisting of a person's last name and three words describing the person. Subjects were instructed to concentrate on imagining the person described by the three words.

A 2-minute delay period preceded recall; during that time, subjects worked on unscrambling anagrams. Subjects then received a booklet containing the last names from the learning task, in randomized order. They were instructed to fill in the

Is Sex a Memorable Attribute?

5

blanks with the words describing the person, using any order they wished.

Finally, subjects received three cards, containing the words MALE, YOUNG, and WHITE. They were told to place the cards in the order they preferred in standard English usage.

Results

Do subjects recall sex more accurately than other attributes? As Table 1 shows, all attributes were recalled equally well. An analysis of variance performed on the recall-accuracy data showed that category had no significant influence on recall, $F(2, 2) = 2.85$, p .25. Thus, sex, age, and race were all recalled equally well. Furthermore, none of the other main effects or interactions was statistically significant.

Insert Table 1 about here

Do subjects recall sex prior to other attributes? We could not perform an analysis of variance because of the nonindependence of the recall-order data. Instead, for all subjects, we calculated an average-recall-position score for each attribute. For example, one subject received scores of 3.0 (sex), 1.1 (age), and 1.9 (race), which indicated that sex was always recalled last, age was typically recalled first, and race was typically recalled second. Age received the lowest (first) position score for 29 subjects, race for 12, and sex for three. A chi-square analysis showed that this was not a chance distribution, $\chi^2(2) = 23.72$, p .001. Thus, age is recalled first, and sex is recalled last--contrary to our hypothesis. A second chi-square analysis showed that females did not differ from males in their tendency to list age first and sex last, $\chi^2(2) = 1.97$, p .10.

Finally, 80% of the subjects placed the adjective cards in the order age, race, sex, indicating that this was the preferred order of the adjectives in English.

Is Sex a Memorable Attribute?

6

Discussion

We had hypothesized that sex would be remembered better than age or race and that sex would be listed prior to the other attributes in recall. The results did not support these hypotheses. The recall-accuracy data showed that all three attributes were recalled equally well, and the recall-order data showed that age and race were recalled prior to sex. The other hypothesis, that the sex of the subject would interact with attribute category, also received no support. Quite honestly, we were surprised with the results because our subject population should have been particularly sensitive to the sex attribute. All subjects were Caucasians under the age of 25, thus eliminating any subjects who might have been especially sensitive to race and age attributes because of their minority status at our overwhelmingly young, White institution. Furthermore, we suspected that our college-student population would be more concerned about sex as an attribute than, for example, the subway-riding population in Grady's first study.

Why did our data fail to match Grady's results on the reporting of the sex attribute? First of all, our competing attributes of age and race were more prominent and permanent than the competing attributes--such as clothing color--that she used in her second study. However, in Grady's first study, age and race could have been mentioned, yet subjects still indicated that sex was the most conspicuous attribute.

We believe that the difference lies in the nature of the task. In both of Grady's studies, subjects were free to attend to any attributes they wished; her results, therefore, seem to reflect selective attention to the attribute of sex. In our study, however, all three attributes were listed verbally and were equally conspicuous. While subjects might have inspected one of the words for a longer period of time, selective attention seems far less likely. Instead, our task primarily tested selectivity in memory. Apparently, when the opportunity for selective attention for sex has been reduced, there is no selective memory for sex. In terms of Erdelyi's

Is Sex a Memorable Attribute?

7

(1974) model, then, selectivity for sex seems to operate during perception but not during memory. Other research efforts should explore other potential loci of selectivity.

Why did the data on recall order show that sex was recalled last? It is possible that recall order is a more sensitive index of selectivity than recall probability and that age and race are stored more accessibly than sex in memory. However, it seems more likely that the recall order simply reflected linguistic patterns. The responses of our subjects on the adjective-arrangement task showed that the predominant order was age, race, sex. The pattern of listing sex last also receives support from linguists. Ziff (1960), for example, proposed that more definite adjectives are placed last in a series. Definiteness, according to Ziff, refers to the range of nouns that could conceivably be modified by the adjective in question. In the case of our adjectives, female and male are used primarily to modify humans and animals; therefore, they would be listed last. The other adjectives--old and young, black and white--can modify a much greater variety of nouns; therefore, they would precede the sex adjectives. Finally, female and male are frequently used as nouns; thus, they may have been forced into the last position in the series in order to occupy the noun position. In short, the interpretation of the recall order data is ambiguous.

Is sex a memorable attribute? The answer to that question is another question: compared to what? Sex is not more memorable than two other conspicuous attributes, age and race. It is probably more memorable than other, less noteworthy attributes, but this remains to be demonstrated.

Is Sex a Memorable Attribute?

8

Reference Note

1. Grady, K. E. <u>The belief in sex differences</u>. Paper presented at the meeting of the Eastern Psychological Association, Boston, April 1977.

Is Sex a Memorable Attribute?

9

References

Donelson, E., & Gullahorn, J. E. Women: A psychological perspective.

    New York: Wiley, 1977.

Erdelyi, M. H. A new look at the New Look: Perceptual defense and vigilance.

    Psychological Review, 1974, 81, 1-25.

Fagot, B. I. Sex differences in toddlers' behavior and parental reaction.

    Developmental Psychology, 1974, 10, 554-558.

Lynn, D. B. Sex differences in masculine and feminine identification.

    Psychological Review, 1959, 66, 126-135.

Nadelman, L. Sex identity in American children: Memory, knowledge, and

    preference tests. Developmental Psychology, 1974, 10, 413-417.

Matlin, M. W., & Stang D. J. The Pollyanna Principle: Selectivity in language,

    memory, and thought. Cambridge, Mass.: Schenkman, 1978.

Rubin, J. Z., Provenzano, F. J., & Luria, Z. The eye of the beholder: Parents'

    views on sex of newborns. American Journal of Orthopsychiatry, 1974, 44,

    512-519.

Ziff, P. Semantic analysis. Ithaca, N.Y.: Cornell University Press, 1960.

Is Sex a Memorable Attribute?

10

Footnote

This paper was presented at the meeting of the American Psychological

Association, Toronto, August 1978.

Is Sex a Memorable Attribute?

11

Table 1

Average Number of Attributes Correctly Recalled

Sex of Subject	Attribute		
	Sex	Age	Race
Female	8.1	8.3	8.8
Male	8.1	8.6	9.0
Combined	8.1	8.4	8.9

Note. Maximum score = 12.

1. Ideas for psychology experiments can come from observation, past research, theory, curiosity, and applied problems.
2. A review of the literature requires an examination of relevant entries in *Psychological Abstracts*. The *Citation Indexes, Annual Review of Psychology,* review articles, and relevant books provide additional channels for finding out what previous research has been conducted.
3. The independent variable raises several potential problems in experimental design. The operational definition must be specified in detail, and the levels for the independent variables must be chosen so that there is sufficient separation—but not too much separation—between the levels.
4. The independent variable can be manipulated in three ways: between subjects, within subjects, or with matched subjects. The problems of a limited subject pool, individual differences, practice, sensitization, carry-over, and range determine which design is preferable.
5. Confounding variables are uncontrolled factors that are present for one condition but absent for other conditions. Confounding variables can be handled by letting the variable vary randomly, by keeping the variable constant, by counterbalancing, or by statistical control.
6. For the dependent variable, the operational definition and the format for the responses must be carefully determined.
7. Several issues must be considered in connection with subjects: representative sampling, subject loss, sample size, and random assignment. Great care must be taken to ensure that the experimental groups are equivalent at the beginning of the experiment.
8. Careful experimental design also requires attention to four other issues: writing the instructions, choosing the apparatus, conducting the pilot study, and debriefing the subjects.
9. The American Psychological Association specifies a precise format for reporting psychology experiments. There are standardized parts for the manuscript and a specified typing format.

3

Social Aspects
of the Psychology
Experiment

OUTLINE

THE EXPERIMENTER

104

In the first two chapters, we talked about many different aspects of the psychology experiment, some theoretical and some practical. However, we ignored one very important aspect: the psychology experiment is actually a social situation. Two or more people are meeting each other, probably for the first time, and they will engage in social interactions. They will have certain expectations of each other, they will communicate with each other, and they will form impressions of each other.

There are two reasons why the social aspects of the experiment are significant enough to deserve a separate chapter: (1) Social factors can be extremely important in determining the outcome of your experiment, even if your experiment does not directly involve social psychology. (2) There have been so many studies on the social aspects of the experiment that it has become a legitimate content area within experimental psychology.

Riecken (1962) has summarized the basic issues that we will consider in this chapter: "those features of persons, situations and events that are unintentionally (from the point of view of the experimenter) present or introduced into the process of data collection and that are responsible for unexpected (and usually, undesired) variation in the behavior of subjects" (p. 25). Ironically, this unexpected variation would be regarded as error by most researchers: subjects vary because of social factors, and we want to reduce this variation. However, one psychologist's "error factor" is another psychologist's "interesting independent variable"; what has traditionally been regarded as undesirable variation by most psychologists has now become a favorite research topic for other psychologists.

Riecken says that the experiment is "an invitation for one person to behave under the scrutiny of another." This social situation, then, is not an evenly balanced one: the experimenter is far more powerful than the subject. Only rarely will the subject try to exert power or try to defy the experimenter. Also, the distribution of information is one-sided. The experimenter may explain the task to the subject, but he or she typically withholds information or hides the purpose of the experiment. Riecken suggests that the experimenter plays a serious game with the subject, and, like the master of ceremonies on a game show, withholds "the right answer" until the end of the program.

Orne (1962) also points out that the strength of the power relationship between experimenter and subject is an unusual one. The experimenter commands some sort of behavior, and the subject behaves. Orne notes that there are very few situations in which such a wide range of requests is carried out obediently, with little or no question. Aside from the experimenter/subject situation, only parent/child or doctor/patient relationships demonstrate such obedience. In fact, Orne believes that almost any request will be obeyed if you first say the magic words, "This is an experiment."

Orne conducted an informal study to demonstrate this principle. He asked a number of casual acquaintances to do him a *favor*. When they said they would, he then asked them to perform five push-ups. They stared at him in amazement and responded "Why?" Then Orne approached other, similar acquaintances and asked them if they could take part in a quick *experiment*. Their typical response to the request to perform five push-ups was "Where?"

Subjects tend to be very obedient. They will continue at meaningless, boring tasks with little sign of hostility. Orne was trying to devise a very boring, long task because he wanted to demonstrate that hypnotized and awake subjects would differ with regard to the control that the experimenter had over them to make them continue with the task. One task he devised involved performing 224 additions on a single sheet of paper, and the subject was given 2000 such sheets. Even this task was not boring enough for normal, awake subjects to give up—they tended to continue for many hours! In fact, Orne has been unable to find an experiment that is so boring that subjects refuse to cooperate. This fact tells us a great deal about the extreme power that experimenters must hold over their subjects. Even your parents couldn't get you to do what an experimenter could! We will consider this issue of power again in the chapter on ethics.

Having looked briefly at the nature of the relationship between experimenters and subjects, let us look more closely at each of these participants. First we will examine the experimenters, to see how their characteristics and expectations can influence subjects' responses. Then we will examine the subjects, to see what "typical subjects" are like and what attitudes toward the experiment they are likely to adopt.

Throughout this chapter, there will be many suggestions about ways in which social aspects of the experiment can be controlled or reduced. Naturally, if you were to include *all* of these suggestions when you design an experiment, the study would be impossibly complex. Instead, be selective. If you are particularly concerned, for example, that experimenters' expectations will influence your subjects' responses, inspect the list of suggestions to see which idea (or ideas) you might include. These suggestions might also be examined if you are reviewing the psychology literature in an area where social aspects may be important: did the authors include any of these precautions to control or reduce social effects? These precautions are especially important to keep in mind for research in the more social areas of psychology. In contrast, psychologists studying reaction times to visual stimuli probably would not be particularly concerned that social factors might contaminate their experiments. It may be, however, that no area of psychology is immune from this potential contamination; we will see, for example, that the strongest demonstration of a phenomenon known as the experimenter-expectancy effect occurs in animal-learning experiments.

THE EXPERIMENTER

Jane Doe does an experiment and finds that the variable she is interested in has a significant effect on behavior. Mary Jones tries to replicate the experiment, and her results are completely different: the variable has absolutely no effect on behavior. What happened?

The problem is that different experimenters often get different results, even if they are each conscientious about trying to follow the experimental procedure exactly. Sometimes the different results can be traced to differences in the characteristics of experimenters. Other times, we find unexplained variability among experimenters' results, even when those experimenters seem to be quite similar in their characteristics.

Characteristics of Experimenters and Their Influence on Experimental Outcome

A wide variety of characteristics is important in determining the outcome of an experiment. We'll examine a number of these characteristics. When you read about research or when you conduct your own research, you should consider whether any of these characteristics could influence the results.

Sex. One important experimenter characteristic that may have occurred to you is sex. Subjects may respond differently, depending on whether the experimenter is male or female. For example, Binder, McConnell, and Sjoholm (1957) conducted a verbal-conditioning study in which subjects were reinforced for saying hostile words. One experimenter was a young, petite woman. The other experimenter was a mature, large, powerful-looking man. The results showed an interaction between the sex of the experimenter and blocks of trials. With the female experimenter, subjects sharply increased the number of hostile responses during the course of the experiment; this increase was much weaker with the male experimenter (see Figure 3-1). Be careful to note, however, that we cannot be certain that this difference is due simply to the sex of the experimenter. There were many other important differences between the two experimenters that may have been responsible.

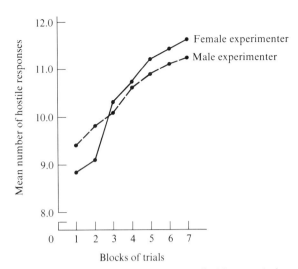

Figure 3-1. The number of hostile words supplied in a verbal-conditioning experiment with a male or a female experimenter. Data from A. Binder, D. McConnell, & N.A. Sjoholm. Verbal conditioning as a function of experimenter characteristics. *Journal of Abnormal and Social Psychology,* 1957, *55,* 309–314.

Often, the influence of the sex of the experimenter on the subject's performance is not a simple one; the influence may depend upon the sex of the *subject.* For example, Stevenson (1961) studied male and female children, using male and female experimenters. With young boys, female experimenters were more influential than males. However, with young girls, male experimenters were more influential than females. In other words, experimenters seemed to have more influence over children of the opposite sex: there was an interaction between the sex of the subject and the sex of the experimenter.

Why does the sex of the experimenter influence the subject's behavior? Rosenthal (1967) suggests that there may be two reasons. There may be an *active effect:* male and female experimenters may actually treat subjects differently, and subjects' responses may be influenced by that treatment. For example, a female experimenter may be more gentle than a male experimenter. There may also be a *passive effect:* subjects may themselves respond differently to female versus male experimenters. For example, a male subject may be more eager to please a female experimenter than a male experimenter.

Race. The experimenter's race is another factor that can influence subjects' responses, although it is not always easy to predict what kind of influence it will have. Sattler (1970) provides a review of the literature on this question. One common finding is that Black children perform better with a Black experimenter than with a White experimenter. For example, in a study by Moore and Retish (1974), 4- and 5-year-old Black children were given the Wechsler Intelligence Scale for Children. Each child was tested by both Black and White experimenters. The children scored significantly higher when the tester was Black.

Personality. Personality characteristics of experimenters often influence subjects' responses. In one experiment (E. E. Smith, 1961), for example, a friendly, permissive experimenter managed to persuade 17 out of 20 Army reservists to try eating grasshoppers, whereas an official-acting, formal experimenter succeeded in persuading only 10 out of 20 subjects to eat the grasshoppers. These results, which were highly significant statistically, suggest that an experimenter's warmth may determine the cooperativeness of subjects.

The experimenter's personality may also interact with the treatment conditions. Chapman, Chapman, and Brelje (1969) were interested in finding out whether homosexual and heterosexual interest could be determined by measuring the dilation of a subject's pupils to photographs of male and female nudes. One experimenter was a "businesslike graduate student." He found no difference in reactions to the male and female pictures. Another experimenter was a "casual, outgoing undergraduate." This experimenter found that males showed significantly greater pupil dilation to the female nudes than to the male nudes.

Additional studies have shown that other personality characteristics such as neuroticism, "adjustment," anxiety, and hostility also influence the subjects' responses. A review of the literature on the personal attributes of experimenters and their influence on experimental outcomes has been conducted by R. F. Q. Johnson (1976).

So far, we have been emphasizing the importance of experimenter characteristics and their influence on subjects' performance. However, variations in the behaviors and attributes of the experimenter do not always produce differences in subjects' performances, even when it seems likely that they should. For example, Bouchard and Hare (1970) studied brainstorming groups, sometimes using a 21-year-old female undergraduate as the experimenter and sometimes using a 30-year-old male professor as the experimenter. The experimenter had no influence on the production of novel ideas. In many cases, then, the attributes of the experimenter may be irrelevant to the particular dependent variable we are examining. We must be cautious and alert for experimenter effects, but we need not assume that they lurk everywhere.

The experimenter variable. What should we do if we suspect that attributes of the experimenter may be relevant to the variable we are studying? McGuigan (1963) proposes that the experimenter should be studied as an independent variable in its own right, just like other variables that influence behavior. If an experiment has used more than one experimenter, he suggests, the variable *experimenter* should be included in the analysis. The analysis can tell us whether the variable *experimenter* interacts with an experimental variable. If it does, we know that experimenter attributes influence the variable we are examining.

Lyons (1964) has suggested that the best solution to the experimenter-effects problem is to replace the human experimenter with some form of automated administration of the experiment, such as a computer. Human contact would still be necessary in recruiting subjects and greeting them when they arrive, but the influence of these humans would presumably be less than the influence of humans who actually administer the experiment. However, this suggestion might create as many problems as it solves. Aronson and Carlsmith (1968), for example, believe that a live experimenter is "not simply a bias-producing machine; he is frequently a necessary ingredient in the experimental process" (p. 52). In other words, human contact during the experiment may well be important for motivational purposes. Subjects may be reluctant, for example, to work on a long, boring task if the human experimenter is replaced by a machine. Furthermore, subjects' reactions to the *machine* might themselves be extremely variable! We might simply replace one kind of variability with another kind of variability. In short, this suggestion has clear drawbacks.

Nondifferentiated Experimenter Influence

We've just seen that experimenters often produce different results because of certain identifiable characteristics. In addition, experimenters often differ from one another for reasons we can't explain. It seems that there is variability among experimenters, even if those experimenters seem quite similar on a number of important characteristics.

For some reason, not many experiments have investigated this effect, which has been called **nondifferentiated experimenter influence** (Kintz, Delprato, Mettel, Persons, & Schappe, 1965). Many researchers *could* have studied this effect, because many experiments are run by more than one person. They could have analyzed their data to see whether subjects responded differently to the different experimenters, but they didn't. Still, there are a number of studies in which the authors did pay particular attention to nondifferentiated experimenter influence. Let's look at a few of these.

Postman and Jarrett (1952) were mainly interested in examining learning. However, they also uncovered information about experimenter effects because they used a total of 30 different experimenters, all of them students in advanced experimental psychology. The experimenters gave the subjects 240 stimulus words and asked them to supply for each word another word that came to mind. Half of the subjects were instructed to guess. The other half were told the "correct" principle for answering, which was to give common associations that would be found in speaking and writing. Postman and Jarrett found that their subjects responded differently, depending on which experimenter they had. In other words, the difference among experimenters was a highly significant source of data variance. Postman and Jarrett remark that it is apparently impossible to obtain complete uniformity in the behavior of experimenters. For this reason, we must sometimes expect to encounter difficulty in trying to replicate the results of other investigators.

Silverman (1974) discusses another good example of nondifferentiated experimenter influence, this time in an investigation of altruism. In this study, the experimenter made telephone calls, pretending that he had used his last coin trying to reach a garage because his car was disabled on a highway. He asked the person who answered the telephone to phone the garage and ask them to come for him. In fact, the "garage" phone number was the experimenter's phone. A published study conducted in New York City found that 60% of the people called the ''garage.'' When a student of Silverman's tried to replicate the study in Toronto, he found a response rate of 90%. It looked as though there were regional differences in altruism! However, a second student repeated the study in Toronto and found a response rate that was even lower than the 60% obtained in New York. In all studies, incidentally, the caller was male.

With the nondifferentiated experimenter influence, then, we find that different experimenters produce different results, and the differences cannot be explained very readily. Experimenters simply differ from one another. This effect is worth knowing about for two reasons. First, it helps explain why replications sometimes fail; keep this in mind when you read articles in the psychology literature. Second, it suggests that we can often improve the generalizability of our studies by using several different experimenters to test the subjects in a study. Silverman (1974) notes that only 20% of the studies in a sample he surveyed used more than one experimenter. Furthermore, only about one-third of those studies included a test to see whether experimenter effects were significant. When you are designing psychology research in an area where experimenter effects are suspected to be important, you should consider using more than one experimenter. (Naturally, you must be meticulously careful to have each experimenter run an equal number of subjects in each condition, to avoid confounding.)

Experimenter Expectancy

In this chapter, we have been looking at characteristics of experimenters that are generally quite permanent—characteristics that the experimenter would bring to every experimental situation. However, there is another kind of experimenter effect that varies from one experiment to the next, and even from one experimental condition to the next. This effect has been called **experimenter expectancy** or **experimenter bias**; it occurs when experimenters' biases influence the outcomes of their experiments.

Rosenthal's research. The experimenter-expectancy effect has been developed largely by Robert Rosenthal and his colleagues. Rosenthal's book, *Experimenter Effects in Behavioral Research* (Enlarged Edition) (1976) provides an excellent survey of the topic. According to Rosenthal (1963), experimenters obtain from their subjects—whether human or animal—the data they want or expect to obtain.

Before we explore some of Rosenthal's studies and other subsequent research, however, let us consider the nature of published research. An understanding of some of the principles that operate in publishing may clarify why the issue of experimenter expectancy is particularly important.

The fact is that most research that is published in journals and books consists of ''positive results.'' In other words, the results obtained in the experiment support the hypothesis proposed by the experimenter. As Jung (1971) has pointed out, we must *not* interpret this fact to mean that experimenters are very clever people who are able to make up hypotheses that are always supported by their data. Instead, journal editors typically do not publish "negative results," in which the independent variable either has no effect on the dependent variable or else has an effect that is exactly the opposite of what was expected. Therefore, if you perform a study and obtain negative results, you may not even bother to submit your article to a journal.

Now imagine that you are a young, starving psychologist, eager to accumulate a long list of published articles. Would you rather find positive results or negative results? It certainly is possible that the experimenter-expectancy effect would be greatly reduced if researchers were not so acutely aware of the benefits of positive results.

Most of Rosenthal's research on experimenter expectancy involves the following kind of design. Rosenthal supplies two or more groups of experimenters with different hypotheses about the results they will obtain from their subjects. In many of the studies, the experimenters use animal subjects, and the animals generally perform according to the experimenters' expectations.

Let us consider Rosenthal's studies on human subjects in more detail. In these studies, the experimenters were asked to obtain ratings of photos from their subjects. The photos were of faces cut from a newsmagazine, selected so that most subjects would normally rate them as occupying a neutral position on a rating scale of success or failure. The rating scale used in the experiment went from −10 (extreme failure) through 0 (neutral) to +10 (extreme success). In a typical set of experiments (for example, Rosenthal & Fode, 1963), the authors told one group of experimenters that they would probably obtain mean ratings of +5 from their subjects and told a second group of experimenters that they would probably obtain mean ratings of −5. It is important to note that all experimenters read identical instructions to their subjects and showed their subjects identical pictures. A total of 30 experimenters ran a total of about 375 subjects. In all three of the studies, every experimenter who expected high ratings in fact *obtained* higher ratings than every experimenter who expected low ratings. Thus, the experimenters obtained from their subjects the data they wanted to obtain!

Again, it must be stressed that the two groups of experimenters read identical instructions to their subjects. The experimenters were told that they must not say anything else other than "Hello" and "Goodbye" to their subjects. How in the world did the experimenters convey their expectations to the subjects when they clearly could not use obvious communications, such as saying to the subject "I expect you are going to rate these people as being fairly successful"?

When people first hear about Rosenthal's animal studies, their first suspicion often is that the experimenters have *cheated,* probably "fudging" the data as they record it. In this particular set of human experiments, however, that was not possible. For the record, Rosenthal (1966, p. 12) describes a study done by his colleagues that concluded that systematic recording errors and computational errors during data analysis are infrequent and trivial. Furthermore, Rosenthal (1976) has analyzed the studies conducted to date and has concluded that the carefully controlled studies—those that use special methods to eliminate cheating—are even more likely to show the experimenter-expectancy effect than those that do not use additional control conditions.

The next obvious hypothesis to account for Rosenthal's finding could be conditioning. Imagine yourself as an experimenter in Rosenthal's picture-rating experiment. Wouldn't you (subtly, of course) nod a little, brighten your expression, perhaps even smile if your subject gave a high rating, just as you had been told to expect? Even without intending to be dishonest, you might convey approval or disapproval. However, Rosenthal found evidence for the experimenter-expectancy effect even on the first trial of the experiment, and, in fact, the experimenter-expectancy effect seemed to *decrease* over trials. This is exactly the opposite of what we would expect if conditioning played an important part. After all, there would be no reinforcement prior to the first response, so there should be no biasing on the first trial. Also, if conditioning were important, the effects should *increase* over trials as the subject learns the appropriate responses.

Rosenthal (1976) proposes that nonverbal communication is largely responsible for the experimenter-expectancy effect. The specific cues, however, have not been identified. "After hundreds of hours of careful observation, no well-specifiable system of unintentional signaling has been uncovered" (p. 301).

The generality of Rosenthal's research. Let us consider evidence for the generality of the experimenter-expectancy effect. In 1966, Rosenthal reported that over 350 different experimenters had been tested, using over 2000 human subjects. He had examined experimenters who were volunteers and nonvolunteers and subjects who were volunteers and nonvolunteers. Experimenters had been drawn from advanced undergraduate courses in experimental, industrial, and clinical psychology and from graduate courses in psychology and education. Some studies had lasted only a few days; one had lasted several months. Some experimenters had run subjects individually; others had run subjects in groups. In other words, the effect had been found with a wide variety of experimenters, subjects, and situations.

More recently, Rosenthal (1976) has surveyed the 311 studies that have been conducted to date on experimenter expectancy. While the early research typically used the "person perception" design we described earlier, more recent research has examined such topics as reaction time, inkblot tests, and psychophysical judgments. There seems to be evidence for experimenter-expectancy effects in all areas, though it is more extreme in animal learning, for example, than in human learning. In all, 35% of the studies reached the $p < .05$ level of significance. (If chance alone were operating, we would have expected only 5% of the studies to have reached the $p < .05$ level of significance.)

It would be unfair, however, to leave you with the impression that experimenter-expectancy effects are inevitable. For example, note two points in the previous paragraph. Yes, 35% of the studies reached statistical significance; however, that means that 65% of the studies (about two-thirds) did not. Also, it is likely that many people have performed experiments on experimenter-expectancy effects without finding the effect and have either failed to submit their findings to a journal or have submitted articles and had them rejected because of nonsignificant results. Thus, the bias in publication practices may have inflated the percentage up to 35%; the "true" percentage is probably much lower.

Theodore X. Barber is probably Rosenthal's most vocal critic. In one paper (Barber & Silver, 1968), he and a colleague argued that the experimenter-expectancy research was weak on several grounds: (1) some of the studies probably permitted fudging of the data; (2) the experimenters were told that certain results were *desirable,* rather than merely *expected;* (3) a majority of studies failed to demonstrate the effect; and (4) the statistical analyses of the data were often inappropriate. Subsequently, Barber (1976) has also argued that: (5) the experiments were not sufficiently standardized in their procedures; and (6) the tasks in these experiments were too ambiguous.

It seems that some people believe in the experimenter-expectancy effect, and some people don't. An interesting irony may be operating: people who believe in the experimenter-expectancy effect may obtain it in their data, whereas people who do not expect to find the experimenter-expectancy effect may fail to find it in their data!

Probably a safe conclusion about experimenter-expectancy effect is this. It does not always occur. However, it occurs often enough for you to be somewhat concerned that significant results in a study *may* be due to the fact that you expected those results.

Early data returns. Let us consider briefly a closely related experimenter-expectancy effect, which has been called the **early-data-returns effect** (Rosenthal, 1963). This effect occurs when the experimenters look at the data they have collected on their first few subjects, and their knowledge of these "early returns" biases the later data. For example, if researchers examine the data from the first five subjects and learn that those data support the experimental hypothesis, the results of later subjects are likely to support the hypothesis. In contrast, if the data from the first five subjects do not support the experimental hypothesis, the results of later subjects are less likely to support the hypothesis.

Rosenthal designed an experiment to test the early-data-returns effect. In this experiment some of the subjects were Rosenthal's confederates (that is, people hired to act a certain way). These confederates supplied either expected or unexpected data to the experimenters. Then the experimenters tested naive subjects—ones who were not confederates. The results showed that the experimenters who had obtained "good" initial data obtained better subsequent data from their naive subjects than did the experimenters who had obtained "bad" initial data.

How can we explain the early-data-returns effect? Probably, when researchers see early data from an experiment, this influences their expectations of the nature of the data that will be obtained later. Once researchers form an expectancy, it can influence the performance of the subjects. It is also possible that the experimenters' mood could be influenced by these early returns and that their mood, in turn, influences the subjects' performance. We can draw a practical conclusion from the research on early data returns: when experimenters look at their early data, they may indirectly influence the responses of later subjects. The preventive is obvious: try to restrain your curiosity!

Applications outside the laboratory. There is additional evidence that the expectancy effect works in the classroom, as well as in the laboratory. Rosenthal and Jacobson (1968) conducted a study that is now a classic in educational psychology. They selected 18 classrooms in San Francisco and gave the students a nonverbal intelligence test. The teachers were told that the test was supposed to predict academic blooming. Then Rosenthal and Jacobson *randomly* selected 20% of the students in each class and told the teachers that these students had scored particularly high on the test of "academic blooming." Thus, the teachers were led to believe that these particular students (who were, in fact, a random sample of the population of all students) would show amazing academic progress throughout the school year. Eight months later, Rosenthal and Jacobson gave the same test again. When they looked at the scores, they found that the selected students obtained significantly higher scores than the rest of the students. This was particularly true of the youngest children: in the first and second grades, the selected students gained an average of 12 IQ points more than the rest of the students. It seems that the teachers communicated their expectations to those students who they believed would do great things, and the students improved to meet these expectations.

Also in the area of education, we can talk about the influence of the test administrator on test performance. It seems likely that test administrators can communicate their expectations to the students taking a test. Perhaps one reason that inner-city Black children score lower on IQ tests than suburban White children is that the person giving the test expects lower performance from Black children.

The expectancy effect is also relevant in the area of clinical psychology. A study by Rosenhan (1973) demonstrates this effect in psychiatric hospitals. Eight "normal" people presented themselves to psychiatric hospitals, complaining that they had been hearing voices. This was their only complaint; in all other respects, they behaved normally. The hospitals admitted them readily, labeling them with the diagnosis of schizophrenia. Once these "pseudopatients" were in the hospital, they stopped showing *any* symptoms of abnormality: they behaved as they would have behaved normally. The interesting finding was that, once a person had been labeled a schizophrenic, the pseudopatient was stuck with that label! In time, all patients were discharged, but upon discharge, they were labeled not "normal" or "cured," but "schizophrenic in remission." In other words, once a label is attached to a patient, the label remains, and all behaviors tend to be interpreted in terms of the original label. Clinicians, like experimental psychologists, tend to derive expectations from past behavior and to judge future behavior in terms of these expectations.

What to do about experimenter expectancy. What are the implications of experimenter effects for designing experiments? There are two reasons why this question is important. First, some suggestions may be helpful as you design your own research or when you serve as the experimenter in someone else's research project. One or more of these ideas should be included if you are concerned that experimenter expectancy may contaminate your study. Second, you can read journal articles more critically if you know some of the techniques that researchers can use to reduce the influence of experimenter effect.

1. *Automation.* Earlier in this chapter, we mentioned one way to reduce experimenter effects; ensure that the subject has very little contact with any people, primarily by automating the experiment. In some cases, the experimenter could be replaced by a computer. Even where this is feasible, however, it would certainly be expensive. Also, subjects may have particular attitudes toward machines that would influence their responses. However, we can consider other, less elaborate machines to replace some of the activities of the human experimenter. For example, Johnson and Adair (1972) found that experimenter-expectancy effects were sometimes reduced by using a tape recorder to give instructions to subjects, instead of having human experimenters read the instructions in person. Similarly, it is better to use electronic counters and timers than to record data by hand. Finally, a screen can be placed between the experimenter and the subject to eliminate visual contact and visual communication of cues.

2. *Blind experiments.* In many cases, experimenter-expectancy effects can be reduced by having a "blind" experimenter. In a **blind experiment,** the experimenter does not know what condition a subject is in or what treatment that subject is to receive. Whenever possible, this technique should be used.

The widest use of the blind technique has been in the field of pharmacology. Many studies in pharmacology use a **single-blind** technique: a single person, the patient, does not know what drug is being administered. The single-blind technique is similar to the design of most psychology experiments. After all, we typically do not tell subjects whether they are in the experimental or the control group.

The **double-blind** technique in pharmacology adds an additional control: the *doctor,* as well as the patient, does not know which drug the patient receives. This technique has been used in pharmacology for over 130 years. It seems to be a wise precaution. Haas, Fink, and Hartfelder (1963), who examined about 100 studies in which the effects of a drug were compared with the effects of a placebo, found that a placebo was most likely to have an effect similar to the real drug if neither the doctor nor the patient knew that it was just a placebo. (A placebo, as you may recall from Chapter 2, is a pill made of an inactive material such as sugar; a subject who takes a placebo pill is therefore an ideal control for another subject who takes a pill containing a drug substance.) With similar expectations for the drug and the placebo, the two substances may have similar effects.

For some reason, psychologists have not adopted the double-blind method very frequently. In other words, psychologists typically *do* know what condition the subject is in, and so they may be able to communicate appropriate cues to the subject. Sometimes, of course, it would be impossible to conduct a double-blind study. For example, if you are trying to observe differences in behavior between adult women and men, it would be difficult to disguise which are the women and which are the men! However, in many cases, it would be easy to use the double-blind method, so that the person who greets the subject, gives the instructions, and records the data knows as little as possible about the expected behavior of the subject being tested.

3. *Professional experimenters*. Rosenthal (1966) suggests that another way to reduce experimenter-expectancy effects is to hire professional experimenters. Just as there are professional interviewers, there should be professional experimenters who hire themselves out to run other psychologists' experiments. These people would not be ego-involved in the hypothesis; they might even be unaware of the hypothesis. Thus, they would be less likely to transmit cues about the hypothesis.

4. *Observers*. Rosenthal (1966) also suggests that the experimenter is less likely to transmit cues when an observer is present.

5. *Multiple experimenters*. Increasing the number of experimenters may also reduce experimenter-expectancy effects. The different experimenters may come to the experiment with different hypotheses, and these might cancel each other out. Also, each experimenter would run fewer subjects, so there would be less time for each one to develop a concrete hypothesis.

6. *Expectancy control groups*. Finally, Rosenthal (1966) suggests using "expectancy control groups." The other five methods we have discussed are designed to *reduce* experimenter-expectancy effects; this method seeks to *increase* them. In the simplest case, one experimenter is told to expect one kind of results, and a second experimenter is told to expect exactly the opposite kind of results. You can then look at the data to see if there is a difference in the performance of the two groups of subjects. If there is a difference, the experimenter can be included as a variable in the analysis; if there is no difference, the data can be combined. (Naturally, the addition of an expectancy control group demands the use of additional subjects and more complex statistical analyses, particularly when the experiment uses several independent variables.)

THE SUBJECT

Now, let's turn away from the experimenter to focus on the other member of the experimental pair—the subject.

Characteristics of Subjects Who Participate in Experiments

In Chapter 2, we mentioned that psychology experiments usually do not involve representative samples of human subjects. Now we can examine that statement in detail. Who are the typical people that are studied in experiments, and how might we expect the results of our studies to be influenced by the characteristics of our subject population?

Adair (1973) provides some answers to these questions. First of all, between 70% and 90% of all research on humans uses college students as subjects. More specifically, most of these subjects are students enrolled in courses in introductory psychology. No wonder skeptics often describe psychology as "the study of the college sophomore and the white rat"! College students are not typical human beings: they are most likely to be young, White, and from relatively wealthy families. College students represent 3% of the population of the United States (U.S. Department of Commerce, 1967); yet we base about 80% of our research on them. We may be willing to agree that their performance in a perceptual-illusions experiment is reasonably representative of the entire population, but it would be naive to assume that their performance in an attitude-change experiment is equally representative.

There is also a clear sex preference for subjects in experiments: about two-thirds of the subjects in published studies are male (Holmes & Jorgenson, 1971). Only about one-third of experiments study both males and females. Some results obtained with male subjects only may be irrelevant for 51% of the population.

We now know that the typical human subject is a male enrolled in introductory psychology. We can be even more specific about our typical subject once we know how the student happens to be participating in the experiment. Jung (1969) found that subjects typically participate in an experiment because it is a course requirement. Somewhat less often, participation in an experiment may be a course option or may be used for extra credit in the course. Only about 7% of the subjects are volunteers, either paid or unpaid. When participation is required, students who show up for experiments are probably representative of all introductory-psychology students. But when participation is optional, or a source of extra credit, it seems likely that those who participate will be higher in achievement motivation, organization, and certain other personality characteristics. At any rate, the participants may constitute a biased sample of the population of college students.

Psychologists have been particularly interested in those 7% of subjects who are volunteers. In fact, Rosenthal has written a book on *The Volunteer Subject* (Rosenthal & Rosnow, 1975). In brief, the volunteer subjects differ from subjects who do not volunteer for experiments in that they are: (1) better educated, (2) of higher social-class status, (3) more intelligent, (4) higher in need for social approval, and (5) more sociable. It seems, then, that volunteer subjects often show an exaggeration of the characteristics of typical college students. The college-student population is already an unusual sample of human beings, but the volunteer population exhibits to an even greater degree those qualities that make college populations unusual. If you use a volunteer population in your study, you can bias the results even more than if you use a sample of the general college population.

As you read about psychological research and as you design your own experiments, it is important to keep in mind that experiments studying college students—particularly volunteers—may have low external validity because they are studying a highly selected group of people. It may be, however, that a growing awareness of this selectivity will encourage psychologists to examine other populations. For example, an increasing number of studies have been concerned with mature adults (for example, Whitbourne & Weinstock, 1979) and with the elderly (for example, Kalish, 1975).

Demand Characteristics of the Experiment

Chances are good that you participated in a psychology experiment when you were taking introductory psychology. Try to recall what that experiment was like. You probably walked into a room, sat down, listened to instructions, and responded. But you probably had a number of thoughts going through your mind: "I wonder what this study is *really* about." "Is there somebody watching me behind that one-way mirror?" "I heard that the second part is more interesting." "Is that tape recorder on?" "Do they expect me to like these words or dislike these words?" "I saw that word more than I saw this other word; I wonder if I'm supposed to remember it better." "That person sitting over there is supposed to make me nervous." Some of your thoughts may have concerned unusual objects or people in the room, some of your thoughts may have been directed to what you had heard about the experiment from others who had taken part in it before, and some thoughts may have concerned what hypothesis the experimenter was testing. Perhaps you had some well-developed ideas about what was going on, but it's more likely that you had some vague hunches.

Orne (1962) has called all the cues that convey the experimenter's hypothesis to the subject the **demand characteristics** of the experimental situation. Demand characteristics include rumors you heard about the experiment, what they told you about it when they wanted you to sign up, the activities of the experimenter, the laboratory setting, and all the communication that goes on in the course of the experiment.

Orne (1969) believes that the entire problem of demand characteristics arises because the human subject is an active organism. (It *is* hard to imagine demand characteristics being relevant for a rat in a Skinner box.) To human subjects, the experiment is basically a problem-solving situation. They are placed in a room, given some directions about what to do, but not told specifically what answers are "right." Subjects, therefore, see the situation as a problem-solving task: it is their job to determine the correct answers, and even the correct *kind* of answers. In some cases, such as in a learning experiment, it may be obvious that you are expected to do well. (Even then, it may be unclear, for example, whether speed or accuracy is preferred.) In other cases, as in a study of attitudes, the correct kind of answer may not be at all clear, and subjects may spend a good deal of time trying to figure out what kind of hypothesis the experimenter has, and therefore what kind of answers they should supply. Incidentally, we will consider in a later section whether or not subjects decide to go along with the hypotheses that they come up with.

Orne suggests that the subjects' behavior in an experiment will be determined by two kinds of variables: (1) those that are traditionally defined as the experimental variables, and (2) the perceived demand characteristics of the experiment. Naturally, we would like the results of an experiment to be caused by the first kind of variable, rather than the second kind. However, we cannot eliminate demand characteristics from experiments. Subjects will always have some thoughts or suspicions about the experiment, and these thoughts will always have some effect. As Orne observes, human beings will ascribe purpose and meaning even in the absence of purpose and meaning. Since we can't eliminate demand characteristics, Orne believes that we should take them into account, study their effect, and manipulate them. (Notice that this strategy is similar to Rosenthal's on experimenter effects: "If you can't beat 'em, join 'em." If you can't get rid of a social effect, you can study it!)

What to do about demand characteristics. Here are some suggestions to consider if you are worried about demand characteristics in your experiment.

1. *The non-experiment.* By now you are familiar with the concept of a control group. This is a group created to handle problems of stimulus *presentation.* Wuebben (1968) talks about creating control groups to handle problems of stimulus *reception*—in other words, to assess the impact of demand characteristics.

An experiment described by Orne (1969) provides a good example of a "nonexperiment" control group. This particular study involves sensory deprivation—a topic we will talk about in Chapter 11. Subjects lay down in a room, deprived of almost all visual, sound, and touch stimulation. After some time in this setting, subjects would often hallucinate, show impaired mental functions, and behave erratically. Orne, however, suspected that much of the reaction to this sensory-deprivation situation was due not to sensory deprivation *per se,* but to the demand characteristics of the situation. To test this hypothesis, he performed an experiment that was identical to the original in as many ways as possible, *except that there was no sensory deprivation.*

This setup is quite similar to the placebo condition we talked about earlier. When you are in the placebo condition, you receive treatment that is identical to the treatment of subjects in the drug condition, with only *one* variable that is different—the substance in the experimental pill is a drug, but the substance in your pill is sugar. The subjects in Orne's study did not receive sensory deprivation, but they did have all the other incidentals that were present in the original sensory-deprivation study. That is, they were treated extremely cautiously, they were screened carefully for mental and physical disorders, they signed extensive release forms, they removed their watches, and there was a prominent "panic (release) button" in the experimental room. Ten tests were given before the subject entered the room, and the same tests were given after they left the room. The only difference was that they had no sensory deprivation. They sat in a room that was well lighted, with two comfortable chairs, ice water, a sandwich, and an optional task of adding numbers. The room was quiet but not soundproof. They remained in the room for four hours.

Now imagine yourself in this situation. In four hours, you would think of all sorts of demand characteristics and come up with many different hypotheses about what was going on. Simply taking the same test after you came out of the room that you took before you went in would be enough to make you suspect that *they* expected your behavior to be changed by the experience.

Orne found that the subjects in his experiment behaved similarly to the subjects in a true sensory-deprivation experiment, even though the sensory deprivation was not introduced. Orne concludes that it was the demand characteristics of the task, rather than the sensory deprivation, that produced the results of earlier research.

One way to examine demand characteristics, then, is to study a control group of subjects that is identical in every way to the experimental group except for the absence of the experimental variable. If the two groups perform identically, we can conclude that the experimental subjects *could* have behaved in a certain way because they guessed how they were supposed to act. However, it is important to be cautious in interpreting results from a nonexperiment group. A study using a nonexperiment group can never *prove* that a given finding in the experimental group must be due to the demand characteristics of the experiment. Instead, it suggests that the demand characteristics *might* have been responsible.

2. *Postexperiment inquiry*. As Orne (1969) points out, the most obvious way to find out about subjects' perceptions of an experiment is to ask them! "It never fails to amaze me that some colleagues go to the trouble of inducing human subjects to participate in their experiments and then squander the major difference between man and animal—the ability to talk and reflect upon experience" (p. 153).

Probably the two main reasons why psychologists have been reluctant to ask subjects what they thought about the experiment are that systematic inquiry is a difficult process and that subjects might not tell them the truth.

Let's consider the first problem. Imagine that you had to design a postexperiment questionnaire to determine what subjects thought was going on in an experiment. How can you find out what they thought, without putting ideas into their heads? Adair (1973) describes some of the characteristics of an ideal postexperiment questionnaire. The initial questions must be broad, designed to find out the subjects' general awareness of the purpose of the study. Later questions are more specific ones about crucial experimental procedures. Each item should be placed on a separate page, so that the later, specific questions will not influence the early answers. A questionnaire designed by Page and Kahle (1976), reproduced in Table 3-1, is an excellent example.

Even if you can design a good questionnaire, the second difficulty may remain: subjects may be reluctant to tell experimenters all that they know. Orne (1969) calls this the "pact of ignorance." Subjects may pretend that they don't know what is going on because (1) they are afraid to disappoint the experimenter by revealing that they figured out the deception, or (2) they are afraid their data will be discarded if they admit that they caught on.

Levy (1967) has demonstrated that subjects do abide by this "pact of ignorance." A confederate, posing as a subject who had just completed the experiment, informed subjects who were waiting for the experiment about the exact nature of the task. The study was a verbal-conditioning procedure in which subjects were reinforced for saying certain pronouns. The confederate

Table 3-1. An example of a postexperiment questionnaire.

Questions

1. Write down anything you thought about the experiment while it was being conducted.
2. What did you feel was the purpose of the experiment?
3. What did you think the hypothesis was (i.e., what did you think we were looking for, trying to study, etc.), and how were you supposed to react?
4. What did you think was the purpose of the word recall test at the time you were filling it out, if anything?
5. What did you think that the food words had to do with the purpose of the experiment, if anything?
6. What did you think was the purpose of the rating scales at the time you were filling them out, if anything?
7. Did you think that the experimenter might have expected that you would rate the nonsense syllables in a particular way? In other words, did the experimenter have a hypothesis about how the average person would tend to work the scales?
8. Why did you rate the nonsense syllables in the way you did? That is, on what basis or for what reason(s) did you rate them toward one end of the scale or the other?
9. In this experiment the nonsense syllables were usually associated with food words. It was expected that if you were hungry you would rate the syllables more on the pleasant side as a result of their association with food. Did you ever have approximately this idea about the purpose of the experiment before this questionnaire was introduced?

Yes——————— No———————

If yes, how certain were you of this?

Guessing ———:———:———:———:———:———: Certain

10. In this experiment some people tend to rate the syllables in such a way as to cooperate with what they believed the experimenter's hypothesis to be. Others, for whatever reason, tend to rate the syllables on a different basis than the experimenter's hypothesis. Rate your own degree of cooperativeness with the experimenter's hypothesis.

Uncooperative——:———:———:———:———:———: Cooperative

11. Please make any other comments that you care to make about your reactions to this experiment, including your reactions to this questionnaire.

From *"Demand Characteristics in the Satiation-Deprivation Effect on Attitude Conditioning,"* by M.M. Page and L.R. Kahle, *Journal of Personality and Social Psychology,* 1976, *33,* 553–562. Copyright 1976 by the American Psychological Association. Reprinted by permission.

said to the waiting subjects, "She wants you to make up sentences using *I* or *We* as the pronoun. . . . Better not say that I told you about it." The waiting subject then completed the experiment and was introduced to an interviewer, who asked questions about how aware the subject was of the "key" to the experiment. Only one of the 16 subjects reported that he had been fully in-formed by the confederate, and only three others admitted that the other sub-ject had told them that they would have to make up sentences but nothing more. Subjects wanted so intensely to preserve the integrity of the experimen-tal situation that even extensive questioning could not drag the truth out of them! Thus, even if we have succeeded in designing a good questionnaire, we cannot be sure that the answers reveal the extent of the subjects' knowledge. (Don't you wonder, though, whether subjects were reluctant to "reveal all" because they didn't want to tattle on the other subject, for fear that the experi-menter might retaliate against that subject?)

Demand characteristics and experimenter expectancy. At the beginning of this chapter, we discussed experimenter-expectancy effects—the idea that experimenters can influence the kind of responses the subjects supply. Now we have been talking about demand characteristics—the idea that sub-jects often supply the kind of responses that the situation (rather than the relevant variable) suggests. These two effects are similar, in that they are artifacts interfering with the true operation of the variable we are interested in. The two effects are also related in the way they operate. Specifically, the *experimenter's expectations* may change the *demand characteristics* for the subject: subjects may perceive subtle cues that tell them how to behave.

Nonetheless, the two processes are really quite different: the motives of the *experimenter* determine experimenter-expectancy effects, whereas the per-ceptions of the *subject* determine demand characteristics. For this reason, experimenter-expectancy effects apply to more situations than do demand characteristics. Geologists, for example, have to worry about experimenter-expectancy effects, to be certain that their hypotheses do not influence the recording of their data. However, you will probably agree that the rocks studied by geologists do not perceive demand characteristics.

Motivation of Subjects

Suppose that the subjects do come up with what they think is the experi-menter's hypothesis; will they provide responses that would fit the hypothesis? This question has four different answers, depending on which article you read.

The cooperative subject. Orne (1962) believes that subjects are basically cooperative. They are positive about experiments before they come into the laboratory, and by signing up for the experiment they agree to cooperate with the experimenter. Orne believes that subjects have a great desire to contribute to the advancement of science—a belief that more skeptical psychologists have questioned. He argues that subjects want to be "good subjects" in order to contribute to science.

Now, think back to some of the experiments you may have taken part in as a student in introductory psychology. You may not have had formal thoughts that you were making a contribution to science, but you may have had vague thoughts such as ''Did I ruin the experiment?'' ''Did I do what I was supposed to?'' ''I hope my results weren't so bad they'll have to throw them out!'' In other words, you may have been hoping that you were a ''good subject''—one who provided data to support the experimenter's hypothesis.

Notice how Orne's concept of the ''good subject'' fits in with his concept of demand characteristics. If the demand characteristics of the experiment make the experimenter's hypothesis obvious, and if the subjects are ''good subjects,'' they will guess the hypothesis and will try to provide data that is consistent with that hypothesis. Thus, the experimenter's hypothesis will be supported because of social factors, rather than because the hypothesis is true.

The negative subject. Other psychologists have argued that subjects are often negative rather than cooperative. According to this view, subjects do not wish to cooperate with the experiment, and they may even try to ruin the experiment. Masling (1966) has provided a colorful label for this attitude—the ''screw-you effect.''

What factors would tend to encourage the ''screw-you effect'' rather than the ''good subject'' attitude? Some subjects may resent being required to participate in experiments and may express their resentment and frustration by trying to wreck the experiment. Argyris (1968) describes a formal evaluation conducted on an introductory-psychology course. The students in the course were asked to choose one of three topics to evaluate, and the overwhelming majority chose to evaluate the requirement of participating in experiments. Their general reactions were criticism, mistrust, and hostility toward the requirement. In many cases, the students described how they had expressed their resentment when participating in the experiments by trying to ''beat the researchers'' in ways that would not be discovered.

Other subjects may not resent the research-participation requirement *per se,* but they may have had bad experiences in earlier experiments. Particularly if an earlier experiment involved deception, subjects may feel that it is perfectly permissible to wreck the next experiment. Still other subjects may be resentful and interested in wrecking an experiment because they hate the course itself. They can't show their anger during lectures, for fear of lowering their grade, so they express their anger and frustration against psychologists by destroying an experiment.

The faithful subject. The ''faithful subject'' is a term coined by Fillenbaum (1966) to describe a third kind of subject. Faithful subjects believe that their major purpose in an experiment is to follow the experimental instructions exactly. They may have suspicions about the experimenter's hypothesis, but they try to avoid acting according to those suspicions. Weber and Cook (1972) describe two different kinds of faithful subjects, and the distinction seems to be a valid one. The passive version of the faithful subject is relatively uninvolved in experiments; this person simply obeys the instructions, apathetically and mechanically. The active version of the faithful subject is similar to the good subject, in that both are anxious to help science. However, an active faithful subject who becomes suspicious about the experimenter's hypothesis deliberately tries to give absolutely honest answers. The active faithful subject is anxious to give honest answers so that the experimenter can draw truthful conclusions.

The unusual thing to note about the faithful subject is that when subjects adopt this faithful role, the results are *not* biased. Good subjects will produce data that will support the experimenter's hypothesis, even though that hypothesis may not be true in reality. Negative subjects will produce data that will go against the experimenter's hypothesis, even though that hypothesis may actually be true in reality. In other words, the first two categories of subjects will cause the experimenter to draw the wrong conclusion. Faithful subjects, in contrast, will bend over backward to do what they would normally do if they were not suspicious; there will be no systematic tendency either to support or to go against the experimenter's hypothesis.

Evaluation apprehension. Cooperative and negative subjects provide responses that will either confirm or contradict the experimenter's hypothesis. Faithful subjects provide responses that ignore the experimenter's hypothesis. A fourth group of subjects is characterized primarily by evaluation apprehension. They aren't particularly interested in the experimenter's hypothesis; they are mostly concerned with trying to look good. After all, it's a psychologist who is running the experiment, and everybody knows that psychologists can tell whether you're mentally healthy or not. Thus, the subjects are *apprehensive* about being *evaluated;* what they seek above all is the approval of the experimenter.

Evaluation apprehension seems to pervade many experiments. I particularly recall an experiment involving word associations. It was a perfectly innocent study of verbal behavior: I was interested in seeing what kind of words subjects would supply for very common words as opposed to very rare words. However, the subjects perceived the task quite differently: they assumed that I was using the word-association test to see whether they were "mentally healthy" or not. Almost every subject, after finishing the experiment, asked a question like "That was to see if I'm normal, right?" or "Did that test show I was crazy?" Perhaps this task was particularly likely to arouse evaluation apprehension because of the popular belief that word associations are powerful tools in diagnosing abnormality.

Other experiments may arouse evaluation apprehension about intelligence. Probably every verbal-learning experiment arouses subjects' concern that they must learn the material quickly and remember it carefully because the experimenter is trying to see how smart they are.

Rosenberg (1969) has written extensively about evaluation apprehension. He is particularly concerned that evaluation apprehension may distort subjects' responses. He has suggested a number of simple ways to reduce the influence of evaluation apprehension in an experiment: (1) Avoid telling subjects that the task will measure their intelligence or their personalities, and avoid telling them what a "normal" response would be. (2) Have the data collected by someone whose evaluative judgment is not relevant for the subjects (not, for example, someone who may have power over them, as in assigning grades). (3) Try an "altered replication" of the experiment, in which evaluation apprehension is reduced, and see if the results are different. (4) Lead the subjects to believe that the experiment concerns a technical matter, rather than some aspect of personality. Along the same line, Jung (1971) suggests: (5) Subjects should be told that the experimenter is interested in the difference between groups, rather than in the performance of individual subjects. One or more of these suggestions should probably be incorporated into any experiment in which evaluation apprehension would otherwise be likely to distort the subjects' responses.

Reconciling various motivations. We now seem to have four different views of the subject: the subject wants to cooperate; the subject wants to rebel against the experiment; the subject wants to provide honest data; and the subject wants to look good. How can they be reconciled? Jung (1971) discusses this issue. One strong possibility is that subjects are motivated primarily by evaluation apprehension. Often, subjects' concern with looking good will make them *appear* cooperative, but this is simply a coincidence. If subjects had to look stupid or ridiculous in order to cooperate and confirm the experimenter's predictions, they would refuse to cooperate. In case of a conflict, subjects would opt for evaluation apprehension. Similarly, we would expect that if negative subjects had to appear stupid or ridiculous in order to wreck an experiment, evaluation apprehension would make them end up cooperating instead.

Weber and Cook (1972), who have written one of the most complete reviews of the subject-role literature, also support the evaluation-apprehension view of the subject. They argue that there is not much evidence for either the good subject or the negative subject. They believe that evaluation apprehension can explain the evidence that is supposed to support the good-subject role and the negative-subject role. Weber and Cook hedge about whether the faithful subject exists: "There is evidence that in certain restricted contexts a faithful subject role may be adopted." These authors strongly believe, though, that evaluation apprehension is the most important motivation.

In light of these conclusions, it would be wise to consider evaluation apprehension when you design an experiment and when you read journal articles. Pay particular attention to ways in which evaluation apprehension could be reduced.

It is important to take into account the motivations of subjects in experiments because their attitudes toward the experiment may determine their responses. However, another reason for considering this area is to make you think of the human subject as an active, thinking person—not merely a passive responder to incoming stimuli. In 1908, Pierce lamented: "Indeed. . . it seems too often as if the subject were now regarded as a stupid automaton " (p. 264). This dehumanized view of human subjects persisted for about half a century, until Orne's article of 1962. The new emphasis on the active, inquiring, *human* qualities of the human subject has probably been important in developing the recent strong emphasis on the ethics of experiments—a topic we will consider in the next chapter.

The Hawthorne Effect. Most of the material in this chapter is relatively recent, involving social aspects of experiments that psychologists generally ignored before 1960. In contrast, the Hawthorne Effect has a long history. A series of studies at the Hawthorne plant of the Western Electric Company (Roethlisberger & Dickson, 1939) was originally intended to study the influence of a number of different factors on the rate of production. The researchers studied factors such as temperature, brightness of the room, hours of work, number of rest periods, salary, and so on. They found that no matter what factor they varied—in either direction—production went up. For example, if they increased the number of rest periods, production went up, as we might expect. However, if they *decreased* the number of rest periods, production also went up—a conclusion we would not have expected.

The authors believe that the explanation for these peculiar findings is that the women who were being studied felt honored to have been chosen for the experiment. They worked as a team, trying hard for the benefit of the whole group.

The **Hawthorne Effect** then, suggests that when we find improvements in performance in an experiment, these improvements may be a result of certain motivational factors, rather than a result of the simple variable we thought we were studying. A second thing that the Hawthorne Effect suggests is that measurement of behavior may be very difficult: simply by *measuring* a behavior, we change that behavior. Thus, we can never really know the true value for some behavior: as soon as we try to measure it, the value will change.

Sommer (1968) describes a relevant study in which motivational factors were important. People took an intelligence test in a quiet room. Then they took another form of the test in a room that had seven bells, five buzzers, a huge spotlight, phonographs, organ pipes, whistles, a photographer taking pictures, and four students doing acrobatics. Naturally, we would expect that people would do better in the quiet room, but in fact, they did equally well in both rooms! What must have happened, according to Sommer, is that people's morale went up as the environment became worse. In other words, the environment affected people's morale, and their morale affected their performance.

The Hawthorne Effect shows us that, once again, we would be foolish to assume there is a simple relationship between the independent variable we are manipulating and the dependent variable we are measuring. Whenever we deal with a human subject, we must consider complex social factors in the experiment that may influence our results.

Postexperimental Communication Patterns of Subjects

Remember when you had just finished taking part in an experiment during introductory psychology? Probably, the last words the experimenter said to you were something like "Please do not tell anybody else about what went on in this experiment." Did you keep completely quiet? Did you talk about it with a friend who was in the experiment at the same time? Did you describe it to your older brother when you went home for vacation?

The amazing thing is that experimenters had been telling subjects for many years "Please do not tell anybody else about what went on in this experiment"—yet it wasn't until the 1960's that psychologists actually tried to find out whether or not subjects obeyed this request. In a study of postexperimental communication patterns of subjects, Wuebben (1974) found that 75% of subjects admitted that they had talked to at least one other person about the study. These data imply that we must routinely assume that word will travel about experiments.

Aronson (1966) suggests one effective technique for reducing intersubject communication. He presents subjects with a long, vivid description of why it is necessary to test only naive subjects—those who do not know what the experiment is about. He stresses the disastrous consequences to science of publishing research based on ''sophisticated'' subjects. This technique has been found to reduce communication among subjects. It is clearly worth considering this technique if you are concerned about intersubject communication.

THE SOCIAL PSYCHOLOGY OF DECEPTION

Psychologists often use deception in order to mislead subjects away from the experimenter's hypotheses. They make up a story about their behavior, about the presence of another person in the experiment, about the equipment, or about the purpose of the experiment.

The purpose of deception, according to Wuebben (1974), is ''to keep subjects ignorant of certain features of an experiment, features which, if known, would prevent effective manipulation of independent variables and/or valid measurement of dependent variables'' (p. 173). As we discussed in Chapter 1, two extremely important goals in designing an experiment are manipulating the independent variable carefully and measuring the dependent variable appropriately. Deception, if correctly used, can help us reach these goals in certain types of experiments.

In many cases, the deception is simply one of *omission:* the experimenter does not tell the subject about everything that is going on, or about the hypotheses underlying the experiment. Sometimes the deception is a bit stronger, but perhaps still innocent. For example, in an incidental-learning experiment, the experimenters tell the subjects to rate English words. Later on, without warning, they ask the subjects to recall the words. Subjects may feel deceived because they were led to believe that the task was simply to rate the words, and they were given no hint that recall would be requested afterwards. (The experimenters would argue, of course, that if they had *told* the subjects they would be tested later, their learning strategies would be entirely different.) In still other cases, the deception may be even stronger. For example, subjects may be told that they will be shocked in the experiment, when the experimenter has no intention of actually delivering the shock.

Obviously, the whole problem of deception opens up the question of ethics: to what extent is it ethically permissible to deceive subjects in order to conduct psychological research? This question will be one of our major concerns in the next chapter. For now, we will concern ourselves with the social-psychological aspects of deception: how do subjects react in an experiment involving deception?

First of all, let's consider how often deception is used and what kind of experiments are most likely to employ this technique. Carlson (1971), reviewing experimental studies published in *The Journal of Personality and Social Psychology* and in *Journal of Personality,* found that 73% of the studies in her sample used deception.

As you might expect, deception is far more common in some areas of psychology than in others. We would not expect to find, for example, that 73% of the studies in *Journal of Comparative and Physiological Psychology* used deception. Deception, like demand characteristics, is a uniquely human problem. Most often, it is used in social-psychology experiments. Within this field, it is used most often in studies of conformity, cognitive dissonance, and experimenter-expectancy effects, and least often in studies of decision making and attitude change.

How effectively are subjects convinced during a deception experiment? Stricker (1967) found that experimenters are not very careful to check up on this question. Only one-fourth of deception studies used a postexperiment questionnaire to find out whether subjects had been suspicious. In Stricker's survey, the highest proportion of suspicious subjects reported in any study was 23%.

In some experimental designs, it may be impossible to avoid suspicion. Stricker, Messick, and Jackson (1969) used a variation of the Asch conformity design. Subjects asked to fill out a questionnaire were supplied with the answers supposedly given by another group of people (in reality the answers were fictitious). Roughly half of the subjects reported that they had suspected their responses were supposed to be influenced by the group's answers. In fact, some experimental designs, like the Asch conformity design, are discussed so frequently in psychology classes that suspicion seems inevitable.

You might think that subjects would be more likely to be suspicious in an experiment if they had been deceived in previous psychology experiments. Actually, this is only partly true. Stricker and his colleagues (1969) reviewed the literature on this question and concluded that prior experience with a deception experiment is relevant only if that previous experiment was similar to the present one. For example, if the first study involved impression formation and the second one involved incidental learning, the experienced subjects were no different from subjects who participated only in the second experiment. However, if they were given false printed norms in one experiment, and then were given false norms from other subjects in the room in a second experiment, the subjects were likely to be suspicious.

What happens if the subjects are, in fact, suspicious? Then the question is thrown back to a topic we discussed earlier: behavior depends on the subjects' motives. They may be ''good subjects'' and provide data in agreement with the experimenter's hypothesis, or they may operate according to the ''screw-you'' ethic. In general, according to Weber and Cook (1972), subjects tend to confirm the prediction of the experimenter in conditioning and persuasion studies and to operate against the prediction in compliance and conformity studies. This last bit of information on compliance and conformity studies makes sense in light of the rule you know about evaluation apprehension: subjects tend to place themselves in a good light. Although people may conform, they don't like to feel that they are being *made* to conform. They may think: "Aha! All these other people here aren't really subjects. They are just saying what the experimenter told them to say, so that I'll go along with them. But I'm not going to be a fool . . . I'll show them!"

We have seen that when subjects are suspicious in deception experiments, the results may be biased: subjects may supply either more or less of the behavior we are interested in. There is another problem with deception experiments. According to Orne and Holland (1968), deception experiments do not have **ecological validity.** In order for an experiment to have ecological validity, the results we obtain in the laboratory should have some application in "real life." In other words, laboratory and "real life" should be similar enough that we can run an experiment in the laboratory and conclude that the same results would occur outside the laboratory. Orne and Holland focus on one very famous deception experiment, Milgram's study in obedience, in order to demonstrate that laboratory deception is not very true to life.

We will examine Milgram's study in more detail in the chapter on ethics, but let's consider it briefly here. Subjects were asked to be "teachers" and to give an electric shock to a confederate "student" every time he made a mistake in the learning task. The confederate, who was in another room, responded with moans and screams, yet the subjects continued to give shocks for errors. Milgram concluded that people will show blind obedience in carrying out instructions, even though it may cause extreme pain for another human being.

Orne and Holland argue that this experiment has little ecological validity. They believe that the Milgram situation is not very realistic, and subjects would not be that obedient outside of the laboratory. Recall that Orne (1962) described the power relationship between the experimenter and the subject as an unusually strong one: experimenters can make any request after saying "This is an experiment," and subjects will obey. Furthermore, subjects really have faith in experimenters. When subjects come into an experiment, they believe that the experimenter is a trustworthy and professional person. They reason to themselves that the experimenter would not really be asking them to do anything that would harm themselves or other people. Imagine yourself in the position of the "teacher" in the learning experiment. If an experimenter told you to do something, wouldn't you assume that it couldn't really hurt anyone?

Orne and Holland conclude, therefore, that the obedience shown by subjects in the Milgram situation is an unusual kind of obedience. Milgram's conclusion that subjects in an experiment will do things that are destructive to themselves and others reflects more upon their willingness to trust the experimenter and the experimental context than on what they would do outside of the experimental situation.

We would expect, then, that if the experiment took place in a setting that was more true to life, obedience would be lower. Orne and Holland note that subjects *were* less obedient when the experiment was conducted in a rented office in a rather disreputable office building in downtown Bridgeport, Connecticut. In this kind of a setting, subjects would be much more likely to abandon the assumption that the experimenter is trustworthy and reliable and that the experiment is safe. When you're sitting in Room 114 of the Psychology Building at the University, it's an experiment, but when you're sitting in a crummy little room in downtown Bridgeport, it's real life!

If deception experiments arouse suspicion, and if they are not ecologically valid, what can be done to improve them? Stricker and his colleagues (1969) provide a number of useful suggestions: (1) Try to make the situation as realistic as possible, both with regard to the realism of the deception and the true-to-life setting of the experiment. (2) Limit the number of different deceptions in an experiment; too many deceptions may alert the subject to the one deception that is really necessary. (3) Use subjects who are naive—perhaps even subjects from less sophisticated populations than college students. (4) Complete the study quickly, so that word doesn't travel about the deception. (5) Give a postexperiment questionnaire to see if people were suspicious; analyze the data separately for the suspicious and nonsuspicious groups.

These suggestions are straightforward and rather modest. There are other, more radical solutions that have been proposed by psychologists who believe that deception studies have so many problems that deception should be eliminated completely. Kelman (1967), for example, believes that deception experiments should be replaced by role playing. In this design, subjects are asked to *pretend* that they are in a deception experiment. We will discuss this method, and its drawbacks, in the next chapter.

Another suggestion for replacing the deception experiment is the field study. We saw in Chapter 1 that field studies, such as the "broken bag caper," can provide useful data in a real-life setting. However, they have their own drawbacks, as we shall see later in this chapter.

Role playing and field studies are unlikely to eliminate the need for deception. It seems that *some* amount of deception may be necessary in most studies. As Wuebben (1974) points out, "Even if subjects are not intentionally deceived, it is a rare study that does not depend upon subject ignorance of the experimental hypothesis" (p. 174). The best answer may be to consider the ethics of the deception to be used and then to follow the suggestions of Stricker and his colleagues, outlined above.

FIELD EXPERIMENTS VERSUS LABORATORY EXPERIMENTS

One suggestion for solving the problems of deception studies was to replace them with field experiments, or "naturalistic research." Clearly, studying behavior in a shopping center or a busy parking lot has far more ecological validity than studying it in Room 114 of the Psychology Building. As we discussed in Chapter 1, cleverly designed field experiments can be effective in obtaining information about human behavior.

The advantage of realism in field studies must be weighed against the disadvantages that crop up whenever you leave the safety and control of the Psychology Building. It seems that the principal disadvantage of the laboratory—its artificiality—is a product of its key advantages—the control and the ability to manipulate variables. Adair (1973) points out that irrelevant variables that can be controlled in the laboratory will confound the relevant variable when the study is done in the field.

As we pointed out in Chapter 1, field studies cannot hope to control these confounding variables in any systematic fashion. For example, in the chapter on cognition, we will discuss a field study conducted by Munson (1962) at a series of public carnivals. He was interested in determining whether income level would influence risk-taking behavior in gambling. He collected data in two wealthy neighborhoods and three poor neighborhoods; his results showed that the two kinds of neighborhoods did not differ.

Consider the large number of variables that present problems for this study: (1) People may travel from other neighborhoods to attend carnivals, thus reducing the contrast in the incomes for the two kinds of neighborhoods. (2) The sample of people who gamble at carnivals may not be representative: perhaps only middle-income people gamble in each neighborhood. (3) The samples may not be representative with respect to other demographic and personality characteristics: in each neighborhood, perhaps only people of a particular sex, ethnic origin, age range, and risk-taking personality gamble. (4) Other factors that influence risk-taking behavior, such as the availability of alcohol, may not be equivalent for the two kinds of neighborhoods. These uncontrolled variables make it impossible to conclude that income has no effect on risk taking. In summary, Munson's study has the advantage of a true-to-life setting, but the disadvantage of the lack of control makes the results difficult to interpret.

Adair (1973) also points out that the power of experimenters is greatly reduced in field studies. They must wait for events to occur, rather than being able to make them happen. For example, one study examined whether there was a relationship between paying for the required automobile tax stamp and displaying a bumper sticker in support of one presidential candidate or another. Obviously, the study could not be done in a nonelection year. Logistic difficulties in such a study may be huge: the experimenters cannot control weather, crowdedness, stray dogs, kind of subjects, and innumerable other factors with the precision that they can in the laboratory. Also, the observers, who are supposed to remain unobtrusive, may unavoidably influence the behavior of those whom they are observing.

Even confederates may be forced to interact with subjects in unexpected ways. Adair describes one experiment in which a young, female confederate and a car with a flat tire were placed on a street in Los Angeles, in order to study helping behavior. Many of the subjects tried to "pick up" the confederate, even after she protested that she was just part of an experiment. (Obviously, this illustration of a disadvantage also highlights the advantages: subjects clearly did not know they were being observed in an experiment, and the situation was indeed realistic!)

Field studies often produce results that are very different from those obtained in laboratory experiments. We have seen that obedience in the Milgram situation was much lower in a more real-life situation than in the laboratory. This is true of other areas as well.

One finding that has been well established in the laboratory is that people favor cognitive consistency: they like their thoughts and beliefs to fit in nicely with each other, rather than contradict each other. However, Bem (1970), reviewing data obtained from surveys conducted outside the laboratory, has found that people don't mind inconsistencies in their real-life beliefs. This difference between field and laboratory results may be a product of the unusual environment of the laboratory. It is so clean and simple, with so many irrelevant stimuli left out, that contradictions become painfully obvious, and it is relatively simple to maintain cognitive consistency. In contrast, real life is cluttered with so many events and facts that we may not even notice inconsistencies.

Clearly, the experimental method and the field-study method each have their own advantages and disadvantages. Ideally, perhaps, psychologists should use the two methods to complement each other. For example, verbal-learning principles established in the laboratory can be tested in a classroom field study to see whether their generality holds for less controlled, more natural environments. Similarly, observations from field studies can be tested in a laboratory: do these observations still hold true when confounding variables are eliminated? In the chapter on psycholinguistics, we will see how observations from naturalistic settings can be translated into experiments in laboratory settings.

One other essential aspect of field studies will be considered in more detail in the next chapter: the ethics of conducting research on people in field studies. We don't ask their permission when we study them, and we don't even give them extra credit in Psych 1. In some field studies, moreover, we should be even more concerned about ethics than we are in the laboratory: our studies may influence subjects' lives, rather than simply the 50 minutes or so that they spend in the laboratory.

WHY SOCIAL ASPECTS ARE IMPORTANT

In this chapter, we have examined several social components of psychology experiments. We have seen that characteristics and expectations of the experimenter may influence the outcome of the experiment. At the same time, aspects of the experiment other than the experimental variable—the demand characteristics of the experiment—may influence how subjects respond. Subjects' motivations may also distort their responses in a systematic fashion. In addition, subjects in experiments are quite unusual, and the experimental setting itself is unusual.

All of these factors must be considered because the aim of research is to discover truth. If an independent variable and a dependent variable are really related to each other, then we want to discover that relationship; if they are *not* related to each other, then we want to discover that the two are independent. The problem, unfortunately, is that other factors may interfere and mislead us, causing us to draw an incorrect conclusion. In Chapters 1 and 2, we explored many of these confounding factors, such as order effects, uncontrolled subject variables, and uncontrolled stimulus variables. In this chapter, we have considered interfering factors associated with human interactions. Sometimes these social factors may be inconsequential, but often they can mislead us from the discovery of the true relationship between our variables.

SUMMARY

1. The relationship between the experimenter and the subject is an unusual one because the experimenter is far more powerful than the subject. Consequently, subjects tend to be very obedient.
2. Characteristics of experimenters such as sex, race, and personality attributes can affect the outcome of an experiment.
3. Because of unexplained variability among experimenters, different experimenters may obtain different results when they conduct the same experiment.
4. Experimenter expectancy occurs when the experimenters' biases influence the outcome of an experiment. The effect is controversial, and it does not always occur, but it occurs often enough for us to be on the alert for it. A related phenomenon is the early-data-returns effect. Effects similar to experimenter expectancy have also been obtained in the classroom and in clinical psychology.
5. Subjects who participate in experiments are not representative of the general population. They are likely to be male, and they are likely to be participating in the experiment because of a college course requirement. Subjects who volunteer for experiments are even less likely to be representative of the general population.
6. Demand characteristics are cues that convey the experimenter's hypothesis to the subject.
7. Psychologists have suggested four different views of subjects' motivations in experiments: the cooperative subject, the negative subject, the faithful subject, and the subject concerned about evaluation apprehension. Evaluation apprehension seems to be dominant in the largest number of experiments.
8. The Hawthorne Effect states that improvements in performance may be produced by motivational factors, rather than by the direct influence of the independent variable.
9. Subjects tell their friends about what happened in psychology experiments, even when they are instructed not to.
10. Deception of subjects is used frequently in some areas of psychology. If the subjects are suspicious, they may produce distorted data. Deception experiments may also have low ecological validity.
11. Field studies have been proposed as a replacement for laboratory experiments. Field studies may have higher ecological validity than laboratory studies, but they are plagued by confounding variables. Ideally, the two approaches should be used to complement each other.

4

Ethical Aspects of the Psychology Experiment

OUTLINE

A study tested whether bystanders would help in an emergency. A confederate of the experimenter walked through a moving subway car, using a cane. At a prearranged location, the person fell down. On some trials, the person simply collapsed; on other trials, "blood" trickled out of his mouth. (The "blood" was a thick red fluid placed in an eye dropper in the person's mouth.) The researchers found that bystanders were less likely to help the bloody victim [Piliavin & Piliavin, 1972].

Men who entered a three-urinal lavatory at a university in the Midwest were the unknowing subjects in an experiment. Some subjects urinated alone, some right next to a confederate of the experimenter, and some several feet away from the confederate. Another researcher, located in a toilet stall, watched with a periscope apparatus and recorded the delay and duration of urination [Middlemist, Knowles, & Matter, 1976].

Local citizens were recruited for a "learning" experiment via newspaper ads. In the laboratory, the subject met another "subject" (in fact, a confederate of the experimenter) who was designated to be the "learner" in the learning experiment. The subject was designated to be the "teacher" and was instructed to administer shocks to the "learner" whenever he made a mistake. Furthermore, the "teacher" was instructed to increase the amount of shock every trial. The shock apparatus was vividly labeled "slight shock," "moderate shock," "extreme intensity shock," and "danger: severe shock." In reality, the confederate received no shocks, but his responses were programmed so that he made many errors. Also, screams came from the confederate's room at appropriate intervals following the "shock." Nonetheless, 25 of the 40 subjects delivered all 450 volts from the area labeled "danger: severe shock" [Milgram, 1963, 1965].

These three examples are not typical psychology experiments, but they are representative of the kind of studies that psychologists are worried about. Are these three experiments ethical? You may think so, or you may think they are atrociously unethical. In fact, no one can provide a clear-cut answer on most ethical questions. It is relatively easy to determine whether a study is plagued by confounding variables; it is far more difficult to determine whether some studies are unethical. Please keep in mind that the majority of psychology experiments are perfectly innocent and that they inconvenience the subject only in terms of time and, perhaps, boredom. Nonetheless, you must be just as careful in considering the ethics of your experiment as you are in considering the methodological factors.

Concern over ethical matters in psychology has had a relatively short history. The American Psychological Association adopted a code of ethics in 1953. In 1963, Cranberg noted that the APA was still the only scientific organization to have adopted a code of ethics. Thus, apathy about ethics seems to have been widespread throughout the scientific community.

The APA revised its code in 1973, using a remarkable empirical method to provide information. They invited about 20,000 APA members to supply ethical problems—actual situations that they themselves had encountered. They received about 5000 descriptions, and these descriptions formed the raw "data" on which the revision was based. The committee drafted a proposed set of principles and distributed them widely at professional meetings and in professional newsletters. The committee then prepared a new set of ten principles, which remain in effect today (American Psychological Association, 1973).

Let's consider the general thrust of the principles before examining them in detail. The primary goal of all ten principles is the welfare of the subject: an experiment should not harm the subject in any substantial way. In reality, as you might guess, it is hard to determine whether a potential harm is substantial or insubstantial. The booklet describing the principles (APA, 1973) suggests that researchers should weigh carefully the advantages and disadvantages of conducting a questionable research project:

> Whether a particular piece of research is ethically reprehensible, acceptable, or praiseworthy—taking into account the entire context of relevant considerations—is a matter on which the individual investigator is obliged to come to a considered judgment in each case, without abdicating this responsibility on the grounds of current practice or judgment by others. In making this judgment, the investigator needs to take account of the potential benefits likely to flow from the research in conjunction with the possible costs, including those to the research participants, that the research procedures entail [p. 11].[1]

In other words, the researcher must weigh the benefit that the research may contribute to humanity against any harm that may result to the individual subject. However, you may have noticed a problem with this cost/benefit analysis. As Baumrind (1971) points out, normally one speaks of risks and benefits in reference to the same person. In this case, the subjects take the risks, and the psychologists and "humanity" get the benefits.

Nonetheless, the weighing of advantages and disadvantages is an important concept. For example, consider the Milgram experiment where subjects gave shocks when ordered to do so by an experimenter. This experiment was undoubtedly temporarily upsetting to the subjects (we'll discuss this aspect later), and so the subjects probably suffered some harm. However, humanity benefited by learning how subjects obey the orders of authorities. We learned that the concentration camps of Nazi Germany and the mass slaughters of Vietnam were not isolated deviations in the course of history. Even pleasant local citizens responding to newspaper advertisements in New Haven, Connecticut, could be ordered to hurt their fellow humans.

The ten ethical principles are reprinted in Table 4-1. Rather than discussing each of them in turn, I would like to approach the various ethical problems chronologically, as they occur for the researcher, and refer to the principles where relevant. We will begin with a discussion of ethical responsibility, a matter that must be considered during the designing of the experiment. The next two aspects of the experiment that may present ethical dilemmas are the recruitment of subjects and obtaining subjects' informed consent to participate. The experiment itself raises questions in three areas: deception, privacy, and

---

[1]This and all other quotations from this source are from *Ethical Principles in the Conduct of Research with Human Participants,* Copyright 1973 by the American Psychological Association. Reprinted by permission.

Table 4-1.

The decision to undertake research should rest upon a considered judgment by the individual psychologist about how best to contribute to psychological science and to human welfare. The responsible psychologist weighs alternative directions in which personal energies and resources might be invested. Having made the decision to conduct research, psychologists must carry out their investigations with respect for the people who participate and with concern for their dignity and welfare. The Principles that follow make explicit the investigator's ethical responsibilities toward participants over the course of research, from the initial decision to pursue a study to the steps necessary to protect the confidentiality of research data. These Principles should be interpreted in terms of the context provided in the complete document offered as a supplement to these Principles.

1. In planning a study the investigator has the personal responsibility to make a careful evaluation of its ethical acceptability, taking into account these Principles for research with human beings. To the extent that this appraisal, weighing scientific and humane values, suggests a deviation from any Principle, the investigator incurs an increasingly serious obligation to seek ethical advice and to observe more stringent safeguards to protect the rights of the human research participant.

2. Responsibility for the establishment and maintenance of acceptable ethical practice in research always remains with the individual investigator. The investigator is also responsible for the ethical treatment of research participants by collaborators, assistants, students, and employees, all of whom, however, incur parallel obligations.

3. Ethical practice requires the investigator to inform the participant of all features of the research that reasonably might be expected to influence willingness to participate and to explain all other aspects of the research about which the participant inquires. Failure to make full disclosure gives added emphasis to the investigator's responsibility to protect the welfare and dignity of the research participant.

4. Openness and honesty are essential characteristics of the relationship between investigator and research participant. When the methodological requirements of a study necessitate concealment or deception, the investigator is required to ensure the partici-

avoiding potential harm. The final ethical considerations involve debriefing, or explaining the experiment to the subject.

ETHICAL RESPONSIBILITY

It seems incongruous that psychologists have carefully developed methods for ensuring that the experimenter has designed the research carefully from the methodological standpoint, yet they devote relatively little professional attention to designing the research carefully from the ethical standpoint. Until recent years, ethics was an unmentioned topic in most experimental-psychology courses. However, just as researchers must assume responsibility for adequate experimental design, they must also assume responsibility for ethically sound experiments.

As Principle 1 states, the investigator is personally responsible for deciding whether an experiment is ethical or not. If the investigator suspects that the experiment might be questionable, he or she should consult with others. The pant's understanding of the reasons for this action and to restore the quality of the relationship with the investigator.

5. Ethical research practice requires the investigator to respect the individual's freedom to decline to participate in research or to discontinue participation at any time. The obligation to protect this freedom requires special vigilance when the investigator is in a position of power over the participant. The decision to limit this freedom increases the investigator's responsibility to protect the participant's dignity and welfare.

6. Ethically acceptable research begins with the establishment of a clear and fair agreement between the investigator and the research participant that clarifies the responsibilities of each. The investigator has the obligation to honor all promises and commitments included in that agreement.

7. The ethical investigator protects participants from physical and mental discomfort, harm, and danger. If the risk of such consequences exists, the investigator is required to inform the participant of that fact, secure consent before proceeding, and take all possible measures to minimize distress. A research procedure may not be used if it is likely to cause serious and lasting harm to participants.

8. After the data are collected, ethical practice requires the investigator to provide the participant with a full clarification of the nature of the study and to remove any misconceptions that may have arisen. Where scientific or humane values justify delaying or withholding information, the investigator acquires a special responsibility to assure that there are no damaging consequences for the participant.

9. Where research procedures may result in undesirable consequences for the participant, the investigator has the responsibility to detect and remove or correct these consequences, including, where relevant, long-term aftereffects.

10. Information obtained about the research participants during the course of an investigation is confidential. When the possibility exists that others may obtain access to such information, ethical research practice requires that this possibility, together with the plans for protecting confidentiality, be explained to the participants as a part of the procedure for obtaining informed consent.

---

reason for outside consultation is clear: the investigator may be too involved to decide objectively. After all, most researchers probably think that their research will provide some benefits to humanity, and they may be likely to overestimate those benefits in comparison to the costs to the subjects. In short, questionable experiments should be examined by an impartial reviewer.

There is another reason that experimenters should consult with others if they question the ethics of their experiment. The experimenters may be too far removed from their subjects in age, as well as in economic, social, and educational background, to judge what situations their subjects might find offensive or dangerous. For this reason, it may be wise to consult with people who are similar to the subjects—questioning college students, factory workers, or local residents, if these populations are the ones to be studied—to determine their reactions to the proposed study. If you suspect that the experiment could be psychologically stressful, you might consult with professional colleagues in personality or psychopathology disciplines. This precaution is particularly important for experiments involving children or others who cannot be expected to give informed consent. Finally, if you are working with a special population, seek out the advice of someone with professional expertise in that area. For example, I would not consider doing a study on migrants without consulting the woman who heads our regional Migrant Center. As you can see, there are no hard-and-fast rules about consulting others, but it is always wise to locate a second opinion.

Principle 2 emphasizes that psychologists are also responsible for the ethical conduct of their assistants and employees. Professors cannot turn their backs and assume that their graduate students are conducting the experiments ethically. The knowledge that they are responsible for what their assistants do ensures that they won't simply hand the assistants a copy of the ten ethical principles and look the other way! At the same time, however, these assistants are also responsible for what they do. This is important to remember if you find yourself helping in a research project after graduation. Whether that project involves experimental psychology, counseling, industry, or education, you must consider whether the research presents any ethical dilemmas.

Please construe the term *ethical responsibility* in the broadest possible sense. It extends also to consideration and courtesy. The subjects you interact with are human beings who expect to be treated decently, politely, and respectfully. Also, they value their time. If they have to wait for you to arrive late—or if you fail to show up at all—you have treated them unethically.

RECRUITMENT OF SUBJECTS

The first opportunity for ethical problems to arise in interacting with subjects occurs when you begin to recruit subjects. Principle 5 is concerned with recruitment: it states that people can decline to participate in research whenever they wish. It is particularly important, then, that subjects should not feel coerced into participating in an experiment.

As Milgram's experiments show, experimenters can convince subjects to perform activities that they probably find distasteful (Milgram, 1963, 1965). It is not surprising, then, that experimenters can exert the same power in recruiting subjects. Subjects should always have the option of saying no. This freedom is particularly important when there are risks or costs that accompany participation.

The problem of coercion is particularly important when the researcher has power over the subjects. The researcher who uses that power to force people to participate against their real preferences runs the risk of exploiting the subjects. Consider, for example, the helpless situation of students whose psychology instructor requires them to participate in his or her research. In this situation, subjects do not really have the option of saying no because they have realistic fears that their nonparticipation might be reflected in their course grade.

In reviewing the history of the current ethical standards, we noted that psychologists sent in approximately 5000 descriptions of ethical dilemmas they had faced. One such dilemma concerned subject recruitment. A psychologist described freshmen students who had participated in several days of hectic activity. Mixed in with the customary testing material were some research questionnaires. The students were told that the questionnaires were optional, but the psychologist questioned whether the students realized that they could refuse to participate, since the circumstances were so rushed. The students were coerced into participating because they had no time to pause, consider the situation, and say no.

Notice that the fifth principle also states that subjects can discontinue the experiment at any time. They are free to leave whenever the situation is unpleasant, and they must not be coerced into continuing. Quite naturally, a subject who drops out in the middle of the experiment is an annoyance to the experimenters. They have spent time in setting up the equipment and reading the instructions, and they have nothing to show for their efforts. Also, subject loss raises the question of a biased sample. The problem is particularly worrisome if subjects drop out of one condition to a greater extent than they drop out of other conditions: two groups that were originally equivalent might become quite different with the loss of subjects from one group, and the experiment would be confounded. This situation is one of many where methodological considerations come into conflict with ethical considerations. However, it is clearly unethical to try to persuade subjects to remain in an experiment against their will.

Let's talk more specifically about several subject populations, because certain special ethical problems arise from the nature of the subject population.

As we saw in the last chapter, most of the human subjects in psychology experiments are students enrolled in introductory psychology. Most of them participate because they are required to do so. The ethical-principles booklet (APA, 1973) presents several arguments for and against such a requirement. Those who support this kind of requirement argue that participation in experiments can be a learning experience, providing students with a realistic idea of how psychologists learn about behavior. They propose that the coercion problem can be avoided by allowing students to choose alternatives to participation in experiments. Others argue that "teachers of psychology have the right to require psychology students to make a contribution to the advancement of the science they are studying" (p. 43). Without subjects, psychologists would be unable to conduct extensive research. Another argument, not mentioned in the booklet, is that professors in colleges without subject pools often find other, less ethical ways of obtaining subjects, such as conducting their own experiments during class time.

Those who oppose the participation requirement argue that it is unethical for someone in power—such as a professor—to require another person to participate in experiments as a condition for enrolling in a course. They argue that experiments are seldom learning experiences for students, as the supporters claim. Furthermore, they point out that the alternatives to participation offered by some colleges are often far more difficult than the short period required for an experiment; consequently, there really is no "freedom of choice."

The answer to the dilemma of the participation requirement seems to lie in the careful management of the requirement. For example, students should be informed about the research requirement before enrolling, and they should be allowed to choose among several equally time-consuming alternatives. Research proposals and requirement procedures should be reviewed systematically. Subjects should be treated with respect and should receive thorough explanations to increase the educational value of the experience. Also, subjects should be informed about the procedures for reporting any mistreatments.

Certain noncollege populations are even more likely than college students to be coerced into participation. The ethical-principles booklet describes workers in an industrial setting whose supervisors asked them to participate in a research project. The psychologist who reported this incident was concerned that nonparticipation might lead to penalties from the supervisor.

Another psychologist reported concern over coercion in prison research:

> We used prison inmates in a number of research projects and always asked for their consent. However, in retrospect, it seems to me that since I also sat on boards that made recommendations for parole and had other important influences on their prison lives, it might be questioned whether they really felt free to refuse in view of their high need in these areas [p. 47].

Civil-rights groups have been concerned about this kind of coercion and have recommended a change in policies. The American Bar Association's Joint Committee on the Legal Status of Prisoners has proposed that no prisoner be compelled to participate in any program except work and that they should not be penalized in any way for refusing to participate ("Prison Research," 1976).

B. Barber (1976) discusses ethical abuses of other relatively helpless populations, especially in the area of medical research. These horror stories are occasionally reported in the newspaper: the live cancer cells injected into geriatric patients, the Black subjects in Alabama whose syphilis was intentionally left untreated, the severely retarded children exposed to hepatitis virus. Quite clearly, researchers must be acutely aware of the coercion problem with special populations.

INFORMED CONSENT

The question of informed consent is closely tied to the question of recruitment: people who are being recruited as subjects must consent to participate after learning what the experiment involves. Principle 3 states that investigators must describe the experiment to potential subjects, mentioning features of the research that might influence the subjects' decisions. After hearing the description, they can refuse to participate.

Informed consent is another area in which ethics may come into conflict with methodology. Often, for an experiment to be methodologically correct, subjects must be either uninformed or misinformed regarding its true nature and purpose.

First, let's talk about uninformed subjects. Very frequently—in fact, almost always—experimenters do not inform the subjects completely about the nature of the experiment prior to participation. For example, if we are conducting a verbal-conditioning study in which we reinforce subjects for saying "I" or "we," we do not *tell* them that we will be reinforcing them for those responses. However, if we interpret the third principle strictly, we should give subjects that information.

Resnick and Schwartz (1973) conducted that experiment in verbal conditioning, using two conditions of information. One group (the "nonethical group") was run under standard conditions. Another group (the "ethical group") was completely informed about the nature of the experiment: they were even told that if they began their sentences with "I" or "we," the experimenter would say "good." You probably will not be surprised to learn that the nonethical group showed the characteristic increase in the number of "I" and "we" sentences, but the ethical group showed a slight *decrease*. Furthermore, Resnick and Schwartz found it extraordinarily difficult to obtain subjects who would consent to participate in the ethical condition: despite intensive recruitment efforts, it took them five weeks to find 14 subjects who would consent to participate.

This study suggests that the results of studies in which subjects are completely informed may be worthless. The answer to the dilemma must be some sort of compromise. Subjects must receive information about tasks that might be unpleasant enough to make them say no, but they do not need to know all the details.

Other subjects are even more uninformed than our traditional laboratory subjects. These are the people who participate in field research without their knowledge. The men in the urinals and the passengers in the subway with the bleeding victim fall into this category. Silverman (1975) summarizes the ethical problems involved:

> No subject gives informed consent, by any interpretation of the concept. There are no contracts, no options to leave the experiment, no briefings or debriefings about the nature and purpose of deception, no opportunities for feedback, no pre-screenings or follow-ups to ensure the subject's welfare [p. 764].

By the very nature of this more naturalistic kind of research, informed consent is impossible. If the subjects were aware of the presence of the experimenter, or if they realized that the situation was a hoax, their behavior would be totally altered. In these cases, you must seriously consider whether you are exposing the subjects to any potential harm or whether you are invading their privacy. (We'll discuss these areas shortly.)

In most cases, however, the involvement of the subjects in field-research studies is minimal. Generally, the research has no positive or negative effects upon them. However, secret observation with hidden cameras and microphones is personally objectionable to many people—whether the information is used for research or not. For example, would you object to the Big-Brother-is-watching-you aspect of this study described in the ethical-principles booklet?

Employees of a public agency copied down license-plate numbers of automobiles that passed designated intersections. Then they located the car owners in official files and sent them a questionnaire asking how often they passed that corner. Some people strongly resent being "spied on"—even for a study of traffic patterns.

Now let's talk about *mis*informed subjects—people who are deliberately given incorrect information about the nature of the experiment and are consequently deceived. Clearly, they cannot give informed consent. We'll discuss deception as part of the experimental procedure in the next section, but we need to talk about deception used in the recruitment of subjects. According to Principle 6, the researcher and the subject must agree about what the experiment involves, and the researcher must keep the promises made in recruiting the subject.

The problem, then, is one of "misinformed consent": subjects are occasionally given promises that the researcher does not intend to keep. The researcher may give these promises to entice the subject to participate. Two alarming examples of this unethical conduct are cited in the ethical-principles booklet. In one case, subjects were asked to choose between a guaranteed $1 payment or a gambling situation in which they could earn up to $10. After the experiment, the researcher explained that he did not have the funds to carry out the gambling-situation option. The other case is more frightening:

> An experimenter interested in creating realism in an experiment convinced subjects that they were being hired for a quasi-permanent job. At the end of one day of "employment," they were told that it was merely an experiment. One subject complained that he had turned down other employment opportunities on the strength of this offer [pp. 37–38].

These situations are unambiguously unethical. However, keep in mind that you must fulfill even those promises that may seem minor to you. If you promise to give the subjects feedback on their test performance, for example, then you must do so. Students sometimes complain that an experimenter promised to send them the results of tests they took, but failed to do so.

Baumrind (1971) has suggested a procedure for determining whether the informed-consent rule can be dropped in cases where it is necessary to have uninformed or misinformed subjects. She proposes that investigators be required to pretest the experiment by asking other, similar subjects whether they would find the concealment reasonable. This proposal has been elaborated by Berscheid, Baron, Dermer, and Libman (1973). They suggest that the experimenters locate a sample of subjects who are similar to the ones they will eventually study. They should provide these subjects with a complete description of the experiment and ask them whether they would be willing to participate. If a large number refuse, the experiment should not be run; if only a small number refuse—perhaps less than 5%—the experiment is justifiable.

This technique of obtaining judgments from people who resemble the subjects has been used by Wilson and Donnerstein (1976). They interviewed passersby, asking them to judge eight field studies. One of the studies was the

Piliavin and Piliavin (1972) study with the bloody victim; other studies involved harassment, unobtrusive observation, and minor annoyances. Many subjects reported that they considered these experiments unethical and would resent being subjects. For example, 47% considered the bloody-victim study to be unethical, and 53% would object to participating in that study. Don't you wonder, incidentally, how the subjects felt about being interviewed in a field study?

The issue of informed consent must also be considered in connection with special populations. Ethically and legally, some potential subjects do not have the competence to give informed consent. These populations include children, the mentally retarded, and psychotic people. In these cases, the legal guardian must give his or her consent after the researcher has provided the necessary information. In addition, however, the researcher should also obtain permission from the subjects whenever they can make a reasonable judgment. The National Commission for the Protection of Human Subjects has recently recommended, for example, that researchers must request permission from all children over the age of 7, as well as from their parents or guardians ("Research on Children," 1977).

DECEPTION

Deception is commonly a part of the research design. It was used in each of the three experiments described at the beginning of this chapter. Another common kind of deception in psychology experiments is false feedback, when subjects are given fake information about how they performed a task. The following study, reported in the APA booklet (1973), is representative:

> In one study with male college freshmen, I returned false test scores to determine effects of success and failure on a subsequent task. Half the subjects were ranked in the top quarter and half in the bottom quarter. In the manipulation, I explained that the test rankings were highly correlated with IQ and probable grade-point average in college. After the second task I revealed the false scores and explained the purpose of the study. The fake test scores, the second task, and the explanation were in a single session so that any anxiety aroused by the manipulation would be quickly dissipated [p. 38].

This particular study involves another ethical issue—producing mental stress in the subject—in addition to deception. For now, though, let's concern ourselves with the problem of deception.

As specified in Principle 4, the relationship between the experimenter and the subjects should be based on openness and honesty. The subjects should be able to trust the experimenter. That trust is broken when subjects discover that they have been deceived.

Sometimes, an experiment employs several different kinds of deception. For example, you will read in Chapter 11 about an experiment in cognitive dissonance performed by Festinger and Carlsmith (1959). Subjects performed a task, and then the experimenters indicated that the experiment was over. The experimenters ''debriefed'' the subjects using false information and then asked the subjects to serve as accomplices in persuading other subjects to participate in the experiment. They were promised either $1 or $20 for their efforts in persuading. In fact, however, the ''other subjects'' were accomplices of the experimenters. Furthermore, the experimenters asked the true subjects to return the money at the true end of the experiment. As Kelman (1967) puts it, ''One wonders how much further in this direction we can go. Where will it all end?'' (p. 212).

We discussed the frequency of deception in Chapter 3. One study, for example, found that 73% of published personality and social-psychology studies used deception (Carlson, 1971). Naturally, the figure is not so high in the areas traditionally associated with experimental psychology. R. J. Menges (1973), for example, found that only 3% of the articles in *Journal of Experimental Psychology* involved supplying the subjects with *incomplete* information. (Menges classified studies as supplying incomplete information if a subject's summary of the experiment would be incomplete.) Is that deception? Subjects probably do not consider most omissions of information to be deceptions, but there may be some situations in which such omissions are construed as deception. For example, recall the experiment on incidental learning described in Chapter 3, and imagine yourself as a subject. The experimenters tell you to rate some English words. Several minutes later, without warning, they ask you to recall those words. Would you feel that the sense of openness and honesty between you and the experimenters had been broken?

We have discussed deception in field research and in experimental laboratory settings. Deception has also been used (or misused) in the case-study technique. Warwick (1975) describes a researcher who gathered information about homosexuals by passing as gay at private gatherings. He posed as a lookout in public restrooms to observe homosexual activity, using a concealed tape recorder. He then traced their license plates through the police and went to their homes to interview them. Clearly, this series of deceptions poses many ethical problems.

What is the answer to the deception problem? Several psychologists have tackled this issue, and they offer a variety of answers. Kelman (1967) suggests that we reduce or eliminate deception whenever possible. He objects to the tendency to accept deception as a matter of course, and he particularly protests the double, triple, and quadruple deceptions involved in some studies. If researchers are sensitized to the ethical problems of deception, they should respond by eliminating deception whenever it is not completely necessary.

Kelman (1967, 1972) has also proposed that psychologists use some of the ingenuity that has been directed toward deception in the past to construct alternative experimental techniques. He describes a new kind of ''contractual'' research in which the subject is asked to role-play the behavior of a person in an experiment. The subject thus becomes a collaborator in the research rather than an object to be studied. Clearly, this proposed technique is ethically sound, but numerous writers have objected to it on the grounds that what subjects *think* they would do may not be related to what they actually *do* do in real situations. Freedman (1969), for example, points out that when people were asked to predict what they would do in the Milgram shock experiment, only 1% reported that they would deliver the full amount of shock. This figure stands in striking contrast to the 62% who were prepared to deliver the full amount of shock in the experiment described at the beginning of this chapter. Still, there may be some areas in which role playing might be acceptable. For further information on this technique, you can consult Forward, Canter, and Kirsch (1976).

Campbell (1969) has suggested a compromise that may be more methodologically attractive. He proposes that subjects should be informed at the beginning of the term that in about half of the experiments they will be deceived either in part or in whole as to the purpose of the experiment. This explanation would further stress the guarantees of anonymity, privacy, and safety. He argues that this technique will simply make explicit a situation that is generally known already. Holmes and Bennett (1974) have provided reassuring data indicating that subjects given this kind of information perform the same as subjects in the standard, no-information condition.

As we discussed in Chapter 3, another replacement for deception studies is the field study. Rather than using elaborate deception to manipulate an independent variable, researchers can go out into the real world to find how the independent variable affects behavior. For example, Baron, Mandel, Adams, and Griffen (1976) studied crowding at the University of Connecticut. Many psychologists have studied crowding in laboratory settings, with the experimenters providing appropriate excuses for the too-cozy conditions. Baron and his colleagues, however, studied students who were forced to live three to a room because of high student enrollment; students in these conditions were compared with students in the standard two-to-a-room living conditions. Although the field-study technique is typically more ethically justifiable than the deception technique, we have seen that it also has clear drawbacks: field studies cannot achieve the control attainable in the laboratory.

PRIVACY

Privacy means that people can decide for themselves whether they want to share their feelings, thoughts, and personal information with others. Principles 5 and 7, in combination, maintain that people should not be coerced into providing material that they consider too personal to reveal. Principle 10 explicitly states that any personal information obtained during research is to be treated confidentially.

We have already discussed one kind of invasion of privacy under the topic of informed consent—the situation in which field research intrudes upon one's private life. Even if the observers never come into direct contact with the subjects, many would find it unnerving to know that they had been watched.

There seem to be three components to the issue of privacy. The first component is the right to refuse to share embarrassing information. Conrad (1967) notes that personality questionnaires ask questions such as ''Are you an illegitimate child?'' ''Does your father or mother drink to excess?'' ''I am no good at anything'' (True or False), and ''My father is really pretty stupid, like my mother'' (True or False). Subjects can validly answer that each of these questions is an invasion of privacy, even if they are not illegitimate, if their parents don't drink, if they are good at everything, and if their parents are brilliant!

It is important to remember that information that is embarrassing to one person may strike another person as perfectly innocent. The ethical-principles booklet (APA, 1973) relates an anecdote about an interviewer asking neighborhood women about the kinds of contraceptives they used. The interviewer had been worried that these questions might be too personal, but the women did not seem concerned. However, they considered the last question in the interview to be an outrageous invasion of privacy; that question was ''What is your family income?'' This story should alert you to the necessity of seeking the advice of similar subjects if you plan to design a questionnaire.

The second component of privacy is **confidentiality**. Any information gathered during research should not be supplied to others. The only exception to this rule occurs if subjects have given their informed consent, prior to the experiment, to the sharing of information. This rule applies even to people who may feel they have a right to the information, such as parents. The APA booklet (1973) cites an example of this dilemma and its ethical resolution:

> It was necessary to obtain parental permission to test the school children, and after the research several parents requested their child's scores on the intelligence test. But we had promised the children that no one outside the research group would be told about their scores, and so we refused to discuss individual children's results with their parents, even in a general way [p. 88].

The ethical-principles booklet discusses other specific problems with loss of confidentiality that can occur when organizations and individuals gain access to information. Babbie (1975) provides another example of this danger:

> I conducted a survey some years back of churchwomen. Ministers in a sample of churches were asked to distribute questionnaires to a specified sample of members, collect them, and return them to the research office. One of these ministers read through the questionnaires from his sample before returning them, and then proceeded to deliver a hellfire and brimstone sermon to his congregation, saying that many of them were atheists and going to hell. Even though he could not know or identify the respondents who gave particular responses, it seems certain that many respondents were personally harmed by the action [p. 464].

There is one final aspect to the confidentiality issue: we have discussed withholding information from others; should information ever be withheld from the *subject*? For example, you might decide that it would be ethically unwise to supply subjects with their scores on a masculinity/femininity scale. This issue is not as clear-cut as it might seem at first glance!

The third component of privacy is **anonymity**: subjects' data are gathered anonymously when the experimenters themselves cannot identify which subjects supplied which data. If you promise your subjects that their responses will be anonymous, then you must keep that promise. Violations of that promise are in conflict with Principles 3 and 6. The APA booklet (1973) provides an example of a situation in which anonymity was violated:

> On a mailed questionnaire, respondents were told that they would be anonymous. The researcher, "For your convenience," included stamped self-addressed envelopes. Each envelope had a commemorative stamp placed at a preselected distance from the upper corner enabling the researcher to identify by name more than 100 respondents [p. 90].

The ethical-principles booklet also provides an illustration of a study that fastidiously ensured privacy for its participants; this example is worth sharing. A psychologist wanted to study sexual behavior of college women. He first described the project to several female and male faculty members, graduate students, and undergraduates. The questionnaire was pretested on this group, and any embarrassing questions were reworded or omitted. Potential subjects picked up the questionnaires anonymously; the procedure did not allow the psychologist to match names with questionnaires. Also, the subjects were informed on a cover sheet that they could refuse to participate whenever they wished.

AVOIDING POTENTIAL HARM

Principle 7 states that participants should not experience physical or mental discomfort, harm, or danger. Let's first consider the portion of this principle that concerns physical pain. Quite clearly, an experiment that is likely to cause permanent harm must be avoided. You may recall reading or hearing in the media of violations of this principle. For example, in 1977, some electric-shock apparatus was reported to be malfunctioning at the State University of New York at Albany. Some inspectors claimed that the shock could have been lethal (R. J. Smith, 1977); others argued that the equipment had been tampered with after the experiment had been completed (Tedeschi & Gallup, 1977). As you can imagine, this episode increased the vigilance and rigor of many ethics review committees throughout the nation!

A rule that you might follow if you must use physical pain in an experiment is to participate in the experiment yourself before testing any subjects. Furthermore, be meticulous about observing all safety precautions, and check the equipment frequently—not simply the first time you use it.

The physical-pain aspect of Principle 7 should be taken in combination with parts of other principles. For example, the informed-consent rule states that subjects must be told what to expect during the experiment. However, this presents a dilemma if you are doing a drug study. If you describe the side effects of the drug to the participants, they may develop these side effects merely because they are expecting them; we saw how expectations can produce physical symptoms when we discussed placebos. If you don't describe the side effects, then the participants cannot supply truly informed consent. The answer, once again, may be a compromise: you might provide a general description, mentioning that the drug might produce discomforts or danger of a certain magnitude.

Also, keep in mind the rule that subjects are free to leave an experiment whenever they wish. They should not be coerced into staying when the situation is unpleasant or painful. The APA booklet (1973) cites an example of a flagrant violation of this rule:

> A researcher was conducting research on pain at a medical school by using a headband with numerous screws that could be tightened by hand to press against the subject's head. According to the experimenter's published report, subjects were solicited mainly from medical students at the university. On the basis of interviews conducted after the experiment, the experimenter reported that the subjects participated for the following reasons: (a) to contribute to science; (b) because they thought it was a requirement for a course they were enrolled in; (c) because they feared the effect refusal to participate might have on their grades; (d) because they wished not to alienate the experimenter, who was also their teacher and had considerable power over them and their fate in medical school. In one experiment reported, the subjects were told to endure the pain inflicted by the head apparatus as long as they possibly could. The instructions stressed the importance of enduring the pain just as long as it was possible to do so. After one of the subjects reported that he could endure the pain no longer, the experimenter mentioned to him that others had endured it much longer and, in various ways, by threatening the subject's masculinity and self-image, he induced the subject to continue to wear the headband for a substantially longer period of time [p. 67].

One final topic to be considered in the context of physical pain is something I call the Arrowsmith Dilemma.

A Sinclair Lewis novel concerns a promising young doctor named Martin Arrowsmith. A medicine had been developed that seemed likely to cure a spreading epidemic, but the medicine had not yet been tested in controlled circumstances. Arrowsmith faced a frightening dilemma. Methodological principles suggested that he give the medicine to the experimental group and leave the control group unmedicated, to face certain death. Ethical principles, on the other hand, suggested that he give the medicine to everyone, thereby possibly saving the control group, too. However, if he gave the medicine to everyone and they all recovered, he would not know whether it was the medicine or some confounding variable that had cured his patients. (Incidentally, he ultimately gave the medicine to everyone, and everyone recovered.) A parallel dilemma could occur in psychology. For example, suppose you devised a procedure that you believed could relieve psychosomatic pain: should you use it on only half of the suffering population at hand or on all of them? As you might suspect, psychologists would find it difficult to agree on a decision.

Let's turn now to the issue of *mental* discomfort and stress. In some cases, invasion of privacy—discussed previously—might become so extreme as to be stress-producing. For example, Koocher (1977) has objected violently to the study conducted by Middlemist et al. (1976) in the urinals. He argues that there is substantial potential harm to "unsuspecting or unstable individuals who might accidentally discover that they were being observed . . . there appear to be serious ethical questions and potential hazards'' (p. 120). Similarly, some questions on personality tests could be considered stressful, beyond the simple invasion of privacy. It is worth noting, once more, that some items may be unintentionally stress-provoking. An innocent-looking question such as "What is the name of your father?" could be devastating to a child whose father is unknown.

Included within the domain of mental stress are mild discomfort and boredom. In Chapter 11, we will discuss sensory-deprivation studies. Such studies, in which subjects are deprived of all sensory stimulation for extended periods of time, examine the most extreme forms of boredom.

More dangerous than boredom is the loss of self-esteem. Often, self-esteem is the independent variable in a study, and the experimenter manipulates this variable by providing false feedback to the subjects. We discussed one example of false feedback—involving scores indicative of IQ—under the topic of deception. Baumrind (1971) cites an example related to her by her own secretary, who had participated in a psychology experiment eight years earlier. The young woman had been instructed to make up stories about pictures; the experimenter had praised her for the stories. Later, the woman discovered that what the experimenter had said was unrelated to her performance; she had simply been assigned at random to the "favorable" condition. She was extremely embarrassed, and the experience helped to convince her that her actual performance was rarely related to the grade or praise she received. That experience, she believed, had helped to lead her into an unfortunate, cyclic achievement pattern that she maintained for a period of five years.

There are other examples of studies in which deception could produce harmful, long-lasting psychological effects. The ethical-principles booklet describes an experiment in which two males competed for the attention of a female, and one subject, chosen at random, experienced an embarrassing defeat. In another group of studies (Bramel, 1962), frequently cited in this context, males were led to believe that they were homosexually aroused by photographs of men. The deception was explained immediately after the experiment, but it is possible that the explanation did not remove all of the fears that had been planted.

The area of mental stress is yet another area in which ethical principles come into conflict with methodological principles. Remember the rule of sufficient separation discussed in Chapter 2? The levels of the independent variable must be sufficiently far apart to demonstrate an effect on the dependent variable. That rule raises no ethical dilemmas in verbal learning, for example, but consider the implications for research in self-esteem. By specifying that the difference in self-esteem must be as large as possible, the rule implies that the high-self-esteem group should be made to have *very* high self-esteem and the low-self-esteem group should be made to have *very* low self-esteem—which could be damaging. In this kind of situation, it is better to modify the rule of sufficient separation. Start with moderate separation—even though you suspect it may be insufficient—and then increase the separation in subsequent experiments if you have determined that the experience was not harmful to the subjects. Another option is to examine only the positive dimension. For example, you could compare high self-esteem with normal self-esteem and eliminate the low-self-esteem group altogether. (Naturally, this reduces the amount of separation.)

One of the ethical problems with the Milgram shock experiment is that the procedure is likely to reduce self-esteem. Imagine yourself in that experiment. You have just delivered 450 volts to a fellow human being. Then the experimenter tells you that the other person really received no shock. How would you react? You might feel extremely foolish for having been deceived, and you might be very embarrassed at your inner struggle over delivering the shock—when, in fact, there was no shock. Furthermore, you might have a very low opinion of yourself, knowing that you yielded to authority in order to hurt someone—and suspecting that you might yield in other circumstances in the future.

A very few experiments are so psychologically stressful that their after-effects may be irreversible. Perhaps the most horrifying example in the APA booklet (1973) is the following:

> The work which seems to me to raise ethical questions of the most serious type occurred in a military setting. It involved taking untrained soldiers, disorienting them, placing them in an isolated situation, giving them false instructions and leading them, as individuals, to believe that they had caused artillery to fire on their own troops and that heavy casualties had occurred. The subjects ran, cried, and behaved in what they could only consider an unsoldierly way, and no amount of debriefing could remove the knowledge that they had done so [p. 74].

Clearly, this experiment should never have been conducted.

Another category of experiments within the area of mental stress are those that encourage antisocial behavior, such as aggression. It is possible that aggression encouraged in the laboratory could be developed further in real life. The ethical-principles handbook describes a potential experiment concerning another antisocial behavior—cheating. A psychologist wanted to observe cheating, but he realized that the observation would need to involve deception. For example, examinations could be returned for "self-grading," and he could count the number of answers that had been changed. The psychologist did not pursue this research because he thought that such deceptive relationships between professor and students were unethical.

So far, we have discussed ethics within the context of human relationships and ideals. It is not *fair* to produce stress in another human being. Silverman (1975) points out another aspect that must also be considered: it may not be *legal* to produce stress in another human being. Silverman provided two lawyers with descriptions of eight field studies (the same ones used by Wilson and Donnerstein, 1976, involving harassment, unobtrusive observation, and minor annoyances). One of the lawyers thought that in three of the cases, a judge could legitimately award "punitive damages" because they involved intentional infliction of mental suffering. One of those cases was the bloody-victim study.

Principle 4 states that investigators are required to explain the reasons for any deceptions. This step is necessary in order to restore subjects to their preexperiment condition and to restore the trust that should exist between experimenter and subject. It is likely that many researchers provide a brief explanation and hope that the problem will disappear. Tesch (1977) notes the care taken in producing the desired effects, in contrast to the carelessness often displayed in dispelling those effects:

> On one hand, we devise marvelous manipulations and hone them for maximum impact upon our participants. On the other hand, we apparently assume that the effects produced conveniently cease when the participants leave our experiments. Have we discovered the best of all possible worlds, in which events happen when we wish and do not when we turn away from them [p. 219]?

Holmes (1976a, 1976b) distinguishes between two aspects of debriefing—*dehoaxing* and *desensitization*. **Dehoaxing** refers to convincing subjects that the information they were given previously was false (for example, that IQ scores had been randomly assigned). **Desensitization** involves helping the subject deal with the new information they have learned about themselves during the experiment (for example, the knowledge that they would obey a dangerous authority).

Holmes (1976a) offers several specific examples of effective methods of dehoaxing. For example, subjects took a fake intelligence test and then placed it in an envelope, which they sealed. The deception involved false feedback on intelligence. During the dehoaxing stage of debriefing, the researchers produced the envelope—still carefully sealed. In a Milgram-type shock experiment, the subject might be shown that the wires do not lead anywhere. Also, subjects could be invited to observe another session of the same experiment.

Now let's talk about desensitization. Holmes (1976b) notes that, unfortunately, there has been little research to determine whether desensitization efforts are successful. Some data have been gathered on the Milgram shock experiment, but these data may not be completely valid. Milgram (1964) sent a questionnaire to his subjects several months after completion of the experiment. Only 1.3% indicated negative feelings. Holmes (1976b) notes, however, that the question reads: "Now that I have read the report, and all things considered, I am very glad; glad; neither sorry nor glad; sorry; very sorry to have been in the experiment." Holmes believes that the strong demand characteristics (recall Chapter 3) of the report and the question may have induced the subjects to respond favorably. Holmes (1976b) presents other data to indicate that desensitization does effectively reduce the subjects' anger, however.

How should experimenters desensitize their subjects? Holmes describes some of the strategies he used in a Milgram-type experiment. He told the subjects that their behavior had been completely normal and that other subjects had performed similarly. He also pointed out that behavior in the laboratory might be completely unrelated to behavior in real life. In addition, Holmes used another strategy that may have involved deception: he told all of the subjects that their behavior had been rather mild when compared with that of other subjects in other experiments. Perhaps this was the case, but what if the subjects had responded extremely: would an experimenter be justified in calming these subjects with a "better than many" explanation? Again, there is no clear answer. Nonetheless, the first two strategies seem excellent, and they should be considered in experiments where subjects are likely to be embarrassed about their behavior.

Psychologists have opposed debriefing on several different grounds: (1) Some psychologists argue that word will travel, and the experimenter might end up testing subjects who have been informed about the experiment. The experimenter can reduce this danger, however, by following the precautions discussed in the last chapter. (2) Others maintain that debriefing is unnecessary unless the subject has been harmed. This argument, however, denies the educational benefit of debriefing, discussed in Chapter 2. Since the subjects are likely to be students in psychology courses, researchers must make every effort to ensure that the experience is as educational as possible. (3) Still others claim that debriefing can be harmful because it will lower the subjects' self-esteem. Baumrind (1971), for one, disagrees with this position and argues that an experiment should not be performed at all if it allows only two possible alternatives:

> *deceptive debriefing* (in which the truth is withheld from the subject because full disclosure would lower the subject's self-esteem or affect the research adversely) or *inflicted insight* (in which the subject is given insight into his flaws, although he is pained and has not bargained for such insight) [p. 892].

This point is worth considering if you are planning an experiment where the debriefing might be psychologically painful: perhaps the study ought to be abandoned.

Several additional points should be considered in connection with debriefing. First, debriefing should take place as soon as possible after the deception. Holmes (1976b) has demonstrated that subjects are substantially less upset by deception if they don't have to ponder the misinformation for a long period of time.

Second, there are many deceptions that are so serious that the effects cannot be undone by a simple explanation. For example, Walster, Berscheid, Abrahams, and Aronson (1967) informed some subjects that they were immature and uncreative and told others that they were mature and creative. After dehoaxing the subjects, they asked all the subjects to rate themselves once more. The subjects' ratings differed significantly. The first group still saw themselves as being relatively immature and uncreative, even though they had been told that the feedback had been false.

Third, how do you figure out what you will say during debriefing so that the subject is treated as ethically as possible? Holmes's (1976b) suggestions for Milgram-type experiments have already been mentioned. Mills (1976) provides some more explicit ideas, including a verbatim scenario that he has developed during 20 years of research using deception techniques. The scenario involves describing the necessity of keeping some information from the subjects. As well as being psychologically helpful to the subject, it provides subjects with an understanding of experimental techniques, thereby increasing the educational value of the experiment. This article, entitled ''A Procedure for Explaining Experiments Involving Deception,'' should be read by anyone using deception techniques in an experiment.

HOW SUBJECTS PERCEIVE THE ETHICS OF EXPERIMENTS

Some psychologists have argued against the adoption of the ten ethical principles. Gergen (1973), for example, argues that we have failed to demonstrate that the procedures used prior to their adoption were actually detrimental to human subjects. He maintains that strict ethical regulations will reduce the amount of research that is conducted and ultimately harm the profession of psychology. He regrets that the APA has adopted the ethical principles before establishing that they were necessary. While his point may be well taken, other psychologists would reply that it is better to err in the conservative direction where the ethical treatment of human beings is involved.

Some data are now available on subjects' perceptions of ethical aspects of experiments. Farr and Seaver (1975) asked subjects to rate a number of hypothetical experimental procedures—procedures that threatened either physical comfort, psychological comfort, or personal privacy. The ratings are valuable because they allow researchers to evaluate the risks of various procedures, rather than merely guessing at their unattractiveness. It is surprising to find, for example, that giving a 5-minute speech on a current topic to a group of other subjects was perceived to be more uncomfortable than having electrodes attached to your scalp suddenly begin to smoke!

Other psychologists have noted that subjects are more tolerant of various kinds of discomfort than we might suspect. Epstein, Suedfeld, and Silverstein (1973) found that more than 70% of their college-student subjects did not expect to be told the purpose of an experiment: the issue of informed consent was not perceived to be a critical problem. Sullivan and Deiker (1973) compared the responses of college students to the responses of professional psychologists on a number of ethical issues. In 18 out of the 20 response categories, the psychologists were much more bothered by ethical problems and more likely to classify an experiment as unethical. For example, when asked whether deception is unethical in experiments involving the alteration of self-esteem, 67% of the psychologists, but only 23% of the students, said yes. Fortunately, psychologists do seem to be quite concerned about the welfare of their subjects.

OTHER ETHICAL CONSIDERATIONS

In this chapter, we have discussed ethics as they concern research with human subjects. You should be aware, however, of other ethical standards governing psychologists.

We have not considered the ethical treatment of animals, for example. The American Psychological Association has adopted nine principles that concern the care and treatment of animals (American Psychological Association, 1971).

In addition, the American Psychological Association has adopted nine principles comprising the revised *Ethical Standards of Psychologists* (APA, 1977a). These standards are concerned with other professional activities of psychologists—other than research with human or animal subjects—such as respecting the integrity of the people with whom psychologists work, using assessment techniques, and making public statements.

The purpose of this chapter has been to alert you to some of the ethical problems that arise whenever you do research with human subjects. The experimenter is in a position of tremendous power, and that power must not be used to exploit the good will and trust of the subject. We defeat ourselves if we harm humans in the process of learning more about them.

SUMMARY

1. In 1973, the American Psychological Association prepared a list of ten ethical principles for the treatment of human subjects in psychology experiments.

2. Investigators are personally responsible for deciding whether their experiments are ethical, and they are also responsible for the conduct of their assistants. They must consult other psychologists and experts if the ethics of an experiment seem questionable.

3. Subjects should not be coerced into participating in experiments; they have a right to say no. Special measures must be taken to ensure that students in college subject pools do not experience coercion. Coercion must also be avoided in recruiting subjects in noncollege settings, such as industries and prisons.

4. Subjects must be given a description of the experiment before consenting to participate. This informed-consent rule presents special problems for subjects in field-research projects and for subjects who have been given misinformation about the experiment. If the design of the experiment prohibits obtaining informed consent, the researcher should consider asking other, similar subjects if they would find the experiment objectionable. Legal guardians must provide consent for special populations, such as children and the mentally retarded.

5. Since deception is commonly used in psychology experiments, psychologists have worked to find more ethically acceptable alternatives. Suggestions include role playing, notifying subject-pool participants that some experiments will use deception, and replacing deception with field studies.

6. The right to privacy has three components: the right to withhold embarrassing information, confidentiality, and anonymity.

7. Subjects should not experience physical or mental discomfort, harm, or danger.

8. Experimenters should debrief their subjects at the end of the experiment, explaining the reasons for any deceptions. Debriefing in deception experiments should involve both dehoaxing and desensitization.
9. Surveys have shown that psychologists are even more conservative than college-student subjects in their judgments of ethics.
10. Ethical considerations are also important in the treatment of animals and in other professional activities of psychologists.

5

Psychological Scaling Methods

OUTLINE

KINDS OF SCALES
    Nominal Scale
    Ordinal Scale
    Interval Scale
    Ratio Scale
SCALING TECHNIQUES
    Rating
    Ranking
    Paired Comparisons
    Scalogram
    Multidimensional Scaling

AN APPLICATION OF SCALING: THE SEMANTIC DIFFERENTIAL 159
FACTORS INFLUENCING SCALING   Psychological
    Stimulus Characteristics   Scaling Methods
    Subject Characteristics
SUMMARY

Scaling has figured into your life from the day you were born. One to five minutes after you were born, the doctor probably gave you an Apgar score. The Apgar score, which ranges from 0 to 10, is an index of a newborn infant's health that takes into account factors such as heart rate and muscle tone (Nelson, Vaughan, & McKay, 1969).

As soon as you learned to talk, you expressed preferences based on informal scales, perhaps similar to the yummy/yucky scale my daughters use (where butter brickle ice cream is yummiest and curried liver is yuckiest).

Throughout your life, your performance has been scaled. Even in kindergarten, you were probably graded on a scale such as E (excellent), S (satisfactory), and U (unsatisfactory). In later years, the rating scale may have had a greater number of categories. You may have received a rank to indicate your overall position in your high school graduating class.

Scales also figure prominently in other aspects of everyday life. You may have rated your college professors on a variety of characteristics. Books are available that rate movies on a scale from 0 to 4 stars; you can consult them if you wonder whether it's worth staying up for the late show. Restaurants are also rated; some authors in search of novelty use a scale from 0 to 4 *forks*.

Less formally, you make dozens of rankings and ratings every day—about the attractiveness of a picture, the intelligence of a friend, the self-confidence of a professor, and so on. We are so accustomed to the frequent process of evaluation that we are usually unaware of the steps involved in arriving at a decision.

This chapter discusses various kinds of scaling methods. We'll focus first on the kinds of scales (nominal, ordinal, interval, and ratio) and then on the techniques for obtaining scales (rating, ranking, and a few more obscure ones). Finally, we'll consider an application of scaling and examine the kinds of variables that can influence ratings and rankings.

First, let's distinguish between this chapter on scaling methods and the next chapter on psychophysical methods. In both cases, we are interested in measuring psychological responses to stimuli. In psychophysics, the stimuli can also be measured *physically*. For example, we could take out a light meter and measure physically the amount of light present in a stimulus. In this chapter on scaling methods, however, we will be discussing stimuli for which there aren't any corresponding physical scales. For example, we might be interested in measuring self-esteem. Unfortunately, we cannot take out a light meter or a ruler and measure anybody's self-esteem. (Most of my own research has involved measuring how much subjects like various stimuli. I've wistfully fantasized how wonderful it would be to peek inside each subject's ear at an imaginary little dial that registers "liking" for each stimulus!)

Thus, the problem in scaling is to assign a number to a psychological reaction to a stimulus—a stimulus that cannot be measured physically. The unavailability of a physical scale is what makes scaling challenging, difficult, and interesting.

In this chapter, we will be talking about scaling both things and people. Suppose we ask four subjects to rate four stimuli and obtain the results shown in Table 5-1. These results tell us something about the things being rated —for example, Professor Jones is rated higher than the other stimuli—and also about the people doing the rating—for example, Susan gives higher ratings than the others.

Table 5-1. Four subjects have been asked to rate four stimuli on a 7-point scale (where 1 = "bad" and 7 = "good").

Stimuli	*Subjects*				*Average*
	Mary	Sam	Joe	Susan	
a pencil	2	1	3	4	2.5
a tree	3	2	4	5	3.5
a rose	5	3	4	5	4.2
Prof. Jones	6	4	5	7	5.5
Average	4.0	2.5	4.0	5.2	

Scales can be used in constructing the independent variable or in assessing the dependent variable. For example, if we were interested in studying imagery as an independent variable, we might use as stimuli a number of English words that have been scaled for imagery. If we wanted to assess preference or liking as a dependent variable, we might ask subjects to rate a number of stimuli that have been presented previously.

KINDS OF SCALES

It is necessary to know what kinds of scales exist so that you can understand the properties of the measures you take. Also, you will need to know what statistics can legitimately be used with the scale you have constructed.

There are four kinds of scales: nominal, ordinal, interval, and ratio. We will begin with the most "primitive" scale (the nominal scale) and move up the hierarchy to the most sophisticated scale—the one with the greatest number of restricting qualities (the ratio scale). As we move up the hierarchy, each scale will have all of the qualities of the preceding one, plus one or more qualities that the more primitive scale does not have.

Nominal Scale

The term **nominal scale** comes from the Latin word for *name:* a nominal scale simply *names* the variables. In a way, the nominal scale isn't a scale at all: it simply names categories, without suggesting any relationship among those

categories. For example, the political parties would represent a nominal scale
because there is no order in which we can accurately place the parties. Even if we could manage to place the Democrats and the Republicans along a liberal/ conservative dimension (and it is unlikely that we could do so without protest), where would we place the Prohibition Party? Since we cannot place the categories in any kind of order, the only basic quality of a nominal scale is that items with the same label share some characteristic in common. For example, all people labeled *Democrat* have something in common. The nominal scale is the least demanding kind of scale: it requires you to say only whether a particular item belongs to one category or another. Is Mr. Brown a Democrat or a Republican? There are no quantities (how much of X?) implied in the nominal scale.

Incidentally, we can assign numbers to categories on a nominal scale (for example, 1 = Democrats, 2 = Republicans), but the numbers do not imply any kind of order. Sometimes the assignment of numbers to categories can be misleading because we are accustomed to associating numbers with quantity. For example, surgical scalpels are numbered. Wouldn't you assume that a #15 was bigger than a #10? In fact, if you look at Figure 5-1, you'll see that there is no apparent systematic pattern in the numbering of scalpels: the scale is simply nominal.

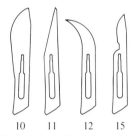

10   11   12   15

Figure 5-1. Surgical scalpels are assigned numbers; this is an example of a nominal scale.

In psychology, the nominal scale is very common. For example, people may be classified as either males or females, smokers or nonsmokers, normal or schizophrenic. The data from a nominal scale can be analyzed, but the analysis will involve a low-power test such as chi-square (see Appendix).[1]

Ordinal Scale

The other three kinds of scales, unlike the nominal scale, all indicate how much you have of a given quality. The **ordinal scale** has an advantage over the nominal scale because it implies *order:* you have placed the items in order along a certain dimension. Thus, if you know that Bill is smarter than Tom and Tom is smarter than Joe, you can place them along an ordinal scale Bill–Tom–Joe.

---

[1] A low-power test is one on which a Type II error is likely; that is, even though there is a true difference between your groups, you are likely to conclude (by mistake) that there is no difference. In contrast, the *t* test and analysis of variance are high-power tests.

You can also *rank* them 1–2–3 in terms of smartness. (Ranking produces ordinal scales, as we shall see later in this chapter.) The ordinal scale also has the properties of the more primitive scale (nominal), in that all items with the same label share some characteristic in common. Thus, if two people receive a ranking of 3, we can consider them to be equivalent on the dimension being ranked.

Notice, however, an important characteristic about the ordinal scale: it tells us order, but nothing more. We *cannot* say anything, for example, about the size of the difference between Bill and Tom or between Tom and Joe. Specifically, we cannot say that the difference in intelligence between Bill and Tom is just the same as the difference between Tom and Joe. Assigning ranks to Bill, Tom, and Joe does not produce equivalence in the differences, even though it might seem that the difference between 1 and 2 should be equivalent to the difference between 2 and 3. In fact, Bill may have an A average, Tom a C average, and Joe a C− average. In other words, when we have an ordinal scale, we cannot draw any conclusions about the size of the intervals between people or objects on that ordinal scale.

One practical point must be remembered about ordinal scales: you cannot use the mean, or average, as the measure of central tendency. In order to use the mean, you need information about the size of the intervals between items on the scale. With an ordinal scale, the **median** is the best measure of central tendency.[2]

Ordinal scales are common in psychology; they are created every time we rank people or things. Suppose we select a group of workers and have them attend an assertiveness-training workshop. Will their subsequent performance be superior to that of a control group? To measure our dependent variable, we might ask someone who is "blind" to the workers' experimental condition to rank their performance.

Now, how can we analyze the data? We cannot use a *t* test because the *t* test involves the mean. We could compare the number of people in the experimental group who are above the median with the number of people in the control group who are above the median. However, a test such as the Mann-Whitney, which compares group ranks (see Appendix), would be more powerful.

Interval Scale

In an **interval scale,** we know the size of the interval between items, as well as the order of the items. Thus, we can make statements about the size of the difference between any two individuals.

In psychology, standardized achievement tests have scores that use an interval scale. For example, you may have taken the Scholastic Aptitude Test

---

[2]The **mean,** as we saw in Chapter 1, is obtained by adding all the scores together and dividing by the number of scores. Thus, the mean of 2, 3, 5, and 7 is 17/4 or 4.25. The **median** is obtained by arranging the scores in order from lowest to highest and locating the midpoint. For the numbers 3, 15, and 65, the median is 15, the middle number. For the numbers 2, 3, 5, and 7, the median is 4—the midpoint between the two middle numbers, 3 and 5.

(SAT) when you applied to college. On that test, we can make statements about the size of the difference between individuals. For example, if Mary receives a score of 520, Judy receives 500, and Anne receives 480, we can say that the difference between Mary and Judy is the same size as the difference between Judy and Anne.

However, the interval scale still lacks certain important attributes: (1) we cannot make any statements about the ratios between items on the interval scale, and (2) we lack an absolute zero point. Thus, if Pete receives a score of 780 and Sam receives a score of 390, we cannot say that Pete is *twice* as smart as Sam. We also cannot specify a zero point on the SAT: a score of zero does not mean that someone has zero aptitude.

How do you decide whether a scale you are using is an interval scale or an ordinal scale? In other words, how do you determine whether your scale has equal intervals? This is actually quite tricky, and "experts" may disagree strongly as to whether a particular scale is ordinal or interval. For example, take a rating scale where 1.00 is "good" and 7.00 is "bad." Let's say that people rate the word *sunshine* as 2.00 on this scale, they rate *tree* as 3.00, and they rate *road* as 4.00. Some people would argue that the interval between *sunshine* and *tree* is the same as the interval between *tree* and *road*. (In other words, *sunshine* is better than *tree* to the same extent that *tree* is better than *road*.) Other people would argue that subjects treat the intervals in different portions of the rating scale as if they were unequal. The theoretical debate is too extensive and too technical to concern us here. In practice, however, psychologists often assume that scales (for example, rating scales) do have equal intervals—that is, that they are interval scales.

There is a distinct advantage to concluding that you are working with an interval scale. You can use the mean as a measure of central tendency and, consequently, can make use of powerful tests such as the *t* test and analysis of variance. You can understand, therefore, why psychologists are particularly eager to conclude that they are working with interval scales. Classically, psychologists were urged to be conservative and to treat their data as only ordinal if they suspected that the intervals were not equal. More recently, however, evidence has been presented (for example, Baker, Hardyck, & Petrinovich, 1966; Jette, Howell, & Gordon, 1977) to show that when *t* tests are conducted with ordinal data, the results are seldom misleading. In other words, the *t* test lets us draw the correct conclusion about our data even if the intervals are somewhat uneven.

In summary, then, it is generally safe to conclude that your data are from an interval scale and to use a *t* test. If you wish to treat your data conservatively, however, consider the data to be from an ordinal scale and use a chi-square or a Mann-Whitney test (see Appendix).

Ratio Scale

A **ratio scale** is even more advanced than an interval scale because it has an additional property: it has a true zero point. Because of the true zero point, we can make meaningful statements about the ratios between two values on a ratio scale. For example, "amount of food eaten" can be measured on a ratio scale. There is a true zero point: someone could eat *no* food. We can also say that Meg ate twice as much as Joe; twice as much food is meaningful, whereas twice as much aptitude (as on the SAT) is not. Angle of orientation is another example of a variable that can be measured on a ratio scale. We can ask a person in a dark room to adjust a line until it is exactly straight up-and-down. Then we measure the deviation from the true upright. One subject may have a deviation of zero degrees—this person's line is perfectly upright. Terry may have a deviation of 5° whereas Pat's deviation is 10°: in this case, we can say that Pat's deviation is twice as big as Terry's. Physical scales such as time, weight, length, and height are also measured on ratio scales.

Recall that each of the scales also has the properties of the less advanced scales. Let's see how this is true of the ratio scale by using the example of amount of food eaten. This scale has nominal properties because everyone who eats 20 grams falls into the same category. It has ordinal properties—Meg ate *more* than Joe. It also has interval properties. If Joe ate 10 grams, Meg ate 20, and Beth ate 30, then the difference between the amount that Beth ate and the amount Meg ate is the same as the difference between the amount Meg ate and the amount Joe ate. Thus, ratio scales also have nominal, ordinal, and interval properties.

What kind of statistics are permissible on data from ratio scales? These data are treated like data from interval scales: *t* tests and analyses of variance can be used.

SCALING TECHNIQUES

In describing the different kinds of scales, we have used the words *rating* and *ranking*. Now let's talk in more detail about these basic scaling techniques, as well as several other, more exotic techniques.

Rating

The most common scaling technique is the **rating scale.** The rating technique asks subjects to judge only a single stimulus at a time. Subjects inspect a rating scale and indicate where along the scale they believe the stimulus belongs. Figure 5-2 provides an example of a simple rating scale.

Usually, the rating scale is divided into a certain number of categories, as in Figure 5-2. How many categories should you use? Obviously, you can't have fewer than two categories. On the other hand, subjects would find it difficult to use a scale with too many categories. For example, imagine a scale with 20 categories, and imagine your indecision as to whether apple pie deserves a 2 or a 3. Chances are that you don't feel you can make discriminations that precise. Typically, psychologists use between five and nine categories: this allows enough choice without being overwhelming. Seven-point scales are probably the most common; they seem to be congruent with subjects' introspections on the number of discriminations they can make.

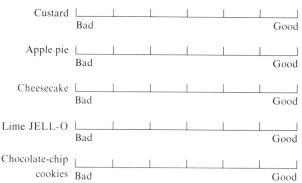

Figure 5-2. An example of a rating scale. Where on the scale would you rate each of these items?

Another factor to consider is whether you want to use an even number or an odd number of categories. This may not sound like a very important decision unless you have ever been asked to rate something that you felt *absolutely* neutral about—and your rating scale contained an even number of categories. For instance, you may have been asked to rate a professor on the dimension "clarity of presentation," using a 6-point scale. Dr. Brown might have deserved a rating exactly in the middle of the scale, yet you were forced to decide whether she was "slightly better than average" or "slightly below average." To avoid imposing this dilemma on your subjects—all else being equal— choose an odd number of categories. In addition, you may want to consider adding another category—one that does not fall along the rating line—labeled "does not apply" or "not enough knowledge to judge." For example, many of my students check this category in rating my statistics class on the attribute "encourages student discussion." (For some reason, rousing discussions on within-subjects analysis of variance shouldn't be encouraged!)

Another decision that must be made is whether the categories should be labeled. In Figure 5-2, the two extreme end points are labeled "good" and "bad," but the intermediate points are not labeled. Another option is to place numbers under each point. Still another option is to place verbal labels under each point; in Figure 5-2, the points might be labeled "very good," "good," "rather good," "neutral," "rather bad," "bad" and "very bad." The problem with verbal labels for every point, however, is that we may not be successful in discovering verbal labels that represent equal intervals. Is the difference between "very good" and "good" the same as the difference between "good" and "rather good"? If subjects do not consider the differences to be equal, the rating scale will clearly lack the interval property. Thus, we can make a better argument for the equal-interval property when there are no verbal labels.

Another variation of the rating scale is the **graphic scale.** This scale has labels on the end points, but there are no divisions or categories along the line. Graphic scales have the advantage that the subject is not restricted to certain numbers and categories. Subjects are also less likely to be influenced by previous judgments. For example, subjects in an attitude-change study may recall that they assigned a 2 to a stimulus the first time they saw it, and they may want to assign a 2 when they see it again to remain consistent. They are much less likely to recall precisely where they placed an X along a graphic scale. The disadvantage to graphic scales is a small one: it takes slightly longer to code the subjects' responses. You can't directly read the number that the subject has marked on the scale. However, a ruler can easily be used to determine the location of the X on the line.

Rating scales have been used heavily in psychology—perhaps most often in the areas of personality and social psychology, but also in more "hard-nosed" areas of experimental psychology. In Chapter 8, for example, you will find examples of learning and memory experiments using words that have been rated on dimensions such as imagery and pleasantness. If you find employment outside of psychology, you will still be likely to use rating scales. For example, you may plan a particular program and ask the participants to rate the effectiveness of the program.

Ranking

The **ranking technique** asks subjects to place items in order, from highest to lowest, according to the amount of some quality they have. Table 5-2 is an example of the ranking technique.

Table 5-2. An example of a ranking scale. Which of these items would you rank as 1 (the best), 2, and so on?

```
____ CHOCOLATE-CHIP COOKIES
____ CHEESECAKE
____ APPLE PIE
____ LIME JELL-O
____ CUSTARD
```

The ranking technique yields an ordinal scale. We may know, for example, that apple pie is liked better than cheesecake, but we know nothing about the size of the distance between the two items. In fact, this is a good example of the noninterval qualities of an ordinal scale: to me, the difference between apple pie and cheesecake is small, but lime JELL-O is so loathesome that the difference between lime JELL-O and custard is huge.

Notice that a low rank does not necessarily mean that you dislike something. For example, I love chocolate chip cookies, but they received a rank of only 3—simply because I like apple pie and cheesecake even better. Thus, we only know where an item stands on the scale *relative* to the other items. We lack knowledge about the *absolute* amount of the quality that is being judged.

In its usual format, the ranking technique forces subjects to make decisions—to say that one item is higher or lower than another. However, a modification of the ranking technique allows ties. In this case, if I like apple pie and cheesecake equally well, I can assign them both a 1.5.

There are some difficulties with the ranking technique. When subjects rank stimuli, all of the stimuli must be present at once and must be kept in mind at once. This task is quite difficult when there are a large number of stimuli. Try ranking the 15 vegetables in Table 5-3. You'll probably feel uncertain about whether the final ranking is accurate. Another problem with the ranking technique stems from not knowing anything about the absolute amount of the relevant quality. Thus, some comparisons between individuals are meaningless. For example, we cannot use the ranking scale in Table 5-2 to find out whether females like to eat desserts more than males do.

Table 5-3. A ranking scale involving 15 items. Do you find it difficult to rank so many different items?

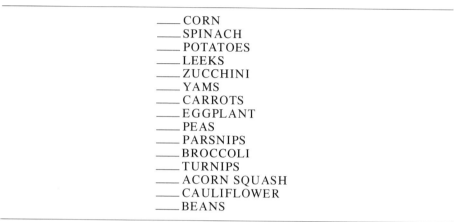

In summary, an advantage of the ranking technique is that it forces decisions. A strong disadvantage of the ranking technique is that it loses a good deal of information that would be available with a rating scale: we don't know how much of the relevant quality the item possesses, and two items that receive similar ranks (say, ranks 4 and 5) may actually be quite different from each other.

As noted earlier, the ranking technique provides ordinal data. Therefore, any statistical analyses must involve tests such as chi-square or the Mann-Whitney test. There is also a mathematical technique for normalizing ranks and converting to an interval scale; this technique is described in Garner and Creelman (1967).

Ranking is not used as much as rating in psychology because of the restrictions on the statistical tests that can be used. However, there are certain areas of applied psychology in which the forced-choice attribute of ranking is useful. For example, an employer faced with the need for staff reduction might rank the employees and keep those with the highest ranks. Ranking may also be preferable to rating because of a problem associated with rating. Often with a rating scale (as we'll see later in this chapter), everyone receives a high rating—perhaps 5 or 6 on a scale where 7 is "good." When everyone receives a high rating, it is impossible to make decisions about relative merit. Thus, ranking scales force those making the judgments to "stretch out" their scales.

The procedure for the **paired-comparisons technique** is just as the name implies: subjects see pairs of stimuli and are asked to choose which member of the pair has more of the relevant quality. In Table 5-4, for example, you must decide whether you prefer cheesecake to apple pie, cookies to cheesecake, and so forth. (In a formal experiment, you would see only one pair at a time.)

Table 5-4. An example of paired comparisons, using all combinations of five items.

Cheesecake—Apple Pie	Apple Pie—JELL-O	JELL-O—Cookies
Cookies—Cheesecake	JELL-O—Cheesecake	Cookies—Apple Pie
Cheesecake—Custard	Custard—JELL-O	Custard—Apple Pie
Apple Pie—Cookies	JELL-O—Apple Pie	Apple Pie—Custard
JELL-O—Custard	Cheesecake—Cookies	Custard—Cheesecake
Apple Pie—Cheesecake	Custard—Cookies	Cheesecake—JELL-O
Cookies—Custard		Cookies—JELL-O

As you can imagine, this method is practical only when you have a small number of items. Each item must be paired with every other item on the list, and this means that there will be a large number of pairs. The formula for the number of different combinations when you take n objects 2 at a time is n $(n-1)/2$. If n is 5, as in Table 5-4, then the number of combinations is 5 (4)/2, or 10 pairs of items. If we decided to add strawberry shortcake to the list, for a total of six items, the number of different pairs would increase to 15. With 15 items, there would be 105 pairs. The time involved in the task and the danger of subject fatigue would make this method impractical.

Now suppose that the subjects are asked to make the comparison "custard–apple pie" in that order only, and not in the reverse order. This may not be fair enough to the apple pie, because subjects may show a slight tendency to choose the first member of each pair, no matter what the items are. Thus, we have to counterbalance order within each pair to avoid confounding: the same pair must also appear in the order "apple pie–custard." Consequently, we have to double the number of judgments the subject must make, and the formula for the total number of judgments becomes n $(n-1)$. With 15 items, there would be 15 (14), or 210 judgments.

Notice that this method has something in common with the ranking method that we just discussed. When you were making decisions about what rank to give to each dessert, you probably made some paired comparisons at several points. For example, your strategy may have been first to set aside the ones you really liked—say, cheesecake and apple pie. Then you had to make a paired comparison between those two items to decide which of those two you liked better. The paired-comparison technique is also similar to the ranking technique in that both involve forced choices. However, notice the important differences. With paired comparisons, you see only two items at a time, whereas with ranking you see all the items at once. It is easier to make decisions with the paired-comparison method, then, because you aren't bothered by many irrelevant stimuli when making decisions about an individual pair. Subjects simply judge the pair that is in front of them; they don't have to consider the pairs that came before or the pairs that will come later. The paired-comparison method is also different from the ranking method because the need to counterbalance means that each pair will be presented twice. With the ranking method, the strategy will differ from one subject to the next, but usually the subject only makes one comparison for each pair.

In Table 5-4, you made 20 paired comparisons. How can you interpret these data? That is, how can they be summarized so that we know which items you like best? Table 5-5 demonstrates this procedure: calculate the total number of times each item was chosen; then rank the items according to these frequencies.

Table 5-5. Summarizing the results of the paired-comparison technique, using sample data from an experimental-psychology class.

Number of Times Each Item Was Chosen

190 Cheesecake	206 Apple Pie	100 Custard	42 JELL-O	198 Cookies

Rank for Each Dessert

3 Cheesecake	1 Apple Pie	4 Custard	5 JELL-O	2 Cookies

What kind of scale of measurement is represented by the totals calculated by the paired-comparison method? It is simply an ordinal scale. If cheesecake was chosen six times and lime JELL-O only twice, all we can say is that you like cheesecake better than lime JELL-O. We cannot make any statements about the size of the interval between cheesecake and lime JELL-O. Thus, the paired-comparison method allows us to put items in *order* according to the amount of a given quality that they possess.

We can also combine the judgments of a number of subjects to see how people judge desserts. Table 5-5 shows these totals for an experimental-psychology class. Like the values you derived for your own judgments, the scale represented by the totals is simply an ordinal scale—we know nothing about the intervals between items. Garner and Creelman (1967) describe a technique for converting this scale to an equal-interval scale.

In psychology experiments, the paired-comparison technique can be used instead of the ranking method when you want to be sure that the subjects are doing a careful job in making judgments. The paired-comparison technique forces subjects to be systematic and to consider all possible pairs in making their judgments. Subjects will often be less systematic and more careless in the ranking method, where they must make up their own strategies for placing items in order.

At the beginning of this chapter, I mentioned that we could scale both subjects and stimuli. The techniques we have examined so far scale either one or the other. **Guttman's scalogram technique** allows us to place both subjects and stimuli on the scale at the same time. The purpose of the scalogram technique is to test whether a characteristic being studied involves only a single dimension, or whether it needs more than one dimension to be adequately summarized. With the scalogram, questions must have only two possible responses, such as yes/no or pass/fail.

Table 5-6 shows some items that might be selected if one wanted to test attitudes toward antimilitarism. We might ask five people to respond to these

Table 5-6. An example of Guttman's scalogram technique: trying to scale antimilitarism.

	Bonnie	*Sam*	*Cynthia*	*Peter*	*Flora*
Risk arrest at a sit-in to protest military spending	+	−	−	−	−
Participate in a vigil to protest military spending	+	+	−	−	−
Write a letter to a Senator or Representative on military spending	+	+	+	−	−
Sign a petition on military spending	+	+	+	+	−
Accept a leaflet on military spending	+	+	+	+	+

items, indicating a "+" if they would perform the activity described and a "−" if they would not. Naturally, when we gather our data, the matrix of responses of the various subjects and the various questions will show a random assortment of +'s and −'s, rather than any noticeable pattern. Rows and columns must be systematically rearranged by moving "easy" questions to the bottom rows and "conservative" respondents to the right-hand columns) to yield the triangular arrangement shown in Table 5-6. Notice how the +'s occupy a triangle in the lower left-hand corner.

If the questions involve only a single dimension (in this example, antimilitarism), then a subject who gives a "+" answer to one question will also give a "+" answer to all questions that involve a *smaller* amount of the characteristic being studied. In this example, for instance, Cynthia answered that she would (+)write a letter to her Senator or Representative on military spending. Note that she also answered "+" to all the "easier" items on the list—signing a petition and accepting a leaflet. Similarly, a subject who gives a "−" answer to one question will also give a "−"answer to all questions that are "more difficult."

If there are a large number of inconsistencies—so that the +'s and −'s are scattered all over the matrix and cannot be arranged in such a way that they cluster together in a triangle—then we can conclude that the test items do not form a one-dimensional continuum, but instead represent two or more subjective dimensions. For example, suppose that we added another question: *"Organize* a vigil protesting military spending." Perhaps this item could not be fit into the continuum. Suppose that Bonnie responded negatively, whereas "less committed" Sam responded positively. This situation would indicate that another dimension had been introduced—perhaps one representing organizational skills.

Koslowsky, Pratt, and Wintrob (1976) used the Guttman scalogram technique to see whether attitudes toward abortion could be scaled. They selected 65 obstetricians/gynecologists and family physicians and asked them whether they would approve of abortion under 11 different circumstances. The 11 questions were found to fit along a single dimension (in other words, the + questions could be arranged into a triangle, with only a few irregularities). When the items on the scale were placed in order, they ranged from "abortion if pregnancy or childbirth is a threat to life," accepted by 77%, to "abortion if career or education would be disrupted," accepted by 40% of the doctors questioned.

Multidimensional Scaling

So far, we have been concerned with scaling objects on a single dimension only. For example, we present subjects with stimuli and ask them to place those stimuli on a seven-point scale for imagery. We then can compare any two stimuli that have been placed on that straight line; differences in where the stimuli have been placed represent differences between those stimuli with respect to imagery.

In real life, however, we make many judgments that cannot be represented by a single line, a single dimension, or a single quality. For example, contemplate the number of dimensions that might be relevant in judging a person's appearance and concluding "Joe looks like John." Another example occurred to me after I saw the movie *Missouri Breaks,* directed by Arthur Penn. It struck me that the movie was similar to *McCabe and Mrs. Miller,* directed by Robert Altman. However, there was no one single scale I could have constructed to represent that similarity; in fact, there were several different scales. Both movies were about Western, pioneer life. Thus, if we made up one scale called "Extent to which film content concerns Western, pioneer life," both films would have received the highest rating (but *Star Wars* would have received a low rating). However, there were many more dimensions, other than content, on which the films were similar. Both films would have received similar ratings on "use of obscenity": both would have been moderately high, lower than *Last Tango in Paris,* but much higher than *Bambi.* The two films would also have received similar ratings on dimensions such as "use of realistic costume," "use of a nonstereotyped female character," and "intelligibility of dialogue."

In other words, there would be no adequate way of demonstrating the similarity of these two movies by using just *one* scale. Similarly, we could not use just one scale to demonstrate how different both of these films are from

Bambi. Judgments of similarity in cases like these are just too complex to be represented by a single dimension. When this occurs, we need **multidimensional scaling**—a process that allows several dimensions to be scaled simultaneously.

Henley (1969) performed an interesting multidimensional scaling of animal names. She presented pairs of animals, one pair at a time, to her subjects and asked them to make a judgment about the amount of similarity between the two members of the pair. A rating of 0 indicated ''no difference,'' whereas a rating of 10 indicated the greatest difference. This rating of degree of similarity is the first step in multidimensional scaling. Next, she used a computer to extract a number of underlying dimensions. She found that animal similarity could be scaled in terms of three dimensions—two of which are represented in Figure 5-3. The first dimension seems to represent size, ranging from elephant to mouse. The second dimension seems to represent ferocity, ranging from cow to tiger. The third dimension (not shown) was harder to label, but it seemed to represent the similarity of each animal to humans: gorilla, chimpanzee, and monkey all scored high on this dimension.

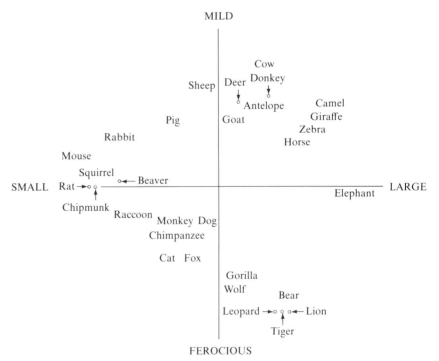

Figure 5-3. Two dimensions of a three-dimensional scaling of 30 animals. From ''A Psychological Study of the Semantics of Animal Terms,'' by N. M. Henley, *Journal of Verbal Learning and Verbal Behavior*, 1969, *8*, 176–184. Copyright 1969 by Academic Press, Inc. Reprinted by permission.

Note, then, that multidimensional scaling assigns a position to each stimulus in a multidimensional space. If two stimuli are near each other in that multidimensional space, we can say that they are similar to each other. Thus, the distance between stimuli in a multidimensional scale represents how differ-ent the stimuli are from each other. In Henley's study, leopard and tiger were right next to each other in a three-dimensional space—a result that probably coincides with your own feelings about leopards and tigers. Incidentally, keep in mind that multidimensional scaling does not need to end up with *three* dimensions. However, it is likely that the dimensions would become weak and difficult to label, in most cases, beyond three dimensions.

AN APPLICATION OF SCALING: THE SEMANTIC DIFFERENTIAL

One of the most widely used applications of scaling techniques is the **semantic differential**—an instrument devised by Osgood (1952) to measure meaning. Think about this for a minute: how would you measure the meaning of words? For example, the words *soft* and *gentle* are quite similar in meaning, but how would we represent their similarity in terms of numbers? (Remember: in scaling, we want to assign a number to a psychological reaction to a stimulus, and meaning is a representative kind of reaction.)

Osgood constructed a large number of 7-point rating scales, each of which was **bipolar**—that is, the end points were opposites in meaning, as in clean/dirty. Subjects were asked to rate a large number of concepts on each of the scales. Osgood then performed a factor analysis (see Appendix) on all the data to identify the most important components of meaning.

The factor analysis showed that three factors could explain most of the meaning. The most important factor—the one that explained most of the way in which words differ from each other—was *evaluation*. That is, the most impor-tant way in which one English word differs from another is in terms of how pleasant or unpleasant that word is. The scales that were most important in determining this factor were good/bad, wise/foolish, kind/cruel, beautiful/ugly, successful/unsuccessful, and true/false.

The second important factor was *potency*. The principal scale with re-spect to potency was hard/soft, although masculine/feminine was also some-what important. Thus, words differ from each other in terms of how potent, or hard and soft, they seem. A boulder is different from silk, although both of them may be equally good. The third factor was *activity:* active/passive was the most important scale here.

Let's consider some specific words. Jenkins, Russell, and Suci (1958) thought it would be useful to obtain semantic-differential profiles on a large number of words, so that these words could be used in later verbal-learning studies. They had subjects rate 360 words on each of 20 7-point scales. (It would be a deadly experience for a single subject to perform a total of 7200 concepts, so they asked each subject to make "only" 400 judgments.) The concepts were usually English words, such as *army, art,* and *continuous,* but some were phrases, such as *birth control, capital punishment,* and *conscien-tious objector,* and some were nonsense words, such as *gojey.* The ratings on all 20 scales for the word *candy* appear in Table 5-7.

Table 5-7. The word *candy*, as rated on 20 semantic scales.

	1	2	3	4	5	6	7	
cruel					X			kind
curved			X					straight
masculine					X			feminine
untimely					X			timely
active				X				passive
savory	X							tasteless
unsuccessful					X			successful
hard				X				soft
wise				X				foolish
new			X					old
good		X						bad
weak			X					strong
important			X					unimportant
angular					X			rounded
calm			X					excitable
false				X				true
colorless					X			colorful
usual		X						unusual
beautiful		X						ugly
slow				X				fast

Data from J. J. Jenkins, W. A. Russell, and G. J. Suci, *American Journal of Psychology,* 1958, *71,* 688–699.

Since the three dimensions of meaning cannot be clearly represented on two-dimensional paper, let's concentrate on the dimensions of evaluation and potency. Specifically, we'll look at how 20 words were rated on the most important scale for each factor—good/bad for evaluation and hard/soft for potency. The results are shown in Figure 5-4.

This spatial arrangement was derived by means of factor analysis rather than multidimensional-scaling techniques, but the result is the same: if two stimuli are near each other on the diagram, their meanings are similar. For example, *tornado* and *sin* should have similar connotative meanings.

The semantic differential has been used to scale words used in verbal-learning experiments—to be discussed in Chapter 8. For example, an experimenter can ask whether the goodness of an item affects how easily that item is learned. In social psychology, the semantic differential is often used to measure attitudes. For example, Majeres (1976) asked subjects to rate the words *youth, adolescent, teenager,* and *adult* on the semantic differential. These words did

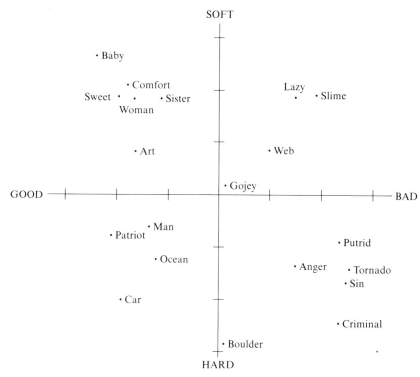

Figure 5-4. Twenty words located on two dimensions of a three-dimensional semantic space. Data from Jenkins, J. J., Russell, W. A., & Suci, G. J. *American Journal of Psychology,* 1958, *71,* 688–699.

not differ on the dimension of evaluation, but the three "young" words did have greater connotations of activity than the word *adult*.

FACTORS INFLUENCING SCALING

When you design a scale, you will probably want to know what factors can influence the results and which will be irrelevant. We'll divide the factors into two sets—those concerned with the scaling instrument (stimulus characteristics) and those concerned with the person doing the scaling (subject characteristics).

Stimulus Characteristics

The serial position of an item is important. Wagner and Hoover (1974) have demonstrated, for example, that the first and last items in a list tend to receive higher ranks than other items. The choice of anchoring labels is also important. For example, imagine that you had to rate desserts on a scale where the end-point labels were "very best possible in the world" and "very worst possible in the world." Your judgments would probably tend to avoid the very extreme labels, and your responses would fall somewhere in the middle. In contrast, the anchoring labels ''good'' and ''bad'' would encourage judgments to be placed at all parts of the scale. Finally, the familiarity of the terms can influence judgment. The reliability of the scales will be reduced if you use unfamiliar anchoring terms (imagine rating words on a scale labeled ''pulchritude'') or if you use unfamiliar concepts to be scaled (imagine rating the nonsense words *gojey* and *pelfel)* (Washington, 1975).

Certain other characteristics of the scaling instrument are *unimportant*—even some characteristics that you might think would have a great influence on the results. For example, the context of other stimuli is typically irrelevant (for example, Daves, 1970). In other words, if you had to rate a neutral term such as *road* for pleasantness, your rating of *road* would not be much different if the other words on the list were all extremely pleasant words than if the words had a wide range of pleasantness. The format of the scale is also rather unimportant. It doesn't seem to make much difference which anchor term is on the left and which is on the right. Nor does it matter whether you choose the customary horizontal scales—the kind that run from left to right, as in Figure 5-2—or vertical scales—the kind that run up and down (for example, Blumberg, DeSoto, & Kuethe, 1966). Finally, suppose you want your subjects to rate 20 concepts on ten different scales. It won't make much difference whether you have them rate one concept at a time on all ten scales, or all 20 concepts on one scale at a time (Blumberg et al., 1966).

Subject Characteristics

One of the most frequently studied subject characteristics is **response style,** or the way that people use rating scales (for example, O'Donovan, 1965). Some people show extreme response style: they rate items as either very good or very bad, and they don't seem to have neutral opinions on anything. Other people have a neutral response style: they tend to choose the intermediate categories and avoid extremes.

Subjects also differ with respect to **leniency effects.** Some raters use the pleasant end of the scale almost entirely, whereas others tend to use the less favorable end more often. In other words, people differ in terms of where their average rating lies. In general, though, there is a **positivity bias:** people use the more pleasant end of the scale the most. In one study (Matlin & Gawron, 1978), for example, subjects were asked to rate their happiness in comparison to the happiness of the average person in the room. A total of 75% of the people rated themselves as happier than the average person in the room—a finding that is mathematically outrageous!

Subjects differ, too, in the extent to which they supply socially desirable responses; there is even a scale to measure this tendency, called the Marlowe-Crowne scale (Crowne & Marlowe, 1964). Social desirability of responses is closely related to evaluation apprehension, discussed in Chapter 3.

Some people in some situations demonstrate a characteristic known as **yea-saying**: they tend to say yes to every question, whether it is phrased in the positive or in the negative. My husband has noticed this tendency among some parents who bring their children to his pediatric practice. He'll ask if the baby has had a fever. Yes. Has the baby had a stuffy nose? Yes. Has the baby had diarrhea? Yes. Vomiting? Yes. After nine or ten yeses, he begins to doubt the validity of the report, and so he asks, "Has your baby sprouted wings and flown around the room?" If the answer is yes, he suspects that he has found a yea-sayer.

Finally, let us consider the **halo effect.** When raters are asked to judge more than one characteristic of a person, the rating on one characteristic may be influenced by the rating on another characteristic. Many professors find that they are influenced by the halo effect when filling out letters of recommendation for students applying to graduate school. If they have rated a student as excellent on "knowledge of material" and "oral expression," they may find that they also give a high rating on other characteristics for which they have no evidence, such as "gets along well with peers" or "creativity." Thus, the halo effect causes people to assign either consistently high or consistently low ratings to a person because of the general, global impression that the person creates. Incidentally, Nisbett and Wilson (1977) have demonstrated that raters are generally unaware that halo effects have been influencing their judgments.

What is the effect of all these factors on ratings? Sometimes these factors lower the *reliability* of judgments. A person may be inconsistent in rating a concept, for example, depending on how the anchoring labels are worded. Sometimes these factors lower the *validity* of judgments. The judgment may not reflect the true reaction to a concept; instead, it may reflect a yea-saying characteristic or a halo effect. Thus, psychologists in search of true relationships between variables must be careful to avoid these contaminating factors.

SUMMARY

1. Scaling methology is concerned with measuring psychological reactions to stimuli for which the relevant attributes cannot be measured physically.
2. A nominal scale involves categories, with no relationship among the categories.
3. An ordinal scale places items in order along a certain dimension. However, no statements can be made about the size of the interval between adjacent items on an ordinal scale.
4. An interval scale provides information about the size of the interval between items.
5. A ratio scale allows us to make meaningful statements about the ratio between two values.
6. The rating technique asks the subjects to place a single stimulus along a scale, typically with labeled end points.
7. The ranking technique asks the subjects to place items in order, from highest to lowest, according to the amount of some quality they have. The ranking technique forces decisions, but it loses information that would be available with the rating technique.

8. The paired-comparisons technique asks subjects to choose which member of each pair has more of a specified attribute. All possible pairs of items are judged. This technique forces systematic judgments, but it is impractical to use with a large number of items.

9. Guttman's scalogram technique allows the experimenter to scale both subjects and stimuli simultaneously. This technique tests whether a characteristic involves a single dimension or more than one dimension.

10. Multidimensional scaling allows several dimensions to be scaled simultaneously.

11. The semantic differential is a scaling instrument used to measure meaning. The most important factors in meaning are evaluation, potency, and activity.

12. Some stimulus characteristics influence scaling: serial position, choice of end points, and the familiarity of terms.

13. Some subject characteristics influence scaling: response style, leniency effects, positivity bias, social desirability, yea-saying, and the halo effect.

6

Psychophysical Methods

179

SIGNAL-DETECTION METHOD
   Theoretical Noise and Signal + Noise Curves
   Four Specific Cases
   Receiver-Operating-Characteristic Curves
   An Application of Signal-Detection Methods
DISCUSSION
SUMMARY

The term **psychophysics**—a combination of *psychology* and *physical stimulus*—refers to the measurement of the relationship between a physical stimulus and the psychological response to that stimulus. A typical problem in psychophysics would be to determine how the psychological response to a light changes as the light grows more intense.

Psychophysical methods have certain features in common with psychological scaling, discussed in the previous chapter. Both approaches present a stimulus and try to assess the psychological response to that stimulus. In a typical scaling study, the psychologist might present a picture and ask the subject to judge how pleasant it is; in a typical psychophysics study, the psychologist might present a light and ask the subject to judge how bright it is.

Psychophysical methods differ from psychological scaling, however, in one important respect. In psychological scaling, we have no *objective* way to measure the quality or dimension we want to assess. For example, there is no objective way, independent of human judgment, to determine how pleasant various objects are. Consequently, we cannot control or manipulate pleasantness with much precision. In psychophysical methods, however, we do have objective methods for measuring physical qualities. For example, we can accurately measure just how much light is being presented to a subject. Furthermore, we *can* control and manipulate light intensity with great precision.

The problems in psychophysics are concerned with how to measure psychological responses to physical stimuli and with the nature of the relationship between the physical stimulus and the psychological response.

What are the applications for psychophysics? One answer is that psychophysics is important as a self-sufficient area of inquiry. If we are concerned with how the mind works, then one concern should be with how the mind processes physical stimuli from the environment.

However, psychophysics is also important because it has produced techniques that can be used in other areas of psychology. In the chapter on perception, you will encounter many experiments in which psychophysical techniques have been used. One experiment by Baker, Rierdan, and Wapner (1974), for example, explores the age-old question: is there a relationship between how valuable an object is and how large people judge that object to be? Psychophysics is relevant to this question because the judgment of size involves a psychological reaction to a physical attribute. The experiment made use of a psychophysical technique called the method of limits: subjects compared coins with comparison stimuli and judged them to be smaller, equal, or larger. (Incidentally, as we shall see, they found that people do judge more valuable objects to be larger than less valuable ones.)

Psychophysics may also be useful to the applied psychologist. For example, a drug company may wish to know how much of a particular sweetener must be added to a bitter cough syrup before people no longer find it bitter. Other applied psychologists may be interested in determining whether drugs or diseases dull a person's sensory capacities. For example, Jones, Moskowitz, Butters, and Glosser (1975) report that alcoholics with a condition known as Korsakoff's psychosis have normal psychophysical scaling for vision and hearing, but abnormal psychophysical scaling for smell.

Essentially, there are two kinds of questions that we can ask about a physical stimulus: (1) Can you detect it? (2) Can you tell the difference between this stimulus and another physical stimulus? The first of these is **detection**; the second is **discrimination.** We have three ways of measuring the answers to each of the two kinds of questions, as summarized in Table 6–1.

Table 6-1. The six classic psychophysical methods.

	Detection	*Discrimination*
Method of limits	See p. 182	See p. 189
Method of adjustment	See p. 185	See p. 191
Method of constant stimuli	See p. 186	See p. 193

In this chapter, we will focus first on the classic psychophysical techniques for measuring detection and discrimination. Next, we will examine how a number of theorists have described the correspondence between physical stimuli and psychological responses. Finally, we will consider the **signal-detection method**—a recently developed technique with some clear advantages over the classic techniques.

DETECTION

Is that milk starting to turn sour? Did the chef use any garlic in the chicken dish? Did somebody put vodka in the punch? Did I hear a buzzer go off? Did something touch my arm just now? Is that a light in the house across the street? Is Judy wearing perfume? In everyday life, you are constantly making decisions about whether you detect something or not. In other words, there is a physical quality (such as sourness of milk), and you are making a psychological judgment about that quality.

You may taste a glass of milk on the day you buy a fresh quart and decide it definitely is not sour. Two weeks later, you taste a glass of milk from the same quart, and you decide that it definitely *is* sour. But if you taste the milk when it is one week old, you may not be sure. One gulp tastes OK, the next one tastes a bit strange, and yet the third gulp again tastes OK. You can't make up your mind about it: half the time it's sour, half the time it's not. In this situation, we say that there is a threshold. A **threshold** is a boundary point, right in the middle between the two conclusions "Yes, I detect sourness" and "No, I do not detect sourness." If the milk were just a day fresher, you probably would conclude "No, I do not detect sourness." If it were just a day older, you probably would conclude "Yes, I do detect sourness." The threshold occurs at the point where you stop saying no and start saying yes, with each response occurring about 50% of the time.

The threshold used to be called the **absolute threshold**. The word *absolute* is now usually dropped, however, because psychologists acknowledge that the threshold is rarely absolute, but somewhat variable. Your ability to detect sourness in milk depends on many factors. For example, if you want to see whether the milk is sour because you want to know if it is safe to serve to important guests, you may be much more sensitive to any little bit of sourness than if you just want to pour the milk over your breakfast cereal. Another term you may run across that has the same meaning as threshold is **limen**—the Latin word for threshold.

Table 6-2 lists some approximate threshold values for each of the five senses. You may be amazed to learn how sensitive humans are!

Table 6-2. Some approximate threshold values.

Sense modality	Stimulus
Light	A candle flame seen at 30 miles on a dark clear night
Sound	The tick of a watch under quiet conditions at 20 feet
Taste	One teaspoonful of sugar in three gallons of water
Smell	One drop of perfume spread out into the entire volume of a three-room apartment
Touch	The wing of a bee falling on your cheek from a distance of one centimeter

From *New Directions in Psychology I: Models of Attitude Change, Contemporary Psychophysics, Ethology: An Approach Toward the Complete Analysis of Behavior Emotion*, by Roger Brown, Eugene Galenter, Eckhard H. Hess, George Mandler, Foreword by Theodore M. Newcomb. Copyright © 1962 by Holt, Rinehart and Winston, Inc. Reprinted by permission of Holt, Rinehart and Winston.

Now let's talk about the three ways to measure detection—that is, how much of a physical quality is necessary to reach the threshold. In each case, we present stimuli that are very weak, and we try to determine whether the stimulus can be detected. In addition to discussing the methods themselves, we will also consider the factors that can interfere and give us a misleading threshold.

The Method of Limits

The **method of limits** is also known as the **method of minimal changes**. In this method, the experimenter presents a very small amount of a physical quality to the subject, and the subject reports whether the stimulus is detected or not. Then the experimenter presents a slightly greater amount, and the subject again reports whether the stimulus is detected. Thus, each trial represents a small increase in the stimulus, compared to the previous trial, and the trials continue until the stimuli are well above threshold level. This series of trials, in which the first stimulus is below threshold and stimulus intensity is gradually increased, is called an **ascending series**. On another series of trials, the experimenter works in the opposite direction. Here, the first stimulus is above threshold, and stimulus intensity is gradually *decreased*. This series is called a **descending series**.

The method of limits has to use both ascending and descending series because subjects typically have different thresholds, depending on which series is used. I discovered this on my own, without really thinking about psychophysics, when I was trying to figure out how to make the volume on the television in the next room as low as possible, and yet avoid my daughters' yelling at me because they couldn't hear their favorite program. When the volume was too loud, I simply turned it down, using the method of descending limits, until my daughters shouted "We can't hear it any more!" But one morning, in a flash of insight, I went in and turned the volume off completely. Then I gradually increased the volume, each time asking them if they could hear. Using the ascending series, we crossed the threshold with the volume much lower than usual.

If you have a cooperative roommate, you might try an informal experiment to familiarize yourself with the method of limits for detection of stimuli. All you need are a flashlight and a stack of plain, white index cards. (Use a flashlight made of metal or some other opaque substance; you want the light to be visible only from the top.) Now, the more index cards you put on top of the flashlight, the less light comes out; by this means, you can informally vary the intensity of the stimulus. Follow the sequence suggested in Table 6-3, using

Table 6-3. Determining the threshold for the perception of light from a flashlight, using the method of limits.

	Number of cards	Series number					
		1 Asc.	2 Des.	3 Asc.	4 Des.	5 Asc.	6 Des.
Very bright	2		Yes				
	3		Yes				Yes
	4		Yes		Yes		Yes
	5	Yes	Yes		Yes	Yes	Yes
	6	No	No	Yes	No	No	Yes
	7	No		No		No	No
	8	No		No		No	
	9	No		No		No	
	10	No		No		No	
	11	No		No		No	
	12			No		No	
	13			No		No	
Very dim	14			No			
Threshold for each series		5.5___	5.5___	6.5___	5.5___	5.5___	6.5___

Overall threshold (Average) = 5.8___

three ascending series and three descending series. On each series, begin with the number of index cards indicated by the asterisk and add or remove cards, as appropriate, until you reach the subject's threshold. Then average the six separate thresholds. The results shown in Table 6-3 were obtained with a subject in normal daylight conditions. Your own results may well be different because your lighting conditions, flashlight, and index cards will undoubtedly be different.

The major purpose of the method of limits in detection is to arrive at a threshold by approaching the threshold region from two directions—above and below. As we have seen, we use both ascending and descending series in order to correct for the human tendency to perceive different thresholds, depending on which stimuli have been presented previously.

There are other human factors that can contaminate the method of limits and can produce an inaccurate threshold unless experimenters are careful to control for them. One such control is illustrated in Table 6-3: each series begins with a *different* number of cards. We vary the intensity of the stimulus with which each series begins in order to avoid a certain problem. Suppose your subjects noticed that they could detect the stimulus around the eighth trial in the first series. If each series thereafter started with the same stimulus, when they reached the eighth trial again, they might simply shout ''I see it!''—without even looking at the stimulus. If you are inconsistent about the starting point for each series, however, the subjects can't get away with simply counting trials.

Subjects in psychophysics experiments may also show two other tendencies. One tendency is known as **errors of habituation.** These subjects operate on the principle that ''the stimulus is likely to be the same as last time, so I'll keep giving the same answer.'' Thus, they tend to keep saying no on ascending trials and to keep saying yes on descending trials, for some time after it is appropriate to change their response. The other tendency is known as **errors of anticipation**. These subjects operate on the opposite principle that ''the stimulus is likely to be different from last time, so I'll change my answer.'' As a result, they ''jump the gun.'' On ascending trials, they claim that they can detect the stimulus when, in fact, they can't quite; on descending trials, they claim that they can no longer detect the stimulus when, in fact, they still can.

How can we correct for errors of habituation and errors of anticipation? If we can assume that a subject who makes errors of habituation is just as likely to make them on ascending trials as on descending trials, the errors will cancel each other out. The threshold we obtain will be too high on ascending trials, but it will be too low on descending trials. If the two are averaged, therefore, we should end up with an accurate threshold. The same kind of cancellation of errors will work for errors of anticipation.

The methods of limits, then, raises three potential problems: (1) Thresholds may be different for ascending series than for descending series. (2) Thresholds may reflect a subject's tendency to change the response on a predetermined trial. (3) Thresholds may reflect a subject's systematic tendency to supply either the same response as the previous one or a different response from the previous one. These problems can be minimized by including an equal number of ascending and descending series in the determination of the threshold and by systematically varying the starting point.

The reason we have reviewed these potential difficulties in such detail is that the basic problem is one shared by all studies and all methods in experimental psychology. Basically, we want to obtain a true picture of reality, and we want to eliminate all those factors that might give us an inaccurate picture. If a threshold reflects a subject's tendency to "jump the gun" and change the response prematurely, for example, then that threshold does not give a true picture of reality: it does not tell us the point at which the subject really perceives the stimulus.

Recall our previous discussions of the "search for truth." In Chapter 1, for example, we saw that a ceiling effect or a floor effect would give us a misleading picture of reality. Similarly, if subjects' responses are influenced by demand characteristics rather than by the independent variable (Chapter 3), we also have a misleading picture of reality. Experimenters must continually search out and eliminate contaminating factors that distort the truth. As we have seen, contaminating factors are present even in something that sounds as precise and clear-cut as psychophysical judgments.

The Method of Adjustment

The **method of adjustment** is also known as the **method of average error**. It differs from the method of limits in that the *subjects* make the adjustments by themselves. Generally, as you might imagine, subjects do not waste time judging stimuli that are way above threshold or way below threshold. Instead, they typically zoom in until they are just about at the threshold, and then they make small adjustments at the threshold level—sometimes adding a bit of the stimulus quality, sometimes taking it away, until they are content with what they have selected as threshold. Notice that in the method of adjustment, subjects are permitted to waver back and forth on both sides of the threshold. In the method of limits, within any series, they could go only from low to high or from high to low.

Usually, in the method of adjustment, the experimenter begins half of the trials with a stimulus level way above threshold (descending series) and half of the trials with a stimulus level way below threshold (ascending series). However, this precaution is not quite so necessary as it is in the method of limits: in the method of adjustments, subjects will spontaneously go both above and below the threshold as they approach their final decision on the threshold.

Similarly, the other problems discussed in connection with the method of limits are less important for the method of adjustment. Subjects will be less likely to change the response on a predetermined trial, and they will be less likely to show errors of habituation or errors of anticipation. After all, they can adjust the stimulus themselves, at their own preferred rate, and they can make fine adjustments as they waver back and forth on either side of the threshold.

To try the method of adjustment, you don't even need a cooperative roommate—just the flashlight and index cards. Following the same sequence of ascending and descending series, as shown in Table 6-4. Notice how quickly you can make a threshold decision, because you skip rapidly over the part of the series that is not close to the threshold. Computation of the threshold is the same as in the method of limits: first compute a threshold for each series as the midpoint between the "yes" and "no" answers. Then take an average of the six separate thresholds and compare your own results with those shown in Table 6-4.

Table 6-4. Determining the threshold for the perception of light from a flashlight, using the method of adjustment.

	Number of cards	Series number					
		1 Asc.	2 Des.	3 Asc.	4 Des.	5 Asc.	6 Des.
Very bright	2		Yes				
	3		Yes				Yes
	4		Yes		Yes		Yes
	5		Yes		Yes		Yes
	6		Yes		Yes		Yes
	7	Yes	Yes		Yes	Yes	Yes
	8	No	Yes	Yes	No	No	Yes
	9	No	No	No		No	No
	10	No		No		No	
	11	No		No		No	
	12			No		No	
	13			No		No	
Very dim	14			No			
Threshold for each series		7.5 ___	8.5 ___	8.5 ___	8.5 ___	7.5 ___	8.5 ___

Overall threshold: 8.1 _____

The Method of Constant Stimuli

The two methods discussed so far have involved presenting stimuli in a systematic sequence in order to determine the threshold. In the **method of constant stimuli**, the stimuli are presented in random order. A subject in an experiment involving detection of light might be exposed first to a very bright light (clearly above threshold), then to a very dim light (clearly below threshold), then to one slightly below threshold, and so on. On each trial, the subject responds either yes or no. Each stimulus intensity is presented several times throughout the experiment, in order to increase the reliability of the measure. As the name of this method implies, the stimulus remains constant—it does not increase or decrease—during any given trial.

Recruit your cooperative roommate to try the method of constant stimuli. On each trial (again, in daylight conditions), cover the flashlight with the

Table 6-5. Determining the threshold for the perception of light from a flashlight, using the method of constant stimuli.

Trial	(a) Raw Data Number of cards to be used	Response	Stimulus	(b)Tabulations Number of "yes" responses	% Yes
1	5	Yes	5	4	100
2	8	No	6	3	75
3	7	No	7	1	25
4	6	Yes	8	0	0
5	9	No	9	0	0
6	8	No			
7	6	Yes			
8	5	Yes	(c) Estimating the threshold		
9	7	No			
10	9	No			
11	6	Yes			
12	5	Yes			
13	7	No			
14	8	No			
15	9	No			
16	5	Yes			
17	8	No			
18	7	No			
19	9	No			
20	6	Yes			

Instructions: For each trial, cover the flashlight with the designated number of cards. Record your subjects' responses next to mine, in part a. Tabulate the number of "yes" responses supplied to each stimulus value, using part b. Next, convert *number* of yes responses to *percentage* of yes responses. Using part c, plot the percentages. Draw a smooth line to fit the points. Draw a horizontal line across the graph at the 50% point. Your estimate of the threshold is the value of the stimulus that corresponds to the point where the horizontal line crosses your curve.

number of cards indicated in Table 6-5. Compare your results with those shown in Table 6-5a. Then, add up the number of yes responses for each level of the stimulus and calculate the percentages, as shown in Table 6-5b.

Now, how do you determine the threshold? The other two methods allowed us to obtain the threshold directly, but we must calculate the threshold indirectly when using the method of constant stimuli. Our goal is to find a midpoint, such that the subject says yes 50% of the time and no 50% of the time. If there is a stimulus intensity that produces a 50% yes response, your troubles are over—that is the threshold. If not, you can use one of several methods to estimate the threshold. One method is to plot the points on a graph and carefully draw a smooth curve to fit the points as closely as possible. Then draw a horizontal line across the graph at the 50% point. The value of the stimulus that corresponds to the point where the horizontal line crosses your curve is your estimate of the threshold.

Notice that none of the problems discussed in connection with the method of limits is applicable to the method of constant stimuli. We don't need to worry about different thresholds for ascending and descending trials. We don't need to worry about a different starting point for each series. We don't need to worry about errors of habituation or errors of anticipation. When all the stimuli are presented in random order, rather than in a systematic series, subjects cannot base their responses on a starting point or on the preceding stimuli. Consequently, the method of constant stimuli does not need to take special precautions to correct for these problems.

DISCRIMINATION

In everyday life, we make discrimination judgments just as often as we make detection judgments. Is this soup saltier than the way Mother makes it? Which half of the candy bar is bigger? Is his voice louder than mine? Which bleach is better at getting clothes whiter-than-white? Which of the two children got to play on the swing longer?

In testing detection, experimenters use very weak stimuli, just at the threshold of perception. In testing discrimination, all stimuli are clearly above threshold.

Detection involves a single stimulus; discrimination involves a comparison of two stimuli. We compare stimulus A with stimulus B and ask: is A more than B, is B more than A, or are they equal? Most often in an experiment, one stimulus stays the same throughout the experiment. This is called the **standard stimulus**. The other stimulus is called the **comparison stimulus**; this one varies throughout the experiment. In discrimination judgments, we ask ''How much can we change the comparison stimulus and still get away with it?'' Suppose, for example, that the standard stimulus is a line 40 cm long. What values can the comparison stimulus have without looking noticeably longer or shorter? The exact answer will depend on many factors, such as lighting conditions and the distance between the two lines. In any case, we would probably judge a comparison line of 36 cm to be shorter and a comparison line of 44 cm to be longer. How about a line of 39 cm, or 42 cm? These lines might be judged to be equal in length to our standard stimulus 40 cm long.

Let us now consider some special terms used in connection with discrimination judgments. The **interval of uncertainty** is the range of values that the comparison stimulus can have and still be judged equivalent to the standard stimulus. It is calculated by subtracting the minimum value for the comparison stimulus from the maximum value for the comparison stimulus. Let's suppose, for example, that subjects judged that a line of 38 cm was equal to the 40-cm standard, but that a line of 37 cm was shorter. Let's suppose that they also judged that a line of 42 cm was equal to the 40-cm standard, but that a line of 43 cm was longer. In this case, the interval of uncertainty would be 42.5 − 37.5, or 5 cm.

The difference threshold is probably the term that we will find most useful. The **difference threshold** is the difference between two stimuli that the subject can just barely tell apart. There are three methods of measuring difference thresholds, and we will spend most of this section discussing these methods. It is also known as the **difference limen**, or **DL**.

Another, related term used in connection with discrimination judgments is the **just noticeable difference**, or **JND**. The full name sounds awkward, but it is descriptive. It is a measure of how different the stimuli can be from each other and have the difference be *just noticeable*. When two stimuli are separated by 1 DL, the psychological reaction is 1 JND. The terms are essentially the same.

Now let's turn to the three methods of measuring discrimination. You are familiar with the basic methods from measuring detection; now you only need to learn how these methods are modified to accommodate two stimuli, rather than one.

The Method of Limits

When the method of limits is used in discrimination experiments, the standard stimulus remains at a constant value, while the comparison stimulus varies along the particular dimension being studied. Again, the experimenter uses both ascending and descending series. In the descending series, the comparison stimulus is much greater than the standard stimulus at the beginning of the series and is progressively reduced until the comparison stimulus is much less than the standard stimulus. In the ascending series, the comparison is initially much less than the standard stimulus and is progressively increased until it is much greater than the standard stimulus.

As noted at the beginning of this section, we are constantly making discrimination judgments in everyday life. One kind of discrimination judgment that we often make involves deciding how many stamps to put on a letter. Is the weight of the letter more than an ounce, equal to an ounce, or less than an ounce (28 grams)? Once again, enlist that cooperative roommate, and try the experiment illustrated in Table 6-6.

Assemble a standard stimulus by placing 12 index cards (3" × 5" or 7.6 cm × 12.7 cm) in a small envelope (3.5" × 6.5" or 8.9 cm × 16.5 cm). Label the envelope *standard stimulus*; it will weigh about one ounce (28 grams). Label a second envelope *comparison stimulus*. For the first series, place 8 index cards in the comparison-stimulus envelope. Have the subject hold the standard stimulus in the right hand and the comparison stimulus in the left hand. Instruct the subject to heft both envelopes and to decide whether the comparison stimulus is heavier, lighter, or equal to the standard stimulus. This first series is an ascending series: add one card to the comparison-stimulus envelope on each trial. Record your subject's responses until they have progressed from "lighter" through "equal" to "heavier." For the next trial series, begin with 16 index cards in the comparison envelope, and remove one card on each trial. On the third and fourth series, begin where indicated by the asterisk.

Note that Series 3 and 4 involve an important change: the standard stimulus is now in the left hand, and the comparison stimulus is in the right

Table 6-6. Determining discrimination for a one-ounce letter, using the method of limits.

Series number:	1	2	3	4
Order:	Ascending	Descending	Ascending	Descending
Position of standard stimulus:	Right	Right	Left	Left

Number of cards in comparison stimulus

	1	2	3	4
8	*Lighter			
9	Lighter	Lighter	*Lighter	
10	Lighter	Equal	Equal	Lighter
11	Equal	Equal	Equal	Equal
12	Equal	Equal	Equal	Equal
13	Equal	Equal	Equal	Equal
14	Equal	Equal	Heavier	Equal
15	Heavier	Heavier		*Heavier
16		*Heavier		

Lower difference threshold: 1.5 _____ (12 − 10.5) 2.5 _____ (12 − 9.5) 2.5 _____ (12 − 9.5) 1.5 _____ (12 − 10.5)

Upper difference threshold: 2.5 _____ (14.5 − 12) 2.5 _____ (14.5 − 12) 1.5 _____ (13.5 − 12) 2.5 _____ (14.5 − 12)

Average lower difference threshold: $\dfrac{1.5 + 2.5 + 2.5 + 1.5}{4} = 2.0$

Average upper difference threshold: $\dfrac{2.5 + 2.5 + 1.5 + 2.5}{4} = 2.25$

Overall difference threshold: 2.12

hand—a reversal of position from the first two trials. When we measure discrimination—whatever method we use—we must introduce a control that was not necessary in the measurement of thresholds. Suppose your subject always held the standard stimulus in the left hand and the comparison stimulus in the right hand. It may be that objects are perceived as slightly heavier by, say, the right hand. Consequently, this confounded design would lead to a systematic overestimate for the comparison stimulus. The confounding must be disentangled by appropriate counterbalancing—by having your subject hold the standard stimulus in the right hand for half of the trials and in the left hand for half of the trials. By this means you are controlling for a confounding of spatial order, or position in space. In other experiments, temporal order, or position in time, may need to be controlled. If the subjects must judge one stimulus prior to another stimulus, that is, then the standard stimulus should precede the comparison stimulus on half of the trials and follow the comparison stimulus on half of the trials.

How do you calculate the difference threshold? First, calculate the **lower difference threshold**, using the following procedure: (1) Take the average of two stimuli—the last one for which the subject responded "lighter" and the first one for which the subject responded "equal." This is the lower boundary of what the subject considers equal to the standard stimulus. (2) Subtract this average from the value of the standard stimulus. (3) Compute the average lower difference threshold by taking the average of the four series.

Now, calculate the **upper difference threshold**, using a similar procedure: (1) Take the average of two stimuli—the last one for which the subject responded "equal" and the first one for which the subject responded "heavier." This is the upper boundary of what the subject considers equal to the standard stimulus. (2) Subtract from this average the value of the standard stimulus. (3) Compute the average upper difference threshold by taking the average of the four series.

Psychologists often report the upper and lower difference thresholds separately because these values often differ. You can calculate the **overall difference threshold**, however, simply by taking an overall average of the average lower difference threshold and the average upper difference threshold, as shown in Table 6-6.

After you have completed the experiment, you might ask your subject whether he or she noticed any tendency to make errors of anticipation or errors of habituation. These errors occur whenever the method of limits is used, whether in measuring detection or discrimination. You should also notice whether the thresholds differed between ascending and descending series. Also notice that we guarded against the subject's tendency to change the response on a predetermined trial by beginning with a different stimulus each time—a precaution we also used in measuring detection thresholds. Finally, remember that in measuring discrimination, a further precaution is necessary—counterbalancing for spatial or temporal order.

The Method of Adjustment

When the method of adjustment is used in measuring *detection*, subjects adjust the stimulus by themselves until it is just barely noticeable. When the method of adjustment is used in measuring *discrimination*, subjects adjust the comparison stimulus by themselves until it seems to match the standard stimulus. They perform this task many times, so that we have many measures of subjective equality.

Notice that the kind of judgment that the subjects make using the method of adjustment is different from the kind of judgment they make using the method of limits. The method of limits focuses on the points at which the subjects begin to report *differences*, whereas the method of adjustment focuses on those points that subjects report are the *same*.

With the method of adjustment, we end up with a number of scores representing values that the subject has judged to be equal to the standard stimulus. Some of the scores may equal the standard stimulus exactly, indicating that the subject has been perfectly accurate in matching the comparison stimulus and the standard stimulus. Other scores will be on the low side, however, and still others will be on the high side. If we take an average of these scores, we obtain the **point of subjective equality**, which is the best guess for the value of the comparison stimulus that the subject believes is equivalent to the standard stimulus.

How do you calculate the difference threshold using the method of adjustment? Remember that the difference threshold represents how much variation the subject will tolerate before reporting that the comparison stimulus is different from the standard stimulus. There are several possible methods of calculating difference thresholds, but one common one is to measure the *standard deviation* of the scores. The **standard deviation** is a measure of variation, and we are trying to measure how much variation the subject can tolerate.

Table 6-7 provides an example of the method of adjustment in measuring discrimination. Try this experiment, using yourself as the subject, to test your own discrimination abilities in the judgment of weights.

Table 6-7. Determining discrimination for a one-ounce letter, using the method of adjustment.

Series number:	*1*	*2*	*3*	*4*
Order:	*Ascending*	*Descending*	*Ascending*	*Descending*
Position of standard stimulus:	*Right*	*Right*	*Left*	*Left*

Number of cards in comparison stimulus				
8	Lighter			
9	Lighter		Lighter	Lighter
10	Lighter	Lighter	Lighter	Equal
11	Equal	Equal	Equal	Equal
12	Equal	Equal	Equal	Equal
13	Equal	Equal	Equal	Equal
14	Heavier	Equal	Equal	Heavier
15		Heavier	Heavier	Heavier
16		Heavier		

Point of subjective equality $= \bar{X} =$ average of all stimuli that the subject considers equivalent =

$$\frac{11 + 12 + 13 + 11 + 12 + 13 + 14 + 11 + 12 + 13 + 14 + 10 + 11 + 12 + 13}{15}$$

Difference threshold =

$$\sqrt{\frac{\Sigma X^2}{N} - \bar{X}^2} =$$

$$\sqrt{\frac{(11)^2 + (12)^2 + (13)^2 + \cdots + (11)^2 + (12)^2}{15} - (12.1)^2} = 1.2$$

(This is the standard deviation of the numbers listed above.)

Remember that the method of constant stimuli differs from the other two methods in that the stimuli, rather than systematically increasing or decreasing in magnitude, are presented in random order.

When the method of constant stimuli is used in measuring discrimination, the experimenter uses a standard stimulus and a set of comparison stimuli that are greater, smaller, and equal to the standard stimulus. As in measuring detection, the comparison stimuli are presented in random order, rather than systematically. Each comparison stimulus is judged several times throughout the testing. On each trial, the subject sees a standard stimulus and a comparison stimulus and must judge whether the latter is greater, smaller, or equal. After the subject has completed all trials, the experimenter counts the number of responses in each of the three categories for each of the comparison stimuli.

How do you determine the discrimination threshold? Recall that when we determined the detection threshold using the method of constant stimuli, we had to engage in certain calculations. A variation of the same method can be used here.

Following the order of presentation shown in Table 6-8a, try this version of the weight-discrimination experiment, recording your subject's responses as shown. Add up the number of judgments in each category; then convert the *number* of each kind of response to the *percentage* of each kind of response, as shown in Table 6-8b.

On a graph, plot the percentage of "lighter" judgments for each level of the comparison stimulus, and connect the points with a smooth curve (see Table 6-8c). From the point where your point crosses the 50% line, drop a vertical line to the *x*-axis, and read the value of the stimulus. This is the *lower* limit of the interval of uncertainty. Follow the same process for the percentage of "heavier" judgments at each level, and read off the *upper* limit of the interval of uncertainty. To find the difference threshold, simply subtract the lower limit from the upper limit and divide the result by 2.

HOW PHYSICAL STIMULI CORRESPOND TO PSYCHOLOGICAL RESPONSES

At the beginning of this chapter, we said that psychophysics is the measurement of the relationship between physical stimuli in the outside world and the psychological reactions on the inside. So far, we have discussed ways to measure some kinds of relationships. Now let us examine what the results of these measurements tell us about the nature of the relationship.

Weber's Law

It may be prohibited by law to write an experimental-psychology textbook and fail to mention **Weber's Law.** Weber's Law concerns the relationship between the just noticeable difference and the standard stimulus.

Table 6-8. Determining discrimination for a one-ounce letter, using the method of constant stimuli.

(a)   Raw Data

Trial	Position of standard stimulus	Number of cards in comparison	Response
1	Right	14	Heavier
2	Left	9	Lighter
3	Right	11	Same
4	Left	15	Heavier
5	Left	10	Same
6	Right	13	Same
7	Right	12	Same
8	Left	12	Same
9	Right	9	Lighter
10	Left	14	Heavier
11	Left	11	Same
12	Right	10	Lighter
13	Left	13	Same
14	Right	15	Heavier
15	Left	9	Lighter
16	Right	13	Same
17	Right	12	Same
18	Left	15	Heavier
19	Right	11	Same
20	Right	14	Heavier
21	Left	10	Lighter
22	Left	11	Same
23	Right	10	Lighter
24	Left	14	Same
25	Right	9	Lighter
26	Left	13	Same
27	Left	12	Same
28	Right	15	Heavier

Imagine that you are asked to judge which is longer, a 1-cm line or a 2-cm line. The task seems ridiculously easy, because 1 cm makes a big difference when you are dealing with small quantities. However, imagine that you are asked to judge which is longer, a 92-cm line or a 93-cm line. Now the task is much more difficult. One cm no longer makes a big difference when you are dealing with large quantities.

Weber was concerned with this question: how much difference does there have to be between two stimuli in order for the difference to be noticed? As it turns out, there is no single number that we can supply as an answer. Instead, the answer depends on the value of the standard stimulus. If the standard stimulus is small, then the comparison stimulus does not have to be much larger before the difference can be detected; if the standard stimulus is large, however, the comparison stimulus has to be quite a bit larger before the difference can be detected.

(b) Tabulation

Number of judgments in each category

	9	10	11	12	13	14	15
Lighter	4	3	1	0	0	0	0
Same	0	1	3	4	4	1	0
Heavier	0	0	0	0	0	3	4

Percentage of judgments in each category

	9	10	11	12	13	14	15
Lighter	100	75	25	0	0	0	0
Same	0	25	75	100	100	25	0
Heavier	0	0	0	0	0	75	100

(c) Estimating the threshold

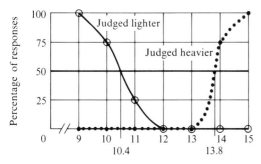

Number of cards in comparison stimulus

Lower limit of interval of uncertainty = 10.4
Upper limit of interval of uncertainty = 13.8
Difference threshold = (13.8 − 10.4)/2 = 1.7

Specifically, Weber's Law states:

$$\frac{\text{JND}}{S} = k.$$

In translation, the formula reads that when we divide the just noticeable difference by the magnitude of the stimulus (S), we will get a constant number, k. This constant, k, will be the same within any given psychophysical task, but will differ from one task to the next. In a task involving the lifting of weights, for example, k equals $^1/_{30}$. This means, for example, that if you use a standard stimulus (S) that weighs 30 grams, the just noticeable difference will be one gram. In other words, a comparison object will have to weigh 31 grams in order to be perceived as being heavier (or 29 grams in order to be perceived as being lighter). However, if the standard stimulus weighs 60 grams, the just noticeable difference will be two grams ($^2/_{60} = {^1/_{30}}$). Adding on a single gram "worked" when we were dealing with 30 grams, but it won't be noticed when we are dealing with 60 grams. Now, the comparison object will have to weigh 62 grams in order to be perceived as being heavier.

A formal psychophysics experiment to demonstrate Weber's Law would involve using one of the three methods for measuring discrimination and measuring the discrimination thresholds for several different standard-stimulus values. Less formally, however, you can demonstrate Weber's Law to yourself using a box of ordinary paper clips.

Put together a chain of 4 paper clips for the standard stimulus and a chain of 5 paper clips for the comparison stimulus. Close your eyes and hold each string of paper clips by the very end. Compare their weights. The chain of 5 should feel noticeably heavier. When you begin with only four clips, then, *one* additional clip is enough of a difference to be noticeable.

Now put together a chain of 8 paper clips for the standard stimulus and a chain of 9 paper clips for the comparison stimulus, close your eyes again, and compare the weights. This time, you are unlikely to detect a difference. Chances are that you will need 10 paper clips in the comparison stimulus (an increase of *two*) to notice the difference.

Finally, try a standard stimulus consisting of 12 paper clips. You will probably find that you need 15 paper clips (an increase of *three*) in order for the difference to be noticeable.

For this range of weights and for this testing method, then, k appears to equal ¼ in the equation $JND/S = k$. Thus, when S equals 4, JND equals 1; when S equals 8, JND equals 2; and when S equals 12, JND equals 3.

How accurate is Weber's Law in predicting the size of the just noticeable difference, given that we have had over a century to test its accuracy? As it turns out, Weber's Law is reasonably accurate when we are examining stimuli in the middle ranges, although it may not hold for stimuli (such as weights) that are extremely small or extremely large.

Fechner's Law

Gustav Fechner, in 1860, developed Weber's Law one step further. Weber had been concerned with the relationship between physical properties (a change in the stimulus) and psychological reactions (the subject noticing that the stimulus had been changed). Fechner, too, was concerned with the relationship between physical properties and psychological reactions, but his goal was to find a scale that would relate the physical properties to the psychological reactions. Basically, he constructed that scale by adding JNDs together.

Let's construct a scale, Fechner-style, for the psychological reaction to a particular physical property—the concentration of some bitter substance in water. Our goal is to end up with a scale of psychological reactions, ranging from 0 to 10, that corresponds to the intensity of the physical stimulus. Think for a moment how this task differs from the tasks we encountered in Chapter 5, on psychological scaling. In that chapter, we needed to find scales of psychological reactions to stimuli—such as happiness—for which there was no objective, physical measure. In psychophysics, however, we *do* have an objective, physical measure. We can measure, for example, how many grams of the bitter substance we mix into 1 liter of water.

In order to construct a Fechner-type scale, we need to know the absolute threshold for a stimulus (for this purpose, we must pretend to believe in absolute thresholds) and the value of the constant, k. Once we have these two pieces of information, we can construct a theoretical scale without any additional psychophysical tests.

Table 6-9 shows the construction of a scale if the absolute threshold is 10 (say, 10 grams of a bitter substance in 1 liter of water) and k is $1/5$. First, we say that if the physical stimulus is 10, we'll call the psychological reaction 0. This is

Table 6-9. Constructing a Fechner-type scale for the psychological reaction to a physical stimulus, where the absolute threshold is 10 and the JND is $1/5$.

Scale of Psychological Reaction	Intensity of Physical Stimulus (Previous stimulus + 1 JND)
0	10
1	12 $[= 10.0 + 1/5 (10.0)]$
2	14.4 $[= 12.0 + 1/5 (12.0)]$
3	17.3 $[= 14.4 + 1/5 (14.4)]$
4	20.8 $[= 17.3 + 1/5 (17.3)]$
5	25.0 $[= 20.8 + 1/5 (20.8)]$
6	30.0 $[= 25.0 + 1/5 (25.0)]$
7	36.0 $[= 30.0 + 1/5 (30.0)]$
8	43.2 $[= 36.0 + 1/5 (36.0)]$
9	51.8 $[= 43.2 + 1/5 (43.2)]$
10	62.2 $[= 51.8 + 1/5 (51.8)]$

our starting point for the scale. Then we ask what physical stimulus corresponds to the psychological reaction whose value is 1. Well, we want that physical stimulus to be *noticeably* different from the previous physical stimulus whose value was 10. What would be noticeably different? Fechner reasoned that if we add 1 JND to the absolute threshold, the result will be noticeably different. If the absolute threshold is 10, then 1 JND is $1/5$ (10), or 2. Therefore, the physical stimulus that is noticeably different from 10 is 10 + 2, or 12. Therefore, a physical stimulus of 12 receives the scale score of 1.

What is the physical stimulus that receives the scale score of 2? Again, this stimulus must be noticeably different from the previous stimulus of 12. Again, 1 JND above 12 should be noticeably different. Now, however, the JND is somewhat larger, because 1 JND is $1/5$ (12), or 2.4. Therefore, the physical stimulus that is noticeably different from 12 is 12 + 2.4, or 14.4. Table 6-9, then, has been constructed by adding 1 JND to each of the previous physical stimuli. We end up with a scale from 0 to 10. Two adjacent numbers on that scale correspond to physical stimuli that can barely be distinguished from each other.

The resulting scale reflects an important aspect of Weber's Law. Notice that the physical stimuli are bunched together at the lower end of the scale: with small values, a small change makes a noticeable difference. However, the physical stimuli are spread out more at the upper end of the scale: with larger values, a larger change is necessary to make a noticeable difference. This relationship is even more clear if we graph the relationship between psychological reactions and physical stimuli, as shown in Figure 6-1.

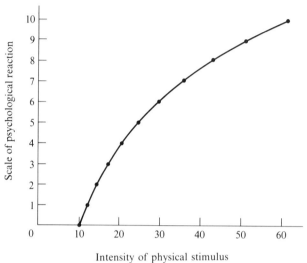

Figure 6-1. The relationship between psychological reactions and physical stimuli.

Fechner derived the equation for curves like these by applying a mathematical technique known as *integration* to Weber's Law. The equation is:

$$R = k \log S$$

In this equation, known as **Fechner's Law**, R equals the psychological reaction to the stimulus. The k represents a constant, just as it did in Weber's Law. Notice that k is multiplied by the *logarithm* of S—the value of the physical stimulus. The important attribute of logarithms that needs to be remembered here is that when you take the logarithm of a number, the logarithmic transformation drastically reduces large numbers—much more so than small numbers. For example, the logarithm of 10 is 1, whereas the logarithm of 1000 is only 3. It makes sense, then, that Fechner's Law uses logarithms, because when the physical stimulus (S) is large, we need to shrink down large differences between physical stimuli into small differences between psychological reactions.

If an equation for a curve has a logarithmic form on the independent-variable side, then the curve becomes a straight line when we express the x-axis in logarithmic form. Notice that the relationship in Figure 6-2 between the psychological reaction and the *logarithm* of the physical stimulus is a straight line.

How accurate is Fechner's Law in predicting psychological reactions to physical stimuli? Recall that it is based on Weber's Law; therefore, it has the

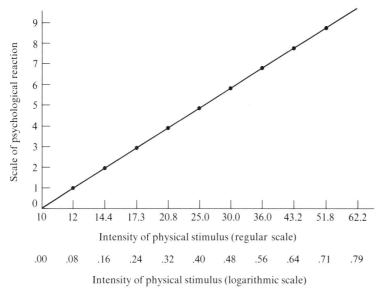

Figure 6-2. The relationship between psychological reactions and the *logarithm* of physical stimuli. (Notice that the logarithmic scale on the *x*-axis shrinks down the larger values so that the relationship is a straight line.)

same accuracies and inaccuracies as the earlier law. Specifically, it seems to hold fairly nicely for moderate values of physical stimuli, but it breaks down when we consider values that are either too large or too small.

Notice that Fechner's Law about the relationship between the physical stimulus and the psychological reaction involves an *indirect*-estimate technique. Aside from the initial direct measurements of the threshold and the JND, we never need to use psychophysical techniques again. We simply sit down with some scratch paper and calculate what those values should be, by adding JNDs to previous stimulus values. This technique is in contrast to the *direct*-estimate technique described in the next section.

Stevens' Power Function

Weber's Law and Fechner's Law remained intact for about 100 years, until S. S. Stevens (1957) proposed a different formula for the relationship between the physical and the psychological. Stevens' method, known as **magnitude estimation**, involves obtaining direct measures of magnitude from subjects by having them make up numbers to correspond with physical stimuli. For example, put your hand into a container of very hot water, the hottest you could tolerate, and imagine that water this hot has a value of 100. Then you place your hand in water that is at room temperature, and the experimenter asks you to supply a number that is appropriate for this temperature, given that the very hot water had a value of 100. In all, you might experience ten physical stimuli and be asked to supply ten numbers to indicate your psychological reaction to those stimuli. (Notice how similar this magnitude-estimation task is to a psychological-scaling task; in both cases, you are asked to supply numbers to correspond to a psychological reaction.)

Stevens (1966) tested subjects using a wide variety of stimuli, including intensity of electric current, strength of handgrip, degree of redness, degree of roughness, number of items, and brightness. On the basis of his experiments, he concluded that the relationship between the psychological response and the physical stimulus is described by the equation:

$$R = kS^n$$

In this equation, R is the psychological response to the stimulus (S). The k in this equation is a constant that depends on the kind of physical stimulus being studied. Notice that S is raised to the nth power. (Recall that the power to which a number is raised tells us how many times a number should be multiplied by itself; for example, $3^2 = 3 \times 3$.) The n is also a number whose value depends on the kind of physical stimulus being studied. Since the equation involves raising the stimulus to a certain power, this equation is referred to as **Stevens' Power Function.**

Stevens has also explored **cross-modality comparisons.** Here, the subject is asked to judge stimuli in one mode of perception (such as hearing) by providing responses from another mode of perception (such as sight). At first, the method may seem somewhat bizarre: you might well stare in amazement at an experimenter who asked you to draw a line that looks as long as the loudness of the sound! However, once you get accustomed to the idea, it's really rather reasonable. You might try, for example, turning up the volume on your radio as loud as possible and drawing a line to represent that loudness. Now turn it down a bit and draw a line to represent that reduced volume. It's not that ridiculous, is it? In fact, it seems just as natural as making up numbers for responses.

In the method of cross-modality comparisons, Stevens simply measures the length of the line that the subject draws to obtain a measure of the subject's psychological reaction (R) to the stimulus (S). The power function $R = kS^n$ fits data obtained by cross-modality comparisons, as well as data obtained from magnitude estimation.

If we perform a logarithmic transformation on both sides of Stevens' power function, the equation becomes:

$$\log R = \log k + n \log S$$

When an equation has a logarithmic form on both sides of the equation, then both the x-axis and the y-axis need to be expressed in logarithmic form in order to obtain a straight line. In Figure 6-3, this "log-log" kind of function is used to demonstrate the similarity of results obtained by the two different methods of magnitude estimation (assigning numbers to brightness) and cross-modality comparisons (representing brightness by the length of a line).

Fechner proposed that the relationship between the psychological reaction and the logarithm of stimulus intensity is a straight line. Stevens proposes that the relationship between the *logarithm* of the psychological reaction and

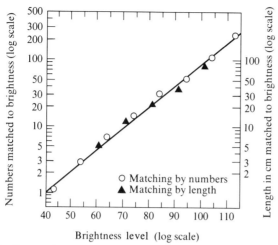

Figure 6-3. Stevens' Power Function ("log-log" function), based on judgments of the brightness of a disc: magnitude-estimation method (open circles) and cross-modality comparisons (dark triangles). Adapted from "On the Operation Known as Judgement," by S. S. Stevens, *American Scientist*, 1966, *54*, 385–399. Used by permission.

the logarithm of stimulus intensity is a straight line. Who is right? To some extent, the different formulas may be a result of different experimental tasks: Fechner obtained his judgments indirectly, whereas Stevens obtained his judgments directly. However, the weight of the evidence seems to favor Stevens' formula: $R = kS^n$ or $\log R = \log k + n \log S$. As Gescheider (1976) concludes in *Psychophysics: Method and Theory*, "There is little doubt that the power function represents the best description of the relationship between an observer's judgments and stimulus intensity" (p. 144).

SIGNAL-DETECTION METHOD

In 1954, Tanner and Swets wrote an article entitled "A Decision-Making Theory of Visual Detection." The **signal-detection method** that they proposed has subsequently been applied widely, both in psychophysics and in other areas of experimental psychology. Many psychologists feel that the signal-detection method has many advantages over classic psychophysics methods.

At the beginning of this chapter, I mentioned that we rarely use the phrase *absolute threshold* any more. We acknowledge that people do not have absolute thresholds for detection. Instead, we realize that a person's likelihood of saying "I detect the stimulus" or "I do not detect the stimulus" depends on his or her past learning, motivation, attention, and many other factors.

Let us suppose that we present a tone to two subjects. The first subject reports "I hear it," and the second subject reports "I don't hear it." Can we say conclusively that the first subject has more sensitive hearing that the second? No, we cannot. It may be that both subjects have equally sensitive hearing, but that they differ in the kind of criterion they use to decide whether they have heard the tone or not. The first subject may operate according to the internal rule: "I'll say 'I hear it' if there's even a vague possibility that I heard the tone, because I want to make certain that I correctly report every single tone that occurs. I will be generous with the 'I hear it' responses and stingy with the 'I don't hear it' responses." The second subject uses a much stricter criterion, following this internal rule: "I'll say 'I hear it' only when I'm absolutely sure that I heard the tone, because I don't want to say that I heard something when no tone occurred. I will be stingy with the 'I hear it' responses and generous with the 'I don't hear it' responses."

One of the advantages of the signal-detection method is that it allows us to distinguish between sensitivity and criterion. **Sensitivity** depends on two factors. One factor is the strength of the stimulus: observers will be more sensitive in detecting a strong stimulus than in detecting a weak stimulus. The other factor is the sensitivity of the observer: observers vary in their ability to detect the same stimulus. The **criterion** depends on many factors. One factor is the probability that the stimulus will actually occur: if you have been told there is a 90% chance that a tone will occur on a given trial, you are much more likely to report "I heard it" than if you have been told there is only a 10% chance that it will occur. Another factor is the **payoff**, or the costs and benefits, associated with saying "I heard it." If you have been told you will be given 10¢ for correctly detecting the tone, you are much more likely to report "I heard it" than if you have been told you will have to give the experimenter 10¢ for saying you heard a tone when no tone occurred. Using classic psychophysics methods, then, the threshold measurements depend on both sensitivity and criterion. Using signal-detection methods, however, we can separate these two factors.

Theoretical Noise and Signal + Noise Curves

Let us imagine that you are trying to determine whether a tone occurred and translate this situation into signal-detection terminology. For trials in which no tone occurs, signal-detection theorists use the term **noise**. Imagine yourself in a back room of your home trying to determine whether the doorbell rang or not. You hear, quite literally, a certain amount of background noise— perhaps music, typing, the television. Your job is to figure out whether you heard noise only, or **signal + noise:** did you hear the appropriate signal (the doorbell) above and beyond the background noise? More generally, *noise* refers to irrelevant stimuli that exist in a situation and that could be mistaken for the stimulus, or *signal*. In this sense, noise need not be auditory; we can speak, for example, of visual noise.

In Figure 6-4, we represent the two situations, noise and signal + noise, in a hypothetical graph. Because the signal + noise creates a larger, stronger sensation than the noise alone, we represent signal + noise as being larger. Why don't we simply choose a single point to represent noise and another point to represent signal + noise? Signal-detection theory proposes that a single point is an inaccurate representation because the observer's perception of each sen-

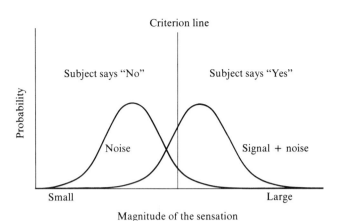

Figure 6-4. A model for signal-detection theory.

sation varies slightly from one moment to the next. For example, a doorbell is perceived sometimes as quite loud and other times as quite soft. Consequently, signal-detection theorists generally represent the distribution of sensations by using a **normal curve.**[1] Notice that both the noise and the signal + noise situations are represented by normal curves.

How far apart are the noise and the signal + noise distributions? The answer to that question depends on how different the two situations are from each other. If the doorbell is very loud and the background, irrelevant noises are very soft, the two distributions will be very far apart. If the doorbell is very soft and the background, irrelevant noises are relatively loud, the two distributions will be quite close together. We'll come back to the distance between the two curves in the next section.

Also notice the vertical line labeled *criterion* in Figure 6-4. The criterion tells us how liberal or how conservative the subject is with regard to decision making, and that criterion may vary with the situation. In Figure 6-4, we see that the subject reports "I hear it" whenever some part of *either* distribution falls into the "Yes" region. Thus if the doorbell (signal + noise) is at least moderately strong *or* if the background noise is very strong, the subject will report "I hear it." The subject reports "I don't hear it" whenever some part of either distribution falls into the "No" region. Thus, if the doorbell is weak or if the background noise is not extremely strong, the subject will report "I don't hear it." With this criterion line, the subject will generally be correct: the signal + noise will generally produce a "Yes" response, and the noise alone will generally produce a "No" response. However, the subject does make some errors: the signal + noise sometimes produces a "No" response, and the noise alone sometimes produces a "Yes" response. We will discuss the concept of criterion in greater detail in the next section.

The four possible situations that can occur in a signal-detection task are represented in Table 6-10. Notice that two of the possible outcomes are correct. In one case, there is a tone and the subject correctly reports it; in the other

[1] A normal curve or normal distribution is bell-shaped and symmetric—that is, the right and left halves of the curve are mirror images.

Table 6-10. The four possible outcomes in a signal-detection trial.

| | | Did the signal truly occur? | |
		No	Yes
The Subject	"No, I don't hear it"	Correct Rejection (Correct)	Miss (Error)
Responds:	"Yes, I hear it"	False Alarm (Error)	Hit (Correct)

case, there is *no* tone and the subject correctly reports "I don't hear it." However, the two other possible outcomes are errors. In one case, there is a tone but the subject incorrectly reports "I don't hear it"; in the other case, there is *no* tone but the subject incorrectly reports "I hear it." (In statistics, these two kinds of errors would be called a Type II and a Type I error, respectively.) Notice how these four possible situations correspond to the regions in Figure 6-6. The terms *hit, miss, false alarm,* and *correct rejection* serve as colorful and accurate representations of each of the four possible outcomes. (When a fire company responds to an alert by sending out a fire truck, but there is no fire—that is, no signal—this is a false alarm!)

Four Specific Cases

How frequently does each of the four possible outcomes occur? There is no single answer to this question. The frequency of the four outcomes depends on the two factors we discussed earlier: sensitivity and criterion.

Four different situations are represented in Figure 6-5. Notice that in the first two cases, the curves are widely separated, with relatively little overlap. We measure sensitivity in terms of the distance between the means of the two curves, represented by the symbol d', or d-prime. Notice that d' is much smaller for the bottom two sets of curves. Here the overlap is great, and it is difficult to detect a difference between the noise curve and the signal-plus-noise curve. The magnitude of d' depends on the strength of the signal (if the signal is strong, d' will be large) and on the sensitivity of the observer (if the observer is sensitive, d' will be large.)

The second factor that determines how often each of the four possible outcomes occurs is the criterion that the observer sets. In the first and third sets of curves, the observers are setting an extremely strict (or conservative) criterion. These observers are being extremely stingy with their "I hear it" reports and extremely generous with their "I don't hear it" reports. In other words, these observers are only going to conclude that they heard the signal if they are absolutely certain that they did. In contrast, consider the second and fourth sets of curves. Here, the observers are setting an extremely lenient (or liberal) criterion. These observers are being extremely generous with their "I hear it" reports and extremely stingy with their "I don't hear it" reports. In

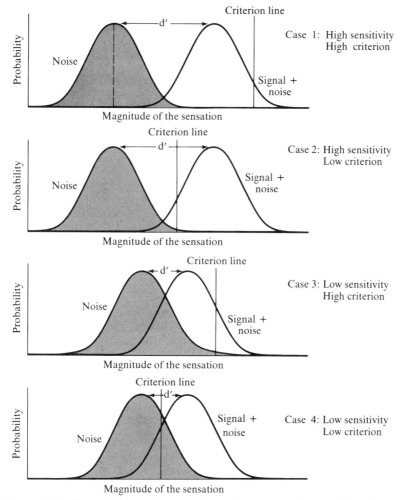

Figure 6-5. Four different observers in a signal-detection experiment.

contrast to the other observers, these observers are willing to conclude that they heard the signal if there is any reasonable possibility that they did.

Now let's look at the correctness of the decisions of these four observers. The proportion of each of the four possible outcomes is represented in Figure 6-6. The first observer has few hits and many misses; at the same time, this person has no false alarms and a perfect correct-rejection rate. The second observer has many more hits and many fewer misses; however, there are some false alarms and a less-than-perfect correct-rejection rate. The third observer has few hits and many misses; this person has a very small number of false alarms and a nearly perfect correct-rejection rate. Finally, the fourth observer has many hits and few misses, but this person has more false alarms and fewer correct rejections than anyone else.

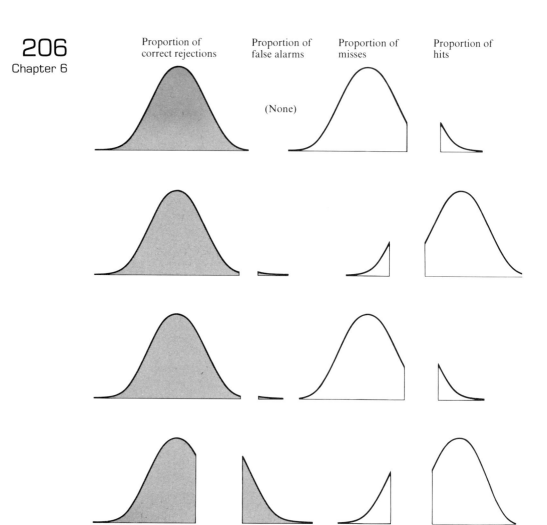

Figure 6-6. Possible outcomes for each of the four observers represented in Figure 6-5.

Which kind of observer is it best to be? Clearly it is best to have a large d'—that is, to have the noise and signal + noise curves as separate from each other as possible. With a large d', the ratio between the hit rate and the false-alarm rate is large. However, is it better to set your criterion high or low? There is no easy answer to this question, because you have to consider the payoff—the relative advantages and disadvantages of each possible outcome. The payoff will depend on the specific situation.

Let us consider a situation in which you might want to set the criterion very high. You are a young police officer, and you have just flagged down a car because you believe that the driver of the car is drunk. You look more closely at the driver, and you realize that he is a U.S. Senator. Your task is to figure out whether the driver is normal (noise) or drunk (signal + noise). If you conclude that he is normal, you send him on with profuse apologies; but if you conclude that he is drunk, you must arrest him. Surely, there would be some advantages to a hit, but contemplate the disadvantages of a false alarm—of arresting the distinguished Senator by mistake when, in fact, he was perfectly normal!

Now let's consider a situation in which you might want to set the criterion rather low. You are a surgeon. You are examining a young child and trying to decide whether the child has appendicitis or not. If you conclude that the child has appendicitis, you will operate. If you conclude that the child does not have appendicitis, you will not operate, and the child will return home. You can make two *correct* decisions: you can decide to operate, and the child turns out to have an inflamed appendix (a hit); or you can decide not to operate, and the child returns home and is better the next day (correct rejection). However, there are also two possible incorrect decisions. One is the false alarm: you decide to operate, and the appendix turns out to be normal. There are clearly disadvantages to a false alarm, because the child has had unnecessary surgery. However, the risks of a miss are far more dangerous: if you decide not to operate, and the appendix ruptures, the child will have to be hospitalized for a long time with serious complications and will run a substantial chance of dying. Surgeons are so concerned with misses that they are willing to tolerate a false-alarm rate of about 20% in diagnosing appendicitis.

It is worth considering what d' means in the case of the surgeon. The value for d', as we noted earlier, depends partly on the strength of the signal. A child who reported abdominal pain, vomiting, and loss of appetite and who, on examination, turned out to have a fever, tenderness over the appendix, and an elevated white blood count would be the case of a very strong signal. On the other hand, a child who reported mild abdominal pain and in whom no other signs of appendicitis were apparent would be the case of a very weak signal. However, d' also depends on the sensitivity of the observer. Just as subjects differ in their ability to detect tones, surgeons differ in their ability to detect appendicitis. If you ever find yourself rushing to the hospital with possible appendicitis, wish for a surgeon with a high d'!

Let's pause for a moment to review what we know of signal-detection theory so far. Signal-detection theory describes a subject's response to two situations—one in which there is a signal (signal + noise) and one in which there are background stimuli alone (noise). There are four possible combinations of situation and response: (1) the signal is presented, and the subject reports it (a hit); (2) the signal is presented, but the subject does not report it (a miss); (3) the signal is not presented, and the subject does not report it (a correct rejection); and (4) the signal is not presented, but the subject *does* report it (a false alarm). In some situations, hits occur frequently, and false alarms occur rarely; in other situations, hits are rare, and false alarms are frequent. We cannot specify how often each will occur because their relative incidence depends on two factors: sensitivity and criterion. Sensitivity (or d'), in turn, depends on two factors: the strength of the signal and the sensitivity of the observer. Criterion depends on many factors, including the probability of occurrence and the payoff. It is always best to have high sensitivity, but the specific situation will determine whether you would like to have a lenient or a strict criterion.

Consider the many applications of signal-detection theory in your everyday life. You often need to decide whether something did or did not occur, or whether something will or will not occur. In each case—though you don't think about it in these formal terms—you are weighing the advantages of a hit or a correct rejection against the disadvantages of a miss or a false alarm.

Receiver-Operating-Characteristic Curves

Our greatest concern in signal detection is with two measures: the proportion of hits and the proportion of false alarms. These numbers summarize the relationship between a subject's accurate and inappropriate responses. A **receiver-operating-characteristic (ROC) curve** plots the relationship between the proportion of hits and the proportion of false alarms. Each curve represents a particular d', and each point along the curve represents the proportions of hits and of false alarms at a certain criterion. Along the curve, then, the observer's sensitivity and the strength of the signal stay the same. The curve is made up of many different points because whenever the criterion changes, the proportions of hits and false alarms change.

Figure 6-7 presents a series of three ROC curves. Look first at the curve marked $d' = 1$. Suppose this observer sets a very strict criterion for saying "I hear it" (like the first and third observers in Figure 6-5). At this criterion, the subject will report the tone when it does occur (a hit) 40% of the time and will report the tone when it does not occur (a false alarm) 10% of the time. This information is plotted as Point A. Now suppose the same observer sets a very lenient criterion for saying "I hear it" (like the second and fourth observers in Figure 6-5); this time, the subject has more hits (say, 90%) but also more false alarms (say, 70%). This combination is plotted as Point B. As the curve im-

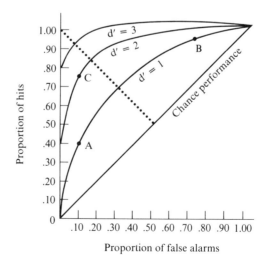

Figure 6-7. Three Receiver-Operating-Characteristic Curves.

plies, there is a trade-off between hits and false alarms: in order to get something good (more hits), you also have to accept something bad (more false alarms).

How do we get subjects to change their criteria when we are performing a signal-detection experiment? One way is by changing the probability that the signal will occur. When a signal occurs frequently, subjects are more willing to say "I hear it," even if they aren't sure: they set their criteria low. When a signal occurs rarely, subjects are more reluctant to say "I hear it": they set their criteria high. Another way to get subjects to change their criteria is to use money: if you pay subjects for every hit, they will set low criteria for saying "I hear it"; if you take away money for every false alarm, they will set high criteria.

We have seen what happens when we hold d' constant and vary only the criterion. Now let's look at what happens when we vary d'. In Figure 6-7, compare the $d' = 2$ curve with the $d' = 1$ curve. Compare, for example, Point C with Point A. The false-alarm rate is identical for these two points (10%). However, when $d' = 2$, the subject is almost twice as accurate: the hit rate is about 75%, rather than 40%.

Figure 6-8 gives an example of data that might be obtained from two subjects, one of whom has better hearing than the other. Note that payment conditions have been varied to encourage each subject to adopt five different criteria. Try plotting ROC curves for these two subjects, and compare them with those shown in Figure 6-7.

	Subject A (good hearing) Prop. of hits/Prop. of f.a.		Subject B (bad hearing) Prop. of hits/Prop. of f.a.	
Lose 10¢ for every false alarm	.65	.00	.20	.10
Lose 5¢ for every false alarm	.83	.02	.54	.28
Lose nothing for false alarms; win nothing for hits	.90	.12	.85	.53
Win 5¢ for every hit	.97	.25	.92	.75
Win 10¢ for every hit	1.00	.30	1.00	.80

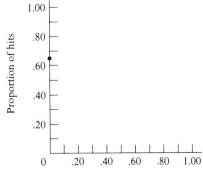

Figure 6-8.

When experimenters use the signal-detection method, they derive an ROC curve by plotting the hit rate and the false-alarm rate associated with each criterion—exactly as you have done. The measure d' is determined by the point at which the dotted diagonal line crosses the curve (see Figure 6-7). Once we know d', we can draw normal curves to represent the noise curve and the signal + noise curve, like the ones shown in Figure 6-7. Incidentally, by varying the position of the criterion line, we can demonstrate that the proportions of hits and false alarms cut off on the normal curves are equivalent to the proportions of hits and false alarms at a point representing that criterion on the ROC.

An Application of Signal-Detection Methods

As we noted at the beginning of this discussion, one clear advantage of signal-detection methods over earlier psychophysical methods is that signal-detection methods allow experimenters to distinguish between sensitivity and criterion—measures that cannot be separated when other psychophysical methods are used. A recent study by Harkins and Geen (1975) demonstrates an interesting application of signal-detection methods in separating the effects of sensitivity from the effects of criterion.

Harkins and Geen discuss a number of earlier studies that showed that introverts (people who turn inward, toward themselves) detect more signals than extroverts (people who turn outward, toward others). However, the authors note that detection has always been measured in terms of the percentage of signals detected. Now, either of two explanations might account for this difference: (1) introverts may be more sensitive than extroverts (this was the commonly accepted explanation); or (2) introverts may have a lower criterion—they may simply be more willing to say "I detect it."

The experiment that Harkins and Geen conducted used a visual detection task, testing ten females who were highly extroverted and ten females who were highly introverted. The data were then analyzed using signal-detection methods. The analysis showed that introverts were significantly better than extroverts in terms of sensitivity: d' was significantly larger for the introverts. At the same time, the analysis showed that introverts had *higher* criterion levels than extroverts. In other words, they were much more conservative with their "I detect it" responses. Clearly, then, we cannot entertain the alternate hypothesis that introverts gain accuracy by using a more liberal criterion.

DISCUSSION

In this chapter, we have explored aspects of the relationship between physical stimuli and psychological reactions. A major concern has been how to measure that relationship, and we have looked at tools for measuring both detection and discrimination. Although psychophysics has a distinct advantage over psychological scaling because of the availability of objective ways to measure the physical stimuli, we have seen that the problem of measurement is still a challenging one. Several confounding factors can interfere and prevent us from obtaining accurate measurements. Furthermore, human judgment often depends on factors other than simple perceptual sensitivity. We have seen how signal-detection theory can provide us with separate measures of sensitivity and decision criterion, thereby offering an improvement over classic psychophysical techniques.

Our other major concern in this chapter has been with the nature of the relationship between the physical and the psychological. Weber's Law made a statement about the relationship between the size of the stimulus and the amount of change in the stimulus that is necessary for discrimination. Fechner and Stevens were more concerned about the scaling of psychological reactions, and their specific predictions differ. The search for the relationship between physical stimuli and the way those stimuli are registered continues; we will look at other aspects of that search in the chapter on perception.

Psychophysical methods have their counterparts in other areas of psychology. For example, the Stanford-Binet test is an intelligence test that you may have heard about in other psychology courses. The method of presenting the items on this test resembles the psychophysical method of limits. The tester, like an experimenter, presents items of a given level of difficulty. If the subject fails these items, the tester presents increasingly easier test items until the subject passes all the items. Note that this series is similar to the descending series in psychophysics. Then the tester presents increasingly more difficult test items until the subject fails all the items—a series similar to the ascending series in psychophysics.

Signal-detection theory also has its counterparts in other areas of psychology. The whole concept of testing is frequently related to decision making. When a firm administers a test to job applicants, for example, the test is valuable to the extent that it produces a relatively large number of hits and correct rejections and a relatively small number of misses and false alarms. In other words, the test should tell the firm who should be accepted and who should be rejected, so that the firm does not hire people who shouldn't be hired and fail to hire people who should be hired. Anastasi (1976, pp. 167–177) includes an excellent discussion of the relationship between testing and decision making.

We will examine other applications of signal-detection theory in the chapters on perception and motivation. A less traditional application of signal-detection theory will be discussed in the chapter on memory. As we will see, asking a subject whether a word has been seen previously is similar to asking a subject whether a signal has been presented. Subjects sometimes have hits (they say they have seen the word before, and they have) and sometimes have false alarms (they say they have seen the word before, and they have not).

Psychophysical techniques are tools that provide some insights into the way the mind processes stimuli. Like all psychological tools, however, they must be used carefully because human factors may render them inaccurate.

SUMMARY

1. Psychophysics is the measurement of the relationship between a physical stimulus and the psychological reaction to that stimulus. Unlike psychological scaling, psychophysical stimuli can be objectively, physically measured.

2. A threshold for detection is a boundary point, such that the stimulus can be detected 50% of the time.

3. In the method of limits in detection studies, the experimenter presents the stimulus in gradually increasing and gradually decreasing series. This method has three potential problems: thresholds may be different for ascending series than for descending series; thresholds may reflect the subject's tendency to change the response on a predetermined trial; and thresholds may reflect errors of anticipation and errors of habituation. Appropriate controls minimize these problems.

4. The method of adjustment in detection differs from the method of limits in that the subjects make the adjustments by themselves.

5. In the method of constant stimuli in detection, the stimuli are presented in random order, with each stimulus intensity presented several times throughout the experiment.

6. Discrimination involves the comparison of two stimuli. The just noticeable difference (JND) measures how different the stimuli can be from each other and have the difference be just noticeable. Discrimination experiments must introduce controls to avoid confounding due to spatial order or temporal order.

7. In the method of limits in discrimination studies, the standard stimulus remains at a constant value while the comparison stimulus is presented in gradually increasing and decreasing series.

8. In the method of adjustment in discrimination, subjects adjust the comparison stimulus by themselves until they think it matches the standard stimulus, and the experimenter notes which stimuli they consider to be the same as the standard stimulus.

9. In the method of constant stimuli in discrimination, the comparison stimuli are presented in random order, with each comparison-stimulus intensity presented several times throughout the experiment.

10. Weber's Law states that the just noticeable difference is equal to some constant number multiplied by the value of the standard stimulus; thus, the JND is larger for larger standard stimuli.

11. Fechner's Law, obtained indirectly by adding JNDs together, states that the psychological reaction to a stimulus is equal to some constant multiplied by the logarithm of the value of the standard stimulus.

12. Stevens used a direct method to obtain psychological reactions to physical stimuli. He found a different equation to describe the relationship between physical stimuli and psychological reactions: $R = kS^n$. This equation is probably closer to the truth than Fechner's Law.

13. Signal-detection theory states that people's responses in a psychophysics task depend on both their sensitivity (d') and their criterion. It is always advantageous to have a high d'. However, the specifics of the situation determine whether it is better to have a strict or a lenient criterion. With a strict criterion, you make few hits but few false alarms; with a lenient criterion, you make many hits but many false alarms. The signal-detection method has many applications in other areas of psychology.

Part 2

The Content of Experimental Psychology: Explorations in Five Research Areas

7

Perception

Perception refers to the way we experience the world of objects and events (Weintraub & Walker, 1966). Perception combines information about the outside world as registered on the sensory organs, such as eyes and ears, with information from memory, such as past experiences. Thus, perception combines aspects of both the outside world and the inside world.

A physical stimulus registered on the sensory organs has no inherent meaning. For example, the song of a bird is registered in your ears in terms of qualities such as loudness and pitch. When you combine that sensory information with information from memory, however, you can perceive that the sound is, in fact, a bird's song.

In this chapter, we will explore a variety of research areas in perception. You will notice that most of the chapter is concerned with vision, because researchers have investigated vision more extensively than the other senses. However, brief sections on hearing, taste, smell, and touch have also been included to give you a feeling for the kinds of questions that are being studied in these areas.

Our methodological emphasis in this chapter will be on the dependent variable—the responses that the subject supplies. The choice of an appropriate dependent variable is particularly important in perception research because the process of perception is typically private and covert. Language, for example, is much more public and overt: we can learn a good deal about the language abilities of humans by listening to them *speak*. In contrast, we cannot learn much by watching or listening while people *perceive*. The challenge in perception, then, is to translate subjects' private responses to perceptual stimuli into public responses that an experimenter can measure. As we will see, some experimenters ask subjects to report their perceptions verbally. Other experimenters use psychophysical techniques to obtain formal, precise measures of perception. Experimenters interested in the perceptual capacities of infants, however, must specify clever, nonverbal responses that their subjects must make in order to ''tell'' us what they perceive. Throughout this chapter, then, we will pay close attention to the methods that experimenters use to measure dependent variables.

A number of different topics will be explored in this chapter. First, we will consider some basic visual abilities: acuity, flicker fusion, and adaptation. Second, we will discuss attributes of stimuli and how these attributes are perceived. Stimuli have color, form, movement, and distance from the observer: how is each of these attributes of objects registered in the perceptions of the observer? Third, we will consider accuracy in perception, noting that perception is not always a perfect mirror of reality. We will see how perceptions can be influenced by constancy, by illusions, and by the pleasantness of the stimulus. Finally, we will look briefly at the other senses: hearing, taste, smell, and touch.

Naturally, a single chapter on perception must omit many topics, as well as many important experiments from those topics that are included. Readers who wish to pursue other studies in perception should read *Sensory Processes* (Alpern, Lawrence, & Wolsk, 1967) and *Perception* (Weintraub & Walker, 1966) for a middle-level coverage of perception, or relevant chapters of *Woodworth & Schlosberg's Experimental Psychology* (Kling & Riggs, 1971) for a more detailed introduction to the field.

VISUAL ABILITIES

Let's begin by looking at three basic visual abilities in humans. **Acuity** is the ability to discriminate between stimuli in space. **Flicker fusion** is the ability to discriminate between stimuli in time. **Adaptation** is the ability to adapt to a change in lighting.

Acuity

When we say that someone has good eyesight, we are referring to visual acuity. Visual acuity is the ability to perceive very fine details—for example, the ability to discriminate two dots placed close together as being two separate objects, rather than a single, blurred object.

How can we measure acuity? Because visual acuity is highly relevant to our everyday lives, ophthalmologists and psychologists have developed a number of different ways of measuring acuity.

The Snellen chart is probably most familiar to you; a miniature version of this chart appears in Figure 7-1. To measure acuity, you stand at a specified distance from the chart—for example, 20 feet (6.6 meters). If you can read the letters that the average person can read at 20 feet (6.6 meters), you have 20/20 vision. If your eyesight is not so sharp, you may have to stand closer in order to read the letters in that line; for example, you may have to stand as close as 10 feet (3.3 meters) from the chart. In this case, we would say that you have 10/20 vision—or, since numbers below 20 are not typically used, 20/40 vision. Notice that this response measure for visual acuity is rather unusual. On the Snellen

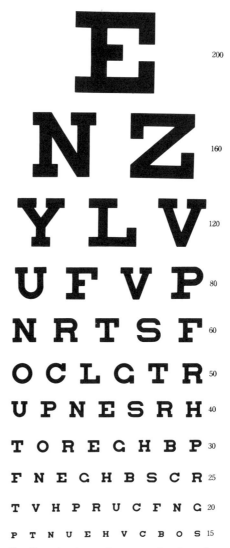

Figure 7-1. The Snellen chart, used to test visual acuity (size reduced).

chart, we record the subject's response in terms of the *distance* from the eye chart at which the verbal report is accurate, rather than the number of errors at some specified distance.

However, there is a problem with the Snellen eye chart, even though it is commonly used: there are too many different letter features that can aid the viewer in arriving at the correct response. Look at the big E at the top, for example. The straight line on the left tells us that the letter cannot be A, C, G, J, and so on; the straight line on top tells us that the letter cannot be C, D, G, H, and so on. Fortunately, there are geometric figures that can do a much better job in measuring acuity. For example, you may have been tested with a variant of the Landolt ring (see Figure 7-2). In this test, you are asked to report

Figure 7-2. The Landolt ring, used to test visual acuity. The observer reports the orientation of the break in the ring.

whether the break in the ring is at the right, left, top, or bottom. A correct report indicates that you can perceive the two separate edges surrounding the break, rather than seeing a continuous, blurred circle. Acuity in the Landolt-ring test is measured in terms of the size of the break in the circle that the viewer can correctly detect. Normal vision has an acuity rating of 1.0, which means that the viewer can detect a break that subtends a 1.0-minute arc. (This is equivalent to a 1-mm break viewed at a distance of 3.2 meters.) If your eyesight is not so sharp, you may require a 3.0-minute break in the circle in order to detect it. In that case, you would receive an acuity rating of 3.0. Naturally, your acuity will vary from one situation to the next, depending on factors such as the amount of light in the room and how dark the ring appears in contrast to its background.

Measuring acuity in adults is a rather easy task—you simply ask them to report what they see. How would you measure acuity in infants? Obviously, you have to rule out verbal reports. The response-measure problem that we considered in Chapter 1 is simply overwhelming here: there is so little that infants can do to demonstrate their true abilities in acuity. Early child psychologists had not developed the appropriate methods to assess acuity in infants; their less refined methods led them to conclude that infants could not see very well. With the development of more recent methods, they have concluded that infants' acuity is quite good. The discovery of new infant skills as a result of the development of new measurement techniques has caused one humorist to remark, "Infants are getting smarter every year."

Fantz's (1961) method of measuring acuity in infants is an excellent example of obtaining information from something an infant *can* do—look at objects. Fantz placed his infant subjects in a crib inside a looking chamber. On the ceiling of the chamber he attached pairs of test objects, slightly separated from each other. The experimenter could look through a peephole in the ceiling and see the tiny images of the test object mirrored in the subjects' eyes. When one of the objects was mirrored in the center of the eye, over the pupil, the experimenter knew that the subject was looking directly at it. The experimenter could record on a timer the amount of attention given to each test object. For example, an infant shown a circle and a square might look at the circle 40% of the time and the square 60% of the time. The important information here is not that the subject preferred one type of object to another, but that the subject could *differentiate* between the objects well enough to spend consistently different amounts of time looking at them. If the subjects were *unable* to differentiate between two figures, then the looking times would turn out to be equivalent—on the average, 50% for each figure. Using this technique, Fantz found that 6-month-old infants could distinguish between a patch of stripes 1/64 inch (4 mm) wide at a distance of 10 inches (25.4 cm) and a patch of gray paper of equivalent brightness (see Figure 7-3). This turns out to be an acuity rating of 5.0—compared to the normal adult rating of 1.0.

Figure 7-3. Infants at 6 months can distinguish between stripes 1/64 inch (4 mm) wide and a gray stimulus of equivalent brightness, when both stimuli are at a distance of 10 inches (25.4 cm).

Flicker Fusion

Acuity measures a person's ability to discriminate between stimuli in *space;* flicker fusion measures a person's ability to discriminate between stimuli in *time.* Look at your desk lamp, for instance. If that light bulb were turned on and off every second, you would clearly be able to discriminate between light and dark. You would even be able to discriminate if it could be turned on and off ten times in each second. However, if the on-and-off cycle were speeded up considerably, the light receptors in your eyes would be unable to fire rapidly enough, and the light would appear to be on continually. The **critical flicker frequency** is the frequency threshold at which a light appears to be steady rather than flickering.

The critical flicker frequency is an example of information obtained in perception by using classical psychophysical techniques. You could measure this threshold using the method of adjustment or the method of constant stimuli, but the method of limits has been used most often. For example, the experimenter might systematically increase the speed at which a light goes on and off, until the subject reports seeing one continuous light. Then the experimenter systematically decreases the speed on the next series until the subject reports a flickering light.

Adaptation

Adaptation is a visual phenomenon that you experience frequently in everyday life. You turn off your light at night, and the world seems pitch dark—you can't even make out the furniture in the room. After several minutes with the light off, however, you can see many objects. It may take 20 to 30 minutes to reach the maximum sensitivity. This is **dark adaptation**—an increase in visual sensitivity with decreased exposure to light. Visual sensitivity increases for two reasons: (1) the pupils dilate to let in more light; and (2) the receptors become more responsive.

Dark adaptation has been well examined in the laboratory. The subject is first exposed to a light for several minutes, with the light intensity and time of exposure precisely controlled. Then the light is turned off, and the threshold for a small spot of light is measured, for example, in an area of the eye that contains both rods and cones (see Figure 7-4). The first rapid decline in the curve is due to dark adaptation of **cones**—the light receptors that are responsible for color vision. The slower decline after the bump in the curve is due to dark adaptation of **rods**—the light receptors that are sensitive to brightness but not color. Notice that it takes about half an hour to reach maximum dark adaptation. (Incidentally, dark-adaptation curves typically represent the performance of a single subject. This is an area where single-subject experiments, discussed in Chapter 2, are the rule rather than the exception.)

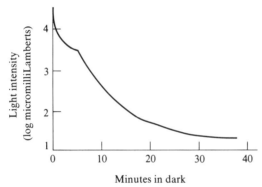

Minutes in dark

Figure 7-4. Dark adaptation to a white disk. The *y*-axis represents how intense a light must be in order to be detected. The *x*-axis represents the passage of time in the dark. Adapted from "Dark Adaptations of Retinal Fields of Different Size and Location," by S. Hecht, C. Haig, and G. Wald, *Journal of General Physiology*, 1935, *19*, 321–327. Copyright 1935 by Rockefeller University Press. Reprinted by permission.

You are also quite familiar with the experience of **light adaptation.** When you emerge from a dark movie theater into bright daylight, you feel blind for a few minutes. Similarly, if a car traveling toward you on a dark night shines its bright lights at you, your vision is impaired.

Adaptation phenomena are among the most impressive visual accomplishments. They permit us to see stimuli varying widely in intensity: some stimuli are one billion times as bright as other stimuli, yet we can see both kinds.

HOW ATTRIBUTES OF STIMULI ARE PERCEIVED

Stimuli are "out there" in the world. How are the attributes of stimuli registered "in here"—in the perception of the observer? We will be concerned with four attributes of stimuli: their color, their form or shape, their movement, and their distance from the observer.

As the saying goes, "In the dark, all cats are gray." In very dim light, only the rods function, and they cannot discriminate color. The light must be brighter in order to perceive color, because cones require more light.

How can all the colors be classified? There are a variety of different methods, but one method that seems logically pleasing is the three-dimensional **color spindle.** Figure 7-5 shows two dimensions of the spindle. The dimension called **hue,** or color names, can be placed around the edge of a circle, in the same order as they appear in the rainbow. The second dimension of color, **saturation,** represents the amount of white a color contains. For example, a rich, bright blue is more highly saturated than a pale, robin's-egg blue. Saturation is represented by the distance from the center of the circle, with a rich (saturated) blue out at the edge and a pale blue in toward the center.

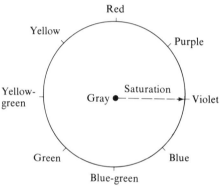

Figure 7-5. The color circle: hue and saturation.

This two-dimensional color circle can be transformed into a three-dimensional color spindle by adding a third dimension, **brightness** (see Figure 7-6). Brightness is represented by the intensity of the light, with the brightest values at the top of the spindle. Keep in mind, however, that this three-dimensional model is only a schematic way of representing the variety of colors; other color models attempt to represent irregularities in the shape of the three-dimensional figure.

One area of interest to color researchers has been the discrimination of colors—specifically, their hues. In these experiments, the subject sees a field divided in half. On one half of the field is the standard stimulus—a color of a given wavelength represented by λ, or *lambda*. On the other half of the field is the comparison stimulus—a color of a slightly different wavelength represented by $\lambda + \Delta\lambda$, or *lambda plus delta lambda*. (The symbol $\Delta\lambda$ means "the change in lambda.") Incidentally, it is important that the standard stimulus and the comparison stimulus be equivalent in brightness. Otherwise, the study might be confounded because the subject might judge in terms of brightness, rather than hue.

The experimenters then use the psychophysical techniques for measuring discrimination described in Chapter 6. Specifically, they note how much λ must

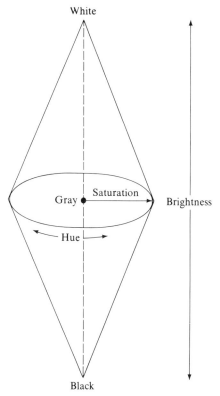

Figure 7-6. The color spindle: hue, saturation, and brightness.

be changed before the subject can discriminate between the two hues. The dependent variable, then, is $\Delta\lambda$. This dependent variable, like others involving psychophysical techniques, involves a verbal report ("same" or "different"). However, this carefully controlled technique allows experimenters to obtain a precise and systematic measure of human discrimination ability.

How much does λ need to be changed before the subject notices the difference between the two halves of the field? As Figure 7-7 demonstrates, $\Delta\lambda$ depends on the color that is being discriminated. Thresholds are low (sensitivity to change is high) for blues tending toward green and for medium yellows; thresholds are relatively high for purples, greens, and reds.

Other aspects of color perception are beyond the scope of this book. Alpern, Lawrence, and Wolsk (1967) and Ganz (1975) may be consulted for information on theories of color vision. Also, Weintraub and Walker's (1966) book on perception includes a chapter on subjective color.

Perception of Form

The topic of form perception includes general issues, such as perceptual organization, as well as specific issues, such as the perception of words.

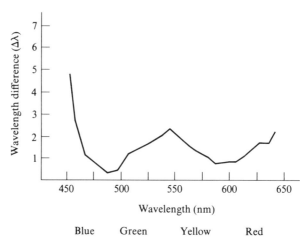

Blue Green Yellow Red

Figure 7-7. The threshold for discriminating a change in hue as a function of the hue of the test light, in nanometers. Adapted from "Chromatic Sensibility to Stimulus Differences," by D. B. Judd, *Journal of the Optical Society of America*, 1932, *22*, 72–108. Used by permission of the Optical Society of America.

Perceptual organization. Look at any two-dimensional picture or shape in your room. What you see does not appear to be a random combination of dots and lines and shapes, lacking in pattern. Instead, it seems well organized. One of the most basic ways in which perception is organized is that objects appear to stand out in contrast to their background, a phenomenon known as the **figure-ground relationship.** Figure 7-8 illustrates a familiar reversible figure, in which you might see a vase as the figure against a black background, or you might see two faces as the figures against a white background. However, you cannot simultaneously see both vase and faces. When one becomes figure, the other insists on becoming ground. The figure-ground relationship is one of the principles identified by Gestalt psychologists as an organizer of perception.

Figure 7-8. The vase/faces reversible figure, illustrating the figure/ground relationship.

Another way in which perception is organized is by **grouping.** Many parts of a two-dimensional picture seem to belong together, rather than in isolation. Figure 7-9 illustrates several of the laws of grouping: **closure, good continuation, similarity,** and **nearness.**

a. Law of closure. This figure will be reported as a triangle,
   although it is not perfectly closed.

b. Law of good continuation. The central bar will be chosen
   to complete the line because it continues in the same
   direction.

```
O O O O O O
X X X X X X
O O O O O O
X X X X X X
O O O O O O
```

c. Law of similarity. This arrangement will be reported as
   a series of rows rather than columns in order to group
   similar items.

```
O  O  O  O  O  O
O  O  O  O  O  O
O  O  O  O  O  O
O  O  O  O  O  O
O  O  O  O  O  O
O  O  O  O  O  O
O  O  O  O  O  O
O  O  O  O  O  O
```

d. Law of nearness. This arrangement will be reported as
   a series of columns rather than rows in order to group
   together items that are near each other.

Figure 7-9. Some of the laws of grouping.

When Gestalt psychologists began examining perceptual organization at
the beginning of the century, the commonly accepted response measure was
verbal report. In Figure 7-9c, for example, subjects report that they see a series
of rows rather than a series of columns.

More recent evidence suggests that infants, as well as adults, are governed by the laws of grouping. T.G.R. Bower (1966) examined infants who
were approximately 2 months old, using a particularly clever method that we
will describe in more detail in the section on perceptual constancies. The infants were conditioned to respond to a wire triangle that was partially covered
by an iron bar. The infants were then tested for generalization to each of four
figures—a complete triangle and three triangles with distortions in the place
where the bar had previously been that violated the laws of grouping. The
infants showed the greatest generalization to the complete triangle, demonstrat-

ing that they had "guessed" that a complete triangle had been hidden behind the bar.

Recognition of objects in pictures. How can we look at a picture and recognize what object it represents? There are some experiments that suggest that this ability does not have to be practiced in order to be acquired. One experiment attests to the persistence of psychologists in pursuing a hypothesis. Hochberg and Brooks (1962) raised a child to the age of 19 months with extremely limited exposure to pictures and no experience with naming pictures. However, at 19 months, the child successfully named both simple and complex line drawings and photographs of familiar objects.

However, Segall, Campbell, and Herskovits (1966) reported that some African natives have had difficulty recognizing objects and people in black-and-white photographs. The photograph's translation of three dimensions into two and the representation of color by shades of black and white seemed too big a jump from the natural object. These authors describe a Bushwoman who "turned a photograph of her own son this way and that, in attempting to make sense out of the shadings of grays on the piece of paper she held. It was only when the details of the photograph were pointed out to her that she was able to perceive the subject" (p.32).

These studies and others summarized by Hagen (1974) suggest that we cannot draw any firm conclusions about whether the perception of pictures must be learned from experience.

Recognition of faces. In this section, we will examine the recognition of faces—particularly, the recognition of faces of one's own race in contrast to faces of other races.

Luce (1974) provides a variant of what most White Americans would recognize as the "Chinese waiter dilemma":

> Twenty years ago, as a young soldier serving in Japan and Korea, I shared with most of my fellow soldiers a belief that all Asians look alike. They seemed interchangeable: short, with straight, black hair and brown eyes. We whites, on the other hand, boasted a rich diversity of eye color, skin tone, hair color and texture. My smug ethnocentrism got a severe blow, though, when a Japanese girl informed me that to her countrymen the first GIs who landed after World War II all looked alike, too, and it was still difficult to distinguish them [pp. 105–106].

Luce's study tested Black students who were familiar with Whites but not Asian-Americans; White students who were familiar with Blacks, but not Asian-Americans; and Asian-Americans (both Chinese and Japanese) who were familiar with both other races. The subjects were asked to study a page of 20 photographs, all from the same racial group. They studied the page for one minute and then were tested with a sheet containing 9 of the original photographs mixed in with 11 new photographs. All subjects judged four sets of photographs: Black, White, Japanese, and Chinese.

The results showed that subjects of all races were most accurate in recognizing photographs of members of their own race. Some of the other results are intriguing but puzzling. For example, Whites were reasonably accurate in recognizing both groups of Asian-Americans, but not Blacks; Asian-Americans were reasonably accurate in recognizing Blacks, but not Whites. Thus, amount of previous contact with a racial group did not determine recognition accuracy. Incidentally, in a supplemental test, Luce found that Asian-Americans could easily categorize photographs of Oriental faces as either Chinese or Japanese.

Galper (1973) has provided some data that show an interesting exception to the rule that people are best at identifying members of their own race. She studied Black and White students enrolled in a psychology course and Black and White students enrolled in a Black-studies course. Her results showed that three of the groups—the Blacks and the Whites in psychology and the Blacks in Black studies—were best at identifying members of their own race, but the White students enrolled in a Black-studies course were more accurate on the Black photographs than on the White photographs. She concludes that "objective" race membership may be less important than allegiance or interest, which she calls "functional race membership." The Whites in Black-studies courses were "functionally" Black; consequently, they performed well on Black photographs.

Recognition of words. From the vast literature on word recognition, we will explore only two topics: the effect of familiarity on word recognition, and perceptual defense. Both of these areas use an instrument called the **tachistoscope** (fortunately abbreviated **T-scope),** which projects visual stimuli such as words for a very brief duration, usually less than one-tenth of a second. The experimenter generally uses a modified method of limits with the tachistoscope, using only ascending series. For example, the experimenter might expose a word for .01 second on the first trial and gradually increase the exposure duration on subsequent trials until the subject reports the word. (Note that descending series would be useless, as the stimulus would be identified on the first trial.) The threshold is typically reported as the minimum exposure duration required for recognition.

Spielberger and Denny (1963) studied the effects of *familiarity* on recognition by choosing words that varied in their frequency of occurrence in the English language. (As we will discuss in Chapter 8, the frequency of English words can be assessed by checking published norms.) For example, a high-frequency word was NECESSARY, a medium-frequency word was SENSATION, and a low-frequency word was HIBERNATE. Appropriately, all the words contained the same number of letters, because word length influences recognition time; if the words had not been equated for length, the experiment would have been badly confounded.

The experimenters presented each word five times at each exposure duration, beginning at .01 second and adding increments of .01 second for each subsequent exposure duration. In this study, threshold was measured by the total number of exposures necessary for the subject to identify the word correctly on two occasions.

As expected, subjects required more exposures for the low-frequency words (approximately 11 exposures) than for the high-frequency words (approximately 7 exposures). An additional finding was an interaction between word frequency and the verbal ability of the subject. Subjects with high verbal ability performed about the same as subjects with low verbal ability when high- and medium-frequency words were tested. However, the high-verbal-ability subjects performed much better than low-verbal-ability subjects on the low-frequency words. Thus, the influence of verbal ability on word recognition depends on the frequency of the stimulus that must be recognized.

Why should familiarity influence the threshold for a word on the tachistoscope? Krueger (1975) suggests that there may be two reasons. First, subjects may be able to *extract* the visual information more readily from familiar words. Second, and perhaps more important, the *interpretation* of familiar words may be easier. With a familiar word, subjects require less evidence in order to supply an answer. They may need to recognize only H—P—Y to guess HAPPY, for example, but may need to see all the letters in MARMOT to guess MARMOT.

Probably the most extensively researched area of word recognition is **perceptual defense**—a term used to describe slower recognition (higher thresholds) for threatening, emotional, or unpleasant material than for more neutral material. Erdelyi (1974), for example, has estimated that at least 1000 research publications have been concerned with perceptual defense.

The classic study in this area was performed by McGinnies (1949). He measured recognition thresholds for neutral words, such as DANCE and BROOM, and for taboo words, mostly sexual, such as RAPED and BITCH. The average recognition threshold for the neutral words was .07 seconds; the average recognition threshold for the taboo words was .12 seconds.

This experiment was promptly criticized by Howes and Solomon (1950), who suggested that the discrepancy in thresholds might be due not to the taboo nature of the emotional words, but to the fact that these words had lower frequencies in the English language. As we have just seen, low-frequency words have higher thresholds than more common English words. Thus, Howes and Solomon proposed that word frequency was a confounding variable.

Others have suggested that the results of perceptual-defense experiments can be explained by response suppression. Perhaps the subjects *see* a taboo word such as RAPED quite readily, but they resist *reporting* the word until they are absolutely certain that the word has been perceived correctly. Recall from Chapter 3 that evaluation apprehension may be an extremely important factor in psychology experiments. Subjects (particularly subjects in the 1940s) may have been reluctant to say the taboo words for fear that the experimenters might evaluate them negatively.

Erdelyi (1974) has reviewed the vast literature in this area. He concludes that there really is evidence for higher thresholds for emotional words, even when the experiments use stimuli controlled for word frequency, and even when response suppression is not a factor. Let's look at one representative study. Johnson, Frincke, and Martin (1961) contrasted the recognition of pleasant words, such as PROSPER, KITCHEN, and JEWEL, with unpleasant words, such as DISMAL, ORDEAL, and TYPHOON. The lists of pleasant words and unpleasant words were equivalent in word frequency and meaningfulness (number of associations produced by a word). The average threshold for the pleasant words was .56; the average threshold for unpleasant words was .90. Looking at the data another way, 16 out of the 17 subjects had lower mean thresholds for pleasant words than for unpleasant words. Thus, there was a significant difference in thresholds even when word frequency could not be a confounding factor. Furthermore, response suppression seems highly unlikely: would you be at all embarrassed to report the word TYPHOON? According to Erdelyi, our attitude toward a word determines how readily we perceive it.

Perception of Movement

The perception of movement is something we take for granted; it seems quite natural that some things should move and others should stand still. However, as Johansson (1975) has pointed out, the perception of movement is really quite remarkable. You are probably familiar with the comparison between the eye and the camera, but the two differ enormously in their reaction to movement. The camera has a shutter that freezes the image, while the eye has no comparable shutter. Without a shutter, the camera would record only a blur. However, as objects pass in front of our eyes, they seem to travel through space with sharp outlines.

Consider the ways in which movement can be registered. First, the object being observed can move. Second, the observer can move. (Often it is difficult to distinguish between these two kinds of movement. Have you ever been seated in a stationary train when a train next to yours begins to move? For a moment, it may seem as though you—the observer—are moving, rather than the object you are observing.) Third, the eye itself can move—sometimes smoothly, as in following the flight of a bird, and sometimes in jerks (**saccadic movement**), as in reading a sentence in a book.

Consider also the complexity of movement that we can perceive at any given moment. Johansson cites an example of his little granddaughter running across the floor of his study to show him a ladybug walking on her finger.

> Perceptually I experience the room as being static, the child as running across the floor, the child's hand and arm as moving relative to her body, the child's finger as moving relative to her hand and the ladybug as moving relative to the child's finger. Thus my visual system abstracts a hierarchical series of moving frames of reference and motions relative to each of them [p. 85].

After a series of experiments, Johansson concluded that the eye resembles a computer with a program of specific rules, rather than resembling a camera. Johansson found, for example, that subjects showed an amazingly strong tendency, when looking at complex motion patterns, to conclude that a single, unified figure was moving through space. In one case, two spots of light followed each other in a perfectly rectangular path. Subjects did not report seeing these spots as isolated from each other; instead, they said that the two spots were lights at the ends of a rigid rod that rotated around a fixed central point. In another case, one corner of a square figure moved inward along a diagonal path. Subjects did not report seeing a shrinking, distorted square; instead, they said that the corner of the square was being lifted up, as illustrated in Figure 7-10. Subjects refuse to abandon the belief that there is a figure, moving through space, that is responsible for what they see.

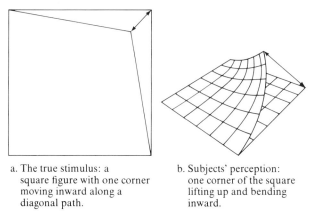

a. The true stimulus: a
   square figure with one corner
   moving inward along a
   diagonal path.

b. Subjects' perception:
   one corner of the square
   lifting up and bending
   inward.

Figure 7-10. Subjects apply a program of rules in perceiving motion. From "Visual Motion Perception," by G. Johansson, *Scientific American*, June 1975, *232*, 76–86. Copyright © 1975 by Scientific American, Inc. All rights reserved.

In another series of experiments, Johansson has explored biological motions—the patterns of motion that people and animals make. For example, he attached flashlight bulbs to the shoulders, elbows, wrists, hips, knees, and ankles of a coworker and took a motion picture of this person moving around a dark room. Subjects viewing the movie were able to identify instantly that the movements of the lights were caused by an otherwise invisible human. In fact, they were able to identify rather subtle changes in the relative movements of the lights—for example, when the person pretended to limp. Further research has determined that a naive observer requires only one-tenth of a second to recognize a familiar biological motion. This time is so short that Johansson concludes that there must be fixed, visual pathways from the retina to the cortex, so that the observer does not have to sort out and decipher the movements each time a new pattern is seen. The observer can recognize the movements quickly, even before these movements reach the level of consciousness.

In everyday life, we commonly make judgments regarding the *cause* of movement. For example, if we observe that person A is sitting at a table and leaves the moment person B arrives at the table, we conclude that person A left because of person B. Visual causality has been explored by the Belgian psychologist Albert Michotte (1963). He found that subjects readily assigned causality to moving spots of light, and not just to social creatures. Michotte used a special apparatus to present two spots. Spot A was stationary, and Spot B moved toward it at a certain speed. As soon as B touched A, A began to move away. Under specified stimulus conditions, subjects reported that B *caused* A to move; for example, causality was perceived only if A moved immediately after being touched by B, but not when there was a delay. (Similarly, if an acquaintance comes up to you when you are seated but were planning to leave, you remain there a few minutes so that the acquaintance does not perceive causality in your leaving.)

Notice that Johansson's study on the interpretation of motion patterns and Michotte's study on the cause of motion both relied on verbal report as the response measure, just as the studies of Gestalt psychologists did at the beginning of the century. When experimenters use verbal report, they trust their subjects to be able to translate their perceptions accurately into words. We can probably trust the correspondence between perception and report when the subjects are verbal adults. What if we wanted to know whether infants perceive causality in motion patterns? Obviously, we would have to abandon verbal report and devise an extremely sensitive response measure instead. We'll see an example of the search for a sensitive response measure in the next section, on the perception of depth.

Depth Perception

One of the oldest questions in the study of perception is this: if the image that falls on the retina is two-dimensional, how can we perceive our world as three-dimensional? Our perceptions tell us that objects vary in their distance from the observer because a large number of cues can provide information about depth. Some cues are muscular, some are **monocular** (involving one eye), and some are **binocular** (involving both eyes).

Muscular cues. Two muscular cues help in the perception of depth. **Accommodation** is the adjustment process managed by the ciliary muscle to change the curvature of the lens of the eye. Accommodation is necessary to bring an object into focus. **Convergence** is the process by which muscles outside the eye cause the eyes to move toward each other to look at a close object. You can easily experience convergence by holding your finger as far away as possible and focusing both eyes on it. Now bring your finger in slowly until it touches your nose, maintaining your focus the entire time. The muscular strain you experience as you feel your eyes "cross" is convergence.

Monocular cues. The remaining cues to depth perception are visual, rather than muscular. First, we'll examine the monocular cues—those that can be seen with one eye.

1. *Size* is one of the best cues to how far away an object is. If you know how big an object really is, then from the size of the object on the retina, you can estimate how far away it is. Relative size may also serve as a cue: if two objects are similar in real size, but object A casts a larger image on the retina, then object A must be closer.
2. *Interposition* is a rule that states that if object A partially hides object B, then object A must be closer. If you look out your window right now, you'll find that this is a very strong depth cue: you cannot convince yourself that a tree is farther away than the building it partly conceals.

3. *Linear perspective* means that parallel lines appear to meet in the distance: the farther away two adjacent points on the parallel lines are, the closer together they will appear on the retina. Linear perspective is strong in Figure 7-11.

4. *Texture gradient* is also apparent in Figure 7-11. Floors, lawns, or railroad ties have distinct patterns which we can see if the surface is close to us. However, if the surface is far away, the pattern is blurred.

Figure 7-11. Linear perspective and texture gradient. (Photo by Jim Pinckney.)

5. *Shadows* give an additional cue to distance. For example, if the sun is behind you and tree A is casting a shadow on tree B, then tree A must be closer—a law similar to interposition. Also, shadows, or shading, can give the impression of depth on an isolated object. If you look at a tree when the sun is shining, the side away from the sun is shaded.

6. *Distance from the horizon* can tell us how far away objects are, even if other monocular cues are missing. In Figure 7-12, there are no shadows, texture gradient, or other cues; yet the circle appears nearest and the triangle farthest away.

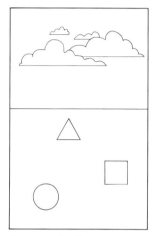

Figure 7-12. Distance from the horizon as a cue to depth perception.

7. *Motion parallax* is one monocular cue that cannot be represented in a picture. It is caused by your own movements, and it involves the apparent direction and speed of motion of objects you watch as you move. To demonstrate this to yourself, go to the window and look at some part of the window. Now move your head to the right. That part of the window will appear to move to the *left*. In contrast, look out the window at a distant object and again move your head to the right. That distant object will appear to move to the *right*—in the same direction as you are moving. (I suspect it was motion parallax that caused my 4-year-old daughter to remark, as we were driving at night, "Mommy, the moon is following us!") Motion parallax can also tell you which of two nearby objects is closer. Hold your right finger 10 cm in front of one eye and your left finger 20 cm in front of the same eye. Close the other eye. Now move your head. The right, or closer, finger rushes by in contrast to the left finger.

We have noted that motion parallax cannot be represented in a picture. In order to perceive depth successfully in a picture, as Gibson (1969) has pointed out, the observer must be willing to ignore the lack of motion parallax. The nearby apple doesn't move any differently from the distant wine bottle as you walk past a picture, but the other depth cues are so strong that you can still perceive depth.

Binocular cues. Now let's talk about a type of cue that involves both eyes—**binocular disparity.** There is a difference, or disparity, in the way an object is represented to the two eyes. To demonstrate this to yourself, hold one finger about 10 cm in front of your nose and hold another finger as far away from you as possible. Look at both fingers with your left eye shut and then with your right eye shut. The finger held close will appear to jump back and forth with respect to the other finger. Similar to motion parallax, a change in the position of the eye that is doing the viewing brings a change in what is seen.

Binocular disparity is a depth cue that we may not appreciate until we are deprived of it. You might occasionally try viewing a scene with one eye closed in order to realize how flat it appears with only monocular vision.

Binocular disparity can be studied on the **stereoscope**—an instrument that typically uses mirrors to represent a different picture to each eye. As a result, the observer sees an object that appears three-dimensional. J. Ross (1976) discusses some of the interesting results that have been obtained with a stereoscope. For example, if the eyes are presented with pictures of two different people, the resulting three-dimensional perception may be of a face that is more attractive than either of the individual pictures.

Depth perception in infants. So far, we have discussed depth perception in adults. How do experimenters measure depth perception in young children, for whom verbal report is not an option? Let's look at two studies that searched for an appropriate response measure.

Are we born knowing how to perceive depth, or is it a skill that must be acquired with experience? This question was explored in a classic series of experiments by Gibson and Walk (1960). They tested a wide variety of species—goats, cats, rats, chicks—but we will concern ourselves only with their results on human infants. They called their apparatus a *visual cliff* (see Figure 7-13). Infants were placed on a center runway that had a sheet of strong glass extending outward on either side. On one side, a textured pattern (for example, a checkerboard design) was placed directly under the glass. On the other side, the same textured pattern, with the same size checks, was placed far below the glass. An adult would perceive depth in this situation because the checks that looked smaller would be interpreted as being farther away. The apparatus was called a visual cliff because the difference between the two sides appeared as a cliff.

In one experiment, Gibson and Walk tested 36 infants between 6 and 14 months of age. The child was placed on the center runway, and the child's mother called to him or her from both the deep side and the shallow side. Of 27 infants who moved off the board, all 27 crawled at least once onto the shallow side; only three crawled onto the deep side. Gibson and Walk's operational definition for *depth perception,* then, was "avoiding crawling to the deep side of the visual cliff."

One drawback to using the visual-cliff apparatus on infants is that they must be old enough to crawl in order to demonstrate depth perception. If only older, crawling infants can be tested, we cannot draw strong conclusions regarding the development of depth perception. Campos, Langer, and Krowitz (1970) decided to abandon crawling behavior as the dependent variable and use cardiac responses instead. By measuring change in heart rate, these research-

Figure 7-13. The visual cliff, designed to test infants' depth perception. Based on Gibson, E. J., & Walk, R. D. The "visual cliff." *Scientific American,* 1960, *202(4),* 64–71.

ers could determine whether younger infants responded differently to the deep and the shallow sides. Testing infants between 2 and 4 months of age, they measured whether the heart rate changed between the prestimulus period and the stimulus presentation period, during which the infant was placed on either the deep or the shallow side of the visual cliff. The infants showed no change in heart rate when placed on the shallow side of the visual cliff, but they showed a significant change in heart rate when placed on the deep side. (In other words, there was an interaction between deep/shallow condition and prestimulus/stimulus condition.) Thus, the use of a sensitive response measure—change in heart rate—showed that even young infants have depth perception and can identify which pattern is further from them.

ACCURACY IN PERCEPTION

In the last section, we talked about how the properties of objects out there in the world are registered by the perceiver. Now let's consider whether the perceiver registers those properties *accurately*. We'll see that perception is sometimes an accurate reflection of reality: we can grasp the true properties of objects, even when the retina provides us with inaccurate information, as in the case of constancy. Sometimes, though, perception is inaccurate: stimuli are distorted in the way they are perceived. Inaccurate perception occurs in illusions and in distortions by stimulus pleasantness.

Pick up this book and move it toward your eyes and then away from your eyes. The image that the book casts on your *retina* grows larger and then smaller as you move the book. However, do you *perceive* the book as changing in size? Does it seem to expand and shrink as you change its distance from you? No—it stays the same size. The tendency for an object to hold its size despite changes in its distance is called **size constancy.**

Subjects find it difficult to ignore size constancy and pay attention to retinal size. Rock (1975) describes a hypothetical experiment that you can try. Cut out a circle 20 cm in diameter and place it 10 m away from you, perhaps at the end of a corridor. Now make some comparison circles, 1 cm, 2 cm, 5 cm, 10 cm, and 20 cm in diameter.

Place the comparison circles 1 m away from you, and choose which one of the comparison circles casts a retinal image that is the same size as the circle at the end of the corridor.[1]

Do infants have size constancy? As an infant's parent moves a bottle toward the infant's eyes, does it seem to stay the same, or does it appear to grow as it moves? T.G.R. Bower (1966) devised a clever way to answer this question. You'll recall that the response-measure problem limits the ways in which we can obtain information from infant subjects. They have such limited ways of responding that we frequently underestimate their abilities in areas such as perception.

Here is the setup devised by Bower to enable infants to "tell" us that they have size constancy. He used the **operant-conditioning method** devised by Skinner, in which the experimenter selects a response that the subject can make and delivers a **reinforcement,** or reward, when the subject makes the designated response. If the subject is a rat, you might deliver a food pellet, particularly if the rat has been starved beforehand. Finding a suitable reinforcement for a baby is a trickier problem, since psychologists frown on starving babies. Bower thought of a delightful alternative reinforcement: peekaboo. When the infant makes a correct response, the experimenter pops up in front of the infant, smiling and nodding, speaking, and patting the infant on the stomach. Infants really enjoy this rich perceptual experience, and they respond for long periods in order to earn a peekaboo.

Now, what response should the infants supply in this conditioning setup? The ideal response would be one that the infant can easily make—that is, one that does not require refined motor ability—and one that is not very tiring. Bower decided on a head-turning response. The infant was placed in a reclining position with its head between two pads. Turning the head as little as one centimeter would be recorded as a response. Even 2-week-olds could give 400 responses like this without getting tired.

In operant conditioning, you may decide to deliver reinforcement for the subject's response only if a particular stimulus is present. For example, the rat

[1]The correct match for retinal-image size would be the 2-cm circle because it is 1/10 as far away as the 20-cm circle. Many observers are unable to resist size constancy and choose the 20-cm circle as the match.

might get a pellet for pressing the lever only if a red light is on; the red light would be called the **discriminated stimulus**. In Bower's experiment, the discriminated stimulus was a white cube. In other words, infants learned that the peekaboo reinforcement would be delivered for their head-turning response only if the white cube was present.

How can operant conditioning be used to test size constancy? Bower tested size constancy by seeing whether infants could recognize that same white cube even when it was farther away. He tested infants from 6 to 8 weeks of age by first training them to turn their heads only when the white cube was in front of them. This cube was 30 cm on each side, and it was placed 1 m from the infants' eyes. The infants responded for a total of one hour.

Next, Bower tested for **generalization**—the tendency to make a learned response to stimuli that are similar to the original stimulus. To the extent that the infant responds to new stimuli, we can conclude that the new stimuli appear similar to the infant. (Similarly, in the rat-conditioning experiment, if the rat pressed the lever frequently when the light was orange, rather than red, we would conclude that the new stimulus appeared similar to the old one.) Figure 7-14 illustrates the conditioned stimulus and three new stimuli.

Now, we expect the infant to make many head-turning responses to the original stimulus; in fact, this stimulus was found to elicit an average of 98 responses. The infants will respond to test stimulus #1 to the extent that they show size constancy, recognizing that the size is the same as that of the original stimulus, even though the distance is different; this stimulus elicited an average of 58 responses. The infants will respond to test stimulus #2 to the extent that

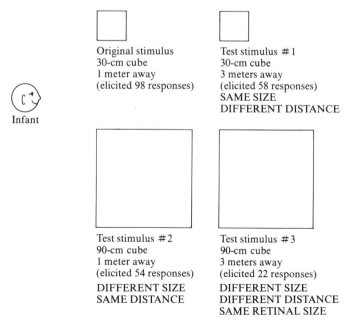

Original stimulus
30-cm cube
1 meter away
(elicited 98 responses)

Test stimulus #1
30-cm cube
3 meters away
(elicited 58 responses)
SAME SIZE
DIFFERENT DISTANCE

Infant

Test stimulus #2
90-cm cube
1 meter away
(elicited 54 responses)
DIFFERENT SIZE
SAME DISTANCE

Test stimulus #3
90-cm cube
3 meters away
(elicited 22 responses)
DIFFERENT SIZE
DIFFERENT DISTANCE
SAME RETINAL SIZE

Figure 7-14. The original (conditioned) stimulus and three new test stimuli used in the experiment by Bower (1966).

they recognize that the distance is the same, even though the size is different; this stimulus elicited an average of 54 responses. Finally, the infants will respond to test stimulus #3 to the extent that they recognize that the retinal size is the same (a 30-cm cube 1 m away and a 90-cm cube 3 m away both produce that same size image on the retina), even though both size and distance are different. This stimulus elicited an average of only 22 responses.

In summary, the infants considered both size and distance to be important in judging similarity. Retinal size, however, was unimportant. Most important here is the relatively large number of responses (58) to test stimulus #1 because this demonstrates that infants do have size constancy—the ability to recognize that the size stayed the same even though the object was farther away. However, by not responding more often than 58 times (still considerably fewer than the 98 responses for the original stimulus), the infants demonstrated that they acknowledged that some attribute of the stimulus, its distance, had been changed.

There are several other constancies in addition to size constancy. For example, how many right angles are there in Figure 7-15? When I first saw this

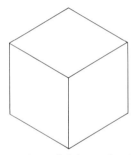

Figure 7-15. Count the number of right angles in this cube.

demonstration, I earnestly began counting four angles for each of the three visible sides. In truth, however, there are *no* right angles in that figure. We *perceive* the figure as a cube, and we count the number of right angles in a cube, ignoring the figure that is truly in front of us. This phenomenon is known as **shape constancy:** an object tends to hold its shape despite changes in its orientation.

T.G.R. Bower (1966) also tested shape constancy in infants, using a rectangle and a trapezoid, which is the retinal image of a rectangle with a changed angle of orientation. The infants showed shape constancy. In fact, they responded just as often to a rectangle placed at an angle as they did to the conditioned-stimulus rectangle, viewed straight on; in other words, in this experiment, they did not discriminate on the basis of the orientation of the object.

Finally, let us consider **brightness constancy**—the tendency for an object to hold its brightness despite changes in its illumination. A white handkerchief still appears white, even in a rather dark room. A piece of coal still appears black, even in the bright sunlight—even though its true brightness might exceed that of the handkerchief in the dark room. The brightness appears constant for a given object because it reflects a constant percentage of the total light, whether that object is viewed in the dark or in the sunlight.

In summary, the constancies allow us to perceive certain attributes of stimuli as remaining constant. This stability is clearly important psychologically. Think for a moment about the chaos you would experience if objects grew and shrank, became regular-shaped and then irregular, and grew light and dark as we moved about in the world. In constancy, then, we tend to perceive the true attributes of objects and disregard the information, such as retinal-image size, that is recorded on the sensory receptors. In terms of constancy, then, perception is a remarkably accurate mirror of the true properties of objects.

Illusions

Illusions, like constancy, disregard sensory information. However, constancy demonstrates that we perceive the true qualities of the stimulus accurately, whereas illusions demonstrate that we perceive the true qualities inaccurately.

Students often report that they are familiar with the classic illusions. Nonetheless, they are amazed by how strongly their performance is influenced by them. For example, try filling in the specified line in each of the illusions illustrated in Figure 7-16, and then measure to see how accurate you were.

Incidentally, the illusions occasionally have practical significance. A friend of mine was constructing a children's gym set that required nails to be driven into the wood at an angle. To his surprise, he kept missing the head of the nail (which was concealed by the descending hammer) and hitting his finger instead. In all probability, he had created a rotated Poggendorf illusion, which made it difficult to estimate where the nail head emerged from between his fingers. You can see this by rotating Figure 7-16d 90° counterclockwise.

One of the most powerful line illusions is the Sander illusion, illustrated in Figure 7-17.

Rock (1975, pp. 405–434) has discussed in detail a number of theories about how the illusions might work. For example, a Gestalt approach would argue that illusions are created by the context in which the stimulus is viewed (for example, the arrowheads at the ends of the Müller-Lyer illusion). A theory of "misapplied constancy" would explain the longer line at the bottom of the Ponzo illusion as the observer's attempt to create size constancy: because the bottom of the diagram is perceived as being closer, a line in that portion of the diagram should be represented as longer. In summary, there is no single, satisfactory theory to explain all of the illusions.

Let's consider for a minute how we might measure the dependent variable in, say, the Müller-Lyer illusion. Figure 7–16a asked you to reproduce a line of equivalent length. In practice, however, judgments of line length are typically obtained by means of classic psychophysical techniques. In effect, we are asking the observer to perform a discrimination task—to compare the length of the line in the standard stimulus with the length of the line in the comparison

a. The Müller-Lyer illusion. Complete the figure on the right by extending the horizontal line and adding arrowheads, making the length of the line match the length of the line on the left. Then measure the two lines.

b. The Ponzo illusion. Complete the line on the bottom, making it the same length as the line on top. Then measure the two lines.

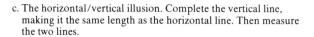

c. The horizontal/vertical illusion. Complete the vertical line, making it the same length as the horizontal line. Then measure the two lines.

d. The Poggendorf illusion. Draw a line where you think the diagonal line will emerge on the other side of the parallel lines. Then use a straightedge to determine whether your prediction was accurate.

Figure 7-16. Four classic illusions.

a. The Sander parallelogram illusion. The two dotted diagonal lines are equal in length.

b. A variant of the Sander parallelogram illusion. The illusion is intensified by removing irrelevant lines and asking the observer to imagine the diagonal lines.

Figure 7-17. Two versions of the Sander parallelogram illusion.

stimulus. Thus, we might use the method of limits, in which the experimenter presents an increasingly larger (or smaller) comparison line; we might use the method of adjustment, in which the subjects adjust the comparison line by themselves; or we might use the method of constant stimuli, in which the experimenter presents a series of lines in random order for comparison with the standard stimulus.

Kanizsa (1976) has recently explored another type of illusion: subjective contours. As Figure 7-18a shows, an illusion of a solid triangle, with well-defined contours, can be created despite the absence of continuous lines. If you look closely at the white space, the contour disappears; when you look at the entire figure, the contour appears. Observers report that the figure bounded by the subjective contour appears brighter than the background, even though the brightness is equivalent as registered on the retina. Also, the figure that is bounded by the subjective contour appears to be in front of the other figures.

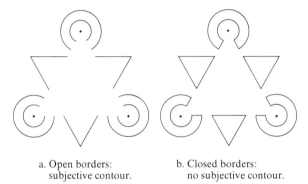

a. Open borders: b. Closed borders:
   subjective contour.   no subjective contour.

Figure 7-18. The illusion of subjective contour. From "Subjective Contours," by G. Kanizsa, *Scientific American*, April 1976, *234(4)*, 48–52. Copyright © 1976 by Scientific American, Inc. All rights reserved.

Kanizsa has found that the one requirement necessary for the perception of subjective contour is that parts of the design must be incomplete. In fact, if the borders are completed, as in Figure 7-18b, the subjective contour is lost. Kanizsa has proposed that subjective contour is created by the visual system, which places an opaque surface on top of the remainder of the design, thus filling in the gaps in the figure. Now, this opaque surface must have borders, so the visual system supplies them as well. The visual system appears to create a good figure by introducing subjective contours.

Distortions Caused by Stimulus Pleasantness

In the section on perceptual defense, we examined how the nature of a word can affect the threshold for that word. Other research has shown that the nature of the stimulus can also influence subjects' estimates of magnitude. In a review of the literature on this topic, Matlin and Stang (1978, Chapter 3) found that people judged valuable objects to be larger than less valuable objects, even when the true sizes were equivalent.

For example, Baker, Rierdan, and Wapner (1974) had subjects judge the size of coins, which could be considered pleasant or valuable, in contrast to plain metal discs, which had no monetary value. The subjects looked at the stimulus, felt it with a blindfold on, and then felt discs in a comparison series. The study used the method of limits, with comparison series ranging from 50% to 150% of the size of the objects. Both ascending and descending series were used. Equivalent judgments were obtained for the plain metal discs as well as for the coins, with appropriate counterbalancing to eliminate practice as a confounding variable.

The results showed that subjects judged the coins to be larger than the metal discs. Furthermore, there was an interaction between the status of the stimulus and the judged size of the stimulus. That is, subjects' overestimates of the size of the coins were greater when they were judging half-dollars than when they were judging quarters—presumably because the contrast in value between half-dollars and metal discs is greater than the contrast in value between quarters and metal discs. The results showed no evidence of a developmental trend with age: all of their subjects, ranging in age from 8 to 18, tended to overestimate coin size to the same extent.

One other study is worth mentioning here. Do you tend to think of high-status people as taller than they really are? Kassarjian (1963) questioned California residents prior to the 1960 Presidential election about whom they favored for president and which of the two major candidates was taller. Of the Kennedy supporters, 68% judged Kennedy as taller and 23% judged Nixon as taller. However, of the Nixon supporters, only 47% judged Kennedy as taller and 43% judged Nixon as taller. This difference was statistically significant. Once again, pleasantness and perceived size were correlated: people overestimated the size of the person they liked better.

THE OTHER SENSES

The emphasis in this chapter on *visual* perception reflects the emphasis of researchers on vision rather than the other senses. Research in hearing, taste, smell, and touch should be mentioned, however, to give you an idea of the kind of questions that are asked in these areas. More extensive summaries of these topics can be found in Kling and Riggs (1971). As we review these studies, you will notice that most of them use a threshold as the dependent measure.

Hearing

Some of the research on hearing covers the same topics as research on vision. For example, we have seen that the frequency of a word in English affects the visual threshold for word recognition: very common words are perceived more rapidly than uncommon words. Rosenzweig and Postman (1957) have demonstrated that word frequency also affects auditory recognition. They made the words difficult to hear by presenting **white noise**—a random mixture of many frequencies, designed to mask the hearing of other material—at the same time as the critical English word. They began by making the white noise very loud in relation to the words, and on each trial, they made the white noise relatively softer—thus using a modification of the method of limits. All of the words were one syllable long; thus, the important variable of word length was appropriately controlled. The words ranged in frequency from common (CHAIR, NEXT) to very uncommon (FLANGE, THRALL). The threshold scores were correlated $-.78$ with word frequency—an impressively high correlation. In another experiment reported in the same article, the authors found that threshold scores and word frequency were also correlated for students at the Sorbonne hearing French words.

The topic of visual illusions also has its parallel in hearing research. Diana Deutsch (1974) reports that people can also experience auditory illusions. She presented a 400-Hz tone (approximately G above middle C) to one ear and an 800-Hz tone (approximately G above high C) to the other ear. Each ¼ of a second, she switched the sounds to the opposite ear. This alternation of sounds continued for 20 seconds. If subjects had perceived the sounds accurately, they would have reported hearing two different tones that frequently switched sides. However, none of the subjects reported this. Instead, most of the subjects thought they had heard a single tone moving from ear to ear, whose pitch also shifted from one octave to another. Notice, incidentally, that Deutsch used verbal report in her study—the same response measure used by researchers for visual illusions.

Have you ever found yourself—at a party, for example—engaged in conversation with someone to your right, but also catching bits of a conversation going on to your left? This type of situation is reproduced in the laboratory in **dichotic-listening** experiments. The subject wears a headphone set that presents a different message to each ear. For example, Moray (1959) presented a list of simple words to one ear and a prose passage to the other ear. He instructed subjects to pay attention to the prose passage and repeat the passage as they were hearing it (''shadowing''). Moray found that subjects were unable to recognize the words on the list, to which they had not paid attention. In fact, the only stimulus he found that would break through the attention barrier was the subject's own name. Again, this may be a phenomenon that is familiar to you. You may be paying close attention to the conversation on your right and be totally unaware of the content of the conversation to your left. However, if your name is mentioned in the conversation to your left, your attention immediately shifts.

Other dichotic-listening studies have focused on the problem of shifting attention from one ear to the other. For example, Axelrod and Guzy (1968) had subjects judge the rate of presentation of clicking noises, using the method of contant stimuli. For some subjects, the standard stimulus was clicking noises shifting from ear to ear (**dichotic**) and the comparison stimulus was clicking noises occurring in one ear only (**monotic**). For other subjects, the standard stimulus was monotic, and the comparison stimulus was dichotic. There were 15 different rates at which the comparison stimuli could be presented—some much faster than the standard stimulus and some much slower. Each of those rates was paired with the standard stimulus on 20 trials. Recall, however, that the method of constant stimuli presents those comparison stimuli in random order. On one trial, the standard might be paired with a very fast rate, and on the next trial, the standard might be paired with a slightly slow rate.

According to the results, subjects thought that the clicks were much more rapid when they occurred in only one ear (monotic) than when the clicks alternated from ear to ear (dichotic). Some of the clicks seemed to be lost when the subject was forced to shift attention from one ear to the other.

Some of the research in hearing has been concerned with subject characteristics that influence performance. Layton (1975) has reviewed the literature on the subject characteristic of age. Some studies show that the elderly cannot handle interfering stimuli as well as younger people can. Dichotic-listening studies have found that the elderly are less accurate than younger subjects for both sets of auditory material—the one presented to the right ear and the one presented to the left ear.

Taste

Most of the research in taste has been concerned with determining thresholds and taste sensitivity. A study by Moore, Linker, and Purcell (1965) used a signal-detection approach to examine taste sensitivity before and after eating. Subjects were asked to taste a sugar solution before and after a lunch and a no-lunch condition. The results showed that eating did not affect sensitivity, but it did affect criterion. (Remember, the criterion is a person's leniency or strictness in reporting "Yes, I taste it.") Specifically, subjects had higher criteria for reporting sweetness if they had just eaten; that is, they were more likely to report "I don't taste it." The advantage of the signal-detection approach is that it provides two response measures, and it therefore allows us to specify which measure is influenced by previous eating. In contrast, a response measure in the form of a threshold is much less informative: we know that people are more likely to report "I don't taste it," but we don't know whether the increase in that report is due to a higher criterion or a lower sensitivity.

Schutte and Zubek (1967) examined taste thresholds following visual deprivation. Subjects lived in darkness for a week but otherwise experienced a normal, varied sensory environment. Other subjects served as controls and continued with their normal daily activities. The experimenters obtained thresholds for both groups of subjects using the ascending method of limits. Think for a moment why only the *ascending* series could be used. Suppose that we tried a descending series for a salty solution and began by giving an extremely salty solution to the subject. That solution would overwhelm the taste buds and make them insensitive to any less salty solution. A threshold obtained on a descending series is therefore extremely misleading in taste research.

Subjects judged salty, sweet, sour, and bitter solutions. The thresholds for salty and sweet solutions were much lower for the subjects who had experienced visual deprivation than for those same subjects prior to visual deprivation or for the control subjects. In other words, subjects reported "I taste it" with much smaller concentrations of salt and sugar in the water. Thresholds for sour and bitter solutions were not influenced by visual deprivation, however. It would be interesting to repeat this experiment using a signal-detection approach to see whether visual deprivation affects the *sensitivity* or the *criterion* for taste.

Smell

Schutte and Zubek (1967) also tested smell thresholds, using a gas called benzene, following visual deprivation. The threshold for detecting the smell of benzene dropped markedly after visual deprivation, just as did the thresholds for taste. The authors propose that people try to maintain an ideal range of sensory variation. When visual sensation is restricted, the other senses become more acute in an attempt to restore the balance. (We will examine other aspects of sensory deprivation in the chapter on motivation.)

Much of the research on smell has been concerned with **adaptation**. When a person is exposed to a smell for a long period of time, adaptation occurs: the threshold for that smell is raised. In other words, the person will need greater concentrations of the smell in order to detect them. This is probably a familiar occurrence for all of us. Recently, for example, I had occasion to make 15 onion-leek quiches. The smell of sautéed onions and leeks seemed overwhelming at first, but as adaptation occurred, I no longer noticed it. Later, I left the house for a while, but when I returned, the smell was again overwhelming. I had returned to my baseline sensitivity.

Engen (1963) has examined a phenomenon called **cross-adaptation**— meaning that adaptation to one smell will produce a higher threshold for a related smell. (For example, after my onion-leek experience, I would have had a high threshold also for sautéed scallions or garlic.) Engen studied chemical liquids in the alcohol family. He first exposed subjects either to an odorless liquid or to one of the alcohol liquids. Then he presented a different alcohol liquid and measured subjects' thresholds, using the ascending method of limits. The thresholds for these new alcohol liquids were far higher when the subjects had first smelled an alcohol liquid than when they had first smelled an odorless liquid. In fact, every subject required a greater concentration of the new alcohol if the first liquid had been an alcohol than if it had been an odorless liquid. In further research, Engen found that the extent of the cross-adaptation was not related in any simple fashion to the similarity in *chemical structure* of the alcohol liquids. Instead, cross-adaptation seemed to be a function of the *psychological similarity* of the alcohol liquids, as assessed by multidimensional scaling. (Remember this from Chapter 5? It is a technique that allows us to scale psychological similarity along several dimensions; we considered an example that scaled the size and the ferocity of animals.)

Touch

You may recall reading in the psychophysics chapter that the threshold for touch can be represented by feeling the wing of a bee falling on your cheek from a distance of one centimeter. S. Weinstein (1968) has used more formal methods to determine the thresholds for touch of various parts of the body. He used special hairs that varied in stiffness to establish thresholds for 20 different body sites. Figure 7-19 shows the thresholds for males. Notice that they are most sensitive for parts of the face and least sensitive for parts of the feet. Weinstein also reported that females were more sensitive than males, and that the interaction of subject's sex and body-part sensitivity was significant. (In other words, males and females differed as to which parts of the body were most sensitive.)

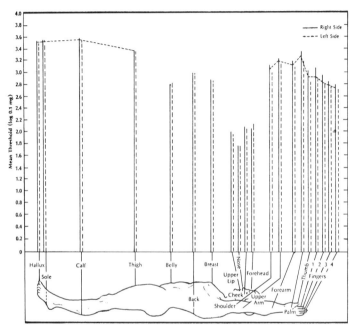

Figure 7-19. Thresholds for touch of various parts of the body: male subjects. From "Intensive and Extensive Aspects of Tactile Sensitivity as a Function of Body Part, Sex, and Laterality," by S. Weinstein. In D. R. Kenshalo (Ed.), *The Skin Senses*. Copyright 1968 by Charles C. Thomas, Publisher. Reprinted by permission.

The Weinstein study examined the pressure component of touch. Studies by Kenshalo (1970) have examined the temperature component of touch. In one study, he found that females had more variable thresholds than males for cold stimuli applied to the skin. In subsequent studies, he found that women show a marked increase in their thresholds at the onset of their menstrual periods and a marked decrease in their thresholds at the time of ovulation. Thus, touch sensitivity depends not only on differences between individuals but also on systematic differences within individuals.

THE DEPENDENT VARIABLE IN PERCEPTION STUDIES

We have examined a wide variety of dependent variables in this chapter. Some studies used a simple verbal report. For example, early Gestalt psychologists presented a triangle containing an opening and asked subjects to report what they saw. Johansson (1975) presented moving spots of lights and asked subjects to report what might cause those movement patterns.

Other studies use psychophysical techniques to obtain precise measures of perceptual abilities. Some experiments measured detection thresholds, such as the threshold for detecting light in a vision experiment, or the threshold for detecting alcohol fragrances in an experiment on smell. Other experiments measured discrimination thresholds, as in discriminating changes in hue. Some experiments used signal-detection techniques, producing separate measures of criterion and sensitivity.

Research on infant perception must employ an appropriate dependent variable in order to avoid the response-measure problem. We have seen several different solutions to the problem. Fantz (1961) used looking time as the dependent variable: if the infants spent different amounts of time looking at two objects, he interpreted this as evidence that they could discriminate between the objects. Gibson and Walk (1960) interpreted infants' avoidance of the "deep" side of a visual cliff as evidence of depth perception. Because this response measure could not be used for noncrawling infants, Campos, Langer, and Krowitz (1970) used cardiac responses instead. Their dependent variable was whether the heart rate changed in comparison to the prestimulus rate. Because infants less than 2 months of age showed a change in heart rate when placed on the "deep" side (but not when placed on the "shallow" side), the authors concluded that these infants had depth perception. Finally, T. G. R. Bower (1966) showed that infants have size constancy. His dependent variable was the number of conditioned head-turning responses the infants supplied to new stimuli.

We need to select the dependent variable carefully in perception experiments because perception is a private process. People perceive quietly; they don't acknowledge their perceptions by making a public response. This presents a challenge to experimenters, who must force the subjects to say something or do something that reveals what the subjects are seeing, hearing, tasting, smelling, or touching.

SUMMARY

1. Perception combines information registered on the sensory organs with information from memory.
2. Acuity, the ability to perceive very fine details, can be measured by determining how big a break in a circle must be in order to be detected.
3. Flicker fusion measures the ability to discriminate between light and dark when a light is rapidly turned on and off (as opposed to seeing a single, ongoing light.)
4. Adaptation is the increase in visual sensitivity that occurs over time when the lights are turned on (light adaptation) or turned off (dark adaptation).
5. Color can be represented by a three-dimensional space showing hue, saturation, and brightness. Hue discrimination is best for blues and yellows and worst for purples, greens, and reds.

6. Perception is organized, rather than random, because of phenomena such as the figure-ground relationship and grouping.

7. We can look at a picture and recognize what object it represents, but it is not clear whether this ability must be learned by experience.

8. People are best at identifying faces for members of their own race.

9. People recognize familiar words faster than unfamiliar words and pleasant words faster than unpleasant words.

10. People can recognize and identify patterns of movement so quickly that certain patterns appear to be built into the visual system.

11. Muscular, monocular, and binocular cues produce depth perception. Even young infants seem to have depth perception.

12. Size constancy means that objects are perceived as holding their size despite changes in distance. Research has shown that infants have size constancy. Two other constancies are shape constancy and brightness constancy.

13. In illusions, people perceive the true qualities of stimuli inaccurately. Some illusions distort the true length of a line; other illusions produce a subjective contour.

14. Valuable or liked stimuli are judged to be larger than valueless or disliked stimuli.

15. Research on hearing shows some of the same phenomena as in vision, including word-frequency effects and illusions. Dichotic-listening studies have shown that people cannot recall information presented to one ear if they are paying attention to information presented to the other ear.

16. The criterion for detection in taste experiments depends on whether the subject has just eaten. The threshold for some tastes is influenced by visual deprivation.

17. The threshold for some smells is influenced by visual deprivation. Other research has shown that adaptation to one smell will produce a higher threshold for a related smell.

18. Touch sensitivity depends on the sex of the subject and the part of the body that is touched. Touch sensitivity in females depends on the time of the menstrual cycle.

19. Studies in perception must take particular care in selecting the appropriate dependent variable because perception is a covert process.

8

Memory and
Verbal Learning

The size of human memory sometimes seems to be huge, almost without limit. Think about the tremendous number of pieces of information that are stored in your memory. There are names, phone numbers, English words, foreign words, facts learned from courses, jokes, things that happened to you. Just focus for a moment on one of those categories—names. You can probably name at least 100 people who attend your college. Or think about the number of performers, movie stars, politicians, and psychologists that you could name. Now think back on a category that you probably have not considered for many years—the kids in your fifth-grade class. Probably, you could name at least five or ten of them. You could probably recognize an even larger number of names. The enormous memory capacity of human beings seems to be one of their most impressive attributes.

However, at other times, the size of human memory seems to be amazingly limited. For example, read this list of letters, close the book, and write the letters down in order on a piece of paper: WHBMPOJDSQTR. All of a sudden, your memory capacity seems to be incredibly small!

How *long* can you keep information in memory? Sometimes, the duration of human memory seems impressively long, even for trivial things. Right now, I can recall the maiden name of my husband's cousin's wife, even though I heard it ten years ago and haven't thought of it since. On the other hand, memory can also have a frustratingly short duration. Tomorrow, I might forget the name of a student who just introduced herself to me one minute ago.

So memory capacity is both large and small, and memory duration is both short and long.

In this chapter, we will focus on memory and learning of verbal items, and we will examine topics such as memory capacity and memory duration. In the first three sections, we'll look at three proposed stages in memory: the sensory register, short-term memory, and long-term memory. Later, we'll discuss whether short-term memory and long-term memory are indeed two separate processes, or whether they are aspects of the same process. The final two sections will be concerned with organization in memory and with factors affecting memory.

We will consider two methodological issues in this chapter. In the first half of the chapter, we will examine a theory of memory and the attempts to test this theory. In the section on factors affecting memory and learning, we will consider the issue of confounding variables.

A three-stage theory of memory has been proposed by psychologists who think of memory in terms of **information processing.** According to this view, people are like computers: they put information into storage, keep it there, and take it out at some later time. Information-processing approaches to memory are rather recent, beginning in the 1950s. Since then, many psychologists have designed information-processing models to represent how information enters the human being and what happens to that information. We will be looking at a typical model, one proposed by Atkinson and Shiffrin in 1968. Like most models designed by information-processing psychologists, it consists of boxes connected by arrows to represent the flow of information through the memory system. The flow diagram was inspired by computer flow diagrams, and many of the terms are also borrowed from computers. The 1968 version of the Atkinson/Shiffrin model appears in Figure 8-1.

Suppose you saw the sentence *William Shakespeare wrote the play Julius Caesar in 1599.* Let's briefly trace what might happen to this sentence, in terms of Figure 8-1. Later, we'll talk about each of the three storage boxes in more detail.

First of all, the sentence on the page is an example of **external input:** it is information from the outside world. If you looked at the words, they went into your **sensory register.** Now, after the words are in the sensory register, two things can happen. The words can be lost from the sensory register: they are forgotten. Or, the words can pass into the short-term store, or *short-term memory.* Information passes through the sensory register very quickly, taking only a few seconds or less.

Information stays in short-term memory a bit longer, maybe as long as a minute. **Short-term memory** contains only the small amount of information that you are currently thinking about. Incidentally, you may run across other terms

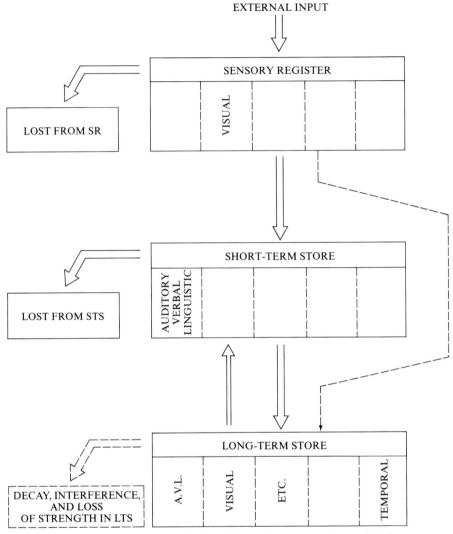

Figure 8-1. Atkinson and Shiffrin's information-processing model of memory. From "Human Memory: A Proposed System and Its Control Processes," by R. C. Atkinson and R. M. Shiffrin. In K. W. Spence and J. T. Spence (Eds.), *The Psychology of Learning and Motivation: Advances in Research and Theory*, Vol. 2. Copyright 1968 by Academic Press, Inc. Reprinted by permission.

for short-term memory, including *short-term store* (Figure 8-1) and *primary memory*. The abbreviation for short-term memory is STM.

Information in short-term memory can go in two directions: it can be lost—forgotten—or it can go into long-term memory. Thus, you may hold the fact about *Julius Caesar* in your short-term memory for 15 seconds and then forget it; or the fact about *Julius Caesar* may make it all the way into long-term memory.

Long-term memory contains memories gathered over long periods of time—in fact, over your whole lifetime. It contains all the information that we talked about in the first paragraph of the chapter—all the miscellaneous facts you have been gathering for years and years. Obviously, this memory is not limited to the extent that short-term memory is; you can put millions of facts into long-term memory. However, you sometimes can't recall information in long-term memory. You've certainly had this experience before: someone asks you for your home phone number, and you draw a blank. Your eyes get a bit glassy, you put your hand to your head, your jaw drops, and you may turn red with embarrassment. You may know that the first three numbers are 334, but what in the world is the rest? Somehow 0983 doesn't sound right; is it 0893? Temporarily, your phone number has been lost from long-term memory. According to the Atkinson/Shiffrin model, information in long-term memory is relatively permanent. Even when the information is present in long-term memory, however, it is sometimes impossible to retrieve information at any one particular time. Other names associated with long-term memory are *long-term store* (Figure 8-1) and *secondary memory*. The abbreviation for long-term memory is **LTM.**

Notice that the model also has two other arrows. The dotted arrow that goes from the sensory register to the long-term store shows that it *may* be possible for information to go directly from the sensory register to the long-term store. Also notice the arrow going from long-term store back to short-term store. This arrow is necessary because we often take information out of long-term store and put it in short-term store in order to think about it. For example, this happened when you took the names of kids in your fifth-grade class out of long-term store and began to think about them.

Now let's look in greater detail at the three stages of memory, as proposed by information-processing psychologists. Keep in mind that these three stages are *theoretical;* many psychologists would not agree with the Atkinson/Shiffrin model. We will take up their arguments in the fourth section.

THE SENSORY REGISTER

Stop for a minute and consider the huge amount of information that is attacking your five senses right now. As I sit at my typewriter and think about everything that makes its way into my sensory register, I'm amazed that I can get anything done! Visually, I have the typewriter in front of me, with all the letters and numbers and signs. I have part of a typed page above that, and finished pages, books, and articles on every side of my desk. Just out the window, in the periphery of my visual field, are a very green woods and a very blue sky. Now if I attend to hearing, I notice that the birds are chirping, the farmer across the road is driving his tractor, and the sump pump is gurgling. As to the sense of touch, the typewriter keys are hard and smooth, and my arm brushes against the chair as I type. Taste and touch are, fortunately, a little more quiet. I can taste just a bit of the rather stale half-piece of spearmint gum in my mouth. I can smell just a trace of spearmint, too, but the smell of tonight's dinner in the oven is stronger.

Now all of this information is going into the sensory register, and it is kept in sensory register for a very brief period. Actually, it would be more accurate to speak of sensory registers, because there are five registers—one for each sense. We saw in the last chapter, however, that psychologists have mostly studied the visual and auditory senses, and so we have the most knowledge about these two registers, or stores.

Iconic Store

Visual information—stimuli that enter through the eyes—goes into the **iconic store** (from *icon*, meaning a picture). Since the iconic store keeps information for such a brief period of time, we have to use very precise instruments to measure memory in this stage. Most often, psychologists use the tachisto-scope, which you know about from the last chapter. The experiments by Sperling (1963) are classics in the study of the iconic store, and we will examine his technique in detail.

Figure 8-2 shows a stimulus card similar to the one used by Sperling. The card is presented for 50 milliseconds, or 1/20 of one second. Now if the card had just three letters on it, you could probably remember all three, even though you saw the card only for that brief period. If the card had four or five letters, you might even be able to remember all of them. But if you saw all 12 letters, chances are that you would only be able to report about four to the experimenter.

Figure 8-2. The stimulus card, used in experiments on the iconic store.

Now look at Figure 8-2 for the shortest period you can, and quickly close your eyes. Did you *see* only four letters? No, you may *report* only four letters, but you think you saw all 12 letters. By the time you've reported those four letters, however, all the others have "faded away." It seems that we see a lot, but we retain only a limited portion of that information. Similarly, if you glance quickly around the room, there are thousands of things that your eye may see, but you certainly could not report much of it. The human information-processing system must simplify what it takes in, or else you would be overwhelmed.

At any rate, Sperling decided that subjects *saw* more than they could *report*. His answer to the problem was a **partial-report technique.** With this technique, the subjects see the card for 50 milliseconds, but they don't have to report all 12 letters—just four of them. The subjects know which four to report because a tone sounds just as soon as the letter presentation is over. If a high tone sounds, the subjects report the top four letters: if it is a medium tone, they report the middle row; if it is a low tone, they report the bottom row. Notice that the subjects do not know in advance *which* tone will sound, so they have to *look* at all 12 letters. Only after the letter presentation is over do they know which of the three rows they will be responsible for.

Let's say that a subject reported all four letters in the row correctly. We can now *estimate* how many letters the subject must have had in the iconic store at the moment the letters disappeared. With four letters available in each of the three rows, we can estimate that there would have been 12 letters in all. Sperling found that if subjects were asked to report all the letters, they correctly reported an average of 4.5. With the partial-report technique, subjects correctly reported slightly more than 3 items from one line. Estimating what the subjects saw on all three lines, then, the average was about 10. Thus, Sperling's experiment with the partial-report technique demonstrates that the iconic store can take in a large amount of information in a short period of time. However, this information is lost from the store very quickly—in just about the period of time it takes to report four letters.

Echoic Store

Auditory information—stimuli that enter through the ears—goes into the **echoic store** (from the word *echo*). The echoic store seems very real. Have you ever heard a clock chime out the hours when you were not really paying attention? If you suddenly ask yourself, ''I wonder what time it is?'' you can ''listen'' to the chimes striking in the echoic store. ''Let's see—BONG, BONG, BONG—it must be three o'clock.'' Or perhaps more often, you're carrying on a conversation with someone who is chattering on while you daydream. Suddenly, the person says, ''You aren't listening to me!'' You reply, ''Oh yes I am. You just said that you think Jim lives in Jones Dormitory.'' In fact, you may amaze yourself with your recall, because in fact you *weren't* paying any attention. The most recent sentence your friend said was in the echoic store, and you can retrieve it from there if you are quick enough.

Echoic store seems to be an appropriate name: it seems that sentences often echo in your head after you've heard them. Notice this the next time you go to a lecture: a sentence, or a part of a sentence, will be sounding for a brief period after it's been spoken. This fortunate storage is what allows you to take notes in class. You don't write down every word as it is spoken; you can draw the sentence out of the echoic store while the professor is pausing.

Darwin, Turvey, and Crowder (1972) demonstrated the existence of the echoic store by using a method inspired by Sperling's partial-report technique. These authors designed lists that were nine items long—for example, B3F-J62-QR8. The first group of three items was presented to the right ear, the second group of three items was presented to the left ear, and the third group of three items was presented to both ears (which made it sound as though it was coming from the middle). All three sequences were presented at the same time. Next, the experimenter indicated to the subjects by means of a visual cue which set of three items they should report. On a screen in front of the subject, a bar on the left meant that the subject should report the three items from the left ear, a bar in the middle indicated the middle channel, and a bar on the right indicated the right channel. Just as in Sperling's technique, then, the sensory information came first, followed by a signal telling which part to report.

With the partial-report method, subjects were estimated to store about 4.9 items. Actually, as Loftus and Loftus (1976) point out, this estimate is probably too low because Darwin et al. could not present all nine items at the exact same time, the way Sperling could. By the time they presented the last item in each of the three channels (F, 2, and 8), the items at the beginning (B, J, and Q) would have faded.

It seemed to take about four seconds for information to fade out of the echoic store. That's much longer than the duration of the iconic store, which was about one-fifth of a second. Maybe that's why it seems much easier to find everyday evidence for the echoic store than for the iconic store.

SHORT-TERM MEMORY

Only a fraction of the material from the sensory registers makes its way into short-term memory. This reduction in information must occur because there would be no way to fit the hundreds of sensory experiences you have each minute into the small storage space that you are allowed in short-term memory.

Before we look at short-term memory in detail, try this informal experiment. Read the list of letters shown in Table 8-1. Then close the book, and try to recall them in any order on a sheet of paper. Repeat with the list of short words, then with the list of longer words. Keep your answers; we'll discuss them later in this section.

Table 8-1. An informal experiment in short-term memory.

N	CAT	WINDOW
Y	JOY	TENDER
R	MAN	TABLE
O	TOE	APPLE
Q	RAY	LIVING
D	MOP	POWER
J	SIT	RUBBER
T	NOT	PAPER
E	GEM	HUMAN
U	MAT	AFTER
X	FUN	HAPPY
F	DOE	SUPPER

Methods

Probably thousands of experiments have been conducted on short-term memory. In the last 20 years, short-term memory has probably been the most popular area of study within the field of memory and verbal learning. One of the reasons for this sudden popularity was the invention, by Peterson and Peterson (1959), of a very simple technique. Basically, they showed subjects three letters and, about 15 seconds later, asked them to recall the letters. To everybody's amazement, subjects typically could not remember all three letters.

The reason that subjects did so poorly on this task was that the Petersons asked the subjects to do an arithmetic task during the period between the presentation of the letters and the recall of the letters. Specifically, subjects were given a three-digit number and asked to count backward by threes from that number, in time to the clicks of a metronome. This task kept the subjects too busy to **rehearse** the letters—that is, to repeat the letters silently to themselves.

If you have a nice, cooperative roommate, you can try a version of the Petersons' method on her or him. Take an index card and write three nonsense words, such as WIPDO, PELFEL, and CIDOB. On the other side, write a number, such as 457. Present the letter side, then flip it over, and have your roommate count backward by threes as quickly as possible. After about 15 seconds, ask for recall. To your roommate's embarrassment, the recall will probably be incomplete.

Incidentally, when psychologists use this technique in the laboratory, subjects typically guess that the reason they have been told to count backward is to make them anxious and irritated. In fact, the real reason for this arithmetic task is to prevent rehearsal. Just for comparison's sake, you might have your roommate try the recall task on other nonsense words, such as NARSIL, BAWTON, and MIPSEE, *without* having to do the arithmetic. After 15 seconds, recall will probably be perfect, because your roommate will have spent the 15 seconds rehearsing, quietly repeating the words over and over. Finally, as an exercise in examining subjects' hypotheses and demand characteristics (see Chapter 3), you might ask your roommate to guess why you included the arithmetic task.

Figure 8-3 illustrates the results obtained with the Petersons' method. Look closely at the two lower curves. First, notice that memory is quite accurate if we ask for recall immediately after presenting the material, but it decreases to only about 20% recall of all three items if we ask for recall 18 seconds later. Second, notice that recall is roughly the same whether the stimuli are three consonants or three words; in either case, recall is much poorer than with a single word. We will discuss this finding in greater detail later in the chapter.

Auditory Characteristics of Short-Term Memory

The evidence from a large number of experiments suggests that items are stored in short-term memory in an auditory form. Even when the material has been presented visually, it is stored in terms of how it *sounds* rather than how it *looks*. Look at the word JANDARA and try to keep it in your short-term memory. How did you do it? Probably by saying it or hearing it, rather than by trying to visualize the word.

The basic study that established the auditory nature of short-term memory was performed by R. Conrad (1964). He presented a string of letters, such

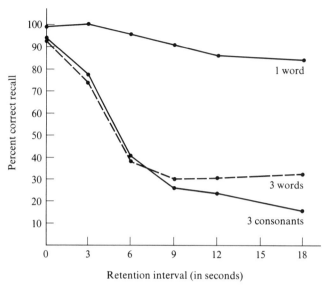

Figure 8-3. Percent correct recall as a function of retention interval for three kinds of verbal material. Data from Murdock, B. B., Jr. The retention of individual items. *Journal of Experimental Psychology*, 1961, *62*, 618–625.

as IBNKERXV, and asked subjects to recall it. There was a clear pattern in the kind of errors subjects made: they tended to substitute another letter that *sounded like* a letter in the string. For example, the subject might recall IPNKERXV—substituting a P for the similar-sounding B.

Another relevant experiment was conducted by Laughery and Fell (1969). In the first part of their study, they presented eight-letter strings, such as IBNKERXV. Some of the strings were presented visually, and some were presented auditorily. After each string, subjects tried to recall the letters.

Then Laughery and Fell gave a mode-preference test to determine which mode each subject preferred. In this test, five letters were presented to the subjects. The subjects *saw* the letters in one order (visual mode) and *heard* the same letters in another order (auditory mode). Subjects were allowed to record the letters in any order they wished. A subject's mode preference could be determined by noticing whether the order of recording the letters resembled the way they had been presented visually or the way they had been presented auditorily. (Note that this experiment is well designed because the mode-preference test was given second. If it had been given first, it might have biased the performance on the other task.)

The results showed that 31 subjects preferred the auditory mode and did better on it. Only two subjects preferred the visual mode and did better on that. When given a choice, then, subjects prefer material that will be stored in short-term memory to be presented auditorily. Furthermore, they are more accurate when the material is presented auditorily. It seems likely that performance is more accurate with the auditory mode because the information can enter short-term memory directly. Material presented in the visual mode, on the other hand, must typically be "translated" first into some sort of auditory code.

Limited Capacity in Short-Term Memory

One of the most important characteristics of short-term memory is that it has a limited capacity: only a few items can be stored at one time. Look now at your answers to the informal experiment presented in Table 8-1. Chances are that you did not get all 12 items correct on any of the three parts. If you got between five and nine items correct on any part, this would be a typical performance.

A famous article by George Miller (1956) was titled "The Magical Number Seven, Plus or Minus Two: Some Limits on Our Capacity for Processing Information." ("Seven Plus or Minus Two" refers to the average memory span of between five and nine items.) Miller suggested, then, that humans cannot keep very many items in short-term memory at one time. If you want to place some new items in short-term memory, some of the items that are already there must be "bumped out." You may have experienced just that kind of sensation when you were trying to memorize one of the lists in Table 8-1. You may have been doing just fine after you read the first three or four items. By the time you had read about five, you probably felt that your short-term memory was getting rather crowded. By the time you read six or more, you probably felt that, for every one item you shoved in, another one dropped out. Now that you think of it, isn't it fortunate that telephone numbers are only seven digits long?

Note, also, that the number of long words you recalled was probably just about the same as the number of short words and the number of letters. Recall seems to depend on the number of distinct items, rather than on the number of letters in each item. We will talk more about this concept later in the chapter.

Forgetting in Short-Term Memory

You've just been introduced to John Jones at a party. You turn around, a moment later, to introduce him to your roommate, and your mind is a complete blank. How could you possibly have forgotten that name within a few seconds? Does it seem to you that his name just "decayed," or faded away during those few seconds, or does it seem to you that you could have remembered his name, only something else got in the way and "interfered"?

Don't feel alarmed if you can't decide which of the two processes seems to make you forget items in short-term memory; in fact, psychologists disagree. Some say that decay is totally responsible, some say that interference is totally responsible, and some take the compromise position that both decay and interference are responsible.

Psychologists who support the **decay** position say that every item that enters short-term memory leaves a memory trace there. As time passes, that trace decays unless you repeat or rehearse the item. Imagine a word written with chalk on the blackboard. An eraser sweeps over that word, gradually wiping away the trace. Within less than a minute, the word is gone, or else so little of it remains (perhaps two smudged letters) that you don't know what the word was. Those who support the decay position think that time is the important factor in forgetting. The mere passage of time causes the erasing of items in short-term memory, and forgetting will occur whether you see one item, five items, or ten items after that word.

Psychologists who support the **interference** position say that forgetting occurs because another item gets in the way, or interferes with the information we want to recall. We try to remember item 1, but we can't because item 2—which we encountered either before or after item 1—gets in the way.

These psychologists argue that interference can explain the forgetting that occurs with the Peterson and Peterson method. One source of interference may be the counting-backward task. That task is included to prevent rehearsal, but, in fact, those numbers may interfere with the recall of the items that the subject is supposed to remember.

Keppel and Underwood (1962) have argued that there was another very important source of interference in the Peterson and Peterson experiments. According to them, the reason that subjects did so poorly in recalling an item such as ZTD was that they had already been tested on other items such as CXP, GQN, HJL, KBW, and SFM. When they tried to remember ZTD, all the other items kept interfering. Thus, the unfortunate subjects trying to recall ZTD had interference both from the items they had learned before ZTD and from the numbers they had to count after ZTD. Keppel and Underwood performed an experiment using the Peterson and Peterson method; their results are shown in Figure 8-4. Look at the curve for the 18-second retention interval. On the first item, recall was close to perfect. By the sixth item, recall was correct less than half the time. Recall depends on the number of prior items: the greater the number of items that can interfere, the greater the forgetting.

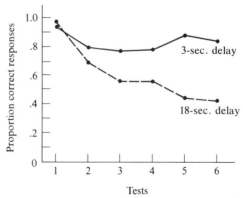

Figure 8-4. Recall in short-term memory as a function of the number of prior tested items and amounts of delay prior to recall. From "Proactive Inhibition in Short-Term Retention of Single Items," by G. Keppel and B. J. Underwood, *Journal of Verbal Learning and Verbal Behavior*, 1962, *1*, 158. Copyright 1962 by Academic Press, Inc. Reprinted by permission.

(Notice, however, that the curve for the 3-second retention interval is not greatly affected by interference.)

Psychologists who believe that both decay and interference cause forgetting in short-term memory find their support from experiments such as one by Reitman (1974). Seeking a task that would prevent rehearsal but cause less interference than the counting-backward task, she used a tone-detection task in which subjects had to listen for a pure tone in a noisy background. She also wanted to study subjects who did not "cheat" and rehearse when they were supposed to be listening to the tone. As you can imagine, subjects were tempted to rehearse surreptitiously—ZTD, listen, listen, ZTD, listen, ZTD—and 42 of her 52 subjects did rehearse. Since they rehearsed, their data cannot tell us much about simple decay. (You may be interested to know how she identified the 10 subjects who presumably did not rehearse. These subjects performed the tone-detection task just as well during the retention interval as during a control period, when they had no items to remember. The other 42 subjects performed the tone-detection task much more poorly during the retention interval because they would miss some signals while rehearsing.)

At any rate, Reitman found that the 10 nonrehearsing subjects forgot 33% of the material. Her conclusion is summarized in the title of her article: "Without Surreptitious Rehearsal, Information in Short-Term Memory Decays." Decay, she argues, accounts for a substantial portion of forgetting.

However, Reitman also found evidence for interference. When the rehearsal-preventing task consisted of detecting syllables rather than tones, the subjects forgot a greater percentage of the material—about 44% more than in the tone condition, or 77% of the total. The syllable-detection task should have caused a lot of interference with the syllables that were to be recalled, and this increased interference caused greater forgetting. In summary, Reitman's experiment suggests that both decay and interference cause forgetting.

LONG-TERM MEMORY

Before the Peterson and Peterson method became popular in the 1960s, virtually all of the research in memory and verbal learning involved long-term memory. Experimenters asked subjects to learn a long list of words—usually a list that was repeated several times—and then the subjects had to recall the words after a delay. The delay was typically a few minutes, but often as long as a day. In some cases, the experimenters waited for several months before asking the subject for recall. Let's begin by examining the methods used in these long-term-memory experiments.

Methods in Long-Term Memory

We will examine two categories of methods in long-term memory: (1) the kinds of tasks used in long-term-memory and verbal-learning studies; and (2) the methods used in measuring retention.

Verbal-learning tasks. There are three classic tasks in verbal learning: free recall, serial learning, and paired-associate learning. Table 8-2 provides an example of each task.

Table 8-2. Examples of three verbal-learning tasks.

Free recall	Serial learning	Paired-Associate learning
BIRD	CAT	GOJEY-KING
WALL	TABLE	WIPDO-CAR
APPLE	WINDOW	BAWTON-SPRING
TOE	LEAF	JANDAR-BOX
CLOCK	BOOK	NANSOM-PENCIL
BUG	GIRL	IKTIT-BABY
SONG	LAKE	SARIC-CUP
PAPER	BLANKET	CIVAD-BEAUTY
CAKE	LIGHT	LOKAN-ROAD
SLEEP	STICK	KADIR-SCHOOL
CHILD	SHEEP	BIWOJ-FARM
RADIO	TRUCK	DILIK-TRAIN

An instrument that is frequently used to present the words in all three tasks is the **memory drum** (see Figure 8-5). What the Skinner box is to the animal-learning psychologist, the memory drum is to the verbal-learning psychologist. The memory drum presents items at a controlled rate. As the experimenter, you can decide how long each item is to be exposed, how long the interval between items should be, and how many items should be exposed at one time. With a memory drum, the experimenters can control many more variables than they could if they simply presented a list of words to subjects, all at once, as in Table 8-2.

Free recall requires the least of the learner. In a free-recall task, the experimenter presents a list of words (perhaps on a memory drum or perhaps with a tape recorder). Typically, the list is presented just once. Then the subjects recall the words in any order they wish. Later in this chapter, we will consider the serial-position curve and organization in memory: the free-recall method has been used to provide information about both of these topics.

Serial-learning tasks require the learner to reproduce the list in the same order in which it was presented. Thus, the learner must memorize not only the words, but the order in which they appear. For example, suppose the words in Table 8-2 are to be presented on a memory drum. First, the symbol * * * * appears, indicating that the list is about to begin: the subject is asked to supply the first word. Then, the memory drum advances, revealing the word CAT and confirming the subject's guess. The word CAT serves not only to confirm the guess, but also to provide the stimulus for the next word: the subject must guess TABLE before it appears in the window. Naturally, the subject would have no way of performing this task correctly on the first trial. During the first trial, therefore, the words are simply presented, and the subject is not required to anticipate the correct next item. On following trials, the subject tries to guess

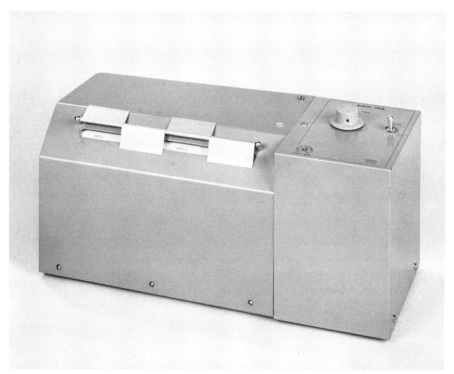

Figure 8-5. A memory drum. Words appear in one or more of the four windows; the rate of presentation is controlled by the knob on the top. Photo courtesy of Lafayette Instrument Company, Inc., Lafayette, Indiana 47902.

the next word whenever possible. Typically, the experimenter repeats the list until the subject can correctly anticipate each item, and the experimenter notes the number of trials to this criterion of one perfect trial. Variations on the serial-learning task include requiring a larger number of perfect trials—perhaps as many as ten—before the end of the learning task. Serial learning was a popular task to use in verbal-learning experiments during the first half of this century, but more recent experiments have used this technique less often.

In **paired-associate learning,** the subject must learn to associate two members of a pair. There are many variations on this task; we will look at the **anticipation method.** In this method, the memory drum first exposes the stimulus—for example, GOJEY—for perhaps 3 seconds. The subject tries to anticipate the correct response, KING. The memory drum rotates, revealing the stimulus and the response together—in this case, GOJEY–KING (see Table 8-2). Then the next stimulus, WIPDO, is exposed, and the subject must anticipate the response CAR. The experimenter continues to present the list (each time in a different order) until the subject can correctly anticipate all of the answers. As with the serial-learning task, a variation would be to require perhaps three perfect trials—rather than only one—before the end of the learning task.

Measuring retention. How can retention be measured for free recall, serial learning, and paired-associate learning? There are three basic measures to show how much of the material the subjects have retained, and they can be used for all three kinds of tasks.

The most common measure of retention is **recall.** After learning the material, subjects must produce what they have learned, according to specific instructions. For example, in a free-recall task, subjects would be instructed to recall as many words as possible from the previous list. Recall is generally measured in terms of the percent of the items that are correctly recalled. As you can imagine, there are many possible variations in scoring when you use recall as a measure of retention. The issue of precise operational definitions was discussed in Chapter 2. For example, what do you do if the word on the list was *chairs* and the subject says *chair?* Does that response constitute correct or incorrect recall?

Recognition, the second measure of retention, is an easier task. Here, the subject sees all the words from the original list again, but those words are mixed in with many new words. The subject must guess which words were on the list and which were not. The difference between recall and recognition is like the difference on an examination between a fill-in-the-blank question and a multiple-choice question. In the first case, you have to come up with the answer, with no hints to limit what that answer might be. In the second case, you know that the right answer must be there somewhere. You don't have to produce the answer by yourself, but you have to be able to recognize which answers are right and which are wrong. Incidentally, the ROC curves discussed in Chapter 6 have been applied to recognition studies. In perception studies, the subject can answer "Yes, I hear it" or "No, I don't hear it." Similarly, in recognition studies, a subject can answer "Yes, I've seen it before" or "No, I've never seen it before." From those responses in recognition studies, we can derive a hit rate (the subject says "Yes, I've seen it," and the word has indeed been presented earlier) and a false-alarm rate (the subject says "Yes, I've seen it," but the word has never been presented before). We can then plot an ROC curve from the information about hit rates and false-alarm rates.

At the beginning of this chapter, we noted that memory sometimes seems very fragile and sometimes seems extremely powerful. A number of studies have shown that memory using the recognition measure of retention is amazingly strong. For example, Shepard (1967) asked subjects to look at 540 stimuli. Then he tested recognition by having subjects indicate which of two stimuli on 60 test cards was familiar and which was unfamiliar. Subjects were 88% accurate when the stimuli were sentences, 90% accurate when the stimuli were words, and 98% accurate when the stimuli were pictures! In other words, subjects were almost perfectly accurate in identifying which pictures they had seen before, even though they had seen 540 pictures previously.

Relearning is the third, and least used, measure of retention. As the name suggests, subjects must relearn the same material that they learned originally. Let's say that subjects were required to learn a list of 15 items in order, so that they could repeat the entire list without an error. Let's suppose it takes subjects an average of ten trials to learn the list. One hour later, we ask subjects to relearn the same list. This time, it takes them an average of three trials. We measure retention during relearning in terms of savings. Savings is the proportion of trials saved in comparison to the first learning session. In this example, the savings would be (10−3)/10, or 70%.

How do these three methods of measuring retention compare? Generally, the recognition measure gives the highest estimate: as we saw from Shepard's (1967) data, subjects are astoundingly accurate in recognizing what they have seen before. The relearning measure is intermediate. The recall measure gives the lowest estimate: with no hints, subjects find it difficult to demonstrate what they remember.

Reconstruction from Long-Term Memory

A number of studies have explored the procedures that subjects use when they are trying to reconstruct some information from long-term memory. For example, Lindsay and Norman (1972) have asked people the question, "What were you doing on Monday afternoon in the third week of September two years ago?" Try to answer this question yourself. It looks ridiculous, perhaps impossible at first, but as you work on the problem, you may be amazed at how much progress you can make. Lindsay and Norman claim that a typical response to the question runs like this:

1. Come on. How should I know? (The experimenter says, "Just try it, anyhow.")
2. O.K., Let's see: Two years ago. . . .
3. I would be in high school in Pittsburgh. . . .
4. That would be my senior year.
5. Third week in September—that's just after summer—that would be the fall term. . . .
6. Let me see. I think I had chemistry lab on Mondays.
7. I don't know. I was probably in the chemistry lab. . . .
8. Wait a minute—that would be the second week of school. I remember he started off with the atomic table—a big, fancy chart. I thought he was crazy, trying to make us memorize that thing.
9. You know, I think I can remember sitting. . . .[p. 379].

Lindsay and Norman discuss this particular protocol. In line 1, the subject argues that the task will be virtually impossible, and he hesitates. When he decides to try, he doesn't try to recall the answer directly, but first decides to figure out what he was doing two years ago, a general answer (lines 2 and 3). He continues with still more specific memories on later lines. Then on line 8, there is a breakthrough with the atomic table, which clearly must have impressed him at the time. By line 9, it seems that the subject is fairly confident about what he was doing at the time. In general, then, the search of memory is active. The task is broken into smaller problems, each to be solved as the search continues. Clearly, this task is not a simple *recall* task. Instead it involves *reconstruction* of the answer. (Incidentally, we will see in the next chapter that reconstruction is also important in memory for sentences.)

King and Pontious (1969) have explored the reconstruction process in an article called "Time Relations in the Recall of Events of the Day." They asked subjects questions such as "What was your meat dish for supper two days ago, which was Monday?" and "Who was the first person you talked to after leaving home four days ago, which was Friday?" Subjects were asked to verbalize what they were thinking as they tried to answer the questions.

The protocols were analyzed and coded according to the time direction used in the reasoning process. The results showed that there was a significant tendency to move from early events to later events. The authors suggest several alternative explanations for these results: (1) Forward chaining occurs more frequently than reverse chaining; that is, an item suggests the item that follows it in a sequence, rather than the item that precedes it. (2) English may be more suited for describing events that occur from past to present, rather than from present to past; the protocols may have been influenced by the nature of the English language. (3) Recall may proceed in the forward direction because an event is more strongly dependent on the event that preceded it than on the event that follows it.

So far, we have been concerned with the route that subjects travel as they try to reconstruct some fact in long-term memory. Neither Lindsay and Norman nor King and Pontious were concerned with determining whether the subjects were *accurate* or not. In contrast, Buckhout (1974) was concerned with the tremendous inaccuracy of people who try to reconstruct a past event.

Buckhout's primary concern is eyewitness testimonies, as in courtroom cases. He suggests that perception and memory are not accurate copiers of events. Instead, he has proposed that observers are active rather than passive perceivers: they reach conclusions based on what they have seen by evaluating fragments of information and then reconstructing them. Buckhout feels that people are ordinarily rather unreliable in recalling past events, and when they are witnesses in a courtroom case, the stress of the situation makes them even less accurate.

In one of Buckhout's studies, he staged an assault in a classroom. A student "attacked" a professor in front of 141 student witnesses. The incident was recorded on videotape so that eyewitness reports could be reliably compared with the actual event. Each witness was asked to give a sworn statement, identifying whatever he or she could recall from the incident.

As Buckhout had predicted, subjects were quite inaccurate. They overestimated the suspect's weight and underestimated his age. Buckhout compiled accuracy scores based on recall of weight, age, height, dress, and so on; the scores generally reached only 25% of the maximum possible score. Interestingly, subjects were most accurate in guessing height. The reason for this accuracy was that the "suspect" was of average height, and when people are uncertain about a judgment, they tend to guess what would be true of the average person.

From what we know about recognition versus recall, we might expect recognition to be quite accurate. Actually, however, it was quite poor. Seven weeks after the event, subjects were asked to identify the suspect from a lineup of six portraits. Only 40% of the witnesses guessed correctly, and even the professor who had been attacked picked out an innocent man.

Buckhout concludes that people are highly unlikely to say "I don't know." They will try to select the suspect, even though they are often wrong. Furthermore, if they are asked to recall information, they will tend to make up the missing details.

Forgetting in Long-Term Memory

Long-term memory is not as fragile as short-term memory, but forgetting occurs nevertheless. You may forget your phone number, your mother's maiden name, or the street you lived on when you were in seventh grade.

We have seen that psychologists disagree about whether forgetting in *short-term memory* is due more to interference or to decay. In *long-term memory,* however, interference seems to be the most widely accepted explanation. A lengthy discussion of interference theory is beyond the scope of this book; a review by Keppel (1968) contains more details.

Let us consider two processes that cause interference: **proactive inhibition (PI)** and **retroactive inhibition (RI).** As Table 8-3 illustrates, both PI and RI involve learning two lists, A and B. In the case of proactive inhibition, subjects have trouble remembering List B on the retention test because items from List A keep getting in the way. In other words, List A items work *proactively,* or forward, to cause forgetting. (The prefix *pro* means forward, as in *progress.*) In the case of retroactive inhibition, subjects have trouble remembering List A on the retention test because items from List B keep getting in the way. Here, List B items work *retroactively,* or backward, to cause forgetting. (The prefix *retro* means backward, as in the phrase, *in retrospect.*)

Table 8-3. Examples of proactive and retroactive inhibition.

	Task 1	*Task 2*	*Retention test*
Proactive inhibition	List A (GAX-TREE)	List B (GAX-PEN)	List B (GAX-PEN)
Retroactive inhibition	List A (GAX-TREE)	List B (GAX-PEN)	List A (GAX-TREE)

We have trouble remembering things, therefore, because other items get in the way. These interfering items may be items we learned earlier (causing proactive inhibition), or they may be items we learned afterward (causing retroactive inhibition).

One of the strongest demonstrations of the two kinds of inhibition that you may have experienced occurs when you drive somebody else's car. The car that you are accustomed to driving is like List A. You have trouble learning and remembering certain aspects of a different car (List B) because A keeps getting in the way. You keep wanting to put the key in with the ridges down, or you reach for the windshield wipers on the right-hand side, because those were the characteristics of A. In this situation, you are experiencing proactive inhibition.

Now suppose after several hours of driving that different car, you go back to your own car. To your surprise, you find that certain aspects of that different car (B) keep getting in the way of your recalling how to drive your own car (A). Now you find yourself putting in the key with the ridges *up*, reaching for the wipers on the *left*-hand side, and so on. This time, you are experiencing retroactive inhibition.

Part of an experiment by Barnes and Underwood (1959) is a classic demonstration of the effects of retroactive inhibition. Subjects learned a paired-associate list until they could see each nonsense-word stimulus and recall the appropriate English word perfectly. Then they learned a second list, in which the old stimuli were paired with new responses. Some subjects saw the second list only once; others saw it 5, 10, or 20 times. After the specified number of exposures on List 2, subjects were given the nonsense-word stimuli and were asked to recall both responses. The results were tabulated according to how many trials they had on List 2.

As you can see in Figure 8-6, the more trials that subjects had on List 2, the better was their recall of List 2 responses. We would expect to find this

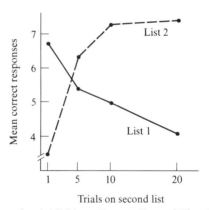

Figure 8-6. Retroactive inhibition. From "Fate of First-List Associations in Transfer Theory," by J. M. Barnes and B. J. Underwood, *Journal of Experimental Psychology*, 1959, *58*, 101. Copyright 1959 by the American Psychological Association. Reprinted by permission.

result. However, notice what happens to List 1 responses. They do not remain at the same high level of accuracy at which they began. Instead, the more of List 2 the subject learns, the more List 1 responses are lost from memory. In fact, Barnes and Underwood conclude that these List 1 responses have been "extinguished": the responses are no longer attached to the stimuli.

The idea of proactive inhibition was slower to develop. After all, it's not quite as obvious that old items will get in the way when you are trying to recall new items. You may recall the Keppel and Underwood (1962) study that demonstrated proactive inhibition in *short-term memory*. Many studies have demonstrated proactive inhibition in *long-term memory*. One by Underwood (1957) is worth noting because of his method of collecting the data. Underwood used the archival method, discussed in Chapter 1. He examined a large number of studies in the verbal-learning literature. For each study, he noted how many previous lists of items had been learned by the subjects and what percentage of the current list was recalled. As Figure 8-7 demonstrates, recall did depend on the amount of proactive inhibition. When subjects had learned no previous lists, they recalled about 80% of the material on the current list. In contrast, subjects who had learned 20 previous lists recalled only about 15% of the material on the current list.

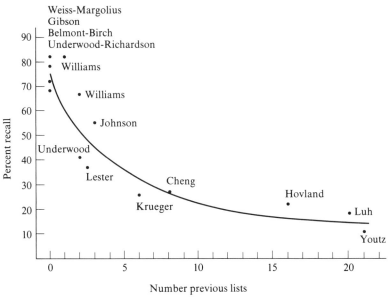

Figure 8-7. Recall as a function of number of previous lists learned. From "Interference and Forgetting," by B. J. Underwood, *Psychological Review*, 1957, *64*, 49–60. Copyright 1957 by the American Psychological Association. Reprinted by permission.

Proactive inhibition and retroactive inhibition are two processes that cause interference and forgetting in long-term memory. Other psychologists have proposed that forgetting can occur because of a **retrieval failure.** According to this view, the desired information is there in long-term memory, but forgetting occurs because the subject is unable to bring forth—or retrieve—that information. Retrieval failure is discussed in more detail in Loftus and Loftus' (1976) book, *Human Memory*.

So far, we have represented short-term memory and long-term memory as two distinctly different processes. A fact goes into short-term memory, and then, after an appropriate stay, it gets hustled off into long-term memory— a separate box in Figure 8-1. However, a great number of psychologists would disagree with Figure 8-1. They would argue that there is only one kind of memory storage, rather than two. Some items have been around for a second, and some have been around for decades, but basically, memory is memory!

Here we encounter an important theoretical conflict in verbal-learning research, with the one-memory-storage psychologists pitted against the two-memory-storage psychologists. This theoretical conflict has stimulated a great deal of research aimed at resolving the conflict. Let's explore some of that research in order to find out how a theory can provide ideas for research; as we saw in Chapter 2, a theoretical problem frequently inspires research ideas.

The question, then, is whether there is sufficient evidence to support a model that has two memory storages: a short-term memory that retains material for less than a minute, and a long-term memory that retains material for longer periods of time. In order to justify a model with two memories, as in Figure 8-1, we would need to demonstrate that certain variables affect short-term memory and long-term memory in different ways. If a variable does work one way for short-term memory and a different way for long-term memory, then we can feel quite comfortable about drawing two different "boxes" to represent two different kinds of memory. On the other hand, if a number of variables have exactly the same kind of effect on items remembered for several seconds as on items remembered for long periods of time, then why should we draw two separate boxes? If the two kinds of items seem to be handled the same way in memory, then we would really only have one type of memory. The law of parsimony dictates that a simple explanation is preferable to a complex one.

Let's look at some of the variables that have been examined. In each case, psychologists have tried to determine whether a variable has different effects on items to be remembered for a short period of time as opposed to items to be remembered for a long period of time.

Interference

Many studies have shown that interference operates in long-term memory. If interference does *not* operate in *short-term* memory, then we can identify interference as a variable that affects short-term memory and long-term memory in different ways. However, recall the study by Keppel and Underwood (1962), whose data are represented in Figure 8-4. They demonstrated that proactive inhibition caused forgetting in short-term memory. When items were stored in memory for 18 seconds, the number of previous items influenced the amount of forgetting. Thus, Keppel and Underwood would favor one-memory storage, because interference operates for both kinds of material.

Atkinson and Shiffrin (1968), whose two-storage model we examined in Figure 8-1, argued that Keppel and Underwood's study was not really very damaging to their theory of two memory storages. After all, they said, 18 seconds is such a long period of time that some of the material is now in long-term memory, where interference can certainly do its damage. In contrast, they point to Keppel and Underwood's results for the 3-second retention interval. As we noted earlier, the influence of interference is only slight for these items. Perhaps, after 3 seconds, all of the material is still in short-term memory, and none of it is in long-term memory. In this short-term memory, argue the two-memory-storage theorists, interference has no effect.

Now you can see one reason why it is so difficult to draw any firm conclusions about the nature of memory: our two kinds of theorists cannot agree on definitions. Supporters of the one-memory-storage model perform experiments in which material must be remembered for 18 seconds and claim that they are studying short-term memory. Supporters of the two-memory-storage model, however, claim that material that must be remembered this long would be mostly in long-term memory. This same difficulty arises when we consider another variable: number of repetitions.

Repetition

An article by Melton (1963) stands as the classic argument for a single kind of memory. According to Melton, we can conclude that there is only one kind of memory if we can find evidence that repeating the stimulus has the same effect on both short and long stimuli. A short, or *subspan,* stimulus would be in short-term memory, whereas a long, or *supraspan,* stimulus would exceed the short-term memory span and would be in long-term memory—if, in fact, there are two different kinds of memory.

The relevant experiment on *short* stimuli was conducted by Hellyer (1962). He used stimuli that were three consonants long, and he presented them 1, 2, 4, or 8 times. The results, as shown in Figure 8-8, demonstrate conclusively that repetition improves performance. This is particularly true when the interval between presentation and recall is the longest, 27 seconds: with eight presentations of the stimulus, subjects are roughly six times as accurate as with only one presentation.

Melton (1963) performed the relevant experiment on *long* stimuli, using 9-digit numbers. (In case you doubt that 9-digit numbers are longer than the short-term memory span, read a 9-digit number to some friends and have them try to repeat it accurately.) We will consider only part of his experiment—the condition in which certain 9-digit numbers appeared four times, with two other irrelevant 9-digit numbers in between. Thus, a subject might see a sequence that began:

```
*142697385
 849152637
 583194726
*142697385
```

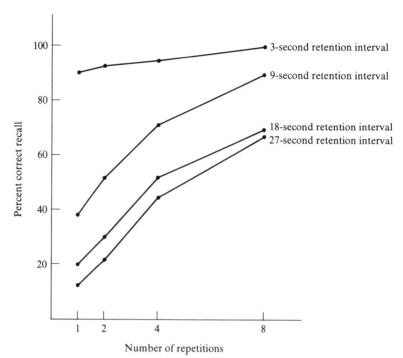

Figure 8-8. The influence of repetition on subspan memory. Data from S. Hellyer. Frequency of stimulus presentation and short-term decrement in recall. *Journal of Experimental Psychology*, 1962, *64*, 650.

After each 9-digit number, subjects tried to recall the number correctly. Figure 8-9 illustrates Melton's results. As in Hellyer's study, recall improves with repetitions: subjects are more accurate after the fourth repetition than after the first. Thus, repetition seems to have the same effect on both short and long stimuli.

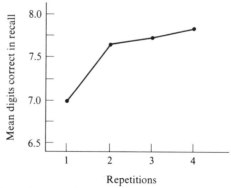

Figure 8-9. The influence of repetition on supraspan memory. From "Implications of Short-Term Memory for a General Theory of Memory," by A. W. Melton, *Journal of Verbal Learning and Verbal Behavior*, 1963, *2*, 18. Copyright 1963 by Academic Press, Inc. Reprinted by permission.

You may be able to guess how supporters of the two-memory model respond to the argument that repetition has the same effect on the two kinds of material. They argue that data obtained on material stored in memory for as long as 27 seconds are not relevant to short-term memory, because material retained this long would be in long-term memory. In fact, some supporters of the two-memory storage model have included this study in a chapter on long-term memory (Loftus & Loftus, 1976). At 27 seconds, they believe, the material is already in long-term memory—where repetition influences recall.

Acoustic versus Semantic Encoding

One argument that is frequently offered in support of the distinction between short-term memory and long-term memory is that short-term memory is primarily acoustic, whereas long-term memory is primarily semantic. In other words, items are stored in short-term memory according to how they *sound*, but items are stored in long-term memory according to what they *mean*. If this generalization were true, we would have a good case for the two-memory model. It would be even more convincing than the other arguments, which simply say that a given variable operates in LTM but not in STM. The acoustic/semantic argument is stronger because it says that sound operates in STM but not LTM and meaning operates in LTM but not STM. However, we will see that this distinction, too, is not a clear-cut one.

Stop and think for a moment whether the acoustic/semantic argument seems reasonable to you. Do you encode something you must recall for a few brief seconds strictly in terms of how it sounds, or does meaning enter, too? Now think about what you have stored in long-term memory: is there any information about how those items sound? Chances are that the acoustic/semantic argument won't seem very reasonable to you. For example, several psychologists have pointed out that there must be acoustic elements in long-term memory, or else we could not recall information about accents or speaking mannerisms. (Think about a phrase that your best friend uses; probably you will note your friend's tone, rhythm, pitch, and other acoustic aspects.)

However, a number of experiments, summarized by Houston (1976), have supported the acoustic/semantic distinction. Specifically, items that *sound* the same are confused with each other in short-term memory but not in long-term memory—supporting the idea that short-term memory uses acoustic features of items in coding. On the other hand, items that *mean* the same thing are confused with each other in long-term memory but not in short-term memory—suggesting that long-term memory uses semantic features in coding.

Representative of these experiments is one by Kintsch and Buschke (1969). They used a serial-learning task, in which subjects had to learn 16 English words in order. They reasoned that the items at the beginning of the list should be in long-term memory by the time recall was requested, whereas the most recent items would still be in short-term memory. They conducted two experiments. The first one tested whether the items at the beginning of the list (presumably in long-term memory) would be influenced by semantic factors;

the second one tested whether the items at the end of the list (presumably in short-term memory) would be influenced by acoustic factors.

In their first study, subjects learned a list of *semantically* related pairs of words—for example, HAPPY, GLOOMY, PLEASED, CAR, DISMAL, AUTO. Notice that this list represents three pairs of synonyms. A control group learned a list of semantically unrelated words. After the subjects had learned the list, the experimenters presented one word from the list—for example, PLEASED—and asked subjects to supply the next word in the list—in this case, CAR. Now if long-term memory is primarily semantic, we would expect that semantic confusions would be greatest for items at the beginning of the list. For example, subjects might supply the word that followed the similar-meaning word—HAPPY—rather than the word that followed PLEASED. Confusions should be minimal at the end of the list, however, because semantic factors should not be important for those items still in short-term memory. As Figure 8-10 shows, the use of semantically related words did influence recall for items at the beginning of the list; however, it had no influence on items at the end of the list. Thus, semantic factors do seem to be important in long-term memory, but not in short-term memory.

In the second study by Kintsch and Buschke (1969), subjects learned a list of *acoustically* related words—for example, LEAD, TACKS, LED, ONE, TAX, WON. Notice that this list represents three pairs of homonyms. A control group learned a list of acoustically unrelated words. As in the first experiment, the experimenters presented one word from the list and asked subjects to supply the word that followed it. If short-term memory is primarily acoustic, then we would expect acoustic confusions to have the greatest effect on items at the end of the list. Confusions should be minimal at the beginning of the list, because acoustic factors should not be important for those items already in long-term memory. Note that this is the case, as shown in Figure 8-10b.

This two-part experiment demonstrates very neatly that semantic confusions disrupt long-term memory, whereas acoustic confusions disrupt short-term memory. Thus, information must be stored in long-term memory in terms of what it *means,* but information must be stored in short-term memory in terms of how it *sounds*.

More recently, however, the distinction has begun to break down. A set of experiments by Wickens (1973), for example, shows that short-term memory also has semantic components. Basically, Wickens used the Peterson and Peterson technique, with subjects retaining sets of three words for 18-second periods. Now, as you know from the Keppel and Underwood (1962) study, as subjects learn many items in that kind of experiment, there is a buildup of proactive inhibition: the greater the number of previous trials, the greater the forgetting. Wickens has found that if you continue to use the same class of stimuli (say, letters), proactive inhibition builds up. However, if you switch to a different class of stimuli (say, numbers) on a certain trial, there will be "release from proactive inhibition." Recall for that new kind of item is unusually high—perhaps even as high as the first item during the learning period.

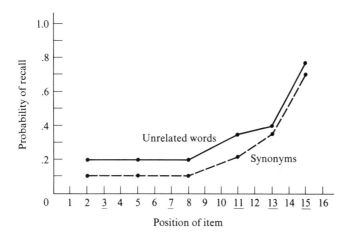

a. Semantic confusions

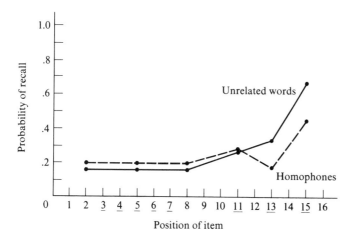

b. Acoustic confusions

Figure 8-10. Demonstrating the acoustic/semantic distinction. From "Homophones and Synonyms in Short-Term Memory," by W. Kintsch and H. Buschke, *Journal of Experimental Psychology*, 1969, *80*, 403–407. Copyright 1969 by the American Psychological Association. Reprinted by permission.

Wickens has found that release from proactive inhibition works not only with stimuli that differ with regard to class (numbers versus letters), but also with words that differ semantically. Table 8-4 shows a setup similar to the one used by Wickens. For the first three trials, subjects must recall words whose semantic nature concerns food. Then, on Trial 4, the semantic content switches to parts of the body. Now if semantic content is completely irrelevant in short-term memory, the switch should not make any difference: meaning would be irrelevant, so it shouldn't matter if we switch meanings.

Table 8-4. A typical setup for testing release from proactive inhibition by changing semantic class, as in experiments by Wickens (1973).

	Subjects see these stimuli	Subjects count backward from a 3-digit number	Subjects recall the three stimuli
TRIAL 1	COOKIE PEAR CHEESE	297	RECALL
TRIAL 2	SOUP BACON PIE	158	RECALL
TRIAL 3	CARROT PANCAKE BREAD	586	RECALL
TRIAL 4	TOE CHIN KNEE	478	RECALL

Figure 8-11 shows the results for the experimental group, where the words were switched from food words to body-part words on Trial 4. Note that on Trial 4, subjects recall substantially more of the material. Wickens also included a control group, which continued with food words on Trial 4. Note that their performance on Trial 4 was even worse than on Trial 3. Think for a moment about why Wickens needed that control group. Otherwise, critics of the experiment could argue that perhaps subjects just normally do better on Trial 4, and the improvement could be unrelated to the semantic change. If we look at the control group, however, we see that subjects normally do worse. Therefore, improvement must be related to the semantic change. Wickens' experiments established, then, that people must be encoding the *meaning* of a word in short-term memory.

If short-term memory has semantic aspects, does long-term memory have acoustic aspects? Nelson and Rothbart (1972) found that information about how a word sounds remains in long-term memory for at least four weeks. They used the relearning method to measure retention. Their subjects learned a list of paired associates, such as 26–AUNT and 73–TAX. Four weeks later, they returned to the laboratory. The experimenters presented the stimuli and asked the subjects to supply the responses. In most cases, as you can imagine, they couldn't. Then, Nelson and Rothbart took a group of stimuli on which subjects had made errors and paired them with homonyms of the old responses—for example, 26–ANT and 73–TACKS. Subjects learned these pairs much more quickly than they learned stimuli paired with new, unrelated words. Thus, some information about how the old response *sounded* must have been in long-term memory in order to boost the learning of the homonym.

In summary, these experiments on the acoustic/semantic distinction leave us uncertain. A number of experiments, of which the Kintsch and Busch-

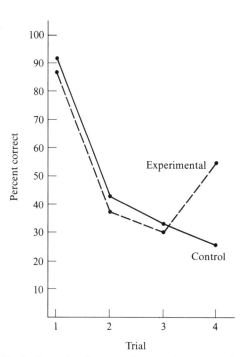

Figure 8-11. Typical results for experiments demonstrating release from proactive inhibition by changing semantic class. From "Some Characteristics of Word Encoding," by D. D. Wickens, *Memory and Cognition*, 1973, *1*, 486. Copyright 1973 by the Psychonomic Society. Reprinted by permission.

ke (1969) experiment is representative, show that acoustic factors are important in short-term memory and semantic factors are important in long-term memory, whereas the reverse is not true. On the other hand, Wickens (1973) has shown that semantic factors are sometimes important in short-term memory, and Nelson and Rothbart (1972) have shown that acoustic factors are sometimes important in long-term memory. Why the conflict? As we noted in the introductory chapters of this book, psychology is a subtle science. It is impossible—at this time—to draw any clear-cut conclusions on this aspect of the one- versus two-memory-storage controversy. The controversy is a theoretical issue that is stimulating a great deal of current research, and a clarification may come soon.

The Serial-Position Effect

Later in this chapter, we will consider a well-known phenomenon in verbal learning called the **serial-position effect.** When subjects perform a free-recall task, we find that they remember the first words of the list very well, the middle items very poorly, and the last items very well. The 0-second delay curve in Figure 8-12 illustrates the typical serial-position curve.

Supporters of the two-memory model were intrigued with why subjects do so well on the *last* items. They proposed that these items are still in short-

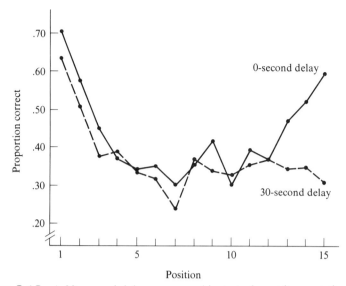

Figure 8-12. A 30-second delay causes subjects to forget items at the end of the list, but it does not affect items at the beginning of the list. Adapted from "Two Storage Mechanisms for Free-Recall," by M. Glanzer and A. R. Cunitz, *Journal of Verbal Learning and Verbal Behavior,* 1966, 5, 358. Copyright 1966 by Academic Press, Inc. Reprinted by permission.

term memory. The reason subjects do so well is that they simply "dump" these words out as soon as they are asked for recall. (It makes sense, doesn't it, that the very recent items should still be in short-term memory, and it should be easy to recover them?)

Glanzer and Cunitz (1966) wondered if they could change that last portion of the serial position curve. Specifically, they hypothesized that a delay prior to recall should make the recall of those last items much poorer. Glanzer and Cunitz, therefore, had one condition in which the experimenter asked for recall as soon as all the words had been presented. This method of 0-second delay produced the typical serial-position curve of Figure 8-12. In another condition, however, Glanzer and Cunitz arranged for a 30-second delay before requesting recall. During this period, subjects counted out loud. As you can see from Figure 8-12, the 30-second delay completely wiped out the peak at the end of the curve for the most recent items. In contrast, the remainder of the curve—representing the words that theoretically should be in long-term memory—is unaffected by the 30-second delay. This experiment, therefore, shows that a variable—in this case, *delay*—affects items in short-term memory, whereas it does not affect items in long-term memory.

As it happens, I once demonstrated the influence of delay on recall for the last items without intending to do so. I was telling an educational-psychology class how they could increase the number of items they could recall in a free-recall task by using the strategy of "dumping" out all the contents of short-term memory before trying to retrieve the words that were in long-term memory. I read the list of words and then said to them, "Now dump out all the words from the end of the list." The class, as a whole, gasped and then glared at me. In the time it had taken me to say that one sentence, I had made them forget the words in short-term memory.

You can demonstrate the influence of delay on recall with a friend. Read one list, and then say a long sentence, such as "Now I want you to recall as many of the words as you can, in any order you want." After your friend has recalled as many words as possible, explain that you are going to read a second list. This time, as soon as you raise your hand, your friend is to recall as many of the words as possible. Read the list, and immediately raise your hand. When you compare the two recall lists, you should find that many more of the recent items were recalled in the second condition.

Conclusions

In the debate over one kind of memory or two, the conclusion must be that the issue remains open. Some psychologists have found the arguments against the two-process theory so convincing that they have rejected it completely. Postman (1975), reviewing the literature on verbal learning and memory for the *Annual Review of Psychology,* went so far as to label a section "The Short and Happy Reign of Dual-Process Theory." He claims that there is an "emerging consensus that this compact and well articulated schema is rapidly losing both face validity and empirical support." (p. 276.) The large number of articles that discuss experimental results in terms of two memories, however, suggests that many psychologists are still pleased with the Atkinson/Shiffrin type of model. These psychologists are not convinced by experiments that seem to demonstrate that the same variables influence both short-term memory and long-term memory, thus implying that there is only one kind of memory. They would point to the experiments by Kintsch and Buschke (1969) and by Glanzer and Cunitz (1966) in support of the two kinds of memory.

Students in my experimental-psychology classes typically react with dismay to these experiments on the nature of memory. They want to know which view of memory is "correct," and I disappoint them by telling them that I don't know. In controversies such as this one, it is doing a disservice to students to claim that the results are clear-cut. This is one area in which the picture is fuzzy. However, current research efforts are attempting to clarify that picture.

Finally, it should be mentioned that other theorists are dissatisfied with both the one-memory-storage and the two-memory-storage views. They argue that memory depends, instead, on the level of processing, or the way in which memory is encoded. This alternative has been discussed by Craik and Lockhart (1972) and Craik and Watkins (1973).

ORGANIZATION IN MEMORY

Let's leave the controversy about the nature of memory and explore another equally important topic: organization in memory. In the section on attributes in memory, we'll discuss various characteristics that are stored in memory. Then we'll examine two organizational strategies, clustering and chunking. Finally, we'll talk about mediation, or memory codes.

Before we look at some of the research on organization, try this informal experiment. In Table 8-5, read List A. Then close the book and try to recall the words on a sheet of paper in any order you wish. Repeat with List B. Then try List C-1, and then list C-2 (the same list in a different order). Keep your answers; we'll discuss them later.

Table 8-5. An informal experiment: organization in memory.

List A	List B	List C-1	List C-2
MONKEY	LIGHT	LIMPET	SYLVAN
DAVID	WOMAN	TROWEL	HOSTAGE
DENTIST	HOT	MARMOT	CATARRH
CARROT	YOUNG	DIPPER	GAUNTLET
MELVIN	BEAUTIFUL	CATARRH	NOSEGAY
BERNARD	SHEEP	ASSAY	BUTCHER
EGGPLANT	DARK	GAUNTLET	DIPPER
POET	OLD	SYLVAN	ASSAY
LION	COLD	OSPREY	MARMOT
GARLIC	MAN	REFLEX	HARPOON
TEACHER	YES	BAGGAGE	CAUSEWAY
TIGER	TABLE	CAUSEWAY	REFLEX
PILOT	LAMB	BUTCHER	TROWEL
LETTUCE	UGLY	HARPOON	OSPREY
GIRAFFE	NO	NOSEGAY	LIMPET
PARSLEY	CHAIR	HOSTAGE	BAGGAGE

Attributes of Material in Memory

Research on attributes in memory demonstrates that subjects often know more than we give them credit for. If we give subjects a recall test and simply mark the items "right" or "wrong," we are underestimating what the subjects know about the material they have learned. For example, when was *Julius Caesar* written? You may not be able to recall the date correctly, but you may have a feeling that you know it and could select the correct answer out of several alternatives. You also know quite a bit about what the answer is *not*. The answer is not "mouse," nor is it "3429," nor is it "1952." You even know where the answer is—it's near the beginning of this chapter. You know how you learned this information—visually through reading this book, rather than auditorily in a class lecture. In short, you can identify many attributes of material in memory.

One area of research on the attributes of material is called the **feeling-of-knowing** phenomenon. Hart (1965) was one of the first to explore this area, even though the feeling-of-knowing sensation is very common. In fact, you probably experienced it on the last test you took that was not a multiple-choice test or on the last quiz show you watched on TV. There was that question—

"Who wrote 'The Pit and the Pendulum'?" You *knew* that you knew the answer, but it just wasn't going to come out of hiding right now. Had somebody offered you the alternatives Robert Burns, Somerset Maugham, Edgar Allan Poe, and Thomas Hardy, it would have been easy, because you knew the answer well enough to recognize it. On the other hand, there was another question, "Who wrote 'The Imaginary Invalid'?" and you knew that you had no idea what the answer to that question was. Even if somebody gave you some alternatives, you could only guess blindly.

Hart's experiment involved just this process. He found that when people said that they had a feeling-of-knowing, they were probably correct. If they were given a multiple-choice question, they were reasonably likely to select the correct alternative. On the other hand, when they said that they did *not* have a feeling-of-knowing, their performance on a multiple-choice question was much poorer.

It seems, then, that people can predict whether they will be able to recognize something that they are unable to recall: this is how we define the feeling-of-knowing. Blake (1973) has explored the feeling-of-knowing further and has demonstrated that it occurs in short-term as well as in long-term memory. Blake used a modification of the Peterson and Peterson method. First, he exposed three consonants. Instead of counting backward, he used Stroop stimuli for the rehearsal-preventing task. (**Stroop stimuli** are color names that are printed in another color; for example, the word *blue* is typed in red ink. Subjects are instructed to read the word, but they experience competition because they tend to read the color of the ink.) After 18 seconds on the Stroop task, subjects tried to recall the three consonants. If the letters were correctly recalled, the subject proceeded to the next item, because the feeling-of-knowing experience was irrelevant. However, a subject who failed to recall one or more letters of the three was asked to indicate whether he or she knew the target well enough to recognize it on a multiple-choice test with eight alternatives. Finally, the subject was asked to choose the correct answer from the eight alternatives.

The results showed that subjects could accurately predict whether or not they could recognize the correct answer. When they had reported a feeling-of-knowing, they were correct in their recognition 64% of the time. When they had reported that they did not have a feeling-of-knowing, they were correct only 38% of the time.

In terms of everyday experience, you can draw a worthwhile conclusion from these feeling-of-knowing studies. If there is an item on a recall examination that you think you must know, you are probably correct! It might even pay to mark those feeling-of-knowing items so that you can come back to them if you have any extra time, rather than wasting time on the items for which you are certain you have no feeling-of-knowing.

You have probably experienced this feeling-of-knowing rather often. It is unpleasant and annoying—it makes you feel anxious. However, another experience is even more intense: the **tip-of-the-tongue phenomenon.** This experience has been discussed by psychologists since the last century, but Brown and McNeill (1966) were the first to investigate it formally.

Here's how Brown and McNeill describe a person experiencing the tip-of-the-tongue phenomenon: "The signs of it were unmistakable; he would appear to be in a mild torment, something like the brink of a sneeze, and if he found the word his relief was considerable" (p. 325). The name *tip-of-the-tongue* always seems amazingly appropriate—can't you feel the target word almost sitting on the end of your tongue, aching to be spoken? One is almost tempted to reach in and try to pull it off! Furthermore, Brown and McNeill's analogy with a sneeze is marvelous. When the tip-of-the-tongue phenomenon is especially strong, it *does* feel like a sneeze that waits, refusing to cooperate. And if you do recall the target word, you're tremendously relieved. So the tip-of-the-tongue involves a familiar experience: you are certain that you know the word you are looking for, yet you cannot quite snatch it into consciousness.

Brown and McNeill produced the tip-of-the-tongue (TOT) state in Harvard and Radcliffe students by giving them the definition for an uncommon English word, such as *nepotism* or *ambergris* or *sampan*. The subjects were asked to supply the word. Sometimes they supplied the word immediately; other times they knew that they did not know the word. However, in 360 cases, the TOT phenomenon occurred. In these cases, the experimenter asked the subjects to supply words that resembled the target in sound but not in meaning, or in meaning but not in sound. For example, when the target word was *sampan*, the similar-sounding words that subjects supplied were *Saipan, Siam, Cheyenne, sarong, sanching,* and *symphoon*. The similar-meaning words that subjects supplied were *barge, houseboat,* and *junk*. (I remember when I was an undergraduate, a professor was showing me how to use a calculator. There was a button labeled *C,* and we both experienced a TOT-state as we tried to recall what the *C* stood for. He quickly said "keyboard," and I quickly said "cabbage." The target word, which we recovered later, was "carriage." He had supplied a similar-meaning word, whereas I had supplied a similar-sounding word.)

The results showed that the similar-sounding words supplied by the subjects were in fact quite similar to the target words they were searching for. In fact, these similar-sounding words had the same number of syllables as the targets in 48% of the cases. They began with the same letter as the target in 49% of the cases. (Of course, in some cases, they could have guessed correctly just by chance, but chance was estimated to be 20% correct in the case of syllables and only 8% correct in the case of letters. Subjects were therefore far more accurate than chance alone would have predicted.) Finally, the similar-sounding words were also very likely to match the target words in terms of which syllable was accentuated.

Subjects were also asked to guess the specific first letter of the target word and the number of syllables in the target word. These specific guesses were even more accurate than the results with the similar-sounding words. For the first letter, they were correct 57% of the time, and for the number of syllables, they were also correct 57% of the time.

The next time you find yourself in the TOT state, try to supply similar-sounding words, and try to guess at the initial letter and at the number of syllables. Then check your accuracy. This process of trying to identify similar-sounding words and the initial letter and number of syllables may prove to be more than an intellectual exercise. You may find that you have identified enough attributes to be able to snatch the target into consciousness!

Brown and McNeill named this recall of the parts of words and the attributes of words *generic recall*. They suggested that memory (in this case, long-term memory) may resemble a dictionary. A word is stored in long-term memory at some particular location. At that location is information about the sound of the word and information about the meaning of the word. In producing the TOT state, Brown and McNeill supplied the definition, or meaning, of the word. When we use a dictionary, we have the sound and look for the meaning; in this case, the subjects took the meaning and tried to find the sound that corresponded to it. In the TOT state, however, subjects cannot retrieve the sound completely—they only have some hints. It's as if the word in the dictionary were somewhat blurred or erased.

Underwood (1969) argues that we know much more about target words we can't recall than simply information about the way they sound. He suggests that items are stored in memory in terms of a group of **attributes**—qualities or context cues belonging to the items. We have seen in the Brown/McNeill data that some attributes involve the sound of the word. Underwood discusses experimental evidence for other attributes. For example, there is the *temporal*, or time, attribute. Sometimes the temporal attribute is quite specific—I can recall, for instance, that I first encountered the word *buoy* in fourth grade. Other times, the temporal attribute simply identifies one event as occurring before or after another event.

The attribute that you are probably most familiar with is the *spatial* attribute—where the item was located in space. For example, if I recall seeing a coupon for a free hamburger in the newspaper, I may have a very strong impression of *where* on the page it was located. In fact, I will leaf through the newspaper, looking only at the lower, left-hand corner of the pages. You've probably had the frustrating experience of not being able to remember a specific fact for a test, but you know exactly where it was in your textbook—on the right-hand page, near the top, just under the picture. A student once told me that as she was trying to answer one question on a test, she could "see" exactly where the information was in the book, but the key sentence was all blurry. She kept squinting, trying to bring that sentence into focus!

Underwood lists many other attributes that people can identify. As in the TOT phenomenon, these are qualities of an item that can be identified correctly, even when you cannot recall the item itself. Some additional attributes are *modality* (whether you have heard a word or seen it), *affective* (whether it has a good or a bad connotation), *class* (whether it is a number or a letter or a word), and *associative* (related antonyms or synonyms).

According to the attribute theory of memory, then, an item is stored according to its many qualities. Often, we cannot recall a target item, but we can recall some of the attributes. In the TOT phenomenon, we can recall some of the attributes that concern the item's sound (and probably others, as well). The feeling-of-knowing experience may be produced by recalling enough attributes of the target that we feel that we can eliminate alternatives on a multiple-choice test that do not have those attributes. When we cannot recall attributes of the target, we report that we do not have a feeling-of-knowing.

Clustering in Free Recall

When people see a list of words and then recall the words in any order, they tend to show some pattern in the organization of the words they remember. For example, the list may contain several words belonging to the same category. Even if the words do not appear together when they are presented, they tend to appear together when they are recalled.

Notice the order in which you recalled the words when you tried the experiment in Table 8-5. Chances are good that the order in which the words came out is different from the order in which they went in. In List A, for instance, you may find that some of the animals are clustered together. In List B, a word may appear next to another word that is related to, or associated with, the first word. List C may also show some pattern of organization, but that pattern will probably vary from one subject to the next; we will describe that kind of organization later in the chapter.

List A is like a list used by Bousfield (1953). He presented subjects with a list of 60 nouns—15 nouns from each of four categories: animals, names, professions, and vegetables. He read the words out loud at the rate of 3 seconds for each word. Then subjects were given 10 minutes to recall all the words. Using a measure that he had devised of the extent to which words cluster together, Bousfield concluded that subjects showed significantly more clustering than could have been expected by chance alone.

Bousfield's experiment provides a classic example of **categorical clustering.** The words in List B, on the other hand, demonstrate **associative clustering.** In associative clustering, a list word evokes a second list word with which it is associated. For example, WOMAN may evoke its associate MAN, and the two will appear next to each other in recall.

Jenkins and Russell (1952) conducted the classic study in associative clustering. They constructed a list by searching through word-association lists to find 24 pairs of words, such as WOMAN-MAN, in which subjects almost always supplied a particular response for the stimulus in a word-association task. The experimenter read the list of words and then requested recall. Again, subjects tended to place words together that were associated with each other. It seems that subjects write down a word, that word reminds them of another word on the list, and then they write down the related word.

Endel Tulving (1962) wrote an article called "Subjective Organization in Free Recall of 'Unrelated' Words." As the title implies, Tulving constructed a list of words that were essentially unrelated to each other. From the *experimenter's* point of view, then, there would be neither categorical nor associative relationships in the list. However, the *subjects* tended to impose their own organization on the list. Tulving called this kind of organization **subjective organization;** this is the third kind of clustering.

Tulving presented 16 unrelated English words and requested recall. Then he presented the same list and asked for recall for 15 additional trials. On each trial, the words were presented in a different order. He found that on Trial 2, subjects tended to place words together in recall that had also been placed together on Trial 1. It seemed, then, that subjects believed that some words "went together" on the first trial, and these words again clustered together on the second trial. Furthermore, subjective organization increased over the 16 trials. On each trial, subjects showed an increasing tendency to cluster together the words that had been clustered together on the previous trial.

Notice that when we test for categorical clustering or associative clustering, we only need to present the list once. We say that there is clustering if the subject puts words together that the experimenter says should go together; the correct answer is defined in terms of the experimenter. However, we can't determine subjective organization from a single trial, because there is no "correct answer" that we can compare with the recall. The only way we can determine the existence of subjective organization is by noticing whether certain words that appear together on one trial tend to stick together on later trials.

Now look at your recall of lists C-1 and C-2 in Table 8-5. Are there some words that you listed next to each other on the first trial that also appear next to each other on the second trial? When I tried this experiment, the words HARPOON and HOSTAGE appeared next to each other in both recalls. This is understandable in that both words begin with the letter H. However, the words DIPPER and GAUNTLET also appeared together in both recalls. This is not a pattern of organization that an experimenter could have predicted: it was a subjective organization that made sense to *me*—but not necessarily to the rest of the world. In subjective organization, then, subjects demonstrate their own unique patterns of organization, and they preserve this organization on the following trials.

Clustering studies are relevant to the question of organization in memory because they show that material is reorganized between the time it is perceived by the human subject and the time it is recalled by that subject. In the case of categorical and associative clustering, subjects rearrange words to agree with commonly accepted organizational patterns. If there is no commonly accepted organizational pattern, they invent their own subjective organization. Furthermore, if we continue in the spirit of "the subjects know more than we give them credit for," it is possible that subjects also tend to use some of their own subjective organization in their treatment of lists intended for categorical and associative clustering. For example, your DENTIST's name might be BERNARD, and so you might put these words next to each other in recall. However, you would not "get credit" for this subjective organization in the experimenter's measure of clustering.

As you were reading this section, you may have wondered whether subjects can improve the number of items they recall by using clustering. It sounds as though it should work: if recalling a word leads you to recall its associate, you get two for the price of one!

A number of experiments have shown that more clustering leads to more recall. For example, Bousfield (1953) found a significant correlation between his measure of clustering and the number of items recalled. More recently,

Shapiro and Bell (1970) examined subjective organization and its relationship to recall. In this experiment, subjects saw and recalled a list of unrelated words for 12 trials. Shapiro and Bell then divided the subjects into three groups on the basis of the extent to which they showed organization in recall. The results showed that subjects who were classified as "high organizers" recalled the most, and subjects who were classified as "low organizers" recalled the least. Bear in mind, however, our argument in Chapter 1 that "correlation is not necessarily causation." We cannot say that increased organization necessarily *causes* increased recall because there may be another factor involved. As this factor (for example, intelligence) increases, that may cause both other factors (organization and recall) to increase. Thus, we know from this study that organization is related to recall. However, we cannot confidently claim that an increase in organization will *cause* an increase in recall.

Chunking

The first time I was exposed to the word *chunking,* it was divided into two parts, at the end of one line of text and the beginning of the next: I read the word as *chun-king* and wondered why a textbook would be talking about this brand of Chinese canned dinners! Ironically, I had failed to make a true *chunk* out of *chunking.*

The term *chunking* was invented by George Miller (1956). A **chunk** is the basic unit in short-term memory, which can hold about seven chunks. Look back at the experiment you tried in Table 8-1. Most likely, you recalled about seven letters. You probably also recalled about seven short words and about seven long words. Notice that the number of items (such as letters) *within* each chunk is generally irrelevant. Humans can recall about seven well-organized units, and it doesn't matter whether each unit has one letter, three, or six—as long as it is well organized. Now look back at Figure 8-3. Notice how similar the two bottom curves are, even though the material to be remembered was sometimes three consonants and sometimes three words. Each of those words was an English word that was already a well-organized unit, or chunk; thus, it took up no more space in memory than each consonant did.

People can expand what they can hold in short-term memory by **recoding,** or rearranging small chunks into larger chunks. For example, I can take five chunks—G, R, A, N, D—and recode them so that they are no longer five separate units, but one chunk—the word GRAND. I can then take that one chunk and combine it with other chunks to form the name of my favorite movie—*Grand Illusion.*

Now look back at your recall on lists A and B of Figure 8-5. Chances are good that you recalled more than seven items from each list. How did you do it? You recoded that list: you reorganized it so that words which were similar were placed near each other. For example, you may have put the vegetables GARLIC, LETTUCE, and PARSLEY next to each other. Rather than three isolated chunks, you now have one single large chunk. If each chunk consisted of three words, you could theoretically store 21 words rather than seven in short-term memory.

We mentioned earlier that it's fortunate that telephone numbers are seven digits long, just at the limit of short-term memory. If you add an area code, however, the length of the telephone number should be ten items—beyond the memory span. However, by now you have probably formed a chunk out of your area code. An area code is no longer 7-1-6, for example; it is one chunk, 716. Furthermore, in many areas, each town has a unique set of three digits at the beginning. In Geneseo, New York, for example, every number starts with 243. This prefix is familiar enough that it, too, has become a chunk. If you plan to phone a friend in Geneseo long distance, and you've just looked up the number, you don't have to remember ten chunks. You simply remember one chunk for the area code, one chunk for the town prefix, and four chunks for the rest of the number. A total of six chunks is within your memory span.

In a free-recall study, subjects recall more and more of a list of words as it is repeated over and over. One thing that may be happening is that, with repetition, people form larger and larger chunks. If you tried to recall the words in List A of Table 8-5 a second time, your chunk of vegetables might contain not only GARLIC, LETTUCE, and PARSLEY, but also EGGPLANT and CARROT. Consequently, your second recall trial would probably have more correct recall than the first, because each chunk contained a greater number of words.

Miller's article received tremendous attention; in fact, it is one of the articles in psychology that is most often cited in other psychology articles. Many people complained, however, that *chunk* was not a well-defined concept. For example, Simon (1974) called Miller's use of the term "artfully vague," and he tried to find out more about chunks. The problem with the term *chunk,* argued Simon, was that it was defined in a circular fashion: "a chunk is what there are seven of in short-term memory." To have more meaning, Simon continued, the concept of the chunk should have some relevance for another psychological task, aside from short-term memory. Simon, therefore, looked at performance on long-term-memory tasks. He hypothesized that if the chunk is a real, legitimate concept, the amount of time it takes to transfer information to long-term memory should increase as the number of chunks increases. In other words, there should be a positive correlation between the number of chunks and learning time. Simon's analysis confirmed the hypothesis: it took between 5 and 10 seconds to fixate each chunk in long-term memory, and it took about twice as long to learn a 20-chunk stimulus as to learn a 10-chunk stimulus. Therefore, the chunk is a legitimate concept—not just an arbitrary term describing the seven units in memory—because it is so closely related to learning time.

Psychologists have also explored Miller's concept of recoding. Bower and Springston (1970), for example, used a series of familiar acronyms and abbreviations, such as PHD, AMA, TWA, LSD, FBI, and XKE. Read over that list to yourself, and try to recall it. You probably will remember most of the items. Now imagine that, instead of hearing those items, you heard the same letters with pauses in different places—for example, PH, DAM, ATW, ALS, DFB, IXK, E. Quite clearly, your performance would not be as accurate. Bower and Springston tested these two conditions—one with pauses between the familiar units, the other with pauses in the middle of the units. As hypothesized, performance was much better when the familiar units stayed intact. Bower and Springston explain their results as follows: During the pause that follows a three-letter sequence, subjects "look up" that sequence in their mental equivalent of a dictionary. If the three letters are there, then the three letters are recoded into a single chunk. If that search of the dictionary fails, however, then the three letters remain as three separate chunks. These three chunks put a greater strain on memory than does the single chunk formed by the familiar unit. Therefore, memory is better for familiar units.

Mediation

Suppose that you had to remember this paired associate: MXB-COFFEE. Would you simply say over and over to yourself "MXB-COFFEE, MXB-COFFEE" until you had memorized it by sheer persistence? More likely, you would try to use a code or memory trick, in a process known as **mediation.** The exact mediator used will vary from one subject to the next. A possible choice in this case might be *Maxwell House*. Thus, MXB would remind you of *Maxwell House,* which would remind you of COFFEE. We could diagram it:

MXB→(Maxwell House)→COFFEE

There are two tricks to finding a good mediator for a paired associate. First, the mediator must follow quite reliably from the stimulus. In this case, *Maxwell House* is a good mediator because it contains two of the letters from the stimulus, rather than just a single letter. Second, we must be able to "decode" the mediator into the response. What good is a mediator if it leaves us dangling there, unable to retrieve the response that it was supposed to remind us of? Thus, you might have a lovely mediator from the standpoint of following from the stimulus—for example, you might be lucky enough to have a friend named Mary Xavier Brown—but Mary will do you little good unless she happens to remind you of coffee.

Prytulak (1971) examined how subjects decode mediators. He presented a list of nonsense words, each composed of a consonant-vowel-consonant arrangement, and asked subjects to write down an English-word mediator for each nonsense word. After they were done, Prytulak gave the mediators back to the subjects and asked them to recall the nonsense words. He found that they were very likely to recall the nonsense word when the mediator used the same letters in the same order. When the mediator did not use all of the letters, or when the order of the letters was mixed up, subjects were much less likely to recall the nonsense word correctly.

Prytulak then figured out a way to classify the transformations, or changes, that a subject used in going from the nonsense word to the mediator. Some transformations involved only one step—for example, adding the letter E to the nonsense word LOV to form the mediator LOVE. To transform the nonsense word KOZ to the mediator COZY, however, requires two steps: in step 1, you replace the K with a C; in step 2, you add a Y.

Prytulak's results showed that subjects recalled the mediators most accurately when only one transformation (or none) was involved. With three or more transformations, recall was decreased to about 20% (see Figure 8-13). Prytulak's explanation for the results is that subjects in search of a mediator work through a stack of transformations, arranged in order of their complexity.

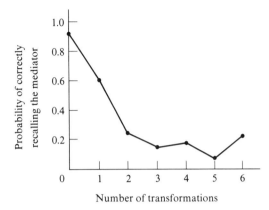

Figure 8-13. Subjects are more likely to be able to recall the mediator when there are few steps involved in transforming a nonsense word into a mediator. Adapted from "Natural Language Mediation," by L. S. Prytulak, *Cognitive Psychology*, 1971, *2*, 19. Copyright 1971 by Academic Press, Inc. Reprinted by permission.

They begin with mediators involving simple transformations and go on to mediators involving complex transformations. They search until they find a mediator that can turn the nonsense word into a familiar word. In later experiments, Prytulak demonstrated that the number of steps involved in the transformation was related to recall in a short-term memory task.

The most extensive series of experiments on mediation has been conducted by Gordon Bower. Bower has explored a number of tricks recommended by **mnemonists**—people who specialize in increasing the size and duration of memory. One trick involves the serial-learning method, when you have to recall a list of items in order. Mnemonists suggest that you construct a story to link together the critical words. For example, if you must recall the serial list JUMP–RUG–CAT–WINDOW–TREE–CAR, you might make up a story such as "I JUMPed on the RUG and scared the CAT, who jumped out the WINDOW, up on to the TREE, and down to the top of the CAR."

Bower and Clark (1969) wanted to see whether this trick used by mnemonists really worked. They instructed one group of subjects (the narrative group) in the art of making up narrative stories to link together the words. Subjects in this group were allowed to spend as long as they wanted making up the story. Subjects in the control group were **yoked** to those in the narrative group: the experimenters measured how long subject 1 in the narrative group took, and they allowed subject 1 in the control group the same amount of time. This yoking process was continued for all 12 pairs of subjects. (Note that the yoked control is excellent in that it allows the narrative-group subjects to spend as long as they want on the task, and no longer, and the control-group subjects spend the identical amount of time on the task. The disadvantage is that the narrative subjects must be tested before the control subjects—or else the experimenters would not know how long to allow for each control subject.)

The control subjects learned the list in the normal way. They were simply told to study and learn each list. Both narrative and control subjects saw identical lists, ten words long. When they were tested for recall immediately after learning, both groups recalled 99% of the material. However, they learned a total of 12 lists of ten words each. After all 12 lists had been presented, Bower and Clark asked for recall from all 12 lists. Figure 8-14 shows the astounding results. As you can see, there is absolutely no overlap. Overall, the narrative subjects recalled 93% of the material—not much less than when they supplied immediate recall. The control subjects recalled only 13% of the material, even though they had spent the same amount of time learning the material.

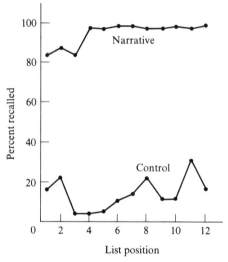

Figure 8-14. Recall as a function of learning condition: narrative versus control. From "Narrative Stories as Mediators for Serial Learning," by G. H. Bower and M. C. Clark, *Psychonomic Science*, 1969, *14*, 181. Copyright 1969 by the Psychonomic Society. Reprinted by permission.

Bower and Winzenz (1970) examined another mnemonic trick—the idea that it is easier to remember something if you picture the items in some kind of vivid interaction. For example, you might try to remember to bring a particular book to class by picturing yourself throwing it at the professor. Does this vivid interaction aid your memory more than simply rehearsing "BOOK–CLASS, BOOK–CLASS"? It seems obvious that it should, but psychologists cannot be satisfied with what *seems* obvious or what has been commonly accepted.

Bower and Winzenz studied paired associates, using concrete nouns. There were four conditions: (1) repetition—subjects repeat and rehearse each pair silently to themselves; (2) sentence reading—subjects see each pair written in a simple sentence, which they read aloud; (3) sentence generation—subjects make up and say aloud a sentence using each pair; and (4) imagery—subjects visualize a mental picture in which the two words are in some kind of vivid interaction. Half of the subjects were tested by cued recall: they saw the stimulus and tried to recall the response. The other half of the subjects were tested by a multiple-choice recognition task. The results are shown in Figure 8-15.

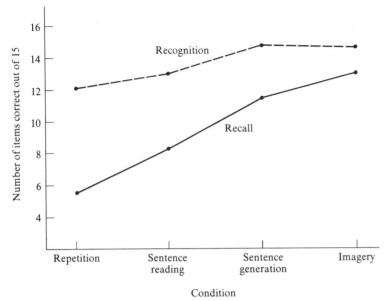

Figure 8-15. Retention as a function of learning condition and method of measuring retention. Data from Bower, G. H., and Winzenz, D. Comparison of associative learning strategies. *Psychonomic Science*, 1970, *20*, 119–120.

First, notice the curve for the recall group. The imagery condition produced more than twice the recall of the repetition condition. The biggest single jump in improvement occurs between the sentence-reading and the sentence-generation conditions. What seems to be important, then, is the active participation of the subject in making up the sentence (or the visual image). Perhaps this is because it allows subjects to choose sentences that are meaningful to themselves, or perhaps it is because it forces the subjects to pay close attention to the task. At any rate, subjects do better when they come up with sentences on their own, rather than having sentences handed to them, ready-made.

Now notice the curve for the recognition group. The method of learning again has an effect on recall, but it is not nearly so impressive as it was for the recall group. This is probably due to a ceiling effect (discussed in Chapter 1). There were only 15 pairs of words, and the worst group recalled 12 words. When the worst group does this well, there is not much room for improvement! The subjects reach the ceiling, so to speak, because the bottom performance is so good and because subjects cannot possibly get more than 15 items correct.

In this section on organization, we have seen some aspects of how memory is organized. An item is not merely tossed into a heap of other items in memory, which lie in confusion. Instead, items seem to be "tagged" with a good deal of information about their attributes. Furthermore, when subjects are asked to recall items from memory, the recall order is not random. Instead, recall order is well-organized, with similar words appearing clustered near each other. Organization also serves to improve memory. One way of improving memory is by chunking, or grouping words together that go together in some way. Finally, using mediation to organize lists helps to recall them more accurately.

Before going on to the next section, try the experiment shown in Table 8-6. Read List A. Then close the book and try to recall the words on a sheet of paper, in any order you wish. Repeat with Lists B, C, and D. Keep your answers; we'll discuss them later.

FACTORS AFFECTING MEMORY AND LEARNING

There are a number of factors that influence learning and memory for verbal items. We can regard some of these factors as *stimulus characteristics*. One word will differ from another in terms of factors such as frequency, meaningfulness, and serial position; consequently, it may be different in terms of how quickly it is learned and how accurately it is remembered. Other factors, however, can be regarded as *subject characteristics*. Subjects differ from one another in terms of factors such as age, social class, and sex; these factors may also determine how quickly verbal material is learned and remembered.

In this section, we will also consider a methodological issue: the control of confounding variables. In particular, we will see how frequency, meaningfulness, pleasantness, and imagery are frequently intertangled with one another. We will also discuss how to avoid confounding in experiments involving the stimulus variable of serial position and the subject variable of age.

Individual Differences among Stimuli

First, let us consider some of the attributes of the verbal items that are permanent—attributes that stay with the items no matter how they are used in an experiment.

Frequency. Look back at your recall of List A of Table 8-6. Which are the words you recalled? Did you remember KITCHEN, DINNER, and OF-FICE? What about LEMUR, CAPSTAN, and ROSTRUM? A wide variety of experiments, summarized by Underwood and Schulz (1960), have shown that high-frequency words are learned and remembered better than low-frequency words.

Let us get sidetracked for a moment to consider how you measure the frequency of an item. Fortunately, there are two books available that list how often each word appears in the English language. The classic one was compiled

Table 8-6. An informal experiment in memory and learning.

List A	List B	List C	List D
KITCHEN	WHP	PRETTY	MAGAZINE
ROSTRUM	ZXQ	TROUBLE	CONTEXT
MONEY	PNK	SENT	INTERIM
CAPSTAN	QJF	HAPPY	TOMAHAWK
DINNER	SNK	WRONG	IDEA
JITNEY	CXJ	HIGHEST	BEGGAR
LEMUR		CHAIR	ORCHESTRA
LEADER		WORRY	PHILOSOPHY
NIMBUS		FIGHT	EXISTENCE
TARTAN		STRENGTH	CHURCH
PEOPLE		METAL	PAPER
OFFICE		ANNOUNCED	SAKE

by Thorndike and Lorge (1944). Thus, if you read a psychology article that says the stimuli were English words with Thorndike-Lorge frequencies of less than 50 times per million, this means that one million words of text were inspected by Thorndike and Lorge, and each of these words appeared fewer than 50 times. The word *jelly,* for example, has a Thorndike-Lorge frequency of 19: in one million words of text, the word *jelly* appeared 19 times. A more recent word count, more generally used today, was compiled by Kučera and Francis (1967). This book, too, lists the number of times a word appeared in a count of approximately one million words.

Now let's return to the influence of word frequency on memory and learning. As we have noted, there is a positive correlation between word frequency and learning. However, the correlation is not very strong, so don't be surprised if you read about a study in which word frequency did not have a significant influence.

Word frequency also has some influence on the order in which items are recalled. The measure of memory that is most frequently used in free recall is simply *recall*—whether the item is remembered or not. However, there is also some more subtle information available in the free-recall data: the order in which an item is recalled, known as its **spew position.** Underwood and Schulz (1960) argue that there is a correlation between frequency and spew position, with high-frequency items being recalled before low-frequency items.

Since frequent words are remembered better, we would also expect to find that they are recognized better. However, this is not the case. Do you recall whether the word SUPPER was in List A of Figure 8-6? How about KUMQUAT? Shepard (1967) found that subjects were significantly more accurate in recognizing low-frequency than high-frequency words. One of the explanations for this paradox is that high-frequency words remind subjects of other, related words that are not on the list, whereas this is not true for low-frequency words. (How many words spring immediately to mind when you see the word CAPSTAN?) Thus, you may think you saw SUPPER because the word DINNER, which was on the list, reminded you of SUPPER. However, no word on the list made you think of KUMQUAT, and so you correctly reported that it was not on the list.

Meaningfulness. Meaningfulness is the association value of an item. It is measured in a variety of ways, but the most common is probably the Noble (1952) method. With this method, the subject sees the item and is allowed one minute to write down all the different words associated with that item. Thus, the nonsense word GOJEY has a meaningfulness rating of .99 (that is, the average subject produced about one association in one minute), whereas the English word KITCHEN has a meaningfulness rating of 9.61. In List B of Figure 8-6, see if your recall was better for the high-meaningful, even-numbered items than for the low-meaningful, odd-numbered items.

Underwood and Schulz (1960) explored the concept of meaningfulness in their book *Meaningfulness and Verbal Learning.* Meaningfulness has a substantial influence on performance in verbal-learning tasks, although the extent of that influence may depend on where the item appears. For example, R.G. Hunt (1959) found that, in a paired-associate task, meaningfulness had a much greater influence on learning for items in the *response* position than for items in the *stimulus* position. Thus, you would learn the pair 23–WHP much better than the pair 46–ZXQ in a study in which we vary response meaningfulness. However, there might not be much difference in your learning of the pair WHP-23 versus ZXQ-46, because stimulus meaningfulness is less important.

Pleasantness. The influence of pleasantness on memory falls under the **Pollyanna Principle,** which states that performance is superior for pleasant items on a variety of tasks. Pollyanna, the heroine of a children's book and a Walt Disney movie, was not the only person to remember the good and forget the bad: we all do it!

One chapter of *The Pollyanna Principle* (Matlin & Stang, 1978) reviews the literature on the relationship between pleasantness and recall. There have been about 100 studies in this area, dating back to the 1890s. Sometimes the studies examine real-life events. (Which do you think you would recall better: something pleasant that happened to you 6 months ago, or something neutral or unpleasant from the same period?) More often, the studies examine English words that vary in pleasantness. (Notice what kind of words you remembered best in List C of Table 8-6.) Incidentally, pleasantness is typically measured by having subjects rate the word on a 7-point scale, like those we looked at in Chapter 5.

In both the real-life events and the English-word experiments, subjects recall the pleasant items best. In general, unpleasant items are recalled next best, and neutral items are recalled worst. Matlin and Stang performed an archival analysis of the literature, trying to see why most experiments showed this selective recall for pleasant items but a few experiments did not. We found that the single most important factor was whether there was a delay period between the learning of the words and the recall test. If the experimenter requested recall immediately after subjects learned the words, there was not much selective recall. After a delay, however, subjects were much more likely to remember the good and forget the bad and neutral. It seems that long-term memory is most influenced by selective recall, whereas short-term memory is much less influenced.

Earlier in this section, we noted that spew position, or order of recall, is an alternate measure of learning. Thus, two items might both be recalled, but we would argue that the one that was recalled first was remembered better than the one that was recalled last. A wide variety of studies have shown that people recall pleasant items before less pleasant items.

In one experiment, for example, Matlin and Stang (1978) asked students to list pairs of adjectives that they might use in describing someone. We found that they tended to supply the more pleasant word of the pair first—for example, FRIENDLY–UNFRIENDLY, PRETTY–UGLY, SMART–STUPID. The next time you are about to say two adjectives together, notice how hard it is to say, for example, ''bad and good'' or ''wrong and right.''

Imagery. Imagery, or the use of a nonverbal method for remembering, is probably the stimulus variable that has received the most attention in recent years. Notice what kinds of words you recalled in List D of Table 8-6. Were they high-imagery words, such as MAGAZINE, TOMAHAWK, and ORCHESTRA, or low-imagery words, such as CONTEXT, INTERIM, and IDEA?

Paivio (1971) is probably the best-known researcher in this area. Paivio and his colleagues asked college students to rate 925 nouns for their ''imagery arousing capacity.''Students gave a high rating, 7, when the word aroused a mental image quickly and easily. They gave a low rating, 1, when a word did not arouse a mental image or when the image came only with difficulty.

We saw in the section on mediation that when subjects try to create a vivid image, they recall the material better than if they do not use imagery. As you might guess, words that naturally have high imagery are recalled and learned better than words that naturally have low imagery.

Frequency, meaningfulness, pleasantness, and imagery as confounding variables. Unfortunately, the four variables we have discussed so far are correlated with one another. Consequently, experimenters will design confounded experiments unless they take special precautions to control for the irrelevant variables.

Let's look again at List A in Table 8-6. In that list, there are six words that are high in frequency and six words that are low in frequency. However, no attempt was made to control those two groups of words so that they would be equivalent in meaningfulness, pleasantness, and imagery. Let's compare the two groups of words on these other three dimensions:

KITCHEN	ROSTRUM
MONEY	CAPSTAN
DINNER	JITNEY
LEADER	LEMUR
PEOPLE	NIMBUS
OFFICE	TARTAN

The two lists are confounded by meaningfulness: you would have many more associations to KITCHEN, for example, than to ROSTRUM. The lists are also confounded by pleasantness: you would probably rate the words on the left as being one or two rating points more positive than the words on the right. (We'll discuss this relationship between frequency and pleasantness in detail in Chapter 11.) Finally, the lists are confounded by imagery: you probably can create extremely vivid images of KITCHEN, MONEY, and DINNER, but it would be much harder and take much longer to find an image for ROSTRUM, CAPSTAN, or JITNEY.

You can anticipate the problem. Suppose you find that the words on the left are recalled better than the words on the right. What can you conclude? Well, perhaps frequency, the selected independent variable, does have an effect on memory. However, one or more of the three confounding variables could really be responsible for the difference in recall. Perhaps the words on the left were recalled better because they are also more meaningful, more pleasant, or higher in imagery, and each of these three factors is related to recall. As you can see, firm conclusions about causality are impossible in a confounded experiment.

As we discussed in Chapter 2, experimenters can try two basic approaches if they suspect that an irrelevant factor may confound their experiment. First, they can try to remove the confounding problem at the outset. For example, they might design their high-frequency and low-frequency lists so that they are equivalent with respect to all other important variables that may influence recall. The experimenters would select the words in such a way that the high-and low-frequency lists are equal in meaningfulness, pleasantness, and imagery. Other potentially confounding factors should also be equal for the two lists. Note that the words in List A are all two-syllable nouns; thus, the high-and low-frequency lists are already equal in word length and part of speech. (Alternately, we could have included several word lengths and parts of speech, but we would have had to be certain that both lists had the same number of 1-, 2-, and 3-syllable words and that both lists had the same number of nouns, verbs, adjectives, and so on.)

Sometimes, however, the design of the experiment does not permit the experimenter to remove the confounding variable at the outset. In such cases, confounding variables must be removed statistically. Recall the experiment described in the section on pleasantness in which people listed pairs of adjectives. Pleasant words tended to be supplied prior to unpleasant words. However, frequent words also tended to be supplied prior to infrequent words. Since pleasant words are also frequent, frequency was a confounding factor. Through statistical analyses, we showed that pleasantness influenced recall order even after controlling statistically for frequency, whereas frequency did not influence recall order after controlling statistically for pleasantness (Matlin & Stang, 1978). Analysis of covariance and multiple regression are two useful tools for the statistical control of confounding variables (see Appendix).

The four characteristics of stimuli that we have discussed so far— frequency, meaningfulness, pleasantness, and imagery—are all qualities of the stimulus that exist before the experiment begins. In contrast, there are other characteristics of stimuli that are a result of the way the stimuli are treated in the experiment.

Serial position. In our discussion of the distinction between short-term memory and long-term memory, we introduced the serial-position curve. Subjects recall items at the beginning and end of a free-recall list very well, but their recall is poor for items at the middle of the list (see Figure 8-16). Now that we are discussing the serial-position effect in greater detail, notice that the curve is not exactly symmetrical—the right and the left sides are not mirror images of each other. The **primacy effect**—the advantage in recall for items at the beginning of the list—is somewhat stronger than the **recency effect**—the advantage in recall for items at the end of the list. Furthermore, the primacy effect holds for the first five positions, in this curve, whereas the recency effect holds for only the last three positions.

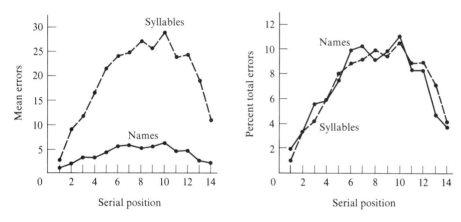

a. Absolute number of errors   b. Relative number of errors

Figure 8-16. Serial-position curves: absolute versus relative number of errors. From "Serial Position Curves in Verbal Learning," by J. W. McCrary and W. S. Hunter, *Science*, 1953, *117*, 131–134. Reprinted by permission of the American Association for the Advancement of Science.

Sometimes if you look casually at free-recall data, there does not seem to be a serial-position effect—the learning may look uniformly good for items at all serial positions. For example, look at the curve for the learning of names in Figure 8-16a. McCrary and Hunter (1953) argued that this curve was really bowed, rather than flat, but the bowing was too subtle to show when performance was measured in terms of the *absolute* number of errors at each position. They measured errors in terms of *relative* errors by noting what percent of the total number of errors was made at each serial position. As you can see in Figure 8-16b, the bowing now looks just the same for names as it does for syllables. Notice that the precise form of the dependent variable has an important effect on experimenters' conclusions.

Earlier in the chapter, we suggested that the recency end of the serial position curve may be due to items being held in short-term memory. Subjects are able to recall the last few items quite accurately because these items have just been placed in short-term memory, and they haven't yet decayed or been displaced by later items.

How can we explain the primacy end of the serial-position curve? Rundus (1971) thought that subjects might be rehearsing the items at the beginning of the curve more frequently. To investigate this question, he devised a method called **overt rehearsal.** Typically, subjects rehearse covertly, or silently to themselves. Rundus asked his subjects to try to learn free-recall lists as they normally would, but to say a word out loud whenever they thought about that word. They were told that the word they said aloud could be the word they were actually looking at, or it could be a word from earlier in the list. The important point is that subjects were encouraged always to say whatever word they happened to be thinking about.

Rundus's results are shown in Figure 8-17. Notice that for the beginning of the curve, the match between the number of rehearsals and the proportion correctly recalled is amazingly close. Subjects rehearse these beginning words frequently, and they recall them very well. The match for the end of the curve is poor. These final items are recalled accurately because they were in short-term memory; we do not need rehearsal to explain the recency effect.

Let's talk about a potential source of confounding in experiments on the serial-position effect. Suppose that a list of words looked like this:

KITCHEN
MONEY
JITNEY
LEMUR
NIMBUS
OFFICE
PEOPLE

If you were asked to recall these words, you would undoubtedly remember the first and the last words best, even if no serial-position effect were operating. The problem is that certain stimuli always appear in certain serial positions, so we don't know whether the superior recall of the first and last items is due to serial position or to the nature of the specific stimuli. In this case, the stimuli are arranged so as to work *in favor of* the serial-position effect. However, confounding variables sometimes operate *in opposition to* the effect that the experimenter has hypothesized. For example, if the list of words looked like this, the experimenter would probably not demonstrate a serial-position effect:

JITNEY
NIMBUS
KITCHEN
MONEY
OFFICE
PEOPLE
LEMUR

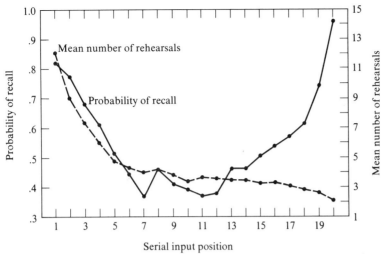

Figure 8-17. Words at the beginning of the list are rehearsed more often; this seems to explain the primacy portion of the serial-position curve. From "Analysis of Rehearsal Processes in Free-Recall," by D. Rundus, *Journal of Experimental Psychology*, 1971, *89*, 66. Copyright 1971 by the American Psychological Association. Reprinted by permission.

In order to avoid confounding, the experimenter must take certain precautions. Some kind of counterbalancing must be used. Complete counterbalancing would probably be logistically difficult, because of the large number of positions. Psychologists typically use some kind of incomplete counterbalancing, such as a modified Latin-square design. A list might be divided into four quarters, and the experimenter might construct four lists, with the stipulation that a word must occupy a different quarter on each of the four lists. Psychologists would also try to minimize the effects of individual stimuli by selecting stimuli that are similar to each other in important stimulus characteristics.

Massed versus distributed learning. Is it better to finish all the learning in a single session (**massed learning**) or to distribute the same amount of learning over a number of sessions (**distributed learning**)? This is a question that has been asked since the days of Ebbinghaus in the 1880s. Again, the answer is not clear-cut, although the bulk of the studies seem to show that some form of distributed learning is generally best. One reason that it is a difficult question to answer is that the conditions of the distributed learning are very important. As you can imagine, there would be no advantage to distributed learning if you had a difficult list of words that was exposed only once in each session, with a month's rest in between.

Underwood, whose name is surely familiar to you by now (because of the distributed practice you have had), has performed several experiments on the massed/distributed issue. Figure 8-18 illustrates his results for 9- to 14-year-old children. Notice that as the number of repetitions of the items increases, the

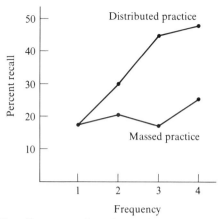

Figure 8-18. Recall as a function of condition—massed versus distributed—and the number of repetitions. From ''A Breakdown of the Total-Time Law in Free-Recall Learning,'' by B. J. Underwood, *Journal of Verbal Learning and Verbal Behavior*, 1970, *9*, 573–583. Copyright 1970 by Academic Press, Inc. Reprinted by permission.

two curves grow further and further apart. With four repetitions, subjects perform about twice as well on distributed practice as on massed practice. In other words, there is an *interaction* between the number of repetitions and the massed/distributed variable.

The von Restorff effect. The von Restorff effect—named for the German Gestalt psychologist who first reported it—occurs when a small number of unusual items are mixed in with a large number of other items that have qualities in common with each other (von Restorff, 1933). In this situation, the unusual items are learned better. For example, if you had to learn the list CAR, GUM, MAT, *book*, TREE, INK, CUP, APPLE, and CARPET, the word that you would learn best would be *book*. Similarly, I learned the name of the one male enrolled in my Psychology of Women class much faster than the names of the 42 females in the class. The explanation for the von Restorff effect seems clear: a distinctive stimulus will receive more attention, and so it will be learned more readily.

Individual Differences among Subjects

As we have seen, verbal-learning psychologists have devoted a great deal of research to the individual differences among stimuli—why one kind of stimulus, or a stimulus in one kind of condition, should be learned better than another kind of stimulus. We looked at seven stimulus variables, and there are numerous others that we didn't have time to cover. In contrast, the individual differences among subjects have been largely ignored by verbal-learning psychologists. They tend to consider the vast area of the differences among people to be merely a source of unwanted variability in their own research and to leave individual differences to personality psychologists. However, as it turns out, personality psychologists have generally not been very interested in verbal learning. Nonetheless, there are some subject variables for which we have a good deal of information.

Age. Age is the subject variable that we know the most about; it would take an entire chapter to summarize adequately the ways in which age influences memory and learning. (For more details, see Chapters 6 and 7 of *Experimental Child Psychology,* Reese & Lipsitt, 1970). In general, however, children are closer to adults in their recognition accuracy than in their recall accuracy. Preschool children who have been shown ten objects may be able to *recognize* all ten objects at a later time. However, they may *recall* only three of the objects.

One of the most important topics in this area concerns children's use of organization in memory. Laurence (1967) was interested in seeing whether children, as well as adults, could use subjective organization. Subjective organization, you'll recall, is the kind of organization that subjects use to help them learn lists of words that are not intentionally related to each other. Laurence chose 16 high-frequency words that were not related to each other and presented them for 16 trials. Her subjects were children 5, 6, 8, and 10 years of age, college students, and older people whose average age was 73. Not surprisingly, the number of words recalled increased steadily with age, reaching a maximum with the college students. Also, the two adult groups showed more subjective organization than did the groups of children. What is perhaps most interesting, however, is that the two adult groups showed a positive correlation between the amount of organization and the amount of recall, but there was no such correlation for the children. In other words, if adults showed a great deal of organization in their recall, they were also likely to recall a large *number* of words. For children, though, the high-organization subjects did not recall any more material than did the low-organization subjects. For children, then, organization is not as important a determinant of recall as it is for adults.

As you can imagine, there are many opportunities for confounding in experiments where age is the independent variable. For example, the samples of elementary school children, college students, and elderly people might differ in terms of social class and intelligence, and they certainly would differ in terms of the number of years of education. It is possible, then, that experimenters might erroneously conclude that age influences memory when the true cause of the difference is a confounding variable.

Some experiments have demonstrated that age is not related to memory when confounding variables have been removed. Hulicka (1965), for example, found that people 60–89 years of age did not differ from people 30–39 years of age in terms of either learning or recall. This lack of a difference may be due to her meticulously careful selection of subjects. Typically, studies of the aged compare healthy, well-educated, young college students with institutionalized, probably unhealthy elderly people. Hulicka, however, selected her younger group of subjects from the medical and surgical wards of a veterans' hospital, so that the comparison group was far more similar to the elderly group than college students would have been. Furthermore, she administered the vocabulary test of the WAIS to her subjects, and both groups received similar scores. Perhaps institutionalization and intelligence have been confounding variables in other studies.

Sex. We also have an abundance of information on the influence of the learners' sex on their performance. However, this variable has not been explored as systematically as the variable of age. The major reason for this is that psychologists seldom design an experiment with sex as the variable that they are most interested in. Most of the time, psychologists run the experiment and, after the subjects have been tested, decide to include the learner's sex as one of the variables in the analysis. If sex does not influence learning, then this finding is frequently not reported. If sex *does* influence learning, then this finding is usually reported. Therefore, an examination of the literature on sex differences in memory may not give an accurate picture of reality.

The most extensive summary of sex differences is an excellent book by Maccoby and Jacklin (1974). They review 21 recent studies on verbal memory and conclude that females have a somewhat better memory for verbal content: 10 studies show that females do better than males, and 11 studies show no difference. However, an examination of studies on memory for objects and digits shows no sex difference: 1 study favors females, 2 studies favor males, and 26 studies show no difference. Thus, males and females seem to be equivalent in terms of memory *capacity.*

Verbal-learning studies, like memory studies, do not show substantial sex differences. In a review of 17 studies of paired-associate learning, Maccoby and Jacklin found that females did better than males in 1 study and that there were no sex differences in the other 16 studies.

We can conclude that sex usually has no effect on verbal learning and on memory for nonverbal objects. Memory for verbal material may be somewhat better for females. However, the tendency to report sex differences and to ignore findings of "no difference" would tend to make any sex differences seem more significant than they are in reality.

Social class. Arthur Jensen is a controversial figure in the area of educational psychology because of his theories on social class, genetics, and intelligence. His theories and research on verbal learning are not so well known, but they are relevant here. Jensen (1969) proposes that intelligence can be classified into two categories: Level I processes represent verbal learning and memory ability, whereas Level II processes represent concept learning and abstract reasoning.

Let us consider Jensen's discussion of Level I processes. A person's Level I processes can be measured by tests of memory span, serial learning, paired-associate learning, and free recall. A series of experiments by Jensen showed that social class had no significant influence on any of these tests. In other words, a child with an average IQ from a poor family would learn a list of paired associates and recall a list of numbers just as well as a child with an average IQ from a middle-class family. Furthermore, Jensen argues that children from different socioeconomic classes not only *start* equal but *stay* equal in their Level I ability.

Intelligence. Earl Hunt and his colleagues have carried out the most extensive research in recent years on the relationship between intelligence and performance on memory and verbal-learning tasks. In particular, they have been concerned with verbal intelligence, as measured by a test of verbal ability given to students in the state of Washington before they enter college. On the basis of scores on this test, they labeled the 25% of students who scored highest as "high verbal" students and the 25% of students who scored lowest as "low verbal" students.

Let's consider some of Hunt's findings (Hunt, Lunneborg, & Lewis, 1975). High-verbal students were significantly better at: (1) searching short-term memory quickly; (2) identifying the order of items in short-term memory; (3) showing release from proactive inhibition—that is, they showed the greatest improvement in recall when the category was shifted; (4) identifying two letters as "same" or "different"; and (5) recalling a greater number of items using the classic Peterson and Peterson (1959) short-term memory technique. Clearly, verbal ability, as measured by a standard intelligence test, is related to learning and memory, as measured in the laboratory.

Mental health. The four subject characteristics we have examined so far—age, sex, social class, and intelligence—have all been concerned with *main effects*. For example, when we focused on sex, we asked whether the sex of the learner influenced the *total* amount that was learned or remembered. In some cases, however, the *interactions* are more interesting than the main effects. We might find, for example, that learner A and learner B recall the same total amount of material, but that learner A recalls certain kinds of words better, whereas learner B recalls other kinds of words better.

When we examine the variable of mental health, comparing normal learners with abnormal learners, the interactions turn out to be very interesting. Let's look at a study by Rychlak, McKee, Schneider, and Abramson (1971). This group of psychologists was interested in examining pleasantness and learning. Recall from the section on stimulus characteristics that pleasant words are generally learned more quickly than unpleasant words. Rychlak and his colleagues wanted to see if this tendency also held true for abnormal subjects.

The subjects in this study were 16 hospitalized schizophrenic patients and 16 normals, who were matched with the patients for sex, age, educational level, social class, and intelligence. All the subjects first rated a large number of three-letter stimuli to indicate how pleasant they thought the stimuli were. Rychlak et al. then constructed pairs of stimuli for each subject—12 pairs of items that the subject had rated pleasant and 12 pairs of items that the subject had rated unpleasant. All subjects learned the lists to a criterion of two consecutive correct trials—in other words, they had to get the entire list correct two times in a row.

Rychlak et al. measured the number of trials that subjects needed to master each list; the results are shown in Figure 8-19. The data analysis showed that normal subjects and schizophrenic subjects did not differ significantly in terms of *total* learning, though normals learned the lists a little faster. The factor that was significant was the interaction of mental health and type of

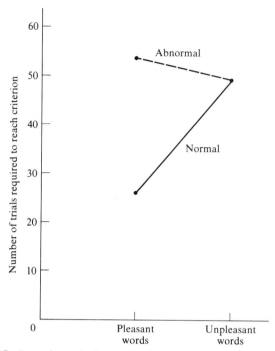

Figure 8-19. Learning of pleasant and unpleasant pairs by normal and abnormal (schizophrenic) subjects. Note that the *y*-axis is trials to criterion, so smaller numbers indicate faster learning. Data from Rychlak, J. F., McKee, D. B., Schneider, W. E., and Abramson, Y. Affective evaluation in the verbal learning styles of normals and abnormals. *Journal of Abnormal Psychology*, 1971, *77*, 247–257.

word. Notice that the normal subjects followed the typical pattern of learning pleasant material faster than unpleasant material; that is, it took them fewer trials to reach criterion for pleasant material. In contrast, the schizophrenic subjects learned unpleasant material, if anything, a little faster than pleasant material.

The discovery of an interaction can be interesting for its own sake, but it also can be interesting in helping us understand some of the factors involved. In this study, for example, it may help us understand why people learn pleasant material more quickly if we know that this tendency does not hold true for abnormal people.

The Atkinson/Shiffrin model illustrated in Figure 8-1 showed material flowing from the sensory register into short-term memory, and then into long-term memory. As we have seen, however, there are a number of factors that influence the likelihood that an item in short-term memory or long-term memory will be recalled. Some of these factors are properties of the stimulus—either permanent properties or temporary properties lasting only the duration of the experiment. Other factors that determine the likelihood of recall are properties of the subject. Still other factors, as we have just seen, depend on a particular combination of stimulus and subject properties.

1. One model of memory involves three kinds of storage systems: the sensory registers, short-term memory, and long-term memory.

2. Information is kept very briefly in the sensory registers, which include the iconic (visual) store and the echoic (auditory) store.

3. Short-term memory is limited in capacity, and a large portion of the information is forgotten. Theorists disagree as to whether decay or interference causes forgetting of information that is to be stored for a short time.

4. There are three classic tasks in verbal learning—free recall, serial learning, and paired-associate learning—and three ways of measuring retention—recall, recognition, and relearning.

5. Studies on long-term memory have demonstrated that people can be surprisingly inaccurate in their recall of details in long-term memory. Forgetting in long-term memory is caused by proactive and retroactive inhibition.

6. There is a theoretical debate as to whether short-term memory and long-term memory are really separate processes or whether there is really only one kind of memory. Despite numerous studies concerning the effects of interference, repetition, acoustic/semantic encoding, and the serial-position effect, we cannot draw firm conclusions on this issue.

7. People store items in memory in terms of their attributes. They have a feeling-of-knowing about whether their answers are correct, and they can identify information for words that are on the tip-of-the-tongue. They can also identify other characteristics of items in memory, such as location in space.

8. Similar items cluster together in memory and appear next to each other in free recall.

9. People seem to remember about seven chunks—whether words, phrases, or letters—in short-term memory.

10. Mediation and other mnemonic tricks can improve recall accuracy.

11. Several characteristics of verbal material influence recall, including frequency, meaningfulness, pleasantness, and imagery. Unfortunately, these variables are correlated with each other, thus presenting problems in designing unconfounded experiments.

12. Other factors that determine how well an item will be recalled are its serial position, whether it was learned by massed or distributed learning, and whether the item was distinctive.

13. Recall is also influenced by subject characteristics, including age, sex, social class, and intelligence. Sometimes, subject characteristics interact with stimulus characteristics. For example, normal subjects learn pleasant material faster than unpleasant material, whereas schizophrenics learn unpleasant material a little faster than pleasant material.

9

Psycholinguistics

Psycholinguistics, or the psychology of language, is an area of research that began to blossom in the 1960s. Previously, language behavior was assigned to an obscure corner of social psychology, and the few psychology studies dealing with language typically limited their scope to the observation of naturally occurring language.

In contrast, psycholinguists today study topics as diverse as language in the chimpanzee, the nature of meaning, and children's understanding of language. We will limit our exploration of language to three topics: language acquisition, memory for sentences, and the Whorfian hypothesis that language influences thought. For information on other topics, I recommend an excellent book by Herbert Clark and Eve Clark (1977) called *Psychology and Language: An Introduction to Psycholinguistics*.

Each of these three topics will be discussed in terms of a different methodological issue. We will look at language acquisition in terms of the various research strategies—naturalistic observation, survey, case study, correlational, and experimental. Memory for sentences will be approached in terms of the search for a model to describe how sentences are stored in memory. The Whorfian hypothesis will be explored as an example of testing a theory.

LANGUAGE ACQUISITION

The acquisition of language is probably the most amazing human accomplishment. Within the first few years of life, children learn thousands of words. Perhaps more impressive, they learn how to combine those words into phrases and sentences that they have never heard before. Furthermore, this activity seems to be relatively effortless. Children acquire language by living with other language-speakers, and they do not have to be carefully instructed or endlessly drilled. Finally, language acquisition is universal: at this very moment, children in every country of the world are rapidly learning and mastering this new skill.

The topic of language acquisition is an enormous one, and an overview of this area could take many different forms. We will approach language acquisition in terms of research strategies, in order to provide more exposure to the techniques that were outlined in Chapter 1. We'll begin with naturalistic observation and the survey method—two research strategies that were widely used in the early history of psycholinguistics. Then we'll look at the case-study method; this method frequently provides helpful information that cannot be obtained from the other methods. Finally, we'll examine the correlational method, which can tell us what factors are related to language, and the experimental method, which provides insights into more subtle, unobservable forms of language behavior.

Naturalistic Observation

Naturalistic observation is the careful observation of behavior in a naturalistic setting. The observer tries not to influence or change the person's normal activities. The aim of naturalistic observation is description rather than causal explanations.

The naturalistic-observation method has been particularly useful in studying the acquisition of language because psychologists have been anxious to *describe* the language spoken by children. It certainly is not the same as adult language, of course, but it must have its own rules and structure. Samples of language spoken in everyday settings are enormously useful for identifying patterns in children's language. This method, therefore, helps us understand *what* they speak, even if it cannot typically clarify *why* they speak.

The early literature on child language contains many examples of naturalistic observation. A representative article is one by Haggerty (1930) called "What a Two-and-one-half-year-old Child Said in One Day." The author simply reports everything that her daughter Helen said from 7:05 A.M. to 7:30 P.M., on April 24, 1930. Here is a short section:

> Where's milk? Milk? (Her father asks if it is too hot.) 'Tis. That milk pretty near burned my hands to pieces. Papa is cooling it. Papa is. I'm looking in the tin. Is there cold water in here? Is there cold water in here? Is there cold water in here? Carrie! Tell me, are you going to scald the dishes? Tell me, Carrie. I'm going to get my bib. I'm looking for my bib. I don't know where it is. I'll have to get one in here (sideboard). Here, this'll do. That's a bib. That will do. Helen just wants to have a little belt. Helen just wants to have a little belt. Helen just wants to have a little belt. Grandma tied the bib on [p. 77].

Even this short segment is sufficient to give us a sense of the language of a 2½-year-old child. It is also sufficient to suggest many hypotheses that could be tested using the experimental method. For example, a researcher might be intrigued with the amount of repetition in this passage and might try to determine what independent variables affect repetition. Is repetition more frequent when the language accompanies an ongoing activity? Is it more frequent when the child's name is part of the sentence? Under what circumstances do children repeat sentences exactly, rather than leaving words out in subsequent repetitions? As we discussed in Chapters 1 and 2, naturalistic observation is a rich source of hypotheses.

The 1960s featured several extensive naturalistic-observation studies of children's language. Researchers became interested not only in transcribing the language but in trying to identify patterns. One project was conducted by Braine (1963), who followed three 18-month-old children as they began to combine words into phrases. For two of the children, parents recorded any spontaneous, comprehensible language, using conventional English spelling rather than attempting to capture the children's pronunciations. For the third child, a tape recording supplemented the written material.

Braine was particularly interested in children's combinations of two words or more. A large number of them seemed to have the same underlying pattern, for example:

all broke	*no bed*	*other bib*
all buttoned	*no more*	*other milk*
all clean	*no pee*	*other side*
all fix	*no fix*	*other bread*

Braine proposed, on the basis of these observations, that there are two kinds of words in children's vocabularies. A small group of words appear only in the first position—for example, *all, other, see,* and *bye-bye*. Braine called these **pivot words.** In contrast, many words can occupy the second position in a phrase. Subsequent psycholinguists have referred to these as **open words.** In the next decade, psycholinguists became disenchanted with "pivot grammar." Nonetheless, Braine is admired for his innovations in abandoning traditional, adult-centered grammatical categories, such as nouns and adjectives, and adopting child-centered grammatical categories based on the language he observed.

The work of Bloom (1970) was most destructive to the theory of pivot grammar. Bloom's technique involved more than recording the spoken language; the psychologist also recorded the context in which the words were spoken. Bloom studied three children, visiting them at 6-week intervals. She obtained samples of language while they played with toys, ate, dressed, and played with a peer.

Bloom found relatively few two-word utterances of the open-word-plus-pivot-word structure that Braine had found so common. Furthermore, when she examined the context in which the utterances appeared, it seemed clear that the child might mean very different things by two phrases that looked structurally similar or identical. For example, one child used the phrase "Mommy sock" in two separate contexts. In one case, the child was picking up her mother's sock; in the other case, the mother was putting the child's sock on the child. The child was apparently describing two different kinds of relationships; simply to record those statements as identical in their surface appearances would be to underestimate the ability of the child. Bloom concluded that pivot-grammar theories were inadequate in describing children's language.

Roger Brown, at Harvard University, is one of the best-known psycholinguists using the naturalistic-observation technique. In one of his earlier studies (Brown & Fraser, 1963), Brown observed that children use a systematically shortened form of adult grammar. He examined the speech records of 13 children between 2 and 3 years of age and coined the phrase **telegraphic speech** to describe his findings. Brown (1973) explained what he meant by *telegraphic:*

> Words in a telegram cost money, and so that is reason to be brief, to say nothing not essential. If the full message were: ''My car has broken down and I have lost my wallet; send money to me at the American Express in Paris'' the telegram would be: ''Car broken down; wallet lost; send money American Express Paris'' [p. 74].

Children, says Brown, operate similarly. **Contentive** words—those that refer to persons, objects, actions, or qualities—are included in children's speech. In contrast, **functors** are more important for grammar than for meaning; these are the inflections, articles, prepositions, conjunctions, and auxiliary verbs such as *is*. Functors are typically omitted in children's speech. Thus, a child might say ''That horsie'' as a telegraphic form of the complete sentence ''That is a horsie.'' Brown and Fraser's observations, using the naturalistic-observation method, inspired another study using the experimental method; we will examine the results of that experiment later.

Brown and his colleagues transcribed the spontaneous speech of three children, observing them from 2 to 6 hours each month as they interacted naturally with their mothers. Each of the children was observed periodically for 8 to 21 months.

The data from these children have been used to examine several questions about language acquisition. For example, Cazden (1968) studied noun and verb inflections such as *-'s, -es,* and *-ed*. Specifically, she calculated what percent of the time the children used each inflection. She found that they mastered plurals before possessives (for example, *girls* before *girl's*) and present progressives before past tenses *(are playing* before *played).*

In another article, Brown (1968) reported on the development of *Wh* questions in the speech of Adam, Eve, and Sarah. (*Wh* questions are those that use *who, what, where, when, why,* and *how.*) Brown found that the most frequently used *Wh* question in early language was ''What dat?'' As the children grew older, they learned to make up more sophisticated questions, but the word order was quite different from the order of standard adult order. Here are some examples:

What John will read?
What that is?
What John will do?

This intermediate stage is interesting because adults never use this kind of word order. Clearly, children do not learn this form merely by imitating their parents. In the last stage, children learn that they must switch the positions of the subject and the verb.

The availability of videotaping equipment in recent years has made it possible to keep excellent records of naturalistic observation, from which researchers can note details such as the context of conversations. In addition, complex conversations can be videotaped and analyzed leisurely at a later time. Wellman and Lempers (1977), for example, recorded the conversations of 2-year-olds in a toddler play group. They found that an average of 80% of the children's remarks were addressed to adults rather than to peers. Perhaps the most interesting finding in the study was that the 2-year-olds were surprisingly good communicators. When the child said something and the listener did not respond, the child repeated the statement 54% of the time. In contrast, when the child said something and the listener responded appropriately, the child repeated the statement only 3% of the time. Furthermore, when the child said something and the listener indicated that he or she had not understood the statement, the child repeated the statement 100% of the time. In summary, children respond appropriately to their listeners.

The Survey Method

The survey method was extremely popular among child psychologists in the first half of the century; this method is used less often today. The relevant literature has been summarized by McCarthy (1954, 1971); here we will discuss only two of the best-known surveys. Strangely, they were conducted by two different people named M. Smith.

M.E. Smith (1926) examined vocabulary comprehension in 273 children ranging in age from 8 months to 6 years, using word samples from Thorndike's 10,000-word list. She found the following estimates: 1 year, 3 words; 2 years, 272 words; 3 years, 896 words; 4 years, 1540 words; 5 years, 2072 words; 6 years, 2562 words. Some psychologists have referred to this dramatic increase in vocabulary as the "language explosion," and the name seems appropriate.

M.K. Smith (1941) surveyed vocabulary size in elementary and high school children, using Seashore and Eckerson's English Recognition Vocabulary Test. This test includes a representative sample of English words; from the raw score, one estimates the total size of the vocabulary. Smith tested a total of 867 pupils from first through 12th grades.

The children were first given the opportunity to define the word in their own terms or to illustrate its proper use in a sentence. If they did not know the word, they were allowed to select the correct meaning from four possible choices. Her results indicate that children in the first grade knew an average of 16,900 words, with a range from 5,500 to 32,800, while 12th-graders knew an average of 47,300 words, with a range from 28,200 to 73,200. McCarthy (1971) and others are astounded at these high estimates and doubt their validity. (Note, for example, that children might have received credit for just guessing, because of the multiple-choice format.) Nonetheless, these figures prompted educators and laypersons to change their ideas about the size of children's vocabularies. Previously, they had estimated informally that children entering school had mastered only 300–400 words. After Smith's study, they conceded that children had probably mastered several thousand words.

The case-study method involves an in-depth study of one person, typically someone with unusual characteristics. Most often, this technique includes information about the person's past history as well as test results.

One of the best-known case studies in psycholinguistics is one reported by Lenneberg (1962). Before we discuss this case study, it is worth quoting Lenneberg on the ethical advantages of the case-study method:

> Our understanding of human behavior is often greatly enlightened by careful investigations of clinical aberrations and in many instances disease or congenital abnormalities provide conditions that may replace the crucial experiments on children that our superego forbids us to plan and perform [p. 419].

Quite clearly, no one would consider producing these abnormalities in children; however, the abnormalities may be observed as they occur naturally.

Lenneberg describes an 8-year-old boy who lacked the motor speech skills necessary to produce language. Nonetheless, the boy was able to understand language. Lenneberg's case report includes a medical history that describes the mother's health during pregnancy, the labor and delivery, and the physical abnormalities at birth. Lenneberg also provides a family history, a report on a physical examination, and the results of standardized intelligence tests. He also includes data on the child's understanding of English. This was assessed by means of commands such as "Take the block and put it on the bottle" and questions such as "Is it time to eat breakfast now?" The child's responses were quite appropriate on this task.

Lenneberg concludes that it is possible to understand language even without prior experience in making sounds. Lenneberg argues that these results contradict theories that claim that language develops by babbling, hearing oneself babbling, and imitating that babbling.

One of the strangest case histories in the recent psycholinguistics literature is that of Genie (Fromkin, Krashen, Curtiss, Rigler, & Rigler, 1974). Genie spent the first 13 years and 9 months of her life in extreme social isolation. (You may be familiar with the cases of other socially isolated children, such as the *Wild Boy of Aveyron,* recently portrayed in Truffaut's film *The Wild Child,* and Kasper Hauser, in Herzog's film *Every Man for Himself and God Against All.*)

Genie had been taken into protective custody by the police and was admitted to the hospital for diagnosis. She suffered from malnutrition and looked about 6 years younger than her age; she could not chew and could not stand. After extensive inquiry, it was determined that she had been isolated in a small closed room, tied into a potty chair. Her father physically punished her for any sounds. No one was allowed to speak to her or spend more than a few moments with her. Investigation of the hospital records established that her birth was relatively normal; however, she had worn a brace for the first year of her life in order to treat hip dislocation. Genie's father believed that this device had caused her "retardation," which he regarded as so severe that he expected her to die at a young age.

As a consultant wrote when Genie was admitted to the hospital, "Genie may be regarded as one of the most extreme and prolonged cases of such deprivation to come to light in this century, and as such she is an 'experiment in nature'" (p. 86). The case study of Genie makes it feasible to answer a question which could not be ethically answered using the experimental method: is it possible to acquire language if a person reaches adolescence without exposure to language? Lenneberg (1967) had proposed that there is a critical period for language, lasting from age 2 to puberty. After puberty, he had argued, the brain is not so "plastic": cerebral dominance has developed completely, and language can no longer be learned.

Genie, however, had reached adolescence without any language development. Would she learn to speak? Fromkin et al. trace her first two years in "civilization." Eleven months after she was discovered, she was able to understand and produce a large number of individual words. However, she had physical difficulties in speaking, which the authors attribute to the fact that she had previously been punished for making noises. The authors also note that Genie's vocabulary size was relatively large; normal children whose sentence-complexity levels were equal to Genie's would typically have had much smaller vocabularies. In general, then, Genie developed an extensive vocabulary in her first two years of exposure to language, but her progress in the combination of words into more complex phrases and sentences was slower than normal. Nonetheless, the implications of Genie for Lenneberg's (1967) theory seem clear: language development *is* possible after puberty.

These two case histories illustrate the value of the case-history technique in contributing to our knowledge of psycholinguistics. For ethical reasons, neither issue could have been tested using the experimental method. However, in each case, a single subject was sufficient to provide important information about the development of language.

The Correlational Method

In the correlational method, psychologists try to determine whether two measures are related to each other. The correlational method seems to be used less in psycholinguistics research than in some other areas of experimental psychology, such as motivation.

The largest number of correlational studies in psycholinguistics concern the relationship between parents' speech and infants' speech. For example, Newport, Gleitman, & Gleitman (1977) studied children between the ages of 12 and 27 months. They calculated several measures of mother and infant speech and found several strong correlations between the two. One measure of mother speech was the number of times the mother identified an object, such as "There is a ball" or "That's your nose." This measure was positively correlated with the size of the child's vocabulary. Another measure of mother speech was the number of times the mother imitated and expanded what the child had just said, as by repeating the child's sentence "That truck" and expanding it into the sentence "That is a truck." This measure of mother speech was also positively correlated with the size of the child's vocabulary. A third measure of mother speech was the number of times the mother repeated what she had just said previously. This measure was *negatively* correlated with the size of the child's vocabulary: mothers who repeated themselves frequently had children with small vocabularies.

Newport et al. point out, very appropriately, that it is difficult to establish which is the cause and which is the effect in these correlations. For example, the mother's speech could influence her child's speech: the more she repeats herself, the fewer new vocabulary words the child learns. On the other hand, the child's speech could influence the mother's speech: the lower the child's vocabulary skills, the more the mother repeats herself in order to be understood. (It is also possible that a third factor caused the correlation, because of its relationship to both mother's and child's speech; can you think of one?) This study provides an excellent example of the principle we discussed in Chapter 1: with a correlation, psychologists can only conclude that two variables are related; they cannot determine which variable is the cause and which is the effect.

A study by Elardo, Bradley, and Caldwell (1977) showed that the home environment, as well as personal attributes of the mother, is related to language ability. These psychologists administered a standardized language test called the Illinois Test of Psycholinguistic Abilities (ITPA) to 74 3-year-olds. Then they rated the family and the home environment on an instrument called the Home Observation for Measurement of the Environment (known by the appropriate acronym, HOME). Overall language ability was significantly correlated with three of the scales on the HOME test: maternal involvement with the child, emotional and verbal responsivity of the mother, and availability of appropriate play material.

Let's leave the area of correlations between mothers' and infants' speech and consider one other example of the correlational method in the study of language acquisition. Carroll and White (1973) were interested in the speed with which adult subjects named various pictured objects (for example, *airplane, clothespin, saxophone*). Specifically, they wondered what kind of variables were most closely related to naming speed. The variables they studied were two estimates of the word's frequency (Kučera-Francis and Thorndike-Lorge, both described in Chapter 8) and two estimates of the age at which the word was learned (one estimate was obtained from published norms and the second from subjects' judgments).

Carroll and White then performed a multiple regression analysis. (Remember from Chapter 1? This is the kind of analysis where several independent variables are related to one dependent variable.) Word frequency turned out not to be related to picture-naming speed. However, both measures of age-of-learning were significantly related. In other words, the younger the age at which a particular word was learned, the more rapidly the word was named when the appropriate picture was exposed. Carroll and White speculate that earlier-learned words are more accessible for retrieval than later-learned words. They even suggest that words learned early in life are stored deeper in the cortex; these words can be named quickly because they are near a central processing element responsible for naming the pictures.

The essential "trademark" of the experimental method is the systematic manipulation of the independent variable. In recent years, the experimental method has become increasingly popular as a tool for studying language acquisition. Consequently, it is particularly difficult to confine a discussion of the experimental method to a small handful of studies.

Let's look at four topics for which the experimental method seems to be the only adequate tool for investigation. (1) The experimental method is useful in confirming suspicions that have been raised in naturalistic-observation studies. (2) It is also the most appropriate method for testing the success of efforts to produce change in children's speech. Finally, it is particularly helpful in assessing covert processes, such as (3) speech perception in young infants, and (4) children's understanding of meaning and grammar. As we noted earlier, the naturalistic-observation method provides many insights about what children *say*—an overt activity—but is less successful in providing insights about what children *think* or *know* about language. To gain these insights, the experimental method is the best tool.

Confirming suspicions from naturalistic observation. Recall the study by Brown and Fraser (1963) on telegraphic speech, in which they found through naturalistic observation that children tended to leave out certain kinds of words. Brown and Fraser (1963) pursued that observation further, using the experimental method. They asked six of the children from the naturalistic-observation study to repeat sentences said by adults. They selected 13 simple sentences of various grammatical types and asked children to repeat each one. The results for the sentence *Do I like to read books?* were two correct imitations plus the following four responses:

To read book?
I read books?
I read books?
I—read book [p. 190]?

Brown and Fraser found that the children almost always repeated the nouns, adjectives, and main verbs; performance for these important words averaged better than 90%. In contrast, they were much less likely to repeat articles (such as *a* and *the*) or auxiliary verbs (such as *shall, am,* and *does);* performance for these kinds of words averaged less than 50%. Brown and Fraser also found that repetition accuracy depended on the position of the word in the initial sentence. Children were most accurate for words that occurred in the final position; notice, for example, the children's relatively accurate repetition of "read books." They were next most accurate for words that occurred in the beginning position, and they were least accurate for words in the middle.

The experimental method allowed Brown and Fraser to draw stronger conclusions about the nature of telegraphic speech than would have been possible with the naturalistic-observation method. They could control the number of contentive and functor words, and they could obtain many children's responses to the same sentences. Consequently, we can be quite confident that telegraphic speech is a characteristic of children's speech.

Producing change. A study by Cazden (1965) is a good example of how the experimental method can be used to produce change. The correlational method provides strong hints: for example, we might conclude from one study that a change in the mother's language *is related to* a change in the child's language. However, systematic manipulation of the independent variable is necessary in order to conclude that an adult's language *causes* the change in the child's language.

Cazden selected 12 Black children, all under 3½ years of age, who were attending a day-care center. She carefully matched four trios of children on the basis of the children's age and initial level of language development. One member of each trio of children was assigned to each of the three conditions: expansion, modeling, or control. The expansion-condition subjects received intensive expansion treatment for 40 minutes each day; for example, if the child said "That horsie," the adult would respond with "Yes, that is a horsie." The modeling-condition subjects received 40 minutes each day of well-formed adult sentences that were not expansions. The control-condition subjects did not receive treatment, but they were exposed to the treatment rooms in order to establish familiarity with the materials.

The children's speech was tape-recorded over a 3-month period and was transcribed by someone who was blind as to the children's experimental conditions. The speech was coded for six different measures of language development, including mean length of utterance, verb complexity, and ability to repeat sentences. The results showed that the expansion treatment did not substantially improve the children's grammar in comparison to the control condition. However, children in the modeling condition showed significant improvement.

Brown (1973) suggests several reasons for these findings. He points out that the 40-minute period of concentrated expansion is an artificial version of the expansion that parents use in a much more natural and leisurely fashion in everyday life. The children may stop paying attention when they find that every sentence they utter will be repeated and expanded. Furthermore, the adults may misconstrue the meaning of the child's fragment and expand it into an inappropriate longer sentence. The more natural conversation of the modeling condition, by avoiding these two dangers, proved more successful in producing improved speech.

Notice that Cazden's use of the experimental method allowed her to draw conclusions about the cause-and-effect relationship between adult language and child language—conclusions that could not have been reached with the correlational method. By appropriate controls and manipulations, she could conclude that the adult language did indeed change the child language. The child language could not have changed the adult language, and the relationship between the two languages could not have been caused by a third, irrelevant factor such as age, initial ability, or race.

Speech perception in young infants. Can infants distinguish among the sounds that adults make? As you can imagine, this is a particularly tricky question to answer; it is a question comparable to many we asked in the chapter on perception (Chapter 7). Infants may well be able to tell the difference among adult sounds, but psychologists will underestimate their abilities unless they select appropriate response measures. Let's discuss three studies that used three different techniques to measure infants' abilities.

Moffitt (1971) selected three groups of 5-month-old infants and used change in heart rate to measure speech perception. One group of subjects heard the syllable *bah* during familiarization sessions and then heard *gah* on a test trial. Another group received just the opposite—*gah* during familiarization sessions and *bah* on the test trial. The control group heard *bah* at all times. Moffitt noted that previous research had established that when infants of this age hear a new noise, their heart rate slows down. However, as the same noise is repeated, habituation may occur, in which case the heart rate does not slow down. Moffitt reasoned that if infants could indeed discriminate between *gah* and *bah,* they would show habituation if the same stimulus were repeated many times, but they would show recovery if the experimenter suddenly switched to the different stimulus.

That is precisely what Moffitt found. Infants in the first group, for example, showed a slowing in heart rate when they first heard *bah*. Gradually, however, habituation took place, and the heart rate slowed less every time *bah* was repeated. After 60 repetitions of *bah,* Moffitt presented the syllable *gah*. Suddenly, the heart rate slowed down again. This recovery indicated that the infant regarded *gah* as a new noise. In Moffitt's study, then, infants as young as 5 months of age demonstrated by their heartbeats that they could distinguish between two similar-sounding syllables.

Eimas, Siqueland, Jusczyk, and Vigorito (1971) also used habituation, but their infants showed discrimination by sucking. Nipples were placed in the mouths of 1- to 4-month-old infants, but no liquid was delivered; this technique is called *nonnutritive sucking*. The experimenters presented a sound, and the infant was required to suck at least two times a second in order to keep the sound going. Typically, babies begin to suck hard in order to keep the sound on, but they stop sucking so hard during habituation; presumably the sound is now "boring," and it's not worth the effort.

Eimas et al. presented a variety of speech sounds using the nonnutritive-sucking technique. The stimuli that they used were synthetic speech sounds that resembled *bah* and *pah*. On some trials, the experimenters tested *bah* versus *pah*—two different-sounding consonants. On other trials, the experimenters tested two consonants that sounded more similar. (These sounds cannot be represented by any English letters, but try to pronounce to yourself two consonants that would fall somewhere in between *bah* and *pah*.) The experimenters might present *bah* for 5 minutes; then they would shift to *pah*. If the infant showed habituation during the initial 5 minutes, but showed increased sucking when the *pah* sounds began, then clearly the infant could discriminate between the sounds.

Figure 9-1 shows the results. As you can see, the infants who were shifted to the different sound showed a significant recovery in sucking rate. The infants who were shifted to a similar sound showed slight recovery. In contrast, the control subjects, who were not shifted, showed no recovery; they continued to show habituation.

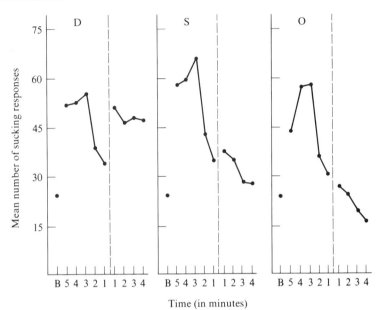

Figure 9-1. Sucking rates for infants who were shifted to a different sound (D), shifted to a similar sound (S), and not shifted at all (O). From "Speech Perception in Infants," by P. D. Eimas, R. Jusczyk, E. R. Siqueland, and J. Vigorito, *Science,* 1971, *171*, 303–306. Copyright 1971 by the American Society for the Advancement of Science. Reprinted by permission.

One of the most fascinating studies in psycholinguistics tested speech perception in even younger infants. This was a study by Condon and Sander (1974) on the relationship between adult speech and the movement patterns of newborns. This study involves a concept called **synchrony**—literally, "moving together." You may not be aware of it, but there is a synchrony between what you say and your body movements as you speak. For example, as you speak the first word in a sentence, your head may rotate slightly and then stop, your right elbow may move slightly to the side and reverse directions at the end of the word, and similar minute movements may occur in your eyes, wrist, and fingers. Thus, people do a small dance—so rapidly and so minutely that they are typically not aware of it—whenever they speak. This **self-synchrony** in adult speech had been established in prior research. Prior research had also established that adult *listeners* do a similar dance in rhythm to the speech they are hearing; this has been called **interactional synchrony.**

Condon and Sander demonstrated that even newborn babies perform this interactional-synchrony dance! They obtained a sample of 16 babies, all younger than 2 weeks of age. Then they took movies of the infants' movements in response to the speech of an adult male, speaking from a location the infant could not see (thus ruling out eye contact). The camera recorded material at the rate of 30 frames per second, and when the movie was matched with the corresponding sound track of the adult's speech, the authors could examine the record one frame at a time.

Condon and Sander describe the dance that the infant performs during the *k* sound of the word *come* in the adult's sentence *Come over and see who's over here*.

> The infant's head moves right very slightly . . . the left elbow extends slightly . . . the right shoulder rotates outward slightly . . . the right hip rotates outward fast . . . the left hip extends slightly . . . and the big toe of the left foot adducts. . . . These body parts sustain these directions and speeds of movement together for these two-thirtieths of a second [p. 460].

Condon and Sander measured the number of times that the body movement changed but the speech sound did not; there were 21 such discrepancies for the dance of one child, for example. Then they matched the same sound track of the adult's speech with a different movie of the child, taken when there was no talking. With this control sample of behavior, we would expect to find many more discrepancies if there is any truth to the interactional-synchrony idea. In fact, Condon and Sander found 119 discrepancies in the control sample—far more than were found in the matched sample. These results suggest that infants have speech-perception abilities within days after they are born!

The structure of this experiment is complex; let's pause for a moment to see why this study can be classified as using the experimental method. Suppose that Condon and Sander had simply seen whether adult speech and infant body movements were related: this would have been a correlational study. With only those data, we would have felt a bit uneasy about concluding that adult speech and infant body movements were clearly related. After all, maybe we could expect to find only 21 discrepancies between speech and body movement just by chance. However, Condon and Sander also analyzed a control sample of infant body movement, obtained when there was no talking, and found 119 discrepancies in that condition. In other words, the speech condition produced 21 discrepancies, whereas the control condition produced 119 discrepancies. The two numbers are different enough (as a statistical analysis would show) that we can be confident that the infants are moving in rhythm to adult speech.

In summary, experimental studies on speech perception have determined that young infants can perceive elements of speech. Through their heartbeats, their sucking, and their body movements, infants have indicated that they can differentiate between sounds and that they can discriminate the boundaries between different sounds.

Children's understanding of meaning and grammar. Numerous studies have used the experimental method to explore what children know about meaning and grammar. For example, E.V. Clark (1971) wrote a paper "On the

Acquisition of the Meaning of *Before* and *After*.'' She asked 3- to 5-year-old children to listen to sentences using the words *before* and *after,* such as ''The boy kicked the rock after he patted the dog.'' Then the children were instructed to demonstrate the action of the sentence, using a number of toys.

Clark found that children were much more accurate in demonstrating the action of sentences using the word *before* than the word *after.* Furthermore, they were more accurate when the order of the phrases duplicated the time order (for example, ''The boy kicked the rock before he patted the dog'') than when the order of the phrases reversed the time order (''Before the boy patted the dog, he kicked the rock''). Specifically, they made errors only 8% of the time when phrase order was the same as time order, but they made errors 58% of the time when the order of the phrases reversed the time order.

Starr (1974) wanted to determine what 2-year-old children know about grammar. One way to pursue this question is to listen to their language. However, Starr believed that children's production of language is less advanced than their knowledge of language. ''The central problem, of course, is the difficulty of testing two-year-olds. They cannot, or will not, tell you what they know'' (p. 381). Earlier researchers had used comprehension as an index of knowledge, but Starr felt that comprehension still underestimates children's knowledge, because comprehension involves other processes such as memory.

Starr therefore chose a unique response measure: children's listening preferences. If children show definite listening preferences for either grammatical or ungrammatical sentences, then they must be able to discriminate. Note that this logic is similar to Fantz's (1961), as described in the perception chapter: if infants look at one form more than another, then they must be able to discriminate between them.

Starr recorded a number of grammatical sentences, such as *The baby wants some of the juice,* on one tape. On another tape, she recorded ungrammatical versions of the same sentences, such as *The baby some of the juice wants*. These tapes were placed in the experimental apparatus containing two tape recorders, two timers, and two levers. By pressing on one lever, the child could play one of the tapes, and the timer would record the total amount of time the tape was played. Starr brought the machine to the children's homes and demonstrated how it worked. She instructed the mothers to ignore it completely, and she left the machine with the children for 3 hours on each of 3 days. Children in the experimental group had grammatical sentences on one tape and ungrammatical sentences on the other tape; children in the control group had grammatical sentences on both tapes.

What were the results? Children in the control group did not show a strong preference for one tape or the other, just as we would have expected. However, the children in the experimental group showed preferences, indicating that they *could* discriminate between the grammatical and the ungrammatical sentences.

Both of these studies illustrate clever uses of the experimental method. Children seem to know a lot about meaning and grammar, but we cannot appreciate how much they know simply by listening to their speech. Instead, we must devise clever ways for children to tell us about their knowledge.

In the last chapter, we talked about memory for isolated words, and we discussed both models of memory and factors that influence accuracy in memory. We also examined memory for groups of words that were related in meaning—a topic that borders on psycholinguistics. Now we turn to the topic of memory for sentences. This question is significantly more complicated: not only must we consider the individual words, but we must consider the grammatical structures and the ideas that bind the words together into sentences. We'll talk about four topics in this section: (1) deep structure in memory, (2) memory for syntax, (3) memory as a constructive process, and (4) memory for stories.

The topic of memory for sentences has generated a great deal of excitement among psychologists as they search for a model to describe how people remember material in sentence form. In the late 1950s and 1960s, psycholinguistics developed and tested a model that proposed that people transform a sentence into its "deep structure": the complexity of the deep structure presumably determines recall accuracy. In the 1970s, a different model has gained support. According to this "constructive" model, syntax and isolated sentences are not stored in memory; instead, people fuse several sentences together into an idea. The whole, rather than the parts, is stored in memory. Finally, the search continues for rules to describe how people remember stories—long groups of related sentences.

Deep Structure in Memory

People generally think of a sentence as an orderly sequence of words, typically lined up in a row on a piece of paper. Chomsky (1957) caused great excitement among psycholinguists by proposing that there is more to a sentence than meets the eye. Specifically, he devised a model that distinguishes between the **surface structure** and the **deep structure** of a sentence. Surface structure is represented by the row of words—the words that are actually spoken or written; the deep structure is the underlying, more abstract meaning of the sentence. Let's look at deep structure in some detail.

Chomsky pointed out that two sentences may have very different surface structures but very similar deep structures. Consider the two sentences:

Sara threw the ball.
The ball was thrown by Sara.

Notice how different the surface structures are: none of the words is in the same position in the two sentences, and three of the words in the second sentence do not appear in the first sentence. However, "deep down," you and I both feel that the sentences have identical meanings.

Chomsky also pointed out that two sentences may have very similar surface structures but very different deep structures, as in these two sentences:

John is easy to please.
John is eager to please.

These sentences *look* almost identical. Both have the same form: noun, verb, adjective, infinitive-form verb. In fact, there is only one word that differs for the two sentences. However, consider how different the deep structures are. We could paraphrase the first sentence:

It is easy to please John.

However, the same kind of paraphrase produces nonsense for the second sentence:

It is eager to please John.

Sometimes, two sentences can have *identical* surface structures but very different deep structures; these are called "ambiguous sentences." Psycholinguists seem particularly amused by these ambiguous sentences, such as the following:

The shooting of the hunters was terrible.
They are cooking apples.
The lamb is too hot to eat.

In each of these cases, the sentence has two possible interpretations. For example, a lamb in a sunny meadow may be too warm to wish to eat. On the other hand, a lamb roast right out of an oven might burn your tongue. One of the best ambiguous sentences I have found was an entry in a *New York* magazine competition many years ago:

Mrs. Nixon found drunk on White House lawn.

In summary, we must consider the deep structure of a sentence as well as its surface structure if we really want to understand what a sentence means.

Psychologists set out to test Chomsky's model. George Miller (of 7 ± 2 fame from Chapter 8) was particularly intrigued with the idea that people understand sentences by transforming the surface structure into a basic deep-structure, or **kernel,** form. To remember a sentence, Miller (1962) reasoned, people store the kernel plus a list of transformations that would be necessary to reproduce the original sentence. More specifically, Miller proposed that people could store these kinds of transformations: active (A), passive (P), negative (N), and question (Q). Consider, for example, the sentences listed in Table 9-1, each of which represents a different kind of transformation of the same deep structure. Miller proposed that people would have more difficulty with sentences that required a greater number of transformations—thereby reworking Chomsky's model into a testable hypothesis.

Mehler (1963) tested this proposal in an experiment. He made up eight kernel sentences, such as *The biologist has made the discovery.* Then he

Table 9-1. Examples of transformations of the same deep structure.

Kind of Transformation	Sentence
A	The biologist has made the discovery.
P	The discovery has been made by the biologist.
N	The biologist has not made the discovery.
Q	Has the biologist made the discovery?
PN	The discovery has not been made by the biologist.
PQ	Has the discovery been made by the biologist?
QN	Hasn't the biologist made the discovery?
PQN	Hasn't the discovery been made by the biologist?

derived seven transformations for each kernel sentence, like those listed in Table 9-1. Subjects listened to various sentences and tried to recall them verbatim. Mehler found that the kernel sentences were the easiest to learn. There was no clear tendency, however, for the P, N, and Q sentences to be easier than the PN, PQ, or QN sentences, nor for the PQN sentences to be most difficult.

Mehler also discovered some interesting information about the recall of the complex sentences. He found that people tended to simplify their form during recall. For example, the PQN sentence

Hasn't the discovery been made by the biologist?

was frequently recalled as being PQ,

Has the discovery been made by the biologist?

or QN,

Hasn't the biologist made the discovery?

In other words, it seems that transformational tags (the N tag in one case and the P tag in the other case) are frequently lost when sentences are stored in memory.

Savin and Perchonock (1965) were also interested in comparing kernel sentences with their transformations. In particular, they wanted to determine how much space the alternate forms of sentences occupied in memory. Now think about how this space might be measured. How nice it would be to hop inside a subject's head, take out your ruler, and measure whether a PQN sentence is taking up more room than an A sentence! Savin and Perchonock didn't manage to do that, but they did devise a clever way to measure memory space. My seventh-grade home-economics teacher taught me that you could measure how much butter was in a lump by seeing how much cold water it displaced in a measuring cup. (Legend has it that Archimedes shouted "Eureka!" from the bathtub on discovering this concept of displacement.) Similarly, Savin and Perchonock measured how much room a sentence occupied by seeing how many words it displaced from memory.

Let's look at their experiment in more detail. They used the same kind of sentences as Mehler (1963). On a given trial, a subject would hear one sentence followed by a list of eight words. They reasoned that a complex sentence, with many transformational tags, would occupy more space in memory than a simple, kernel sentence. If a sentence took up more space, it would displace a larger number of the eight extra words, forcing them out of memory. Consequently, we can construe the number of extra words forgotten to be a measure of the amount of memory space a sentence occupies.

Table 9-2 shows the average number of words forgotten as a function of the complexity of the sentences. Notice the reasonably consistent tendency for sentences with a greater number of transformational tags to occupy more space in memory.

Table 9-2. The average number of words forgotten as a function of sentence complexity.

Sentence Type	Room Occupied in Memory (Number of Words Forgotten)
simple	2.73
Wh—question	3.22
question	3.33
passive	3.45
negative	3.56
negative question	3.61
exclamation	3.70
passive negative question	3.92
passive question	4.15
passive exclamation	4.26
negative passive	4.52

Data from H. B. Savin & E. Perchonock. Grammatical structure and the immediate recall of English sentences. *Journal of Verbal Learning and Verbal Behavior*, 1965, *4*, 348–353.

Later experiments tried to replicate the Savin/Perchonock experiment. These experiments generally showed that performance factors unrelated to linguistics might be responsible for the results. For example, Boakes and Lodwick (1971) substituted digits for the isolated words and asked subjects to recall either the sentence before the digits or the digits before the sentence. When subjects recalled the sentence first, they forgot some of the digits. When they recalled the digits first, the memory for the sentence was unaffected. It seems, then, that interference during *recall* of the material may have produced Savin and Perchonock's results, rather than displacement during *storage* of the material.

Unfortunately, the issue has never been fully resolved. A further reason for confusion is that Chomsky later revised his own transformational model (Chomsky, 1965). According to this new model, active and passive sentences are equally complex—leaving the earlier enthusiasts in an embarrassing position.

Other psycholinguists have studied the deep-structure model in different ways. For example, Blumenthal (1967) focused on the idea that two sentences that have similar surface structures can have different deep structures. He devised two sets of passive sentences. Some of the sentences had a standard passive form, such as

Gloves were made by tailors.

Other sentences lacked the agent (in this case, *tailors),* replacing it with an adverbial phrase using *by,* as in

Gloves were made by hand.

These two kinds of sentences were mixed in with other, nonpassive sentences in order to reduce demand characteristics (see Chapter 3). The experimenter read each sentence, instructing the subject to repeat each sentence after hearing it. After all the sentences had been read and repeated, the experimenter supplied a list of prompt words—words selected from the sentences. Sometimes the prompt word was the last word of the sentence, such as *tailors* or *hand.* Other times, the prompt word was the first word of the sentence, such as *gloves.*

Blumenthal found that first-word prompts produced equivalent recall in the two kinds of sentences: subjects achieved about 70% accuracy whether the sentences were standard passives or replaced-agent passives. However, a standard passive-agent prompt, such as *tailors,* produced sentence recall 72% of the time, whereas a replaced-agent prompt, such as *hand,* produced sentence recall only 39% of the time. In other words, a minor change in the surface structure of a sentence produces a major change in the degree to which a word prompts the recall of a sentence. This difference in recall must be due to the differences in deep structure for the two kinds of sentences. In this study, then, memory depends on deep structure rather than surface structure.

Other psychologists (for example, Martin & Roberts, 1966) rose to protest the deep-structure concept. They argued that complex deep structure is reflected in complex surface structure: for example, the surface structure for

Hasn't the discovery been made by the biologist?

is more complex than the surface structure for

The biologist has made the discovery.

They contended that it was the surface structure, rather than the deep structure, that had produced differences in performance in earlier psycholinguistic studies.

Rohrman (1968) defended deep structure by producing more data. In one of his experiments, for example, half of the items were subject nominalizations, such as *growling lions,* and half of the items were object nominalizations, such as *digging holes*. Rohrman demonstrated, using linguistic diagrams, that object nominalizations have more complex deep structures than subject nominalizations. However, their surface structures are equivalent in difficulty. Rohrman also made certain that the word length and word frequency for the two kinds of items were equivalent, another necessary control. His results showed that subjects were significantly more accurate in recalling the subject nominalizations. Once again, deep structure, rather than surface structure, determines how well items will be recalled.

In this section, we have seen a variety of attempts to test Chomsky's model that sentences are transformed into deep structure to be stored in memory. Although the evidence is not clear-cut, several studies have demonstrated that the underlying, abstract meaning frequently influences the ease with which people remember sentences.

Memory for Syntax

How well do people recall **syntax,** or sentence structure? Before we investigate this question, try a little experiment on yourself. Read the following story:

> There is an interesting story about the telescope. In Holland, a man named Lippershey was an eye-glass maker. One day his children were playing with some lenses. They discovered that things seemed very close if two lenses were held about a foot apart. Lippershey began experimenting and his ''spyglass'' attracted much attention. He sent a letter about it to Galileo, the great Italian scientist. Galileo at once realized the importance of the discovery and set about to build an instrument of his own. He used an old organ pipe with one lense curved out and the other in. On the first clear night he pointed the glass toward the sky. He was amazed to find the empty dark spaces filled with brightly gleaming stars! Night after night Galileo climbed to a high tower, sweeping the sky with his telescope. One night he saw Jupiter, and to his great surprise discovered near it three bright stars, two to the east and one to the west. On the next night, however, all were to the west. A few nights later there were four little stars [Sachs, 1967, pp. 438–439].

Now cover the story. Did you read this sentence? ''A letter about it was sent to Galileo, the great Italian scientist.'' Check whether your answer was correct; we'll discuss the result later.

Suppose I gave you the sentence

> *John liked the painting and bought it from the duchess.*

Would you be able to select it as the only familiar sentence among these choices if you were tested about a minute later?

> *John liked the painting and the duchess sold it to him.*
> *The painting pleased John and he bought it from the duchess.*
> *John liked the painting and bought it from the duchess.*
> *The painting pleased John and the duchess sold it to him.*

In other words, would you remember the transformational tags necessary to translate the kernel, deep structure back into the appropriate surface structure?

We have already had some hints about memory for syntax in the last section. Recall that Mehler (1963) asked subjects to remember transformations of kernel sentences such as *The biologist has made the discovery*. He found that people tended to forget transformational tags and to end up with a simpler sentence.

Johnson-Laird and Stevenson (1970) wondered if people would be more likely to remember syntax if they knew they were going to be tested. Subjects in one group were told that they would be given a memory test on one sentence in a passage; subjects in another group received no memory instructions, so their learning was "incidental." The subjects then listened to a tape-recorded paragraph that included the sentence *John liked the painting and bought it from the duchess*. One minute later, they were asked to select the sentence that they had heard from a group of eight sentences, including the four sentences listed above. As you can see, the three wrong answers are very similar in meaning (or deep structure) but different in syntax (or surface structure). The four other sentences in the recognition test were different in meaning—for example, *The duchess liked the painting and bought it from John*.

The results showed that knowledge of testing was an important determinant of memory for syntax. Of the subjects who knew that they would be tested, 58% selected the correct sentence; of the incidental-learning group, only 17% were correct. The subjects who were correct often remarked that the sentence they had chosen "sounded right" to them; the authors therefore speculate that the memory instructions may have led the subjects to keep an acoustic trace of the sentence for an unusually long time.

The accuracy of the incidental-learning group seems surprisingly low: merely by guessing, they would have been correct 12% of the time. Keep in mind that the condition for the incidental-learning group is similar to our everyday situation: in daily life, no one tells us to remember the sentence we have just heard. In everyday life, then, our memory for syntax is probably quite poor.

One final observation is necessary on this experiment. Notice that Johnson-Laird and Stevenson used only one sentence and its variants. In Chapter 2, we discussed the advantages of testing many stimuli, and I remarked that testing a large number of stimuli is just as important as testing a large number of subjects. Unfortunately, we cannot be very confident about the generality of this experiment: subjects might recall syntax with greater than 17% accuracy if they were tested on other sentences.

Now look back at your answer on the story-reading experiment. Were you accurate in recalling the sentence about the letter to Galileo? Sachs (1967) asked subjects to listen to paragraphs such as this one. Each paragraph contained a critical sentence, and Sachs interrupted the story either zero, 80, or 160 syllables after that critical sentence. At this point, she gave subjects a sentence, such as the following:

He sent a letter about it to Galileo, the great Italian scientist.
(no change: same word order, same syntax, same meaning)

A letter about it was sent to Galileo, the great Italian scientist.
(change from active to passive: different word order, different syntax, same meaning)

He sent Galileo, the great Italian scientist, a letter about it.
(formal change: different word order, same syntax, same meaning)

Galileo, the great Italian scientist, sent him a letter about it.
(semantic or meaning change: different word order, same syntax, different meaning)

Now, if subjects were perfectly accurate, they would say that only the first sentence had appeared in the paragraph; they would respond "no" to each of the other three sentences.

Sachs found, however, that subjects did not pay much attention to word order or syntax. As Figure 9-2 shows, subjects were reasonably accurate if they were tested immediately after they had heard the sentence. (Still, it is surprising to see that 10–15% were inaccurate, even though no time had passed.) As time passed, though, their performance quickly deteriorated to chance level for the first three kinds of sentences. Notice, however, that performance remained relatively high for the semantic-change sentences. Subjects seemed to be quite confident about the *meaning* of a sentence, and they could not be tricked into thinking they had heard that Galileo sent the letter to Lippershey. Sachs' study fits neatly with the other results we have discussed in this section: people remember what a sentence means, but they easily forget the exact form, or syntax, of the sentence.

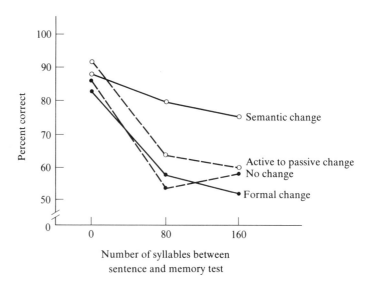

Figure 9-2. Sentence recognition as a function of delay and the type of sentence in the recognition test. From "Recognition Memory for Syntactic and Semantic Aspects of Connected Discourse," by J. Sachs, *Perception and Psychophysics*, 1967, *2*, 437–442. Copyright 1967 by the Psychonomic Society. Reprinted by permission.

Before going on to the next section, try the experiment shown in Table 9-3. Check your results; we'll discuss them shortly.

Table 9-3. An experiment in memory as a constructive process.

Sentence	Question
Acquisition sentences: Read each sentence, count to five, answer the question, go on to the next sentence.	
The girl broke the window on the porch.	Broke what?
The tree in the front yard shaded the man who was smoking his pipe.	Where?
The hill was steep.	What was?
The cat, running from the barking dog, jumped on the table.	From what?
The tree was tall.	Was what?
The old car climbed the hill.	What did?
The cat running from the dog jumped on the table.	Where?
The girl who lives next door broke the window on the porch.	Lives where?
The car pulled the trailer.	Did what?
The scared cat was running from the barking dog.	What was?
The girl lives next door.	Who does?
The tree shaded the man who was smoking his pipe.	What did?
The scared cat jumped on the table.	What did?
The girl who lives next door broke the large window.	Broke what?
The man was smoking his pipe.	Who was?
The old car climbed the steep hill.	The what?
The large window was on the porch.	Where?
The tall tree was in the front yard.	What was?
The car pulling the trailer climbed the steep hill.	Did what?
The cat jumped on the table.	Where?
The tall tree in the front yard shaded the man.	Did what?
The car pulling the trailer climbed the hill.	Which car?
The dog was barking.	Was what?
The window was large.	What was?

STOP—Cover the preceding sentences. Now read each sentence below and decide if it is a sentence from the list given above.

Test set . . . How many are new?

The car climbed the hill.	(old—, new—)
The girl who lives next door broke the window.	(old—, new—)
The old man who was smoking his pipe climbed the steep hill.	(old—, new—)
The tree was in the front yard.	(old—, new—)
The scared cat, running from the barking dog, jumped on the table.	(old—, new—)
The window was on the porch.	(old—, new—)
The barking dog jumped on the old car in the front yard.	(old—, new—)
The tree in the front yard shaded the man.	(old—, new—)
The cat was running from the dog.	(old—, new—)
The old car pulled the trailer.	(old—, new—)
The tall tree in the front yard shaded the old car.	(old—, new—)
The tall tree shaded the man who was smoking his pipe.	(old—, new—)

Table 9-3. *(continued)*

The scared cat was running from the dog.	(old—, new—)
The old car, pulling the trailer, climbed the hill.	(old—, new—)
The girl who lives next door broke the large window on the porch.	(old—, new—)
The tall tree shaded the man.	(old—, new—)
The cat was running from the barking dog.	(old—, new—)
The car was old.	(old—, new—)
The girl broke the large window.	(old—, new—)
The scared cat ran from the barking dog that jumped on the table.	(old—, new—)
The scared cat, running from the dog, jumped on the table.	(old—, new—)
The old car pulling the trailer climbed the steep hill.	(old—, new—)
The girl broke the large window on the porch.	(old—, new—)
The scared cat which broke the window on the porch climbed the tree.	(old—, new—)
The tree shaded the man.	(old—, new—)
The car climbed the steep hill.	(old—, new—)
The girl broke the window.	(old—, new—)
The man who lives next door broke the large window on the porch.	(old—, new—)
The tall tree in the front yard shaded the man who was smoking his pipe.	(old—, new—)
The cat was scared.	(old—, new—)

STOP. Count the number of sentences judged "old."
See text for answer.

From "Remember That Old Theory of Memory? Well, Forget It," by J. J. Jenkins, *American Psychologist,* 1974, *29,* 791. Copyright 1974 by The American Psychological Association. Reprinted by permission.

Memory as a Constructive Process

Sachs (1967) showed that we remember meaning—that is, we store the meaning of a sentence even if we forget syntactic information. Another group of psychologists has demonstrated that meaning is so important that we will claim that we have heard sentences before—even if we have not—when the meaning makes sense.

Look back at your own responses to the experiment in Table 9-3. How many of the sentences in the second half looked familiar to you? Actually, you hadn't seen a single one of them before.

This experiment is like one performed by Bransford and Franks (1971). They asked subjects to listen to 24 sentences that belonged to four different stories. Then the subjects were given a recognition test, including many new sentences that were combinations of the earlier sentences. Subjects frequently responded that they were certain they had already heard the new sentences. This tendency was particularly strong for complex sentences, such as *The tall tree in the front yard shaded the man who was smoking his pipe.* Subjects generally rated their certainty of having seen this sentence at either 4 or 5 on a scale of 5. It seems that people construct the four stories as they hear more and more information. For example, they might take the sentence *The tree in the front yard shaded the man who was smoking his pipe,* and the sentence *The tree was tall,* and fuse these together into a single sentence in their mind: *The tall tree in the front yard shaded the man who was smoking his pipe.*

Bransford and Franks proposed a **constructive** model of memory. According to this model, people fuse sentences together when they hear them. Once the sentences are fused, people cannot untangle them later into the two original sentences. Thus, memory is a constructive process in which we continually build ideas by integrating new information with old information.

Bransford, Barclay, and Franks (1972) pursued this idea of storing more in memory than is presented in either the surface structure or the deep structure of sentences. "Essentially these experiments ask whether sentence memory is primarily a function of the deep structural information underlying the input sentences or a function of the semantic descriptions that such inputs suggest" (p. 194).

Bransford et al. gave some subjects a sentence such as:

(1) *Three turtles rested beside a floating log, and a fish swam beneath them.*

They gave other subjects a sentence such as:

(2) *Three turtles rested on a floating log, and a fish swam beneath them.*

Notice that the only difference is in the word *beside* or *on.* Later, subjects were given a recognition test with the sentence:

Three turtles rested (beside/on) a floating log, and a fish swam beneath it.

Bransford et al. point out that this recognition sentence with the word *it* substituted for *them* is derivable from sentence 2 because of our knowledge of spatial relations. If we know that the turtles are on the log and a fish is beneath them, then the fish must be beneath the log as well.

The results showed that the people who had seen sentence 2 frequently said that they recognized sentence 3, whereas people who had seen sentence 1 (where it is ambiguous whether the fish swims beneath the log) were much less likely to say that they recognized sentence 3. Bransford et al. believe that these results show that people have constructed an idea by combining sentence 2 with what they know about the world. As in the Bransford and Franks (1971) experiment, people have trouble reconstructing the original elements after they have constructed a new idea.

Paris and Carter (1973) have shown that children also construct an idea that contains more information than what has been presented in individual sentences. They read sentences to their subjects that came from seven unrelated stories. For example, one story might consist of these three sentences interspersed among the others:

The bird is inside the cage.
The cage is under the table.
The bird is yellow.

During the recognition period, subjects heard sentences like these:

The bird is inside the cage. (True premise)
The cage is over the table. (False premise)
The bird is under the table. (True inference)
The bird is on top of the table. (False inference)

Paris and Carter tested second-graders and fifth-graders on this task and found that children in both age groups showed the same pattern of errors. They made the greatest number of errors on the true-inference problems. More than 60% of the children claimed that they had heard "The bird is under the table." They had *not* heard this sentence, but this sentence would be a correct inference from their knowledge that the bird was inside the cage and the cage was under the table. In contrast, their performance was relatively accurate on false-premise and false-inference sentences. Both of these sentences violated the idea that they had constructed from the other three sentences, and so they typically concluded (correctly) that they had not seen these sentences. Once again, people retain the meaning of what they hear, and this tendency is true for children as well as adults.

In this section, we have seen that people take isolated sentences and combine them with other sentences or with other information they know about the world. In experiments we find that this construction process has a disadvantage: people cannot recall the original sentences. In real life, however, that disadvantage is seldom relevant: experimenters don't run around asking you to recover the original sentences. Instead, the construction process permits people to synthesize many bits of information into a well-organized whole rather than store many isolated fragments in memory.

Before you go on to the next section, try another experiment. This one has an added bonus—it requires you to take a break! Read the story printed below; then do something else for 15 minutes. Then write down the story as you remember it.

The War of the Ghosts

One night two young men from Egulac went down to the river to hunt seals, and while they were there it became foggy and calm. Then they heard war-cries, and they thought: "Maybe this is a war-party." They escaped to the shore, and hid behind a log. Now canoes came up, and they heard the noise of paddles, and saw one canoe coming up to them. There were five men in the canoe, and they said:

"What do you think? We wish to take you along. We are going up the river to make war on the people."

One of the young men said: "I have no arrows."

"Arrows are in the canoe," they said.

"I will not go along. I might be killed. My relatives do not know where I have gone. But you," he said, turning to the other, "may go with them."

So one of the young men went, but the other returned home.

And the warriors went on up the river to a town on the other side of Kalama.

The people came down to the water, and they began to fight, and many were killed. But presently the young man heard one of the warriors say: "Quick, let us go home: that Indian has been hit." Now he thought: "Oh, they are ghosts." He did not feel sick, but they said he had been shot.

So the canoes went back to Egulac, and the young man went ashore to his house, and made a fire. And he told everybody and said: "Behold I accompanied the ghosts, and we went to fight. Many of our fellows were killed, and many of those who attacked us were killed. They said I was hit, and I did not feel sick."

He told it all, and then he became quiet. When the sun rose he fell down. Something black came out of his mouth. His face became contorted. The people jumped up and cried.

He was dead.[1]

Now try a second experiment in story remembering. Read the story that follows, close the book, and try to write down the story as exactly as possible.

If the balloons popped, the sound wouldn't be able to carry since everything would be too far away from the correct floor. A closed window would also prevent the sound from carrying, since most buildings tend to be well insulated. Since the whole operation depends on a steady flow of electricity, a break in the middle of the wire would also cause problems. Of course, the fellow could shout, but the human voice is not loud enough to carry that far. An additional problem is that a string could break on the instrument. Then there would be no accompaniment to the message. It is clear that the best situation would involve less distance. Then there would be fewer potential problems. With face to face contact, the least number of things could go wrong [p. 719].[2]

Both of these experiments will be discussed in the course of the next section.

Memory for Stories

So far, we have talked about memory for single sentences. In those studies, experimenters ask subjects either to recall a specified sentence or to recognize it. Now let's talk about memory for groups of sentences that are organized into a story. First we'll discuss Bartlett's (1932) classic study on remembering stories and later research testing his theories. Then we'll explore several factors that influence recall accuracy. Finally, we'll look briefly at story structure.

Look at the story you recalled after reading "The War of the Ghosts." How accurate were you? Bartlett (1932) adapted this story from a North American Indian folktale. Subjects read the story and reproduced it after vary-

---

[1]From F. C. Bartlett, *Remembering*, Cambridge, England: Cambridge University Press, 1932, p. 65. This and all other quotations reprinted by permission.

[2]From "Contextual Prerequisites for Understanding: Some Investigations of Comprehension and Recall," by J. D. Bransford and M. K. Johnson, *Journal of Verbal Learning and Verbal Behavior*, 1972, *11*, 717–726. Copyright 1972 by Academic Press, Inc. Reprinted by permission.

ing intervals. Here, for example, is the story as one subject remembered it 8 days later:

The War of the Ghosts

Two young men from Edulac went fishing. While thus engaged they heard a noise in the distance. ''That sounds like a war-cry,'' said one, ''there is going to be some fighting.'' Presently there appeared some warriors who invited them to join an expedition up the river.

One of the young men excused himself on the ground of family ties. ''I cannot come,'' he said, ''as I might get killed.'' So he returned home. The other man, however, joined the party, and they proceeded in canoes up the river. While landing on the banks the enemy appeared and were running down to meet them. Soon someone was wounded, and the party discovered that they were fighting against ghosts. The young man and his companion returned to the boats, and went back to their homes.

The next morning at dawn he was describing his adventures to his friends, who had gathered round him. Suddenly something black issued from his mouth, and he fell down uttering a cry. His friends closed around him, but found that he was dead [p.67].

This reproduction illustrates some of the tendencies Bartlett found during recall. First of all, the story is substantially shorter, mostly because of omissions—for example, the name ''Kalama.'' Second, the phraseology becomes more idiomatic—for example, ''excused himself on the ground of family ties.'' Finally, the story is more coherent and rational than it was originally.

It is interesting to see how Bartlett's rules predict what happens to folk ballads as they are transmitted orally from one generation to another. For example, there is a British ballad about Queen Jane Seymour called ''The Death of Queen Jane.'' In one of the classic versions, the first verse begins:

Queen Jane lay in labour for six weeks and some more—
Her women grew weary and the midwife gave o'er.

Now the idea of being in labor for six weeks or more has always struck me as totally irrational, and others must have thought so, too. Another version of the same song goes:

Queen Jane lay in labour full nine days or more,
Till the women were so tired, they could stay no longer there.

Presumably, nine days makes much more sense! Another solution to this irrationality is this American version of the song:

O Jane was a neighbor for six months or more,
Till the neighbors grew weary and left her alone.

Ballads seem to become more rational as they are passed from one singer to another, just as stories become more rational as they are retold.

Gauld and Stephenson (1967) were interested in pursuing Bartlett's ideas on memory for stories, and they designed four experiments to examine subjects' errors in story recall.

In the first experiment, they varied the instructions to the subjects. They thought that Bartlett's instructions were too vague, and subjects might not have understood that they were supposed to strive for accuracy in recalling details. Therefore, they simply instructed one group of subjects to write down the story as exactly as possible. Two other groups received much more explicit instructions. The second group was told to leave blanks and to avoid writing down information that was not in the original story; the third group received these instructions plus additional urgings to be scrupulously honest. As you can imagine, a conscientious scoring of the responses demands an elaborately precise operational definition for "correct response." The authors decided, for example, to accept synonyms but to reject inversions such as "up river" for "down river." The results showed that subjects in the first group were significantly less accurate than subjects in the other two groups. These findings were replicated in a second study using a different story.

In a third experiment, the authors read "The War of the Ghosts" and asked subjects to answer ten written questions on the text, indicating their degree of certainty about their responses. Certainty was found to be related to accuracy. In other words, subjects knew when they were guessing.

In a final experiment, Gauld and Stephenson obtained measures of "conscience strength" in their subjects. This measure, whose validity had been determined previously, assessed factors such as the tendency to suffer from guilt feelings and remorse. They found that the number of errors on "War of the Ghosts" was significantly related to the conscience-strength measure. In contrast, the number of errors was unrelated to intelligence-test scores.

The authors conclude from these studies:

> The striking ability to pick out their own errors which subjects display, the distinct inverse correlation between error rate and conscientiousness, and the fact that strict instructions to be accurate decidedly reduce the error rate, all combine to suggest rather strongly that the ordinary subject in experiments of the Bartlett kind does not do his best to *remember*. On the contrary, he probably bridges gaps in his memory with a great deal of more or less conscious guessing and inventions [p. 47].

Instructions to be careful in remembering the story, then, influence recall accuracy. Other researchers have investigated other potential determinants of recall accuracy.

For example, Bransford and Johnson (1972) studied the influence of contextual knowledge on subjects' abilities to understand and recall stories. How was your recall for the story about the balloons? Would your recall have been better if you had seen the picture in Figure 9-3 beforehand? Bransford and Johnson found that subjects performed much more accurately when they were supplied with the picture as context for the story *prior* to hearing the story. In contrast, when the picture was supplied *after* hearing the story, performance

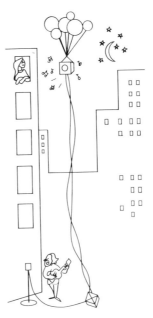

Figure 9-3. Does this picture help you understand the story about the balloons? From "Contextual Prerequisites for Understanding: Some Investigations of Comprehension and Recall," by J. D. Bransford and M. K. Johnson, *Journal of Verbal Learning and Verbal Behavior*, 1972, *11*, 717–726. Copyright 1972 by Academic Press, Inc. Reprinted by permission.

was not substantially improved. Bransford and Johnson believe that the picture creates a context that can be used to help subjects understand incoming information. Passages must be understood in order to be recalled at a later time.

Kintsch and Monk (1972) examined the effects of story complexity. In a simple version of the story, the propositions were expressed as directly as possible. In a complex version of the same story, the material was transformed in both syntax and meaning. In one condition, subjects were allowed to read the material at their own rate. As you might suspect, subjects took longer to read the complex version. Surprisingly, however, subjects were just as quick and just as accurate in drawing inferences about complex passages as they were in drawing inferences about simple passages. The authors conclude that simple and complex passages are stored similarly in memory. If subjects answer questions about complex passages quickly and accurately, then the information about those passages must be stored in a form similar to the information about simple passages.

In recent years, psychologists have begun to study other aspects of stories. In particular, they have tried to determine the structure of stories. For example, Mandler and Johnson (1977) have derived a set of rules for the structure of stories and have found that these rules predicted Bartlett's subjects' recall of "The War of the Ghosts." Thorndyke (1977) has found that recall probability depends on how central a fact is to the structure of the story: central facts are remembered, but low-level details are forgotten. This new area of research has been summarized best by G. H. Bower (1976), who draws some other conclusions about the structure of stories and folktales: (1) Simple stories have definite, regular structures. (2) People acquire this structure, and they use it to sort out any new stories they hear and to reconstruct stories that they have heard. (3) If a text violates some critical rule—for example, by leaving out the main goal of the central character—then the story is forgotten more readily. (4) Recall depends on the concreteness of the characters and their actions. (5) Understanding some sentences frequently requires the listener to make inferences based on information learned earlier.

We have come a long way from traditional studies on memory for isolated words. We have seen how linguistic relationships between words in the sentence—the deep structure—can influence recall in several tests of Chomsky's (1957) model of sentence structure. We have also seen how the exact wording of sentences is not accurately recalled. Next, we found that people often construct an idea in memory, based on the sentences they have heard. Finally, we found that subjects tend to make sensible patterns out of stories. All of these findings have shown us that memory for sentences involves more than mere rote memory for strings of words. In each case, we see that subjects take an active role in processing and restructuring the sentences they hear or read. The meaning of what they hear is frequently remembered long after the exact sequence of words is forgotten.

THE WHORFIAN HYPOTHESIS: LANGUAGE AND THOUGHT

Does the language that you speak determine how you think? This is a question that has excited psychologists, linguists, and anthropologists for some time. Think about this for a moment. If your native language were Japanese, for example, would you still think the same thoughts, or would your language shape and restrict your thoughts into different forms? Are certain thoughts possible with some languages, but impossible with other languages that lack the appropriate words?

You may have had some experience with this notion if you have ever studied a foreign language. At some point, inevitably, the instructor must have said, "There is really no good way to translate this word into English." The implication is that a particular thought—captured by a single word in that other language—cannot be grasped by someone speaking English, because English words are not suitable. If you have ever read Leo Rosten's (1970) *The Joys of Yiddish,* you may have experienced this "nontranslatability." For example, Rosten defines the word *chutzpa* as follows:

Gall, brazen nerve, effrontery, incredible "guts"; presumption-plus-arrogance such as no other word, and no other language, can do justice to [p. 93].

Perhaps because Rosten believes that English words are inadequate to capture the essence of *chutzpa,* he provides several examples, such as:

``Chutzpa'' is that quality enshrined in a man who, having killed his mother and father, throws himself on the mercy of the court because he is an orphan [p. 93].

This notion, taken to its extreme, argues that two people who have grown up speaking different languages can never communicate with each other. Others strongly protest this viewpoint, arguing that any concept can be translated: it may take many words, and the definitions may be very elaborate, but any thought can be translated into another language. For example, it took five synonyms and one example for Rosten to translate *chutzpa* for us, but we probably now have a fairly clear interpretation of this thought.

These are the issues involved in the **Whorfian hypothesis,** named after Benjamin Lee Whorf. The Whorfian hypothesis has two parts: (1) **linguistic determinism**—the idea that the structure of language determines the structure of thought, and (2) **linguistic relativity**—the idea that speakers of different languages have different thought structures.

Whorf himself was an unusual person. He was a fire-prevention inspector for the Hartford Fire Insurance Company. However, in his spare time he worked on his hobby, linguistics; he was particularly interested in American Indian languages.

Whorf (1956) describes how the formulation of ideas differs from one language to another:

> We dissect nature along lines laid down by our native languages. The categories and types that we isolate from the world of phenomena we do not find there because they stare every observer in the face; on the contrary, the world is presented in a kaleidoscopic flux of impressions which has to be organized by our minds—and this means largely by the linguistic systems in our minds. We cut nature up, organize it into concepts, and ascribe significances as we do, largely because we are parties to an agreement to organize it in this way—an agreement that holds throughout our speech community and is codified in the patterns of our language [p. 213].

For example, the Eskimos have three different words for snow (designating soft snow, wet snow, and hard-packed snow), whereas we have only one. The Hopi have only one word for three different things that fly that we label with three entirely different names—pilot, airplane, and flying insect.

Whorf presented a hypothesis, and he provided some naturalistic-observation data in support of that hypothesis. Others have followed through with experiments to test the hypothesis. Let's look at several lines of attack that have been pursued in this research.

Codability and Recognition

The first major test of the Whorfian hypothesis was conducted by Roger Brown and Eric Lenneberg (1954), two people whose names are familiar to you from the language-acquisition section of this chapter. They explored the relationship between codability, a language attribute, and recognition, a thought attribute.

Let's talk about how they measured codability. They selected 24 colors
and exposed each of them very briefly to a group of subjects, all of whom spoke English as a native language. The subjects were asked to name each color quickly. Some of the subjects returned one month later to repeat the color-naming task. Brown and Lenneberg derived for each word five measures of **codability**, or the ease with which a color can be named: (1) the number of syllables used to describe the color; (2) the number of words used to describe the color; (3) the average reaction time; (4) the extent to which different subjects agreed upon a name for the color; and (5) the extent to which the subjects who repeated the color-naming task agreed with their own first name for the color. All of these measures turned out to be highly correlated with each other. However, interpersonal agreement (the fourth measure) produced the strongest intercorrelations. Therefore, interpersonal agreement was selected as the measure of codability for the second phase of the study.

Before we discuss this second phase, let's think about codability for a moment. Some colors are highly codable—consider a bright, true red, for example. That color can be coded in terms of a single, one-syllable word, and we would supply the name *red* very quickly. Many different people would agree with each other in supplying the name *red* to that color. Finally, they would tend to supply that same name *red* the next time they saw the color. In contrast, imagine the brownish-green color of the inside of an avocado after it has been left exposed to the air for a day. That seems to be a highly uncodable color in terms of all five measures of codability.

Brown and Lenneberg proposed that codability—the availability of a language label—would be related to a particular measure of thought—recognition. In the second phase of their study, therefore, they assembled 120 color chips, including the 24 for which codability measures had been obtained. All of the chips were mounted on a large white board. Brown and Lenneberg tested recognition in four different conditions. (None of the subjects had participated in Phase 1 of the study.) The simplest recognition task involved presenting one color to the subjects, waiting 7 seconds, and then asking the subjects to select that color from the 120 color chips. The next easiest task involved four colors with a 7-second delay. The two hardest tasks involved four colors with either a 30-second or a 3-minute delay. Brown and Lenneberg predicted that codability would not be closely related to recognition in the simplest task: subjects might retain a mental image of the single color they had seen; therefore, a verbal label would not be necessary. In the more difficult tasks, however, codability should be increasingly critical. After all, subjects could not retain an image of four different colors for a period of 3 minutes. In this case, it would be particularly helpful to have a nice, readily available name for a color.

The results confirmed their predictions. For the easiest task, there was no correlation between codability and recognition: highly codable colors were not recognized any better than low-codable colors. However, the strength of the correlation increased as the difficulty of the task increased. For the four-color, 3-minute-delay task, codability and recognition were correlated +.52. In other words, a highly codable color such as red was recognized very accurately, whereas a low-codable color such as day-old-avocado-insides was not recognized very accurately. In short, differences in language are related to differences in thought.

Communication Accuracy and Recognition

Lenneberg (1961) performed an archival analysis in which he found that there was a *negative* correlation between codability and recognition when different color samples were used. With these samples, then, the more codable a color was, the *less* recognizable it was. This discovery caused disenchantment among those who had been excited about Brown and Lenneberg's (1954) results that codability and recognition were positively correlated.

Fortunately, Lantz and Stefflre (1964) came to the rescue by arguing that the operational definition for codability—the agreement among various people about the name for a color—was the source of the problem. Therefore, they devised a new measure of codability, which they called **communication accuracy.** One group of subjects, called the "encoders," were instructed to "name each color using the word or words you would use to name it to a friend so that he or she could pick it out" (p. 475). A different group of subjects, called the "decoders," tried to pick out the colors from an array, using the names that had been provided previously by the encoders. A color with high communication accuracy would be one for which the names supplied by the encoders allowed the decoders to identify the color accurately. For example, if I am the encoder and you are the decoder, my name *red* would probably allow you to identify the particular red I am looking at right now: this color has high communication accuracy. However, my name *brownish-green avocado insides exposed to the air for a day* might not allow you to identify the particular brown-green I am looking at: this color would have low communication accuracy.

Lantz and Stefflre obtained communication-accuracy scores for two sets of colors—the ones used by Brown and Lenneberg (1954) and the ones studied by Lenneberg (1961). They also obtained measures of the agreement among various people about the name for a color, which had been Brown and Lenneberg's operational definition for codability. Finally, they obtained several measures of recognition.

For both sets of colors, communication-accuracy scores were highly correlated with recognition. In other words, if a color can be named so appropriately that people can describe that color accurately to other people (high communication accuracy), then they can also describe that color accurately to themselves (high recognition accuracy).

Incidentally, Lantz and Stefflre also found that codability in terms of interpersonal agreement was correlated with recognition for the Brown and Lenneberg (1954) colors, but it was not correlated with recognition for the Lenneberg (1961) colors. For some reason, then, the operational definition of codability in terms of interpersonal agreement is not very systematic. In contrast, the communication-accuracy measure systematically revealed a relationship between language and thought: if a color is one that can be given a name that will be useful to others, then this color is one that can be stored in memory quite accurately.

The Universality of Color Systems

The studies we have discussed so far have used only English-speaking subjects. These studies assumed, as Brown (1976) points out, that English divides the color space in an arbitrary way and that there are other, non-English-speaking communities that divide up the color space in a different way. In some other community, for example, red might be a low-codable color and brownish-green-avocado a highly codable color. At any rate, recognition for colors would presumably be highly correlated with the codability scores of those colors in that particular community, just as the two measures are correlated in English.

In the late 1960s, however, it became increasingly apparent that color space is not divided in an arbitrary way. Berlin and Kay (1969) examined 20 extremely different languages, such as Arabic, Thai, and Hungarian. Their approach was anthropological rather than psychological: they typically asked a single informant to provide judgments about colors in his or her native language. They asked informants to name colors and then to select the best instance of each color on a color chart. Berlin and Kay found that the best instances of colors in the various languages seemed to be located in similar positions. For example, the best instance of our color red might be very similar to the best instance that a speaker of Thai selected for one of their basic colors. Far from being an arbitrary division of color space, color names are instead assigned rather consistently in many different cultures. The "best instances" seem to be reasonably universal. Linguistic codes seem to be devised to fit those "good colors," in English as in other languages. Thus, Berlin and Kay's study showed that Whorf's statement "We dissect nature along lines laid down by our native languages" does not seem to hold true for colors because all languages seem to have laid down the same lines.

Heider (1972), a student of Roger Brown's, provided further information for the universality of color systems. She conducted a series of experiments; only some of her results will be considered here. She chose eight **focal colors,** or "best instances" colors, and 13 **boundary colors**—those that occur at the boundaries between focal colors. In one study, her subjects were 23 speakers of 23 languages other than English. She defined codability in terms of the length of the name given to the color and the amount of time taken to name the color. (Recall that Brown and Lenneberg used these measures, too.) Her results showed that focal colors were *more codable* than boundary colors across all languages.

In another experiment in the same series, Heider (1972) found that these same focal colors were *recognized better* than the other, boundary colors. This was true for a group of native English speakers. More important, it was also true for 21 members of the Dani tribe of New Guinea. Now the interesting thing about the Dani language is that it only has two color terms, roughly equivalent to ''dark'' and ''light.'' In fact, when Heider tried to obtain codability scores for her Dani subjects, she found that it was an impossible task! In naming the colors, the Dani tended to ''chant'' the two names—*mili* for dark colors and *mola* for light colors—at a constant rate. Consequently, colors did not differ in the length of their names, nor in the amount of time taken to name the colors. In other words, all colors had identical codability. Nonetheless, the focal colors were recognized better than boundary colors, even though there was no difference with respect to codability.

Roger Brown, in a recent review of the literature (1976), concludes that Heider's studies reduce the value of the original Brown and Lenneberg (1954) findings. He concludes that focal areas are human universals, and that these ''focal colors are more memorable, easier to recognize, than any other colors, whether the subjects speak a language having a name for the focal colors or not'' [p. 151].

What are we to conclude? Can all of the relationships between codability and recognition be explained by the universality of color systems? Schönbach (1977) thinks not. He thinks that Brown has been too harsh on himself; indeed, his article is titled ''In Defense of Roger Brown Against Himself.'' He feels that Brown neglected to emphasize one important aspect of the Brown and Lenneberg (1954) paper. You may recall that codability was not significantly correlated with recognition for easy tasks, but the correlation became stronger as task difficulty increased. That finding cannot be explained by the argument of universality. After all, if focal colors are more memorable, they should be more memorable whenever they are encountered. Schönbach argues that in more difficult tasks, ''the linguistic codes available to a particular group of speakers do enter more forcefully as partial determinants of cognitive processes'' [p. 182]. The answer may be, then, that certain universal tendencies partially explain why some colors are recognized better than others; however, language does influence thought when we consider more complicated tasks.

Language and Classification

So far, we have discussed only those experiments that deal with the way people divide up the world of color into areas that have different names. In fact, the great majority of studies on the Whorfian hypothesis have examined color.

In contrast, Carroll and Casagrande (1958) pursued a different line of attack to test the Whorfian hypothesis. They wondered if language would influence the way people classify verbs and objects. Their first experiment dealt with members of the Hopi tribe in Arizona. Verbs in the Hopi language have structures that are quite different from verbs in English. For example, the Hopi use two verbs to talk about *breaking*: one verb is used if the object breaks into two pieces, and a different verb is used if the object breaks into many pieces. Also, the Hopi use a different verb for a *spilling* or *pouring* action depending on whether the material is liquid or nonliquid. In English, we don't distinguish on the basis of liquid versus nonliquid, but on the basis of accident (*spilling*) versus intention (*pouring*).

Carroll and Casagrande assembled sets of three drawings of various physical actions. For example, one set represented (1) a person pouring fruit out of a box, (2) a coin accidentally falling out of a person's pocket, and (3) a person accidentally spilling some water. Subjects were instructed to point out which two of the three pictures "went together." The Hopi, in this example, tended to classify pictures 1 and 2 together, whereas English-speaking subjects tended to classify pictures 2 and 3 together.

Carroll and Casagrande tabulated all the results, eliminating those items that had been misinterpreted by the subjects, and found that the Hopi did classify the pictures differently from the English-speaking subjects. They concluded that language influences one aspect of thought—classification.

In a second experiment, Carroll and Casagrande (1958) studied the way Navajo children classified objects. The children were given ten pairs of objects, such as colored wooden blocks, sticks, and pieces of rope. Each of the pairs differed on two attributes—for example, a yellow rope and a blue stick. Then the child was given a third object, such as a blue rope, and was asked to indicate which member of the pair "went with" this new object. The Navajo language uses different verb endings depending on whether the object of the verb is rigid (like a stick) or flexible (like a rope). Carroll and Casagrande argued, therefore, that Navajo children would classify the blue rope with the yellow rope: importance in language would be reflected in importance in thought.

Carroll and Casagrande tested a group of children who were either monolingual in Navajo or Navajo-predominant and contrasted their performance with a group of Navajo children who were either monolingual in English or English-predominant. The two groups differed significantly in the predicted direction on most of the pairs. For example, the Navajo-speaking group placed the blue rope with the yellow rope, whereas the English-speaking group placed the blue rope with the blue stick.

So far, then, the results are delightfully straightforward and supportive of the Whorfian hypothesis. However, Carroll and Casagrande then tested a group of White American children living in the Boston area. Their results no doubt disappointed them: these children tended to select the "Navajo" response to an even greater extent than the Navajo children. The authors attribute the results on the Boston children to their greater experience with toys that emphasize forms and shapes, and they argue that these Boston children do not constitute an appropriate control group for the Navajo children because of the large differences in cultural background and experience. They maintain that the contrast between their two well-controlled and well-matched groups of Navajo children is more noteworthy. Nonetheless, the results on the Boston children do weaken a Whorfian-hypothesis interpretation of the findings.

Shape Names and Cognition

A number of other studies are often cited in support of the Whorfian hypothesis. Specifically, these studies examine whether cognition is affected by providing a label for a shape. For example, in a classic experiment, Carmichael, Hogan, and Walter (1932) showed several stimulus shapes to subjects. Subjects received one of two different names for the objects. For example, a picture of two circles joined together by a short, straight line was called "eyeglasses" for some subjects and "dumbbells" for other subjects. Later on, the subjects were asked to reproduce the figures. Subjects who had received the label "eyeglasses" tended to reproduce the figure with the central line bent, more closely resembling eyeglasses than the original picture did. Subjects who had received the label "dumbbells" tended to draw it with a thick central line, more closely resembling dumbbells than the original picture did.

More recently, Santa and Ranken (1972) tested the influence of a label on memory for solid, many-sided shapes. All subjects received practice in discriminating these shapes. However, some subjects received a name for each object (for example, "cat" for a ten-sided figure that vaguely resembled a cat), while other subjects received no names. Later, the subjects in the label-present condition recognized the shapes more accurately than did subjects in the label-absent condition. Furthermore, the advantage of the label was particularly strong when the subjects were required to remember a large number of the nonsense shapes—a finding that parallels Brown and Lenneberg's (1954) finding that codable language labels are more helpful as the task becomes more difficult. Thus, language influences the memory aspect of cognition: words determine the way a particular shape is stored in memory.

Conclusions

In general, there is some support for a "weak interpretation" of the Whorfian hypothesis. The words we use have some influence on how well we remember and recognize certain colors and shapes. Furthermore, the words we use may influence how we classify objects. However, all of these experiments have been rather modest. None of them has been ambitious enough to determine whether differences in language produce differences in "world view"—a requirement for a "strong interpretation" of the Whorfian hypothesis. Yes, Hopi verbs may "dissect" the world of action differently from English verbs, but we have no real evidence that Hopi Indians therefore view the world differently. Language may influence thought, but so far the experimental evidence limits that influence to rather specific cognitive tasks—memory and (perhaps) classification. Experiments on "world view" are naturally harder to design and execute, but we must wait for these results before drawing any final conclusions on the Whorfian hypothesis.

In looking at the Whorfian hypothesis, we have seen that researchers have approached this theoretical issue from several different angles. However, there are still many other angles to be explored, and a clear answer about the validity of the Whorfian hypothesis has not been obtained. Sometimes, psychologists do find clear answers—for example, we saw in the previous section that people have poor memory for syntax. Just as often, a single experiment or set of experiments provides a hint but not a clear answer. Laypeople sometimes assume that psychologists have all the answers to human behavior. In reality, however—as we see again in the case of the Whorfian hypothesis—many unresolved issues remain.

345
Psycholinguistics

SUMMARY

1. Language acquisition has been studied by means of all five different research approaches: naturalistic observation, the survey method, the case-study method, the correlational method, and the experimental method.
2. Naturalistic observation has proved to be a useful technique for psycholinguists who want to describe the language spoken by children—for example, their tendency to use telegraphic speech. The development of videotaping equipment has expanded the usefulness of naturalistic observation, enabling researchers to record details such as the context of conversations.
3. The survey method has not been used extensively in psycholinguistics, though it has been used to estimate children's vocabulary size.
4. The case-study method has been useful in examining the language development of abnormal children and answering questions that could not be ethically conducted with the experimental method. This method has provided information about the possibility of language development without the motor ability to speak and without early exposure to language.
5. The correlational method is used by psycholinguists primarily to determine what factors are related to language ability. For example, the quality of the mother's speech is correlated with her infant's language development.
6. The experimental method is now the most popular method among developmental psycholinguists. It is particularly useful in pursuing hypotheses generated by naturalistic observation, in establishing what factors can produce a change in language, in examining speech perception in young infants, and in studying children's understanding of language.
7. A number of different models have been proposed to describe how sentences and groups of sentences are stored in memory.
8. There is some evidence that the transformational form of a sentence influences how well the sentence will be remembered.
9. Many studies have demonstrated that memory for the syntax of sentences is astonishingly poor.
10. Memory for the meaning of sentences, in contrast, is quite accurate. Meaning is so much more important than syntax that people seem to use a constructive process to fuse together several sentences into an idea, from which the original sentences cannot be recovered.
11. Memory for stories seems to be governed by certain rules; for example, the reproduced story is generally more coherent than the original version.
12. The Whorfian hypothesis, or linguistic-relativity hypothesis, states that the language we speak determines how we think: because languages differ in the way they organize the world into concepts, people in different countries differ in their view of the world. This theory has been tested only partially.
13. Brown and Lenneberg (1954) have shown that the colors that are most

memorable are those for which subjects can agree on a color name; thus, words are related to an aspect of thought.

14. Other research has shown that colors for which names can be communicated accurately to others are those that can be retained most accurately in memory.

15. Heider (1972) has argued that correlations between language and thought arise because there are certain universal focal colors that happen to be more codable and more memorable than other colors.

16. Carroll and Casagrande (1958) have found that speakers of Hopi and English differ in the way they classify pictures, and that speakers of Navajo and English differ in the way they classify objects. However, their results are not clear-cut.

17. Several studies have demonstrated that language labels influence the way a shape is remembered.

18. Research on the Whorfian hypothesis has provided some evidence that language can influence thought, but no study has demonstrated that differences in language produce differences in world view.

10

Cognition

OUTLINE

Cognition is the process of knowing or thinking. In this chapter, we will consider three topics in experimental psychology that fall under the heading of cognition: problem solving, concept identification, and decision making. As different as these topics may seem, they all involve thinking about information that has been gathered from perception and memory.

As you might imagine, an area as broad as cognition encompasses a wide variety of topics. Textbooks on cognitive psychology—for example, Manis's (1971) *An Introduction to Cognitive Psychology*—include topics such as learning, memory, language, and cognitive dissonance. Though I have dealt with these topics in separate chapters, all of them can be included in the area of cognition because they involve knowledge or thought.

Psychologists frequently distinguish between cognition and perception. Perception involves the awareness of sensory stimulation—a very immediate process—whereas cognition involves the *interpretation* of those perceptions. Julesz (1975) defines this distinction as follows: "Any visual task that cannot be performed spontaneously, without effort or deliberation, can be regarded as a cognitive task rather than a perceptual one" (p. 34). Thus, in Figure 10-1, the figures on the left can be distinguished from each other by "pure perception"; this task can be performed spontaneously. In the figures on the right, however, cognition is required to determine that one figure is a continuous line and the other is not: effort, deliberation, and thought are required for this task.

Figure 10-1. Are the figures on the left formed by one continuous line, or do they have two separate parts? How about the figures on the right? From "Experiments in the Visual Perception of Texture," by B. Julesz, *Scientific American*, April 1975, *232*, 34–43. Copyright © 1975 by Scientific American, Inc. Reprinted by permission.

The structure of this chapter on cognition differs from that of the other four chapters in this part of the book: it is organized in terms of the four different kinds of independent variables. In Chapter 1, I described these kinds of independent variables: stimulus characteristics, environmental characteristics, subject characteristics, and manipulated subject differences. However, in

Chapter 1, we inspected only a few examples in each of these four categories. In this chapter, we'll have time for a more leisurely examination of independent variables.

Each of the four kinds of variables represents a different method of attack chosen by experimental psychologists trying to unravel the complex processes involved in knowing and thinking. Classically, experimental psychologists have been interested in stimulus characteristics—for example, whether the pleasantness of the stimulus influences the subject's judgment of how probable that stimulus is. Classically, too, experimental psychologists have examined manipulated subject differences—for example, whether a hint facilitates problem solving. More recently, however, psychologists interested in individual differences have asked whether subject characteristics influence performance on cognitive tasks—for example, whether age influences risk taking in decisions. Finally, the recent interest in environmental psychology has prompted additional investigation of environmental characteristics—for example, whether noise affects problem solving.

There is an additional reason for focusing on independent variables. One day you may find it necessary to design an experiment—during this course in experimental psychology, in later psychology courses, or in "real life." As mentioned in Chapter 2, one way in which psychologists find ideas for experiments is by focusing on a particular behavior (the dependent variable) that interests them and asking what *independent variables* might influence that behavior. This chapter can give you some ideas about the kind of independent variable you might select. We will spend a portion of the next chapter on the variety of *dependent variables* that have been studied in connection with a particular area of motivation—namely, sensory deprivation.

The topics we will consider within the framework of the independent variable are three areas that have had rather different histories. Problem solving has had a long history, dating back to such classic problems as Maier's rope problem (1931) and Luchins' water-jar problem (1942); recently, interest in this area seems to be dwindling. Concept identification has had a long history, too, but interest in this area seems to remain high. Decision making is the newest of the three fields, and interest in this field appears to be growing yearly.

PROBLEM SOLVING

Each of the examples in Figure 10-2 represents a task that has been studied in **problem-solving** experiments. According to Davis (1966), "Virtually any semicomplex learning task which does not clearly fall into a familiar area of learning can safely be called 'problem solving'" (p. 36). One common property of problem-solving tasks is that they are solved by "insight": at first, the parts of the problem seem unrelated to each other, but all of a sudden, the parts fit together into a solution. You may have had this sensation as you gazed at one of the anagrams: GRITE looked as though it could never be rearranged into a word, and then, all of a sudden, TIGER flashed out at you. (In contrast, most verbal-learning tasks do not involve a sudden, insightful solution.)

GRITE   RGTAE   NEIAN   GLTIH

a.   An anagram task: Rearrange each of these anagrams into an English word.

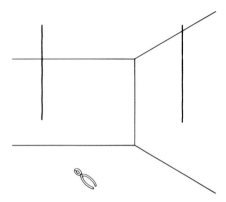

b.   Maier's (1931) rope problem: The subject is instructed to tie together the two ropes, even though they are too far apart to reach simultaneously. The solution involves tying the pair of pliers to one rope and swinging it like a pendulum.

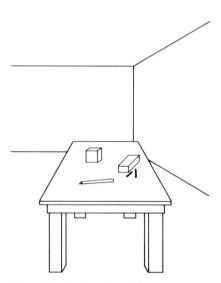

c.   The candle problem: The subject is instructed to affix the candle to the wall of the room, using only the equipment on the table—a candle, matches, and a box of tacks.

Figure 10-2. Examples of problem-solving tasks.

Incidentally, the area of cognition known as *concept learning* is frequently included under the heading of problem solving. We will consider concept learning separately in the next section of this chapter.

We'll see that a number of stimulus characteristics can influence problem solving. The presence or absence of labels on the stimuli can make a difference in solving the classic candle problem. Stimulus characteristics, such as the frequency of the letter combinations in the anagram and the frequency of the word from which the anagram was constructed, are also important in anagram problem solving.

Look back at the candle problem in Figure 10-2. If you still have not been able to solve it, would it help if the various items were labeled with the words *candle, matches, box,* and *tacks?* Glucksberg and Weisberg (1966) found that subjects solved the problem in an average of 36 seconds when all four objects were labeled, but they took an average of nearly 9 *minutes* when there were no labels. The problem's solution, incidentally, is to use the box as a candle holder, affixing it to the wall by the tacks. If the box is perceived merely as part of the tacks, as it seems to be with no label, subjects have trouble imagining it as a holder of other objects. With a label *box,* however, the subjects break the **set**—or familiar pattern of responding—and quickly discover the solution.

Other studies have shown that the frequency of two-letter combinations **(bigram frequency)** affects anagram solution time. A nonsense sequence like GRITE has high bigram frequency, because each bigram (GR, RI, IT, and TE) appears quite often in English words. If the sequence had been written RGTEI, bigram frequency would have been low. Mayzner and Tresselt (1959) found that stimuli like GRITE were harder to solve than stimuli like RGTEI. It seems to be more difficult to move letters around if they are presented in a familiar setting. However, Stachnik (1963) was unable to replicate this experiment. Stachnik attributed this nonreplication to the fact that his subjects were allowed to use paper and pencil in solving the anagrams. Subjects could proceed from each subsequent revision of the letters without returning to the original stimulus—thereby minimizing the influence of the form of the original stimulus. The reason for contrasting these two studies here is to point out how a difference in methodology that may appear quite trivial—such as allowing the use of paper and pencil—may actually have important consequences for the outcome of an experiment.

Other studies have focused on the frequency of the solution words, rather than the frequency of the stimulus. Dominowski (1967) chose words from the Thorndike and Lorge counts (described in Chapter 8), using some words high in frequency (for example, GREAT), some medium (for example, LUMP), and some low (for example, INANE). Word frequency had a strong effect on the number of problems solved, with high-frequency words being the easiest to solve. This finding is similar to some of the studies discussed in Chapter 8, where the frequency of the response can determine how easily a pair of words is learned. A familiar answer is easier to reach than an unfamiliar answer.

Gavurin and DeVito (1973) combined two of the stimulus variables that we have been discussing—bigram frequency of the anagram presented to the subject, and the frequency of the solution word. The best predictor of the ease of solving an anagram was a measure derived by taking the frequency of the solution word *minus* bigram frequency. Thus, RGTAE would be easy to solve, and NEIAN would be difficult.

The fact that the frequency of the solution word influences performance suggests that any variable that makes the response more obvious should be effective. However, this is not always the case. For example, one of the variables that Jablonski and Mueller (1972) examined was imagery (described in Chapter 8). They selected four high-imagery words (such as KNIFE) and four low-imagery words (such as FAITH). In one experiment, high imagery items were solved more rapidly, but imagery had no effect in a second experiment. It is possible that imagery would have had a more reliable effect if a greater number of different stimuli had been used. As we discussed in Chapter 2, it is just as essential to test a large number of stimuli as it is to test a large number of subjects—words can differ almost as much as people can!

Environmental Characteristics

In contrast to stimulus characteristics, relatively few studies have examined the importance of environmental characteristics in determining problem-solving ability. We will discuss two kinds of relevant studies in the next chapter—problem solving in sensory deprivation, and problem solving in the presence of another person.

Several other kinds of environmental characteristics are worth mentioning here. The results are not always what you would have expected! For example, Fine, Cohen, and Crist (1960) examined the effects of climate on complex mental performance. Wouldn't you suspect that you accomplish about twice as much in the way of "complex mental performance" on a cool, crisp autumn day as on a steamy afternoon in August? However, when these experimenters studied anagram-solving behavior, they found that performance was slightly *better* after 6.5 hours in the most hot, humid condition. These results are reminiscent of the study mentioned in Chapter 3 where performance on intelligence tests was not affected by buzzers buzzing, organ pipes piping, or photographers photographing (Sommer, 1968).

As I sat down to write about problem solving, an unseen cricket was chirping so vigorously that I moved my typewriter into another room and closed the door behind me. I was convinced that auditory distraction would hinder my "complex mental performance"! Do the experimental data support these intuitions? The answer seems to depend on the nature of the task and on the predictability and loudness of the noise. Glass and Singer (1972) conclude from reviews of the literature: "There is no compelling evidence of adverse effects of noise, *per se*, on mental and psychomotor performance, providing the tasks do not involve auditory communication" (p. 15). This conclusion certainly contradicts the reports of dozens of newspaper accounts and magazine stories! Glass and Singer note, however, that when the noise is unpredictable, performance may be hindered. It seems that noise, in itself, is not harmful. However, when cognitive processes must interpret the noise—as they did

when I had to think about when the cricket was next going to chirp—
performance may be affected.

Loud noise may also hinder performance. Kurz (1964) and Woodhead (1964) showed that multiplication and other arithmetic problem-solving tasks are relatively unaffected by the presence of soft or moderate noise. Only intensities above 90 decibels hindered performance.

Glass, Singer, and Friedman (1969) explored the effects of noise on a different aspect of problem solving—persistence in solving insoluble puzzles. The subjects were given stacks of cards containing line diagrams. They were instructed to trace over all the lines of the diagram without tracing over any line twice and without lifting the pencil from the figure. Two of the puzzles could be solved, but there was no possible solution for the other two. The noise used in the experiment was a tape recording of a mimeograph machine, a desk calculator, and a typewriter, all rattling on at the same time, with two people speaking Spanish and one person speaking Armenian. There were four noise conditions, in which the tape was played either loud or soft and either predictably (for 9 seconds at the end of every minute) or unpredictably (sporadically throughout each minute).

The authors found that subjects in the four noise conditions did not differ from each other in the number of trials necessary to solve the two problems that were soluble. However, they differed dramatically in their persistence on the two problems that could not be solved. Figure 10-3 shows how long they persisted on both problems, as measured by the average number of trials taken on each problem. Quite clearly, subjects are more persistent when noise is predictable than when it is unpredictable. Also notice the interaction: loudness is not important when the noise is predictable, but it does influence persistence

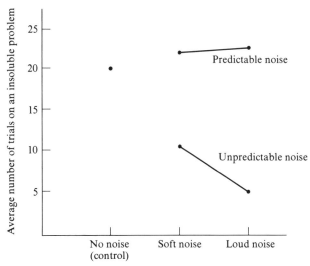

Figure 10-3. Persistence at an insoluble problem with soft and loud noise that is either predictable or unpredictable. Data from Glass, D. C., Singer, J. E., & Friedman, L. N. Psychic costs of adaptation to an environmental stressor. *Journal of Personality and Social Psychology*, 1969, *12*, 200–210.

when the noise is unpredictable. Finally, notice that subjects are somewhat *more* persistent when the noise is predictable (whether loud or soft) than when there is no noise at all! These findings reinforce Glass and Singer's (1972) conclusion that random or unpredictable noise is harmful, but predictable noise has little or no effect.

Shifting to another kind of environmental variable, let us consider the effects of high altitude. Phillips, Griswold, and Pace (1963) found that high altitude affected different problem-solving tasks in different ways. Subjects performed better on arithmetic problems at an altitude of 14,250 feet than they did at moderate altitudes. However, they performed worse in solving word-rhyme problems at high altitudes than at moderate altitudes. As you can see, environmental variables produce subtle and often unpredictable results.

Manipulated Subject Differences

Two classic studies in psychology examined the effect of manipulated subject differences on problem-solving ability. One of them was Maier's rope problem (1931), illustrated in Figure 10-2. In this experiment, subjects were led, one at a time, into a room that contained two ropes—one hanging from the center of the room and one hanging near the wall. The subjects were instructed to tie the ends of the cords together. Now this would be an easy task, except for one problem: if you were to hold one rope in one hand, you could not reach the other rope. (Can you picture yourself running to one rope and trying to grasp the other rope, then running over to the other rope in exasperation?) The only available piece of equipment in the room was a pair of pliers; the solution to the problem involved tying the pliers onto one rope as a weight, swinging it, and catching it while holding the other rope. Maier supplied a "hint" to some subjects: as he walked past, he "accidentally" brushed against one of the ropes, causing it to swing. Subjects who were given the hint solved the problem quite readily.

Luchins (1942) offered a much more general hint in his classic water-jar problem. The setup for that problem is illustrated in Table 10-1. Now, the best way to solve the first problem is to fill up jar B, and then remove one jarful with jar A and two jarful with jar C. Problems 1 through 5, therefore, were designated by Luchins as the Einstellung, or set, problems. Problems 6 and 7 can

Table 10-1. Try this experiment, similar to the Luchins water-jar problem.

Given the following empty jars as measures, *obtain* the following amount of water:

	A	B	C	
1.	23	129	3	100
2.	9	42	6	21
3.	20	57	3	31
4.	14	160	25	96
5.	18	43	9	7
6.	23	49	3	20
7.	18	48	4	22

also be solved by the same laborious procedure, but an alternate, simpler solution would be to use only jars A and C—subtracting for problem 6 and adding for problem 7. Which solution do you think subjects would adopt? In one extensive series of experiments, 81% of the subjects persisted in applying the same B - A - 2C solution. Another group of subjects, who were instructed to write the words "Don't be blind" on their papers before beginning problem 6, persisted in the familiar solution only 55% of the time. Thus, a difference in instructions produced a difference in performance. Note, however, that even this hint was not sufficient to convince most of the subjects to abandon an inefficient strategy.

The interest in hints has persisted in more recent problem-solving studies. Colgrove (1968) presented her subjects with a problem involving three workers on an assembly line. Some subjects received standard instructions, but other subjects received instructions that said:

> You have the reputation of being a very original person and of being good at coming up with answers to difficult problems. That's why Gus came to you. Keep this in mind while studying the problem [p. 1208].

A significantly greater number of subjects came up with the designated creative solution when they received the very-original-person instructions. Colgrove concludes that the mere suggestion that a person has the reputation of being an original thinker is sufficient to create a mental set that improves performance. The data do not allow her to determine *why* the instructions work, however. It is possible that subjects either concern themselves directly with producing clever responses, or else that they intentionally inhibit the obvious responses.

The two other studies to be discussed in the area of manipulated subject differences involve problem-solving strategy. Hilgard, Irvine, and Whipple (1953) examined memorization versus understanding strategies in solving a card-trick problem. One group of subjects learned a trick by rote memorization, while another group of subjects was taught a rational method. Both groups were tested for retention the next day, and then both groups were tested for transfer to another, similar problem. The results showed that the understanding group took longer to learn the task than did the memorization group, and the two groups did not differ in retention the next day. The understanding group, however, showed greater transfer to the new problem. So, which is better, memorization or understanding? It depends on your measure of performance: memorization may work better in the short run, but understanding may be more effective in the long run. Clearly, this study underscores the necessity of operational definitions for performance. In this case, the definition chosen determines the nature of the conclusion.

Gagné and Smith (1962) examined the effects of requiring subjects to verbalize, or state aloud, why they were making each individual move. Subjects worked on a problem that involved moving disks, one at a time, in order to end up with a specified arrangement of disks. The verbalization group performed significantly better, both in terms of the number of moves required and in terms of amount of time required. Gagné and Smith speculate that when subjects are required to verbalize during practice, they are forced to think of new reasons for their moves. This thought process makes it easier to discover general principles and to use these principles later in the problem.

Subject Characteristics

The subject characteristic of age has been a popular variable in problem-solving studies. First, let's look at a developmental study contrasting the strategies of elementary school children. Mosher and Hornsby (1966) studied the strategies that children use when they try to solve a problem by asking questions in a game similar to 20 Questions. First of all, imagine yourself as a subject in an experiment. The experimenter poses the following problem: "A man is driving down the road in his car, the car goes off the road and hits a tree. How come?" You are allowed to ask questions that can be answered either "yes" or "no." What would your first question be? It is likely that your question would be classified as a **constraint-seeking** question—the kind of question in which you try to eliminate about half of the alternatives. For example, you might ask "Did it happen at night?" or "Did it have anything to do with the car?" The opposite strategy—one adopted typically by young children—is called **hypothesis scanning.** With this strategy, each question tests a specific hypothesis—for example, "Did the driver get stung in the eye by a bee and lose control and go off the road into the tree?" Ocasionally the questioner using the hypothesis-scanning strategy can "get rich quick," but typically this strategy is less efficient.

In one experiment, Mosher and Hornsby showed 6-, 8- and 11-year-olds a display of 42 pictures of common objects, such as a saw, an apple, and a doll. The children were first asked to identify the pictures to make sure they knew them all. (Note that this step was necessary to make sure that familiarity with the objects' names was not a confounding variable.) Then they were instructed to find out which one of the 42 objects the experimenter had in mind. The experimenter recorded all questions and classified them into three categories: (1) constraint, in which the question was general enough to refer to two or more pictures—for example, "Is it a toy?" (2) hypothesis scanning, in which the child named a particular object—for example, "Is it a boat?" and (3) pseudoconstraint, in which the child referred to only one item in the array (hypothesis scanning) but phrased the question like a constraint question—for example, "Does it have a sail?"

Figure 10-4 shows the dramatic change in the kind of strategy adopted as a function of age. As children grow older, they appreciate the relative efficiency of constraint-type questions. Interestingly, pseudoconstraint questions also increase with age: the child has learned to make the question sound right, without always knowing how to use the logic behind the constraint-type question.

Mosher and Hornsby followed the game with an inquiry, asking the children if they had any system for getting the answers. Only 23% of the youngest group answered yes, with the typical response sounding like a charming line out

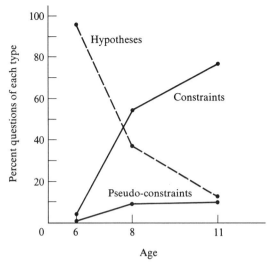

Figure 10-4. Percent questions of each type asked by children at three different ages. From "On Asking Questions," by F. A. Mosher and J. R. Hornsby. In J. S. Bruner et al. (Eds.), *Studies in Cognitive Growth*. Copyright 1966 by John Wiley & Sons, Inc. Reprinted by permission.

of A.A. Milne's *Winnie the Pooh:* "Well, I just say them in my mind, and then I start to think about them, as I say them in my mind, so then I say the words and that's what it is" (p. 98). Most (73%) of the 8-year-olds had an explanation, such as "Think of the most likely things to happen" (p. 99). Almost all of the 11-year-olds mentioned a strategy, typically involving asking questions that would "eliminate big things quickly." In summary, then, the maturing child learns to plan questions carefully, constructing the questions so that the answers will provide the maximum amount of information. Thus, age has an important influence on the strategy of problem solving.

Sex is another demographic variable that has been examined in problem-solving experiments. The literature on this topic has been summarized in Maccoby and Jacklin's (1974) superb book *The Psychology of Sex Differences*. They find that males often do better on set-breaking problems, such as the Luchins jar problem described in Table 10-1. Females, however, often do better on anagram problems. Other kinds of problems show no sex differences. Thus, there does not seem to be a consistent, reliable sex difference in problem-solving ability.

It is also possible that sex interacts with other variables to produce a difference in problem-solving ability. Maier and Burke (1967), for example, found that males were superior on a problem-solving task when certain alternatives were available. When the problem was rephrased, however, the sex differences disappeared. Thus, sex may be an important variable in some conditions, but not in other conditions.

Many experiments have examined ability or personality characteristics as determinants of problem-solving ability. For example, word fluency, as measured by a standardized vocabulary test, was found to be correlated with number of anagrams solved (Mendelsohn & Covington, 1972).

The results on word fluency are not surprising—fluency *should* be correlated with behavior on a word task. How well can we predict performance on other problem-solving tasks? Burke and Maier (1965) obtained some disappointing results. They used Maier's hatrack problem, in which subjects are asked to build a structure to hold a coat, using only two sticks and a C-clamp. (The correct solution involves clamping the two sticks together, and wedging the structure between the floor and the ceiling, using the clamp as a hook.) The experimenters recorded whether the subject solved the problem within the 15-minute time limit. Then they examined the subjects' scores on 18 different tests, including SAT-Verbal, SAT-Mathematics, object naming, "achiever personality," and a number of creativity tests. They adopted the .05 level of significance in deciding whether each of the 18 factors was significantly correlated with problem-solving ability. Now, if we adopt the .05 level of significance, approximately 1 in 20 correlations would be expected to be significant on the basis of chance. Thus, we might expect that 1 of Burke and Maier's 18 correlations would be significant, by chance alone. As it turned out, Burke and Maier found only 1 significant correlation—between a single-item task asking for uses for a brick and problem-solving ability. Since this is what we would expect by chance alone, we must conclude that problem-solving ability cannot be reliably predicted by any of a large number of likely subject characteristics.

When we looked at sex differences in problem solving, we concluded that sex, in itself, does not seem to be a reliable predictor of problem-solving ability, but sex may interact with other variables. The same may be true for ability tests. For example, Murray and Denny (1969) examined scores on the Gestalt Transformation test. This test, which asks subjects to think of unusual uses for a number of standard items, was not significantly related to problem-solving ability in Burke and Maier's study described above. However, Murray and Denny divided their subjects into two groups. A continuous-work group worked on a problem-solving task continuously for up to 20 minutes. Subjects in the interpolated-activity group worked on the problem for 5 minutes, then performed a paper-and-pencil task for 5 minutes, then returned to work on the problem for up to 15 minutes. Figure 10-5 shows the results.

Is the main effect of continuous-versus-interpolated work significant? No. Is the main effect of score on the Gestalt Transformation test significant? Again, no. However, look at the interaction, which is significant. High-ability people, as measured by that particular test, perform *better* (take less time to find the solution) than low-ability people on a problem-solving task when they work continuously on the problem. However, high-ability people perform *worse* (take more time) than low-ability people when they are interrupted. Murray and Denny propose that people of different abilities use different problem-solving processes. A high-ability person has many ideas, and the interpolated activity disrupts those ideas. A low-ability person "blocks" on generating new ideas, and the old, inadequate ideas may weaken during the interpolated activity, leaving room for new ideas.

Finally, let us consider a subject characteristic called **conceptual tempo,** or **reflection/impulsivity.** Suppose you were given the figures in Figure 10-6 and

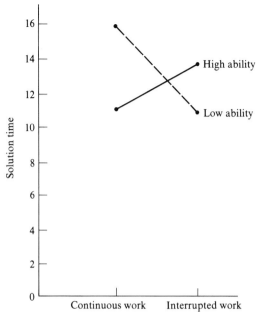

Figure 10-5. Performance on a problem-solving task for subjects of high and low ability, as measured by scores on the Gestalt Transformation test, as a function of continuous or interrupted work. Data from Murray, H. G., and Denny, J. P., Interaction of ability level and interpolated activity (opportunity for incubation) in human problem solving. *Psychological Reports*, 1969, *24*, 271–276.

were asked to match the beast at the top with one of the six at the bottom. Some people (particularly children) are impulsive: they respond quickly and often make mistakes. Other people are reflective: they carefully consider the options, taking longer on the task but making fewer mistakes. Messer (1976) has reviewed the literature on the relationship between reflection/impulsivity and problem-solving ability. In particular, he considers four studies that used the Mosher and Hornsby (1966) 20 Questions game. As you might expect, reflective subjects were more likely to use constraint questions—a more profitable strategy in the long run—whereas impulsive subjects were more likely to use hypothesis-scanning questions.

In this section, we have seen that a variety of subject characteristics influence problem-solving ability. Sometimes, however, the influence operates through an interaction rather than a main effect. Occasionally, too, a variable that should have an influence—according to our common sense—in fact is unimportant.

Discussion

Many of the situations examined in problem-solving studies have high ecological validity because they are similar to situations we encounter in daily life. For example, Maier's rope problem and the candle-and-tacks problem are both situations that require using the equipment that *is* available for new,

Figure 10-6. Which of the six beasts at the bottom matches the beast at the top? This is a sample item from the Matching Familiar Figures Test. From "Reflection-Impulsivity: A Review," by S. B. Messer, *Psychological Bulletin*, 1976, *83*, 1026–1052. Copyright 1976 by the American Psychological Association. Reprinted by permission.

creative purposes—because the ideal tools are not available. Similarly, in daily life, we frequently find ourselves stranded in new settings without our customary tools—forced to make the best of it with what we have. If you've ever gone camping, for instance, you can probably recall several examples of your own resourcefulness. Maybe you didn't use a tacks box for a candle holder, but you did use a large stone for a hammer, a coffee can to boil water, or a large leaf for an impromptu umbrella.

Problem solving, however, is a difficult area to examine. In most cases, psychologists have not been very successful in examining the covert, unobservable thought processes that lie behind the overt, observable actions of problem solvers. Psychologists often seem to be more interested in designing clever new problems and focusing on the problems, rather than on the problem solvers.

An approach to problem solving that many psychologists have adopted is the computer-simulation approach. They construct information-processing models of problem-solving behavior and program the computer to respond according to the theory. Then the particular problem is given to the computer, and the psychologist compares the theory's predictions with the computer's responses. Details of this approach can be found in Newell and Simon (1972) and in Manis (1971).

A **concept** is the same response made to a class of stimuli that share similar characteristics; **concept identification** involves discovering what those similar characteristics are. Thus, in Figure 10-7a, the subject must learn that all square stimuli are to be called BUFs, while all round stimuli are to be called DIVs. In this particular task, the subject must learn that attributes other than shape (such as size and surface pattern) can be ignored. The experiment typically involves the experimenter presenting a stimulus, the subject responding BUF or DIV, and the experimenter saying "right" or "wrong."

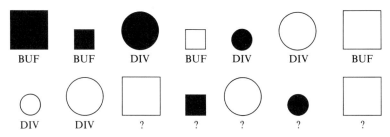

a. If you have been presented with the first nine stimuli, can you guess the appropriate response for the last five stimuli?

NOL				BEF			
1. cloud	potato	desk	star	1. red	type	rank	club
2. bean	book	ask	snake	2. pretty	now	yellow	pretend
3. never	chair	carrot	fish	3. blue	tea	plain	clay
4. paper	corn	letter	forgive	4. friend	ever	green	ask

b. If you have been presented with the first three cards containing four words, with one of them underlined to indicate the correct response to be associated with the nonsense word NOL, what would be your response on the fourth card? Can you guess the correct response for BEF?

circle	feather	speck	pudding
silk	ball	sheep	freckle
dot	crumb	doughnut	plate

c. Guess the appropriate adjective for each of these words. Four of these words can be described by a single word, four others by another word, and four others by a third word.

Figure 10-7. Examples of concept-identification tasks.

Notice that the experiments often use verbal skills. In Figure 10-7a, the responses are verbal, and the task is a bit like a paired-associate task. In Figure 10-7b, the subject must know that the stimuli *potato, bean, carrot,* and *corn* all belong to the class *vegetable*. In Figure 10-7c, the subject must find the adjective that is associated with the four stimuli *circle, ball, doughnut,* and *plate*.

Think for a moment of the task faced by a child learning concepts. From adult speech, the child must extract the stimulus attributes that are relevant. For example, a cup is something that has a particular shape, a handle, and is made of plastic, china, or metal. (However, if the height-to-width ratio is greater, if it lacks a handle, and if it is made of glass, it should be called a glass.)

The child learns that some attributes, such as color and design, are irrelevant. Sometimes, the child meets additional difficulties in trying to learn the correct response, even after the concept has been mastered. Dr. Eleanor Maccoby told her child-psychology class at Stanford University about a small child who thought that the appropriate name for toast was "jamonit." Apparently, his mother would hand the child a piece of toast each morning and say, "Would you like some jam on it?"

A few words about methodology are in order before we proceed to the variables that influence concept identification. What do we use as the dependent variable in a concept-identification task? The most frequently used measures assess learning speed. For example, we could measure how many trials are needed before the subject responds correctly (for example, says BUF to all square stimuli) six times in a row. We might also ask the subjects to tell us their hypothesis as soon as they think they have learned a concept; our measure here would be the trial on which the subjects guessed the hypothesis correctly. Another dependent variable would be subjects' confidence ratings. Coltheart (1973), for example, asked subjects to make a response and then to rate how confident they were of the correctness of their response. The ratings ranged from 1 ("no idea—response is a guess") to 5 ("quite certain response is correct"). One of her findings was that subjects were more confident in the correctness of a response if their *previous* response had been correct than if it had been an error. Still another dependent variable could be response latency—the amount of time between the presentation of the stimulus and the subject's response. Fink (1972) used this measure and found that one group of subjects showed a decrease in response latency on the trial that immediately followed their last error. Thus, the dependent variable may be number of trials to criterion, trial on which the hypothesis was verbalized, confidence rating, or response latency.

Stimulus Characteristics

Try an experiment devised by Heidbreder (1946), shown in Figure 10-8. She was interested in studying the influence of class of stimuli on concept identification. She found that concrete objects (faces, buildings, and trees) were learned fastest. Spatial forms (the circle, the intersecting diagonal lines, and the figure that looks like a broken, sideways figure 8) were learned next fastest. Abstract numbers (2, 5, and 6) were learned slowest. Heidbreder reasoned that subjects have preferences for what they attend to, with abstract concepts such as numbers being the least preferred.

Another kind of experiment that has been popular in the area of concept identification involves positive versus negative examples. Suppose an experimenter gave you a small plain circle, a medium striped circle, and a large plain circle and told you that these were all examples of the concept DIJ. In contrast, suppose the experimenter gave you a small plain triangle, a medium plain square, and a large striped triangle and told you that these were *not* examples of the concept DIJ. Which task would be easier? Experimenters seem to agree

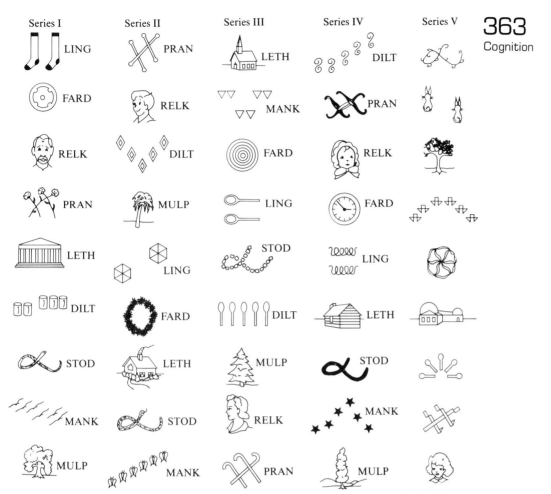

Figure 10-8. Try this concept-identification task. Given the set of stimuli and responses in Series I, II, III, and IV, what would your responses be for Series V? From "The Attainment of Concepts: I. Terminology and Methodology," by E. Heidbreder, *Journal of General Psychology*, 1946, *35*, 173–189. Copyright 1946 by The Journal Press. Reprinted by permission.

that positive examples (the first task, where you are told what a DIJ *is*) are easier than negative examples (the second task, where you are told what a DIJ is *not*). This was originally demonstrated by Smoke (1932), who found that negative examples were almost useless in the learning of concepts.

Why are negative examples so useless? Hovland and Weiss (1953) proposed that positive examples may convey more information than negative examples. (It is typically much more useful to know what something is than what it isn't!) In their experiments, they made sure that the positive and negative examples conveyed the same amount of information. The subjects still learned faster with positive examples. In one condition, for example, 100% of the subjects in the positive-examples condition learned the concept, but only

17% of the subjects in the negative-examples condition learned it. The authors concluded that negative examples are harder because subjects find it more difficult to *make use of* negative information, even when that information is just as useful as positive information.

Can subjects learn from negative examples in any circumstances? Freibergs and Tulving (1961) showed that they could if they received extensive training. Figure 10-9 shows the results for two groups of subjects—one learning with only positive examples and one learning with only negative examples.

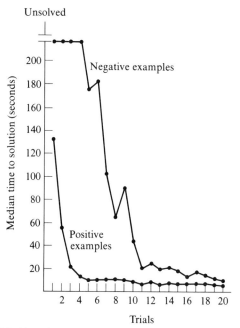

Figure 10-9. Median times to solution of concept-identification problems, as a function of practice: negative versus positive examples. From "The Effect of Practice on Utilization of Information from Positive and Negative Instances in Concept Identification," by V. Freibergs and E. Tulving, *Canadian Journal of Psychology*, 1961, *15*, 101–106. Copyright 1961, Canadian Psychological Association. Reprinted by permission.

Notice that on the first few trials, the subjects in the negative-examples condition failed to solve the problem within the time limit. After about 11 trials, however, their performance became nearly as fast as that of the positive-examples subjects. Perhaps subjects can learn to make use of negative information.

Environmental Characteristics

Laughlin, Chenoweth, Farrell, and McGrath (1972) examined an unusual kind of environmental characteristic—videotaping performance. The subjects in this experiment performed a concept-identification task that involved arranging two rows of cards appropriately. In the video condition, videotaping of the subjects' performance began as soon as the instructions were finished. The subjects were told that the session was being videotaped in order to obtain a record of performance. In the control condition, subjects performed the same tasks, except that no portion was videotaped. The authors found that the videotape variable affected one dependent variable but not the other. Specifically, the videotape-condition subjects, compared with the control subjects, gave a larger proportion of hypotheses that were inconsistent with the available information. However, the videotape-condition subjects did not differ from the control subjects in terms of the number of trials to solution. The authors concluded that "proportion of inconsistent hypotheses" is a more sensitive measure of performance.

Shrauger (1972) showed that environmental variables can interact with subject variables. The subjects, all female undergraduates, worked on a concept-identification task that involved figures varying along five dimensions, such as number, color, and shape. Some of the subjects performed the task alone, but some performed with an "audience"—a male and a female who were said to be interested in the experiment. Shrauger also included the subject variable of self-esteem—whether the subjects had scored high or low on a scale of self-esteem that asked 16 questions such as "What percentage of people of your own age and sex have a more pleasing personal appearance than you?" Thus, the experiment represented a 2 x 2 factorial design.

Figure 10-10 shows the results of the experiment. Notice that there is a strong main effect for self-esteem: high-self-esteem subjects made fewer errors on the task. However, notice also that the effect of an audience is different for the two kinds of subjects: people with low self-esteem performed much worse when an audience was present, but people with high self-esteem performed

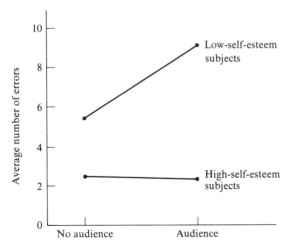

Figure 10-10. Number of errors made in a concept-identification task by high- and low-self-esteem subjects, in "no audience" and "audience" conditions. Data from Shrauger, J. S., Self-esteem and reactions to being observed by others. *Journal of Personality and Social Psychology*, 1972, *23*, 192–200.

about the same with or without an audience. We'll return to this topic— performance in the presence of other people—in the next chapter.

Manipulated Subject Differences

What is the effect of experimentally manipulated subject differences on the identification of concepts? Some experiments manipulate the instructions given to the subjects. For example, Underwood and Richardson (1956) used a task similar to the one shown in Figure 10-7c. Thus, the subject would learn that *round* was the appropriate response for *circle, ball, doughnut,* and *plate*. Subjects received one of three kinds of instructions. One group of subjects was told to supply responses freely, as in a word-association task. A second group received more information: they were told what kinds of descriptive words were correct and were given examples. A final group was given the six correct responses printed on cards: their task was simply to fit each stimulus with the appropriate response. Underwood and Richardson also included a stimulus variable in their design. Some of the stimuli had high-dominance association with the response (for example, *round* to *ball*), as established by previous norms. Other stimuli had medium dominance (for example, *white* to *frost*), and still others had low dominance (for example, *big* to *forest*). Thus, the experiment used a 3 × 3 design, with three levels of instructions and three levels of dominance.

The results are shown in Figure 10-11. Notice that the nature of the instructions had a strong effect on the number of correct responses. However,

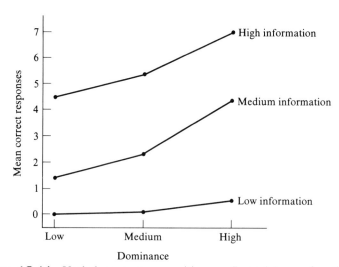

Figure 10-11. Verbal concept recognition on first trial as a function of dominance level and nature of instructions. From "Verbal Concept Learning as a Function of Instructions and Dominance Level," by B. J. Underwood and J. Richardson, *Journal of Experimental Psychology*, 1956, *51*, 229–238. Copyright 1956 by the American Psychological Association. Reprinted by permission.

also notice the interaction. In the high-information and medium-information groups, response dominance is an important factor. In the low-information group, response dominance has no effect. Thus, the strength of the connection between the stimulus and the response is only important if subjects have some idea of what to look for as a response.

Other experiments have involved manipulating the amount of information that subjects must remember. For example, Bourne, Guy, Dodd, and Justesen (1965) manipulated the amount of information available to subjects in the period following feedback. Some subjects did not have to remember any information: they were given both the stimulus pattern and the feedback signal during this period. Other subjects had to remember some information: they were given either the stimulus or the feedback. Other subjects had to remember everything: they received no information. When the period following feedback was short (less than 15 seconds), performance was equivalent for all groups. However, with longer delays, the subjects who had the stimulus available performed significantly better. Thus, concept identification involves memory: for accurate performance, the stimulus should not be forgotten.

Information about *previous* stimuli also influences performance on a concept-identification task. Bourne, Goldstein, and Link (1964) used cards with drawings of geometric forms that varied on six dimensions. Six groups of subjects differed in the number of cards from previous trials that the subject was allowed to keep. Thus, subjects who kept zero cards had no concrete record of previous trials. At the other extreme were the subjects who kept five cards from previous trials. The number of cards available had a strong effect on identifying the concept: subjects who kept zero cards took about three times as long to master the task as subjects who kept five cards. Both these Bourne et al. experiments point to the importance of memory in concept-identification tasks: subjects seem to perform better when the information is in front of them, so that they do not need to reconstruct the information from memory.

Subject Characteristics

Age is the subject characteristic that has been studied most thoroughly by psychologists interested in concept formation. The results show that children differ from adults in the speed with which they learn a concept and in their strategy of responding when the pattern of reinforcement is changed.

Kendler and Kendler (1970) demonstrated both of these characteristics, using the procedure diagrammed in Figure 10-12. Their subjects were kindergarteners, second-graders, sixth-graders, and college students. The IQs for the elementary school children were equal, but the IQs for the college students were about 15 points higher.

The first task was a kind of concept learning called **discrimination learning,** in which the subject must choose which of two stimuli is the "correct" one. On the first trial, for example, the subjects might have a choice of a green circle or a red triangle (see Figure 10-12). If they select the green circle, they receive a marble as a reward; if they select the red triangle, they receive no

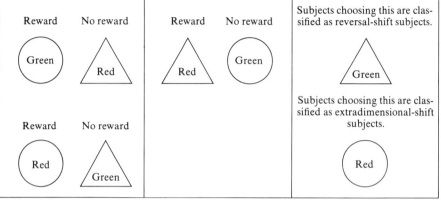

Figure 10-12. Setup of experiments used to test whether subjects use reversal shifts or extradimensional shifts.

reward. Learning continues until the subject has made ten correct responses in a row.

Before describing the rest of the experiment, let's consider the results on just that first task. Age had a very strong effect on the number of trials necessary to reach the criterion of ten correct responses. In one condition, for example, the kindergarteners needed 68 trials to master the task, whereas second-graders needed 34, sixth-graders needed 20, and college students needed only 8.

After subjects mastered the first task, they began the **shift-discrimination** task. During this period, subjects saw only two stimuli, and the red triangle was always the correct response. Now, if you were a subject in this experiment, imagine what you might think. One strategy you might adopt would be to say, "Earlier, circles were right, and triangles were wrong. Now they have simply reversed the correct kind of stimulus: now circles are wrong, and triangles are right." This kind of strategy is referred to as a **reversal shift**, because subjects reverse the concept that had been correct. However, another strategy you might adopt would be to say, "Earlier, circles were right; now red is right." This strategy is called an **extradimensional shift** because the subject changes dimensions—in this case, from shape to color.

How can we determine which strategy the subjects have adopted? We could ask them to tell us their strategies, but young children would be unlikely to describe how they had been operating. Instead, Kendler and Kendler (1970) ran a test series that included a green triangle and a red circle. If subjects choose the green triangle, we can conclude that they have made a reversal shift, because they now believe that triangles are correct. If subjects choose the red circle, we can conclude that they have made an extradimensional shift, because they now believe that red things are correct.

All of the subjects were classified on the basis of the first ten responses in
the test series. If they made eight or more responses that would be consistent with a reversal shift, they were classified as *reversal-shift subjects*. If they made eight or more responses that would be consistent with an extradimensional shift, they were classified as *extradimensional-shift subjects*. Subjects who were not consistent in their responding were classified as *nonselective subjects*.

Figure 10-13 shows how the strategies change as a function of age. Notice that the subjects are more likely to make reversal shifts as they grow older. Furthermore, they are less likely to make either extradimensional shifts or nonselective responses. Kendler and Kendler propose that older subjects are more likely to make reversal shifts because they are more likely to develop mediators, or concepts summarizing the situation. Developing the concept in the first task that shape is relevant allows the older subjects to respond on the basis of shape in future tasks. Once shape is relevant, it is easy to reverse the choice of which shape (triangle or circle) is correct.

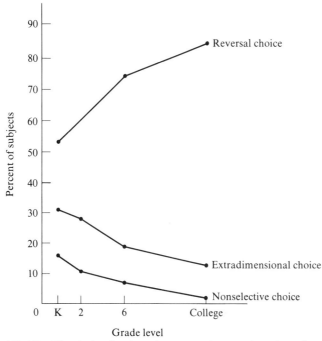

Figure 10-13. Discrimination learning strategies as a function of age. Data from Kendler, T. S., & Kendler, H. H., An ontogeny of optional shift behavior. *Child Development,* 1970, *41,* 1–28.

Other studies concerned with age have contrasted performance of the elderly with the performance of young adults. Nehrke (1973), for example, compared the performance of college students, middle-aged people (35–50 years old), and elderly people (55 years or older). (It seems likely that these subjects were not equivalent in intelligence, because the older two groups were recruited from community groups, and general populations like these are less likely to have the intelligence of the college group.) The task was similar to Kendler and Kendler's (1970) discrimination-learning task, except that Nehrke arranged the stimuli so that subjects were forced to learn either a reversal-shift task or an extradimensional-shift task. The most interesting comparison was between the number of errors made on the first task and the number of errors made on the reversal-shift task. The college subjects and the middle-aged subjects made fewer errors on the reversal-shift task than on the original task—even though they had to "unlearn" their original response in order to master the reversal shift. The elderly subjects, however, made more errors on the reversal-shift task than on the original task. Nehrke suggests that with increasing age, the subjects perform more like young children who lack mediators. The elderly in this experiment may have failed to develop concepts to guide their choices during the original task, and so they found it difficult to reverse the choice of which item was correct. It is important to remember, however, that we should be cautious about attributing these differences to age, because age might have been confounded with intelligence in this study.

Intelligence is another stimulus characteristic that has received some attention. Kendler and Kendler (1970), whose study we examined earlier, also looked at IQ scores for their elementary-school subjects. They found that intelligence was not related to the number of trials to criterion required on the first task. In other words, bright children performed no better than the less bright children on the first task shown in Figure 10-12. Moreover, there was no relationship between IQ and the strategies that the subjects adopted. We might have expected to find that bright children would be more likely to make reversal shifts and less likely to make extradimensional shifts and nonselective responses, but this pattern was not found.

However, a study by Osler and Fivel (1961) has demonstrated that bright children differ from less bright children in their use of other kinds of strategies. Their task also involved selecting the correct member of each pair. However, the concepts represented in the tasks were verbal concepts—bird, animal, or living thing. For example, a subject in the living-thing condition might see an umbrella and a flower. A marble hidden under the flower indicated that it was the correct response. Both age and intelligence influenced the proportion of children who mastered the concepts. However, a more interesting analysis examined the percentage of correct responses in the ten trials preceding mastery of the concept. Subjects who made a large number of errors were classified as *sudden learners:* their performance quickly shifted from being very poor to being very accurate. Subjects who made fewer errors during that period before mastery were classified as *gradual learners.* Osler and Fivel found that the sudden learners were brighter than the gradual learners. Gradual learners—those with average or below-average intelligence—acquire concepts slowly but surely, gradually learning which cue is relevant. Sudden learners may use hypothesis testing, trying first one hypothesis, then another—all of which leads to many errors—until suddenly they select the correct hypothesis. After they arrive at the correct concept, their performance is close to errorless.

Finally, what is the effect of sex on concept learning? Maccoby and Jacklin (1974) have summarized the findings on discrimination learning—that special kind of concept learning in which the subject must select the correct response from each pair of stimuli. Of the 28 studies they found in the literature between 1967 and 1972, 5 favored females, 2 favored males, and 21 found no sex differences. Clearly, there is no consistent sex difference in discrimination learning.

Discussion

Research on concept identification has been more successful than research on problem solving in probing covert thought processes. For example, Kendler and Kendler (1970) were able to identify the strategy that subjects had adopted in shifting from one task to a second task by observing the kinds of responses they made on a third task. Mayer (1977) points out another advantage of the concept-identification approach to cognition: "One advantage of concentrating on an agreed-upon task and method is that researchers have been able to amass an impressive amount of detailed and thorough information about human thinking with respect to concept learning" (p. 53). In contrast, the diversity of problems studied in problem-solving experiments makes a systematic approach more difficult.

Mayer also acknowledges, however, that the concept-identification approach has its disadvantages. One problem, for example,

> concerns the finding that subjects tend to use "rules" and "strategies" in problem solving; in the concept learning task the rules and structure are built into the task by the experimenter (e.g., defining red as positive, or making a structural tree), and therefore it is not entirely surprising that the subjects display some effects of the experimenter's rules and structure [p. 53].

In addition, concept-identification tasks are somewhat artificial. In real life, objects that must be classified are not simply circles or triangles that are large or small and black or white. Objects have many more attributes, some of which may be correlated with other attributes. Furthermore, objects do not come only in black or white, but in every shade of gray. Consider, for example, the task of botany students learning to classify plants. They must consider whether the leaves are borne singly or in pairs, whether the veins on the leaves are parallel or not, the number of petals, the number of stamens, the symmetry of the petals, whether the petals are joined, and where the plant is growing. The size and color of the flower may be important, but often these characteristics are irrelevant.

At present, then, psychologists have detailed information on how people identify simple, well-structured concepts. Given the current level of enthusiasm for concept identification, it seems likely that they will soon be unraveling the process of identifying complex, unstructured concepts.

Decision making is an important part of our everyday lives. We have to decide whether it is likely enough to rain that we should bring an umbrella—"Maybe I shouldn't because the weather forecaster said there was only a 20% chance of rain." We have to decide whether to bring a book to class—"I think I will because the professor has referred to it in each of the last four lectures." We have to decide whether to wait for the bus or walk the seven blocks—"I think I'll walk because that will only take 10 minutes and it's likely to take 15 minutes for the bus to arrive." There are also less trivial decisions to make: whether to take Job A or Job B; whether to accept Graduate School A's offer or hope for a more attractive offer from Graduate School B; whether to marry John or not.

In recent years, the decision-making process has been carefully examined in the laboratory. Some experiments require subjects to choose between two alternatives; other experiments ask subjects to judge the relative probability of various alternatives. Recent research in the laboratory has changed psychologists' views of humans as decision makers. Humans used to be viewed as "intuitive statisticians," capable of rationally applying the laws of statistics and probability (see, for example, Peterson & Beach, 1967). However, Slovic, Fischhoff, and Lichtenstein (1977) have reviewed some recent evidence that people are really quite inaccurate at decision-making tasks; they quote statements from the literature such as " 'man's cognitive capacities are not adequate for the tasks which confront him' " and " ' people systematically violate the principles of rational decision making when judging probabilities, making predictions, or otherwise attempting to cope with probabilistic tasks' " (p. 3). We will see evidence for these claims in the studies that follow. In particular, people often make decisions according to inappropriate, informal rules, rather than according to more rational, scientific strategies. Furthermore, people are often inappropriately conservative in their decisions.

Stimulus Characteristics

Suppose that some people came up to you with a coin, saying that they would give you $5.00 if the coin landed heads up, but that you would lose $5.00 if the coin landed tails up. Objectively, you know you have a 50% chance of winning (or losing), but *subjectively* the probability of winning may seem much higher. The subjective probability of pleasant stimuli seems higher than the subjective probability of unpleasant stimuli.

Marks (1951) demonstrated this relationship between stimulus pleasantness and subjective probability in fifth- and sixth-grade children. The concept of probability was conveyed to the children through a card game. Each child played ten card games, each game consisting of choosing a single card out of a deck of ten cards. Some cards were blank, and some had a picture on the reverse side. In five of the games, picking a picture card meant that the subject won a point; in the other five games, a picture card meant that the subject lost a point. For each of the two sets, there were five probabilities of choosing a picture card: .10, .30, .50, .70, and .90. Each time, Marks announced the number of picture and blank cards in the deck she held, as well as the outcome for the subject if a picture card was chosen. For example, she might say, "There are 7 dogs and 3 blank cards. If you pick a dog, you'll get a point." Then Marks asked subjects whether they expected to pick a dog on this trial. To avoid influencing expectations, Marks did not tell the children what card they had actually picked.

Marks' results are straightforward. At all true probability levels, children perceived pleasant outcomes to be significantly more probable than unpleasant outcomes. In fact, as Figure 10-14 shows, the effect was so strong that a pleasant outcome that would truly occur only 10% of the time was judged to occur only slightly less often than an unpleasant outcome that would truly occur 90% of the time!

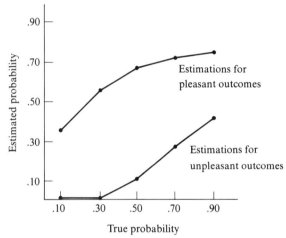

Figure 10-14. Children's estimates of probability of pleasant and unpleasant outcomes (percentage of the time the children thought that each particular outcome was likely to occur). Data from R. W. Marks, The effect of probability, desirability, and "privilege" on the stated expectations of children. *Journal of Personality*, 1951, *19*, 332–351.

Pruitt and Hoge (1965) showed that undergraduates also overestimate the probability of pleasant outcomes. Subjects watched two lightbulbs flash in random order 24 times. Then they were asked to guess whether light A or light B would be illuminated the 25th time. The authors varied the value of light A, from "win 50 cents" to "win or lose nothing" to "lose 50 cents." Subjects used one of four methods to guess the probability of light A: one was simply guessing A or B (as Marks' subjects had done); another was rating the probability of A on an 11-point scale, with a cash reward promised to the most accurate subjects. With all four methods, subjects guessed that light A was more likely when it was worth a gain of 50 cents than when it was worth a loss of 50 cents. However, the effect was much stronger in the guessing condition than in the rating-with-accuracy-stressed condition.

Both of these studies are examples of the Pollyanna Principle in cognition (Matlin & Stang, 1978). Just as pleasant items are recalled better in memory and judged larger in perception, they are judged more likely to occur than unpleasant items. However, instructions to be accurate can reduce the influence of pleasantness on subjective probability.

Other researchers have studied the importance of the decision as a stimulus characteristic. Alker and Hermann (1971) examined **Bayesian decisions**, which require subjects to modify their original probability estimates after being supplied with new information. Studies in this area typically find that subjects are not good decision makers because they are too conservative. That is, they do not modify the probability estimates as much as they should in light of the new information. Alker and Hermann proposed that this conservatism might be especially strong when the decision is an important one. One of their judgment tasks involved an unimportant decision—the number of different colors of poker chips contained in a bookbag. Two other judgment tasks involved important decisions: one concerned the reasons for a hypothetical increase in birth defects, and the other concerned responsibility for an atomic explosion. As predicted, subjects were substantially more conservative when making decisions about important problems than when making decisions about unimportant problems.

So far, we have seen that the *kind* of information the subjects receive influences their decision. Other studies have investigated the *amount* of information that subjects receive. Jacoby (1975) reviewed his own research program in consumer psychology. Subjects were asked to make choices from among a number of hypothetical brands of laundry detergent. They were given a total of 4, 8, 12, or 16 items of information about each kind of detergent. Jacoby found that there was a curvilinear relationship between amount of information supplied and the accuracy of the decision; that is, as the information increased, there was first an increase and then a decrease in accuracy. In other words, extra information is helpful up to a point, but too much information hinders. Jacoby also asked subjects how they felt about the decision-making process in each of the information conditions. As the amount of information increased, the consumers became more satisfied, less confused, and more certain in the decision-making task. Thus, a vast amount of information makes consumers feel good about their decisions, even though it seems to hinder the accuracy of those decisions.

Oskamp (1965) found a comparable pattern in his data. He asked 32 judges, including eight professional clinical psychologists, to read some background information about a psychological case. The background information was divided into four sections. The judges read each section and then answered 25 questions about the attitudes and behaviors of the subject. They also supplied a confidence rating for each answer. The results showed that, as the amount of information increased, the judges' accuracy remained at about the same level. However, the judges' confidence increased markedly as the amount of information increased. Once again, with piles of information, we have the illusion of confidence about our decisions, even though that information does not improve our accuracy.

The most extensive studies on stimulus characteristics in decision making have been performed by two psychologists at Hebrew University in Israel— Daniel Kahneman and Amos Tversky. Their impressive series of studies has shown that people are influenced by some stimulus characteristics that are really irrelevant, but they are not influenced by some other stimulus characteristics that are really important.

Kahneman and Tversky (1972) have found that subjects regard representativeness as a very important factor in determining subjective probability. If an event is **representative**, (1) it is similar in important characteristics to the population from which it was selected, and (2) it demonstrates the important features of the process by which it was selected from the population. For example, if I toss a coin eight times and find the sequence H H H H H H H H (where H = heads), this sequence would not be representative of the population from which it was selected, which contains an equal number of heads and tails. If I found the sequence H H H H T T T T, it would be representative of the number of heads and tails in the population, but it would not be representative of the random sequence we would expect to result from the process by which it was selected. However, the sequence H T H H T H T T would be representative according to both criteria for representativeness. That last sequence *seems* likely because it has the randomness that is supposed to be characteristic of the coin-tossing procedure. In actuality, however, the *specific* sequence H H H H T T T T is just as likely as the *specific* sequence H T H H T H T T.[1] Once again, humans are not accurate "intuitive statisticians": they are not aware of the laws of chance.

Look at the problem in Table 10-2, which is similar to a problem posed to subjects by Kahneman and Tversky (1972). Of their 52 subjects, 36 believed that Group A distributions would occur more often than Group B distributions.

Table 10-2. If marbles are distributed at random among five children, which distribution would you consider to be most likely?

Group A		Group B	
Alice	5	Alice	5
Betsy	5	Betsy	5
Carol	4	Carol	5
Diane	5	Diane	5
Eleanor	6	Eleanor	5

In reality, however, the statistically most likely outcome is the Group B distribution. Kahneman and Tversky conclude: "People view chance as unpredictable but essentially fair. Thus, they expect that in a purely random allocation of marbles each child will get approximately (though not exactly) the same number of marbles" (p. 435). Thus, a slight deviation from an exactly equal

[1] The reason that this is puzzling is that the probability of an outcome *like* H T H H T H T T (for example T H H T H T T H) is far greater than the probability of H H H H T T T T. However, we are speaking here of the probabilities of those two specific sequences, H T H H T H T T and H H H H T T T T, and those two probabilities are identical, each one chance in 256.

distribution (5 marbles per child) is viewed as more representative of randomness, and hence as more probable.

In everyday life, we are often fooled by the inappropriate use of representativeness in determining probabilities. For example, suppose you added up some numbers on a calculator and came up with the sum 12345. That number seems so unlikely (that is, unrepresentative of the randomness you expect to result from the addition process) that you would be tempted to conclude that you'd made a mistake. However, the specific number 12345 is no less likely than another specific, but more representative-looking number, such as 85769. Similarly, it surprises most people to learn that a group of 23 people is likely to include at least two people with the same birthday (that is, the same day of the same month). In other words, given a total of 365 days, people believe that the most representative solution is to have each person born on a separate day. However, the statistically most likely solution is to have 2 people born on the same day and 21 people born on different days.

Kahneman and Tversky (1972) discuss a final example of the inappropriate use of representativeness in real-life situations. In World War II, London was intensively bombed. It was generally believed that there was a pattern to the bombing because some sections of town were hit several times, whereas many others were not hit at all—the pattern did not seem representative enough to be due to chance alone. However, when statisticians compared the bombing pattern with the pattern that would be expected by chance alone, the fit was remarkably good. By chance, a pattern that allows for duplicates (such as duplicate birthdays or duplicate bomb strikes) is often more likely than a pattern without any duplicates.

People also use **availability**—the ease with which instances can be brought to mind—to determine how probable an outcome is, even though this stimulus cue can be just as inappropriate as representativeness. Tversky and Kahneman (1974) give an example of how people use availability in everyday life. If you were asked to judge the risk of heart attack among middle-aged people, you would probably try to think of middle-aged friends who had experienced heart attacks. The number of instances that you could bring to mind would determine your judgment. Often, availability is a useful clue for judging probabilities, because examples of frequent events can usually be recalled better and faster than examples of less frequent events. However, there are other, psychological factors that influence availability—availability is not always an accurate measure of frequency.

Let's consider one of those psychological factors. Imagine that you were asked to sample words at random from this book, looking at all words that are three or more letters long. Is it more likely that the word starts with an *r* or that *r* is the third letter? It is likely that you would base your judgment on availability—on the ease with which examples come to mind. Words starting with an *r* leap to mind—red, road, rod, rent, and so on. It is far more difficult to think of words in which *r* is the third letter. Tversky and Kahneman (1974) found that subjects guessed that words were more likely to have *r*'s as their first letter than as their third letter. In reality, however, *r* is more likely to appear in the third-letter position. (Check this out by counting the number of *r*'s in each position on this page.) Thus, availability influences estimates, even though availability is not an accurate measure of frequency.

We have seen that two stimulus characteristics, representativeness and availability, have a significant influence on subjects' frequency judgments, even though they are often inappropriate cues. Another stimulus characteristic, sample size, does *not* have a significant influence on subjects' frequency judgments, even though it is an appropriate cue. Imagine that you were asked this question in an experiment:

> A certain town is served by two hospitals. In the larger hospital about 45 babies are born each day, and in the smaller hospital about 15 babies are born each day. As you know, about 50% of all babies are boys. However, the exact percentage varies from day to day. Sometimes it may be higher than 50%, sometimes lower.
>
> For a period of 1 year, each hospital recorded the days on which more than 60% of the babies born were boys. Which hospital do you think recorded more such days?
> * The larger hospital
> * The smaller hospital
> * About the same (within 5% of each other) [Tversky & Kahneman, 1974, p. 1125].

Now, the correct answer to the problem is that the smaller hospital would be more likely to report the deviant sample: as can be demonstrated with statistics formulas, small samples are more likely to deviate from the expected mean. However, only 22% of the subjects gave the correct answer, another 22% answered that the larger hospital would be more likely to report the deviant sample, and 56% answered "about the same." In other studies, Kahneman and Tversky (1972) found that subjects ignored sample size when they estimated word length for small and large samples and when they estimated adult male height for small and large samples. Thus, the stimulus characteristic of sample size is not an important determinant of frequency judgments.

Environmental Characteristics

Studies on decision making have been conducted in a wide variety of environmental settings, as summarized in two excellent reviews of this literature (Kogan & Wallach, 1967; Lee, 1971). However, studies do not typically include environmental setting as one of the independent variables. Consequently, information on environmental characteristics is much more scanty than information on stimulus characteristics.

Wright (1974) wondered if noise distractions would influence decision making—in particular, whether noise would influence the amount of attention that subjects paid to negative attributes. He asked subjects to read descriptions of 30 hypothetical car models. They received information on five attributes of each car: selling price, ease of handling, cost of maintenance, styling, and riding comfort. Their task was to judge each car according to the likelihood that they would buy it. Subjects in the high-distraction condition heard a radio talk show, complete with commercials, at moderately high volume while they made their decisions. Subjects in the moderate-distraction condition heard the same radio show at low volume. Subjects in the low-distraction condition heard music from an FM station. Ratings in response to the question "How distracting did you find the noise from the tape recording while making your judgments?" showed that the subjects perceived the high-distraction condition as more distracting than the moderate-distraction condition, which in turn was perceived as more distracting than the low-distraction condition. When Wright examined the decisions, however, the results were puzzling. The subjects who gave the heaviest weighting to negative evidence were the subjects in the *moderate-distraction* group. Thus, subjects paid more attention to what was bad about an alternative when they were distracted by a low-volume talk show than when they were distracted by a high-volume talk show or music from an FM station. These findings reinforce the suspicion, discussed in the other sections of this chapter, that noise has complex and inconsistent effects on cognitive performance.

What effect does the presence of other individuals have on decision making? Preston and Baratta (1948) conducted a gambling experiment in which subjects played in groups of either two or four. These authors found that subjects in the four-person groups valued the low-probability, high-payoff bids more highly than did subjects in the two-person groups. People seem to be more willing to take risks in large groups. This finding may help to explain why betting at race tracks—clearly a group setting—is generally high-risk, whereas betting in the laboratory—almost always without others present—is generally conservative. A related phenomenon in social psychology, called the **risky shift,** has been discussed by Wrightsman (1977). When groups discuss an issue and reach a decision, that decision is typically more extreme than the decisions made by the group members as individuals. Thus, group decisions shift to the risky side.

Manipulated Subject Differences

Many studies that examine manipulated subject differences are concerned with the issue of conservatism. As we have seen, subjects are often inappropriately conservative—they don't revise their subjective probabilities as much as they should in the light of new evidence. Researchers have asked whether experimental conditions can force subjects to become less conservative.

For example, Phillips and Edwards (1966) thought that the method of responding might influence conservatism. Perhaps subjects give conservative responses because extreme responses such as ".95 probability" are near the upper boundary of the probability scale, close to 1.00. Phillips and Edwards thought that the unbounded-odds method of responding, in contrast, might encourage subjects to be less conservative; subjects might be willing to say "19 in 20 chances" because no boundary is involved. However, when these two

methods of responding were compared, the unbounded-odds group was only
slightly less conservative.

Can subjects be trained to be less conservative? Messick and Campos (1972) studied manipulated subject differences by varying the training experiences of their subjects. Their task was a Bayesian decision task—that is, a task that required subjects to modify their original probability estimates after they had received new information. Subjects were asked to imagine two jars, each filled with 100 poker chips. One jar contained 80 red and 20 blue poker chips; the other jar contained 20 red and 80 blue poker chips. The subject was then shown 5 poker chips (for example, 3 reds and 2 blues) and asked to make bets on which jar the chips were most likely to have been drawn from. Messick and Campos let subjects try this task for several trials. Then, each of three groups received a different treatment. One group received training in what is called *posterior distributions*: they were given a sample of chips and told how likely it was that the sample came from each of the two distributions. For example, they were given 3 reds and 2 blues, and then they saw the word *red* listed 27 times and the word *blue* listed 7 times—indicating that the odds were 27:7 that the sample came from the predominantly red jar. The second group of subjects received training in sampling distributions: they saw 100 random samples of chips from each of the two jars. For the predominantly red jar, for example, they might see 3 reds and 2 blues, 4 reds and 1 blue, 3 reds and 2 blues, and so on. The third group of subjects served as controls: they simply rested for about one minute. (Note, however, that this is not an ideal control group, because the two groups with the training experiences undoubtedly took longer than one minute on their tasks.) Then all subjects continued with the Bayesian decision task.

Messick and Campos found that both groups with the training experience were less conservative than the control group. However, the two training groups did not differ from each other. In other words, training in posterior distributions was no more helpful than training in sampling distributions for performance on Bayesian decision tasks, even though it was directly relevant to the task.

Another study of manipulated subject differences has examined whether the starting point has an influence on probability estimates. Tversky and Kahneman (1974), as we saw earlier, have demonstrated that subjects are often influenced by factors that should be irrelevant when they make probability estimates. Starting point is another factor that should be irrelevant. Imagine that you have been asked to guess the percentage of African countries in the United Nations, and you are given a starting point of 65. Would your estimate be different from a condition in which you were given a starting point of 10? Tversky and Kahneman found that subjects given a starting point of 65 gave a final estimate of 45, whereas subjects given a starting point of 10 gave a final estimate of 25. They called this tendency to be influenced by the starting point the **anchoring effect.**

Another manipulated-subject-differences variable that has been studied is involvement. Langer and Roth (1975) asked one group of subjects to predict the outcome when a coin was tossed; another group of subjects merely watched while these subjects predicted the outcome. The involved subjects had higher expectations for future success than did the uninvolved subjects. Furthermore, the involved subjects gave themselves more positive evaluations of their past performance than did the uninvolved subjects.

Another way to manipulate involvement is to compare real versus imaginary payment for gambling choices. Slovic (1969) told one group of subjects to choose which gamble from each pair they would prefer to play in a "real gambling situation." However, the subjects knew that they would not actually get to play these gambles. Another group of subjects received $1.50 at the beginning of the experiment, and they used this money to play the gambles they selected. Subjects in the real gambling situation were more cautious—they chose better odds, and they chose gambles in which the losses were smaller—whereas subjects in the imaginary situation took greater risks. (Incidentally, this is an example of how results in a real-life situation can be different from results in a role-playing situation—a discrepancy we noted in the ethics chapter.)

Subject Characteristics

Think for a moment about the ways in which people you know differ with regard to decision making. Some people make decisions that you might consider too risky—they buy a new house even though it seems likely that they will have to move in a year. Other people seem too conservative—they are reluctant to make a decision until they are 100% certain that there is no risk. Are there consistent ways in which subject characteristics can account for these kinds of individual differences?

Age has a significant effect on many different measures of decision making. Wallach and Kogan (1961) conducted a very carefully controlled study comparing young adults with elderly subjects. In many of the studies discussed in this chapter, the variable of age has been confounded with the variable of intelligence. Samples of elderly subjects gathered from old-age homes and other institutions are likely to have lower intelligence and less education than the highly selected samples of young adults found in college subject pools. However, Wallach and Kogan selected their elderly subjects from a carefully chosen group of healthy people who were not institutionalized. They were equivalent to the college subjects in terms of the number of years of education and in terms of scores on an intelligence test. "Relative to college students," claim Wallach and Kogan, "the present sample of older subjects probably represents as similar a comparison group as one can obtain in practice" (p. 26).

Wallach and Kogan used three dependent measures to assess decision making: (1) Extremity of judgment was assessed by asking subjects to judge the likelihood of various events. Questions took the form, "The chances that such-and-such event will occur are about _____ in 100" (p. 27). Extremity was measured in terms of deviation from 50; thus, people who estimated that events would occur either extremely often or extremely rarely received high extremity scores. (2) A confidence index was derived from subjects' ratings on a 5-point confidence scale for the questions in the judgment task. (3) A deterrence-of-failure index was derived from subjects' estimates of risk in 12 hypothetical situations. For example, one situation described an engineer currently holding a safe job with a modest salary who must decide whether to accept a high-paying job with a new company whose future is uncertain. Subjects were asked to select the lowest probability that they would consider acceptable to make it worthwhile for the engineer to take the job, with probabilities ranging from "The chances are 1 in 10 that the company will prove financially sound" to "Mr. A should *not* take the new job no matter what the probabilities."

Wallach and Kogan found that young adults had higher extremity scores than the elderly; that is, the elderly more often gave judgments close to 50. Young adult males were more confident than elderly males, but age was not an important factor for females. Young people were less likely to be deterred by failure; they were more likely to accept the risky job even if there was only a small chance that the company would prove financially sound.

The conclusion that age is related to decision making has important consequences for other findings in experimental psychology. For example, in a hearing test, elderly people may be reluctant to say "I hear the tone" because they want to be absolutely sure that they hear it before they report it. Also, elderly people may be reluctant in a memory experiment to say "I've seen that word before" unless they are absolutely sure that the word appeared before. It seems, then, that elderly people differ from young adults in terms of the *criterion* they use in judgment—to use a term from signal-detection theory. Because elderly people use more conservative criteria, they show lower "hit rates." Any attempts to measure the sensitivity of the elderly, therefore, would do well to use a signal-detection approach, because this approach would isolate the confounding variable of criterion.

The variable of sex often has a significant effect on decision making, but the nature of the effect depends upon the kind of decision to be made. Wallach and Kogan (1959) studied college males and females in the Boston area. Unfortunately, the males attended a different college from the females. Even though Wallach and Kogan argue that the samples are similar, we would have to consider the possibility of confounding variables. All subjects performed the same three tasks used in the study of age difference.

The results showed an interesting pattern of sex differences. Men had higher confidence indexes than women. However, there was no simple sex difference on extremity of judgment. As Figure 10-15 shows, in cases where the subjects were anything less than sure (that is, moderately sure, slightly sure, or not at all sure), men gave more extreme judgments than women.

Do wealthy people take more risks in gambling situations than people with lower incomes? Munson (1962) used a real-life gambling game to study this question. A series of public carnivals was held in a Midwestern city, and the same gambling game was conducted in two neighborhoods where the median yearly income was high and in three neighborhoods where the median yearly income was low. Both groups preferred the small but frequent rewards of the low-risk offer and avoided the high-risk offer. Thus, low-income subjects did not differ from high-income subjects. It is important to notice, however, that

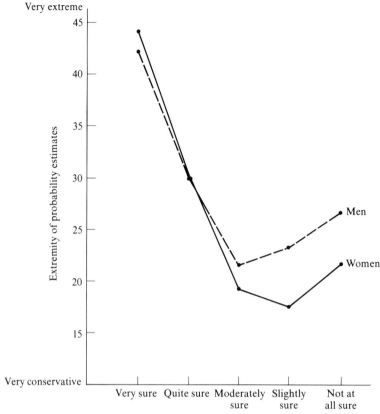

Figure 10-15. Probability estimates for male and female subjects at each of five certainty levels. Data from Wallach, M. A., & Kogan, N. Sex differences and judgment processes. *Journal of Personality*, 1959, *27*, 555–564.

Munson may not have manipulated the income variable very effectively; a number of factors may have caused the two groups of subjects to be reasonably similar in terms of income. For example, the sample of people who gamble at carnivals may not be representative of the two populations from which they are selected; it may be that those who like to gamble are the wealthiest people from the poor neighborhoods and the poorest people from the wealthy neighborhoods. Furthermore, people may leave their own neighborhoods to travel to carnivals. Consequently, measuring the income of the neighborhood is probably an inaccurate way to measure the income of the subjects.

So far, we have discussed three demographic variables as subject characteristics: age, sex, and income. Personality characteristics can also influence decision making. A study conducted by Liverant and Scodel (1960), for example, compared internally controlled subjects with externally controlled subjects. This personality variable is measured by the **Internal-External, or I-E, Scale** (Rotter, 1954), which assesses the extent to which people believe that external events control their lives. A typical question on the I-E Scale would be: "I more strongly believe that: (a) People are responsible for their actions, both good and bad. (b) Many people could be described as victims of circumstances beyond their control" (Liverant & Scodel, 1960). People who provide answers like (a) are classified as internally controlled, whereas people who provide answers like (b) are classified as externally controlled.

The subjects in Liverant and Scodel's experiment completed the I-E Scale and then played a gambling game in which they betted on the outcome of the toss of a pair of dice. The results showed that internally controlled subjects were more likely to select intermediate-risk bets, whereas externally controlled subjects were more likely to select high-risk bets. Furthermore, internally controlled subjects wagered a greater *amount* of money on safe bets, whereas externally controlled subjects wagered a greater amount of money on risky bets. Liverant and Scodel conclude:

> In this case, the internal-external control variable under consideration apparently does make a difference in the manner in which the same objective situation is categorized, and knowledge of this differential categorization is necessary for increased predictability in the study of decision making under conditions of risk [p. 67].

We have seen in other sections of this chapter that research into subject characteristics that *should* influence cognitive processes often proves to be disappointing. The same is true of decision making. Alker and Hermann (1971), whose article on the effect of the importance of decisions we discussed earlier, also examined subject characteristics. They obtained six measures of individual differences for their 120 subjects: two measures of risk taking, similar to those used in the Wallach and Kogan (1959, 1961) studies; a measure of integrative complexity; a measure of verbal intelligence; a measure of humanistic tendencies; and a measure of dogmatism. They calculated a correlation coefficient relating each of these measures to conservatism in making decisions. The correlations ranged from $-.07$ to $+.15$; none of the correlations was significant.

Discussion

Slovic, Fischhoff, and Lichtenstein (1977), in their review of the literature on decision making, include this imaginary dialogue:

> "If behavioral decision theory researchers are so smart, why aren't they rich?"
> "They're not in business."
> "Then why aren't people who are in business falling over themselves to utilize their results?" [p. 17]

Slovic et al. proceed to describe the growing trend in various other professions to make use of some of the information gathered by decision theorists, though they admit that the psychological research has not yet swept the world's decision makers like wildfire. Among those who have shown an interest in the research findings are weather forecasters, the Department of Defense, U.S. intelligence analysts, accountants, and radiologists.

Similarly, psychologists have shown an increased interest in bridging the gap between the laboratory and real-life decision-making situations. Some of the topics that have been studied include the decisions of jurors at a trial, the performance of lab technicians in performing blood-cell counts, choices made by gamblers at Las Vegas, and decisions made by U.S. Senators. Many psychologists interested in decision making have apparently decided that the advantages of ecological validity in real-life settings outweigh the advantages of rigorous control in laboratory settings.

SUMMARY

1. Cognition is the process of knowing or thinking; it includes, among other areas, problem solving, concept identification, and decision making. These areas have been studied using all four types of independent variables: stimulus characteristics, environmental characteristics, manipulated subject differences, and subject characteristics.

2. Studies of stimulus characteristics in problem solving have shown that the presence of labels influences problem solving, and that anagrams are solved most easily if the letter combinations in the anagram are low frequency and the anagram solution is high frequency.

3. Studies of environmental characteristics in problem solving have shown that noise may hinder performance if it is loud and unpredictable and that environmental characteristics often have unexpected influences on behavior.

4. Studies of manipulated subject differences have shown that hints aid problem solving, as does requiring subjects to state their strategies out loud.

5. As to subject characteristics, children are more likely than adults to use a hypothesis-scanning strategy in solving a problem. Sex interacts with other variables to influence problem-solving ability. Word fluency influences anagram-solving ability, but other personality characteristics have no main effect on problem-solving ability.

6. Studies of stimulus characteristics in concept identification have shown that some classes of stimuli are learned more quickly than others, and that subjects learn more readily from positive examples than from negative examples.

7. Studies of environmental characteristics in concept identification have shown that subjects propose a larger number of inconsistent hypotheses when their performance is being videotaped. Moreover, low self-esteem people make more errors in the presence of an audience.

8. In the area of manipulated subject differences, subjects perform better on a concept-identification task when the information is in front of them than when they must reconstruct the information from memory.

9. As to subject characteristics, adults are more likely than children to make

reversal shifts; they also learn concepts faster. Bright children are more likely to have sudden insight, whereas less bright children learn gradually.

10. Studies of stimulus characteristics in decision making have shown that pleasant stimuli are judged to be more probable than unpleasant stimuli. A large amount of information makes people feel good about their decisions, but it may hinder decision accuracy. People use two inappropriate factors, representativeness and availability, to make judgments; they ignore an appropriate factor, sample size.

11. Studies of environmental characteristics in decision making have shown that subjects give the heaviest weighting to negative evidence in a condition involving moderate noise distraction, and that people seem willing to take greater risks in large groups.

12. Studies of manipulated subject differences have shown that the starting point influences probability estimates. Task involvement is also an important variable.

13. As to subject characteristics, young people give more extreme judgments and are less likely to be deterred by the possibility of failure than elderly people. Men are more confident of their decisions than women. Externally controlled subjects are more likely to choose high-risk bets and to wager a greater amount of money on high-risk bets than are internally controlled subjects.

11

Motivation

Why did you eat breakfast this morning? Why did you suddenly want orange juice more than ever, when the person before you in line took the last one? Why did the tomato juice you ended up with taste pretty good after all? Why did you eat another roll when you were sitting with others, when you suspected that you would have eaten just one if you had been by yourself? And why did you leave the table to go upstairs and open your experimental-psych textbook?

These questions belong to the topic of **motivation**—a word that literally means "the process of being moved" (Wilkening, 1973). More generally, motivation refers to the "why" of behavior. Why do we do what we do, and why do we do it with such intensity and for so long? Why don't we just lie in a limp heap for the rest of our lives?

Some of the research on motivation has been concerned with individual variation in motivational systems. People differ, for example, in the intensity with which they pursue certain motives, such as hunger, achievement, and power. Researchers in these areas typically concentrate on subject characteristics as the independent variable—though some researchers study the characteristics of nations or historical periods rather than the characteristics of individuals. Other areas of research concentrate on less permanent circumstances that motivate behavior. We will examine these other influences on motivation—events, stimuli, and environmental factors—in the second part of this chapter.

In this chapter we will consider a wide variety of methodological issues. In the section on hunger and obesity, we will see many examples of interactions; this is a research area in which the interactions are more striking than the main effects. The section on achievement motivation focuses on testing a theory of need achievement and on the measurement of reliability and validity. One focus of the section on power motivation will be on archival analysis as a research strategy. Several methodological problems will be considered in the section on sensory deprivation: the variety of dependent measures; biased samples; between-, within-, and matched-subjects designs; problems in manipulating the independent variable; and problems in measuring the dependent variable.

INDIVIDUAL DIFFERENCES IN MOTIVATION

People differ. In some areas of psychology, individual differences serve only to produce unwanted variation—variation that might conceal the effect that the researcher is most concerned about. In these areas, individual differences have not been explored systematically. In the chapter on memory, for example, we saw that relatively few experimenters have concentrated on individual differences in memory capacity.

In contrast, experimenters in the area of motivation have systematically explored a number of areas in which individuals differ. Some of these areas involve so-called biological drives. In this chapter, we will cover only the hunger drive and the related characteristic of obesity. Other biological drives have been discussed by Birch and Veroff (1966). Individual differences have also been identified in so-called higher-level drives—drives that are social or confined to higher animals. Of these, we will cover achievement and power. Harrison (1976) can be consulted for information on aggression and affiliation, two other important drives.

Hunger and Obesity

Food is enormously important to us, as can be demonstrated by a journey down the aisles of a supermarket or by an inspection of the entries under "Restaurants" in any telephone book. In light of its importance, it is surprising that research on why humans eat has been rather slow to develop. Stanley Schachter and his colleagues have been primarily responsible for the current abundance of information in this area. Schachter contrasted obese people with normal-weight people to determine whether they eat for different reasons. He has found that obese and normal people differ on a number of dimensions: response to internal states of hunger, cue prominence, taste of the food, and working to obtain food. We'll look at these four topics in that order.

As you read through this section on hunger and obesity, pay particular attention to interactions in the results. In most cases, the main effect (obese versus normals) is not particularly interesting. Instead, we are interested in the interaction: normal people may eat more than obese people in some circumstances, but less than obese people in other circumstances.

Responses to internal states of hunger. A number of studies have shown that obese people are not as sensitive as normal people are to their internal states of hunger. Stunkard and Koch (1964), for example, found that obese subjects were not very accurate in labeling their bodily states—they simply do not know when they are physiologically hungry! In this study, the experimenters asked subjects to report to the laboratory at 9 A.M., without eating breakfast. Half of the subjects were normal weight, and half were obese.

The subjects swallowed gastric balloons, which provided the experimenters with a measure of stomach contractions. Meanwhile, the subjects reported every 15 minutes on the state of their stomachs; they were asked if they were hungry, and they simply answered yes or no. Stunkard and Koch found that the obese and normal subjects did not differ in the number of times their stomachs contracted. Furthermore, obese and normal subjects did not differ in their hunger reports when their stomachs were *not* contracting; both groups reported hunger about 38% of the time. The important difference between the two groups was their hunger reports when their stomachs *were* contracting. Normal subjects reported that they were hungry 71% of the time, whereas obese subjects reported that they were hungry only 48% of the time.

Intrigued by these results, Schachter, Goldman, and Gordon (1968) decided to manipulate experimentally their subjects' internal states. The subjects were led to believe that the experiment was concerned with the effects of tactile stimulation on taste. They came to the laboratory without having eaten the previous meal. The subjects' internal state was manipulated by varying the amount of food they ate upon arrival at the laboratory. Subjects in the empty-stomach condition ate nothing; subjects in the full-stomach condition ate roast beef sandwiches. Thus, one of the independent variables was empty stomach versus full stomach; the other independent variable was obese versus normal.

Schachter et al. used an unobtrusive measure for their dependent variable. They placed five bowls of crackers in front of each subject and asked them to rate each kind of cracker on a number of dimensions, such as salty and garlicky. The subjects were told to taste as many crackers of each type as they wished. The experimenters counted the number of crackers each subject ate. What effect did internal state have on the eating responses of the subjects? As Figure 11-1 shows, normal subjects did precisely what we would have expected: they ate *more* when they were empty than when they were full. However, the behavior of the obese subjects showed a remarkable contrast: they ate *slightly less* when they were empty than when they were full! As you might

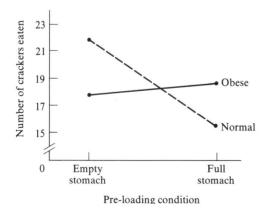

Figure 11-1. The effects of hunger on eating. From "Some Extraordinary Facts about Obese Humans and Rats," by S. Schachter, *American Psychologist,* 1971, *26*, 130. Copyright 1971 by the American Psychological Association. Reprinted by permission.

imagine, the interaction was highly significant. Thus, when normal people should be hungry, they report that they are hungry, and they eat more; they seem to be guided by internal cues. However, when obese people should be hungry, they don't report much hunger, and they eat, if anything, less; internal cues aren't particularly relevant for them.

If internal cues don't trigger the eating responses of obese people, what does? Schachter (1971) has proposed that *external* cues are important for obese people. Two kinds of external cues are the physical presence of food (cue prominence) and the taste of food.

Cue prominence. So far, we have considered laboratory evidence for differences between obese and normal people. Goldman, Jaffa, and Schachter (1968) conducted one of many field studies in this area. Taking advantage of a food-related holiday, they studied fasting on Yom Kippur among a sample of religious Jewish college students. On Yom Kippur, orthodox Jews are supposed to fast for 24 hours, spending many hours in the synagogue. In the synagogue, there are no external cues concerning food. Therefore, Goldman et al. reasoned, obese subjects would not miss the food—in fact, they should be more likely to fast than normal subjects. The results showed that 83% of the obese subjects fasted, in contrast to only 69% of the normal subjects. (Notice that subject-confounding variables could contaminate this study. Obese subjects may differ from normal subjects with regard to their religious convictions. Thus, obese people may be more likely to fast than normal people because they are more religious, rather than for food-related reasons.) For obese subjects, moreover, the more time they spent in the synagogue, the less unpleasant they considered the fasting period; when external food cues were absent, there was no real urge to eat. However, for normal subjects, there was no relationship between time in the synagogue and unpleasantness of fasting; external cues did not influence hunger pangs for them.

W. G. Johnson (1974) used a different kind of dependent variable to assess food-related behavior: how hard people will work to get food. Subjects, who had refrained from eating for 4 hours before the experiment, were instructed to ''earn their meal''—a delicious, delicatessen-type sandwich. The task involved using the index finger to pull a ring, to which was attached a weight of about seven pounds. After about 50 responses, they were allowed to eat one-quarter of the sandwich. Johnson varied the prominence of the cues in the following manner. Some subjects had double cues: they were allowed to taste the sandwich before beginning the task, and the sandwich, wrapped in a transparent covering, was placed next to them during the task. Other subjects had a single cue: for example, they might taste the sandwich first, but the sandwich would be wrapped in a nontransparent covering during the task. The last group of subjects had minimal cues: they did not taste the sandwich, and the sandwich was in a nontransparent covering. Johnson recorded the number of times subjects pulled the ring during the 12-minute duration of the experiment. The results showed a striking interaction between subjects' weight category and cue prominence. The normal subjects, if anything, worked less when external cues were prominent, whereas obese subjects made close to twice as many responses when external cues were prominent.

Cue prominence has also been investigated by Ross (1974), who manipulated this variable simply by varying the level of illumination in the experimental room. When a 7½-watt red bulb was used, obese subjects ate fewer cashews than normal subjects. When a 40-watt bulb was used, obese subjects ate almost twice as many cashews.

Taste of the food. Nisbett (1968) reasoned that the taste of a food is an external stimulus, because the taste sensations are external to the stomach. Therefore, taste should have a greater influence on eating for obese subjects than for normal subjects. In this experiment, subjects were allowed to eat as much as they wanted of vanilla ice cream. Half of the subjects were given high-quality, French vanilla ice cream. The other subjects were given a loathesome mixture of cheap vanilla ice cream and quinine. Subjects rated the ice cream on a 6-point scale, and Nisbett measured how many grams of ice cream had been eaten. When subjects disliked the ice cream, obese subjects ate about the same amount as normal subjects. However, when subjects liked the ice cream, obese subjects ate far more than normal subjects. Once again, we see an interaction between subjects' weight category and the experimental condition.

Another study on taste and its relationship to obesity was an ingenious field study. Goldman, Jaffa, and Schachter (1968) examined a phenomenon that must be universal wherever there is dormitory food: getting out of the contract to eat in the dining hall. At Columbia University, students could cancel their food contracts and pay a penalty; then they would eat for the rest of the semester in neighborhood restaurants. Goldman et al. made the reasonable assumption that dormitory food was less tasty than food in restaurants. If this is so, then we would expect more contract cancellations among people to whom taste matters—obese students. The data showed that 87% of obese students cancelled their contracts, in comparison to 67% of normal students. Once again, external cues, such as taste, are more relevant for obese than for normal people. (As in many field studies, however, other confounding variables could explain the difference. For example, obese people may begin diets and cancel their contracts because they want to avoid starchy dormitory food.)

Working to obtain food. Another important difference between obese and normal people is how hard they will work to obtain food. Contrary to what you might expect, obese people won't work as hard as normal people when other factors are equal. Schachter and Friedman (1974) varied the work involved in eating by using almonds without shells for some subjects and almonds with shells for other subjects. The deception involved having the subjects complete some personality tests. However, in addition to the typical litter on the desk, there was a bag of nuts. The experimenter casually invited the subjects to help themselves to the nuts. Afterwards, the bag of nuts was weighed to determine whether any had been eaten. The data are shown in Figure 11-2. Schachter (1971) notes elsewhere that these data are too perfect: they look like data produced by someone who is faking the data and making the differences unrealistically large. Schachter is right: seldom in psychology do we find results as clearcut as those for the obese subjects—95% of whom ate nuts when the shells were off, and only 5% of whom ate nuts when the shells were on. In

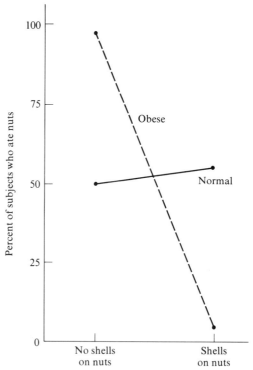

Figure 11-2. Percentage of normal and obese subjects who ate nuts, with and without shells. Data from Schachter, S., & Friedman, L. N. The effects of work and cue prominence on eating behavior. In S. Schachter and J. Rodin (Eds.), *Obese humans and rats*. Potomac, Md.: Lawrence Erlbaum Associates, 1974.

contrast, normal people ate the same amount in both conditions. Thus, we see yet another unusually strong interaction.

"Who Eats with Chopsticks?" is the intriguing title of another relevant paper (Schachter, Friedman, & Handler, 1974). The experimenters visited 14 different Chinese and Japanese restaurants and observed 493 different eaters. They had previously trained themselves in estimating weight, and each eater was classified as normal, chubby, or obese. A total of 18% of the normal subjects ate with chopsticks, according to these observations, in contrast to only 3% of the chubby or obese subjects. Unfortunately, there is a potential source of experimenter bias in this study: the observer might have tended to err in the direction of classifying chopstick-eaters as normal and silverware-eaters as obese.

Finally, Nisbett and Gurwitz (1970) found that subjects' weight influences how hard they will work for food, even when the subjects are infants. Newborn infants were divided into groups on the basis of their weight/length ratios. Mothers bottle-fed their infants, using either a regular nipple or a nipple with smaller holes. (Mothers were not told which nipple had smaller holes, but since this study used a within-subjects design, the mothers might have noted the difference.) Small and normal infants consumed about the same amount in the two nipple conditions. Big infants, however, drank 21% less when the nipple had small holes. In summary, normal subjects obtain food, even if they have to work to get it. For obese subjects, it often isn't worth the effort.

Other research on obesity. Additional studies have identified numerous other ways in which obese subjects differ from normal subjects. Rodin, Herman, and Schachter (1974), for example, examined reaction time, immediate recall, shock sensitivity, and recognition thresholds. Yaremko, Fisher, and Price (1975) studied galvanic skin response conditioning. An experiment by Grossberg and Grant (1976) is worth mentioning because it used the signal-detection method. (As I mentioned in Chapter 6, the signal-detection method seems to work its way into virtually every area of psychology.) Obese and normal subjects were seated in front of a tachistoscope and told that they would see either the word *sugar* or the word *board*. On each trial, a word was presented, and they had to guess which word it was. Obese subjects showed lower *sensitivity* (or detection ability) than normal subjects at short exposure times. At longer exposure times, however, they showed greater sensitivity than normal subjects. The *criterion* did not differ for the two groups: both groups were equivalently lenient in saying "I see it."

In summary, we have seen that obese people differ from normal people in a number of ways. The differences are much more subtle than simple main effects. For example, if we combine the conditions in Figure 11-1, obese people do not differ from normal people in the total amount of food eaten. Instead, we see that weight category interacts with the experimental condition. The experimental condition has different effects on the two kinds of people. Obese people eat somewhat more with a full stomach, whereas normal people eat much less with a full stomach. Similar kinds of interactions appear in all the areas we have examined. Looking over this section, we find that: (1) normal people are influenced more by hunger than obese people are; (2) obese people are influenced more by cue prominence than normal people are; (3) obese people are influenced more by taste than normal people are; and (4) obese people are discouraged more by conditions that make it difficult to obtain food.

Achievement Motivation

In Chapter 2, we discussed sources of ideas for research hypotheses. One of these sources of ideas was theory. A theory may suggest a certain relationship among variables, and the psychologist wants to test that relationship. We saw one example of a theory that has generated an enormous amount of research in Chapter 8, when we looked at the question of whether short-term memory is different from long-term memory.

Achievement motivation is another area where a theory has made specific predictions that can be tested experimentally. We'll explore the theory, the predictions, and the data shortly. First, however, we must look at the tools that are used to measure individual differences in need achievement.

Measuring need achievement. Think about the variety of ways in which you could measure differences among people in their tendency to seek success in an achievement situation. You could watch people, either overtly or unobtrusively, to see how they behave in situations. You could have people answer questions about how they have acted in the past, how they typically act, or how they might act in the future. All of these methods would be direct assessments, and they would each have their advantages and disadvantages. Alternately, you could use a **projective technique**, which Wilkening (1973) describes as

> an indirect, standardized method for obtaining a diagnosis of personality organization by interpreting the subject's responses to relatively unstructured and ambiguous stimuli. The responses (fantasies, associations, etc.) are considered as projections, or the throwing forth in disguised fashion of unconscious attitudes, needs, or fears that ordinarily would not be expressed in direct, conscious, controlled language [p. 128].

A projective technique developed by H. A. Murray (1936) has been used most often in studying achievement motivation. Murray developed the Thematic Apperception Test (TAT), a series of pictures for which subjects make up stories. The stories can then be scored, assigning a +1 for achievement imagery, a 0 for doubtful imagery, and a −1 for imagery unrelated to achievement. The total score is presumed to reflect one's need for achievement, or *n* Ach. Thus, a picture of a man sitting at a desk, with a picture of his family at one side, might elicit a story about an engineer trying to design a bridge from a high *n* Ach person. In contrast, a low *n* Ach person might write a story about a man thinking about the pleasant weekend he recently enjoyed with his family.

Before using this measure of achievement to test hypotheses, it would be wise to see whether the scores are valid—whether they measure what they are supposed to measure. (We discussed the concept of validity in Chapter 1.) To answer this question, McClelland, Atkinson, Clark, and Lowell (1953) manipulated the achievement orientation of the setting in which subjects took the TAT and then examined the *n* Ach scores to see whether they reflected reality. They used six conditions: (1) In the *relaxed* condition, a college class took tests that were reported to be in a developmental stage, administered by an informal, graduate student experimenter. (2) In the *neutral* condition, the TAT was administered normally in a college classroom. (3) In the *achievement-oriented* condition, the TAT was introduced as a test of important abilities, and students were urged to do their best. (4) In the *success* condition, subjects took the TAT after having been told that they had achieved high scores on previous tests. (5) In the *failure* condition, subjects took the TAT after having been told that they had achieved low scores on previous tests. (6) In the *success/failure* condition, subjects took the TAT after having been told that they had achieved high scores on the first test and low scores on the last test. The mean *n* Ach score for the relaxed condition was about 2; for the neutral, achievement-oriented, and success conditions, it was about 8; and for the failure and success/failure conditions, it was about 10. Clearly, achievement-oriented settings produced higher *n* Ach scores; students who are concerned about achieving write stories about people who are concerned about achieving.

Achievement-motivation theory. J. W. Atkinson (1964) has described the
theory of achievement motivation that he, McClelland, and other cowork-ers have developed. He maintains that the tendency to approach success (T_s) for an individual in a given situation depends on three factors, as illustrated by this equation:

$$T_s = M_s \times P_s \times I_s$$

Let's look at each of those three factors. M_s is the **motive to achieve success**. This is presumed to be a stable characteristic—one that you carry about with you from one situation to the next. An index of your M_s is your n Ach score. P_s is the perceived probability of success—how likely you think it is that you will succeed on a given task. For example, if you are trying to toss a ring around a stake that is 2 feet away, your P_s will be higher than if the stake is 20 feet away. I_s is the incentive value of success on a given task. While M_s is relatively stable, P_s and I_s vary from task to task.

The theory provides more information about I_s. Specifically,

$$I_s = 1 - P_s$$

What this means is that the incentive of a task is inversely related to the probability of success on that task. For small values of P_s, when the task is difficult, I_s is high. For example, the incentive when the stake is 20 feet away is very high; you would be very proud of succeeding. For large values of P_s, when the task is easy, I_s is low. Thus, the incentive when the stake is 2 feet away is very low; you would hardly click your heels with joy at the prospect of success.

One of the most attractive features of the Atkinson/McClelland theory is that it suggests a number of testable hypotheses. Let us insert some hypotheti-cal values and see what relationships are implied. In Table 11-1, we can look at the tendency to achieve success for a person who has a low M_s and for a person

Table 11-1. Tendency to achieve success as a function of probability of success and incentive of success for two people—one with low motive to achieve success, and one with high motive to achieve success (where $T_s = M_s \times P_s \times I_s$).

Task	P_s	I_s	For a Person whose $M_s = 1$	For a Person whose $M_s = 10$
Very Difficult	.10	.90	.09	.90
Difficult	.30	.70	.21	2.10
Moderate	.50	.50	.25	2.50
Easy	.70	.30	.21	2.10
Very Easy	.90	.10	.09	.90

who has a high M_s, using the arbitrary M_s values of 1 and 10, respectively. We can look at each subject's performance on five tasks, from very difficult to very easy. Figure 11-3 is a graphic representation of the values for T_s for these two people.

Perhaps the most striking feature of the graph is that T_s is greatest for a moderately difficult task. In other words, people are most likely to try to succeed when the probability of success is about .50—where half of the time

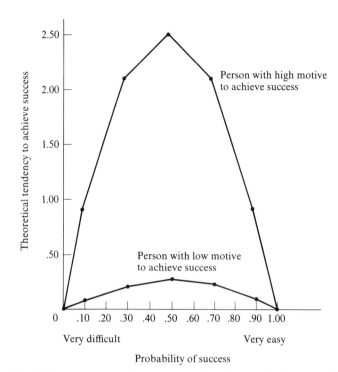

Figure 11-3. Tendency to achieve success, based on calculations in Table 11-1.

they will succeed and half of the time they will fail. This preference for moderate risks is true to some extent for a person with a low motive to achieve success, but it is particularly true for a person with a high motive to achieve success. That person is about three times as likely to try to succeed when the task is moderately difficult as when the task is either very easy or very difficult. (In a way, this is contrary to intuition. You might have expected that high achievers would try hardest when the task is most difficult.)

McClelland (1958) performed an experiment that confirmed this hypothesis. In this study, children were asked to toss a ring over a stake located on the floor. They were allowed to choose how far away they wished to stand from the stake. The distance they selected was interpreted as an index of the task-difficulty level that they preferred. Children with the highest achievement motive were most likely to choose an intermediate distance—thus indicating the preference for tasks of intermediate difficulty predicted by Figure 11-3.

The motive to avoid failure. Atkinson (1964) has proposed, however, that there are other motives—in addition to the achievement motive—that determine performance in an achievement task. For example, there is the **motive to avoid failure**. Whereas the motive to achieve is associated with pride in accomplishment, the motive to avoid failure is associated with shame following failure. A person may be concerned about failure when he or she knows that performance on a task will be evaluated and that failure is likely. The person will become anxious and tend to withdraw from the situation. This motive to avoid failure is operationally defined as the score on the Mandler-Sarason Test Anxiety Questionnaire, a standard test of anxiety.

The equations describing the tendency to avoid failure are covered in detail in Atkinson (1964). In general, however, the effect of this tendency to avoid failure is to interfere with positive motivation. Performance in an achievement task is a function of the tendency to achieve success *minus* the tendency to avoid failure. Furthermore, a person with a high motive to avoid failure tends to *avoid* tasks of intermediate difficulty. This person may be more likely to select an easy task (where there is not much chance of failure) or a difficult task (where failure is not as embarrassing).

Atkinson and Litwin (1960) tested these hypotheses about the motive to avoid failure, using college men playing a ring-toss game. The subjects were categorized as being either high or low on achievement motivation and either high or low on test anxiety; thus, there were four groups of subjects. Each subject was instructed to choose where he wanted to stand in relation to the stake, anywhere from 1 to 15 feet away; each was allowed ten shots.

Figure 11-4 shows the percentage of shots selected by each of the four groups. The results confirm the hypotheses. First of all, look at the group that is *high* in achievement motivation and *low* in test anxiety (motive to avoid failure). These people should be most likely to select a moderately difficult task, because of the relationship we saw in Figure 11-3 and because they are not afraid of failing on this task. Notice that they do show an overwhelming tendency to select a moderately difficult task—in fact, they almost never

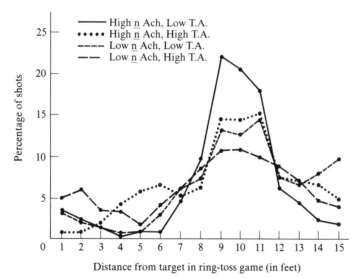

Figure 11-4. Distribution of throwing distances chosen in a ring-toss game by college males who were either high or low in *n* Ach and either high or low in test anxiety. From "Achievement Motivation and Test Anxiety Conceived as Motive to Approach Success and Motive to Avoid Failure," by J. W. Atkinson and G. H. Litwin, *Journal of Abnormal and Social Psychology*, 1960, *60*, 52-63. Copyright 1960 by the American Psychological Association. Reprinted by permission.

selected a distance less than 7 feet or greater than 13. Now look at a very different group, the one that is *low* in achievement motivation and *high* in test anxiety. These people should be the least likely of all four groups to select a moderately difficult task, because, as we saw in Figure 11-3, they show only a mild preference for a moderately difficult task from the standpoint of a tendency to achieve success, and because their motive to avoid failure is greatest for a moderately difficult task. Notice that these subjects are, in fact, the least likely to choose a moderately difficult task. They stand 10 feet away only 10% of the time. Instead, they are reasonably likely to stand 1 or 2 feet away, where they know they can't fail, or 14 or 15 feet away, where losing is not embarrassing. The other two curves, representing the groups who are high in both motives or low in both motives, are intermediate—as they should be.

In Chapter 2, we mentioned that people frequently do research in order to discover the limit conditions for a theory. An experimenter may speculate that the theory holds true only if certain conditions are met. Raynor (1970) proposed that motives are related to achievement only if that particular achievement is relevant for future career plans. Specifically, Raynor asked college students enrolled in a course whether they considered a good grade in that course to be related to their future career plans. Among those who answered yes, approach-oriented students—those whose motive to achieve success exceeded their motive to avoid failure—received higher course grades than avoidance-oriented people—those whose motive to avoid failure exceeded their motive to achieve success. However, among those who answered no (for whom the course was irrelevant to future career plans), there was no relationship between motives and achievement.

The archival approach to achievement motivation. Most of the research on achievement motivation has used the experimental method. However, some studies have used the archival method. McClelland (1961) proposed that a nation's need achievement would be related to its rate of development; his study, therefore, examined individual differences among nations. In this study, he gathered children's books that were available in various developed countries in 1925 and rated the stories for *n* Ach. Then he obtained data on the growth in electricity production in each of those countries for the years 1929–1950. The correlation between need achievement and rate of development was +.53. Thus, the countries whose folktales and children's stories showed a need for achievement were the countries that showed the highest rate of development.

More recently, Finison (1976) tried to replicate the McClelland study, using *n* Ach data from 1950 and electrical production data from 1950–1971. Finison found a correlation of −.02 between the two measures, thus failing to replicate the earlier study. As we discussed in Chapter 2, a failure to replicate a study may mean that in the earlier study the experimenter was "lucky" and found a statistically significant relationship even though no relationship existed in reality (a Type I error). It may also mean that the second experimenter was "unlucky" and found no statistically significant relationship even though a relationship did exist in reality (a Type II error). Finally, as Finison proposes, both studies may have reflected reality, but certain other variables may have changed in the time between the two studies. There are probably many factors that influence electrical production today that were irrelevant in the first half of the century.

The reliability of **n** *Ach measures.* The topic of achievement motivation has stimulated a huge number of studies. As M. S. Weinstein (1969) has observed, "Few areas of personality research and theory have endured with the vigor, following, and influence of achievement motivation" (p. 153). Although the early research found abundant support for achievement-motivation theory, some more recent research has raised important questions. For example, Entwisle (1972) has written an article titled "To Dispel Fantasies About Fantasy-Based Measures of Achievement Motivation." She believes that measures of *n* Ach are not reliable. Let's review for a moment what *reliability* means in this context. Reliability means consistency; one kind of consistency would be demonstrated if two scorers agreed on the scores they assigned to a particular response. McClelland, Atkinson, Clark, and Lowell (1953) measured this kind of reliability and found it to be extremely high. Even though the scorers had relatively little training, the correlations between two scorers were above +.90.

However, there is another kind of reliability or consistency that we must also pay attention to: will a subject receive the same score on various parts of the *n* Ach test? If a test is reliable, a person who receives a high score for the story written about one picture should also receive a high score for the story written about another picture. Entwisle (1972) reviewed both published and unpublished reports of this homogeneity reliability and found that these correlations seldom exceeded +.30. Another related measure of test reliability is called test-retest reliability. This measure of reliability assesses the extent to which a person who receives a high score on the first test will receive a high score when the same test is administered at a later time. Entwisle also found that test-retest reliability was very low for the *n* Ach test. Entwisle's article was clearly worrisome to researchers in achievement motivation; if the test itself was unreliable, how could they trust it to assess individual differences?

Several researchers have come to the defense of these tests. For example, Winter and Stewart (1977) have proposed that the test produces low reliability scores because of the demand characteristics of the task. Thematic Apperception Test instructions request the subject to make up an "imaginative story." Suppose you are being shown the same picture you were shown last week, and you are asked again to make up an "imaginative story." In all likelihood, you will want to demonstrate your imagination by producing a story as different as possible from last week's story. Winter and Stewart argue that the demand characteristics encourage people to write about different motives; consequently, the correlations between the two tests will necessarily be low. They conducted an experiment in which they specifically instructed subjects not to worry about whether the stories were similar to or different from the stories they wrote earlier. The test-retest correlation with these instructions was +.58. In contrast, instructions to write stories as different as possible from the previous stories produced a test-retest correlation of +.27, which is quite close to the correlations normally found in these studies. The authors conclude that subjects normally try to write different stories on a retest.

Achievement motivation in women. One of the most important limiting conditions for Atkinson's and McClelland's achievement-motivation theories is that the theories predict behavior for *men*, but not for *women*. For various reasons, the early research in achievement motivation used male subjects almost exclusively. For example, an important book on achievement motivation (Atkinson, 1958) contains 800 pages on the theories and facts of achievement motivation in men, with one footnote devoted to women.

Attempts to replicate classic studies using female subjects rather than male subjects have generally been unsuccessful. For example, Veroff, Wilcox, and Atkinson (1953) tried to replicate the study described at the beginning of this section by McClelland, Atkinson, Clark, and Lowell (1953). With female subjects, however, the achievement orientation of the setting did not affect the *n* Ach.

Achievement motivation in women has now become a "hot topic," and there is scarcely an article on the psychology of women in popular magazines that fails to mention it. Horner (1972) has suggested that there is an important motive that operates for women called the **motive to avoid success**. This motive involves the fear that success in competitive achievement situations will lead to unpleasant consequences, including unpopularity, loss of femininity, and inability to find a husband. Horner proposes that this motive to avoid success has acted as a psychological barrier to achievement in women: when women are faced with the possibility of success, they become anxious and try to avoid succeeding.

Horner used a variant of the TAT, in which subjects completed a story based on a beginning sentence, rather than a picture. The females completed a story that began "After first term finals, Anne finds herself at the top of her medical school class," and the males completed a story that began "After first term finals, John finds himself at the top of his medical school class." The stories were scored for imagery involving fear of success. Among college freshmen and sophomores, 65% of females showed fear of success, in contrast to 9% of males. Women wrote stories in which Anne turns out to be very lonely, in which everyone hates and envies her, in which she drops out of medical school, and in which Anne does not really exist (Anne simply being a code name for a nonexistent person created by a group of med students). In an extreme story, Anne starts proclaiming her surprise and joy, and her classmates are so disgusted with her behavior that they jump on her and beat her, leaving her maimed for life. In contrast, men tended to be delighted at John's success and predicted a grand and glorious future for him.

Horner (1972) also tested the validity of the motive to avoid success. If the measurement of the motive to avoid success is valid, then people who score high in that motive should differ in their behavior from people who score low. The behavior Horner chose to examine was performance on achievement tasks in a competitive situation in comparison to performance in a noncompetitive situation. Of the 17 women who were high on the motive to avoid success, 13 scored lower when they were competing against men than they did in the noncompetitive situation. Of the 13 women who were low in motive to avoid success, only 1 scored lower in competition against men. As you might guess, the difference between these groups was statistically significant.

The extensive research and controversy that followed Horner's original research cannot be summarized here, but summaries are available in Deaux (1976) and Zuckerman and Wheeler (1975). Some researchers have questioned the scoring system; others have found the motive to avoid success to be unrelated to other behavior; still others have failed to find substantial sex differences on the measure. Other psychologists (for example, Stein & Bailey, 1973) have proposed that women achieve in different areas than men do; for women, they suggest, it is consistent with the female sex role to achieve in social, rather than intellectual, skills.

Karabenick (1977) argues that research on the motive to avoid success has typically failed to consider other motives that could influence behavior. After all, Horner proposed the motive to avoid success within the context of other motives; thus, all the motives should be considered at the same time. Karabenick's experiment is complex, but his results show that women's performance in a competitive situation, in contrast to a noncompetitive situation, is related both to fear of success and to need for affiliation.

Achievement motivation and attribution. Recent research in achievement motivation has been expanding in new directions. One of these directions concerns attributions, or causes for past events. Weiner and his colleagues have explored people's interpretations of their past success.

> Approximately seven years ago a doctoral student came into my office and said that she was interested in finding out what people believe are the causes for their successes and failures. She planned to induce different achievement outcomes, and then merely ask the subjects what caused these events. I urged her to change topics. The psychological study of achievement motivation had advanced far beyond this introspective and unscientific stage. But the more I considered the proposed study, the more I realized how little was known about the experiential or phenomenological aspects of achievement. Eventually I, rather than the student, changed research topics [Weiner, 1974, p. 3].

Some of Weiner's research has examined whether subjects attribute success to internal or external causes. Think about a recent success you have had. Do you think that your success was due to internal causes—because you worked hard, for example—or to external causes—because the task was easy? Weiner and Kukla (1970) studied children in grade school and high school. They found that boys whose motive to achieve success was higher than their motive to avoid failure ($M_s > M_{af}$) were more likely than boys with the reversed motives ($M_{af} > M_s$) to believe that their success was due to internal causes. In other words, boys motivated primarily by a desire to achieve success believe that they, themselves, are responsible for their success; in contrast, boys motivated primarily by a desire to avoid failure think that external factors are responsible for their success.

In other publications, Weiner has examined causal stability. Sometimes people attribute their success to stable causes; for example, you might say that you were successful on a task because you have high ability—a relatively permanent and stable characteristic. Other times, people attribute their success to unstable causes; for example, you might say that you were successful on a task because you tried hard that time—a factor that could vary from one attempt to the next.

Weiner proposes that people differ from one another with respect to causal stability. Furthermore, these differences are related to expectations of success. In one study, Weiner, Nierenberg, and Goldstein (1976) divided their subjects into high-causal-stability and low-causal-stability groups on the basis of their responses to questions such as " Did you succeed on this task because you are always good at these kinds of tasks or because you tried especially hard on this particular task? (p. 61)" Subjects made specified designs out of blocks for a number of trials and were given feedback that indicated that they had been successful. Then they were asked to estimate how many of the next ten designs they believed they would solve successfully. The high-causal-stability subjects gave higher estimates than the low-causal-stability subjects. If you think you succeeded because you are good at something—a rather permanent characteristic—you are more likely to expect success in the future than if you think you succeeded because you tried hard.

Power Motivation

Several motivational systems that involve interpersonal relationships have been studied in humans. Two of these systems, affiliation and aggression, have been carefully examined in social-psychology textbooks (for example, Harrison, 1976; Wrightsman, 1977). In this section, we will be concerned with another interpersonal motivation—power. When a person is high in **power motivation**, she or he is interested in having an impact on someone else, in being able to influence that other person's decision.

Veroff (1957) developed a TAT measure of power in much the same way as the TAT measure of achievement was developed, by comparing an aroused and a nonaroused group in their responses to TAT pictures. He used a between-subjects design, in which the aroused group were college students who were on the ballot at a college election. These students responded to the TAT on the evening of ballot counting, a time when they would presumably have been particularly concerned with power. The nonaroused group of subjects were students in a college classroom. When the stories were coded for n Power, the students involved in the election received higher scores than the students in the classroom. Thus, n Power scores reflected a difference that existed in reality. You may have anticipated a problem, however, that is also discussed by Birch and Veroff (1966). The selection of subjects for the two groups was not random, because people who seek election are probably very different from students in a typical classroom. Thus, we only know that office seekers have higher n Power scores, but we don't know whether this difference is due to initial personality differences or to circumstantial differences at the time of measurement. Other studies have established that the circumstances in which *n* Power scores are measured can influence the scores (for example, Steele, 1977).

Winter (1973) has summarized the literature on power motivation. Studies have demonstrated that people who are high in power motivation are, for example, more likely to influence people in small-group discussions, to participate in athletics, and to hold office in organizations. In this section, we will explore two areas related to power motivation—historical events and personal relationships.

Power as a predictor in history. Several studies have attempted to explore power in a historical context. These studies are particularly intriguing because, if a relationship can be demonstrated in the past, it is tempting to try to predict future historical events. As in the study by McClelland (1961) on the relationship between achievement motivation in various countries and their electricity production, these studies use the archival approach.

Donley and Winter (1970) wanted to measure the need for power and the need for achievement among public officials. How could this be done, since public officials would not smile warmly at the prospect of giving up an hour or so to take a Thematic Apperception Test? Donley and Winter ingeniously proposed an excellent source of information about important public officials—the inaugural addresses of U.S. Presidents. Usually, of course, these addresses are examined for statements about new policies and programs. However, as J. D. Barber (1968) has remarked, news analysts' predictions about a candidate's political style and performance—based only on these policy statements—have been incorrect so frequently that an examination of the psychological imagery of political speeches might have better predictive value.

Prior to scoring the inaugural addresses, Donley and Winter classified U.S. Presidents from 1905 to 1965 along the dimensions of power and achievement, using a variety of sources compiled by historians. Thus, on the power dimension, high-power Presidents were Theodore Roosevelt, Woodrow Wilson, Franklin Roosevelt, John Kennedy, and Lyndon Johnson; low-power Presidents were Howard Taft, Warren Harding, Calvin Coolidge, Herbert Hoover, and Dwight Eisenhower. Next, each inaugural address was scored by Donley, with Winter checking a large sample of the decisions. (Donley could often guess the identity of the Presidents from key phrases and events mentioned in the speeches, but Winter performed the scoring "blind"; their high agreement of 85% indicates that experimenter-bias effects could not have been large.) A passage from Franklin Roosevelt's first address, for example, read: "These are the lines of attack. I shall presently urge upon a new Congress in special session detailed measures for their fulfillment." This statement was scored positively for *n* Power. The need for power per 1000 words was then compared for all Presidents, and the Presidents were classified as either high or low in *n* Power with respect to the median. The results were impressive. Every President rated high in power by historians also received a high power score on the Donley/Winter analysis. Every President rated low in power by historians also received a low power score on the Donley/Winter analysis.

McClelland (1975) was interested in predicting war and peace over the course of U.S. history. He postulated that a combination of high n Power and low n Affiliation in a sample of literature would precede a period of war. On the other hand, low n Power and high n Affiliation should precede a period of peace. McClelland gathered literature from each decade from 1780 to 1970. The samples consisted of children's textbooks, popular novels, and hymns. The samples were scored, and measures of n Power and n Affiliation were assigned to each decade. If we look at the period from 1780 to 1900 and assume, as McClelland did, that there should be about a 15-year lag between sentiments expressed in literature and the nation's foreign policy, the results are impressive. For example, in 1785, n Power was low in relation to n Affiliation, and 1800, 15 years later, was a peaceful period in history. However, in 1795, n Power was high in relation to n Affiliation, and then came the War of 1812. For this whole period, 11 of the 13 predictions were correct. Unfortunately, the model works for the 20th century only if we assume a lead time shorter than 15 years—an assumption that McClelland does not justify in his discussion of the experiment.

Power as a predictor in personal relationships. Other studies concerned with power have a much more modest aim than predicting the course of history. The aim of these studies is to predict certain aspects of the relationship between two people. Stewart and Rubin (1974), for example, investigated the power motive in the dating couple. If the power motive involves the desire to have an impact on someone else, then we would expect power to be influential in intimate relationships. Stewart and Rubin identified 63 dating couples in the Boston area. Subjects responded to a TAT-type test, with verbal leads substituted for the usual TAT pictures. They also answered questions regarding their satisfaction with their current dating relationship. The written stories were then scored for power motivation, with power being demonstrated if a character in the story took a strong action that affected another person, expressed concern with his or her reputation, or aroused a strong emotional response in others.

Let's look at the results. When the male in the relationship was high in power motivation, both members of the pair were likely to be dissatisfied with the current relationship. The male was also likely to anticipate problems in the relationship in the next year. Two years after the initial testing, Stewart and Rubin contacted at least one member of each couple to determine what had happened to the relationship. The couples were equally divided among three categories: broken up, married, and still dating. When the male in the couple was high in power motivation, 50% of the couples had broken up, and only 9% of the couples had married. When the male was low in power motivation, only 15% had broken up, and 52% had married. Interestingly, the power motivation of the female was not related to the anticipation of problems, nor to the fate of the relationship.

Winter, Stewart, and McClelland (1977) performed a correlational study on the relationship between a husband's power motivation and his wife's career level. It is worth examining this study to see why the causality in correlational studies is typically unclear. The authors first obtained TAT measures of power for males graduating from "a prestigious Eastern university." Ten years later, the authors sent out a questionnaire regarding wives' current occupations, and they received 51 responses. (Recall that one problem with questionnaires is that many people fail to return them, and this may bias the sample.) The wives' occupations were classified into categories ranging from "no work outside the home" to "professional" (doctor, lawyer, professor, executive, and the like). The correlation between the men's power motivation and their wives' occupation was $-.42$. In other words, if a husband had high n Power, his wife was *less* likely to pursue work outside the home.

Now let's see why it is difficult to interpret cause-and-effect relationships from that correlation. Winter et al. propose three possible interpretations of the relationship: (1) The husband's power motive could cause him to discourage his wife's choice of competitive work outside the home. (2) The husband's power motive could influence the kind of wife he chooses, with high-power men choosing women who do not wish to pursue competitive work outside the home. (3) The wife could choose a husband suitable for her own career plans, with ambitious women choosing low-power men. Which is the correct answer? With a correlation, we only know that a relationship exists; we do not know what factor caused what. Other research would be needed to clarify the direction of causality.

SITUATIONAL DETERMINANTS OF MOTIVATION

So far, we have focused on individual differences in motivation. People differ from one another in the intensity with which they pursue food, achievement, and power. We have also seen that nations and periods in history show individual differences, and these differences can be studied using the same tools that are used to examine differences among individual human beings.

Now we will shift our attention toward less permanent circumstances that motivate behavior. This research downplays individual differences that may be responsible for the variation in the intensity with which people do things. Here individual differences only produce unwanted variation; we are more interested in determining common patterns of response to other kinds of variables. In this half of the chapter, we will examine how events, stimuli, and environmental factors influence motivation.

In particular, we will be seeking answers to five questions: (1) How do people react when other people are present? (2) How do people react when their freedom is reduced? (3) How do people react when they have been given inconsistent information? (4) How do people react when they have been rewarded for performing an activity they like and the reward is then removed? (5) How do people react to novel versus familiar stimuli? Thus, the five topics in this section will be: (1) presence of others, (2) reactance, (3) cognitive dissonance, (4) overjustification, and (5) sensory variation.

You may have wondered whether having someone else in the same room helps or hinders you when you are trying to accomplish something. For example, when you are studying for a final in statistics, would you do better if your roommate were not there? How does the presence of someone else affect you if you are typing a paper? Do you think you could do better on an exam if you were alone in the room?

Robert Zajonc (1965) wrote a paper called "Social Facilitation," in which he examined the influence of the presence of others on performance. He inspected 70 years of research on the problem and found that an impressive variety of subjects had been studied—including ants, puppies, chickens, cockroaches, and National Guard trainees. In some cases, the presence of others seemed to improve performance, but in other cases, it hindered performance. For example, subjects do better on multiplication tasks or vigilance tasks when someone else is present. However, they do worse on verbal-learning and maze-learning tasks when someone else is present.

How can the conflicting results be reconciled? Zajonc noticed a general relationship in the literature. When the task is an easy one, involving well-learned responses, the presence of others *improves* performance; in other words, social facilitation occurs. However, when the task is a difficult one, involving new or poorly learned responses, the presence of others *hinders* performance.

Zajonc develops this idea further, focusing on the kinds of responses made at different stages of learning. Specifically, he notes that if you are just beginning to learn something, your responses are most often incorrect. In other words, your dominant (or most likely) response is an error. However, after you become skilled at that task, your responses are most often correct. In other words, your dominant response is now a correct response.

Zajonc proposes that the presence of other people influences the dominant response. In particular, other people serve to increase arousal or drive; with others present, you are more excited. Now this idea fits in quite neatly with something else that is well documented in the literature about drive: as drive increases, the probability of the dominant response increases. To summarize, the presence of others produces an increase in drive, and an increase in drive produces an increase in the probability of occurrence of the dominant response.

On a difficult, new task, the dominant response will be an error. Thus, when you are performing a difficult task, the presence of others increases the probability of an error. Consequently, your performance will be worse when others are present. On a well-learned task, however, the dominant response will be a correct response. Thus, when you are performing this easy task, the presence of others increases the probability of a correct response. Thus, your performance will be even better when others are present.

So, should you study alone or with your roommate? It all depends on the particular task. On easy material, you will perform better with someone else present; on difficult material, you will perform worse with someone else present. Here is the advice of Zajonc (1965):

> If one were to draw one practical suggestion from the review of the social-facilitation effects which are summarized in this article he would advise the student to study all alone, preferably in an isolated cubicle, and to arrange to take his examinations in the company of many other students, on stage, and in the presence of a large audience. The results of his examination would be beyond his wildest expectations, provided, of course, he had learned his material quite thoroughly [p. 274].

You might try to notice whether Zajonc's generalization seems to hold true for you in everyday life. I recall my first experiences with trying to use an IBM keypunch machine. If other people were present, I seemed to make many more errors. This fits Zajonc's generalization: this was a new task, and I made many errors; therefore, the presence of others should produce even more errors. In contrast, I find that I type much faster and more accurately if someone else is present. Typing is a familiar, easy task for me now; therefore, the presence of others should produce even more accurate performance.

Zajonc's hypothesis, that the presence of others increases the likelihood that the subject will supply the dominant response, summarized the prior research quite nicely. Subsequent research has provided further tests for Zajonc's hypothesis. For example, let's look at a study on word associations conducted by Matlin and Zajonc (1968). We've talked about word associations in other chapters. Basically, the experimenter presents a stimulus, such as the word TABLE, and the subject provides an association, such as CHAIR. Sometimes people provide very common responses, like CHAIR, to the stimulus TABLE, but other times they provide very unusual responses—for example, MUDBALL. Now, dominant responses are common responses. We can measure the number of dominant or common responses that a subject makes in a free-association task by looking in the Palermo/Jenkins word association norms (1964). These norms list all the responses that a large group of subjects supplied to a number of stimuli. For example, for the stimulus TABLE, 691 people responded CHAIR, 23 people responded EAT, and 7 people responded WOOD. However, no one responded MUDBALL. If the response that the subject supplied was listed in the norms, Matlin and Zajonc classified the response as a dominant response. In other words, this response was a reasonably common response—someone else had also given that response in the norms.

Subjects were asked to supply free associations to a large number of stimuli. Half of the time, the subjects were alone in the room, and half of the time, another student was present as an observer. (Counterbalancing was used to avoid the confounding variable of practice in this within-subjects design. That is, half of the subjects performed alone first and then with an observer; the other half of the subjects performed first with an observer and then alone.) The results showed that the subjects supplied a significantly greater number of dominant responses when the observer was present. Thus, the presence of others makes the dominant response more likely; people are more likely to give common responses when someone else is present.

Other literature on social facilitation has been summarized by Cottrell (1972). Cottrell, however, believes that evaluation apprehension is an important component of social facilitation. (Recall our discussion of evaluation apprehension in Chapter 3.) Specifically, he believes that the presence of others influences performance only when people are concerned about being evaluated. Thus, if we wanted to explain the Matlin and Zajonc results in terms of evaluation apprehension, we would say that subjects supplied common responses when someone else was present because they were worried about how that person might evaluate them. Presumably, subjects would be reluctant to supply unusual responses like MUDBALL because they would seem too weird.

In this section, we have seen that people are influenced by the presence of another person. However, we cannot specify the nature of that influence unless we know something about the task. If the task is easy, they do better. If the task is hard, they do worse. In general then, the presence of others makes people intensify their normal tendencies.

Reactance

Last winter we decided to escape from snowy Upstate New York and go to some island in the Caribbean, though we weren't sure where. After looking over the brochures, we casually decided on St. Lucia, though Barbados was a close runner-up. We phoned the travel agent, only to learn that there were no remaining seats on the flight to St. Lucia. We were outraged! Suddenly, St. Lucia became by far the most attractive island in the entire Caribbean, and we began to investigate alternate flights to St. Lucia that would have cost hundreds of dollars more. In other words, we resented the loss of freedom and sought to regain that freedom; a weak preference was instantly transformed into a strong preference.

We had experienced **reactance**. According to Brehm (1966), "if a person's behavioral freedom is reduced or threatened with reduction, he will become motivationally aroused. This arousal would presumably be directed against any further loss of freedom and it would also be directed toward the re-establishment of whatever freedom had already been lost or threatened" (p. 2).

Here is a representational study that Brehm discusses in his book, *A Theory of Psychological Reactance*. Subjects were told that they would be rating four phonograph records for a distributing company. They were also told that they could keep one of the records for their efforts. They listened to the records and rated them on a favorability scale. On the next day, they returned to the laboratory for a second session. They were told that the complimentary records had just arrived but, for some unknown reason, no copies had been sent of one of the four records. This unavailable record, by prearrangement, was the subject's third choice on the previous day. After this explanation, subjects heard and rated the records a second time. An additional group of control subjects completed the same tasks, except that they did not have one of the records eliminated.

How did the subjects in the experimental group respond in their rating of the Rank 3 record—the one that was no longer available? They rated it much more positively than they had before, and this increase in rating was much greater than the increase for the other two records. Also, the increase was greater than the increase awarded by the control subjects to the Rank 3 record.

A book by Wicklund (1974) examines many variables that influence reactance. One variable is the subject's competence. In one study, subjects answered questions about some biographical sketches. The experimenter provided false feedback from these answers, telling half of the subjects that they had high social-judgment ability and half of them that they had low social-judgment ability. (In this connection, recall the earlier discussions of the social psychology and ethics of deception.) In the second part of the study, subjects were asked to make judgments about two job applicants, Al and Paul. Midway through this part, all of the subjects received a note, presumably from another subject, saying either "Paul is the best advisor" (low threat) or "There is no question about it. Paul is the best advisor" (high threat). Subjects who believed that they had high social-judgment ability showed reactance in the high-threat condition: they *lowered* their rating of Paul. In contrast, the subjects who believed that they had low social-judgment ability did not change their rating of Paul. Wicklund concludes: "An increase in social pressure to adopt a new judgment arouses reactance only to the degree the subject is highly competent to form his own judgments on the matter" (p. 48).

Cognitive Dissonance

The reactance we experienced when we could not go to St. Lucia was soon replaced by another motivation. Here we were holding tickets to Barbados when we really wished we were going to St. Lucia! But then, gradually, we found that one guidebook claimed that Barbados' beaches were the most glorious in the Caribbean, that there were fewer interesting sights in St. Lucia, and so on. On our return trip, we assured ourselves complacently that Barbados was surely superior to St. Lucia in the temperature of the water, the quality of the snorkeling, the friendliness of the inhabitants—in short, Barbados had clearly been the right place to visit.

In 1957, Leon Festinger proposed the term **cognitive dissonance** to describe the uncomfortable situation in which a person holds two cognitions, or thoughts, that are inconsistent with each other. For example, the cognitions "I want to go to St. Lucia" and "I am going to St. Lucia" would be *consistent* with each other. However, the cognitions "I want to go to St. Lucia" and "I am going to Barbados" produced cognitive dissonance. Festinger maintained that cognitive dissonance is unpleasant; like hunger, it is an aversive motivational state. He proposed that people experiencing cognitive dissonance will try to reduce the dissonance and achieve consistency, or *consonance*. Consonance can be achieved by (1) increasing the number or the importance of consonant cognitions or (2) decreasing the number or importance of dissonant cognitions. Thus, we ultimately achieved consonance by discovering good things about Barbados, consonant with our cognition "We are going to Barbados," and by learning less pleasant things about St. Lucia, decreasing the number of dissonant cognitions.

Cognitive-dissonance theory does not sound particularly extraordinary; yet in a review of social-psychology theory, Zajonc (1968a) notes that it has produced more investigation than any other theory in social psychology. Probably one reason that the theory generated such excitement is that some of the studies produced some very unexpected results. The best known study is one by Festinger and Carlsmith (1959). The basic question they were investigating was this: what happens when you are asked to say something publicly that you do not privately believe?

In this study, college students spent one hour doing repetitive, boring tasks, such as turning pegs one-quarter of a turn. The authors believed that the task was dull enough for the subjects to adopt the private cognition "That was a terrible experiment." Then came the deception. Subjects were told that they were to describe the experiment to the subjects scheduled for the next time slot. Specifically, they were to stress that the tasks were exciting and fun; thus, the private belief would be in conflict with the public statement. Subjects in a low-reward condition were told that they would be paid $1 for talking to the new subjects; subjects in a high-reward condition were told that they would receive $20 for talking to the new subjects. A third group of subjects served as controls and just rested for the appropriate amount of time. Then another experimenter questioned the subjects about their attitudes toward the dull tasks.

If you are not already familiar with this experiment, you might try to guess who liked the experiment best. A first guess might be one derived from reinforcement theory: the more reinforcement you get, the better you like it. Thus, the $20 subjects should have liked it better than the $1 subjects. However, the reverse was found: *the $1 subjects liked it the best!* The explanation for these strange results comes from cognitive-dissonance theory. The subject is faced with two cognitions: "That was a terrible experiment" and "I have just told someone that it was an exciting experiment." The dissonance will be resolved if the subject can come up with some positive attitudes toward the experiment, and this is what the $1 subjects did. However, the $20 subjects could resolve the dissonance quite readily because they had a *reason* for saying that the experiment was exciting; after all, $20 is fantastic pay (particularly in the 1950s) for a few minutes' work. Thus, the $20 subjects did not have to modify their attitudes toward the boring task. Figure 11-5 shows the average rating for each of the three groups on several of the attitude questions. (Incidentally, as I mentioned in the chapter on ethics, all subjects were asked to return the money to the experimenter. The subjects were reported to have returned the money willingly, but the experiment might be questionable in light of current ethical standards.)

Sometimes we do something contrary to our beliefs because we will receive a reward for it. Other times we can justify dissonance because "he's a

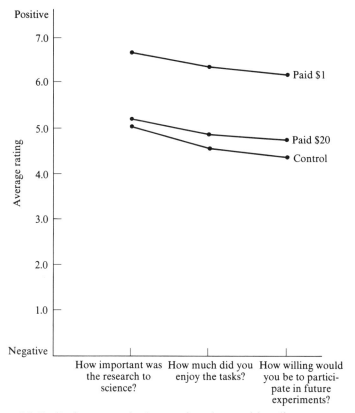

Figure 11-5. Ratings on attitude questions in cognitive-dissonance experiment. Data from L. Festinger and J. M. Carlsmith, Cognitive consequences of forced compliance. *Journal of Abnormal and Social Psychology*,
1959, *58*, 203–210.

nice guy." Zimbardo, Weisenberg, Firestone, and Levy (1969) examined the
effects of experimenter characteristics in an article enticingly titled "Changing
Appetites for Eating Fried Grasshoppers with Cognitive Dissonance." These
authors measured attitudes toward fried grasshoppers (by pretest, the most
awful of a large variety of unusual foods). The ratings were made once at the
beginning of the experiment and a second time after a session in which they
were urged to eat the grasshoppers, which about half of them did. The authors
expected to find that those who had eaten the grasshoppers would improve
their opinion of fried grasshoppers more than those who had not eaten the
grasshoppers. However, they wanted to see whether attitude change would be
different for those subjects who had a pleasant experimenter than for those who
had an unpleasant experimenter. Now, as Zajonc (1968a) has noted, the experiments testing dissonance theory often "involve the resources of a minor theat-
rical production" (pp. 390–391). In this experiment, the pleasant experimenter
interacted pleasantly with his "assistant"; he was polite, friendly, and forgiving
of a mistake. The same person acted the role of the unpleasant experimenter for
other subjects; he was snobbish, bossy, and hostile, and he blew up when his

"assistant" made a mistake. The results showed that people who ate grasshoppers grew more positive toward them than those who had refused to eat them. However, the contrast in attitudes was much greater in the case of the unpleasant experimenter. With a pleasant experimenter, subjects had a good excuse for eating grasshoppers: they ate them because the experimenter was a nice guy, not because the grasshoppers were tolerable. With an unpleasant experimenter, subjects had no such excuse. The only way in which they could reduce the dissonance was by believing "Fried grasshoppers aren't that bad after all!"

An excellent chapter by Sherwood, Baron, and Fitch (1969) summarizes the theory and research on cognitive dissonance. An inspection of this overview gives a good feeling for the variety of approaches to a research problem. For example, if we look at the variety of dependent variables used in dissonance research, we find: (1) changes in opinion, (2) exposure to information; (3) recall of information; (4) perceptual distortion; (5) changes in overt behavior; and (6) changes in evaluations of people, groups, objects, activities, foods, sensory qualities, and subjective experiences.

Overjustification

An old man lived on a street where boys played noisily. One day when the noise was overwhelming, he called them over and asked them to play noisily in front of his house, for which he would pay them a quarter. They did so, and he paid them. They returned the next day, and he paid them only 20 cents, because he was running out of money. The next day, they received only 15 cents. "Furthermore, the old man told them, he would have to reduce the fee to five cents on the fourth day. The boys became angry, and told the old man they would not be back. It was not worth the effort, they said, to make noise for only five cents a day" (Casady, 1974, p. 52).

This story, which is probably fictional, illustrates the principle of **overjustification**. Overjustification occurs when people who are performing an activity they like receive a reward for that activity. There is now too much justification for performing that activity—there is overjustification. What frequently happens is that the persons' **intrinsic motivation**, or internal interest, in that activity decreases. If these people are later given a choice, and no rewards are offered, they will be less likely to perform that activity.

Lepper and Greene (1975) examined overjustification experimentally in an article called "Turning Play Into Work." In this study, 4- and 5-year-old children played with puzzles that had previously been found to be interesting to children their age. One group of children was told that they could play with some attractive toys if they did a good job on the puzzles. Another group of children had no information about any reward. Two weeks later, the children were observed from behind a one-way mirror to see how often they played with puzzles when there was no reward. Lepper and Greene found that the children who had played with the puzzles in order to win a reward now played with the puzzles much less than the children who had not known about the reward. It seems that when a person performs an activity for a reward, that activity becomes a means to an end. Because of the reward, the person now has a different, external reason for taking part in the activity. Now, if you take away the reward, the person will be less likely to perform the activity spontaneously.

The topic of intrinsic motivation has been carefully examined in a book by Edward Deci (1975). One study in Deci's investigation involved college students working on a spatial-relations puzzle called Soma, a game that they found very interesting. Students in two groups worked on the puzzle for three 1-hour sessions. Subjects in the control group never received any reward for any of their puzzle solving. Subjects in the experimental group, however, received a reward of $1 for each puzzle they solved during the second session; they received no reward during the first or the third session.

In each session, the experimenter left the room for 8 minutes between the second and the third puzzle, using a cover story that he was going to the computer to feed in data from the first two puzzles in order to set up the rest of the experiment. In fact, he went outside the room to observe through a one-way mirror. Thus, he could record how long each group played with the third puzzle during each of the three sessions.

Deci found that subjects in the experimental group—those who had received money in the second session—played with the game much less in the observation period of the third session than they had in the first session. However, the controls did not show any decrease in their interest between the first and the third sessions. It seems that the payment for solving the puzzles led to a decrease in intrinsic motivation for the experimental group to solve puzzles. When the reward was removed, they no longer solved puzzles as much as they had originally.

Although Deci, his colleagues, and other researchers have performed numerous studies in support of the concept that reward can decrease intrinsic motivation, other psychologists are skeptical. Scott (1976), for example, believes that the data can be explained within the context of traditional learning theory. His article can be consulted for an alternate interpretation of the over-justification hypothesis.

Sensory Variation

What kind of stimulus conditions encourage the best performance? Would you function best if there were very little variability in what you could see and hear—in a "sensory deprivation" setting—or if your sensory world were continually changing? Furthermore, if our dependent variable is *preference*, rather than *performance*, how much sensory variation would you find most desirable?

Psychologists have been extremely interested in this question, and the theory and research evidence have been extensive (for example, Berlyne, 1967, 1970; Fowler, 1965; and Walker, 1970, 1973). In this section, we will focus on only two issues: sensory deprivation, and novelty versus familiarity.

The issue of sensory variation is interesting to psychologists concerned with motivation because it seems to contradict some motivational theories. According to these theories, organisms are motivated to reduce certain drives and sources of stimulation, such as hunger, sexual urges, pain, and anxiety. Organisms try to reduce these drives in order to return to a balance, or **homeostasis.** However, research in the 1950s began to show that both animals and people often try to *increase,* rather than decrease, the amount of stimulation. Furthermore, as the research on sensory deprivation shows, people find low levels of stimulation extremely unpleasant.

Sensory deprivation. Imagine that you have volunteered for an experiment that will pay you extremely well to do virtually nothing. You will be lying on a bed. Your eyes will be covered with goggles that will let light in, but you won't be able to see any distinct shapes. You will be wearing earphones that will present a constant buzzing noise. Cardboard shields will cover your arms and hands, to reduce tactile sensations. You will have plenty of food and water. Since your biological drives have been satisfied, some theories would predict that you would be delighted with your surroundings. However, according to Suedfeld (1975), who has summarized the research on sensory deprivation, subjects found the experience to be extremely unpleasant. Subjects showed decreased intellectual functioning, shifts in mood, alterations in EEG (brain-wave patterns), and visual and auditory hallucinations. Thus, it seems that people need some sensory stimulation in order to function properly.

The area of sensory deprivation is worth examining in a textbook on experimental psychology for two reasons. First, a wide variety of psychological processes have been examined with this technique. Second, sensory-deprivation research seems to have more than its share of methodological problems, and these problems can serve as examples of some of the issues raised in the first chapters of this textbook.

First, let's examine the three kinds of sensory-deprivation situations that are most common. The bed-confinement situation, described above, was the one used in the original McGill University experiments; it is diagrammed in Figure 11-6. Notice that the room is equipped with an air conditioner, exhaust fan, and microphone. The subject wears goggles, earphones, cardboard shields; EEG leads are attached to his head. The subject is supposed to stay in the room for two to three days. Meals are brought in, and the subject can request to go to another room for toilet facilities.

Other subjects have experienced sensory deprivation in a respirator. As Figure 11-7 illustrates, the subject lies in a tank-type respirator. The subject's arms and legs are placed in rigid cylinders to prevent tactile stimulation. During the experiment, the door to the enclosure around the head is closed, so that only a blank interior is present. The subject hears only a dull noise from the respirator motor. He can drink an eggnog mixture from a tube near his mouth and can request a bedpan.

Suspension in a water tank is probably the most severe of all the sensory-deprivation situations. The subject wears a head mask and is immersed

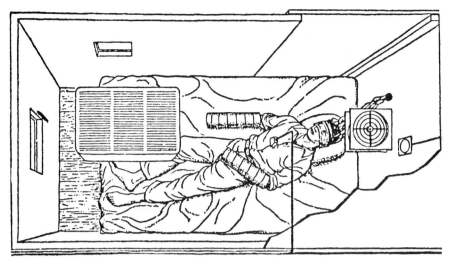

Figure 11-6. Sensory deprivation by bed confinement. From *Sensory Deprivation*, by P. Solomon et al. Copyright 1961 by the President and Fellows of Harvard College. Reprinted by permission of Harvard University Press.

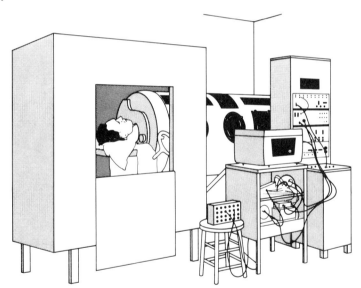

Figure 11-7. Sensory deprivation by confinement in a tank-type respirator. From *Sensory Deprivation*, by P. Solomon et al. Copyright 1961 by the President and Fellows of Harvard College. Reprinted by permission of Harvard University Press.

in a pool of warm water. He is instructed to inhibit all movement. This situation is diagrammed in Figure 11-8.

One dependent measure that is frequently taken in sensory-deprivation studies is simply endurance. How long do subjects remain in isolation in each

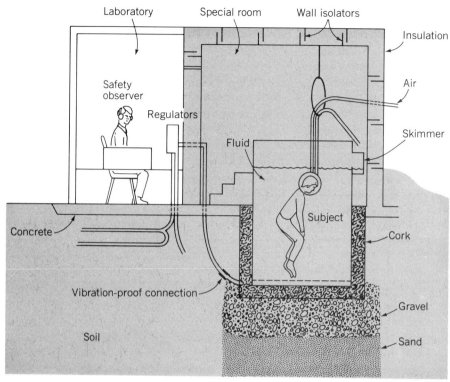

Figure 11-8. Sensory deprivation by confinement in a water tank. Redrawn from J. Shurley, Proceedings of the Third World Congress of Psychiatry, Vol. 3. Toronto: University of Toronto Press, 1963.

of the three situations? As shown in Figure 11-9, which summarizes the results of several studies, endurance is by far the best in bed confinement and by far the worst in the water tank.

Myers (1969) has discussed endurance as a dependent measure in sensory-deprivation studies. It is easy to see why this measure is a popular one, because it is easy to score. However, irrelevant factors, such as the relationship of the subject to the experimenter, probably have a great influence on how long the subject remains in the deprivation situation. Also, endurance time is not a sensitive index of behavior in short-term deprivation studies (with the exception of water-tank studies) because of a ceiling effect. A ceiling effect, you may recall, occurs when the dependent variable—endurance time, in this example—is extremely high in all conditions.

In its favor, however, endurance time may be a valid measure of tolerance for sensory deprivation because it is related to a number of other measures. As Myers summarizes the literature, people who last only a short time in sensory deprivation studies have: (1) high motor restlessness on the second day of deprivation; (2) greater time overestimation; (3) greater seeking of stimulation via a viewing box; and (4) higher stress ratings. Because simple endurance time is related to so many other behaviors that are thought to be hallmarks of

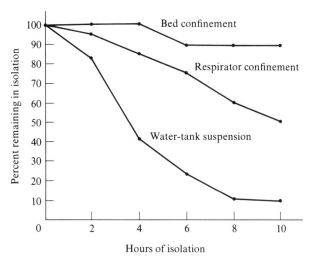

Figure 11-9. Endurance in three kinds of sensory deprivation. From "Variables Affecting Deprivation Results," by M. Zuckerman. In J. P. Zubek (Ed.), *Sensory Deprivation: Fifteen Years of Research*. Copyright 1969 by Appleton-Century-Croft. Reprinted by permission of Irvington Publishers, Inc.

isolation, endurance time can serve as a single critical index of tolerance for sensory deprivation.

Perceptual performance often serves as the dependent measure in sensory-deprivation studies. In the perception chapter, we discussed a study by Schutte and Zubek (1967) that involved visual deprivation, rather than the more severe deprivation of all sensory input. In that study, visual deprivation led to more sensitive taste and smell. Zubek (1969) has reviewed the literature on other perceptual effects. It seems, for example, that depth perception, visual acuity, and the constancies are not affected by deprivation. However, performance on the Müller-Lyer illusion and reversible figures is affected by deprivation.

Suedfeld (1969) has reviewed the literature on intellectual performance as a dependent measure in sensory-deprivation studies. Subjects seem to show some improvement in memory for nonsense syllables and figures after sensory deprivation. For material such as arithmetic and logical reasoning, there is slight impairment. For material such as verbal fluency and free associations, there is strong impairment.

The dependent measure in sensory-deprivation studies that attracted the most attention was the reporting of hallucinations. Zuckerman (1969a) notes that most variables have no influence on the frequency of hallucinations. For example, subjects whose movements are confined are no more likely to report hallucinations than subjects who are not confined. Also, anxiety does not seem to have any strong effect on reporting hallucinations.

With many of the dependent measures that we have considered so far, sensory deprivation has led to an impairment in the dependent measure. Suedfeld (1975), in contrast, has discussed "the benefits of boredom." He conducted a series of experiments that demonstrated that sensory deprivation helped to reduce addiction to smoking. In one study, for example, subjects were randomly divided into four conditions: deprivation plus antismoking messages, deprivation only, messages only, and a no-treatment group. The deprivation groups experienced 24 hours of sensory deprivation, in a single session. Both deprivation groups reduced their smoking significantly more than the other two groups. Two years after the treatment, the deprivation-groups subjects were smoking 55% less than originally, while the subjects from the other groups were smoking 18% less. (The deprivation-plus-antismoking-messages and the deprivation-only groups did not differ from each other.)

A book entitled *Sensory Deprivation: Fifteen Years of Research* (Zubek, 1969) and an article by Suedfeld (1975) contain summaries of research on other dependent measures, including biochemical secretions, galvanic skin responses, group interaction, conformity, and attitude change. In summary, psychologists have information about the influences of sensory deprivation on dozens of different dependent variables, which include higher mental processes, social behaviors, and physiological measures.

Let us turn to the methodological problems with sensory-deprivation research. These can be divided into four basic groups: (1) subjects, (2) manipulating the independent variable, (3) measuring the dependent variable, and (4) obtaining control data.

We discussed one of the problems involving subjects in the chapter on the social psychology of the experiment. As Orne (1969) pointed out, the demand characteristics of sensory-deprivation experiments may be sufficient to produce the unusual effects. As I stressed in that chapter, however, the fact that effects similar to sensory deprivation were found with a group of nonexperiment subjects simply means that demand characteristics *could* have produced the effects, not that they *did* produce the effects.

Another problem concerning subjects in sensory-deprivation studies may be one that you have already anticipated: people who volunteer to participate in a sensory-deprivation study are extremely unusual. They must have free time available. They may be people who desperately need the money (even in the early 1950s, subjects were paid $20 a day). Their personality characteristics have been found to differ from nonvolunteers: they are higher in thrill seeking and lower in phobic reactions, and they have MMPI scores that indicate somewhat better than average mental health (Myers, 1969). In conclusion, then, subjects in sensory-deprivation experiments constitute an extremely biased sample. As we discussed in Chapter 2, a biased sample arises when the people who serve in an experiment are not representative of the entire population. Conclusions based on these unusual people should not be interpreted as representing the behavior of all humans.

There are many problems with manipulating the independent variable in sensory-deprivation studies. First of all, as we have seen, there is no one, single way to produce sensory deprivation. Consequently, different results may be obtained with different methods—and, in fact, we have already seen that endurance times vary with the three methods. Another problem is that it seems nearly impossible to produce complete sensory deprivation. Even in the water-tank situation, subjects can hear water ripples, blood pounding in their ears, and their own swallowing sounds (Rossi, 1969). There are also enormous problems of maintenance that must be solved in order to guarantee that the subjects experience only sensory deprivation, and not physical and physiological difficulties. The subjects must somehow be fed and toileted in deprivation experiments that last more than a few hours. In the more severe water-tank situation, the experimenter must also be concerned with problems such as wrinkling of the skin, changes in fluid, and electrolyte imbalance (Rossi, 1969).

Problems involved with measuring the dependent variable have also been discussed by Rossi (1969). The problem is that the measures taken in sensory-deprivation studies are seldom unobtrusive. As a consequence, we find the same problem we discussed in the beginning chapters of this book: in measuring behavior, we change that behavior. For example, if we attach electrodes to the subjects, the subjects may suspect that they will be shocked. If we measure intellectual functioning, we must introduce a test; this test will provide stimulation and reduce the sensory deprivation. Subjects are often asked to report their sensations, but this allows them to stimulate their vocal chords. There are so many problems with some dependent variables that researchers often use measures that are selected because they solve these problems rather than because of their adequacy and appropriateness in measuring psychological changes (Rossi, 1969). Often, too, measures are selected mostly because they are available, rather than because they are appropriate.

Rossi (1969) also discusses problems with obtaining control data. Recall our discussion in Chapter 2 of between-subjects, within-subjects, and matched-subjects designs, where we concluded that each of these designs had advantages and disadvantages. The problem of deciding which kind of design to use is an important one in sensory-deprivation studies, and there is no ideal answer. In between-subjects designs, control subjects are people who leave the laboratory for a period of time equal to the period of deprivation. Experimenters rarely inquire into what the subjects were doing during this period, merely hoping that their experiences will be randomized. Consequently, the two groups may be far from equivalent. Furthermore, individual differences may be so overwhelming that they diminish the impact of the independent variable— and individual differences are considerable in sensory-deprivation studies.

Are within-subjects designs any better? When subjects serve as their own control, we don't need to worry as much about individual differences. However, recall the disadvantages of this design that we discussed in Chapter 2. For example, if a test is repeated, subjects will have had more practice during the second session. Also, there may be a sensitization problem: subjects are no longer naive if the first session involved deception.

Is a matched-subjects design the answer to sensory-deprivation researchers' dreams? Individual differences could theoretically be reduced by matching each subject in the control group with a subject in the experimental group. However, what attributes should the experimenter consider when matching subjects? Typically, experimenters have used demographic variables such as age, sex, and education. Unfortunately, none of these variables has proved to be important in sensory-deprivation research. Rossi concludes about matched-subjects designs: "Thus, matched controls in sensory deprivation re-search are more often based on hope than fact that the matched variables are relevant" (p. 35). In summary, each of the three kinds of designs presents its own, unique problems.

Before going on to the next section, try another informal experiment. Rate each of the ten words shown in Figure 11-10 on the 7-point scale provided. Then assign a number to each rating, ranging from 1 for "good" to 7 for "bad." The results will be discussed shortly.

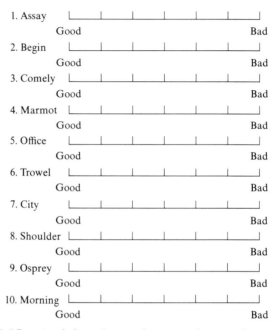

Figure 11-10.   An informal experiment: rating words as "good" or "bad."

Novelty versus familiarity. Which kind of stimulus should people prefer—something novel, which they have never seen before, or something familiar, which they have seen on many occasions? As we shall see, the answer to this question depends on the operational definition that the experimenter chooses for the dependent variable, preference. The answer also depends on the kind of stimuli used.

Berlyne's (1958) classic experiment is often mentioned in psychology textbooks as proof that people like novelty. In this experiment, subjects viewed pairs of pictures of animals. A pair was shown for 10 seconds, and an observer recorded the amount of time that each of the two members of the pair was examined. In all, there were ten of these viewing trials. However, one member of the pair appeared in the same position on all ten trials, whereas the other member of the pair changed on every trial. Thus, a subject might see a rooster on the left-hand side on all ten trials, with a bird, an elephant, a cat, and so on, on the right-hand side. (Naturally, the side on which the familiar figure appeared was counterbalanced.)

Which member of the pair did subjects prefer to look at—the novel one or the familiar one? By the tenth trial, Berlyne found that subjects spent about three times as long looking at the novel picture. Thus, if preference is measured in terms of the amount of time that the subject spends examining a stimulus, novelty is preferable to familiarity.

However, another area of research has reached quite a different conclusion on the issue of novelty versus familiarity. Look over the ratings you supplied in the experiment shown in Figure 11-10. Did you supply different ratings for novel, unfamiliar words, as opposed to common, familiar words? Specifically, take an average for words 1, 3, 4, 6, and 9. Compare this average with the average for words 2, 5, 7, 8, and 10. If you are like the subjects in one study (Matlin, 1970), your ratings of the infrequent words will be at least one point lower than your ratings of the frequent words. This relationship occurs even though there is nothing inherently unpleasant about the infrequent words.

There are examples of this relationship between familiarity and liking in everyday life. Harrison (1977), for example, remarks upon the initial reaction to the Eiffel Tower, an unfamiliar structure that aroused "a storm of protest from Frenchmen who considered it an unforgivable profanation of the arts and a slap in the face for a nation which previously upheld the banner of civilization and refinement" (p.40). However, as the structure became more familiar, it became better liked. No longer distasteful, it became the "subject of lyrical raptures" and a sight that would "cause Louis XIV to die of envy."

An article by Zajonc in 1968 titled "Attitudinal Effects of Mere Exposure" (Zajonc, 1968b) inspired dozens of experimental studies in this area. According to Zajonc, mere repeated exposure of an object is sufficient for a person to become more positive about that object. Zajonc's research took several forms. Some of the research was correlational. For example, he asked college students to circle the more favorable of each of 154 antonym pairs such as *better-worse, reward-punishment,* and *love-hate.* Then he checked the frequency of each word in the Thorndike-Lorge word counts (1944), described in Chapter 8. For 126 of the 154 antonym pairs, subjects had circled the more frequent member of the pair as being more positive. In other correlational studies, Zajonc found that more frequent words were also rated more positively for lists of trees, fruits, vegetables, countries, and cities. (Which did you rank more positively in Chapter 5, *corn* or *leek*?)

However, these results are another excellent example of the problem with the correlational method that we discussed in Chapter 1. If *corn* is liked better than the lower-frequency *leek*, it could indeed be the case that frequent exposure to corn causes greater liking of corn. However, the reverse seems even more likely: we like corn, and as a result we talk about corn frequently, which causes a high word frequency in word counts.

Because of the ambiguity of the correlational data, Zajonc used the experimental method in another study. Zajonc assembled some nonsense words, such as JANDARA, IKTITAF, and LOKANTA. Each subject saw two of these words at each of six frequencies: 25, 10, 5, 2, 1, and 0. Zajonc was careful to counterbalance the words across the six frequencies. For example, Subject 1 might see JANDARA 25 times, Subject 2 might see it 10 times, Subject 3 might see it 5 times, and so on. By systematic counterbalancing, Zajonc guaranteed that all of the words had been exposed at all of the frequencies.

After seeing all of the words, the subjects were told to guess how pleasant each of the words was on a 7-point, good-bad scale. The results are shown in Figure 11-11. Note that words that were seen 25 times were liked much better than words that were seen less often. (Suppose, however, that Zajonc had *not* counterbalanced the words, and JANDARA had been presented 25 times to all subjects and IKTITAF had been presented 0 times to all subjects. The more positive rating for stimuli seen 25 times might have been due to the fact that JANDARA as a stimulus is more positive than IKTITAF.) As Figure 11-11 shows, the same effect held true when Chinese characters were used as stimuli.

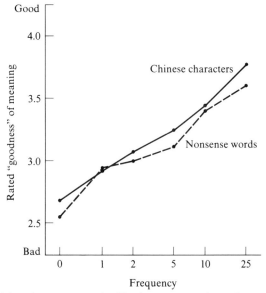

Figure 11-11. Average rated affective connotation of nonsense words and Chinese-like characters as a function of frequency of exposure. From "The Attitudinal Effects of Mere Exposure," by R. B. Zajonc, *Journal of Personality and Social Psychology*, 1968, 9(2), 14. Copyright 1968 by the American Psychological Association. Reprinted by permission.

The results of the mere exposure research may seem to contradict the results of Berlyne's research that we discussed earlier. Berlyne found that people tend to *explore* unfamiliar stimuli more than familiar stimuli, but Zajonc found that people tend to *give higher ratings* to familiar stimuli than to unfamiliar stimuli. On an intuitive level, both exploration and giving high ratings would seem to reflect a positive attitude, and so we would expect both measures to respond similarly to variation in stimulus novelty.

The research of Harrison (1968) helped to resolve this apparent contradiction. Harrison asked subjects to rate stimuli—nonsense words, Chinese characters, and photographs of men's faces—on 7-point, good-bad scales.

Other subjects looked at each stimulus for as long as they wanted, thus supplying a measure of exploration time. The results showed a negative correlation between rating and exploration time: the more pleasant the stimulus was, the less it was explored. Thus, it makes sense that subjects spend a long time exploring novel stimuli (perhaps because they want to understand them), even though they do not like novel stimuli. This area of research, incidentally, points out why it is important to choose independent variables carefully: rating and exploration time respond in very different ways to variation in novelty.

In later research, Berlyne (1970) identified other factors that influence whether people prefer novel or familiar stimuli. In Berlyne's earlier study (Berlyne, 1958), the familiar stimulus was shown over and over, with no other stimuli in between. In Zajonc's (1968) studies, however, the 25 exposures of a particular stimulus were distributed throughout the exposure period. It makes sense that seeing a stimulus 25 times in a row would be boring! In fact, Berlyne (1970) *did* find that subjects were more likely to find the repetition of a stimulus unpleasant when the stimulus was presented many times in a row.

Also, the *kind* of stimulus tested influences whether subjects prefer novel or familiar stimuli. Simple stimuli tend to be liked *less* as they are repeated, whereas complex stimuli tended to be liked *more* (Berlyne, 1970). In other research, Underhill (1977) has shown that the meaningfulness of the stimulus is important. Meaningful pictures, such as a drawing of a staircase, grow unpleasant and boring as you see them repeatedly. On the other hand, meaningless pictures, such as an 11-sided geometric figure, grow more pleasant as you see them repeatedly.

In summary, we cannot demonstrate any simple relationship between preference and novelty/familiarity. Instead, the relationship depends on many factors, including (1) the operational definition of preference, (2) whether repetition is continuous or distributed, and (3) characteristics of the stimuli. It is possible that Zajonc's finding that preference increases as familiarity increases is a phenomenon that occurs only in certain, unusual circumstances. Perhaps the more general relationship between preference and familiarity is that a moderate amount of familiarity is most preferred—that very novel and very familiar stimuli are not as pleasant as moderately familiar stimuli (see, for example, Walker, 1973).

SUMMARY

1. Normal and obese people differ in several ways: normal people are influenced more by hunger, whereas obese people are influenced more by cue prominence and by taste and are discouraged more by conditions that make it difficult to obtain food.
2. Need achievement is measured by projective techniques such as the Thematic Apperception Test (TAT). One theory states: $T_s = M_s \times P_s \times I_s$. One implication of this theory is that the tendency to approach success is greatest when the probability of success and the incentive value of success are both .50.

3. Other motives than the motive to achieve success are important in determining achievement behavior. For example, the motive to avoid failure interferes with positive motivation. The motive to avoid success, a controversial topic, may explain a portion of achievement behavior in women. Other research has focused on people's reactions to achievement behavior; people differ, for example, in whether they attribute success to internal or external causes.

4. Power motivation, which can also be measured by a TAT, is related to historical events; for example, high need for power has generally been expressed in U.S. literature during periods preceding wars. Power motivation is also related to personal relationships; for example, if the male member of a dating couple is high in need for power, the couple is more likely to break up.

5. Social-facilitation literature indicates that the presence of another person leads to improved performance on a familiar task and impaired performance on a difficult or unfamiliar task.

6. Reactance theory states that when a person's freedom is reduced, he or she will become motivationally aroused and will attempt to restore the lost freedom.

7. Cognitive-dissonance theory states that people experiencing cognitive dissonance will try to achieve consistency by inflating the consonant cognitions and decreasing dissonant cognitions.

8. According to overjustification theory, rewarding people for an activity they enjoy will lead to a decrease in their intrinsic motivation. Later, if the reward is removed, they will be less likely to perform that activity.

9. Sensory deprivation influences perceptual performance, intellectual performance, the reporting of hallucinations, smoking behavior, and physiological measures. Sensory-deprivation studies are plagued by many methodological problems.

10. One area of research on the novelty/familiarity question has found that people look at novel pictures longer than familiar ones. Another area of research has found that people prefer familiar stimuli to novel ones. The discrepancy may be explained by the difference in the dependent variables.

Appendix:
Statistical
Analysis

There are four reasons for including an appendix on statistical analysis in this textbook: (1) to refresh your memory on statistical procedures; (2) to give you guidelines for analyzing data from simple experiments conducted in your experimental-psychology course or in your later work in psychology; (3) to help you understand statistical tests referred to in this textbook; and (4) to help you understand statistical analyses referred to in journal articles. This appendix is *not* intended to serve as your only exposure to statistics; it is only a brief "how-to" guide. For a more thorough understanding of statistical theory, consult a statistics textbook such as Kirk (1978) or Horowitz (1974).

This guide will cover the basic tests used in psychology. In each case, there is a brief description of the test and a representative problem. Please note that the problems show only a small number of subjects being tested in each group. I have done this to make it easier for you to see where the numbers are inserted in the formulas. In reality, however, experimenters usually test much larger groups of subjects.

In this section, we will consider the major tests: the t test, the Mann-Whitney test, analysis of variance, correlation, and the chi-square test. The next section contains a brief description of other, less common tests.

How to Use This Section for Analyzing Data

Suppose that you have gathered data from an experiment. With your data in front of you, look through the descriptions of the five basic problems listed below to see which description fits your data. Three of the problems supply the answer for the statistical analysis immediately, referring you to the appropriate page. For the two other problems, you must answer other questions before being referred to the appropriate page. Turn to the specified page and check out the example to confirm that the description of the problem is similar to your own data. There is a step-by-step solution for an example listed there. Please note that an explanation of the symbols follows this section on the five basic problems.

Problem 1: You have one group of numbers, and you want to see if the numbers are significantly different from a well-established population mean.

Answer: See p. 428, the t test/testing a hypothesis about a single mean.

Problem 2: You have two groups of numbers, and you want to see if the numbers are significantly different from each other.

Ask yourself:

a. Is it a within-subjects or a matched-subjects design? (*Within-subjects:* each subject participates in both conditions; *matched-subjects:* a subject in one group is matched with a subject in another group.)
If so,

Answer: See p. 430, the t test/testing a hypothesis about two means, within-subjects or matched-subjects design.

b. Is it a between-subjects design with the scores normally distributed? (*Between-subjects:* each subject participates in only one condition; *normally distributed:* the scores are distributed so that most of them cluster together in the middle of the distribution, with relatively few high or low scores; it is bell-shaped and symmetrical.)
If so,

Answer: See p. 432, the t test/testing a hypothesis about two means, between-subjects design.

c. Is it a between-subjects design with the scores *not* normally distributed?

If so,

Answer: See p. 434, the Mann-Whitney test.

Problem 3: You have more than two groups of numbers, and you want to see if the numbers are significantly different from each other.

Ask yourself:

a. Is it within-subjects or a matched-subjects design? (*Within-subjects:* each subject participates in all conditions; *matched-subjects:* subjects are matched so that each subject is similar to one subject in each of the other groups.)

If so,

Answer: See p. 436, analysis of variance, within-subjects or matched-subjects design.

b. Is it a between-subjects design? (*Between-subjects:* each subject participates in only one condition.)

If so,

Answer: See p. 439, analysis of variance, between-subjects design.

Problem 4: You have two scores for each of your subjects, and you want to see if the scores are related to each other in a systematic fashion.

Answer: See p. 441, correlation.

Problem 5: Your data are expressed in terms of the number of items or people in each category (that is, they are nominal); you do not have individual scores on your subjects.

Answer: See p. 443, the chi-square test.

What the Symbols and Letters Stand For

Unfortunately, statistics often resembles alphabet soup, with the addition of a few Greek symbols. Here is a brief explanation of the symbols and letters used in the section that follows.

Σ (Greek letter *sigma*) This means that you must add together whatever follows. Thus, ΣX means to add up all the X scores.

χ^2 (Greek letter *chi*) This is the number summarizing your results in a chi-square test.

F This is the number summarizing your results in an analysis of variance.

D This is a score obtained by taking the difference between two other scores.

df   This is the degree of freedom, or the number of independent scores used to calculate your statistic. It is used in determining whether your results are significant.

N (or n) This refers to number, as in the number of scores in a group.

p This refers to the probability of finding results as extreme as the results you found by chance alone. Thus, $p < .05$ means that there is less than a .05 (or 1 in 20) chance that results so extreme could be due to chance alone.

r_{XY} This is the number summarizing your results in a correlation test.

$s_{\overline{D}}$ This is the standard error of the difference between two means. It tells us how much the difference between two means is likely to vary.

$s_{\overline{X}}$ This is the standard error of the mean. It tells us how much the mean is likely to vary.

t This is the number summarizing your results in a t test.

U This is the number summarizing your results in a Mann-Whitney test.

X This stands for any score in a group.

$\overline{X}$ This stands for the mean of the scores in a group of X scores, calculated by taking the total of the scores and dividing by the number of scores.

Y This stands for any score in a group (generally in contrast to the scores in another group represented by X).

$\overline{Y}$ This stands for the mean in a group of Y scores.

DESCRIPTIONS AND EXAMPLES

I. The t Test

There are three different situations in which you would want to use a t test: testing a hypothesis about a single mean; testing a hypothesis about two means, within-subjects or matched-subjects design; and testing a hypothesis about two means, between-subjects design.

A. Testing a hypothesis about a single mean

Sometimes, there is a well-established population mean for a particular measure. You test a group of subjects and find their mean score. Is the mean score for your subjects significantly different from that well-established population mean?

Example: On an 8-point rating scale for the question "How happy are you with your job?" you know that the mean in the population is 5 (as established by a nationwide survey). You test the five employees at a particular industry and obtain the scores listed below. Are these scores significantly different from the population mean of 5?

1. Calculate the mean $(\overline{X})$ for your sample.

$$X$$
$$4$$
$$5$$
$$6$$
$$7$$
$$8$$
$$\overline{}$$
$$\Sigma X = 30$$

$$\frac{\Sigma X}{N} = \overline{X} = \frac{30}{5} = 6$$

2. Subtract the mean from each of your scores. Check your accuracy; the sum of these $(X - \overline{X})$ scores should be 0.

X	$X - \overline{X}$
4	$4 - 6 = -2$
5	$5 - 6 = -1$
6	$6 - 6 = 0$
7	$7 - 6 = +1$
8	$8 - 6 = +2$
	$\Sigma (X - \overline{X}) = 0$

3. Square each of the $(X - \overline{X})$ scores and then add them up.

$$(X - \overline{X})^2$$
$$(-2)^2 = 4$$
$$(-1)^2 = 1$$
$$(0)^2 = 0$$
$$(+1)^2 = 1$$
$$(+2)^2 = 4$$
$$\Sigma (X - \overline{X})^2 = 10$$

4. Calculate the standard error of the mean $(s_{\overline{X}})$ by inserting the appropriate values in this equation:

$$s_{\overline{X}} = \frac{\sqrt{\dfrac{\Sigma (X - \overline{X})^2}{N - 1}}}{\sqrt{N}}$$

(Remember: N = the number of scores)

$$s_{\overline{X}} = \frac{\sqrt{\dfrac{10}{4}}}{\sqrt{5}} = \frac{1.58}{2.24} = .71$$

5. Calculate t by dividing the difference between the sample mean and the population mean by the standard error of the mean.

$$t = \frac{\text{sample mean} - \text{population mean}}{s_{\overline{X}}}$$

$$t = \frac{6 - 5}{.71} = 1.41$$

6. Calculate the degrees of freedom (df) by subtracting 1 from the number of scores.

$$df = N - 1$$

$$df = 5 - 1 = 4$$

7. Check statistical tables to see whether your t is significant, given your degrees of freedom. If your t is smaller than the cutoff listed in the table for the .05 level of significance, write $p > .05$: your mean is not significantly different from the population mean. If your t is larger than the cutoff listed for the .05 level of significance, write $p < .05$: your mean *is* significantly different from the population mean. In this case, 1.41 is smaller than the cutoff listed for df = 4 (they list 2.78); therefore, $p > .05$.

8. State your results in APA format, with the degrees of freedom in parentheses, then your t, then the level of significance.

$$t(4) = 1.41, p > .05$$

B. Testing a hypothesis about two means, within-subjects or matched-subjects design

In a within-subjects design, each subject serves as his or her own control: you test subjects in one condition, and then you test the same subjects in another condition. In a between-subjects design, each subject in one condition is matched with another similar subject in the other condition. (These two designs are discussed in Chapter 2.) The analysis for both designs is identical. It involves finding the mean-difference score for the two conditions. Is this mean-difference score significantly different from zero?

Example: You have six pairs of identical twins, and you randomly assign one member of each pair to the experimental condition and the other member to the control condition. (This is a matched-subjects design.) You are studying problem-solving ability. The control group solves the problems after receiving standard instructions. The experimental group solves the problems after receiving instructions to "be creative." You obtain the latency scores listed below. Are these scores significantly different from each other?

1. Calculate a difference score (D) for each pair of scores (that is, the two scores received by the same person in a within-subjects design, or the two scores received by the members of a matched pair in a matched-subjects design) by subtracting the score for one condition from the score for the other condition. Be sure you are consistent about which score is subtracted from which.

Control	Experimental	$D = C - E$
43	40	+3
45	40	+5
50	48	+2
54	49	+5
60	55	+5
70	60	+10

2. Calculate the mean of the D scores, $\overline{D}$.

$$\frac{\Sigma D}{N} = \overline{D} = \frac{+3 + 5 + 2 + 5 + 5 + 10}{6} = \frac{+30}{6} = +5$$

3. Subtract $\overline{D}$ from each of your scores. Check your accuracy. The sum of these $(D - \overline{D})$ scores should be 0.

$$(D - \overline{D})$$

$$+ 3 - 5 = -2$$
$$+ 5 - 5 = 0$$
$$+ 2 - 5 = -3$$
$$+ 5 - 5 = 0$$
$$+ 5 - 5 = 0$$
$$+10 - 5 = +5$$
$$\Sigma (D - \overline{D}) = 0$$

4. Square each of the $(D - \overline{D})$ scores and then add them up.

$$(D - \overline{D})^2$$

$$(-2)^2 = 4$$
$$(0)^2 = 0$$
$$(-3)^2 = 9$$
$$(0)^2 = 0$$
$$(0)^2 = 0$$
$$(+5)^2 = 25$$
$$\Sigma (D - \overline{D})^2 = 38$$

5. Calculate the standard error of the mean for the difference scores ($s_{\overline{D}}$) by substituting the values for $\Sigma (D - \overline{D})^2$ and N in this formula:

$$s_{\overline{D}} = \frac{\sqrt{\dfrac{\Sigma(D - \overline{D})^2}{N - 1}}}{\sqrt{N}} = \frac{\sqrt{\dfrac{38}{5}}}{\sqrt{6}} = \frac{2.76}{2.45} = 1.13$$

Please note that N is the number of *pairs* of scores (also, the number of difference scores) rather than the number of actual scores.

6. Calculate t by dividing the mean difference score by the standard error of the mean for the difference scores.

$$t = \frac{\overline{D}}{s_{\overline{D}}}$$

$$t = \frac{+5}{1.13} = 4.42$$

7. Calculate the degrees of freedom (df) by subtracting 1 from the number of pairs of scores.

$$df = N - 1$$

$$df = 6 - 1 = 5$$

8. Check statistical tables to see whether your t is significant, given your degrees of freedom. If your t is smaller than the cutoff listed in the table for the .05 level of significance, write $p > .05$: your two conditions are not significantly different from each other. If your t is larger than the cutoff listed for the .05 level of significance, write $p < .05$: your two conditions *are* significantly different from each other. In this case, 4.42 is larger than the cutoff listed for df $= 5$ (they list 2.57); therefore, $p < .05$.

9. State your results in APA format, with the degrees of freedom in parentheses, then your t, then the level of significance.

$$t(5) = 4.42, p < .05$$

C. Testing a hypothesis about two means, between-subjects design

The classic, simple experiment involves two separate groups, an experimental group and a control group. Each subject participates in only one of the two groups; thus, the experiment is a between-subjects design (see Chapter 2). You obtain a mean for the experimental group and a mean for the control group. Are the two means significantly different from each other?

Example: Five subjects in a control group learn a list of English word pairs after receiving standard instructions. Seven subjects in an experimental group learn the same words after receiving instructions to visualize the word pairs. You obtain the scores listed below. Are these scores significantly different from each other?

1. Calculate the mean for each group.

Control X	Experimental Y
2	7
3	8
4	9
5	10
6	11
	12
	13
$\Sigma X = 20$	$\Sigma Y = 70$

$$\frac{\Sigma X}{N} = \overline{X} = \frac{20}{5} = 4 \qquad \frac{\Sigma Y}{N} = \overline{Y} = \frac{70}{7} = 10$$

2. Subtract the mean from each of the scores in the appropriate group. Check your accuracy: the sum of the $(X - \overline{X})$ scores should be 0, and the sum of the $(Y - \overline{Y})$ scores should be 0. Then square each $(X - \overline{X})$ score and square each $(Y - \overline{Y})$ score. Calculate $\Sigma (X - \overline{X})^2$ and $\Sigma (Y - \overline{Y})^2$.

X	$X - \overline{X}$	$(X - \overline{X})^2$	Y	$Y - \overline{Y}$	$(Y - \overline{Y})^2$
$2 - 4 =$	-2	4	$7 - 10 =$	-3	9
$3 - 4 =$	-1	1	$8 - 10 =$	-2	4
$4 - 4 =$	0	0	$9 - 10 =$	-1	1
$5 - 4 =$	$+1$	1	$10 - 10 =$	0	0
$6 - 4 =$	$+2$	4	$11 - 10 =$	$+1$	1
			$12 - 10 =$	$+2$	4
			$13 - 10 =$	$+3$	9
$\Sigma (X - \overline{X}) = 0$		$\Sigma (X - \overline{X})^2 = 10$	$\Sigma (Y - \overline{Y}) = 0$		$\Sigma (Y - \overline{Y})^2 = 28$

3. Calculate s^2 by substituting the values for $\Sigma(X - \overline{X})^2$ and $\Sigma(Y - \overline{Y})^2$ and N_X and N_Y in this formula.

$$s^2 = \frac{\Sigma (X - \overline{X})^2 + \Sigma (Y - \overline{Y})^2}{(N_X - 1) + (N_Y - 1)}$$

$$s^2 = \frac{10 + 28}{4 + 6} = \frac{38}{10} = 3.8$$

4. Calculate the standard error of the mean for the difference scores $(s_{\overline{D}})$ by substituting the values for s^2, N_X and N_Y in this formula. Please note that you have already calculated s^2 (rather than s) in Step 2, so you do not need to square that number before inserting it in the formula.

$$s_{\overline{D}} = \sqrt{\frac{s^2}{N_X} + \frac{s^2}{N_Y}}$$

$$s_{\overline{D}} = \sqrt{\frac{3.8}{5} + \frac{3.8}{7}} = \sqrt{.76 + .54} = \sqrt{1.30} = 1.14$$

5. Calculate t by dividing the difference between your two group means by the standard error of the mean for the difference scores.

$$t = \frac{\overline{X} - \overline{Y}}{s_{\overline{D}}}$$

$$t = \frac{4 - 10}{1.14} = \frac{-6}{1.14} = -5.26$$

6. Calculate the degrees of freedom (d.f.) by subtracting 1 from the number of scores in each group and adding the results together.

$$df = (N_X - 1) + (N_Y - 1)$$

$$df = (5 - 1) + (7 - 1) = 10$$

7. Check statistical tables to see whether your t is significant, given your degrees of freedom. If your t is smaller than the cutoff listed in the table for the .05 level of significance, write $p > .05$: your two means are not significantly different from each other. If your t is larger than the cutoff listed for the .05 level of significance, write $p < .05$; your two means *are* significantly different from each other. In this case, 5.26 is larger than the cutoff listed for df = 10 (they list 2.23); therefore, $p < .05$.

8. State your results in APA format, with the degrees of freedom in parentheses, then your t, then the level of significance.

$$t(10) = 5.26, p < .05$$

(Note that the minus sign in front of the value for t is traditionally omitted.)

II. The Mann-Whitney Test

Use the Mann-Whitney test when you would like to use a between-subjects t test, but the scores are not normally distributed. The Mann-Whitney test asks whether two groups are significantly different from each other. It is also used for ranked data.

Example: You are studying whether word associations are influenced by the emotionality of the stimulus word. One group of subjects supplies word associations to neutral stimulus words, and a separate group of subjects supplies word associations to emotional stimulus words. The amount of time taken to respond is listed for the two kinds of words. Are the latencies for neutral words different from the latencies for emotional words?

1. Take all the scores of both groups and rank them with respect to their standing among all the scores. Give the lowest score a rank of 1 and the highest score a rank of N (the total number of scores).

| Group A (emotional words) | Group B (neutral words) |
Ranks	Ranks
$(10) \leftarrow$ 32 sec	40 sec $\rightarrow$ (11)
$(9) \leftarrow$ 25 sec	12 sec $\rightarrow$ (7)
$(8) \leftarrow$ 19 sec	8 sec $\rightarrow$ (6)
$(5) \leftarrow$ 6 sec	4 sec $\rightarrow$ (3)
$(4) \leftarrow$ 5 sec	3 sec $\rightarrow$ (2)
	2 sec $\rightarrow$ (1)

2. Sum the ranks for A and call it R_A. Sum the ranks for B and call it R_B.

$$R_A = 10 + 9 + 8 + 5 + 4 = 36 \qquad R_B = 11 + 7 + 6 + 3 + 2 + 1 = 30$$

3. Compute U_A and U_B using these formulae:

$$U_A = (N_A)(N_B) + \frac{(N_A)(N_A + 1)}{2} - R_A$$

$$U_A = (5)(6) + \frac{(5)(6)}{2} - 36 = 9$$

$$U_B = (N_A)(N_B) + \frac{(N_B)(N_B + 1)}{2} - R_B$$

$$U_B = (5)(6) + \frac{(6)(7)}{2} - 30 = 21$$

4. Which is smaller, U_A or U_B? Call this U.

$$U_A \text{ is smaller; } U = 9$$

5. Look up your U value in the tables to find the exact probability that U is this small or smaller. Call the smaller of the two numbers N_1 and the larger of the two numbers N_2. If the exact probability listed for your U value is greater than .05, your two groups are not significantly different from each other. If the exact probability listed for your U value is smaller than .05, your two groups are significantly different from each other. In this case, $N_1 = 5$; $N_2 = 6$; $p = .16$. This is larger than $p = .05$; therefore, the two groups are not significantly different from each other.

6. State your results in APA format, with the degrees of freedom in parentheses, then your U, then the level of significance.

$$U(5, 6) = 9, p = .16$$

III. Analysis of Variance

Analysis of variance tests hypotheses about more than two groups of numbers. We will cover only one-way analysis of variance, involving only one independent variable. For two-way analysis of variance (involving two independent variables), consult Kirk (1968). There are two kinds of analyses of variance, depending on whether you are using a within-subjects or a between-subjects design.

A. Testing a hypothesis about more than two means, within-subjects or matched-subjects design

Use this kind of analysis if you have more than two groups and if each subject participates in each of the conditions (a within-subjects design) or if subjects are matched so that each subject is similar to one subject in each of the other groups (a matched-subjects design). In an analysis of variance, you ask whether the means are significantly different from each other, when all means are considered together.

Example: In a frequency-estimation study, your subjects see pleasant, unpleasant, and neutral words ten times each and then estimate how often they have seen the words. Each subject participates in all three conditions. You obtain the scores listed below. Are the means for the three groups significantly different from each other?

1. Calculate for each condition: (1) the sum of the scores [ΣX], (2) the average score [$\overline{X}$], and (3) the sum of the squared scores [ΣX^2]. (The average score is not used in further calculation, but it should be reported in the results section of your report.)

Pleasantness of Words

	Pleasant	*Unpleasant*	*Neutral*
Subject 1	9	8	7
2	8	7	6
3	8	6	5
4	5	6	4
$\Sigma X =$	30	= 27	= 22
$\overline{X} = \dfrac{\Sigma X}{N} =$	7.5	= 6.8	= 5.5
$\Sigma X^2 =$	234	= 185	= 126

2. Calculate a "grand sum" [$\Sigma\Sigma X$] by adding together the sums of the scores for all of the conditions.

$$\Sigma\Sigma X = 30 + 27 + 22 = 79$$

3. Calculate a "grand sum of squares" [$\Sigma\Sigma X^2$] by adding together the sums of the squared scores for all of the conditions.

$$\Sigma\Sigma X^2 = 234 + 185 + 126 = 545$$

4. Calculate a "sum of squares total" [ss_T] using the formula:

$$ss_T = \Sigma\Sigma X^2 - \frac{(\Sigma\Sigma X)^2}{N}$$

$$ss_T = 545 - \frac{(79)^2}{12} = 545 - 520.08 = 24.92$$

5. Calculate a "sum of squares between conditions" [ss_{BC}]. Take each of the condition totals [ΣX] that you calculated in Step 1, square each condition total, then add them together. Divide that sum by the number of scores in each condition. From that number, subtract $\frac{(\Sigma\Sigma X)^2}{N}$, which you already calculated as part of Step 4.

$$ss_{BC} = \frac{\Sigma(\text{total for each condition})^2}{n \text{ in that condition}} - \frac{(\Sigma\Sigma X)^2}{N}$$

$$= \frac{(30)^2 + (27)^2 + (22)^2}{4} - 520.08 = 528.25 - 520.08 = 8.17$$

6. Calculate a total score for each subject.

$$\text{Total for Subject 1} = 9 + 8 + 7 = 24$$
$$\text{Total for Subject 2} = 8 + 7 + 6 = 21$$
$$\text{Total for Subject 3} = 8 + 6 + 5 = 19$$
$$\text{Total for Subject 4} = 5 + 6 + 4 = 15$$

7. Calculate a "sum of squares between subjects" [ss_{BS}]. Take each of the totals for the subjects, square each, then add them together. Divide that sum by the number of scores for each subject. From that number, subtract $\frac{(\Sigma\Sigma X)^2}{N}$, which you already calculated as part of Step 4.

$$ss_{BS} = \frac{\Sigma(\text{total for each subject})^2}{N \text{ for each subject}} - \frac{(\Sigma\Sigma X)^2}{N}$$

$$= \frac{(24)^2 + (21)^2 + (19)^2 + (15)^2}{3} - 520.08 = 534.33 - 520.08 = 14.25$$

8. Calculate a "sum of squares residual" [ss_R] by simply subtracting ss_{BC} and ss_{BS} from ss_T.

$$ss_R = ss_T - ss_{BC} - ss_{BS}$$

$$ss_R = 24.92 - 8.17 - 14.25 = 2.50$$

9. Calculate degrees of freedom [df]. The degrees of freedom associated with the total is the number of scores minus 1. The degrees of freedom associated with "between conditions" is the number of conditions minus 1. The degrees of freedom associated with "between subjects" is the number of subjects minus 1. The degrees of freedom associated with "residual" is calculated by subtracting the degrees of freedom for "between conditions" and "between subjects" from the degrees of freedom for "total."

df for total = number of scores − 1
= 12 − 1 = 11
df between conditions = number of conditions − 1
= 3 − 1 = 2

$$\text{df between subjects} = \text{number of subjects} - 1$$
$$= 4 - 1 = 3$$

$$\text{df residual} = \text{df total} - \text{df between conditions}$$
$$- \text{df between subjects}$$
$$= 11 - 2 - 3 = 6$$

10. Construct a table to display your sums of squares and degrees of freedom. All further calculations can also be entered in this table.

Source	Sum of squares	df	Mean square	F	p
Total (T)	24.92	11			
Between conditions (BC)	8.17	2	4.09*	9.74**	<.05***
Between subjects (BS)	14.25	3			
Residual (R)	2.50	6	.42*		

*(see Step 11)
**(see Step 12)
***(see Step 13)

11. Calculate the "mean square between conditions" by dividing the "sum of squares between" by the "degrees of freedom between." Calculate the "mean square residual" by dividing the "sum of squares residual" by the "degrees of freedom residual."

$$\text{Mean square between conditions} = \frac{\text{sum of squares between conditions}}{\text{degrees of freedom between conditions}}$$

$$ms_{BC} = \frac{8.17}{2} = 4.09$$

$$\text{Mean square residual} = \frac{\text{sum of squares residual}}{\text{degrees of freedom residual}}$$

$$ms_R = \frac{2.50}{6} = .42$$

12. Calculate the F ratio by dividing "mean square between conditions" by "mean square residual."

$$F = \frac{\text{mean square between conditions}}{\text{mean square residual}}$$

$$= \frac{4.09}{.42} = 9.74$$

13. Check statistical tables to see whether your F is significant, given the "degrees of freedom between" and the "degrees of freedom residual." If your F is smaller than the cutoff listed in the table for the .05 level of significance, write $p > .05$: the difference among your means is not significant. If your F is larger than the cutoff listed for the .05 level of significance, write $p < .05$: the difference among your means is significant. In this case, 9.74 is larger than the cutoff listed for 2 and 6 degrees of freedom (they list 5.14); therefore, $p < .05$.

14. State your results in APA format, with the degrees of freedom between conditions and the degrees of freedom residual listed in parentheses, then your F, then the level of significance.

$$F(2, 6) = 9.74, p < .05$$

B. Testing a hypothesis about more than two means, between-subjects design

Use this kind of analysis if you have more than two groups and if each subject participates in only one of the groups (a between-subjects design). In an analysis of variance, you ask whether the means are significantly different from each other, when all the means are considered together.

Example: In a verbal-learning experiment, you have a list of ten nonsense words. You present the list two times to one group, four times to a second group, and eight times to a third group. You obtain the scores listed below. Are the three means—3, 6, and 7—significantly different from each other?

1. Calculate for each condition: (1) the sum of the scores, (2) the average score, and (3) the sum of the squared conditions. (The average score is not used in further calculations, but it should be reported in the results section of your report.)

	Number of presentations		
	2	4	8
	3	4	7
	4	6	6
	3	6	7
	2	8	8
$\Sigma X =$	12	= 24	= 28
$\overline{X} = \dfrac{\Sigma X}{N} =$	3	= 6	= 7
$\Sigma X^2 =$	38	= 152	= 198

2. Calculate a "grand sum" $[\Sigma\Sigma X]$ by adding together the sums of the scores for all of the conditions.

$$\Sigma\Sigma X = 12 + 24 + 28 = 64$$

3. Calculate a "grand sum of squares" $[\Sigma\Sigma X^2]$ by adding together the sums of the squared scores for all of the conditions.

$$\Sigma\Sigma X^2 = 38 + 152 + 198 = 388$$

4. Calculate a "sum of squares total" $[ss_r]$ using the formula:

$$ss_T = \Sigma\Sigma X^2 - \frac{(\Sigma\Sigma X)^2}{N}$$

$$ss_T = 388 - \frac{(64)^2}{12} = 388 - 341.33 = 46.67$$

5. Calculate a "sum of squares between conditions" (ss_{BC}). Take each of the condition totals [ΣX] that you calculated in Step 1, square each condition total, then add them together. Divide that sum by the number of scores in each condition. From that number, subtract $\dfrac{(\Sigma\Sigma X)^2}{N}$, which you already calculated as part of Step 4.

$$ss_{BC} = \frac{\Sigma(\text{total for each condition})^2}{n \text{ in that condition}} - \frac{(\Sigma\Sigma X)^2}{N}$$

$$= \frac{(12)^2 + (24)^2 + (28)^2}{4} - 341.33 = 376 - 341.33 = 34.67$$

6. Calculate a "sum of squares within" (ss_W) by simply subtracting ss_B from ss_T.

$$ss_W = ss_T - ss_B$$
$$ss_W = 46.67 - 34.67 = 12.00$$

7. Calculate degrees of freedom [df]. The degrees of freedom associated with the total is the number of scores minus 1. The degrees of freedom associated with "between conditions" is the number of conditions minus 1. The degrees of freedom associated with "within conditions" is calculated by subtracting the degrees of freedom for "between conditions" from the degrees of freedom for "total."

df for total $\quad = $ number of scores $- 1$
$\quad\quad\quad\quad\quad\quad\quad = 12 - 1 = 11$
df for between conditions $=$ number of conditions $- 1$
$\quad\quad\quad\quad\quad\quad\quad = 3 - 1 = 2$
df for within conditions $\quad =$ df total $-$ df between conditions
$\quad\quad\quad\quad\quad\quad\quad = 11 - 2 = 9$

8. Construct a table to display your sums of squares and degrees of freedom. All further calculations can also be entered in this table.

Source	Sum of squares	df	Mean square	F	p
Total (T)	46.67	11			
Between conditions (BC)	34.67	2	17.33*	13.03**	<.05***
Within conditions (W)	12.00	9	1.33*		

*(see Step 9)
**(see Step 10)
***(see Step 11)

9. Calculate "mean square between conditions" by dividing the sum of squares between conditions by the degrees of freedom for between conditions. Calculate "mean square within conditions" by dividing the sum of squares within conditions by the degrees of freedom for within conditions.

Mean square between conditions $= \dfrac{\text{sum of squares between conditions}}{\text{degrees of freedom between conditions}}$

$$= \dfrac{34.67}{2} = 17.33$$

Mean square within conditions $= \dfrac{\text{sum of squares within conditions}}{\text{degrees of freedom within conditions}}$

$$= \dfrac{12.00}{9} = 1.33$$

10. Calculate the F ratio by dividing "mean square between conditions" by "mean square within conditions."

$$F = \dfrac{\text{mean square between conditions}}{\text{mean square within conditions}}$$

$$= \dfrac{17.33}{1.33} = 13.03$$

11. Check statistical tables to see whether your F is significant, given the "degrees of freedom between conditions" and the "degrees of freedom within conditions." If your F is smaller than the cutoff listed in the table for the .05 level of significance, write $p > .05$: your means are not significantly different from each other. If your F is larger than the cutoff listed for the .05 level of significance, write $p < .05$: your means are significantly different from each other. In this case, 13.04 is larger than the cutoff listed for 2 and 9 degrees of freedom (they list 4.26); therefore, $p < .05$.

12. State your results in APA format, with the degrees of freedom between conditions and the degrees of freedom within conditions listed in parentheses, then your F, then the level of significance.

$$F(2, 9) = 13.03, p < .05$$

IV. Correlation (Pearson product-moment correlation)

You compute a correlation when you would like to see whether two sets of measures on the same individuals are related to each other. (The correlational method is discussed in Chapter 1.) The correlation test asks whether two sets of measures are positively correlated (with high scores on one measure associated with high scores on the other measure), negatively correlated (with low scores on one measure associated with high scores on the other measure), or not related in any consistent fashion.

Example: You are trying to determine whether anxiety is related to the amount of time people spend looking at pictures of disaster scenes. You obtain a measure of anxiety on each of your five subjects, and then you obtain a measure of the amount of time spent looking at the disaster scenes. Is there a relationship between the two measures?

1. For the X measures, calculate (1) the sum of the scores $[\Sigma X]$, (2) that same sum squared $[(\Sigma X)^2]$, and (3) the sum of the squared scores $[\Sigma X^2]$. Repeat this process for the Y measures.

	X *Anxiety*	Y *Amount of time spent looking*
Subject 1	1	6
2	2	6
3	3	4
4	6	5
5	8	2
	$\Sigma X = 20$	$\Sigma Y = 23$
	$(\Sigma X)^2 = 400$	$(\Sigma Y)^2 = 529$
	$\Sigma X^2 = 114$	$\Sigma Y^2 = 117$

2. Calculate ΣXY. Take each person's X score and multiply it by his Y score to obtain XY. Now add together the XY scores for all your subjects.

	X	Y	XY
Subject 1	(1)	(6)	$= 6$
2	(2)	(6)	$= 12$
3	(3)	(4)	$= 12$
4	(6)	(5)	$= 30$
5	(8)	(2)	$= 16$
		ΣXY	$= 76$

3. Figure out N, which is the number of subjects (also, the number of *pairs* of scores).

$$N = 5$$

4. Calculate r_{XY} using this formula.

$$r_{XY} = \frac{N\Sigma XY - (\Sigma X)(\Sigma Y)}{\sqrt{N\Sigma X^2 - (\Sigma X)^2}\sqrt{N\Sigma Y^2 - (\Sigma Y)^2}}$$

$$= \frac{5(76) - (20)(23)}{\sqrt{5(114) - 400}\sqrt{5(117) - 529}} = \frac{380 - 460}{\sqrt{170}\sqrt{56}} = \frac{-80}{(13.04)(7.48)} = \frac{-80}{97.54} = -.82$$

5. Calculate the degrees of freedom [df] by subtracting 2 from the number of pairs of scores.

$$\text{df} = \text{number of pairs} - 2$$
$$= 5 - 2 = 3$$

6. Check statistical tables to see whether your r_{XY} is significant, given your degrees of freedom. If the value of your r_{XY} (either positive or negative) is less

than the cutoff listed in the table for the .05 level of significance, write $p > .05$: there is no relationship between your two measures. If the absolute value of your r_{XY} is greater than the cutoff listed in the table for the .05 level of significance, write $p < .05$: there is a relationship between your two measures. If there is a plus sign (+) in front of your r_{XY}, you have a positive correlation. If there is a minus sign (−) in front of your r_{XY}, you have a negative correlation. In this case, .82 is larger than the cutoff listed for 3 degrees of freedom (they list .81); therefore $p < .05$. Also, you have a *negative* correlation.

7. State your results in APA format, with the degrees of freedom in parentheses, then your r_{XY}, then the level of significance.

$$r_{XY}(3) = -.82, p < .05$$

V. The Chi-square (χ^2) Test

Use the chi-square test when your data are expressed in terms of the number of items or number of people in each category. You do not have individual scores on your subjects; you simply know how many subjects fall into each category. In other words, the chi-square test is appropriate for nominal data (see Chapter 5). The chi-square test asks whether the people (or items) are evenly distributed throughout the categories or whether the people (or items) seem to be more heavily concentrated in some categories than in other categories.

Example: You would like to know whether a film on the dangers of smoking influences the number of people who light up a cigarette within one hour of seeing the film. Sixty subjects, who have identified themselves as smokers, view that film. Fifty other subjects, who have also identified themselves as smokers, view a control film. The number in each group who do smoke and who don't smoke within one hour are listed below. Did the film make a difference? That is, did those who saw the smoking film end up in the "don't smoke" category, whereas those who saw the control film ended up in the "smoke" category?

1. Enter the data in a table like this and label it *Observed*. Calculate a total for each of the columns and for each of the rows.

	Observed Smoke	Don't smoke	(Totals)
Smoking film	10	50	(60)
Control film	30	20	(50)
(Totals)	(40)	(70)	(110)

2. Calculate the number of entries that you would expect to occur in each cell if the entries were distributed *by chance alone* throughout the categories. For

each cell, locate the appropriate totals for the row and column in which the cell is located. Multiply those two numbers by each other, and divide that number by the "grand total" number of entries. Repeat this process for each of the cells.

Number expected for smoking film/smoke category $= \dfrac{(60)\,(40)}{110} = 22$

Number expected for control film/smoke category $= \dfrac{(50)\,(40)}{110} = 18$

Number expected for smoking film/don't smoke category $= \dfrac{(60)\,(70)}{110} = 38$

Number expected for control film/don't smoke category $= \dfrac{(50)\,(70)}{110} = 32$

3. Prepare a table of "expected" values, using the numbers you calculated in Step 2. The labels and the totals should be the same as in your table of observed values. Check to see that the sum of the entries equals the total for each of the rows and for each of the columns.

| | Expected | | |
	Smoke	Don't smoke	(Totals)
Smoking film	22	38	(60)
Control film	18	32	(50)
(Totals)	(40)	(70)	(110)

4. Calculate the chi-square. For each cell, subtract the expected value from the observed value, and square this number. Then divide the result by the expected value. Repeat this procedure for each of the cells, and add those numbers together.

$$\chi^2 = \Sigma\,\frac{(\text{observed} - \text{expected})^2}{\text{expected}}$$

$$= \frac{(10 - 22)^2}{22} + \frac{(50 - 38)^2}{38} + \frac{(30 - 18)^2}{18} + \frac{(20 - 32)^2}{32}$$

$$= \quad 6.55 \quad + \quad 3.80 \quad + \quad 8.00 \quad + \quad 4.50 \quad = 22.85$$

5. Calculate the degrees of freedom [df]. Subtract 1 from the number of rows, and then subtract 1 from the number of columns. Multiply these two numbers together.

$$df = (\text{number of rows} - 1)\,(\text{number of columns} - 1)$$
$$= (1)\,(1) = 1$$

6. Check statistical tables to see whether your χ^2 is significant, given your degrees of freedom. If your χ^2 is smaller than the cutoff listed in the table for the .05 level of significance, write $p > .05$: the entries are evenly distributed throughout the categories. If your χ^2 is larger than the cutoff listed in the table for the .05 level of significance, write $p < .05$: the people (or items) are more heavily concentrated in some categories than in other categories. In this case, 22.85 is larger than the cutoff listed for 1 degree of freedom (they list 3.84); therefore, $p < .05$. (In other words, those who see the smoking film are more likely to end up in the non-smoking category, whereas those who see the control film are more likely to end up in the smoking category.)

7. State your results in APA format, with the degrees of freedom listed in parentheses, then your χ^2, then the level of significance.

$$\chi^2(1) = 22.85, p < .05$$

GLOSSARY OF OTHER STATISTICAL TESTS AND PROCEDURES

The following are some other statistical tests and procedures you might encounter in reading journal articles. This list does not include terms commonly encountered in an introductory statistics course. For those terms, you should consult a statistics textbook such as those by Kirk (1978) and Horowitz (1974).

Analysis of Covariance—A type of analysis of variance that allows you to remove, statistically, a confounding variable.

Canonical Correlation—A statistical analysis that attempts to explain how several independent variables are related to several dependent variables.

Crosstabulation—A tabulation of items with respect to two kinds of classification variables (for example, sex and religion).

Factor Analysis—An analysis, based on correlation, that allows you to isolate a small number of common factors from a large number of measures.

Kendall's Tau—A test using rank orders to determine whether two variables are related (similar to Spearman's rho).

Kruskal-Wallis Test—A test used with more than two experimental conditions, used instead of an analysis of variance when scores are not normally distributed.

Multiple Correlation—An analysis that shows the correlation between the dependent variable and a combination of two or more independent variables.

Multiple Regression—An analysis involving two or more independent variables that allows you to isolate the unique influence of each variable on the dependent variable.

Multivariate Analysis—An analysis that allows you to analyze data for two or more dependent variables.

Partial Correlation—An analysis involving three or more variables that shows the correlation between two of those variables when other variables are held constant.

Path Analysis—An analysis that examines a group of variables that are correlated with each other in order to determine the causal relationship among the variables.

Regression Equation—An equation for predicting a person's score on one measure from his or her score on another measure.

Sign Test—A test used to determine whether there are an equal number of plus and minus signs in a group of difference scores.

Spearman's Rho—A test using rank orders to determine whether two variables are related (similar to Kendall's tau).

Wilcoxon Matched-pairs Signed-ranks Test—A test used to determine whether two groups are significantly different from each other, used instead of a within-subjects *t* test when the scores are not normally distributed.

References

Adair, J. G. *The human subject: The social psychology of the psychological experiment*. Boston: Little, Brown, 1973.

Alker, H. A., & Hermann, M. G. Are Bayesian decisions artificially intelligent? The effect of task and personality on conservatism in processing information. *Journal of Personality and Social Psychology,* 1971, *19,* 31–41.

Alpern, M., Lawrence, M., & Wolsk, D. *Sensory processes.* Monterey, Calif: Brooks/Cole, 1967.

American Psychological Association. *Guidelines for non-sexist language in APA journals.* Washington, D. C.: Author, 1977 (b).

American Psychological Association. *Ethical principles in the conduct of research with human participants.* Washington, D. C.: Author, 1973.

American Psychological Association. *Publication manual of the American Psychological Association* (2nd ed.). Washington, D. C.: Author, 1974.

American Psychological Association. *Ethical standards of psychologists* (1977 Revision). Washington, D. C.: Author, 1977 (a).

American Psychological Association. *Principles for the care and use of animals.* Washington, D.C.: Author, 1971.

447

Anastasi, A. *Psychological testing* (4th ed.). New York: Macmillan, 1976.

Argyris, C. Some unintended consequences of rigorous research. *Psychological Bulletin*, 1968, *70*, 185–197.

Aronson, E., & Carlsmith, J. M. Experimentation in social psychology. In G. Lindzey & E. Aronson (Eds.), *Handbook of social psychology* (2nd ed.). Reading, Mass.: Addison-Wesley, 1968.

Astin, A. *Preventing students from dropping out*. San Francisco: Jossey-Bass, 1975.

Atkinson, J. W. *Motives in fantasy, action, and society*. Princeton, N.J.: Van Nostrand, 1958.

Atkinson, J. W. *An introduction to motivation*. Princeton, N.J.: Van Nostrand, 1964.

Atkinson, J. W., & Litwin, G. H. Achievement motive and test anxiety conceived as motive to approach success and motive to avoid failure. *Journal of Abnormal and Social Psychology*, 1960, *60*, 52–63.

Atkinson, R. C. Reflections on psychology's past and concerns about its future. *American Psychologist*, 1977, *32*, 205–210.

Atkinson, R. C., & Shiffrin, R. M. Human memory: A proposed system and its control processes. In K. W. Spence & J. T. Spence (Eds.), *The psychology of learning and motivation: Advances in research and theory* (Vol. 2). New York: Academic Press, 1968.

Avery, D. D., & Cross, H. A. *Experimental methodology in psychology: Everyone needs it*. Monterey, Calif.: Brooks/Cole, 1978.

Axelrod, S., & Guzy, L. T. Underestimation of dichotic click rates: Results using methods of absolute estimation and constant stimuli. *Psychonomic Science*, 1968, *12*, 133–134.

Babbie, E. R. *The practice of social research*. Belmont, Calif.: Wadsworth, 1975.

Baker, A. H., Rierdan, J., & Wapner, S. Age changes in size-value phenomena. *Child Development*, 1974, *45*, 257–268.

Baker, B. O., Hardyck, C. F., & Petrinovich, L. F. Weak measurements vs. strong statistics: An empirical critique of S. S. Stevens' proscriptions on statistics. *Educational and Psychological Measurement*, 1966, *26*, 291–309.

Barber, B. The ethics of experimentation with human subjects. *Scientific American*, 1976, *234*(2), 25–31.

Barber, J. D. Adult identity and presidential style: The rhetorical emphasis. *Daedalus*, 1968, *97*, 938–968.

Barber, T. X. *Pitfalls in human research*. New York: Pergamon Press, 1976.

Barber, T. X., & Silver, M. J. Fact, fiction, and the experimenter bias effect. *Psychological Bulletin Monograph*, 1968, *70* (6, Pt. 2).

Barker, R. G., & Wright, H. F. *One boy's day: A specimen record of behavior*. New York: Harper & Row, 1951.

Barnes, J. M., & Underwood, B. J. "Fate" of first-list associations in transfer theory. *Journal of Experimental Psychology*, 1959, *58*, 97–105.

Baron, R. M., Mandel, D. R., Adams, C. A., & Griffen, L. M. Effects of social density in university residential environments. *Journal of Personality and Social Psychology*, 1976, *34*, 434–446.

Bartlett, F. C. *Remembering: An experimental and social study*. Cambridge, England: Cambridge University Press, 1932.

Baumrind, D. Principles of ethical conduct in the treatment of subjects: Reaction to the draft report of the committee on ethical standards in psychological research. *American Psychologist*, 1971, *26*, 887–896.

Bem, D. *Beliefs, attitudes, and human affairs*. Monterey, Calif.: Brooks/Cole, 1970.

Berlin, B., & Kay, K. *Basic color terms: Their universality and evolution*. Berkeley and Los Angeles: University of California Press, 1969.

Berlyne, D. E. The influence of complexity and novelty in visual figures on orienting responses. *Journal of Experimental Psychology, 1958, 55,* 289–296.

Berlyne, D. E. Arousal and reinforcement. In D. Levine (Ed.), *Nebraska Symposium on Motivation.* Lincoln: University of Nebraska Press, 1967.

Berlyne, D. E. Novelty, complexity and hedonic value. *Perception and Psychophysics, 1970, 8,* 279–286.

Berscheid, E., Baron, R. S., Dermer, M., & Libman, M. Anticipating informed consent: An empirical approach. *American Psychologist, 1973, 28,* 913–925.

Binder, A., McConnell, D., & Sjoholm, N. A. Verbal conditioning as a function of experimenter characteristics. *Journal of Abnormal and Social Psychology, 1957, 55,* 309–314.

Birch, D., & Veroff, J. *Motivation: A study of action.* Monterey, CA: Brooks/Cole, 1966.

Blake, M. Prediction of recognition when recall fails: Exploring the feeling-of-knowing phenomena. *Journal of Verbal Learning & Verbal Behavior, 1973, 12,* 311–319.

Bloom, L. *Language development: Form and function in emerging grammars.* Cambridge, Mass.: M.I.T. Press, 1970.

Blumberg, H. H., DeSoto, C. B., & Kuethe, J. L. Evaluation of rating scale formats. *Personnel Psychology, 1966, 19,* 243–259.

Blumenthal, A. L. Prompted recall of sentences. *Journal of Verbal Learning and Verbal Behavior, 1967, 6,* 203–206.

Boakes, R. A., & Lodwick, B. Short-term retention of sentences. *Quarterly Journal of Experimental Psychology, 1971, 23,* 399–409.

Bouchard, T. J., & Hare, H. Size, performance and potential in brainstorming groups. *Journal of Applied Psychology, 1970, 54,* 51–55.

Bourne, L. E., Jr., Goldstein, S., & Link, W. E. Concept learning as a function of availability of previously presented information. *Journal of Experimental Psychology, 1964, 67,* 439–448.

Bourne, L. E., Jr., Guy, D. E., Dodd, D., & Justesen, D. R. Concept identification: The effects of varying length and informational components of the intertrial interval. *Journal of Experimental Psychology, 1965, 69,* 624–629.

Bousfield, W. A. The occurrence of clustering in the recall of randomly arranged associates. *Journal of General Psychology, 1953, 49,* 229–240.

Bower, G. H. Experiments on story understanding and recall. *Quarterly Journal of Experimental Psychology, 1976, 28,* 511–534.

Bower, G. H., & Clark, M. C. Narrative stories as mediators for serial learning. *Psychonomic Science, 1969, 14,* 181–182.

Bower, G. H., & Springston, F. Pauses as recoding points in letter series. *Journal of Experimental Psychology, 1970, 83,* 421–430.

Bower, G. H., & Winzenz, D. Comparison of associative learning strategies. *Psychonomic Science, 1970, 20,* 119–120.

Bower, T. G. R. The visual world of infants. *Scientific American, 1966, 215*(6), 80–92.

Braine, M. D. S. The ontogeny of English phrase structure: The first phase. *Language, 1963, 39,* 1–13.

Bramel, D. A dissonance theory approach to defensive projection. *Journal of Abnormal and Social Psychology, 1962, 64,* 121–129.

Bransford, J. D., Barclay, J. R., & Franks, J. J. Sentence memory: A constructive versus interpretive approach. *Cognitive Psychology, 1972, 3,* 193–209.

Bransford, J. D., & Franks, J. J. The abstraction of linguistic ideas. *Cognitive Psychology, 1971, 2,* 331–350.

Bransford, J. D., & Johnson, M. K. Contextual prerequisites for understanding: Some investigations of comprehension and recall. *Journal of Verbal Learning and Verbal Behavior, 1972, 11,* 717–726.

Brehm, J. W. *A theory of psychological reactance*. New York: Academic Press, 1966.

Brown, R. The development of Wh questions in child speech. *Journal of Verbal Learning and Verbal Behavior,* 1968, *7,* 277–290.

Brown, R. *A first language*. Cambridge, Mass.: Harvard University Press, 1973.

Brown, R. Reference: In memorial tribute to Eric Lenneberg. *Cognition,* 1976, *4,* 125–153.

Brown, R., & Fraser, C. The acquisition of syntax. In C. N. Cofer & B. S. Musgrave (Eds.), *Verbal behavior and learning*. New York: McGraw-Hill, 1963.

Brown, R., Galanter, E., Hess, E. H., & Mandler, G. *New directions in psychology*. New York: Holt, Rinehart & Winston, 1962.

Brown, R., & Lenneberg, E. H. A study in language and cognition. *Journal of Abnormal and Social Psychology,* 1954, *49,* 454–462.

Brown, R., & McNeill, D. The ''tip of the tongue'' phenomenon. *Journal of Verbal Learning and Verbal Behavior,* 1966, *5,* 325–337.

Buckhout, R. Eyewitness testimony. *Scientific American,* 1974, *231*(6), 23–31.

Burke, R. J., & Maier, N. R. F. Attempts to predict success on an insight problem. *Psychological Reports,* 1965, *17,* 303–310.

Campbell, D. T. Reforms as experiments. *The American Psychologist,* 1969, *24,* 409–429.

Campbell, D. T., & Stanley, J. C. *Experimental and quasi-experimental designs for research*. Chicago: Rand McNally, 1963.

Campos, J. J., Langer, A., & Krowitz, A. Cardiac responses on the visual cliff in prelocomotor human infants. *Science,* 1970, *170,* 196–197.

Carlson, R. Where is the person in personality research? *Psychological Bulletin,* 1971, *75,* 203–219.

Carmichael, L., Hogan, H. P., & Walter, A. A. An experimental study of the effect of language on the reproduction of visually perceived form. *Journal of Experimental Psychology,* 1932, *15,* 73–86.

Carroll, J. B., & Casagrande, J. B. The function of language classifications in behavior. In E. E. Maccoby, T. M. Newcomb, & E. L. Hartley (Eds.), *Readings in social psychology* (3rd ed.). New York: Holt, Rinehart & Winston, 1958.

Carroll, J. B., & White, M. N. Word frequency and age of acquisition as determiners of picture-naming latency. *Quarterly Journal of Experimental Psychology,* 1973, *25,* 85–95.

Casady, M. The tricky business of giving rewards. *Psychology Today,* August 1974, p. 52.

Cazden, C. B. *Environmental assistance to the child's acquisition of grammar*. Unpublished doctoral dissertation, Graduate School of Education, Harvard University, 1965.

Cazden, C. B. The acquisition of noun and verb inflections. *Child Development,* 1968, *39,* 433–448.

Chapman, L. J., Chapman, J. P., & Brelje, T. Influence of the experimenter on pupillary dilation to sexually provocative pictures. *Journal of Abnormal Psychology,* 1969, *74,* 396–400.

Chomsky, N. *Syntactic structures*. The Hague: Mouton Publishers, 1957.

Chomsky, N. *Aspects of the theory of syntax*. Cambridge, Mass.: M.I.T. Press, 1965.

Christensen, L. B. *Experimental methodology*. Boston: Allyn & Bacon, 1977.

Clark, E. V. On the acquisition of the meaning of *before* and *after*. *Journal of Verbal Learning and Verbal Behavior,* 1971, *10,* 266–271.

Clark, H. H., & Clark, E. V. *Psychology and language: An introduction to psycholinguistics*. New York: Harcourt Brace Jovanovich, 1977.

Clarkson, F. E., Vogel, S. R., Broverman, I. K., Broverman, D. M., & Rosenkrantz, P. S. Family size and sex-role stereotypes. *Science,* 1970, *167,* 390–392.

Colgrove, M. A. Stimulating creative problem solving: Innovative set. *Psychological Reports,* 1968, *22,* 1205–1211.

Coltheart, V. Confidence rating as a response index in concept identification. *Journal of Experimental Psychology,* 1973, *97,* 46–50.

Condon, W. S., & Sander, L. W. Synchrony demonstrated between movements of the neonate and adult speech. *Child Development,* 1974, *45,* 456–462.

Conrad, H. S. Clearance of questionnaires with respect to "invasion of privacy," public sensitivities, ethical standards, etc. *American Psychologist,* 1967, *22,* 356–359.

Conrad, R. Acoustic confusions in immediate memory. *British Journal of Psychology,* 1964, *55,* 75–84.

Cottrell, N. B. Social facilitation. In C. G. McClintock (Ed.), *Experimental social psychology.* New York: Holt, Rinehart & Winston, 1972.

Craik, F. I. M., & Lockhart, R. S. Levels of processing: A framework for memory research. *Journal of Verbal Learning and Verbal Behavior,* 1972, *11,* 671–684.

Craik, F. I. M., & Watkins, M. J. The role of rehearsal in short-term memory. *Journal of Verbal Learning and Verbal Behavior,* 1973, *12,* 598–607.

Cranberg, L. Ethical code for scientists? *Science,* 1963, *141,* 1242.

Cronbach, L. J. The two disciplines of scientific psychology. *American Psychologist,* 1957, *12,* 671–684.

Cronbach, L. J. Beyond the two disciplines of scientific psychology. *American Psychologist,* 1975, *30,* 116–127.

Crowne, D. P., & Marlowe, D. *The approval motive: Studies in evaluative dependence.* New York: Wiley, 1964.

Darwin, C. J., Turvey, M. T., & Crowder, R. G. An auditory analogue of the Sperling partial-report procedure: Evidence for brief auditory storage. *Cognitive Psychology,* 1972, *3,* 255–267.

Daves, W. F. Absence of a context effect in rated pleasantness of concrete and abstract words. *Perceptual and Motor Skills,* 1970, *31,* 688.

Davis, G. A. Current status of research and theory in human problem solving. *Psychological Bulletin,* 1966, *66,* 36–54.

Deaux, K. *The behavior of women and men.* Monterey, Calif.: Brooks/Cole, 1976.

Deci, E. L. *Intrinsic motivation.* New York: Plenum Press, 1975.

Deutsch, D. An auditory illusion. *Nature,* 1974, *251,* 307–309.

Dominowski, R. L. Anagram solving as a function of bigram rank and word frequency. *Journal of Experimental Psychology,* 1967, *75,* 299–306.

Donelson, E., & Gullahorn, J. E. *Women: A psychological perspective.* New York: Wiley, 1977.

Donley, R. E., & Winter, D. G. Measuring the motives of public officials at a distance: An exploratory study of American presidents. *Behavioral Science,* 1970, *15,* 227–236.

Eimas, P. D., Siqueland, E. R., Jusczyk, R., & Vigorito, J. Speech perception in infants. *Science,* 1971, *171,* 303–306.

Elardo, R., Bradley, R., & Caldwell, B. A longitudinal study of the relation of infants' home environment to language development at age three. *Child Development,* 1977, *48,* 595–603.

Engen, T. Cross adaptation to aliphatic alcohols. *American Journal of Psychology,* 1963, *76,* 96–102.

Entwisle, D. R. To dispel fantasies about fantasy-based measures of achievement motivation. *Psychological Bulletin,* 1972, *77,* 377–391.

Epstein, Y. M., Suedfeld, P., & Silverstein, S. J. The experimental contract: Subjects' expectations of and reactions to some behaviors of experimenters. *American Psychologist,* 1973, *28,* 212–221.

Erdelyi, M. H. A new look at the New Look: Perceptual defense and vigilance. *Psychological Review,* 1974, *81,* 1–25.

Erlebacher, A. Design and analysis of experiments contrasting the within- and between-subjects manipulation of the independent variable. *Psychological Bulletin,* 1977, *84,* 212–219.

Evans, P. Some practical problems of applied psychology. *APA Monitor,* March 1977, pp. 12–13.

Fantz, R. E. The origin of form perception. *Scientific American,* 1961, *204*(5), 66–72.

Farr, J. L., & Seaver, W. B. Stress and discomfort in psychological research: Subject perceptions of experimental procedures. *American Psychologist,* 1975, *30,* 770–773.

Festinger, L. *A theory of cognitive dissonance.* Stanford: Stanford University Press, 1957.

Festinger, L., & Carlsmith, J. M. Cognitive consequences of forced compliance. *Journal of Abnormal and Social Psychology,* 1959, *58,* 203–210.

Fillenbaum, S. Prior deception and subsequent experimental performance: The "faithful" subject. *Journal of Personality and Social Psychology,* 1966, *4,* 532–537.

Fine, B. J., Cohen, A., & Crist, B. Effect of exposure to high humidity at high and moderate ambient temperature on anagram solution and auditory discrimination. *Psychological Reports,* 1960, *7,* 171–181.

Finison, L. J. The application of McClelland's national development model to recent data. *Journal of Social Psychology,* 1976, *98,* 55–59.

Fink, R. T. Response latency as a function of hypothesis testing strategies in concept identification. *Journal of Experimental Psychology,* 1972, *95,* 337–342.

Forward, J., Canter, R., & Kirsch, N. Role enactment and deception methodologies: Alternative paradigms. *American Psychologist,* 1976, *31,* 595–604.

Fowler, H. *Curiosity and exploratory behavior.* New York: Macmillan, 1965.

Freedman, J. L. Role playing: Psychology by consensus. *Journal of Personality and Social Psychology,* 1969, *13,* 107–114.

Freibergs, V., & Tulving, E. The effect of practice on utilization of information from positive and negative instances in concept identification. *Canadian Journal of Psychology,* 1961, *15,* 101–106.

Fromkin, V., Krashen, S., Curtiss, S., Rigler, D., & Rigler, G. The development of language in Genie: A case of language acquisition beyond the "critical period." *Brain and Language,* 1974, *1,*81–107.

Gagné, R. M., & Smith, E. C. A study of the effects of verbalization on problem solving. *Journal of Experimental Psychology,* 1962, *63,* 12–18.

Galper, R. E. "Functional race membership" and recognition of faces. *Perceptual and Motor Skills,* 1973, *37,* 455–462.

Ganz, L. Vision. In B. Scharf (Ed.), *Experimental sensory psychology.* Glenview, Ill.: Scott, Foresman, 1975.

Garner, W. R., & Creelman, C. D. Problems and methods of psychological scaling. In H. Helson & W. Bevan (Eds.), *Contemporary approaches to psychology.* Princeton, N.J.: Van Nostrand, 1967.

Gauld, A., & Stephenson, G. M. Some experiments relating to Bartlett's theory of remembering. *British Journal of Psychology,* 1967, *58,* 39–49.

Gavurin, E. I., & DeVito, G. Correlation of anagram solving to transition probability and word frequency. *Journal of General Psychology,* 1973, *88,* 135–140.

Gawron, V. J. *Stress, personal space and sex role identification.* Unpublished master's thesis. S.U.C. Geneseo, Department of Psychology, 1977.

Gergen, K. J. The codification of research ethics: Views of a doubting Thomas. *American Psychologist,* 1973, *28,* 907–912.

Gescheider, G. A. *Psychophysics: Method and theory.* Hillsdale, N.J.: Lawrence Erlbaum Associates, 1976.

Gibson, E. J. *Principles of perceptual learning and development.* New York: Appleton-Century-Crofts, 1969.

Gibson, E. J., & Walk, R. D. The "visual cliff," *Scientific American,* 1960, *202*(4), 64–71.

Glanzer, M., & Cunitz, A. R. Two storage mechanisms in free-recall. *Journal of Verbal Learning and Verbal Behavior,* 1966, *5,* 351–360.

Glass, D. C., & Singer, J. E. *Urban stress.* New York: Academic Press, 1972.

Glass, D. C., Singer, J. E., & Friedman, L. N. Psychic cost of adaptation to an environmental stressor. *Journal of Personality and Social Psychology,* 1969, *12,* 200–210.

Glucksberg, S., & Weisberg, R. W. Verbal behavior and problem solving: Some effects of labeling in a functional fixedness problem. *Journal of Experimental Psychology,* 1966, *71,* 659–664.

Goldman, R. L., Jaffa, M., & Schachter, S. Yom Kippur, Air France, dormitory food, and the eating behavior of obese and normal persons. *Journal of Personality and Social Psychology,* 1968, *10,* 117–123.

Grady, K. E. *The belief in sex differences.* Paper presented at the meeting of the Eastern Psychological Association, Boston, April 1977.

Greenwald, A. G. Within-subjects designs: To use or not to use? *Psychological Bulletin,* 1976, *83,* 314–320.

Greive, D. M., & Matlin, M. W. *Is sex a memorable attribute?* Paper presented at the meeting of the American Psychological Association, Toronto, August 1978.

Grossberg, J. M., & Grant, B. F. Obese-normal differences in visual stimulus detection as a function of cue salience. *Journal of Personality,* 1976, *44,* 645–653.

Haas, H., Fink, H., & Härtfelder, G. The placebo problem. *Psychopharmacology Service Center Bulletin,* 1963, *2,* 1–65.

Hagen, M. A. Picture perception: Toward a theoretical model. *Psychological Bulletin,* 1974, *81,* 471–497.

Haggerty, L. C. G. What a two-and-one-half-year-old child said in one day. *Journal of Genetic Psychology,* 1930, *37,* 75–101.

Harkins, S., & Geen, R. G. Discriminability and criterion differences between extroverts and introverts during vigilance. *Journal of Research in Personality,* 1975, *9,* 335–340.

Harlow, H. G. Experimental analysis of behavior. *American Psychologist,* 1957, *12,* 485–490.

Harrison, A. A. Response competition, frequency, exploratory behavior and liking. *Journal of Personality and Social Psychology,* 1968, *9,* 363–368.

Harrison, A. A. *Individuals and groups.* Monterey, Calif.: Brooks/Cole, 1976.

Harrison, A. A. Mere exposure. In L. Berkowitz (Ed.), *Advances in experimental social psychology* (Vol. 10). New York: Academic Press, 1977.

Hart, J. T. Memory and the feeling-of-knowing experience. *Journal of Educational Psychology,* 1965, *56,* 208–216.

Hecht, S., Haig, C., & Wald, G. Dark adaptation of retinal fields of different size and location. *Journal of General Physiology,* 1935, *19,* 321–337.

Heidbreder, E. The attainment of concepts: I. Terminology and methodology. *Journal of General Psychology,* 1946, *35,* 173–189.

Heider, E. R. Universals in color naming and memory. *Journal of Experimental Psychology*, 1972, *93*, 10–20.

Hellyer, S. Frequency of stimulus presentation and short-term decrement in recall. *Journal of Experimental Psychology*, 1962, *64*, 650.

Henley, N. M. A psychological study of the semantics of animal terms. *Journal of Verbal Learning and Verbal Behavior*, 1969, *8*, 176–184.

Hersen, M., & Barlow, D. H. *Single case experimental designs*. New York: Pergamon Press, 1976.

Hilgard, E. R., Irvine, R. P., & Whipple, J. E. Rote memorization, understanding, and transfer: An extension of Katona's card trick experiment. *Journal of Experimental Psychology*, 1953, *46*, 288–292.

Hochberg, J. E., & Brooks, V. Pictorial recognition as an unlearned ability: A study of one child's performance. *American Journal of Psychology*, 1962, *75*, 624–628.

Holmes, D. S. Debriefing after psychological experiments: I. Effectiveness of post-deception dehoaxing. *American Psychologist*, 1976, *31*, 858–867. (a)

Holmes, D. S. Debriefing after psychological experiments: II. Effectiveness of postexperimental desensitizing. *American Psychologist*, 1976, *31*, 868–875. (b)

Holmes, D. S., & Bennett, D. H. Experiments to answer questions raised by the use of deception in psychological research. *Journal of Personality and Social Psychology*, 1974, *29*, 358–367.

Holmes, D. S., & Jorgensen, B. W. Do personality and social psychologists study men more than women? *Representative Research in Social Psychology*, 1971, *2*, 71–76.

Horner, M. S. Toward an understanding of achievement-related conflicts in women. *Journal of Social Issues*, 1972, *28*, 157–175.

Horowitz, L. M. *Elements of statistics for psychology and education*. New York: McGraw-Hill, 1974.

Houston, J. P. *Fundamentals of learning*. New York: Academic Press, 1976.

Hovland, C. I., & Weiss, W. Transmission of information concerning concepts through positive and negative instances. *Journal of Experimental Psychology*, 1953, *43*, 175–182.

Howes, D. H., & Solomon, R. L. A note on McGinnies' "Emotionality and perceptual defense." *Psychological Review*, 1950, *57*, 229–234.

Hulicka, I. M. Age differences for intentional and incidental learning and recall scores. *Journal of the American Geriatrics Society*, 1965, *13*, 639–649.

Hunt, E., Lunneborg, C., & Lewis, J. What does it mean to be high verbal? *Cognitive Psychology*, 1975, *7*, 194–227.

Hunt, R. G. Meaningfulness and articulation of stimulus and response in paired-associate learning and stimulus recall. *Journal of Experimental Psychology*, 1959, *57*, 262–267.

Jablonski, E. M., & Mueller, J. H. Anagram solution as a function of instruction, priming and imagery. *Journal of Experimental Psychology*, 1972, *94*, 84–89.

Jacoby, J. Perspectives on a consumer information processing research program. *Community Research*, 1975, *2*, 203–215.

Jenkins, J. J., & Russell, W. A. Associative clustering during recall. *Journal of Abnormal and Social Psychology*, 1952, *47*, 818–821.

Jenkins, J. J., Russell, W. A., & Suci, G. J. An atlas of semantic profiles for 360 words. *American Journal of Psychology*, 1958, *71*, 688–699.

Jensen, A. R. Intelligence, learning ability and socio-economic status. *Journal of Special Education*, 1969, *3*, 23–35.

Jette, A., Howell, D. C., & Gordon, L. R. *Effect of non-interval scales on conclusions from the t-test*. Paper presented at the meeting of the Eastern Psychological Association, Boston, April 1977.

Johansson, G. Visual motion perception. *Scientific American,* 1975, *232*(6), 76–86.

Johnson-Laird, P. N., & Stevenson, R. Memory for syntax. *Nature,* 1970, *227,* 412.

Johnson, R. C., Frincke, G., & Martin, L. Meaningfulness, frequency, and affective character of words as related to visual duration threshold. *Canadian Journal of Psychology,* 1961, *15,* 199–204.

Johnson, R. F. Q. The experimenter attributes effect: A methodological analysis. *Psychological Record,* 1976, *26,* 67–78.

Johnson, R. W., & Adair, J. G. Experimenter expectancy vs. systematic recording error under automated and nonautomated stimulus presentation. *Journal of Experimental Research in Personality,* 1972, *6,* 88–94.

Johnson, W. G. The effects of cue prominence and obesity on effort to obtain food. In S. Schachter & J. Rodin (Eds.), *Obese humans and rats.* Potomac, Md.: Lawrence Erlbaum Associates, 1974.

Jones, B. P., Moskowitz, H. R., Butters, N. A., & Glosser, G. Psychophysical scaling of olfactory, visual, and auditory stimuli by alcoholic Korsakoff patients. *Neuropsychologia,* 1975, *13,* 387–393.

Judd, D. B. Chromatic sensibility to stimulus differences. *Journal of the Optical Society of America,* 1932, *22,* 72–108.

Julesz, B. Experiments in the visual perception of texture. *Scientific American,* 1975, *232*(4), 34–43.

Jung, J. Current practices and problems in the use of college students for psychological research. *Canadian Psychologist,* 1969, *10,* 280–290.

Jung, J. *The experimenter's dilemma.* New York: Harper & Row, 1971.

Kahneman, D., & Tversky, A. Subjective probability: A judgment of representativeness. *Cognitive Psychology,* 1972, *3,* 430–454.

Kalish, R. A. *Late adulthood.* Monterey, Calif.: Brooks/Cole, 1975.

Kanizsa, G. Subjective contours. *Scientific American,* 1976, *234* (4), 48–52.

Karabenick, S. A. Fear of success, achievement and affiliation dispositions, and the performance of men and women under individual and competitive conditions. *Journal of Personality,* 1977, *45,* 117–149.

Kassarjian, H. H. Voting intentions and political perceptions. *Journal of Psychology,* 1963, *56,* 85–88.

Kelman, H. C. The problem of deception in social psychological experiments. *Psychological Bulletin,* 1967, *67,* 1–11.

Kelman, H. C. The rights of the subject in social research: An analysis in terms of relative power and legitimacy. *American Psychologist,* 1972, *27,* 989–1016.

Kendler, T. S., & Kendler, H. H. An ontogeny of optional shift behavior. *Child Development,* 1970, *41,* 1–28.

Kenshalo, D. R. Psychophysical studies of temperature sensitivity. In W. D. Neff (Ed.), *Contributions to sensory physiology.* New York: Academic Press, 1970.

Keppel, G. Retroactive and proactive inhibition. In T. R. Dixon & D. Horton (Eds.), *Verbal behavior and general behavior theory.* Englewood Cliffs, N.J.: Prentice-Hall, 1968.

Keppel, G., & Underwood, B. J. Proactive inhibition in short-term retention of single items. *Journal of Verbal Learning and Verbal Behavior,* 1962, *1,* 153–161.

King, D. L., & Pontious, R. H. Time relations in the recall of events of the day. *Psychonomic Science,* 1969, *17,* 339–340.

Kintsch, W., & Buschke, H. Homophones and synonyms in short-term memory. *Journal of Experimental Psychology,* 1969, *80,* 403–407.

Kintsch, W., & Monk, D. Storage of complex information in memory: Some implications of the speed with which inferences can be made. *Journal of Experimental Psychology,* 1972, *94,* 25–32.

Kintz, B. L., Delprato, D. J., Mettel, D. R., Persons, C. E., & Schappe, R. H. The experimenter effect. *Psychological Bulletin,* 1965, *63,* 223–232.

Kirk, R. E. *Experimental design: Procedures for the behavioral sciences.* Monterey, Calif.: Brooks/Cole, 1968.

Kirk, R. E. *Introductory statistics.* Monterey, Calif.: Brooks/Cole, 1978.

Kling, J. W., & Riggs, L. A. *Woodworth & Schlosberg's experimental psychology* (3rd ed.). New York: Holt, Rinehart & Winston, 1971.

Kogan, N., & Wallach, M. A. Risk taking as a function of the situation, the person, and the group. In *New directions in psychology III.* New York: Holt, 1967.

Koocher, G. P. Bathroom behavior and human dignity. *Journal of Personality and Social Psychology,* 1977, *35,* 120–121.

Koslowsky, M., Pratt, G. L., & Wintrob, R. M. The application of Guttman scale analysis to physicians' attitudes regarding abortion. *Journal of Applied Psychology,* 1976, *61,* 301–304.

Krueger, L. E. Familiarity effects in visual information processing. *Psychological Bulletin,* 1975, *82,* 949–974.

Kučera, H., & Francis, W. N. *Computational analysis of present day American English.* Providence, R.I.: University Press, 1967.

Kurz, R. B. Effects of three kinds of stressors on human learning and performance. *Psychological Reports,* 1964, *14,* 161–162.

Langer, E., & Roth, J. Heads I win, tails it's chance: The illusion of control as a function of the sequence of outcomes in a purely chance task. *Journal of Personality and Social Psychology,* 1975, *32,* 951–955.

Lantz, D., & Stefflre, V. Language and cognition revisited. *Journal of Abnormal and Social Psychology,* 1964, *69,* 472–481.

Lashley, K. S. Persistent problems in the evolution of mind. In F. A. Beach, D. O. Hebb, C. T. Morgan, & H. W. Nissen (Eds.), *The neuropsychology of Lashley.* New York: McGraw-Hill, 1960.

Laughery, K. R., & Fell, J. C. Subject preferences and the nature of information stored in the short-term memory. *Journal of Experimental Psychology,* 1969, *82,* 193–197.

Laughlin, P. R., Chenoweth, R.E., Farrell, B. B., & McGrath, J. E. Concept attainment as a function of motivation and task complexity. *Journal of Experimental Psychology,* 1972, *96,* 54–59.

Laurence, M. W. A developmental look at the usefulness of list categorization as an aid to free recall. *Canadian Journal of Psychology,* 1967, *21,* 153–165.

Layton, B. Perceptual noise and aging. *Psychological Bulletin,* 1975, *82,* 875–883.

Lee, W. *Decision theory and human behavior.* New York: Wiley, 1971.

Lenneberg, E. H. Color naming, color recognition, color discrimination: A reappraisal. *Perceptual and Motor Skills,* 1961, *12,* 375–382.

Lenneberg, E. H. Understanding language without ability to speak: A case report. *Journal of Abnormal and Social Psychology,* 1962, *65,* 419–425.

Lenneberg, E. H. *Biological foundations of language.* New York: Wiley, 1967.

Lepper, M. R., & Greene, D. Turning play into work: Effects of adult surveillance and extrinsic rewards on children's intrinsic motivation. *Journal of Personality and Social Psychology,* 1975, *31,* 479–486.

Levy, L. H. Awareness, learning and the beneficent subject as expert witness. *Journal of Personality and Social Psychology,* 1967, *6,* 365–370.

Lin, N., & Ensel, W. *Public perceptions of social institutions*. Paper presented at the Conference on Community and Policy Research, SUNY-Albany, April 1976.

Lindsay, P. H., & Norman, D. A. *Human information processing: An introduction to psychology*. New York: Academic Press, 1972.

Liverant, S., & Scodel, A. Internal and external control as determinants of decision making under conditions of risk. *Psychological Reports*, 1960, *7*, 59–67.

Loftus, G. R., & Loftus, E. F. *Human memory: The processing of information*. Hillsdale, N.J.: Lawrence Erlbaum Associates, 1976.

Luce, T. S. Blacks, Whites, and Yellows: They all look alike to me. *Psychology Today*, November 1974, pp. 105–108.

Luchins, A. S. Mechanization in problem solving. *Psychological Monographs*, 1942, *6, 54* (Whole No. 248).

Luria, A. R. *The mind of a mnemonist: A little book about a vast memory*. New York: Basic Books, 1968.

Lyons, J. On the psychology of the psychological experiment. In C. Scheerer (Ed.), *Cognition: Theory, research, promise*. New York: Harper & Row, 1964.

Lyons, J. *A primer of experimental psychology*. New York: Harper & Row, 1965.

Maccoby, E. E., & Jacklin, C. N. *The psychology of sex differences*. Stanford, Calif.: Stanford University Press, 1974.

Maier, N. R. F. Reasoning in humans: II. The solution of a problem and its appearance in consciousness. *Journal of Comparative Psychology*, 1931, *12*, 181–194.

Maier, N. R. F., & Burke, R. J. Response availability as a factor in the problem-solving performance of males and females. *Journal of Personality and Social Psychology*, 1967, *5*, 304–310.

Majeres, R. L. Semantic connotations of the words "adolescent," "teenager," and "youth." *Journal of Genetic Psychology*, 1976, *129*, 57–62.

Mandler, J. M., & Johnson, N. S. Remembrance of things passed: Story structure and recall. *Cognitive Psychology*, 1977, *9*, 111–115.

Manis, M. *An introduction to cognitive psychology*. Monterey, Calif.: Brooks/Cole, 1971.

Marks, R. W. The effect of probability, desirability, and "privilege" on the stated expectations of children. *Journal of Personality*, 1951, *19*, 332–351.

Martin, D. W. *Doing psychology experiments*. Monterey, Calif.: Brooks/Cole, 1977.

Martin, E., & Roberts, K. H. Grammatical factors in sentence retention. *Journal of Verbal Learning and Verbal Behavior*, 1966, *5*, 211–218.

Marx, M. *Theories in contemporary psychology*. New York: Macmillan, 1963.

Masling, J. Role-related behavior of the subject and psychologist and its effects upon psychological data. In D. Levine (Ed.), *Nebraska Symposium on Motivation* (Vol. 14). Lincoln: University of Nebraska Press, 1966.

Matlin, M. W. Response competition as a mediating factor in the frequency-affect relationship. *Journal of Personality and Social Psychology*, 1970, *16*, 536–552.

Matlin, M. W. *Relationship between affect and estimate of English word frequency*. Paper presented at the meeting of the American Psychological Association, Chicago, August 1975.

Matlin, M. W. The relationship between English word length and short-term memory. *Journal of General Psychology*, 1976, *94*, 47–57.

Matlin, M. W., & Gawron, V. J. Individual differences in Pollyannaism. *Journal of Personality Assessment*, in press, 1979.

Matlin, M. W., & Stang, D. J. *The Pollyanna principle: Selectivity in language, memory, and thought*. Cambridge, Mass.: Schenkman, 1978.

Matlin, M. W., & Zajonc, R. B. Social facilitation of word associations. *Journal of Personality and Social Psychology,* 1968, *10,* 455–460.

Mayer, R. E. *Thinking and problem solving: An introduction to human cognition and learning.* Glenview, Ill.: Scott, Foresman, 1977.

Mayzner, M. S., & Tresselt, M. E. Anagram solution times: A function of transition probabilities. *Journal of Psychology,* 1959, *47,* 117–125.

McCarthy, D. Language development in children. In L. Carmichael (Ed.), *Manual of child psychology.* New York: Wiley, 1954.

McCarthy, D. Language development. In A. Bar-Adon & W. F. Leopold (Eds.), *Child language.* Englewood Cliffs, N.J.: Prentice-Hall, 1971.

McClelland, D. C. Risk taking in children with high and low need for achievement. In J. W. Atkinson (Ed.), *Motives in fantasy, action, and society.* Princeton, N.J.: Van Nostrand, 1958.

McClelland, D. C. *The achieving society.* Princeton, N.J.: Van Nostrand, 1961.

McClelland, D. C. *Power: The inner experience.* New York: Irvington, 1975.

McClelland, D. C., Atkinson, J. W., Clark, R. W., & Lowell, E.L. *The achievement motive.* New York: Appleton-Century-Crofts, 1953.

McCrary, J. W., & Hunter, W. S. Serial position curves in verbal learning. *Science,* 1953, *117,* 131–134.

McGinnies, E. Emotionality and perceptual defense. *Psychological Review,* 1949, *56,* 244–251.

McGuigan, F. J. The experimenter: A neglected stimulus object. *Psychological Bulletin,* 1963, *60,* 421–428.

Mehler, J. Some effects of grammatical transformation on the recall of English sentences. *Journal of Verbal Learning and Verbal Behavior.* 1963, *2,* 346–351.

Melton, A. W. Implications of short-term memory for a general theory of memory. *Journal of Verbal Learning and Verbal Behavior,* 1963, *2,* 1–21.

Mendelsohn, G. A., & Covington, M. V. Internal processes and perceptual factors in verbal problem solving: A study of sex and individual differences in cognition. *Journal of Personality,* 1972, *40,* 451–471.

Menges, R. J. Openness and honesty versus coercion and deception in psychological research. *American Psychologist,* 1973, *28,* 1030–1034.

Messer, S. B. Reflection-impulsivity: A review. *Psychological Bulletin,* 1976, *83,* 1026–1052.

Messick, D. M., & Campos, F. T. Training and conservatism in subjective probability revision. *Journal of Experimental Psychology,* 1972, *94,* 335–337.

Michotte, A. *The perception of causality.* New York: Basic Books, 1963.

Middlemist, R. D., Knowles, E. S., & Matter, C. F. Personal space invasions in the lavatory: Suggestive evidence for arousal. *Journal of Personality and Social Psychology,* 1976, *33,* 541–546.

Milburn, T. W., & Bell, N. Values and estimation of word frequencies. *Psychological Reports,* 1972, *31,* 47–56.

Milgram, S. Behavioral study of obedience. *Journal of Abnormal and Social Psychology,* 1963, *67,* 371–378.

Milgram, S. Issues in the study of obedience: A reply to Baumrind. *American Psychologist,* 1964, *19,* 848–852.

Milgram, S. Some conditions of obedience and disobedience to authority. *Human Relations,* 1965, *18,* 57–76.

Miller, G. A. The magical number seven, plus or minus two: Some limits on our capacity for processing information. *Psychological Review,* 1956, *63,* 81–97.

Miller, G. A. Some psychological studies of grammar. *American Psychologist,* 1962, *17,* 748–762.

Miller, G. A. Psychology as a means of promoting human welfare. *American Psychologist*, 1969, *24*, 1063–1075.

Mills, J. A procedure for explaining experiments involving deception. *Personality and Social Psychology Bulletin*, 1976, *2*, 3–13.

Moffitt, A. R. Consonant cue perception by twenty- to twenty-four week old infants. *Child Development*, 1971, *42*, 717–731.

Moore, C. L., & Retish, P. M. Effects of the examiner's race on Black children's Wechsler preschool and primary scale of intelligence. *Developmental Psychology*, 1974, *10*, 672–676.

Moore, M. E., Linker, E., & Purcell, M. Taste sensitivity after eating: A signal detection approach. *American Journal of Psychology*, 1965, *78*, 107–111.

Moray, N. Attention in dichotic listening: Affective cues and the influence of instruction. *Quarterly Journal of Experimental Psychology*, 1959, *11*, 56–60.

Mosher, F. A., & Hornsby, J. R. On asking questions. In J. S. Bruner, R. R. Oliver, & P. M. Greenfield (Eds.), *Studies in cognitive growth*. New York: Wiley, 1966.

Munson, R. F. Decision-making in an actual gambling situation. *American Journal of Psychology*, 1962, *75*, 640–643.

Murray, H. A. Techniques for a systematic investigation of fantasy. *Journal of Psychology*, 1936, *3*, 115–143.

Murray, H. G., & Denny, J. P. Interaction of ability level and interpolated activity (opportunity for incubation) in human problem solving. *Psychological Reports*, 1969, *24*, 271–276.

Myers, T. I. Tolerance for sensory and perceptual deprivation. In J. P. Zubek (Ed.), *Sensory deprivation: Fifteen years of research*. New York: Appleton-Century-Crofts, 1969.

Naeye, R. L., Ladis, B., & Drage, J. S. Sudden infant death syndrome. *American Journal of Diseases of Children*, 1976, *130*, 1207–1210.

Nehrke, M. F. Age and sex differences in discrimination learning and transfer of training. *Journal of Gerontology*, 1973, *28*, 320–327.

Nelson, T. O., & Rothbart, R. Acoustic savings for items forgotten from long-term memory. *Journal of Experimental Psychology*, 1972, *93*, 357–360.

Nelson, W. E., Vaughan, V. C., & McKay, R. J. *Textbook of pediatrics* (9th ed.). Philadelphia: Saunders, 1969.

Newell, A., & Simon, H. A. *Human problem solving*. Englewood Cliffs, N.J.: Prentice-Hall, 1972.

Newport, E. L., Gleitman, H., & Gleitman, L. R. Mother, I'd rather do it myself: Some effects and non-effects of maternal speech style. In C. E. Snow & C. A. Ferguson (Eds.), *Talking to children*. Cambridge, England: Cambridge University Press, 1977.

Nisbett, R. E. Taste, deprivation, and weight determinants of eating behavior. *Journal of Personality and Social Psychology*, 1968, *10*, 107-116.

Nisbett, R. E., & Gurwitz, S. Weight, sex, and the eating behavior of human newborns. *Journal of Comparative and Physiological Psychology*, 1970, *73*, 245–253.

Nisbett, R. E., & Wilson, T. D. The halo effect: Evidence for unconscious alteration of judgments. *Journal of Personality and Social Psychology*, 1977, *35*, 250–256.

Noble, C. E. An analysis of meaning. *Psychological Review*, 1952, *59*, 421–430.

O'Donovan, D. Rating extremity: Pathology or meaningfulness? *Psychological Review*, 1965, *72*, 358–372.

Orne, M. T. On the social psychology of the psychological experiment: With particular reference to demand characteristics and their implications. *American Psychologist*, 1962, *17*, 776–783.

Orne, M. T. Demand characteristics and the concept of quasi-controls. In R. Rosenthal

& R. L. Rosnow (Eds.), *Artifact and behavioral research*. New York: Academic Press, 1969.

Orne, M. T., & Holland, C. H. On the ecological validity of laboratory deceptions. *International Journal of Psychiatry*, 1968, *6*, 282–293.

Osgood, C. E. The nature and measurement of meaning. *Psychological Bulletin*, 1952, *49*, 197–237.

Oskamp, S. Overconfidence in case-study judgments. *Journal of Consulting Psychology*, 1965, *29*, 261–265.

Osler, S. F., & Fivel, M. W. Concept attainment: I. The role of age and intelligence in concept attainment by induction. *Journal of Experimental Psychology*, 1961, *62*, 1–8.

Page, M. M., & Kahle, L. R. Demand characteristics in the satiation-deprivation effect on attitude conditioning. *Journal of Personality and Social Psychology*, 1976, *33*, 553–562.

Paivio, A. *Imagery and verbal processes*. New York: Holt, Rinehart & Winston, 1971.

Palermo, D. S., & Jenkins, J. S. *Word association norms*. Minneapolis: University of Minnesota Press, 1964.

Paris, S. G., & Carter, A. Y. Semantic and constructive aspects of sentence memory in children. *Developmental Psychology*, 1973, *9*, 109–113.

Peterson, C. R., & Beach, L. R. Man as an intuitive statistician. *Psychological Bulletin*, 1967, *68*, 29–46.

Peterson, L. R., & Peterson, M. J. Short-term retention of individual verbal items. *Journal of Experimental Psychology*, 1959, *58*, 193–198.

Phillips, L. D., & Edwards, W. Conservatism in a simple probability inference task. *Journal of Experimental Psychology*, 1966, *72*, 346–357.

Phillips, L. W., Griswold, R. L., & Pace, N. Cognitive changes at high altitude. *Psychological Reports*, 1963, *13*, 423–430.

Pierce, A. H. The subconscious again. *Journal of Philosophy, Psychology, and Scientific Methods*, 1908, *5*, 264–271.

Piliavin, J. A., & Piliavin, I. M. Effect of blood on reactions to a victim. *Journal of Personality and Social Psychology*, 1972, *23*, 353–361.

Postman, L. Verbal learning and memory. In M. R. Rosenzweig & L. W. Porter (Eds.), *Annual review of psychology* (Vol. 26). Palo Alto, Calif.: Annual Reviews, 1975.

Postman, L., & Jarrett, R. F. An experimental analysis of learning without awareness. *American Journal of Psychology*, 1952, *65*, 244–255.

Postman, L., & Underwood, B. J. Critical issues in interference theory. *Memory and Cognition*, 1973, *1*, 19–40.

Poulton, E. C. Unwanted range effects from using within-subject experimental designs. *Psychological Bulletin*, 1973, *80*, 113–121.

Preston, M. G., & Baratta, P. An experimental study of the auction-value of an uncertain outcome. *American Journal of Psychology*, 1948, *61*, 183–193.

Prison research: Rearranging the deck chairs on the Titanic. *APA Monitor*, July 1976, pp.1; 4.

Pruitt, D., & Hoge, R. Strength of the relationship between the value of an event and its subjective probability as a function of method of measurement. *Journal of Experimental Psychology*, 1965, *69*, 483–489.

Prytulak, L. S. Natural language mediation. *Cognitive Psychology*, 1971, *2*, 1–56.

Raynor, J. O. Relationships between achievement-related motives, future orientation and academic performance. *Journal of Personality and Social Psychology*, 1970, *15*, 28–33.

Reese, H. W., & Lipsitt, L. P. *Experimental child psychology*. New York: Academic Press, 1970.

Reitman, J. S. Without surreptitious rehearsal, information in short-term memory decays. *Journal of Verbal Learning and Verbal Behavior,* 1974, *13,* 365–377.

Research on children. *APA Monitor,* November 1977, p. 21.

Resnick, J. H., & Schwartz, T. Ethical standards as an independent variable in psychological research. *American Psychologist,* 1973, *28,* 134–139.

Riecken, H. W. A program for research on experiments in social psychology. In N. F. Washburn (Ed.), *Decisions, values, and groups.* Elmsford, N.Y.: Pergamon Press, 1962.

Rock, I. *An introduction to perception.* New York: Macmillan, 1975.

Rodin, J., Herman, C. P., & Schachter, S. Obesity and various tests of external sensitivity. In S. Schachter & J. Rodin (Eds.), *Obese humans and rats.* Potomac, Md.: Lawrence Erlbaum Associates, 1974.

Roethlisberger, F. J., & Dickson, W. J. *Management and the worker.* Cambridge, Mass.: Harvard University Press, 1939.

Rohrman, N. L. The role of syntactic structure in the recall of English nominalizations. *Journal of Verbal Learning and Verbal Behavior,* 1968, *7,* 904–912.

Rosenhan, D. L. On being sane in insane places. *Science,* 1973, *179,* 250–258.

Rosenthal, R. On the social psychology of the psychological experiment: The experimenter's hypothesis as unintended determinant of experimental results. *American Scientist,* 1963, *51,* 268–283.

Rosenthal, R. *Experimenter effects in behavioral research.* New York: Appleton-Century-Crofts, 1966.

Rosenthal, R. Covert communication in the psychological experiment. *Psychological Bulletin,* 1967, *67,* 356–367.

Rosenthal, R. *Experimenter effects in behavioral research* (Enlarged ed.). New York: Halsted Press, 1976.

Rosenthal, R., & Fode, K. L. Psychology of the scientist: V. Three experiments in experimenter bias. *Psychological Reports,* 1963, *12,* 491–511.

Rosenthal, R., & Jacobson, L. *Pygmalion in the classroom.* New York: Holt, Rinehart & Winston, 1968.

Rosenthal, R., & Rosnow, R. L. *The volunteer subject.* New York: Wiley, 1975.

Rosenzweig, M. R., & Postman, L. Intelligibility as a function of frequency of usage. *Journal of Experimental Psychology,* 1957, *54,* 412–422.

Ross, J. The resources of binocular perception. *Scientific American,* 1976, *234*(3), 80–86.

Ross, L. Effects of manipulating salience of food upon consumption by obese and normal eaters. In S. Schachter & J. Rodin (Eds.), *Obese humans and rats.* Potomac, Md.: Lawrence Erlbaum Associates, 1974.

Rossi, A. M. General methodological considerations. In J. P. Zubek (Ed.), *Sensory deprivation: Fifteen years of research.* New York: Appleton-Century-Crofts, 1969.

Rosten, L. *The joys of Yiddish.* New York: Pocket Books, 1970.

Rotter, J. B. *Social learning and clinical psychology.* New York: Prentice-Hall, 1954.

Rundus, D. Analysis of rehearsal processes in free-recall. *Journal of Experimental Psychology,* 1971, *89,* 63–77.

Rychlak, J. F., McKee, D. B., Schneider, W. E., & Abramson, Y. Affective evaluation in the verbal learning styles of normals and abnormals. *Journal of Abnormal Psychology,* 1971, *77,* 247–257.

Sachs, J. Recognition memory for syntactic and semantic aspects of connected discourse. *Perception and Psychophysics,* 1967, *2,* 437–442.

Santa, J. L., & Ranken, H. B. Effects of verbal coding on recognition memory. *Journal of Experimental Psychology,* 1972, *93,* 268–278.

Sattler, J. M. Racial "experimenter effects" in experimentation, testing, interviewing, and psychotherapy. *Psychological Bulletin,* 1970, *73,* 137–160.

Savin, H. B., & Perchonock, E. Grammatical structure and the immediate recall of English sentences. *Journal of Verbal Learning and Verbal Behavior,* 1965, *4,* 348–353.

Schachter, S. Some extraordinary facts about obese humans and rats. *American Psychologist,* 1971, *26,* 129–144.

Schachter, S., & Friedman, L. N. The effects of work and cue prominence on eating behavior. In S. Schachter & J. Rodin (Eds.), *Obese humans and rats.* Potomac, Md.: Lawrence Erlbaum Associates, 1974.

Schachter, S., Friedman, L. N., & Handler, J. Who eats with chopsticks? In S. Schachter & J. Rodin (Eds.), *Obese humans and rats.* Potomac, Md.: Lawrence Erlbaum Associates, 1974.

Schachter, S., Goldman, R., & Gordon, A. Effects of fear, food deprivation, and obesity on eating. *Journal of Personality and Social Psychology,* 1968, *10,* 91–97.

Schönbach, P. In defense of Roger Brown against himself. *Cognition,* 1977, *5,* 181–183.

Schutte, W., & Zubek, J. P. Changes in olfactory and gustatory sensitivity after prolonged visual deprivation. *Canadian Journal of Psychology,* 1967, *21,* 337–345.

Scott, W. E. The effects of extrinsic rewards on "intrinsic motivation": A critique. *Organizational Behavior and Human Performance,* 1976, *15,* 117–129.

Segall, M., Campbell, D. T., & Herskovits, M. J. *The influence of culture on visual perception.* Indianapolis: Bobbs-Merrill, 1966.

Shapiro, S. I., & Bell, J. A. Subjective organization and free recall: Performance of high, moderate and low organizers. *Psychonomic Science,* 1970, *21,* 71–73.

Shepard, R. N. Recognition memory for words, sentences and pictures. *Journal of Verbal Learning and Verbal Behavior,* 1967, *6,* 56–163.

Sherwood, J. J., Baron, J. W., & Fitch, H. G. Cognitive dissonance: Theory and research. In R. V. Wagner & J. J. Sherwood (Eds.), *The study of attitude change.* Monterey, Calif: Brooks/Cole, 1969.

Shrauger, J. S. Self-esteem and reactions to being observed by others. *Journal of Personality and Social Psychology,* 1972, *23,* 192–200.

Shurley, J. *Proceedings of the Third World Congress of Psychiatry* (Vol. 3). Toronto: University of Toronto Press, 1963.

Sidman, M. *Tactics of scientific research.* New York: Basic Books, 1960.

Sidowski, J. B. *Experimental methods and instrumentation in psychology.* New York: McGraw-Hill, 1966.

Siegel, M. H., & Zeigler, H. P. (Eds.). *Psychological research: The inside story.* New York: Harper & Row, 1976.

Sigman, M., Kopp, C. B., Parmelee, A. H., & Jeffrey, W. E. Visual attention and neurological organization in neonates. *Child Development,* 1973, *44,* 461–466.

Silverman, I. The experimenter: A (still) neglected stimulus object. *Canadian Psychologist,* 1974, *15,* 258–270.

Silverman, I. Nonreactive methods and the law. *American Psychologist,* 1975, *30,* 764–769.

Simon, H. A. How big is a chunk? *Science,* 1974, *183,* 482–488.

Skinner, B.F. A case history in scientific method. *American Psychologist,* 1956, *2,* 221–233.

Slovic, P. Differential effects of real versus hypothetical payoffs on choices among gambles. *Journal of Experimental Psychology,* 1969, *80,* 434–437.

Slovic, P., Fischhoff, B., & Lichtenstein, S. Behavioral decision theory. In M. R. Rosenzweig & L. W. Porter (Eds.), *Annual Review of Psychology,* 1977, *28,* 1–39.

Smith, E. E. *Relative power of various attitude change techniques*. Paper presented at the meeting of the American Psychological Association, New York, September 1961.

Smith, M. E. An investigation of the development of the sentence and the extent of vocabulary in young children. University of Iowa, *Studies in Child Welfare*, 1926, No. 5.

Smith, M. K. Measurement of the size of general English vocabulary through the elementary grades and high school. *Genetic Psychology Monographs*, 1941, *24*, 311–345.

Smith, R. J. Electroshock at Albany violates ethics guidelines. *Science*, 1977, *198*, 383–386.

Smoke, K. L. An objective study of concept formation. *Psychological Monographs*, 1932, *42*(4, Whole No. 191).

Solomon, P., et al. *Sensory deprivation*. Cambridge, Mass.: Harvard University Press, 1961.

Sommer, R. Hawthorne dogma. *Psychological Bulletin*, 1968, *70*, 592–595.

Sperling, G. A model for visual memory tasks. *Human Factors*, 1963, *5*, 19–39.

Spielberger, C. D., & Denny, J. P. Visual recognition thresholds as a function of verbal ability and word frequency. *Journal of Experimental Psychology*, 1963, *65*, 597–602.

Stachnik, T. Transitional probability in anagram solution in a group setting. *Journal of Psychology*, 1963, *55*, 259–261.

Starr, S. Discrimination of syntactical errors in children under two and one-half years. *Developmental Psychology*, 1974, *10*, 381–386.

Steele, R. S. Power motivation, activation, and inspirational speeches. *Journal of Personality*, 1977, *45*, 53–64.

Stein, A. H., & Bailey, M. M. The socialization of achievement orientation in females. *Psychological Bulletin*, 1973, *80*, 345–366.

Stevens, S. S. On the psychophysical law. *Psychological Review*, 1957, *64*, 153–181.

Stevens, S. S. On the operation known as judgment. *American Scientist*, 1966, *54*, 385–399.

Stevenson, H. W. Social reinforcement with children as a function of CA, sex of E and sex of S. *Journal of Abnormal and Social Psychology*, 1961, *63*, 147–154.

Stewart, A. J., & Rubin, Z. The power motive in the dating couple. *Journal of Personality and Social Psychology*, 1974, *34*, 305–309.

Stricker, L. J. The true deceiver. *Psychological Bulletin*, 1967, *68*, 13–20.

Stricker, L. J., Messick, S., & Jackson, D. N. Evaluating deception in psychological research. *Psychological Bulletin*, 1969, *71*, 343–351.

Stunkard, A., & Koch, C. The interpretation of gastric motility: I. Apparent bias in the reports of hunger by obese persons. *Archives of General Psychiatry*, 1964, *11*, 74–82.

Suedfeld, P. Changes in intellectual performance and in susceptibility to influence. In J. P. Zubek (Ed.), *Sensory deprivation: Fifteen years of research*. New York: Appleton-Century-Crofts, 1969.

Suedfeld, P. The benefits of boredom. *American Scientist*, 1975, *63*, 60–69.

Sullivan, D. S., & Deiker, T. E. Subject-experimenter perceptions of ethical issues in human research. *American Psychologist*, 1973, *28*, 587–591.

Tanner, W. P., Jr., & Swets, J. A. A decision-making theory of visual detection. *Psychological Review*, 1954, *61*, 401–409.

Taylor, D. W., et al. Education for research in psychology. *American Psychologist*, 1959, *14*, 167–179.

Tedeschi, J. T., & Gallup, G. G. Human subjects research. *Science, 1977, 198,* 1099–1100.

Tesch, F. E. Debriefing research participants: Though this be method there is madness to it. *Psychological Bulletin, 1977, 35,* 217–224.

Thorndike, E. L., & Lorge, I. *The teacher's wordbook of 30,000 words.* New York: Columbia University Press, 1944.

Thorndyke, P. W. Cognitive structures in comprehension and memory of narrative discourse. *Cognitive Psychology, 1977, 9,* 77–110.

Trouton, D. S. Placebos and their psychological effects. *Journal of Mental Science, 1957, 103,* 344–354.

Tulving, E. Subjective organization in free-recall of "unrelated" words. *Psychological Review, 1962, 69,* 344–354.

Tversky, A., & Kahneman, D. Judgment under uncertainty: Heuristics and biases. *Science, 1974, 185,* 1124–1131.

Underhill, W. *Effects of stimulus complexity and meaningfulness on the mere-exposure phenomenon.* Paper presented at the meeting of the Eastern Psychological Association, Boston, April 1977.

Underwood, B. J. Interference and forgetting. *Psychological Review, 1957, 64,* 49–60.

Underwood, B. J. *Experimental psychology.* Englewood Cliffs, N.J.: Prentice-Hall, 1966.

Underwood, B. J. Attributes of memory. *Psychological Review, 1969, 76,* 559–573.

Underwood, B. J. A breakdown of the Total-Time Law in free-recall learning. *Journal of Verbal Learning and Verbal Behavior, 1970, 9,* 573–580.

Underwood, B. J., & Richardson, J. Verbal concept learning as a function of instructions and dominance level. *Journal of Experimental Psychology, 1956, 51,* 229–238.

Underwood, B. J., & Schulz, R. W. *Meaningfulness and verbal learning.* Chicago: Lippincott, 1960.

United States Department of Commerce. *200 million Americans.* Washington, D.C.: United States Government Printing Office, 1967.

Veroff, J. Development and validation of a projective measure of power motivation. *Journal of Abnormal and Social Psychology, 1957, 54,* 1–8.

Veroff, J., Wilcox, S., & Atkinson, J. W. The achievement motive in high school and college age women. *Journal of Abnormal and Social Psychology, 1953, 48,* 108–119.

von Restorff, H. Über die Wirkung von Bereichsbildungen im Spurenfeld: Analyse von Vorängen im Spurenfeld. *Psychologische Forschung, 1933, 18,* 229–342.

Wagner, E. E., & Hoover, T. O. The effect of serial position on ranking error. *Educational and Psychological Measurement, 1974, 34,* 289–293.

Walker, E. L. Complexity and preference in animals and men. *Annals of the New York Academy of Science, 1970, 169,* 619–652.

Walker, E. L. Psychological complexity and preference: A hedgehog theory of behavior. In D. E. Berlyne & K. B. Madsen (Eds.), *Pleasure, reward, preference: Their nature, determinants and role in behavior.* New York: Academic Press, 1973.

Wallach, M. A., & Kogan, N. Sex differences and judgment processes. *Journal of Personality, 1959, 27,* 555–564.

Wallach, M. A., & Kogan, N. Aspects of judgment and decision making: interrelationships and changes with age. *Behavioral Science, 1961, 6,* 23–36.

Walster, E., Berscheid, E., Abrahams, D., & Aronson, V. Effectiveness of debriefing following deception experiments. *Journal of Personality and Social Psychology, 1967, 6,* 371–380.

Warwick, D. P. Deceptive research: Social scientists ought to stop lying. *Psychology Today,* February 1975, pp. 38–40; 105–106.

Washington, W. N. A methodology for response style analysis of the semantic differential index. *Journal of General Psychology,* 1975, *93,* 289–294.

Webb, E. J., Campbell, D. T., Schwartz, R. D., & Sechrest, L. *Unobtrusive measures: Nonreactive research in the social sciences.* New York: Rand McNally, 1966.

Weber, S. J., & Cook, T. D. Subject effects in laboratory research: An examination of subject roles, demand characteristics, and valid inference. *Psychological Bulletin,* 1972, *77,* 273–295.

Weigel, R., Weigel, V. M., & Hebert, J. A. Non-volunteer subjects: Temporal effects. *Psychological Reports,* 1971, *28,* 191–192.

Weiner, B. *Achievement motivation and attribution theory.* Morristown, N.J.: General Learning Press, 1974.

Weiner, B., & Kukla, A. An attributional analysis of achievement motivation. *Journal of Personality and Social Psychology,* 1970, *15,* 1–20.

Weiner, B., Nierenberg, R., & Goldstein, M. Social learning (locus of control) versus attributional (causal stability) interpretations of expectancy of success. *Journal of Personality,* 1976, *42,* 52–68.

Weinstein, M. S. Achievement motivation and risk preference. *Journal of Personality and Social Psychology,* 1969, *13,* 153–172.

Weinstein, S. Intensive and extensive aspects of tactile sensitivity as a function of body part, sex, and laterality. In D. R. Kenshalo (Ed.), *The skin senses.* Springfield, Ill.: Charles C. Thomas, 1968.

Weintraub, D., & Walker, E. *Perception.* Monterey, Calif.: Brooks/Cole, 1966.

Wellman, H. M., & Lempers, J. D. The naturalistic communicative abilities of two-year-olds. *Child Development,* 1977, *48,* 1052–1057.

Whitbourne, S. K., & Weinstock, C. S. *Adult development: The differentiation of experience.* New York: Holt, Rinehart & Winston, 1979.

Whorf, B. L. Science and linguistics. In J. B. Carroll (Ed.), *Language, thought and reality: Selected writings of Benjamin Lee Whorf.* Cambridge, Mass.: M.I.T. Press, 1956.

Wickens, D. D. Some characteristics of word encoding. *Memory and Cognition,* 1973, *1,* 485–490.

Wicklund, R. A. *Freedom and reactance.* Potomac, Md.: Lawrence Erlbaum Associates, 1974.

Wilkening, H. E. *The psychology almanac.* Monterey, Calif.: Brooks/Cole, 1973.

Wilson, D. W., & Donnerstein, E. Legal and ethical aspects of nonreactive social psychological research: An excursion into the public mind. *American Psychologist,* 1976, *31,* 765–773.

Winter, D. G. *The power motive.* New York: Free Press, 1973.

Winter, D. G., & Stewart, A. J. Power motive reliability as a function of retest instructions. *Journal of Consulting and Clinical Psychology,* 1977, *45,* 436–440.

Winter, D. G., Stewart, A. J., & McClelland, D. C. Husband's motives and wife's career level. *Journal of Personality and Social Psychology,* 1977, *35,* 159–166.

Wispé, L. G., & Freshley, H. B. Race, sex, and sympathetic helping behavior: The broken bag caper. *Journal of Personality and Social Psychology,* 1971, *17,* 59–65.

Woodhead, M. M. The effect of bursts of noise on an arithmetic task. *American Journal of Psychology,* 1964, *77,* 627–633.

Wright, P. The harassed decision maker: Time pressures, distractions and the use of evidence. *Journal of Applied Psychology,* 1974, *59,* 555–561.

Wrightsman, L. *Social psychology.* Monterey, Calif.: Brooks/Cole, 1977.

Wuebben, P. L. Experimental design, measurement, and human subjects: A neglected problem of control. *Sociometry,* 1968, *31,* 89–101.

Wuebben, P. L. Dissemination of experimental information by debriefed subjects: What is told to whom, when. In P. L. Wuebben, B. C. Straits, & G. I. Schulman (Eds.), *The experiment as a social occasion.* Berkeley, Calif.: Glendessary Press, 1974.

Yaremko, R. M., Fisher, M. L., and Price, J. M. Pavlovian GSR conditioning in overweight and normal weight women. *Journal of Abnormal Psychology,* 1975, *84,* 429–432.

Zajonc, R. B. Social facilitation. *Science,* 1965, *149,* 269–275.

Zajonc, R. B. Cognitive theories in social psychology. In G. Lindzey & E. Aronson (Eds.), *The handbook of social psychology* (2nd ed.). Reading, Mass.: Addison-Wesley, 1968. (a)

Zajonc, R. B. The attitudinal effects of mere exposure. *Journal of Personality and Social Psychology Monograph,* 1968, *9*(2). (b)

Zajonc, R. B., Crandall, R., Kail, R. B., & Swap, W. Effect of extreme exposure frequencies on different affective ratings of stimuli. *Perceptual and Motor Skills,* 1974, *38,* 667–678.

Zimbardo, P. G. (Ed.). *The cognitive control of motivation.* Glenview, Ill.: Scott, Foresman, 1969.

Zimbardo, P. G., Weisenberg, M., Firestone, I., & Levy, B. Changing appetites for eating fried grasshoppers with cognitive dissonance. In P. G. Zimbardo (Ed.), *The cognitive control of motivation.* Glenview, Ill.: Scott, Foresman, 1969.

Zubek, J. P. Sensory and perceptual-motor processes. In J. P. Zubek (Ed.), *Sensory deprivation: Fifteen years of research.* New York: Appleton-Century-Crofts, 1969.

Zuckerman, M. Hallucinations, reported sensations and images. In J. P. Zubek (Ed.), *Sensory deprivation: Fifteen years of research.* New York: Appleton-Century-Crofts, 1969. (a)

Zuckerman, M. Variables affecting deprivation results. In J. P. Zubek (Ed.), *Sensory deprivation: Fifteen years of research.* New York: Appleton-Century-Crofts, 1969. (b)

Zuckerman, M., & Wheeler, L. To dispel fantasies about the fantasy-based measure of fear of success. *Psychological Bulletin,* 1975, *82,* 932–946.

Name Index

Subject Index